READINGS ON FINANCIAL INSTITUTIONS AND MARKETS

READINGS ON FINANCIAL INSTITUTIONS AND MARKETS

1994–1995 Edition

Edited by
Peter S. Rose
Texas A&M University

IRWIN

Chicago • Bogota • Boston • Buenos Aires • Caracas
London • Madrid • Mexico City • Sydney • Toronto

©RICHARD D. IRWIN, INC., 1980, 1984, 1987, 1990, 1993, 1994, and 1995

All rights reserved. No part of this publication may be reproduced, stored in a retrieval system, or transmitted, in any form or by any means, electronic, mechanical, photocopying, recording, or otherwise, without the prior written permission of the publisher.

Senior sponsoring editor: James M. Keefe
Senior marketing manager: Ron Bloecher
Project editor: Karen J. Nelson
Production supervisor: Bob Lange
Designer: Larry J. Cope
Art coordinator: Heather D. Burbridge
Compositor: Precision Typographers
Typeface: 10/12 Times Roman
Printer: Malloy Lithographing, Inc.

Library of Congress Cataloging-in-Publication Data

Readings on financial institutions and markets / [edited by] Peter S.
  Rose. 1994–1995 Edition
      p.   cm. — (Irwin series in finance)
  Includes bibliographical references.
  ISBN 0-256-14526-1
  1. Financial institutions—United States. 2. Finance—United
States. I. Rose, Peter S. II. Series.
HG181.F633   1995
332.1′0973—dc20   94-30043

Printed in the United States of America
1 2 3 4 5 6 7 8 9 0 ML 1 0 9 8 7 6 5 4

THE IRWIN SERIES IN FINANCE

Stephen A. Ross
Sterling Professor of Economics and Finance
Yale University
Consulting Editor

FINANCIAL MANAGEMENT

Block and Hirt
Foundations of Financial Management
Seventh Edition

Brooks
PC Fingame: *The Financial Management Decision Game*

Bruner
Case Studies in Finance: *Managing for Corporate Value Creation*
Second Edition

Fruhan, Kester, Mason, Piper, and Ruback
Case Problems in Finance
Tenth Edition

Harrington
Corporate Financial Analysis: *Decisions in a Global Environment*
Fourth Edition

Helfert
Techniques of Financial Analysis
Eighth Edition

Higgins
Analysis for Financial Management
Fourth Edition

Jones
Introduction to Financial Management

Kallberg and Parkinson
Corporate Liquidity: *Management and Measurement*

Nunnally and Plath
Cases in Finance

Ross, Westerfield, and Jaffe
Corporate Finance
Third Edition

Ross, Westerfield, and Jordan
Fundamentals of Corporate Finance
Third Edition

Schary
Cases in Financial Management

Stonehill and Eiteman
Finance: *An International Perspective*

White
Financial Analysis with an Electronic Calculator
Second Edition

INVESTMENTS

Bodie, Kane, and Marcus
Essentials of Investments
Second Edition

Bodie, Kane, and Marcus
Investments
Second Edition

Cohen, Zinbarg, and Zeikel
Investment Analysis and Portfolio Management
Fifth Edition

Hirt and Block
Fundamentals of Investment Management
Fourth Edition

Lorie, Dodd, and Kimpton
The Stock Market: *Theories and Evidence*
Second Edition

MarketBase, Inc.
MarketBase-E
Annual Edition

Shimko
The Innovative Investor

FINANCIAL INSTITUTIONS AND MARKETS

Rose
Readings on Financial Institutions and Markets
1994-95 Edition

Rose
Money and Capital Markets: *The Financial System in an Increasingly Global Economy*
Fifth Edition

Rose
Commercial Bank Management: *Producing and Selling Financial Services*
Second Edition

Rose and Kolari
Financial Institutions: *Understanding and Managing Financial Services*
Fifth Edition

Saunders
Financial Institutions Management: *A Modern Perspective*

REAL ESTATE

Berston
California Real Estate Principles
Seventh Edition

Berston
California Real Estate Practice
Sixth Edition

Brueggeman and Fisher
Real Estate Finance and Investments
Ninth Edition

Smith and Corgel
Real Estate Perspectives: *An Introduction to Real Estate*
Second Edition

FINANCIAL PLANNING AND INSURANCE

Allen, Melone, Rosenbloom, and VanDerhei
Pension Planning: *Pensions, Profit-Sharing, and Other Deferred Compensation Plans*
Seventh Edition

Crawford
Law and the Life Insurance Contract
Seventh Edition

Crawford
Life and Health Insurance Law
LOMA Edition

Hirsch and Donaldson
Casualty Claim Practice
Fifth Edition

Kapoor, Dlabay, and Hughes
Personal Finance
Third Edition

Kellison
Theory of Interest
Second Edition

Rokes
Human Relations in Handling Insurance Claims
Revised Edition

Preface

We live in a world of change and the process of change seems to be accelerating as we approach the 21st Century. Nowhere is change more evident than within the *global financial system*—that vast collection of financial institutions, financial markets, and financial services accessed every day by millions of businesses, households, and governments around the world. New financial services and new service delivery methods are proliferating with incredible speed. Thanks to rapid advances in the technology of communication, financial institutions today can interact with their customers over hundreds or thousands of miles, faxing loan applications, executing customer orders, and giving customers access to their checking, savings, and credit accounts via computer, electronic wire, and by satellite from the most distance places on the globe.

The financial system truly has become a worldwide financial-services marketplace, offering a growing menu of financial products supplied by thousands of service providers. At the same time financial institutions—banks, insurance companies, mutual funds, finance companies, and thousands of other financial-service providers—are experiencing wrenching changes as competition between these financial businesses continues to intensify. Breakthroughs in communications technology are not only reshaping the production and delivery of financial services, but are also overcoming the geographic barriers that used to isolate and protect many financial institutions from each other. Falling political and economic barriers in Europe, with the welding together of the European Economic Community (EEC), and in North America, with passage of the North American Free Trade Agreement (NAFTA), have thrust distant financial institutions into the same market areas, forcing them to compete head to head. The risk of failure among financial-service institutions has grown proportionally, often shaking public confidence in those institutions the public must depend upon for credit, insurance, savings, investment, and other key financial services. Financial-service providers are rapidly consolidating into much larger, more complex businesses, while small, locally-owned financial institutions find it increasingly difficult to compete for capital and to hold onto their most valuable customers.

In addition, the public these institutions serve is itself undergoing remarkable changes. All over the world people are becoming better educated about the financial marketplace, more aware of what financial services are available from different suppliers, and more knowledgeable about how to seek out the best terms available to them. Increasingly sophisticated financial-service customers are demanding better quality, more convenient, and more reasonably priced financial services. This trend has placed enormous competitive pressure on financial-service providers to lower their operating costs and continuously update the methods they use to produce and deliver services to the public.

At the same time the rules of the financial-services game are changing all over the globe. The key trend of the past two decades has been *deregulation*—the movement towards less regulation in order to allow financial firms to compete more freely, to enter each other's traditional markets, and to face the strong winds of change blowing through the financial-services marketplace without heavy government protection. In country after country the legal and regulatory walls that separate financial-service providers selling insurance and security brokerage and underwriting services from providers of loans, checking, and savings instruments are falling away. Thanks to deregulation of the financial-services sector, financial institutions today face an increasingly uncertain environment in which there are few safe harbors any more. Even the global environmental quality movement has impacted the financial-services markets, threatening to punish lending institutions that ally themselves with customers who fowl the air, water, and soil and fail to clean up the damage to the environment that they cause. Some institutions appear to be losing out in this increasingly "no holds barred" market environment and new dominant financial-service suppliers are emerging—tough, lean, multiservice firms that can cross continents and oceans in search of new markets and withstand unstable economies and volatile currency prices and interest rates.

All of the foregoing changes and more are captured in the articles that comprise this newest edition of *Readings in Financial Institutions and Markets*. This new seventh edition is divided into five parts.

Part One, Bank and Nonbank Financial Institutions, includes articles dealing with the important issue of decline in the banking industry, the spread of interstate banking in the United States, the persistence of excess profits in certain segments of the banking industry, the risks faced by lenders due to tougher environmental laws and regulations, and the remarkable growth of the mutual fund industry which appears to be capturing a greater financial market share at the expense of commercial banks.

Part Two, Regulation of Banks and Other Financial Institutions, contains articles devoted to the market-value accounting controversy in banking, to the new Basle Agreement on international bank capital standards, and to recent proposals to force banks to raise new capital in order to cover the risks of fluctuating security prices, interest rates, and currency values. This section also examines the impact of the "prompt corrective action" doctrine passed by the U.S. Congress in 1991 on depository institutions and the federal deposit insurance fund, the phase out of the "too-big-to-fail" doctrine as the result of recent U.S. banking legislation, the swirling controversy surrounding the Community Reinvestment Act that requires many U.S. financial institutions to make an affirmative effort to serve all neighborhoods within their local communities, and the procedures used by the Federal Reserve and other bank regulatory agencies to approve or deny applications for bank mergers and acquisitions.

Part Three, Interest Rates, Financial Instruments, and Financial Markets, encompasses a wide range of interesting articles covering such topics as the impact of recent population changes and government deficits on national savings rates in the United States and other countries, the yield curve (term structure of interest rates) and its applications in the fields of investor decision-making and public policy, and the pattern of growth in private debt during the 1980s and 1990s. This portion of the book also looks at attempts to predict the volatility of stock prices, at the unusual behavior of the market for pricing new public stock issues, and at the ever-changing market for derivatives (futures, options, swaps, and mortgage-backed securities) whose special features and policy implications are covered in a whole series of articles that close this section of the book.

Part Four, Monetary and Fiscal Policy, contains articles devoted to the controversial issue of how independent a central bank needs to be in order to be effective in promoting noninflationary economic growth, the procedures used by the Federal Reserve to smooth and stabilize interest rates, the changing role of reserve requirements as a tool of central bank policy in the United States and other leading countries, the impact of the federal government's budget on saving, investment, and the growth of the economy, an exploration of the limits on a borrowing government's ability to continually issue new debt to refund old debt, and an exploration of the benefits and costs of different possible methods that the U.S. Treasury might use to auction off its huge debt.

Part Five, International Finance, includes articles examining the worldwide expansion of trading in stocks, futures, and options, the potential diversification benefits stemming from asset portfolios that include securities from several different countries, the possible linkages between interest rates in the United States and Japan, the barriers and opportunities emerging from the gradual formation of the European common market for financial services, and the opportunities open to banks and other financial-service firms to enter Mexico now that NAFTA has been adopted by Canada, Mexico, and the United States.

As before, *Readings in Financial Institutions and Markets* has not one, but many authors who have contributed their talents and valuable insights through the many articles included in this book. My deepest gratitude goes to all those writers who consented graciously to having their research contributions reprinted in this new edition. Special thanks must also be extended to Cynthia Briggs and Lisa Matthews who labored to type the numerous drafts of the preface and the introductions to all five parts of this new book and to Jim Keefe and Beth Kessler, editors at Irwin, who encouraged and supported this project from beginning to end. Gratitude must also be extended to the author's family who, without complaint, granted him the time to assemble this collection of articles and see the project through to its ultimate completion. Hopefully, the reader will be the ultimate beneficiary of the skill and energy expended by so many dedicated professionals to make this book a reality.

Peter S. Rose

Acknowledgements

Article 1: "Is Banking a Declining Industry? A Historical Perspective," George G. Kaufman and Larry R. Mote, Federal Reserve Bank of Chicago, *Economic Perspectives*, May/June 1994, pp. 2–21.

Article 2: "Interstate Banking: A Status Report," Donald T. Savage, Board of Governors of the Federal Reserve System, *Federal Reserve Bulletin,* December 1993, pp. 1075–1089.

Article 3: "The Proconsumer Argument for Interstate Branching," Paul S. Calem, Federal Reserve Bank of Philadelphia, *Business Review*, May/June 1993, pp. 15–29.

Article 4: "Competitive Forces and Profit Persistence in Banking," Mark E. Levonian, Federal Reserve Bank of San Francisco, *FRBSF Weekly Letter*, January 29, 1993, pp. 1–3.

Article 5: "Lenders and Environmental Policies," Eleanor H. Erdevig, Federal Reserve Bank of Chicago, *Economic Perspectives*, November/December 1991, pp. 2–12.

Article 6: "Recent Trends in the Mutual Fund Industry," Phillip R. Mack, Board of Governors of the Federal Reserve System, *Federal Reserve Bulletin*, November 1993, pp. 1001–1012.

Article 7: "Banks and Mutual Funds," Elizabeth Laderman, Federal Reserve Bank of San Francisco, *FRBSF Weekly Letter*, December 17, 1993, pp. 1–3.

Article 8: "Market Value Accounting for Commercial Banks," Thomas Mondschean, Federal Reserve Bank of Chicago, *Economic Perspectives*, January/February 1992, pp. 16–31.

Article 9: "Market Risk and Bank Capital: Part I," Mark E. Levonian, Federal Reserve Bank of San Francisco, *FRBSF Weekly Letter*, January 7, 1994, pp. 1–3.

Article 10: "Market Risk and Bank Capital: Part 2," Mark E. Levonian, Federal Reserve Bank of San Francisco, *FRBSF Weekly Letter*, January 14, 1994, pp. 1–3.

Article 11: "Interest Rate Risk and Bank Capital Standards," Jonathan A. Neuberger, Federal Reserve Bank of San Francisco, *FRBSF Weekly Letter*, November 6, 1992, pp. 1–3.

Article 12: "The Effects of Legislating Prompt Corrective Action on the Bank Insurance Fund," R. Alton Gilbert, Federal Reserve Bank of St. Louis, *Review*, July/August 1992, pp. 3–22.

Article 13: "Too-Big-To-Fail After FDICIA," Larry D. Wall, Federal Reserve Bank of Atlanta, *Economic Review*, January/February 1993, pp. 1–14.

Article 14: "The Community Reinvestment Act: Evolution and Current Issues," Griffith L. Garwood and Dolores S. Smith, Board of Governors of the Federal Reserve System, *Federal Reserve Bulletin*, April 1993, pp. 251–267.

Article 15: "Competitive Considerations in Bank Mergers and Acquisitions: Economic Theory, Legal Foundations, and the Fed," Christopher L. Holder, Federal Reserve Bank of Kansas City, *Economic Review*, January/February 1993, pp. 23–26.

Article 16: "Saving and Demographics: Some International Comparisons," Stephen A. Meyer, Federal Reserve Bank of Philadelphia, *Business Review*, March–April 1992, pp. 13–23.

Article 17: "Interpreting the Term Structure of Interest Rates," Timothy Cogley, *FRBSF Weekly Letter*, Federal Reserve Bank of San Francisco, April 16, 1993, pp. 1–3.

Article 18: "Understanding the Term Structure of Interest Rates: The Expectations Theory," Steven Russell, Federal Reserve Bank of St. Louis, *Review*, July/August 1992, pp. 36–50.

Article 19: "Debt in the 1990s," Francesca Eugeni, Steven Strongin, and Paula R. Worthington, Federal Reserve Bank of Chicago, *Chicago Fed Letter*, May 1993, pp. 1–4.

Article 20: "Predicting Stock-Market Volatility," D. Keith Sill, Federal Reserve Bank of Philadelphia, *Business Review*, January/February 1993, pp. 15–28.

Article 21: "The IPO Underpricing Puzzle," James Booth, Federal Reserve Bank of San Francisco, *FRBSF Weekly Newsletter*, March 11, 1994, pp. 1–3.

Article 22: "Derivative Markets and Competitiveness," Janet A. Napoli, Federal Reserve Bank of Chicago, *Economic Perspectives*, July/August 1992, pp. 13–24.

Article 23: "Determining Margin for Futures Contracts: The Role of Private Interests and the Relevance of Excess Volatility," James T. Moser, Federal Reserve Bank of Chicago, *Economic Perspectives*, March/April 1992, pp. 2–18.

Article 24: "The Convexity Trap: Pitfalls in Financing Mortgage Portfolios and Related Securities," James H. Gilkeson and Stephen D. Smith, Federal Reserve Bank of Atlanta, *Economic Review*, November/December 1992, pp. 14–27.

Article 25: "Index Amortizing Rate Swaps," Lisa N. Galaif, Federal Reserve Bank of New York, *Quarterly Review*, Winter 1993–94, pp. 63–70.

Article 26: "The Pricing and Hedging of Index Amortizing Rate Swaps," Julia D. Fernald, Federal Reserve Bank of New York, *Quarterly Review*, Winter 1993–94, pp. 71–74.

Article 27: "Central Bank Independence and Economic Performance," Patricia S. Pollard, Federal Reserve Bank of St. Louis, *Review*, July/August 1993, pp. 21–36.

Article 28: "Is There a Cost to Having an Independent Central Bank?" Carl E. Walsh, Federal Reserve Bank of San Francisco. *FRBSF Weekly Letter*, February 4, 1994, pp. 1–3.

Article 29: "What Hath the Fed Wrought? Interest Rate Smoothing in Theory and Practice," William Roberds, Federal Reserve Bank of Atlanta, *Economic Review*, January/February 1992, pp. 12–24.

Article 30: "The Changing Role of Reserve Requirements in Monetary Policy," Stuart E. Weiner, Federal Reserve Bank of Kansas City, *Economic Review*, Fourth Quarter 1992, pp. 45–63.

Article 31: "The Federal Budget Deficit, Saving and Investment, and Growth," Adrian W. Throop, Federal Reserve Bank of San Francisco, *FRBSF Weekly Letter*, September 17, 1993, pp. 1–3.

Article 32: "Can the Government Roll Over Its Debt Forever?" Andrew B. Abel, Federal Reserve Bank of Philadelphia, *Business Review*, November/December 1992, pp. 3–18.

Article 33: "Auctioning Treasury Securities," E. J. Stevens and Diana Dumitru, Federal Reserve Bank of Cleveland, *Economic Commentary*, June 15, 1992, pp. 1–4.

Article 34: "Globalization of Stock, Futures, and Options Markets," Peter A. Abken, Federal Reserve Bank of Atlanta, *Economic Review*, July/August 1991, pp. 1–22.

Article 35: "Measuring the Gains from International Portfolio Diversification," Kenneth Kasa, Federal Reserve Bank of San Francisco, *FRBSF Weekly Letter*, April 8, 1994, pp. 1–3.

Article 36: "Interdependence: U.S. and Japanese Real Interest Rates," Michael M. Hutchison, Federal Reserve Bank of San Francisco, *FRBSF Weekly Letter*, June 18, 1993, pp. 1–3.

Article 37: "The Path to European Monetary Union," Paula Hildebrandt, Federal Reserve Bank of Kansas City, *Economic Review*, March/April 1991, pp. 35–48.

Article 38: "How the 1992 Legislation Will Affect European Financial Services," K. Alec Chrystal and Cletus Coughlin, Federal Reserve Bank of St. Louis, *Review*, March/April 1992, pp. 62–77.

Article 39: "U.S. Banks, Competition and the Mexican Banking System: How Much Will NAFTA Matter?" William C. Gruben, John H. Welch, and Jeffery W. Gunther, Federal Reserve Bank of Dallas, *Financial Industry Studies*, October 1993, pp. 11–25.

Contents

PART ONE
Bank and Nonbank Financial Institutions 1

1. Is Banking a Declining Industry? A Historical Perspective   George G. Kaufman and Larry R. Mote   *4*
2. Interstate Banking: A Status Report   Donald T. Savage   *24*
3. The Proconsumer Argument for Interstate Branching   Paul S. Calem   *39*
4. Competitive Forces and Profit Persistence in Banking   Mark E. Levonian   *54*
5. Lenders and Environmental Policies   Eleanor H. Erdevig   *57*
6. Recent Trends in the Mutual Fund Industry   Philip R. Mack   *68*
7. Banks and Mutual Funds   Elizabeth Laderman   *80*

PART TWO
Regulation of Banks and Other Financial Institutions 83

8. Market Value Accounting for Commercial Banks   Thomas Mondschean   *86*
9. Market Risk and Bank Capital: Part 1   Mark E. Levonian   *102*
10. Market Risk and Bank Capital: Part 2   Mark E. Levonian   *105*
11. Interest Rate Risk and Bank Capital Standards   Jonathan A. Neuberger   *108*
12. The Effects of Legislating Prompt Corrective Action on the Bank Insurance Fund   R. Alton Gilbert   *111*
13. Too-Big-to-Fail After FDICIA   Larry D. Wall   *131*
14. The Community Reinvestment Act: Evolution and Current Issues   Griffith L. Garwood and Dolores S. Smith   *145*
15. Competitive Considerations in Bank Mergers and Acquisitions: Economic Theory, Legal Foundations, and the Fed   Christopher L. Holder   *162*

PART THREE
Interest Rates, Financial Instruments, and Financial Markets 177

16. Saving and Demographics: Some International Comparisons   Stephen A. Meyer   *180*
17. Interpreting the Term Structure of Interest Rates   Timothy Cogley   *191*
18. Understanding the Term Structure of Interest Rates: The Expectations Theory   Steven Russell   *194*
19. Debt in the 1990s   Francesca Eugeni, Steven Strongin, and Paula R. Worthington   *209*
20. Predicting Stock-Market Volatility   D. Keith Sill   *213*
21. The IPO Underpricing Puzzle   James Booth   *227*

22. Derivative Markets and Competitiveness   Janet A. Napoli   *230*
23. Determining Margin for Futures Contracts: The Role of Private Interests and the Relevance of Excess Volatility   James T. Moser   *242*
24. The Convexity Trap: Pitfalls in Financing Mortgage Portfolios and Related Securities   James H. Gilkeson and Stephen D. Smith   *259*
25. Index Amortizing Rate Swaps   Lisa N. Galaif   *273*
26. The Pricing and Hedging of Index Amortizing Rate Swaps   Julia D. Fernald   *281*

PART FOUR
Monetary and Fiscal Policy   *285*

27. Central Bank Independence and Economic Performance   Patricia S. Pollard   *288*
28. Is There a Cost to Having an Independent Central Bank?   Carl E. Walsh   *304*
29. What Hath the Fed Wrought? Interest Rate Smoothing in Theory and Practice   William Roberds   *307*
30. The Changing Role of Reserve Requirements in Monetary Policy   Stuart E. Weiner   *320*
31. The Federal Budget Deficit, Saving and Investment, and Growth   Adrian W. Throop   *339*
32. Can the Government Roll Over Its Debt Forever?   Andrew B. Abel   *342*
33. Auctioning Treasury Securities   E. J. Stevens and Diana Dumitru   *358*

PART FIVE
International Finance   *363*

34. Globalization of Stock, Futures, and Options Markets   Peter A. Abken   *365*
35. Measuring the Gains from International Portfolio Diversification   Kenneth Kasa   *387*
36. Interdependence: U.S. and Japanese Real Interest Rates   Michael M. Hutchison   *390*
37. The Path to European Monetary Union   Paula Hildebrandt   *393*
38. How the 1992 Legislation Will Affect European Financial Services   K. Alec Chrystal and Cletus C. Coughlin   *407*
39. U.S. Banks, Competition, and the Mexican Banking System: How Much Will NAFTA Matter?   William C. Gruben, John H. Welch, and Jeffery W. Gunther   *423*

READINGS ON FINANCIAL INSTITUTIONS AND MARKETS

Part One

Bank and Nonbank Financial Institutions

We rely on banks and other financial institutions, such as insurance companies and mutual funds, to provide a wide range of essential financial services at prices close to cost. In recent years competition among *all* financial institutions has sharply intensified, driving some of these important financial-service suppliers into bankruptcy, while others have been absorbed by merger or acquisition, resulting in fewer but much larger financial-service firms. At the same time changing public preferences for financial services have led to marked differences in the growth of different financial-service industries. During the current decade, for example, banks—the dominant financial firm in most financial systems—appear to have lost market share to their nonbank financial-service competitors, especially to mutual funds and other financial-service firms that offer higher-yielding but more risky investments in stocks, bonds, and other popular financial instruments. A major motivation for this trend appears to be the public's increasing interest in better returns on its savings in preparation for retirement, for the purchase of a new home, or to fund higher education for their children. Another causal factor appears to be regulation, which severely limits the services most banks can offer.

In the first article in this section, entitled "Is Banking a Declining Industry?," Dr. George G. Kaufman, the John F. Smith, Jr. Professor of Economics and Finance at Loyola University in Chicago, and Larry R. Mote, economic adviser and vice president at the Federal Reserve Bank of Chicago, question whether bank decline is really underway. They find that the nature of the banking business has changed so much in recent years with the unbundling of many services, the expansion of activities off bank balance sheets, the growth of security underwriting and brokerage activities, and the offering of mutual fund shares that *new* measures of bank size and growth are needed. While banks' share of the total assets of all financial institutions appears to have declined in recent years, measurements of bank size that focus upon such indicators as total bank employment, revenues, or value added yield a mixed picture of either no decline or only a slight decline in banking's importance relative to other financial institutions. Economists Kaufman and Mote do a particularly excellent job in their article of tracing recent service innovations in banking, including the servicing and securitization of loans, the expansion of bank standby credit guarantees, the development of security brokerage services, and the growth of sales of shares in mutual funds.

One of the leading structural trends in the U.S. banking industry of the past decade is the spread of *interstate banking*. As Dr. Donald T. Savage, economist with the Federal Reserve Board, observes in his article "Interstate Banking: A Status Report," restrictions at the state level against interstate banking have undergone drastic changes in recent years. All states except Hawaii have now passed legislation allowing bank holding companies to cross state lines and acquire banks and bank holding companies subject to a variety of restrictions. Moreover, at least eight states have voted to allow state-chartered banks not members of the Federal Reserve System to set up cross-border branch offices under stipulated conditions. By mid-1993 there were nearly 180 interstate banking companies, collectively representing just over 21 percent of all U.S. domestic banking assets.

Nevertheless, as Dr. Savage notes, important barriers to nationwide banking in the United States still remain, though a new federal bill allowing greater authority to branch and acquire other banks across state lines appeared to be moving toward passage in 1994. By 1993 fifteen states were still restricting entry only to banks from their region and even more states required that banks based in their territory be extended entry privileges from other states before they would allow outside bankers to come in. Moreover, because most states have permitted entry into their territory only through holding company acquisitions and not by the simple expedient of establishing branch offices, this restriction has tended to drive up organizational costs and weaken the performance of interstate acquirers. As Dr. Savage notes, most authorities in the field argue that allowing nationwide branching would *lower* bank operating costs, other factors held equal, and perhaps result in more service convenience for the customer.

This conclusion is echoed by Paul S. Calem in his article, "The Proconsumer Argument for Interstate Branching." Dr. Calem points out that restrictions against branching across state lines not only increase the cost of interstate expansion, but also limit potential benefits to consumers. He believes that interstate branch networks would make it much easier for consumers to gain access to their deposit accounts when they travel or move across state lines, facilitate the nationwide flow of capital into areas where credit is most in demand, and promote greater competition, particularly in those markets previously dominated by a small number of entrenched financial-service providers. Paul Calem argues that fears over domination of local markets by large multistate banking organizations and concerns that bigger banking organizations would be insensitive to local community credit needs are overstated. He believes that strong competitive pressures would force all service providers—interstate and intrastate—to be more responsive to the consumer's financial-service needs.

Next, in a short article entitled "Competitive Forces and Profit Persistence in Banking," prepared for the Federal Reserve Bank of San Francisco, research officer Mark E. Levonian contends that government regulation of banking may have an unwanted, but perhaps unavoidable side effect—above-normal profits that are higher and longer-lasting than would be true in a fully competitive, less regulated industry. To determine if this might be true, Dr. Levonian estimates the speed of adjustment of bank profits, using financial and stock price data from 126 U.S. banks and bank holding companies. He finds that excess bank profits tend to approach normal profit levels over time, but that profit adjustment is relatively slow—substantially slower, in fact, than seems to prevail in other industries. Below-normal profits also appear to be slow to correct in banking, but tend to return to a more normal level considerably faster than is true of excess bank profits. Economist Levonian believes that *regulation* may, at least partially, account for the slow adjustment in bank profits. However, he points out that the persistence of above-normal profits may stimulate innovations in financial services that ultimately benefit consumers.

Concern over the quality of the environment and environmental damage has reached into virtually every sector of the economy in recent years and the banking and financial-services sector has been no exception, creating potential drains on the profits of banks and other financial institutions that lend money to business firms. Passage of key federal legislation (most notably the Comprehensive Environmental Response, Compensation, and Liability Act of 1980, known widely as the Superfund Act) has created the prospect that lenders can be held liable for environmental damage and environmental cleanup costs that result from the business activities of their borrowing customers. Economist Eleanor H. Erdevig of the Federal Reserve Bank of Chicago, in her article "Lenders and Environmental Policies," explores the nature of this new form of lender risk and points out that banks and other lenders must be especially careful in the future to avoid becoming involved in the management of a business firm, especially if it has contaminated property that it has pledged as collateral for a loan. Dr. Erdevig calls for further clarification of environmental rules so that lenders can more accurately assess the risks they face today in the environmental field.

Finally, we turn in the last portion of this section of the book to one of the most successful financial institutions of the past decade—the *mutual fund* or investment company which typically acquires large pools of stocks, bonds, and other securities. In a detailed and thoroughly researched article entitled "Recent Trends in the Mutual Fund Industry" Philip R. Mack from the Division of Research and Statistics of the Federal Reserve Board explores the causes and consequences of the recent dramatic growth of mutual funds. He finds that many former depositors in banks have been lured away by perceived higher returns offered by mutual funds compared to record lows in bank deposit interest rates. Moreover, mutual funds have attracted thousands of new customers by offering an expanding menu of services (including checking, savings, credit, and investment advisory services) while, in many cases, charging lower sales commissions.

Dr. Mack believes that the growth of mutual funds has improved the efficiency of the financial system by lowering transactions costs. These investment firms have given corporations interested in increasing their capital base greater access to the money and capital markets. Dr. Mack contends that the growing importance of mutual funds has altered the relationship between money and economic activity by contributing to a decline in the role of banks and other depository intermediaries in providing credit.

This last trend is also explored in the final article in this section, prepared by Elizabeth Laderman of the Federal Reserve Bank of San Francisco. She points out in her article, "Banks and Mutual Funds," that banks' growing involvement in offering mutual funds to their customers is really part of a broad trend covering more than two decades in which banks' share of household assets and their share of the total volume of credit provided in the economy has been falling. Dr. Laderman believes that the trend toward less bank intermediation of funds and greater mutual fund intermediation within the financial system is likely to continue on a long-term basis (albeit with fluctuations from year to year), though some banks may be able to slow the decline in their market share by offering attractive mutual-fund programs of their own.

Is banking a declining industry? A historical perspective

George G. Kaufman and Larry R. Mote

Regulation has been widely blamed for contributing to the decline of the commercial banking industry in the United States. Before one can evaluate the truth or falsity of this accusation, it is necessary to determine whether banking is indeed a declining industry. To answer this question, we examine a number of different measures of changes in the size of the banking industry in the United States during the twentieth century.

Few industries are as closely associated in the public image with the growth of modern economies as is commercial banking. Bankers have been widely caricatured as pulling the strings behind the "bosses of industry" and have been viewed with suspicion or fear in many quarters. Indeed, it would be difficult to understand the elaborate set of regulations intended to restrict the growth and thereby the power of commercial banks in the United States without first understanding the widespread distrust of banks and banking dating back to early U.S. history. In the 1800s, some states even went so far as to ban banks altogether.

But the image of bankers as all-powerful has changed dramatically in recent years, especially among bankers themselves, their regulators, and the business community. Over the past decade, banking in particular and depository institutions in general have come to be viewed as declining. This widespread perception is based primarily on their declining share of some measure of assets or liabilities for all financial institutions. An example is provided by figure 1, which shows the decline since 1952 in the combined total assets of U.S.-chartered commercial banks and U.S. offices of foreign banks as a percentage of the assets of all financial institutions. Several presentations at the Federal Reserve Bank of Chicago's 1993 Conference on Bank Structure and Competition noted this decline (Federal Reserve Bank of Chicago 1993).

The common view is that banks are losing out to a wide range of nonbank competitors such as finance companies, mutual funds, and private pension funds that are offering traditional types of banking products more efficiently, either because technological advances have eliminated advantages previously enjoyed by banks or because these competitors are free of costly regulations imposed on banks. The source of any decline is important in judging its welfare implications. If banking were a declining industry because of market forces, as was the fate of horse-drawn carriages, the railroads, and coal mining, then it would be of concern to bankers who lose their jobs but of little public policy concern.[1] Indeed, attempting to prevent the decline would reduce aggre-

---

George G. Kaufman is the John F. Smith, Jr. Professor of Economics and Finance at Loyola University of Chicago and consultant to the Federal Reserve Bank of Chicago. Larry R. Mote is an economic adviser and vice president at the Federal Reserve Bank of Chicago. The authors wish to thank Lisa Hardesty for compiling data for the study. They also gratefully acknowledge the helpful contributions of Doug Evanoff and Steven Strongin.

gate economic welfare. On the other hand, if the decline were attributable to excessive regulation that prevents banks from operating more effectively, or from introducing newer products for which demand is growing rapidly, then aggregate economic welfare would be reduced and the decline would be a legitimate public policy concern.

However, before anyone writes the banking industry's epitaph, it may be useful to look a little more closely at the evidence. This article examines a number of data series to determine whether banking is or is not a declining industry and, if it is, whether the decline is the result of market forces or of excessive and discriminatory regulation. Although the evidence is not clear-cut, several of the alternative measures examined in this article suggest that banking may not be declining.

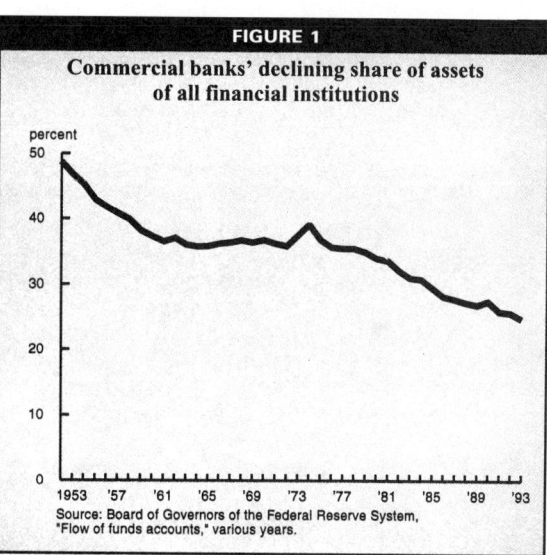

FIGURE 1
Commercial banks' declining share of assets of all financial institutions

Source: Board of Governors of the Federal Reserve System, "Flow of funds accounts," various years.

Alternative measures of the size of the banking industry

There are serious conceptual and practical problems in measuring the output of any industry.[2] Because of the intangible nature of the output provided by service industries generally, and banks in particular, the problem of measuring output has occupied banking scholars for decades. The problem arises in a number of contexts—for example, in calculating shares of output in local markets for antitrust purposes, in measuring banking output and costs for the purpose of determining the relationship between size and efficiency, and in calculating the industry's contribution to gross domestic product (GDP). Some of the issues related to choosing the most appropriate measure of the size of the banking industry are discussed in the accompanying box.

Because each of the measures used in past studies appears to contain conceptual or practical problems—difficulties in obtaining appropriate data, shortcomings in the quality of available data, lack of comparability of data over time, or a failure of the data to correspond closely to the theoretical concept they are used to measure—this article analyzes a number of them. Among the most frequently used measures of the size of the banking industry are 1) assets; 2) employment; and 3) revenues, earnings, and value added. We present data for each of these measures in turn, together with an indication of their strengths and shortcomings. Because assets and related balance sheet data have been, by far, the most frequently used measures of the size of the banking industry, we consider them first.

Assets

Total assets, earning assets, and total deposits have all been used at one time or another as measures or indexes of banking output. Such measures accord with the common perception of banks as firms that use "inputs" such as deposits, labor, and capital to produce "outputs" primarily in the form of loans and investments. This more or less commonsense view has greatly influenced the analysis of banks as firms and the measurement of bank output.

It is therefore not surprising that total assets or deposits, or some variant thereof, has long been the most popular measure of the size or output of the banking industry. Balance sheet data for banks are readily available at frequent intervals and serve as the basis for the widely used flow of funds data published quarterly by the Federal Reserve.[3] Moreover, in contrast with most other businesses, the products and services of banks have traditionally been closely related to the size and composition of their asset and liability portfolios. Throughout the nineteenth century and the first half of the twentieth century, the activities of commercial banks were largely limited to accepting and processing deposits and making loans and investments. Indeed, those functions still account for a substantial if declining proportion of the typical bank's activities.

Issues in the measurement of bank output

Analysts have tried to measure bank output for two purposes: to assess economies of scale in banking, and to calculate banks' contribution to gross domestic product (GDP). Earning assets or total assets were the most widely used measures of bank output in early studies of the relationship between scale—that is, size measured in terms of output—and cost in banking. However, critics pointed out that an equal number of dollars of credit extended for a given period of time, as would be reflected in asset measures, do not necessarily imply equal output in an economic sense. For example, a given dollar amount of consumer installment loans does not necessarily represent the same output as the same dollar amount of loans to a large corporate customer. A consumer loan is likely to require much more risk-bearing, information gathering, credit analysis, and bookkeeping per dollar of loan principal than a loan to a large corporate customer (Benston 1965; Greenbaum 1967). Thus, simply adding the dollar amounts of all the loans on a bank's books would be adding apples and oranges. The only dimensions of output that could be said to be identical for loans of different types but equal dollar amounts outstanding are the amount and duration of the postponement of consumption by one group of economic units that is a prerequisite for making a loan enabling another economic unit to consume beyond its current income. A similar objection applies to adding the outstanding values of loans of the same type but of different sizes.

Another relatively obvious criticism of balance sheet measures of output is that output is a flow, measured in quantity or value per unit of time, whereas assets are a stock at a particular point in time. Only in banking and related financial industries have assets been widely used as a measure of output and relative importance. In other industries, sales or revenues are the preferred measure for some purposes, including the calculation of market shares for antitrust analysis. For most other purposes, there is fairly general agreement among economists that the most relevant measure of the size of an industry is its value added, or contribution to the total output of the economy. Although there may be issues affecting the industry for which assets or liabilities or employment are more useful measures—for example, changes in the importance of banking as a channel for monetary policy or banking's role in creating new jobs—the contribution of banking to GDP is a more general measure of the industry's importance in the economy.

In the search for a single index of banking output, considerable progress had been made by the late 1960s toward achieving consensus that some variant of bank revenue, rather than assets, was the preferred measure of final output. Of course, if one wishes to measure commercial banks' contribution to final output as measured by value added, rather than the value of final output per se, it is necessary to subtract from revenues the value of purchased inputs. Nevertheless, the persistence of conflicting views concerning the nature of the output of financial institutions led to a continuing debate over which measure of value added was most appropriate. Serious questions were raised about the "liquidity principle" used by the U.S. Commerce Department's Office of Business Economics to measure the contribution of banks and other financial intermediaries to GDP. According to the liquidity principle, bank output consists only of interest and other services to depositors, not to borrowers (Hodgman 1969). However, as Hodgman pointed out,

> a closer examination of banking activity and banking costs will reveal that *financial services* (rather than deposits or loans) are the products of banking.... When banks are viewed as financial service firms we see that the banking product sold to *borrowers* is not only credit but intermediation and that a portion of a bank's interest receipts is paid by the borrower to cover the costs of intermediation rather than as a payment for liquidity or consumption foregone by the ultimate lender. This portion of "interest" received by banks should be regarded as part of their gross value product in the national accounting sense. The remainder of interest paid to banks will, under competitive conditions, be paid in turn by the banks to the ultimate lenders who are depositors and

Support for the view that banking is declining in relative importance is typically based on the downward trend in the share of total assets at all financial institutions (see figure 1),

stockholders. Conceptually, therefore, the *net* interest received by banks should be included in gross product originating rather than set to zero by definition.*

But while Hodgman and others were gaining considerable support for some variant of revenue as the single index of output in banking, the literature on bank costs moved in a very different direction. First, researchers began to estimate separate cost functions for individual functional areas within the bank (Benston 1965; Bell and Murphy 1968). Later, they began to use the translog and related multi-product cost functions (Benston, Hanweck, and Humphrey 1982). Neither of these approaches required using a single index of banking output.

The objections noted above to using assets as the measure of banking output apply fully only to attempts to aggregate many different types of loans or other banking products into a single index of banking output. As long as each category of loans is relatively homogeneous—for example, consumer loans that do not vary greatly in size or riskiness—it may be unobjectionable to use total loans outstanding as a measure of the output associated with that category. The reason is that, if all the loans in a particular category are identical in size, maturity, risk, and other important characteristics, then the number of loan accounts, total revenue, and other alternative measures of output associated with that category would be proportional to the amount outstanding. Thus, asset measures may be a reasonable choice for the estimation of multi-product cost functions that utilize a large number of output categories rather than a single index of overall output. Indeed, recent studies comparing the performance of stock and flow measures of output in bank cost studies have concluded that there is not much empirical evidence to favor one over another (Humphrey 1992). But it is still true that this approach finesses the issue rather than addressing it; there is no presumption that a dollar of consumer loans represents the same output as a dollar of commercial and industrial loans.

---
*Hodgman 1969, p. 191.

or particular categories of assets accounted for by commercial banks or by all depository institutions. As table 1 shows, the decline in banks' share of short-term business credit, the traditional bread and butter lending activity of commercial banks, has been even more dramatic than that of banks' share of total assets. The data are frequently presented with such a sense of urgency that one might be led to believe that the decline in asset share is a sudden, recent development that requires an immediate response.

However, a closer review of the evidence shows that neither this decline nor the concern over it is of recent origin. A pioneering study of U.S. financial institutions conducted by Raymond Goldsmith in the 1950s and 1960s reported that commercial banks' share of total assets of financial intermediaries had declined from 71 percent in 1860 to 63 percent in 1900 and 32 percent in 1963 (Goldsmith 1958, 1969).[4] Table 2 shows commercial banks' share of the total assets of financial institutions for selected dates from 1860 through 1993. Thus, the more recent decline in the market share of commercial banks should not be overly surprising. Much of it simply reflects the fact that, because banks were the first major financial institution in the United States, it was virtually inevitable that they would lose market share over time to newer types of financial institutions offering previously unknown products, for example, pension funds and mutual funds.

Nor is evidence of a decline in banks' market share limited to the United States. As the data in table 3 indicate, banks' share of total liabilities of financial intermediaries in the United Kingdom also declined between 1913 and 1991. Similar declines have occurred in most of the 30 major foreign countries analyzed by Goldsmith (1969).

But even before Goldsmith's study, bankers lamented that the traditional business of banking was shrinking and that if banks were to survive they would have to expand the scope of their activities. Thus, as corporations relied increasingly on internal sources of funds and less on bank loans in the 1920s, banks expanded their lending to include consumer and residential real estate loans. The same decade also saw the rapid expansion of banks and bank securities affiliates into the underwriting and distribution of corporate securities. Retrospec-

TABLE 1

Composition of short-term credit market debt of nonfinancial corporate business
(1950-92)

	1950	1960	1970	1980	1990	1992
	(------------------------percent----------------------)					
Bank loans	91	87	83	71	59	59
Nonbank finance loans	6	9	9	14	17	18
Commercial paper	1	2	6	9	12	12
Foreign loans	--	--	--	1	9	9
Bankers' acceptances	2	2	2	5	3	2
Total	100	100	100	100	100	100
Billion dollars	20	43	125	324	951	882

Source: Board of Governors of the Federal Reserve System, *Balance Sheets for the U.S. Economy, 1945-92*, March 10, 1993.

tively, and almost certainly incorrectly, some blamed the banking collapse of the early 1930s on the entry by banks into some of these new and unfamiliar activities.

The 1950s were marked by renewed concern over banks' loss of business, this time to then rapidly growing nonbank depository institutions, such as savings and loan associations, which at the time were free of such regulatory restrictions as interest rate ceilings on deposits and reserve requirements. Indeed, the widely discussed Gurley-Shaw thesis held that if regulation continued to restrain traditional banks relative to their nonbank competitors, the result would be the development of more and more "near monies" such as time and savings deposits at thrift institutions, and the continued shrinkage of the banking industry (Gurley and Shaw 1955, 1956, 1960). Eventually, a point would be reached at which monetary policy, if it continued to operate only through traditional banks, would lose its effectiveness. A quick examination of table 2 shows that, rather than preempting commercial banks, savings and loan associations and savings banks are themselves now declining rapidly in importance. A history of the Office of the Comptroller of the Currency published in 1968 also remarked on the loss of market share by commercial banks in the postwar period and attributed it to excessive regulation of banks in combination with tax and other incentives enjoyed by some nonbank competitors (Robertson 1968). Like most other research on the issue, both the Gurley and Shaw study and that of the Comptroller's office relied on balance sheet data to support the thesis that banking was in decline.

Improving the asset measure

Assets probably give an adequate picture of the size of the banking industry in the nineteenth century. However, there is reason to believe that even for the first half of the twentieth century and certainly for more recent decades, reported assets give a distorted and incomplete view of the output of the commercial banking industry. The asset figures typically used in these analyses include only bank-owned or "on-balance-sheet" assets. But banks also manage or otherwise service assets owned by others. These activities are referred to as "off-balance-sheet." The economics of banking, as opposed to accounting conventions, suggests that banks should be measured by some measure that reflects the full range of their activities, such as revenues, income, or value added. However, because on-balance-sheet assets are the most readily available and frequently used yardstick of the size of the banking industry, it may be worthwhile to try to correct banks' aggregate balance sheet for a number of failings, in particular its exclusion of important off-balance-sheet activities, and bring it closer to what might be called an "economic balance sheet." We will discuss some of these exclusions and the adjustments needed to correct for them in the following sections.

Bank trust services

Among the most important off-balance-sheet activities are bank trust services, perhaps the oldest off-balance-sheet activities engaged in by banks in the United States. Indeed, a number of banks began as strictly trust companies providing only trustee or fiduciary services and expanded into deposit and other banking services primarily as an accommodation to their customers. Today, few strictly trust com-

TABLE 2
Share of assets of financial institutions in the United States (1860-1993)

	1860	1880	1900	1912	1929	1939	1948	1960	1970	1980	1993
	(------percent------)										
Commercial banks	71.4	60.6	62.9	64.5	53.7	51.2	55.9	38.2	37.9	34.8	25.4
U.S.-chartered banks and bank holding companies	71.4	60.6	62.9	64.5	53.7	51.2	55.3	37.6	37.2	32.4	21.7
U.S. offices of foreign banks	--	--	--	--	0.0	0.0	0.6	0.6	0.7	2.4	3.7
Thrift institutions	17.8	22.8	18.2	14.8	14.0	13.6	12.3	19.7	20.4	21.4	9.4
Savings and loan associations	0.0	2.2	3.1	3.0	6.0	4.2	4.7	11.8	13.0	15.5	7.4[a]
Savings banks	17.8	20.6	15.1	11.8	8.0	9.2	7.4	6.9	6.0	4.2	
Credit unions	--	--	--	--	0.0	0.2	0.2	1.1	1.4	1.7	2.0
Insurance companies	10.7	13.9	13.8	16.6	18.6	27.2	24.3	23.8	18.9	16.1	17.4
Life insurance	1.8	9.4	10.7	13.6	14.8	23.5	20.6	19.4	15.1	11.5	12.8
Property/casualty	8.9	4.5	3.1	3.0	3.8	3.7	3.7	4.4	3.8	4.5	4.6
Investment companies	--	--	--	--	2.4[c]	1.9[c]	1.3[c]	2.9	3.5	3.6	14.9
Mutual funds	--	--	--	--	--	--	--	2.9	3.5	3.4	14.2
Stock and bond	--	--	--	--	--	--	--	2.9	3.5	1.5	10.2
Money market	--	--	--	--	--	--	--	--	--	1.9	4.0
Closed-end funds	--	--	--	--	--	--	--	b	b	0.2	0.7
Pension funds	--	--	0.0	0.0	0.7	2.1	3.1	9.7	13.0	17.4	24.4
Private	--	--	--	--	0.4	0.8	1.6	6.4	8.4	12.5	16.7
State and local government	--	--	0.0	0.0	0.3	1.3	1.5	3.3	4.5	4.9	7.6
Finance companies	--	0.0	0.0	0.0	2.0	2.2	2.0	4.6	4.8	5.1	4.7
Securities brokers and dealers	0.0	0.0	3.8	3.0	8.1	1.5	1.0	1.1	1.2	1.1	3.3
Mortgage companies	0.0	2.7	1.3	1.2	0.6	0.3	0.1	b	b	0.4	0.2
Real estate investment trusts	--	--	--	--	--	--	--	0.0	0.3	0.1	0.1
Total (percent)	100.0	100.0	100.0	100.0	100.0	100.0	100.0	100.0	100.0	100.0	100.0
Total (trillion dollars)	.001	.005	.016	.034	.123	.129	.281	.596	1.328	4.025	13.952

[a] The end of the first quarter of 1993 was the last date for which data for savings and loan associations and savings banks were reported separately. The figures for that date were: savings and loans, 6.0 percent; savings banks, 1.9 percent.

[b] Data not available.

[c] Breakdown between open- and closed-end funds not available.

Sources: Data for 1860-1948 from Raymond W. Goldsmith, *Financial Structure and Development*, Studies in Comparative Economics, New Haven, CT: Yale University Press, 1969, Table D-33, pp. 548-9. Data for 1960-1993 from Board of Governors of the Federal Reserve System, "Flow of funds accounts," various years.

TABLE 3
Share of total liabilities of intermediaries, United Kingdom (1913-91)

Year	Banks	Building societies	Insurance companies	Pension funds
		(----------percent----------)		
1913	64	4	32	--
1930	61	8	31	--
1939	55	12	32	n.a.
1960	43	12	30	14
1970	32	17	27	16
1980	30	20	25	21
1990	28	17	26	26
1991	27	18	27	26

Note: n.a. indicates data not available.
Source: Harold Rose, "The changing world of finance and its problems," working paper no. 167-93, Institute of Finance and Accounting, London Business School, 1993, p. 29.

panies exist. To serve customers who wish to invest in securities other than bank deposits, many banks have long operated trust departments in which they provide fiduciary, investment, managerial, and custodial services for a fee. Trust department assets are assets that the bank manages or otherwise services but does not own, and that therefore do not appear on the bank's balance sheet.

Trust accounts come in various types and require different amounts of servicing by the bank; accordingly, they generate different amounts of fee income for banks. Most trusts can be classified as personal trusts, estates, or employee benefit trusts. The trust contracts with the trustee bank for the kind of services that it requires. Almost all trust contracts call for custodial and recordkeeping services, including performance measurement, timely valuation, portfolio analysis, Employee Retirement Income Security Act (ERISA) and other required disclosure assistance, benefit disbursement, cash management, and proxy monitoring.

Some banks also provide investment management services, either as an agent or as a trustee.[5] Trust accounts whose assets are managed by the bank are generally referred to as discretionary, while accounts that are in the custody of the bank but managed by others are referred to as nondiscretionary. At year-end 1992, bank trust departments, trust companies, and thrift institutions held $1.8 trillion of discretionary assets and $7.7 trillion of nondiscretionary assets; the commercial bank share was 87 percent of the former and 94 percent of the latter (Federal Financial Institutions Examination Council 1992). Total trust assets serviced by commercial banks at year-end 1992 totaled $8.8 trillion, more than 2.5 times the assets on the balance sheets of banks. Moreover, bank trust assets have expanded rapidly in recent years, rising from $283 billion at year-end 1968 to $4.1 trillion in 1985 and $8.8 trillion in 1992. As figure 2 shows, the most rapid growth in recent years has been in nondiscretionary assets.

Banks face little competition for custodial trust services. Few if any financial institutions other than banks or trust companies offer them,

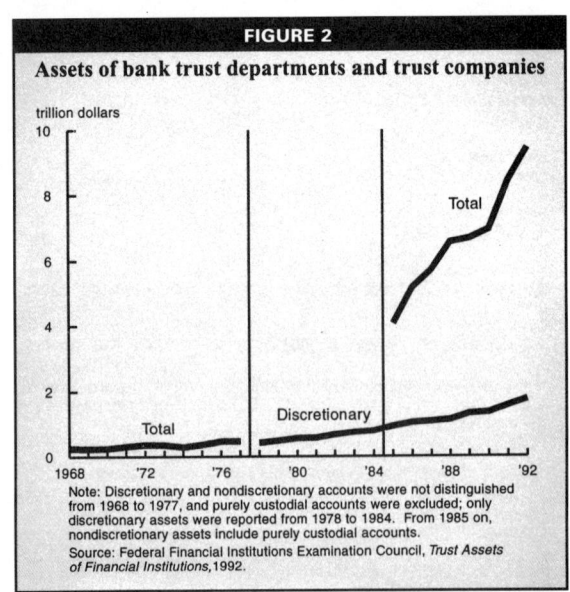

FIGURE 2
Assets of bank trust departments and trust companies

Note: Discretionary and nondiscretionary accounts were not distinguished from 1968 to 1977, and purely custodial accounts were excluded; only discretionary assets were reported from 1978 to 1984. From 1985 on, nondiscretionary assets include purely custodial accounts.
Source: Federal Financial Institutions Examination Council, *Trust Assets of Financial Institutions*, 1992.

TABLE 4
Ten largest bank trust departments, personal and employee benefit accounts
(1992)

	Trust assets			Bank assets	Discretionary trust assets/ bank assets	Total trust assets/ bank assets
	Discretionary	Nondiscretionary	Total			
	(-------------------- billion dollars --------------------)				(---------------- ratio ----------------)	
State Street Bank (Boston)	113	1,165	1,278	16.5	6.8	77.5
Morgan Guaranty (New York)	38	695	733	76.7	0.5	9.6
Bank of New York	30	685	715	36.5	0.8	19.6
Citibank (New York)	23	399	422	163.8	0.1	2.6
Northern Trust (Chicago)	37	341	378	11.9	3.1	31.8
Mellon Bank (Pittsburgh)	37	323	361	29.6	1.3	12.2
Bankers Trust (New York)	128	222	351	55.8	2.3	6.3
Chase Manhattan (New York)	17	339	356	74.5	0.2	4.8
Boston Safe Deposit	19	217	236	8.3	2.3	28.4
Bank of America (San Francisco)	112	107	219	133.4	0.8	1.6

Source: Federal Financial Institutions Examination Council, *Trust Assets of Financial Institutions*, 1992.

and only a few trust companies are not chartered as banks. The ten largest bank trust departments according to assets in personal and employee benefit accounts are listed in table 4. Two of the institutions—State Street Bank and Boston Safe Deposit—are basically trust companies rather than banks, although both have bank charters. As the data in the table make clear, the trust assets held by each of these institutions greatly exceed the assets on its balance sheet.

Banks also provide corporate trust services. Such services include serving as trustee for the holders of corporate and municipal securities and as registrar, paying agent, transfer agent, and recordkeeper for publicly issued securities, including mutual funds. As trustee for the debt security holders, the bank trust department monitors scheduled payments for timeliness and represents the holders' interests in disputes. The largest bank trust departments in each corporate trust activity are listed in table 5. Only as mutual fund transfer agents do commercial banks appear to face serious competition.

When personal trust assets held by bank trust departments are added to balance sheet assets for the years since 1900, the share of assets held by banks increases somewhat, but the downward trend is basically unaltered. For the period since 1968, adding personal trusts increases commercial banks' share of total assets by an amount ranging from 4.5 percentage points to 9 percentage points. However, the downward trend remains and is in fact intensified in percentage terms, since the ratio of banks' personal trust assets to total assets of financial institutions fell by 50 percent over that period, whereas banks' share of balance sheet assets fell only about a third. As figure 3 shows, essentially the same conclusion holds when other assets are included over which bank trust departments exercise managerial discretion. These assets, which include roughly one-third of employee benefit trust assets, were nearly three times as large as personal trust assets at year-end 1992 but have grown at roughly the same pace in recent years. Thus, while their inclusion substantially increases banks' average share of the market over the period, it does little to moderate its downward trend. Including trust assets over which banks do not exercise managerial discretion would moderate the decline, but because a narrower range of services is provided in conjunction with such accounts, they should not receive the same weight as discretionary assets.

TABLE 5
Largest bank providers of corporate trust services
(1992)

Corporate and municipal security trusteeship	Securities, principal amount (billion dollars)
Citibank (New York)	222
First National Bank (Chicago)	197
Bank of New York	160
Chemical Bank (New York)	149
Bankers Trust (New York)	132
Texas Commerce (Houston)	99
Chase Manhattan (New York)	94
State Street (Boston)	92
Bank of America (San Francisco)	91
United States Trust (New York)	87

Stock or bond transfer agent	Number of issues
Citibank (New York)	16,030
Chemical Bank (New York)	12,109
Bank of New York	8,124
Bankers Trust (New York)	2,961
Seattle-First National	2,849
Ameritrust Texas (Dallas)	2,360
American National (St. Paul)	2,223
Security Pacific (New York)	1,905
First Chicago Trust (New York)	1,542
First National of Boston	1,347

Mutual fund transfer agent	Number of issues
PNC National (Wilmington, DE)	427
Investors Fiduciary Trust (Kansas City)	241
Firstar (Milwaukee)	132
Putnam Fiduciary (Boston)	71
Investors Trust (Boston)	44
NationsBank (Dallas)	32
Norwest Bank (Minnesota)	23
Wells Fargo (San Francisco)	22
Fifth-Third Bank (Cincinnati)	8
Wilmington Trust	7

Source: Federal Financial Institutions Examination Council (1992).

The reentry of banks into securities activities

Primarily through the nonbank subsidiaries of their parent holding companies, banks have also been entering or reentering areas of activity long considered off-limits to banks, at least since the enactment of the Glass-Steagall Act in 1933. Although banks' own aggressiveness and inventiveness have been the driving force in this development, much of it would have been impossible without a series of rulings by the Comptroller of the Currency and the Board of Governors of the Federal Reserve System (Kaufman and Mote 1990). As of today, banking organizations, subject to some quantitative restrictions that are more onerous for smaller institutions, may serve as full-service or discount securities brokers, may underwrite and deal in a full range of municipal and corporate debt, futures, options, swaps, and other derivative securities as well as corporate equities, and may manage or broker (but not underwrite or sponsor) mutual funds.

In recent years, commercial banks have made significant inroads into the underwriting of new securities. In 1993, two bank holding companies—J. P. Morgan and Citicorp—ranked among the top 15 underwriters of all new domestic securities sold in the United States. The remaining 13 were investment banks. Three banks ranked among the top 15 underwriters of both investment-grade and junk bonds and also among the top five underwriters of asset-backed securities. It is of interest to note that only one commercial bank ranked among the top 15 underwriters of municipal revenue bonds, most of which they were not permitted to underwrite until recent years. But this is the same number of banks that rank among the top 15 underwriters of municipal general obligation bonds, which banks have always been permitted to underwrite. As we have noted elsewhere, it is only since the late 1970s that banks have become aggressive in pursuing securities underwriting activities (Kaufman and Mote 1990). In part this may reflect differences in corporate culture between these activities and more traditional commercial banking activities.

Banks and mutual funds

Mutual funds are one of the newer and, since the late 1970s, more rapidly growing types of financial institutions. As figure 4 shows, mutual funds have increased their share of assets of all financial institutions from 1.8 percent in 1977 to 14.2 percent in 1993. This rapid increase is the result of both a rapid inflow of new funds into mutual funds, in part reflecting the introduction of money market funds in the early 1970s, and the sharp increase in stock and bond prices in recent years. Ex-

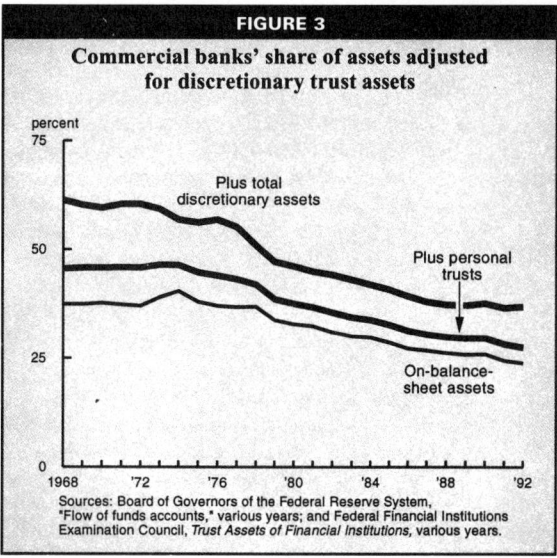

FIGURE 3
Commercial banks' share of assets adjusted for discretionary trust assets

Sources: Board of Governors of the Federal Reserve System, "Flow of funds accounts," various years; and Federal Financial Institutions Examination Council, *Trust Assets of Financial Institutions*, various years.

cept for money market funds, mutual funds are valued at market prices. In contrast, the assets of depository institutions, insurance companies, and finance companies are typically measured by book value.

Mutual funds are open-ended investment funds sponsored (organized) by an entity called an investment company that sells shares to raise a third-party pool of funds for investment in securities. The shares represent an interest in the pool and are generally valued at the day-end net asset price of the asset portfolio. The fund stands ready to buy and sell shares continuously at this price. The sponsor investment company may manage the fund by providing investment advice, provide the necessary back-room operations including recordkeeping, custodial, and transfer services, and/or market and sell the shares directly to the public, or it may hire one or more third parties to do so. Thus, mutual funds consist of a sponsor, investment manager, share distributor, and operations agent. These four functions may be conducted by a single entity, four different entities, or something in between.

Commercial banks are traditionally portfolio investors that raise funds by selling primarily debt instruments (deposits) to second parties. Thus, unlike the case with mutual funds, most bank investors are creditors rather than owners, whose returns are fixed. But many bank customers also wish to invest in securities offering greater risks and hopefully higher returns than can be obtained on bank deposits. This has been especially true in recent years as households have become wealthier and older and have placed increasing emphasis on saving for retirement through pension plans. As indicated above, banks have long provided some of these services through their trust departments. It has been common practice for trust departments to commingle trust accounts for investment purposes in order to reduce transaction costs and realize operating economies.

In 1965, however, the Comptroller of the Currency permitted the First National Bank of New York, the predecessor of Citibank, to commingle its managing agency accounts and to advertise them to the general public. Customers would receive participation units in the pool. This change was challenged by the

FIGURE 4
The rise in mutual funds' share of assets of all financial institutions

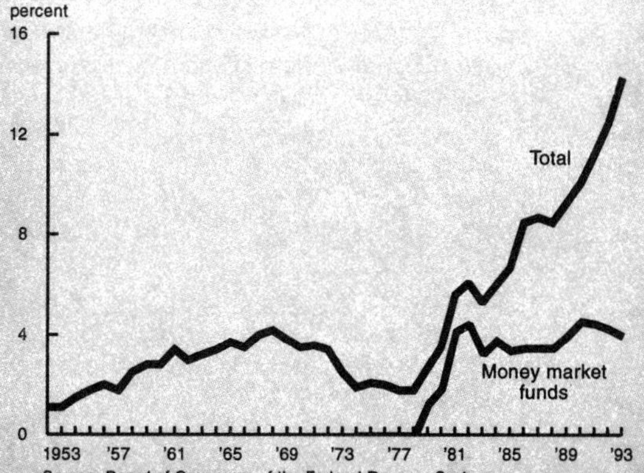

Source: Board of Governors of the Federal Reserve System, "Flow of funds accounts," various years.

securities industry and ultimately struck down by the Supreme Court, which ruled that it violated the provisions of the Glass-Steagall Act separating commercial and investment banking. The court ruled that commingling managing agency accounts and selling participation shares in them was in effect dealing in securities, which was prohibited. The court concluded that such a "bank investment fund finds itself in direct competition with the mutual fund industry" (Fischer, Gram, Kaufman, and Mote 1984). The decision temporarily stalled banks' efforts to offer a competitive investment product. However, a 1972 decision by the Board of Governors of the Federal Reserve System that explicitly permitted banks to act as investment managers for mutual funds, while prohibiting them from brokering such funds, helped banks to enter this market.

Although the Glass-Steagall Act prohibited banks from dealing in private securities for their own account, it did not prohibit them from purchasing and selling private securities without recourse upon order of their customers. While some banks offered brokerage services as an accommodation to their customers, few viewed them as a profitable activity. Indeed, in 1936, the Comptroller of the Currency explicitly authorized national banks to offer brokerage services, but only as an accommodation to their customers and not on a profit-making basis. The increase in securities activities and the end of fixed commissions on the New York Stock Exchange in 1975 caused banks to reconsider their interest in brokerage activities. In 1981, BankAmerica Corporation announced its intention to acquire Charles Schwab, the country's largest discount broker. Shortly thereafter, Security Pacific National Bank initiated a cooperative arrangement with the Fidelity Group to broker securities, including mutual funds, to its customers and then organized its own discount broker as a subsidiary of the bank. Both activities were undertaken with the approval of the regulatory agencies. Thus, banks could broker mutual funds either directly through the bank or bank holding company or indirectly through a cooperative agreement with a third-party broker. Some banks began to offer their customers "private-label" mutual funds managed by others. At the same time, some banks also started "proprietary funds" that were managed by the organizing bank but distributed by others. In 1992, the Federal Reserve liberalized its regulations to permit banks and bank holding companies to broker funds that they also managed. Thus, banks could effectively engage in all aspects of mutual fund operations except sponsoring and distributing (underwriting) the shares directly.

Banks have moved relatively slowly into the mutual fund business and were not overly aggressive in lobbying the regulators to lower the barriers. Not until the substantial runoff of time deposits in search of higher yields when market interest rates declined sharply in the early 1990s did many banks awaken to the possibilities of offering money market and other mutual funds to their customers. Nevertheless, by 1992 more than 90 percent of all banks offered mutual funds in some way, more than double the proportion in 1985. Data on bank-managed and proprietary mutual funds since 1983 are presented in table 6. As late as 1987, banks managed less than 5 percent of all mutual fund assets, and by early 1993 this had increased to only 11 percent. Banks made much more substantial gains in money market funds, managing 23 percent of the assets of such funds in 1993, compared with only 6 percent of stock and bond mutual funds. When brokered private-label and other funds are included, banks sold more than one-third of the dollar volume of all mutual funds in the first half of 1992, nearly all of which were money market funds. The ten banking organizations that managed the largest amounts of mutual fund assets in 1993 are shown in table 7.

In recent years, some banks have tried to increase their participation in the mutual fund industry by acquiring large mutual fund investment companies or entering into exclusive joint agreements with them. In 1993, for example, Mellon Bank, the twelfth largest bank in the country, announced its intention to purchase the Dreyfus Funds, the third largest sponsor of money market funds and tenth largest sponsor of other mutual funds. At the same time, NationsBank entered into a partnership that gave Dean Witter Financial exclusive rights to market proprietary NationsBank funds as well as other funds to bank customers from locations in the bank's offices. On the other hand, Chemical Bank and Liberty Financial broke off their attempted joint venture.

TABLE 6
Bank-managed mutual funds: dollar amount, number of funds, and percent of industry (1983-93)

	Money market				Other funds				Total			
	Assets		Number		Assets		Number		Assets		Number	
	$[a]	%[b]	#	%[b]	$[a]	%[b]	#	%[b]	$[a]	%[b]	#	%[b]
1993	134	23.1	461	39.9	85	6.0	954	20.2	219	11.0	1,415	24.2
1992	111	19.4	382	36.0	47	4.6	502	14.7	158	9.9	884	19.9
1991	95	16.9	316	32.8	27	3.4	359	12.7	122	10.3	675	17.9
1990	67	13.1	256	33.1	13	2.4	271	11.4	80	7.9	527	16.7
1989	50	11.5	191	28.8	10	1.8	213	9.5	60	7.0	404	13.9
1988	38	11.3	154	26.2	6	1.3	166	8.0	44	5.4	320	12.0
1987	31	10.3	109	21.8	4	0.9	104	6.2	35	4.6	213	9.8
1986	28	10.1	80	19.0	4	0.9	65	4.9	32	4.5	145	8.3
1985	19	8.3	56	15.1	2	0.8	52	4.9	21	4.3	108	7.6
1984	17	7.8	48	15.4	1	0.7	39	4.7	18	5.0	87	7.6
1983	14	8.2	42	15.0	1	0.8	24	3.6	15	5.2	66	7.0

[a]Billion dollars.
[b]Percent of industry.
Source: Courtesy of Lipper Analytical Services.

Although the flow of funds data incorporate the assets of mutual funds managed by banks, they do not attribute those assets to the commercial banking sector. Rather, assets of all mutual funds, regardless of their managers, are listed under a separate mutual funds sector. Adding the data on bank-managed mutual funds from table 6 to banks' total assets for each of the eleven years for which data are available reduces the decline in banks' share of assets over the past decade by nearly 2 percentage points. Taking account of both trust department and bank-managed mutual fund assets would further reduce the downward bias in asset measures of banks' share of financial institutions' output over the past decade.

Unfortunately, because the trust asset data include a large but not precisely determinable portion of the assets of mutual funds managed by banks, the two sets of data cannot be simply added.

In addition to trust, securities, and mutual fund activities, banks also engage in a number of other activities either directly or through nonbank subsidiaries of their parent holding companies that are reported in the "Flow of funds accounts" as part of other financial industries. These subsidiaries include consumer and commercial finance companies, mortgage companies, and savings associations. For example, in September 1993, bank holding companies owned 154 thrift institutions with assets of $107 billion. Citicorp operated Citibank

TABLE 7
Banking organizations with largest managed mutual funds (1993)

	Assets		
Bank holding company	Money market	Other	Total
	(-------bilion dollars-------)		
PNC (Pittsburgh)	18.0	2.7	20.7
NationsBank (Charlotte)	8.3	5.5	13.7
BankAmerica (San Francisco)	11.8	1.1	12.9
Wells Fargo (San Francisco)	2.5	5.6	8.1
Banc One (Columbus)	3.3	4.1	7.4
Northern Trust (Chicago)	5.7	1.2	6.9
NBD (Detroit)	3.4	2.3	5.7
State Street (Boston)	3.3	1.8	5.1
Chase Manhattan (New York)	3.0	2.1	5.0
Norwest (Minneapolis)	3.9	0.8	4.7

Source: Yvette D. Kantrow, "Bank-managed funds grew by 34% in 1993," *American Banker*, February 9, 1994, p. 14.

TABLE 8
Nonbank assets held by large bank holding companies (1992)

Activity	Billion dollars	Percent
Securities brokerage and underwriting	77	36
Thrift institutions[a]	34	16
Mortgage banking	19	9
Commercial finance	16	8
Consumer finance	12	6
Leasing	6	3
Small business investment companies	4	2
Data processing	2	1
Insurance underwriting and insurance agency	2	1
Other nonbank	41	19
Total[b]	212	100

[a] Excludes institutions supervised by the Federal Deposit Insurance Corporation, such as state-chartered savings banks
[b] Columns may not total because of rounding.
Source: Board of Governors of the Federal Reserve System.

Savings, which is the eighth largest savings association in the country. Similarly, at year-end 1992, twelve of the fifty largest finance companies were owned by bank holding companies. These include CIT, the ninth largest company, which is owned by Dai-Ichi Kangyo Bank (Japan). The total assets of non-banking subsidiaries owned by reporting large bank holding companies (which are estimated to be roughly 95 percent of those of all bank holding companies) were $212 billion in 1992.[6] As table 8 shows, over one-third of these are in securities brokerage and underwriting subsidiaries. Despite their absolute importance, the nonbank assets of bank holding companies are dwarfed by the reported assets of banks. If the total assets of the nonbank subsidiaries of bank holding companies are added to reported bank assets, the market share of banks in 1992 increases only from 25.8 percent to 27.5 percent. But even after one adjusts reported assets for assets either owned by subsidiaries of bank holding companies or managed by banks but reported under other institutions in the "Flow of funds" data, there is still a growing volume of bank activities which are unrelated to either owning or managing assets but which generate income for banks, for example, lines of credit, letters of credit, and futures, options, and swaps.

Noninterest income

Although the growing importance of off-balance-sheet activities is not captured by traditional asset measures, it does show up in the growth of noninterest or fee income. While fee income has received much attention over the past two decades, it is not of recent origin or importance, as figure 5 indicates. When loan demand collapsed and interest rates fell to extremely low levels in the 1930s, commercial banks' ratio of fee income to interest income increased sharply. However, because of the steady rise in interest rates in the post-World War II era, the growing importance of fee income was obscured until the early 1980s.[7]

The trend towards an increase in fee income relative to interest income is present not only in the United States but in nearly all developed countries. The percentages of gross bank income derived from fees in fifteen major countries for selected years from 1980 to 1990 are shown in table 9. (Note that these data are

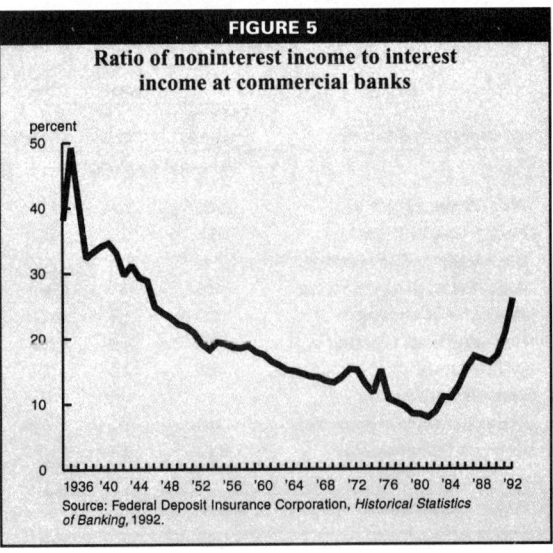

FIGURE 5
Ratio of noninterest income to interest income at commercial banks

Source: Federal Deposit Insurance Corporation, *Historical Statistics of Banking*, 1992.

TABLE 9
Fee income as a percent of gross income of banks, 15 major countries[a]
(1980-90)

Countries	1980-82	1984-86	1990
United States[b]	30.0	31.4	38.0
Japan[b,c]	20.4	24.6	35.9
Germany[b]	30.6	28.6	34.9
France[b]	14.6	15.3	24.9
Italy	26.0	30.3	26.8
United Kingdom[b]	28.5	36.9	41.1
Canada[c]	21.6[d]	23.7	31.0
Australia[c]	32.1	33.5	34.0
Belgium[c]	19.6	23.4	23.0
Finland	48.8	58.3	46.9
Netherlands	25.0	24.7	29.7
Norway	27.3	35.2	25.9
Spain[b]	15.7	18.1	22.3
Sweden	29.8	33.5	26.2
Switzerland	46.6	47.5	49.1

[a]Share of noninterest income in the gross income of commercial banks; the data are not fully comparable across countries.
[b]Large commercial banks.
[c]Fiscal years.
[d]1982.
Source: Bank for International Settlements, *Annual Report*, 1992, p. 196.

not fully comparable with the data for U.S. banks described above nor across countries.) In all countries except Finland, the importance of fee income increased during this period. Although fee income is relatively more important in the United States than in most other countries, it is considerably less important than in Switzerland or Finland and somewhat less important than in the United Kingdom.

The unbundling and securitization of financial services

The rise in fee income is in part a consequence of another phenomenon. The 1970s witnessed an acceleration of a trend that had been evident for some time, namely the "unbundling" of financial services. Unbundling is the separation of complex banking services, including such fundamental and traditional banking services as real estate and commercial lending, into their component steps or functions and the performance of some of those functions by separate entities. The oldest and most obvious example of unbundling was separating the origination and servicing of residential mortgage loans from the portfolio investment function through the sale of the mortgage from the originator to an institutional investor. Pioneered by mortgage companies decades before, this practice has since been adopted by banks and other mortgage lenders.

A major development in this unbundling was the introduction of the mortgage-backed security by the Federal Home Loan Mortgage Association and the Government National Mortgage Association. This was also the first step in the now familiar process of "securitization," the issuance of securities whose principal and interest payments reflect the behavior of a pool of underlying assets. The 1980s saw an enormous enlargement of the scope of securitization, which now encompasses automobile loans, credit card receivables, and other consumer credit, and is even making inroads into commercial loans, a type of asset that is much more difficult to securitize because of the greater heterogeneity of loan agreements and covenants. The banks receive fees for origination and possibly servicing but frequently do not hold the asset in their portfolios and thus do not receive interest revenue from it.

Sanford Rose, a former associate editor of the *American Banker*, argued vigorously in the early 1980s that costly regulation, inadequate compensation for lending risks, and the futility of trying to outguess the market regarding increasingly volatile interest rate movements were bringing about a fundamental transformation of the banking environment (Rose 1981). He asserted that the most prudent strategy for banks was to reduce their emphasis on portfolio investment, hedge or sell off their interest rate risk, and rely on origination and servicing fees to provide the bulk of their earnings. Indeed, he argued that mortgage companies, which have long operated in this manner, were the model for the financial firm of the future. In the years since this analysis appeared, commercial banking organizations have come more and more to resemble Rose's vision: They originate a large volume of loans—although even here they have lost ground to other institutions—and sell off a growing proportion of them. They also use their financial expertise, reputation, and capital to provide guarantees of financial performance, mostly in the form of standby letters of credit, but increasingly encompassing a growing variety of new and exotic instruments.

The Boyd-Gertler approach

Two somewhat different approaches to the adjustment of bank assets for off-balance-sheet activities were recently presented by Boyd and Gertler (1994). Both involved developing estimates of the asset equivalents of bank off-balance-sheet and fee-for-service activities. The first approach adjusted for loan commitments and letters of credit, two of the most important types of off-balance-sheet guarantees offered by banks, using the risk weights developed in the Basel risk-weighted capital standards. These weights were used to calculate the level of assets that would represent the same risk exposure to the bank as the off-balance-sheet activities. These asset equivalents were then added to each institution's on-balance-sheet assets to obtain a more complete asset measure of banks' market share. The shortcoming of this approach is that it takes account only of loan commitments and letters of credit and omits such important activities as trust services and mutual funds.

Boyd and Gertler's second procedure was to convert all noninterest income—from loan servicing, asset management, and other services (including trust and securities activities), as well as off-balance-sheet guarantees—into a balance sheet equivalent. Using net interest income (interest income less interest expense and loan losses) as a measure of the return from on-balance-sheet assets, and assuming that the same rate of return is earned in off-balance-sheet activities, the authors capitalized fee income at that rate to generate "imaginary" asset equivalents. They then added the asset equivalents of the noninterest income to on-balance-sheet assets to obtain a more comprehensive measure of bank output for the years since 1971. When they did so, virtually all evidence of a downward trend in banks' share of financial institutions' assets over the period 1957-1990 disappeared, although there was some decline from the 1974 peak. Commercial banks' share of the assets of all financial institutions, both unadjusted and as adjusted by

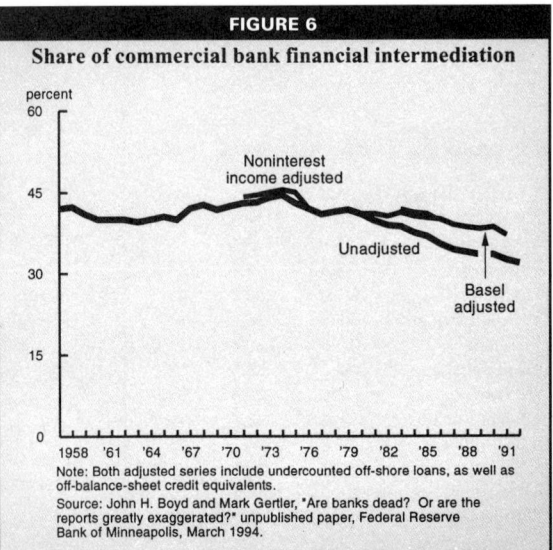

FIGURE 6
Share of commercial bank financial intermediation

Note: Both adjusted series include undercounted off-shore loans, as well as off-balance-sheet credit equivalents.
Source: John H. Boyd and Mark Gertler, "Are banks dead? Or are the reports greatly exaggerated?" unpublished paper, Federal Reserve Bank of Minneapolis, March 1994.

Boyd and Gertler's two alternative methods, is shown in figure 6.

Summary of asset measures

This section has described a number of approaches to adjusting data on bank assets to take account either of assets that are managed by the bank but do not show up on its accounting balance sheet or of activities that are done for a fee and are not associated with assets either owned or managed by the bank. One of the problems with trying to "fix" banks' balance sheets is that the problems associated with them are not limited to banking. For example, life insurance companies also engage in a large volume of off-balance-sheet activities. Thus, to obtain a meaningful measure of banks' relative importance in the financial system, it would be necessary to perform similar adjustments on the balance sheets of other financial industries. Together with the conceptual shortcomings of assets as a measure of output—that is, it is a stock rather than a flow measure, and different levels of output may be associated with the same value of assets of different kinds—this suggests the desirability of also looking at alternative measures of the relative size of the banking industry.

Employment

A second measure of banking's size or importance is the number of employees in the industry. For some purposes, employment may be the most relevant and useful measure. This is most obviously true in regard to the industry's impact on the economy of a particular city or region. However, because employment is a measure of input rather than output, it is much less appropriate as a measure of the size or competitiveness of an industry relative to other industries producing similar products or services. Moreover, employment does not adjust for differences in productivity between sectors of the economy or changes in productivity over time. Nevertheless, it may serve as a useful check on the accuracy of other measures.

As figure 7 indicates, between 1934 and 1977, employment in the commercial banking industry more than kept pace with that in the entire financial, insurance, and real estate sector. Thereafter it declined by roughly one-fourth through 1992. As a percentage of total employment in the private nonfarm economy, employment in commercial banking continued to rise through 1983, when it peaked at 1.67 percent. Since then, that number has fallen as well. The absolute level of employment in the industry continued to rise through 1986, peaking at 1.56 million. By 1992, it had fallen to 1.48 million.

The decline in employment in the banking industry in recent years is not surprising given the large number of bank closings and consolidations in the 1980s and the acceleration of consolidation in the early 1990s. However, the rise over the preceding decades suggests two possibilities: either commercial bank productivity was falling continuously over that period, as the declining ratio of bank assets to employment would suggest,[8] or total assets is an inadequate measure of financial institution output. Although a decline in the productivity of banking extending over five decades cannot be dismissed as a logical possibility, it seems inconsistent with the increased use of computers and other advanced technology by banks and with the continued rise of productivity in the economy as a whole. Moreover, the great expansion of off-balance-sheet activities in banking described in detail in the preceding sections casts further doubt on the hypothesis

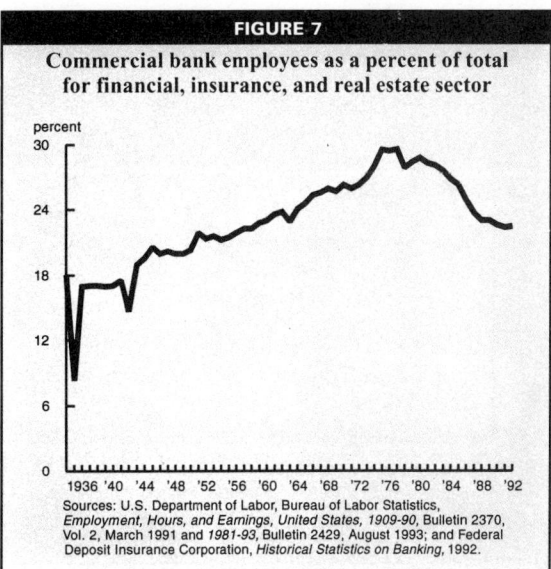

FIGURE 7
Commercial bank employees as a percent of total for financial, insurance, and real estate sector

Sources: U.S. Department of Labor, Bureau of Labor Statistics, *Employment, Hours, and Earnings, United States, 1909-90*, Bulletin 2370, Vol. 2, March 1991 and *1981-93*, Bulletin 2429, August 1993; and Federal Deposit Insurance Corporation, *Historical Statistics on Banking*, 1992.

that productivity in banking has declined over any extended period in recent years.

Revenues, earnings, and value added

A third set of measures of the importance of banking is based on revenue and earnings data that reflect the full range of services offered. Such measures have the advantage of being flow rather than stock measures of output. Indeed, in most industries, market share is typically measured by revenues, sales, or value added rather than assets. These measures are also used by the Department of Justice in antitrust actions. Revenue and value added measures are available for banks and other depository institutions from data reported to the bank regulatory agencies in their periodic *Reports of Income and Dividends* or from data reported on a regular basis to the Internal Revenue Service (IRS). Virtually since the IRS was established in 1916, it has published annual compilations of income and expenses of corporations and individuals. For the earliest years, these reports were based on the universe of federal income tax returns; more recently, they have been based on a sample. The advantage of the IRS data is that they can be obtained on a relatively uniform basis for all categories of financial institutions.

A measure of the size of the banking industry based on IRS data that takes account of both lending and off-balance-sheet activities is

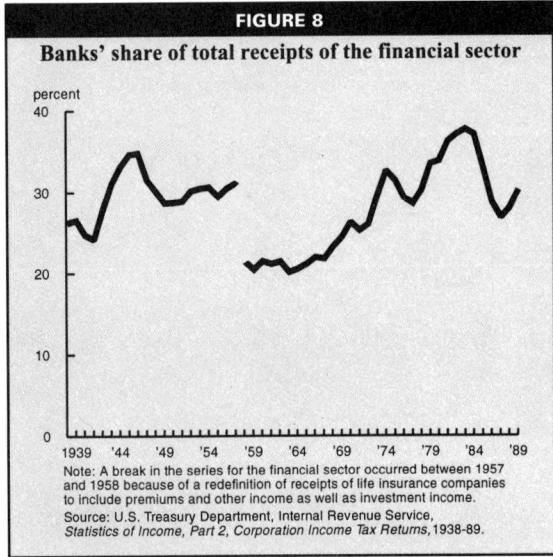

FIGURE 8
Banks' share of total receipts of the financial sector

Note: A break in the series for the financial sector occurred between 1957 and 1958 because of a redefinition of receipts of life insurance companies to include premiums and other income as well as investment income.
Source: U.S. Treasury Department, Internal Revenue Service, Statistics of Income, Part 2, Corporation Income Tax Returns, 1938-89.

simply total receipts or revenues. Figure 8 shows the ratio of total receipts for banks to those for the entire financial sector, including insurance, for the years 1938-82. Unfortunately, this measure is strongly influenced by movements in the general level of interest rates, and its volatility tends to obscure the basic trend in the data. Moreover, as was suggested in the earlier discussion of the conceptual problems in measuring the importance of banking in the financial services industry, there is much to be said for using a measure of value added—the value of the products sold by an industry less the value of intermediate goods and raw materials purchased by it.

The IRS data permit the calculation of commercial banks' share of a variable that closely approximates a measure of value added for total financial institutions proposed by Donald Hodgman (see box). This is the difference between total receipts, including interest received, and interest paid. The netting of interest received and paid greatly reduces but does not eliminate the enormous variation in bank revenues stemming from changes in the level of market interest rates. Unfortunately, because of changes in definitions and reporting categories and the amount of detailed information published by the IRS, the measure is available only from 1938 on.

As figure 9 shows, this measure of commercial banks' share of the total output of the financial sector gives a considerably different picture than reported asset measures. Rather than declining monotonically over the entire period like the asset measure, it averages around 25 percent in the late 1930s, rises to the low 30 percent range in the 1940s and early 1950s, declines to just over 15 percent in the 1960s, rises above 20 percent in the mid-1970s and again in the early 1980s, and declines to about 16 or 17 percent by the late 1980s. There was clearly a decline in the banking industry's share of the output of all financial institutions through the mid-1960s, although the greater part of the apparent sharp decline between 1957 and 1958 was spurious, reflecting a change in the reporting of revenues of life insurance companies. However, there has been no obvious trend since then.[9]

Relative to the entire economy, the output of both banks and the entire financial sector has increased over the past half-century. As

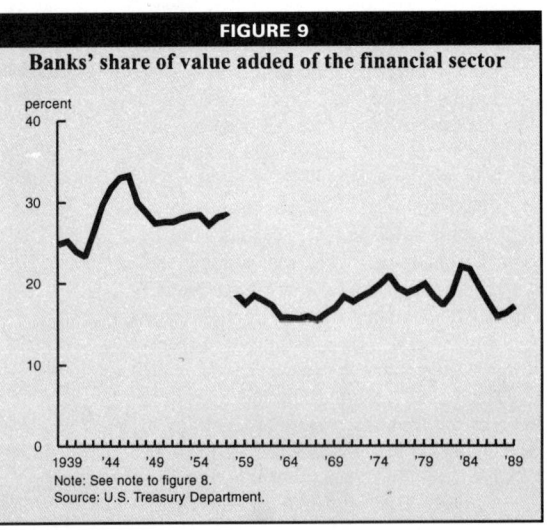

FIGURE 9
Banks' share of value added of the financial sector

Note: See note to figure 8.
Source: U.S. Treasury Department.

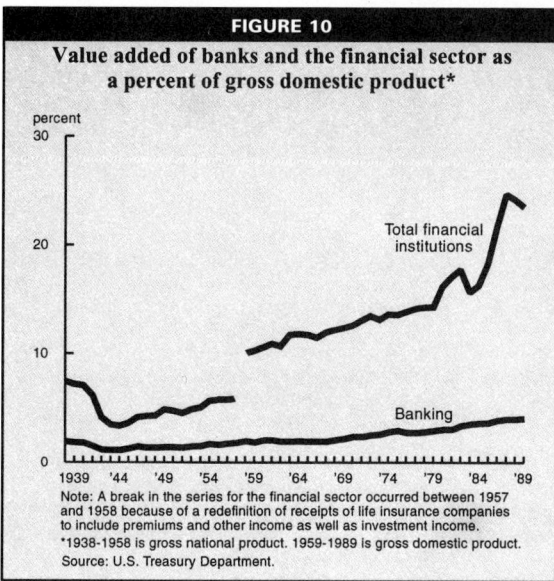

FIGURE 10
Value added of banks and the financial sector as a percent of gross domestic product*

Note: A break in the series for the financial sector occurred between 1957 and 1958 because of a redefinition of receipts of life insurance companies to include premiums and other income as well as investment income.
*1938-1958 is gross national product. 1959-1989 is gross domestic product.
Source: U.S. Treasury Department.

figure 10 shows, the value added of the financial sector as a proportion of GDP rose from 7.5 percent in 1938 to 23.5 percent in 1989, while that for commercial banks increased from 1.9 percent to 4.0 percent.

Conclusion

Is banking a declining industry? There is a widespread perception that the size of the commercial banking industry relative to that of all financial institutions in the United States has been declining rapidly in recent years. Restrictive regulations imposed primarily in earlier years when banking was relatively more important are often blamed as contributing to the decline. Most of the evidence for the belief that banking is declining consists of data on commercial banks' share of reported assets or of specific categories of assets, such as commercial loans. Similar results obtain for banks in countries with greatly different regulatory environments, such as the United Kingdom. However, when one analyzes other measures of the size of the banking industry, such as employment, revenues, and value added, the same conclusion does not always emerge. In part, this is because the nature of bank activities has changed drastically over the past several decades and many of the newer activities are not reflected in balance sheet assets. When asset figures are adjusted to incorporate some measure of the new activities, they show either no decline or a much attenuated rate of decline for banking in recent years.

In summary, the evidence does not clearly support the widespread perception that banking has declined, either absolutely or relative to the financial services industry or the entire economy, since the early 1960s. Nonetheless, this conclusion is consistent with the belief that banking has not grown as rapidly as it might have if banks had not been constrained from providing new products quickly in response to changes in market conditions. Unfortunately, we do not know how rapidly banking would have grown under alternative regulatory regimes, or what the social costs and benefits of those alternatives would have been. Nor do our measures of the relative size of the banking industry shed light on whether the regulations, by preventing individual banks from expanding or opening branches across state boundaries, have restricted the efficiency of banks and thereby increased the cost of banking to consumers. Those, however, are the types of questions that need to be answered in order to improve public policy towards banking.

FOOTNOTES

[1] It has been argued that a major decline in the size of the banking industry, regardless of its cause, would create problems for the implementation and effectiveness of monetary policy. This article does not attempt to address this issue.

[2] The National Bureau of Economic Research has sponsored a number of conferences on this and related issues (National Bureau of Economic Research 1961, 1969).

[3] Board of Governors of the Federal Reserve System, "Flow of funds accounts."

[4] A recent book by Robert E. Litan (1987) also presents data for 1835 (figure 2.2, p. 18). These data were obtained from a Census publication (U.S. Bureau of the Census 1975).

[5] The major difference between an agent and a trustee is that in an agency relationship the principal (customer) retains legal title to the assets, whereas in a trust relationship, legal title passes to the fiduciary. In addition, a trust relationship will involve more duties and responsibilities on the part of the fiduciary even in the absence of specific written authority and, unlike an agency relationship, which terminates on the death of the principal, may continue beyond the death of the grantor of the trust.

[6] The data on nonbank subsidiaries of bank holding companies reported here were obtained from the FR-Y11Q and FR-Y11AS reports, which are filed with the Federal Reserve by all bank holding companies with consolidated assets of more than $1 billion and by those with assets of more than $150 million that have nonbank activities exceeding specified levels. These figures are larger than reported in table 8 because they include FDIC-supervised savings banks that are excluded from the data used to construct the table.

[7] In the early 1960s, many of the larger banks sought to increase the variety and volume of services that they offered on a fee-for-service basis. A series of favorable rulings by then Comptroller of the Currency James Saxon encouraged national banks in their efforts to expand their activities. The services that they, or subsidiaries of their bank holding companies, began to offer included such relatively minor extensions of existing activities as providing investment advice, payroll accounting, data processing, armored car and courier services, and insurance agency services. Because the courts eventually disallowed many of these activities as violating the National Banking Act, the Banking Act of 1933 (Glass-Steagall Act), or the Bank Holding Company Act, the activities did not contribute greatly to banks' fee income.

[8] Bert Ely of Ely Associates, Inc., a financial institutions consulting firm, has argued that, largely as a consequence of regulatory constraints, the efficiency of the entire financial system has declined and that many widely heralded "innovations" in finance represent nothing more than "regulatory arbitrage" (Ely 1992).

[9] This result accords with that of Boyd and Gertler (1994), who also presented data on value added. They found a slight upward trend in the share of value added of bank-related industries relative to that for the entire finance, insurance, and real estate sector over the period 1947 to 1990. However, their "bank-related industries" category contained all depository institutions.

REFERENCES

Bank for International Settlements, *Annual Report*, 1992.

Barth, James R., R. Dan Brumbaugh, Jr., and Robert E. Litan, *The Future of American Banking*, Armonk, NY: M. E. Sharpe, Inc., 1992.

Bell, Frederick W., and Neil B. Murphy, *Costs in Commercial Banking: A Quantitative Analysis of Bank Behavior and its Relation to Bank Regulation*, Federal Reserve Bank of Boston, Research Report No. 41, April 1968.

Benston, George J., "Economies of scale and marginal costs in banking operations," *National Banking Review*, Vol. 2, June 1965, pp. 507-49.

Benston, George J., Gerald A. Hanweck, and David B. Humphrey, "Scale economies in banking: a restructuring and reassessment," *Journal of Money, Credit, and Banking*, Vol. 14, November 1982, pp. 435-56.

Board of Governors of the Federal Reserve System, *Balance Sheets for the U.S. Economy, 1945-92*, March 10, 1993.

_____, "Flow of funds accounts," Washington: Board of Governors, 1952-93.

Boyd, John H., and Mark Gertler, "Are banks dead? Or are the reports greatly exaggerated?" unpublished paper, Federal Reserve Bank of Minneapolis, March 1994.

Ely, Bert, "Commercial banks are not obsolete and the federal government should stop trying to make them so," *Credit Markets in Transition*, Proceedings of a Conference on Bank Structure and Competition, Chicago: Federal Reserve Bank of Chicago, 1992, pp. 356-90.

Federal Deposit Insurance Corporation, *Historical Statistics on Banking*, 1992.

Federal Financial Institutions Examination Council, *Trust Assets of Financial Institutions*, various years.

Federal Reserve Bank of Chicago, *FDICIA: An Appraisal*, Chicago: Federal Reserve Bank of Chicago, 1993.

Fischer, Thomas G., William H. Gram, George G. Kaufman, and Larry R. Mote, "The securities activities of commercial banks," *Tennessee Law Review*, Vol. 51, Spring 1984, pp. 467-518.

Goldsmith, Raymond W., *Financial Intermediaries in the American Economy since 1900*, a study by the National Bureau of Economic Research, Princeton, NJ: Princeton University Press, 1958.

_____, *Financial Structure and Development,* Studies in Comparative Economics, New Haven, CT: Yale University Press, 1969.

Greenbaum, Stuart I., "A study of bank costs," *National Banking Review*, Vol. 4, June 1967, pp. 415-34.

Gurley, John G., and Edward S. Shaw, "Financial aspects of economic development," *American Economic Review*, Vol. 45, September 1955, pp. 515-38.

_____, "Financial intermediaries and the saving-investment process," *Journal of Finance*, Vol. 11, May 1956, pp. 257-76.

_____, *Money in a Theory of Finance*, Washington, DC: Brookings Institution, 1960.

Hodgman, Donald R., "Discussion," *Production and Productivity in the Service Industries*, National Bureau of Economic Research Studies in Income and Wealth, Vol. 34, New York: Columbia University Press, 1969, pp. 189-95.

Humphrey, David B., "Flow versus stock indicators of banking output: effects on productivity and scale economy measurement," *Journal of Financial Services Research*, Vol. 6, August 1992, pp. 115-35.

Kantrow, Yvette D., "Bank-managed funds grew by 34% in 1993," *American Banker*, February 9, 1994, pp. 1, 14-16.

Kaufman, George G., and Larry R. Mote, "Glass-Steagall: repeal by regulatory and judicial reinterpretation," *Banking Law Journal*, Vol. 107, September/October 1990, pp. 388-421.

Litan, Robert E., *What Should Banks Do?* Washington, DC: The Brookings Institution, 1987.

National Bureau of Economic Research, *Output, Input and Productivity Measurement,* Studies in Income and Wealth, John W. Kendrick (ed.), Vol. 25, Princeton, NJ: Princeton University Press, 1961.

_____, *Production and Productivity in the Service Industries,* Studies in Income and Wealth, Victor R. Fuchs (ed.), Vol. 34, New York: Columbia University Press, 1969.

Powers, John A., "Branch versus unit banking: bank output and cost economies," *Southern Economic Journal*, Vol. 36, October 1969, pp. 153-64.

Robertson, Ross M., *The Comptroller and Bank Supervision*, Washington, DC: Office of the Comptroller of the Currency, 1968.

Rose, Harold, "The changing world of finance and its problems," working paper no. 167-93, Institute of Finance and Accounting, London Business School, 1993.

Rose, Sanford, "'De-intermediation': a word for the '80s," *The Future of the Financial Services Industry*, Proceedings of a conference, Atlanta: Federal Reserve Bank of Atlanta, 1981, pp. 157-64.

U.S. Bureau of the Census, *Historical Statistics of the United States, Colonial Times to 1970*, Part 2, Washington, DC: U.S. Government Printing Office, 1975.

U.S. Department of Labor, Bureau of Labor Statistics, *Employment, Hours, and Earnings, United States, 1909-90,* Bulletin 2370, Vol. 2, March 1991, and *1981-93,* Bulletin 2429, August 1993.

U.S. Treasury Department, Internal Revenue Service, *Statistics of Income, Part 2, Corporation Income Tax Returns,* annual, 1938-89.

Article 2

Interstate Banking: A Status Report

Donald T. Savage, of the Board's Division of Research and Statistics, prepared this article.

In the late 1980s, about a decade after Maine became the first state to permit some form of interstate banking, thirty states had interstate bank holding company laws in effect and another seven had enacted laws that had not yet taken effect. Fifty-one multistate bank holding companies were in operation, but only 6 percent of domestic commercial banking assets were held by banks owned by out-of-state bank holding companies.[1]

The picture has changed considerably over the past several years. All states except Hawaii now have interstate bank holding company laws in effect, and several states have interstate branch banking laws. The number of multistate bank holding companies has risen to 178 (as of June 30, 1993), and the share of domestic commercial banking assets held by out-of-state organizations has increased to 21.3 percent (as of December 31, 1992).

This article reports on the status of interstate banking laws, discusses the issues involved in the choice between interstate bank holding companies and interstate branch banking as alternative means of geographic expansion, provides some data on interstate banking organizations, and reviews the effect of interstate banking on bank concentration.

HISTORICAL BACKGROUND

Before 1956, federal laws and regulations did not prohibit bank holding companies from owning subsidiary banks in more than one state, although both federal and state laws did prohibit banks from establishing branches across state lines. Despite the lack of statutory barriers to the expansion of bank holding companies across state lines, only nineteen multistate bank holding companies were operating in 1956.

The Bank Holding Company Act of 1956 introduced barriers to the interstate expansion of bank holding companies. The Douglas Amendment to the bill, introduced in floor debate, prohibits a holding company from acquiring a bank outside its home state unless the acquisition is specifically permitted by the statutes of the home state of the bank to be acquired. In 1956, no state had a statute permitting bank acquisitions by out-of-state holding companies; therefore, no new multistate organizations could be formed.

Although it effectively prohibited new interstate banking organizations, the Bank Holding Company Act of 1956 did provide grandfather rights for the nineteen existing multistate companies. Most of the grandfathered companies were quite small; the four largest together held 86 percent of the total deposits of the nineteen.

The 1956 act regulated only holding companies that owned more than one bank. The smaller multibank, multistate companies chose to reorganize and give up their grandfathered rights to operate in more than one state so as to avoid the new federal regulations being applied to multibank holding companies. Over time, the number of grandfathered multistate bank holding companies decreased to seven.

The states' option to allow bank acquisitions by out-of-state holding companies, provided by the Douglas Amendment, went unused until 1975. In that year, a general revision of the Maine state banking code made it possible for out-of-state bank holding companies, beginning in 1978, to acquire Maine banks. The Maine legislation was motivated in large measure by a desire to attract new investment capital to the state. The law initially required reciprocity: Bank holding companies headquartered in another state, Massachusetts, for example, could acquire Maine banks only if bank holding companies headquartered in Maine were allowed

---

[1]. The early stages of interstate banking were described in Donald T. Savage, "Interstate Banking Developments," *Federal Reserve Bulletin*, vol. 73 (February 1987), pp. 79–92.

to acquire Massachusetts banks. Because of this reciprocity requirement, no acquisitions of Maine banks were possible until another state enacted a statute allowing the acquisition of its banks by Maine bank holding companies.

Other interstate banking statutes began appearing in the early 1980s, with Alaska, Massachusetts, and New York passing laws that became effective in 1982. Since then, all the remaining states except Hawaii have enacted some form of interstate bank holding company law.

Despite congressional consideration of various changes in federal laws, the movement to interstate bank holding companies has largely been a product of state action. However, after several unsuccessful attempts to pass such legislation, the Garn–St Germain Depository Institutions Act of 1982 amended the Bank Holding Company Act of 1956 to allow for the interstate acquisition of large failed banks, regardless of state laws. This provision had been sought, especially by the federal bank regulatory agencies, for many years. Its purpose was not to promote interstate banking, but rather to increase the number of firms that would be eligible to acquire a large failed bank. In many states, the argument went, there would be few potential buyers if one of the state's largest banks were to fail; expanding the number of potential purchasers would, supporters contended, lower the cost of resolving the failure.

In February 1991, the U.S. Department of the Treasury, as required by the Financial Institutions Reform, Recovery and Enforcement Act of 1989, produced a report to the Congress on reforming and strengthening the banking system. The report, *Modernizing the Financial System: Recommendations for Safer, More Competitive Banks*, recommended that three years after enactment of enabling legislation, bank holding companies be allowed to acquire banks in all states, regardless of state laws. Further, the report recommended that national banks immediately be allowed to branch into those states in which their parent holding company could acquire a bank. The report also recommended that state banks be given any necessary federal permission to branch across state lines, and that the states retain control over branching within states. Although many of the other proposals made in the report were included in the Federal Deposit Insurance Corporation Improvement Act of 1991, that act contained no provisions for the deregulation of geographic expansion by banks and bank holding companies.

Although the Congress has not made any major changes in the federal statutes regarding branching or bank holding company expansion since 1956, the issue continues to be under active consideration. John P. LaWare, member of the Board of Governors of the Federal Reserve System, has in recent months presented the Board's views on various aspects of several interstate banking bills before committees of both the U.S. Senate and the U.S. House of Representatives.[2]

THE INTERSTATE BANK HOLDING COMPANY LAWS

The interstate bank holding company laws enacted by the states and the District of Columbia since 1975 differ in several respects. The states' reasons for passing the laws also vary.

The Forces of Change

Why did so many states decide to permit entry by out-of-state bank holding companies, especially considering that some of them still restricted in-state branching and bank holding company expansion? The events leading to passage of the legislation in each state probably were unique to that state. Several factors that may have played a role in changing the opinions of bankers and state legislators are identified below, but undoubtedly the list is not exhaustive.

• In some states, legislators believed that interstate banking would lead to an inflow of investment capital.

• Large banks in major financial centers wanted to expand geographically, but the states they wanted to expand into required reciprocity; the

---

2. Statements before the Subcommittee on Financial Institutions Supervision, Regulation and Deposit Insurance of the Committee on Banking, Finance and Urban Affairs, U.S. House of Representatives, June 22, 1993, *Federal Reserve Bulletin*, vol. 79 (August 1993), pp. 772–77; and before the Committee on Banking, Housing and Urban Affairs, U.S. Senate, October 5, 1993, appearing on pp. 1093–97 of this issue.

changes in their home state laws accommodated the wishes of the large banks. Elsewhere, the views of large banks, which traditionally favored geographic expansion, came to outweigh the views of smaller banks, which traditionally opposed expansion.

• Many bankers, especially at medium-sized, regional banks, believed that their banks could survive and attain competitive operating cost levels only by growing larger. Wanting to enhance their banks' ability to compete, some states decided to allow interstate banking.

• Interstate activity allows expansion into markets that may be considered more attractive than markets within a bank's home state. Funds may be less expensive than in the home state, or the investment opportunities may promise higher yields at lower risk or offer portfolio diversification. Many banks wanted the right to explore these opportunities.

• Many banks wanted to be able to establish offices throughout a market area made up of parts of two or more states. Some wanted to follow their customers to suburbs in adjacent states or to their homes in popular retirement states.

• Some banking organizations may have argued for interstate banking because they expected to be acquired. For a bank that expects to be acquired in a consolidation of the industry, there is an advantage to increasing the number of potential purchasers.

• In some states, imitation and "level playing field" effects played a role as bankers argued that to be competitive with banks in neighboring states, they too had to have interstate banking rights.

• The views of some opponents of change were countered by the argument that large out-of-state companies would not enter the smaller local banking markets served by many of the small banks, but instead would be competitors for the state's large banks. In addition, some smaller banks thought the out-of-state bankers would not know the local market and would not be able to compete as effectively as the banks that were being acquired.

• Everyone in the industry increasingly recognized that interstate banking was occurring despite laws prohibiting it. The proliferation of loan production offices, nonbank subsidiaries of bank holding companies, nonbank banks, and interstate thrift institutions, the widespread use of credit cards, and the provision of financial services by nonfinancial firms not subject to geographic limitations all made the traditional restrictions on the geographic expansion of banks more difficult to explain and justify. If so many financial services could be provided across state lines by these various means, why shouldn't deposit-taking institutions be allowed to expand as well?

• Finally, many in the industry came to believe that interstate banking was inevitable, and that the banks in their states should be permitted to participate in the evolution to a new financial structure, lest they be left behind.

Characteristics of the Laws

Provisions of the interstate banking laws of forty-nine states and the District of Columbia are listed in table 1. Thirty-four states now allow acquisition of banks in their state by holding companies headquartered in any other state. Many of these thirty-four states at first allowed acquisition by holding companies headquartered in only a limited number of states; later, either on a predetermined "trigger" date or by subsequent legislation, they began to allow entry from all other states.

Twenty-one of the thirty-four states that allow entry from all other states require reciprocal entry rights for bank holding companies headquartered in their state. For example, New York has a nationwide reciprocal interstate banking law; a bank holding company headquartered in any other state can acquire banks in New York if its home state allows acquisition of that state's banks by New York bank holding companies. Because not all states allow entry by New York holding companies, not all holding companies can enter New York. The thirteen states whose interstate banking laws do not require reciprocity can be entered by bank holding companies headquartered in any other state, regardless of the law of the home state of the entering holding company.

Fifteen states and the District of Columbia allow entry only by bank holding companies headquartered in selected states within a region. Currently defined regions range from areas as small as the six adjacent states to areas as large as sixteen states and the District of Columbia. All the states that

1. State legislation on interstate bank holding companies, November 1, 1993[1]

State	Area covered and reciprocity requirement	State	Area covered and reciprocity requirement
Alabama	Reciprocal, 13 states (AR, FL, GA, KY, LA, MD, MS, NC, SC, TN, TX, VA, WV) and DC	Missouri	Reciprocal, 8 states (AR, IA, IL, KS, KY, NE, OK, TN)
Alaska	National, no reciprocity	Montana	Reciprocal, 7 states (CO, ID, MN, ND, SD, WI, WY)
Arizona	National, no reciprocity	Nebraska	National, reciprocal
Arkansas	Reciprocal, 16 states (AL, FL, GA, KS, LA, MD, MO, MS, NC, NE, OK, SC, TN, TX, VA, WV) and DC	Nevada	National, no reciprocity
		New Hampshire	National, no reciprocity
California	National, reciprocal	New Jersey	National, reciprocal
Colorado	National, no reciprocity	New Mexico	National, no reciprocity
Connecticut	National, reciprocal	New York	National, reciprocal
Delaware	National, reciprocal	North Carolina[2]	Reciprocal, 13 states (AL, AR, FL, GA, KY, LA, MD, MS, SC, TN, TX, VA, WV) and DC
District of Columbia	Reciprocal, 11 states (AL, FL, GA, LA, MD, MS, NC, SC, TN, VA, WV)	North Dakota	National, reciprocal
		Ohio	National, reciprocal
Florida	Reciprocal, 11 states (AL, AR, GA, LA, MD, MS, NC, SC, TN, VA, WV) and DC	Oklahoma	National, no reciprocity for initital entry; after initial entry, bank holding company must be from state offering reciprocity or wait 4 years to expand
Georgia	Reciprocal, 10 states (AL, FL, KY, LA, MD, MS, NC, SC, TN, VA) and DC		
Idaho	National, no reciprocity	Oregon	National, no reciprocity
Illinois	National, reciprocal	Pennsylvania	National, reciprocal
Indiana	National, reciprocal	Rhode Island	National, reciprocal
Iowa	Reciprocal, 6 states (IL, MN, MO, NE, SD, WI)	South Carolina	Reciprocal, 12 states (AL, AR, FL, GA, KY, LA, MD, MS, NC, TN, VA, WV) and DC
Kansas	Reciprocal, 6 states (AR, CO, IA, MO, NE, OK)		
Kentucky	National, reciprocal	South Dakota	National, reciprocal
Louisiana	National, reciprocal	Tennessee	National, reciprocal
Maine	National, no reciprocity	Texas	National, no reciprocity
Maryland	Reciprocal, 14 states (AL, AR, DE, FL, GA, KY, LA, MS, NC, PA, SC, TN, VA, WV) and DC	Utah	National, no reciprocity
		Vermont	National, reciprocal
		Virginia	Reciprocal, 12 states (AL, AR, FL, GA, KY, LA, MD, MS, NC, SC, TN, WV) and DC
Massachusetts	National, reciprocal		
Michigan	National, reciprocal	Washington	National, reciprocal
Minnesota	Reciprocal, 16 states (CO, IA, ID, IL, IN, KS, MI, MO, MT, ND, NE, OH, SD, WA, WI, WY)	West Virginia	National, reciprocal
		Wisconsin	Reciprocal, 8 states (IA, IL, IN, KY, MI, MN, MO, OH)
Mississippi	Reciprocal, 13 states (AL, AR, FL, GA, KY, LA, MO, NC, SC, TN, TX, VA, WV)	Wyoming	National, no reciprocity

1. Not listed in the table is Hawaii, which has not enacted interstate bank holding company legislation.
2. On July 1, 1996, will become national, reciprocal.

SOURCE. Financial Structure Section, Division of Research and Statistics, Board of Governors of the Federal Reserve System.

allow entry only by bank holding companies headquartered in a limited region require reciprocity for their bank holding companies.

Although regions such as New England and the southeast were initially thought of as interstate compact areas, states in these regions did not develop formal compacts or treaties among themselves. Instead, each state defined its region as it thought best. Today, only states in the southeast are a somewhat cohesive unit, generally allowing entry from the other states in the region and generally excluding entry from states outside the region.

Even within the southeast, however, the states differ in their definition of "region." For example, some of the states include Texas and Arkansas in their region, but others do not. Also, some states permit a holding company headquartered in their region to enter only if a certain high percentage of the holding company's deposits (in most cases, 80 percent) are in banks in states in the region. With such a restriction, a state is able to prevent entry by bank holding companies that are headquartered in its region but have more than a minor part of their operations in states outside the region.

As the states have crafted their legislation, they have placed a variety of other conditions on interstate banking activity.

• Many states restrict de novo entry. Out-of-state bank holding companies may not enter these states by forming a new bank, but must acquire a bank that has been in existence for a certain period, typically between three and six years. Although few large bank holding companies have chosen to enter new markets within their home state by forming a de novo bank, a desire to protect the franchise value of existing bank charters has prompted many states to erect barriers to the formation of new banks by out-of-state holding companies.

• Eighteen states place a cap on the share of state deposits that may be controlled by any single banking organization (in most states, the cap applies to in-state as well as out-of-state organizations). These restrictions were prompted by the arguments of many opponents of interstate banking that the entering out-of-state bank holding company would have major operating advantages over local banking organizations or would use unfair tactics to acquire an overwhelming share of the state's deposits.

The cap on the share of state deposits that may be held by any one organization ranges from as low as 10 percent in Iowa to as high as 30 percent in Minnesota. The base against which the cap is measured also differs among states: In some states the cap is stated as a percentage of deposits at banks, but in other states the base includes deposits at thrift institutions and credit unions as well as banks.

- Some states promote specific forms of economic activity. For example, Delaware encourages holding companies from other states to establish banks in that state for the purpose of issuing credit cards and processing credit card transactions. Many of these special-purpose banks concentrate on their defined purpose and do not compete generally with local banks.
- A few states allow individual banks to "opt out" of the interstate banking provisions, making them ineligible for acquisition by an out-of-state organization. In some cases, banks choosing to avoid acquisition in this way are themselves not allowed to acquire banks in other states.
- Some states differentiate between out-of-state bank holding companies and foreign banking organizations. Foreign ownership of a full-service, state-chartered commercial bank is prohibited in a number of states. Other states require that a certain percentage of the directors of a bank must be citizens of the United States or impose requirements on foreign banks that are not applied to banks chartered in the United States.

Although not all states allow nationwide entry yet, the laws have become more permissive over time. As more states allow entry from all states, bank holding company expansion opportunities increase. Treating each pair of states (and the District of Columbia) as a combination results in 2,550 possible two-state combinations (for example, Alabama entry into Alaska is one combination, and Alaska entry into Alabama is a second). At this time, entry is permitted in 1,570 (62 percent) of the 2,550 possible instances. The percentage would increase significantly if the states in the southeast region were to allow nationwide entry. In mid-1993, North Carolina established a mid-1996 date for allowing nationwide entry; whether this change will lead to similar action by other southeastern states and to a breaking down of the regional system is uncertain.

THE INTERSTATE BRANCHING LAWS

The likely final step in the geographic expansion of banking will be interstate branch banking. Historically, both the federal government and the states have prohibited interstate branch banking. However, eight states have enacted laws that permit some degree of interstate branching for state nonmember banks (state-chartered banks that are not members of the Federal Reserve System) (table 2). The main reason the interstate branching laws have been enacted is a belief among bankers that interstate branch banks could provide bank services at a lower cost than interstate bank holding companies.

The process of deregulating interstate branch banking will be different from that for interstate bank holding companies. The Douglas Amendment provided the states with the means of controlling the expansion of interstate bank holding companies. However, the states do not have such wide authority to control interstate expansion via branch banking. The states can permit interstate branching only by state-chartered banks that are not members of the Federal Reserve System. The McFadden Act of 1927 as amended, which sets the branching laws for national banks and for state-chartered banks that are members of the Federal Reserve System, prohibits these banks from branching outside their home state.

2. State legislation on interstate branch banking, November 1, 1993

State	Effective date	Area covered and reciprocity requirement
Alaska	January 1, 1994	National, reciprocal
Massachusetts	Currently	National, reciprocal
Nevada	Currently	Permitted in counties with population less than 100,000
New York	Currently	National, reciprocal
North Carolina	Currently	National, reciprocal
Oregon	November 4, 1993	National, reciprocal
Rhode Island	Currently	National, reciprocal
Utah	Currently	National, no reciprocity

If branching across state lines is to grow substantially, federal legislation granting interstate branching powers to national banks and state-chartered Federal Reserve System member banks will be necessary. These banks typically are larger, and have more branch offices, than state nonmember banks. At the end of 1992, 3,555 national banks and 1,001 state member banks were in operation; the average national bank had $507.7 million in domestic banking assets and 7.9 branches, and the average state member bank had $509.0 million in domestic banking assets and 7.5 branches. In contrast, the averages for the 6,873 insured state nonmember banks were $120.6 million in domestic banking assets and 2.7 branches. Because the nation's larger banks, which have a greater propensity to branch, are not state nonmember banks, interstate branch banking is likely to be limited until the McFadden Act is further amended or repealed—unless banking organizations are willing to give up their national charter or Federal Reserve System membership.

A change in the McFadden Act could take one of two courses. Under one approach, national banks could be allowed to branch nationwide. Removal of the McFadden Act's restrictions on national bank branching would provide uniform branching rights for all national banks, regardless of their home state; state member banks would remain subject to the interstate branching restrictions imposed by their home state. If national banks were permitted to branch across state lines, the states likely would be pressured to provide equal opportunities for state-chartered banks, and this pressure would almost surely result eventually in changes in state laws.

Alternatively, a change in the McFadden Act could leave control over branching with the states, as the Douglas Amendment left to the states the decision about bank holding companies. This option would follow the dual banking system's approach to regulating branching within states. National and state-chartered member banks would be allowed to branch interstate to the same extent that their home state allowed state nonmember banks to branch, just as national and state member banks are currently allowed to branch within a state to the same extent that state-chartered nonmember banks are allowed to branch within that state.

INTERSTATE EXPANSION: WHICH APPROACH IS BEST?

Most of the benefits of interstate banking will be achieved regardless of whether holding company expansion across state lines or interstate branching is ultimately the main vehicle for interstate expansion. Either way, interstate banking will increase customer convenience and will enable banking organizations to diversify their loan portfolios over a wide geographic area. The removal of barriers to entry into new banking markets will also help promote and protect competition; the knowledge that any other bank in the nation can, if it chooses, enter its market area should serve as a significant deterrent to anticompetitive practices on the part of an existing bank.

The means by which these gains are to be achieved have been discussed extensively. Many observers believe that holding companies that own more than one bank, whether within one state or in multiple states, are merely a product of restrictions on branch banking. By this line of thought, interstate bank holding companies serve only as a transition between a system that limits interstate banking and a full nationwide branch banking system. Other observers believe that multibank holding companies offer advantages and argue that such companies would continue to exist even if full interstate branch banking were permitted. Several issues have emerged in the debate about the best way to achieve interstate banking.

Customer Service

The original issue in the discussion of the relative merits of the two forms of interstate banking is that of customer convenience. Although two banks may be owned by the same holding company, they are not "branches" of each other, and there are limits on the services that one bank can provide to the customers of the other. For example, a customer moving from one state to another would most likely need to move his or her account to the subsidiary bank located in the new state of residence. Interstate branch banking would eliminate that need; the customer would be able to obtain services at any branch office of the bank. Opponents of branching, whether within one state or across state lines, note that in this case only branch office services would be available, instead of the full line of services typically provided at the main office of a bank.

The ability to provide customers with easy access to cash from their account while they are away from home was once a major argument for allowing branching. This pressure for geographic deregulation has been alleviated by the spread of automated teller machine (ATM) networks that can connect a consumer with his or her bank account from machines all over the nation, and in a growing number of foreign countries as well. Most likely, no one bank would ever be able to provide a branch office network comparable in size or coverage to the major ATM networks. The development of ATM networks has also reduced the magnitude of one of the claimed advantages of banks that have many branches; through ATM networks, a small bank can provide customers with access to funds over just as wide an area as can a large bank that has many branches.

Cost of Operation

Cost is a second issue in the debate about the best approach to geographic expansion. Proponents of interstate branching argue that it is much less expensive to operate branches than to maintain a large number of separately incorporated subsidiary banks. Branching should offer savings on administrative costs because only one bank must be examined and one set of regulatory reports filed, and because the bank has only one board of directors and one set of officers. Although a bank holding company can centralize some operating functions—such as personnel management and training, data processing, and advertising—in the parent organization, each bank is a separate legal entity, and some functions must be performed at each subsidiary.

Research findings raise questions about the claim that the operating costs of branch banking organizations are indeed lower than those of multibank holding companies. If one form of organization were substantially less costly than an alternative form, the difference would be reflected in profitability and long-run survival; the bank organized in the less efficient manner would not be able to compete. The fact that, within states, some banks choose the branching format while others choose the multibank holding company format suggests that there may be little cost difference between the two approaches.

Even if there are cost differences between the two formats, there may also be offsetting revenue differences. The multibank format, though requiring separate boards of directors for each bank owned by the holding company, may give the banking organization greater identification with the local market; each bank is essentially a local bank rather than a branch of an out-of-town bank. Likewise, although multiple boards of directors must be paid, the separate board may increase the bank's income by bringing in new loan customers, and may lower the bank's costs by providing information on the local market that reduces loan losses.

Although questions concerning the least costly means of providing interstate banking services are interesting to researchers, different banking organizations may find different organizational structures more efficient. Some organizations might choose to have one bank with numerous branch offices in many states. Others might choose to be multibank holding companies having perhaps one bank in each state and branches radiating from that bank. If one form of organization were vastly superior to others, the market would lead all banking organizations to adopt that structure. More likely, however, cost differences are not significant across forms of organization, and banks should be free to find the structure that leads to the achievement of their organizational goals. In the long run, a variety of organizational structures probably would coexist.

Effect on Small Banks

A third issue in the debate over interstate branch banking versus interstate bank holding companies is their potentially different impact on small banks. Some small banks believe that requiring a new organization to enter a community by opening a full-service bank, rather than a branch, would reduce the likelihood that the new organization would be able to lower prices, cut services, and drive out the small bank. However, this point of view is undercut by the demonstrated ability of many small banks to compete with large banks within their home state. Out-of-state banking organizations should pose no new problems. In addition, small banks typically earn a rate of return on assets as high as, or higher than, that earned by large banks, and there is no evidence that they are any less competitive when they are competing with a branch office than when they are competing with a full-service bank.

Service to the Local Community

Another issue in the debate is service to the local community and the measurement of that service. Community groups often argue that large banks from outside the area drain funds from the local community, collecting deposits but not extending loans to local businesses and consumers. To an extent, service to the local community is easier to measure in the context of interstate bank holding companies. Banks report on deposits held by individual branch offices once a year, but they are not required to report loans originated on a branch office basis. For that reason, monitoring of lending at the local level (absent additional reporting requirements) would be more difficult with branch banking. In contrast, each bank owned by a holding company must report quarterly on both its deposits and its loans.

Funds flow into and out of communities according to the forces of supply and demand. Measuring the flow is difficult because bank loans and investments can be local or nonlocal. For example, a bank invests in its local community when it makes loans to local businesses and consumers, but it invests local deposits outside the market when it purchases government securities or sells federal funds.

Although the Community Reinvestment Act requires banks to serve their community or communities, the market also plays a major role in this cause. A bank or branch that does not serve its community is likely to face competition from one that provides better service. So long as new banking organizations are allowed to enter the market and the costs of entry are low, the failure of existing banks to make worthwhile loans and to provide other needed services to the community should attract new banking institutions into the market.

New entry occurs via acquisition of an existing bank, formation of a new branch, or the chartering of a new bank. Since 1979, more than 3,500 new banks have been chartered, though more than 5,000 existing banks have been absorbed by mergers; in addition, more than 24,000 new branches have been opened, while 10,500 existing branches have been closed. These numbers suggest that the industry does respond to the needs of markets. If, as is likely the case, entry via the opening of a new branch is less costly than entry via the chartering of a new bank, the achievement of community reinvestment objectives may be accomplished more easily by lowering restrictions on branching.

The Dual Banking System

Finally, the debate about the best way to achieve interstate banking has implications for the preservation of the dual banking system. Many observers believe that a bank with branches in more than one state would be chartered as a national bank. If that were the case, all the bank's branches would be regulated by the federal authority, the Comptroller of the Currency. If, on the other hand, a bank with branches in more than one state were to be state-chartered, it would be subject to regulation by each of the states in which it had a branch. Although the banking authorities of the various states could make agreements as to how such an organization would be examined and which state's regulations would prevail, many issues would have to be resolved. An individual bank, having a choice of regulators, might find it less costly to deal with the national bank regulators.

Although banks planning multistate branch networks might find it more efficient to be regulated as national banks, the rate of formation of interstate banks thus far suggests that relatively few large multistate organizations will be formed. Because of the apparent lack of significant scale economies, as evidenced by direct studies of the subject as well as the observed profitability of small banks, thousands of banks will probably survive into the future. Some of these institutions will likely choose to be state-regulated banks, and the dual banking system will continue.

In summary, several important issues will be debated as policymakers continue to discuss potential changes in the geographic regulation of banking. The resolution of these issues will determine the structure of the banking system of the future. Regardless of the method of geographic expansion, however, the current large number of financial institutions and the evidence suggesting that smaller institutions are surviving seem to ensure that the U.S. banking system will continue to be characterized by a large number of financial institutions.

THE INTERSTATE BANKING ORGANIZATIONS

This section turns from the issues involved in a geographic restructuring of the banking system to an examination of progress in the development of interstate banking.

Interstate Branch Banking

The few state laws permitting interstate branch banking have not yet been widely utilized. As of June 30, 1992, 146 branches were being operated across the borders of states, territories, or possessions, according to the Summary of Deposits, an annual survey conducted by the Federal Deposit Insurance Corporation (FDIC) that reports the amount of deposits each bank has at each of its offices. These 146 branches represent only a tiny fraction of the more than 56,000 branch offices operated by commercial and savings banks insured by the FDIC. Most of the 146 were branches of U.S. banks headquartered in the United States but operating branches in territories and possessions of the United States (for example, a branch on Guam of a bank headquartered in California). Others were U.S. branches of banks headquartered in a U.S. territory or possession (for example, a New York branch of a Puerto Rican bank).

Only 43 of the 146 branches were operating across state lines. These branches exist as a result of a variety of historical exceptions to the general prohibitions: Some were grandfathered from earlier periods, some were permitted as a means of resolving a bank failure or potential failure, and some are branches of banks serving more than one military installation.

Interstate Bank Holding Companies

Beyond the few interstate branches, the remaining interstate banking activity is conducted through multistate bank holding companies. As of June 30, 1993, 170 U.S. bank holding companies and 8 foreign bank holding companies owned banks in more than one state. These 178 companies represent only 3.2 percent of the 5,509 bank holding companies currently active in the United States. Although many of these companies are major banking organizations, as suggested by their average holdings of U.S. deposits of just over $8 billion, 71 of the 178 companies have domestic deposits of less than $1 billion.

Many of the multistate bank holding companies—111 of the 178—have subsidiary banks in only two states, their home state and one other state. Another 45 have banks in three or four states, and 17 have subsidiaries in five to nine states. Only 5 holding companies have subsidiary banks in ten or more states, and 2 of these 5 were among the grandfathered interstate bank holding companies that had acquired some of their out-of-state subsidiary banks before the Bank Holding Company Act of 1956. Clearly, only a few banking organizations have used the state interstate banking laws to make significant progress toward becoming truly nationwide banks.

EXTENT OF INTERSTATE BANKING

Although the share of deposits held by out-of-state bank holding companies nationwide has grown in recent years, the record differs from state to state. In some states, interstate banking activity is still insignificant, but in others, nearly all deposits are held by banks that are owned by out-of-state holding companies.

Share at the National Level

The share of domestic commercial banking assets controlled by interstate bank holding companies has expanded substantially over time, though not as rapidly as many observers, particularly the opponents of change, had expected. In February 1987, 6 percent of domestic banking assets were held by banks controlled by out-of-state bank holding companies, compared with 21.3 percent at the end of 1992. Looking at a different measure of activity, at the end of June 1993, 22.8 percent of domestic banking deposits were held by insured commercial banks that were subsidiaries of out-of-state bank holding companies.

The slower-than-expected increase in interstate banking activity may be due to several factors. The financial problems encountered by some of the nation's largest banks during the period when many states were enacting their interstate bank holding company laws provide one explanation. Many of the holding companies that had been expected to expand rapidly did not have the resources to grow at the anticipated rate. Therefore, as the condition of the banking system continues to improve, additional interstate expansion can be expected.

Research on the post-acquisition performance of bank holding companies provides another possible explanation for the slower-than-expected growth in interstate banking. Although some holding companies have been able to make numerous large acquisitions, integrate the new banks into their organizations, and in the process increase their profit rate, studies of hundreds of mergers within and across state boundaries suggest that, on average, mergers do not increase the profitability or efficiency of the combined firm. As noted earlier, studies have not found the economies of scale that would require firms to become very large in order to be competitive and profitable. Thus, smaller banks are not under great pressure to be acquired; the vast majority can remain independent and still be profitable.

The slow growth of interstate banking may also be explained by the fact that most acquisitions must be negotiated. Only a relatively few bank holding companies have publicly traded stock that could be acquired in a hostile takeover. Therefore, if the target firm does not want to be acquired, or is not willing to accept the per share price offered by the acquiring firm, the takeover attempt is usually unsuccessful.

Share at the State Level

State-by-state data reveal large differences among states in the percentage of domestic banking deposits held by insured commercial banks that are sub-

3. Share of domestic banking deposits held by insured commercial banks owned by out-of-state bank holding companies, by state, June 30, 1993[1]
Percent

State	Share
Alabama	3.19
Alaska	23.55
Arizona	89.69
Arkansas	1.99
California	1.10
Colorado	56.89
Connecticut	49.40
Delaware	37.96
District of Columbia	58.70
Florida	50.04
Georgia	42.19
Hawaii	8.42
Idaho	56.67
Illinois	15.31
Indiana	53.42
Iowa	23.16
Kansas	10.15
Kentucky	35.44
Louisiana	5.34
Maine	78.15
Maryland	24.60
Massachusetts	29.81
Michigan	3.58
Minnesota	3.15
Mississippi	2.18
Missouri	.18
Montana	31.14
Nebraska	10.15
Nevada	89.41
New Hampshire	23.43
New Jersey	21.12
New Mexico	32.93
New York	6.46
North Carolina	.25
North Dakota	30.66
Ohio	3.36
Oklahoma	12.69
Oregon	48.23
Pennsylvania	10.66
Rhode Island	26.85
South Carolina	64.15
South Dakota	52.96
Tennessee	29.46
Texas	53.01
Utah	27.45
Vermont	4.40
Virginia	39.73
Washington	81.19
West Virginia	26.97
Wisconsin	16.66
Wyoming	53.58
National average	22.81

1. Based on Reports of Condition and Income for June 30, 1993, but covers acquisitions approved and reported in the *Federal Reserve Bulletin* through September 1993. Excludes data for foreign banks, except foreign-owned bank holding companies that have bank subsidiaries in two or more states; also excludes special-purpose banks, nonbank banks, and nondeposit trust companies.

sidiaries of out-of-state bank holding companies. In four states, more than 75 percent of domestic banking deposits are held by banks owned by out-of-state holding companies (table 3). In nine states, 50 percent to 75 percent of deposits are under out-of-state ownership; in twenty-five states, 10 percent to 50 percent; and in the remaining thirteen states, less than 10 percent.

The states in which banks owned by out-of-state holding companies hold more than 75 percent of domestic banking deposits are Arizona, Maine, Nevada, and Washington. Before they allowed interstate banking, these four states had relatively few banking organizations and relatively few large banking organizations, and a relatively high percentage of deposits were held by the largest banks. Thus, only a few acquisitions by out-of-state firms were required to bring more than 75 percent of banking deposits under out-of-state control.

Bank failures are another important factor explaining levels of out-of-state ownership. In a few states, most notably Texas, the relatively high percentage of deposits held by out-of-state holding companies (53 percent) is due in large part to the failure of one or more major banking organizations in the state and their subsequent acquisition by out-of-state holding companies.

Several possible explanations can be offered for the low percentages of out-of-state control of deposits in some states. Some states may be viewed as not particularly attractive for entry because of their low income levels or low rates of economic growth. Other states, such as New York, are home to many very large banks; few out-of-state entrants would be able to acquire one of these large banks and gain a large share of the state's deposits. Finally, in some of the states the largest banks hold relatively small shares of total deposits; several of the largest banks in those states could be acquired without transferring a large percentage of total deposits in the states to out-of-state firms.

Thirty-nine states (including the District of Columbia) are home to at least one banking organization that has acquired an out-of-state subsidiary (table 4). In most of these states, the ratio of out-of-state deposits to total deposits held by the state's multistate bank holding companies is not particularly high. In a few states, such as Minnesota, North Carolina, Georgia, Rhode Island, and Ohio, the state's multistate banking organizations obtain a large share of their total deposits through their out-of-state subsidiaries.

4. Multistate bank holding companies, by state, June 30, 1993

State	Number	Total domestic deposits (billions of dollars)	Share of total domestic deposits held by out-of-state subsidiary banks (percent)
Alabama	5	30.72	26.85
Arkansas	4	4.99	20.84
California	5	183.75	35.01
Connecticut	1	15.58	46.98
District of Columbia	1	3.67	13.35
Florida	2	32.35	3.49
Georgia	7	38.66	60.87
Hawaii	1	4.87	1.64
Idaho	1	5.37	48.79
Illinois	14	58.43	13.18
Indiana	5	6.22	24.60
Iowa	3	.67	22.42
Kansas	5	6.22	20.28
Kentucky	3	3.92	8.52
Maryland	7	24.52	16.64
Massachusetts	3	29.20	19.32
Michigan	6	80.65	29.65
Minnesota	8	51.07	55.00
Mississippi	4	9.55	21.99
Missouri	11	47.40	33.38
Nebraska	8	3.81	12.31
New Jersey	7	52.88	29.80
New Mexico	2	3.35	43.02
New York	11	243.25	23.70
North Carolina	7	166.40	74.23
North Dakota	1	1.05	68.57
Ohio	10	126.09	48.97
Oklahoma	1	.18	27.78
Oregon	1	15.10	48.54
Pennsylvania	7	78.95	18.07
Rhode Island	1	31.41	83.06
South Carolina	1	.38	65.79
South Dakota	1	.23	13.04
Tennessee	5	11.84	8.07
Utah	2	8.37	32.38
Virginia	4	24.84	22.95
Washington	2	1.11	10.81
West Virginia	5	2.70	10.44
Wisconsin	6	19.73	23.18

SOURCES. Reports of Condition and Income, June 30, 1993, and NIC (the Federal Reserve's National Information Center for Systemwide Structure and Financial Information).

INTERSTATE BANKING AND DEPOSIT CONCENTRATION

Critics of the concept of interstate banking have argued that the removal of traditional barriers to nationwide banking would result in a more concentrated banking system. Over time, they have maintained, the number of banks would decline and the remaining banks would control an increasingly large share of total banking system deposits. In this more concentrated system, the users of bank services—consumers and businesses—would be harmed because the few remaining firms would be free to charge higher prices than would prevail in a more competitive environment.

Banking concentration has been examined on a number of levels. Nationwide concentration has been of historical interest because of a concern about the overall control of credit in the United States that dates back to the earliest years of the nation. Concentration at the state level has been examined because, traditionally, banking organizations could expand only within the boundaries of their home state. As these barriers are broken down, the relevance of state concentration decreases. Concentration at the local level is of paramount concern because the local banking market is where most bank customers—such as households and small businesses—seek out financial services. To the extent that these customers are restricted to the local banking market, the preservation of unconcentrated markets that provide a high level of competition for banking services is critical.

In discussing banking concentration, especially changes in concentration over time, it is important to note that the concentration data reported in this section are based on insured commercial banks. The numbers do not capture any increase in financial activity by other depository and nondepository institutions. To the extent that other institutions perform financial services that were once the exclusive province of commercial banks, an increase in a concentration ratio that is based solely on banking will almost surely overstate the actual change in financial concentration.

National Concentration

At the national level, banking has become much more concentrated over the period during which interstate banks have been formed. The increased concentration is particularly noticeable for the nation's 100 largest insured commercial banking organizations (as measured by volume of deposits). For several decades, the percentage of total domestic deposits held by the 100 largest banking organizations hovered just below 50 percent (table 5). Now, that percentage is 64 percent. The rise is a result of both interstate mergers asso-

5. Shares of domestic commercial banking deposits held by largest U.S. banking organizations, selected years, 1960–93 [1]
Percent

Year	Largest 10	Largest 25	Largest 50	Largest 100
1960	20.4	31.7	40.3	49.6
1965	21.3	32.7	40.9	49.8
1970	20.0	30.8	38.9	48.1
1975	19.9	30.6	38.7	48.2
1980	18.6	29.1	37.1	46.8
1985	17.0	28.5	40.5	52.6
1986	17.6	29.6	42.4	55.6
1987	18.1	31.1	44.1	57.4
1988	19.2	33.2	47.5	59.9
1989	19.9	34.1	48.1	60.5
1990	20.0	34.9	48.9	61.4
1991	22.7	37.5	49.6	61.3
1992	24.1	39.2	51.7	62.6
1993	25.0	40.4	53.1	64.0

1. Banking organizations are ranked by volume of domestic commercial banking deposits. Rankings and shares for 1960–92 are as of December 31; for 1993, as of June 30.
SOURCES. Reports of Condition and Income and NIC database.

ciated with the formation and growth of multistate bank holding companies and large mergers in which the merged banks were headquartered in the same state.

The percentage of domestic deposits held by the ten largest banking organizations has risen more slowly. As recently as 1990, the ten largest organizations held a smaller percentage of deposits than they did in 1960. Over the past two and one-half years, however, the ten largest banking organizations have increased their share of deposits. This recent growth reflects several events. Some of the fastest growing organizations have moved into the top ten, replacing banks that were acquired by other bank holding companies or that, in spite of their size, were not able to maintain their relative rank in a dynamic industry. In addition, improvements in their financial condition removed a barrier to the expansion of some major bank holding companies. Finally, mergers occurred between some very large banking organizations.

The relative importance of in-state and interstate acquisitions in the increase in national concentration can be seen in data on turnover, over time, among the 100 largest banking organizations. Beginning with the largest 100 organizations as of June 1985 and tracing these firms forward in time, 49 had been acquired by mid-1993. Of the 49 firms, 34 were acquired by an out-of-state bank holding company, while 15 were acquired by another firm in their home state.

Concentration at the State Level

Concentration at the state level has also increased substantially. Table 6 gives data for 1980 and mid-1993, by state, on the shares of domestic banking deposits in the state held by the three largest banking organizations, individually and as a group. In eleven states and the District of Columbia, the three-firm share decreased; in the other states, the share increased. The average of the state three-firm concentration ratios increased from 42.0 percent in 1980 to 50.5 percent in June 1993.

Table 6 also identifies the banking organizations among the largest three in each state that are owned by out-of-state bank holding companies. In 1980, these organizations were the subsidiaries of the multistate bank holding companies that were grandfathered by the Bank Holding Company Act of 1956. By the end of June 1993, the number of instances in which one or more of the three largest firms were controlled by an out-of-state bank holding company had increased substantially.

Although in many states one or more of the three largest banks are owned by out-of-state bank holding companies, this does not mean that concentration has increased as a result of interstate banking. It simply means that an out-of-state owner has replaced the in-state owner of the bank; the bank's share of state deposits has not necessarily changed. Thus, to the extent that out-of-state firms have merely gained control of shares previously held by in-state firms, interstate banking has not led to increased concentration at the state level. Concentration in a state increases when the out-of-state firm is able to increase the share of state deposits held by its subsidiary, or when the out-of-state firm subsequently acquires additional banks in the state so as to increase its state share. Evidence suggests that firms entering new markets by acquiring large banks in the market are not, on average, able to increase the market share of the acquired bank.

The data in tables 3 and 6 appear to suggest a positive relationship between the percentage of out-of-state ownership and the level of state concentration. Many of the states where concentration is high also have a relatively high level of out-of-state ownership. The high level of statewide concentration may have contributed to a high percentage of out-of-state ownership, because in the highly concentrated states only a few acquisitions were necessary to bring a high percentage of the state's deposits under the control of out-of-state bank holding companies.

Local Banking Market Concentration

Most bank customers are concerned with competition at the local level, rather than the national or state level. A large business might seek banking services over a wide geographic area, but a household or small business typically does not search the nation or the state for banking services. The relevant banking market for the vast majority of households and small businesses is a local banking market.

The 1989 Survey of Consumer Finances demonstrated the importance of the local market to households.[3] Nearly 96 percent of the households surveyed indicated that their primary financial institution was a local bank, thrift institution, or credit union. Fewer than 20 percent of the households reported using a nonlocal financial institution for any services.

The importance of the local market for small businesses was revealed by the 1988–89 National Survey of Small Business Finances.[4] The survey concluded that the vast majority of small businesses rely on local firms for the bulk of their financial needs. Only 20 percent of the firms surveyed reported using a financial institution located thirty miles or more from the firm's home office.

Because households and small businesses rely so heavily on local financial institutions, the local banking market is generally considered the appropriate market for analysis under antitrust laws. Although a more exact definition of the market is

---

3. Gergory E. Elliehausen and John D. Wolken, "Banking Markets and the Use of Financial Services by Households," *Federal Reserve Bulletin*, vol. 78 (March 1992), pp. 169–81.

4. Gregory E. Elliehausen and John D. Wolken, "Banking Markets and the Use of Financial Services by Small and Medium-Sized Businesses," *Federal Reserve Bulletin*, vol. 76 (October 1990), pp. 801–17.

6. Shares of domestic commercial banking deposits held by largest banking organizations in state, by state, 1980 and 1993[1]
Percent

State	Largest organization		Second largest organization		Third largest organization		Sum of three largest organizations		Change in share for three largest organizations, 1980 to 1993
	1980	1993	1980	1993	1980	1993	1980	1993	
Alabama	15.3	18.3	11.6	17.6	11.3	17.2	38.2	53.1	14.9
Alaska	30.9	42.3	22.5	25.5	10.3	18.6*	63.7	86.3	22.6
Arizona	42.1	31.5*	27.3*	25.0*	15.5	21.7*	84.8	78.2	-6.6
Arkansas	6.7	13.1	3.2	10.3	3.1	4.7	13.0	28.0	15.0
California	35.1	36.5	12.9	17.3	10.0	7.2	58.0	61.1	3.1
Colorado	15.8	24.1*	15.3	16.6*	9.9	9.1*	41.1	49.7	8.6
Connecticut	19.1	32.3	18.7	24.3*	9.3	9.4**	47.1	66.1	19.0
Delaware	34.3	16.2	21.8	15.5*	18.1	11.0*	74.1	42.6	-31.5
District of Columbia	32.3	33.1	28.4	21.4*	10.5	12.7*	71.2	67.2	-4.0
Florida	10.5	26.1	9.2	17.9*	7.3	14.0*	27.0	58.0	31.0
Georgia	16.5	13.6*	11.9	13.1	11.5	12.9*	39.8	39.5	-.3
Hawaii	38.6	42.5	32.5	37.1	8.2**	9.3**	79.2	88.9	9.7
Idaho	36.6	35.0	26.0*	28.3*	11.6*	12.5*	74.2	75.8	1.6
Illinois	16.8	13.5	12.0	7.1	4.5	5.2**	33.3	25.8	-7.5
Indiana	6.4	18.3*	6.1	11.7*	4.9	8.5*	17.4	38.5	21.1
Iowa	7.4*	12.3*	5.9	6.7*	5.3	5.2	18.6	24.1	5.4
Kansas	4.7	14.9	2.7	4.1*	1.8	3.8	9.1	22.8	13.7
Kentucky	9.5	12.3*	8.9	10.8*	4.4	10.3	22.8	33.4	10.6
Louisiana	6.7	15.1	4.1	12.1	3.8	9.5	14.6	36.6	22.0
Maine	18.4	32.3*	16.5	28.3*	14.0	14.2*	48.9	74.8	25.9
Maryland	20.9	19.2	13.3	12.9**	10.7	10.4	44.9	42.4	-2.5
Massachusetts	23.9	23.8	12.6	15.7	10.9	13.1*	47.5	52.7	5.2
Michigan	15.4	19.9	11.6	19.3	9.4	14.6	36.4	53.8	17.4
Minnesota	26.1	25.6	24.8	22.4	2.4	2.6	53.3	50.5	-2.8
Mississippi	12.1	16.2	10.9	15.1	4.2	8.6	27.2	39.9	12.6
Missouri	11.1	21.9	10.0	12.2	8.5	10.9	29.5	45.0	15.5
Montana	24.0*	16.9*	12.0*	11.0*	5.9	10.3	41.9	38.2	-3.7
Nebraska	7.8*	14.8	6.5	11.8	5.1	10.0*	19.4	36.6	17.2
Nevada	47.5*	34.6*	22.4	32.9*	13.6*	9.6*	83.5	77.1	-6.4
New Hampshire	15.5	23.4*	11.7	18.7	7.3	14.9	34.5	57.0	22.5
New Jersey	8.5	20.4**	8.4	11.2	7.9	10.5	24.7	42.1	17.3
New Mexico	23.1	25.1*	11.9*	14.7	8.9	11.0	43.9	50.8	6.8
New York	15.3	20.2	12.7	15.1	12.2	12.7	40.1	48.0	7.9
North Carolina	19.9	18.8	19.3	18.4	11.9	14.0	51.2	51.3	.1
North Dakota	16.2*	13.7*	15.8*	10.7*	6.8*	6.3*	38.8	30.7	-8.1
Ohio	9.2	15.9	8.7	14.9	7.1	14.5	25.0	45.3	20.3
Oklahoma	7.8	9.1	6.4	7.0	4.7	4.8*	18.9	20.9	2.0
Oregon	34.4	37.8	33.8*	24.9*	7.8	12.3*	76.0	75.0	-1.0
Pennsylvania	12.3	16.7	6.3	15.0	4.7	8.7	23.2	40.3	17.1
Rhode Island	41.5	57.5	25.1	28.2*	24.0	8.3**	90.6	94.0	3.4
South Carolina	19.1	24.5*	13.4	24.0*	12.8	8.6*	45.4	57.0	11.7
South Dakota	23.0*	26.7*	17.0*	18.3*	3.2	4.4*	43.2	49.5	6.2
Tennessee	11.5	15.0	8.1	12.1	7.9	10.2*	27.5	37.2	9.7
Texas	9.0	16.4*	8.2	11.8*	8.1	10.0*	25.3	38.2	12.9
Utah	27.8	31.5	20.6	23.6	11.2*	9.1*	59.6	64.2	4.6
Vermont	17.2	27.0	13.2	20.9	12.8	15.4	43.2	63.2	20.0
Virginia	13.7	16.4*	10.8	14.6	10.1	12.3*	34.5	43.4	8.9
Washington	37.0	35.8*	18.7	17.0*	8.6*	14.4*	64.3	67.1	2.8
West Virginia	3.8	14.3*	2.6	14.2	1.8	7.7	8.2	36.1	28.0
Wisconsin	13.3	15.8	8.3	13.4	7.0	10.5*	28.7	39.7	11.0
Wyoming	16.0	23.7*	12.9*	7.9*	9.7	6.8	38.7	38.4	-.3

1. Banking organizations are ranked by volume of domestic commercial banking deposits. Rankings and shares for 1980 are as of December 31; for 1993, as of June 30. Components may not sum to totals because of rounding.

* Out-of-state bank holding company.
** Foreign bank holding company.
SOURCES. NIC database and Reports of Condition and Income.

necessary when an application for a specific bank merger or bank holding company acquisition is being reviewed, the local banking market is frequently approximated by a metropolitan statistical area, as defined by the federal government, or by a nonmetropolitan county.

7. Average share of domestic commercial banking deposits held by the three largest banking organizations in metropolitan statistical areas and nonmetropolitan counties, 1976–92

Year	Metropolitan statistical areas	Nonmetropolitan counties
1976	68.5	90.0
1977	67.9	89.9
1978	67.4	89.9
1979	66.8	89.7
1980	66.4	89.6
1981	66.1	89.4
1982	65.9	89.4
1983	66.0	89.4
1984	66.4	89.4
1985	66.7	89.5
1986	67.5	89.5
1987	67.7	89.5
1988	67.8	89.7
1989	67.5	89.7
1990	67.3	89.6
1991	66.7	89.3
1992	67.5	89.2

SOURCE. Federal Deposit Insurance Corporation, Summary of Deposits, 1976–92.

These local banking markets have not, on average, become more concentrated over recent years (table 7). In spite of the thousands of mergers that have occurred, the average concentration in local banking markets has remained remarkably stable over time. Because many of the banks involved in mergers had not been competitors in the same local banking market, their combination did not increase local market concentration. In some cases in which the merging banks were major competitors in the same local market, divestitures were used to limit the impact of the merger on local market concentration.

SUMMARY

Nearly all states now have some form of law permitting interstate bank holding companies, some have laws allowing interstate branch banking, and more will be considering the liberalization of their laws in coming years. The debate in the next few years will likely focus on the relative merits of interstate bank holding companies and interstate branch banking as a means of geographic expansion. Today, however, there are still relatively few interstate banking organizations. Although the share of deposits owned by out-of-state bank holding companies has grown substantially, it is less than many had predicted. Interstate banking has contributed to an increase in the concentration of deposits at the national level, but, thus far, local banking markets have not become more concentrated. □

Article 3

The Proconsumer Argument for Interstate Branching

*Paul S. Calem**

Interstate banking in the United States, an impossibility for many years, became a reality in the 1980s with the passage of state laws authorizing bank holding companies to expand across state lines. All but two states now allow an out-of-state holding company to acquire an in-state bank, and most large banking organizations now have subsidiaries in several states. However, a significant barrier to interstate expansion still exists. It is not yet permissible for individual banks to establish branch networks that cross state boundaries. Interstate expansion is possible only at the holding company level.

This remaining obstacle to interstate banking is critical because it can raise banks' costs of expanding interstate and also limit the potential benefits to consumers. Maintaining an independent, out-of-state subsidiary can be more costly for an institution than operating a

---

* Paul Calem is a senior economist and research adviser in the Research Department of the Philadelphia Fed. He thanks Gary Bosco of the Conference of State Bank Supervisors for providing information on states' branching laws.

cross-state branch network.[1] And branch networks provide particular convenience benefits to consumers. Most important, while consumers can deposit funds into their accounts at any branch of their bank, they cannot make deposits via an out-of-state affiliate of their bank.

Removal of the legal impediments to interstate branching surely would lead to the creation of interstate branch networks, in part because some bank holding companies currently operating interstate would choose to merge subsidiary banks. This geographic expansion would benefit consumers of banking services. Consumers in multistate areas would gain easier access to their bank accounts and related services. In addition, interstate branching would be procompetitive. For instance, blanket repeal of federal interstate branching restrictions would enable national banks to enter out-of-state markets by establishing new branches there.[2] Such de novo entry (as opposed to entry via acquisition) would tend to make a market more competitive, especially in the case of markets that, prior to entry, had been dominated by a small number of institutions. As a result, consumers in these markets would likely be offered more favorable rates and fees.[3]

Despite these potential benefits to consumers, interstate branching proposals have generally been opposed by consumer advocates.[4] In part, this opposition has arisen because the benefits have not been thoroughly articulated. More important, opponents of interstate branching fear that it would lead to domination of local markets by large multistate banks. They are concerned that these institutions would be less willing to lend to small local businesses and would be less responsive to community needs in general.

This article examines the various pros and cons of geographic deregulation, focusing on the potential impact of interstate branching on consumer convenience, competition, and credit availability. There are, of course, other matters relevant to interstate branching. For example, by lowering the costs of geographic expansion, interstate branching may enable banks to reduce the riskiness of their loan portfolios through further geographic diversification.[5] My intention, however, is to examine only those issues that directly affect retail and small-business customers. Indeed, recent debate over interstate branching has emphasized such consumer issues.[6]

THE CURRENT STATUS OF INTERSTATE BANKING

Banking deregulation during the 1980s loosened the constraints on interstate banking considerably. Unlike other major regulatory initia-

---

[1] For elaboration on this point, see Mengle (1990) and Svare (1992).

[2] Whether restrictions on interstate branching by national banks will be repealed without conditions remains to be seen. Some proposals would repeal existing federal restrictions but allow individual states to pass laws that restrict interstate branching. Given such authority, some states might opt to forbid the establishment of de novo interstate branches. See Mengle (1990) for discussion of alternative proposals.

[3] The relationship between structure, conduct, and performance in banking markets has been studied extensively. There is general agreement that markets dominated by a few institutions tend to be less competitive, with banks in those markets offering lower deposit rates and having higher fees and loan rates. See, for example, Calem and Carlino (1991) and Hannan (1991).

---

[4] See, for example, the statements by representatives of the Consumers Union, the Consumer Federation of America, and the U.S. Public Interest Research Group before the Subcommittee on Consumer Affairs and Coinage, U.S. House of Representatives (U.S. Congress 1991).

[5] For discussion of this issue and other considerations related to interstate branching, see Mengle (1990) and U.S. Congress (1991).

[6] See U.S. Congress (1991).

tives during this period, such as the lifting of ceilings on deposit interest rates, interstate banking reform occurred at the state rather than the federal level. Since 1956, the Douglas Amendment to the federal Bank Holding Company Act has prohibited interstate acquisitions by bank holding companies, except where authorized by the acquired bank's home state. During the 1980s, most states changed their laws to permit entry by out-of-state bank holding companies.

Only two states, Hawaii and Montana, have yet to adopt a law allowing entry by an out-of-state holding company.[7] Thirty-five states now permit entry on a nationwide basis, with the stipulation (in most cases) that the entering bank's home state have a reciprocal law. Fourteen states (plus the District of Columbia) allow entry on a regional reciprocal basis.[8]

One significant limitation of these interstate banking laws is that most states do not allow out-of-state holding companies to establish de novo bank subsidiaries in the state. Rather, entry by out-of-state banking organizations is restricted to acquisitions of existing banks. Only 19 states allow de novo entry.[9]

Geographic deregulation during the 1980s resulted in numerous interstate mergers and acquisitions, transforming the structure of the banking industry. One dramatic consequence of this merger activity has been the creation of so-called "superregionals." Huge multistate organizations emerged from consolidations involving two or more large banks, as in the case of NationsBank Corporation in the South, or through the acquisition of many smaller banks by a major institution, as in the case of Banc One Corporation in the North Central region.

A list of the 25 largest banking organizations in the U.S. and the states in which they operate bank subsidiaries (Table 1) shows that almost all large banking organizations now have subsidiaries in several states.

Many smaller organizations also have expanded interstate. For example, 14 bank holding companies headquartered in Pennsylvania or New Jersey operate out-of-state bank subsidiaries. These institutions (Table 2) range in size from $240 million to $52 billion in assets; seven of them have less than $2 billion in assets.

Restrictions on Interstate Branching. While bank holding companies can now cross state lines, various legal obstacles preclude interstate branching by commercial banks.[10] Foremost among these is the McFadden Act, a federal law dating from 1927 that rules out interstate branching by national banks.[11] The

---

[7] Hawaii permits entry by institutions from Guam, American Samoa, and several other Pacific territories, subject to reciprocity.

[8] The District of Columbia also allows entry on a nationwide basis for institutions outside the D.C. region that meet certain community reinvestment and job creation requirements. For details on each of the state laws, see "State Laws Gain Renewed Significance as Congress Stumbles," Banking Policy Report, January 6, 1992, pp. 10-14, and "A Look at Laws Granting Interstate Powers to Banks," *American Banker*, March 20, 1992, p. 8.

[9] The states allowing de novo entry are Arizona, Colorado (effective July 1, 1993), Connecticut, Maine, Maryland, Massachusetts, Michigan, Minnesota, Nevada, New Hampshire, New Jersey, New Mexico, New York, Ohio, Pennsylvania, Rhode Island, South Dakota, Texas, and Vermont.

[10] Federally chartered thrifts, on the other hand, are no longer subject to such a restriction. The Office of Thrift Supervision, in April 1992, adopted a rule allowing full nationwide branching for healthy federally chartered savings and loan institutions.

[11] For an overview of the history of branch banking in the U.S., including further discussion of the McFadden Act, see Mengle (1990). A loophole in the act allows a national bank to relocate its headquarters up to 30 miles, even across a state line. U.S. Bancorp recently exploited this loophole to branch from Oregon into Idaho. See "Fed Gives Interstate Issue a Push by Easing Bank Relocation Rule," *American Banker*, February 27, 1992, p. 1.

TABLE 1
25 Largest Banking Organizations and States in Which They Operate Bank Subsidiaries
(as of 12/31/92)

	Name of Institution	Total Assets (millions $)	Region[a]
1	Citicorp	213,701.0	AZ, CA, CO, DE, FL, MD, ME, NV, NY, SD
2	BankAmerica Corp.	180,814.0	AZ, CA, ID, NV, OR, TX, WA
3	Chemical Banking Corp.	134,655.0	DE, NJ, NY, TX
4	NationsBank Corp.	119,805.0	DC, FL, KY, MD, NC, SC, TN, TX, VA
5	J.P. Morgan & Co., Inc.	102,941.2	DE, NY
6	Chase Manhattan	95,862.3	AZ, CT, DE, FL, MD, NY
7	Bankers Trust New York Corp.	72,448.0	DE, FL, NY
8	Banc One Corp.	61,331.6	IL, IN, KY, MI, OH, TX, WI
9	Wells Fargo & Co., Inc.	52,536.9	CA
10	PNC Financial Corp.	51,523.0	DE, KY, NJ, OH, PA
11	First Union Corp.	51,326.6	FL, GA, NC, SC, TN
12	First Interstate Bancorp, Inc.	50,863.1	AK, AZ, CA, CO, ID, MT, NV, NM, OR, TX, UT, WA, WY
13	First Chicago Corp.	49,281.0	DE, IL, WI
14	Fleet Financial Group, Inc.	47,121.5	CT, MA, ME, NH, NY, RI
15	Norwest Corp.	44,557.1	CO, IA, MN, MT, ND, NE, SD, WI, WY
16	Bank of New York Co., Inc.	41,023.0	DE, NY
17	NBD Bancorp, Inc.	40,843.2	FL, IL, IN, MI, OH
18	Barnett Banks, Inc.	39,631.0	FL, GA
19	SunTrust Banks, Inc.	36,647.2	FL, GA, TN
20	Wachovia Corp.	33,356.1	DE, GA, NC, SC
21	Bank of Boston Corp.	32,346.1	CT, FL, ME, MA, RI
22	Mellon Bank Corp.	31,540.7	DE, MD, PA
23	First Fidelity Bancorporation	31,481.6	NJ, NY, PA
24	National City Corp.	28,963.5	FL, IN, KY, OH
25	Comerica, Inc.	26,660.0	CA, MI, OH, TX

[a] Except in the case of PNC Financial and Mellon, the Delaware subsidiaries of institutions listed in the table are limited-purpose banks.

TABLE 2
Banking Organizations Headquartered in NJ or PA That Have Out-of-State Bank Subsidiaries[a]
(as of 12/31/92)

Name of Institution	Total Assets (millions $)	Locations of Subsidiaries
PNC Financial	51,523.0	DE, KY, MA*, NJ, OH, PA
Mellon Bank Corp.	31,540.7	DE, MA*, MD, PA
First Fidelity Bancorporation	31,481.6	CT*, NJ, NY, PA
CoreStates Financial Corp.	23,774.4	NJ, PA
Midlantic Corp.	14,423.1	NJ, NY, PA
UJB Financial Corp.	13,794.6	NJ, PA
Meridian Bancorp, Inc.	12,221.1	DE, NJ*, PA
Susquehanna Bancshares	1,727.9	MD, PA
F.N.B. Corporation, Inc.	1,698.6	OH, PA
Commerce Bancorp, Inc.	1,428.0	NJ, PA
B.M.J. Financial Corp.	655.1	NJ, PA
State Bancshares	557.4	NJ, PA
Vista Bancorp	336.9	NJ, PA
Glendale Bancorporation	236.7	NJ, PA

[a] Limited-purpose banking subsidiaries are not considered.

*As of this writing, this institution has signed a deal to acquire a bank in this state. Total assets reported in the table do not reflect this proposed transaction.

Federal Reserve Act applies this constraint to state-chartered banks that are members of the Federal Reserve System. Moreover, all but five states generally prohibit the operation of in-state branches by out-of-state banks.[12]

Proposals to permit nationwide interstate branching were considered by Congress during 1991. These measures were included as part of comprehensive proposals to restructure regulation of the banking industry. For instance, the Treasury Department submitted a banking reform bill that would have authorized interstate

---

[12] According to the Conference of State Bank Supervisors, out-of-state banks are allowed to establish branches in Alaska, Massachusetts, Nevada, New York, and Rhode Island (but in Massachusetts and Rhode Island, only entry via branch acquisition is permissible). These laws, in effect, authorize entry by state-chartered banks that are not members of the Federal Reserve System. In addition, "Florida

branching by national banks. In addition, the bill would have allowed banking organizations to engage in a broader range of financial activities, and it would have permitted nonfinancial firms to own banks within a "diversified holding company" structure. But comprehensive restructuring was put on hold. Instead, Congress decided to grapple with the more pressing issues of deposit insurance reform and recapitalization of the FDIC's bank insurance fund.

In 1992, Treasury tried to rally support for a narrower bill that would have permitted nationwide branching and limited insurance activities. Because of disagreements among bankers and between the banking and insurance industries over the specifics of such a bill, no bill was introduced. Nevertheless, interstate branching remains a key topic on the banking reform agenda, one which Congress is likely to revisit in the future.

INTERSTATE BRANCHING AND CUSTOMER CONVENIENCE

One need not be an economist to surmise that branch networks provide convenience in the form of greater access to accounts and related services across the geographic area covered by the network. Clearly, then, interstate branching would enhance the convenience of bank customers who frequently cross state lines. In addition, interstate branching would benefit businesses that require banking services at diverse locations in more than one state. A further potential convenience benefit is somewhat more subtle. Economic reasoning and empirical evidence indicate that interstate branching will tend to have a favorable impact on branch coverage, i.e., on the total number of bank branches serving a given area.

Enhanced Convenience for Consumers in Multistate Areas. Anyone who frequently crosses a state line, for work, for shopping, for business or pleasure, stands to benefit from interstate branching. Interstate branching would provide these customers with convenient access to their accounts and related banking services.

Current restrictions on interstate branching adversely affect such customers in two ways. First, these restrictions may keep some banking institutions from expanding interstate, since expansion at the holding company level can be more costly. Second, interstate banking at the holding company level cannot provide the same level of convenience as interstate branching. In particular, a consumer cannot deposit funds into his or her account through an out-of-state affiliate of his or her bank, and certain account-specific services such as check-cashing may not be obtainable at branches of an affiliate.[13]

Bank branching is important to customers for a number of reasons. First, small-business customers are very dependent on branch banking, both for teller transactions and for special

---

allows an outsider to branch into the state via merger or acquisition if its home state has a reciprocal law" (*American Banker*, December 16, 1992, p. 2.)

I am aware of at least one instance in which a state regulatory agency approved an interstate branch acquisition in a state where such transactions are permitted only under exceptional circumstances. This was the case in Pennsylvania in February 1992, when the state Department of Banking and the FDIC allowed Wilmington Trust Company, a Delaware Bank, to merge with a failed Pennsylvania bank and operate its sole office as a branch. The department has not yet ruled on whether current state law would allow Wilmington Trust to establish additional branches in Pennsylvania now that it has obtained a foothold.

There are a few interstate bank branches around the country that were established before either state or federal laws forbade them and that have been "grandfathered," i.e., permitted to remain in operation. For instance, Midlantic Bank, a New Jersey bank, operates a "grandfathered" branch in downtown Philadelphia.

[13] The McFadden Act (as it has been interpreted) also prevents a bank from accepting deposits through out-of-state ATMs. Thus, repeal of the act would enable consumers to deposit funds into their bank accounts at out-of-state locations through ATMs.

services such as night depository, account reconciliation, and financial counseling.[14] Second, despite teller machine networks, the typical retail customer regularly visits a brick-and-mortar branch to conduct transactions.[15] Third, consumers may save on transactions fees by using automated teller machines located at branches of their banks, since banks usually charge higher fees for transactions at ATMs that are "nonproprietary" (owned by other banks).[16]

The number of people in the U.S. living and working in multistate areas who are apt to benefit from interstate branching is substantial. Six consolidated metropolitan statistical areas (CMSAs) and an additional 28 metropolitan statistical areas (MSAs) cross state boundaries, and approximately 66 million people reside in these multistate metropolitan areas, according to the 1990 U.S. Census.[17]

In addition to benefiting bank customers in localities that straddle state boundaries, interstate branching would be advantageous to customers who require banking services at diverse locations in two or more states, primarily businesses with multistate operations. Under current branching restrictions, such a customer may be pressed to maintain relationships with multiple banks. For instance, a business may have to maintain checking accounts at several banks, which may complicate the firm's cash management and increase its fee expenses.[18]

Increased Branch Coverage. The value to a bank of adding a branch at a particular location depends on the branch's potential to attract new depositors and borrowers and its potential convenience benefits to current customers. Legal restrictions on branching may prevent some banks from realizing their full branching potential. Locations where these banks would have established branches will be left unserved, unless other banks are willing and able to locate there, which will not always be the case.[19] Under current restrictions on interstate branching, an out-of-state bank holding company can create a new bank subsidiary to operate a branch. But creating a new bank subsidiary can be more costly and of less convenience value

---

[14] According to a 1989 survey, more than 20 percent of small-business owners or officers visit their branch daily on behalf of the company. Forty percent are in the branch once a week or more; 88 percent report that branch employees know them by name; only 3 percent never visit a branch. Other small-business employees also make frequent branch visits on behalf of their company. See Trans Data Corporation (1989a).

[15] According to a 1989 survey, 95 percent of consumers visit a branch at least once each month to conduct transactions. Per household, the average number of trips to a branch is about three per month; branch visits are more frequent among higher income households. Close to half of the respondents (47 percent) reported that they do not use teller machines, and of these households, almost 60 percent indicated that "nothing could get them to use an ATM." See Trans Data Corporation (1989b).

[16] According to a 1988 survey, less than 20 percent of ATM-offering banks and thrifts (having more than $750 million in deposits) charged "us-on-us" transaction fees, and only 1 percent planned to add such fees in 1989. However, over 60 percent of such institutions charged for "us-on-others" transactions, and 12 percent more planned to begin charging such fees in 1989. The mean "us-on-us" transaction fee for institutions charging such fees was 21 cents, while the mean "us-on-other" fee for institutions charging such fees was 70 cents. See Trans Data Corporation (1988).

[17] Consolidated metropolitan statistical areas and metropolitan statistical areas are constructs defined by the U.S. Office of Management and Budget.

[18] According to Nakamura (1993), "in general, large firms have multiple relationships with banks. [Surveys of large corporations] show how complex these relationships can be." In part, these multiple banking relationships are a consequence of restrictions on bank branching.

[19] Other banks may not attach as much value to the additional branch or may have to incur higher costs to operate the branch.

than adding a branch to an existing network.

Thus, branching restrictions tend to reduce total branch coverage. By this reasoning, we can expect that repeal of interstate branching restrictions would have a beneficial impact on branch coverage because banks would establish branches at previously unserved locations as they expand interstate.

Empirical support for this line of reasoning is found in studies that investigate the factors determining bank branch coverage. Evanoff (1988) analyzes 1985 data on branch coverage for each county in the 48 contiguous states. He finds fewer branches per square mile in states with legal restrictions on branching, holding constant other factors such as whether the county is rural or urban. Similarly, Calem and Nakamura (1993), using 1990 data and controlling for a wide range of factors, find reduced branch coverage in states with highly restrictive branching laws. They find that, on average, branching restrictions entailed one less branch in non-MSA counties and 13 fewer branches in urban counties, holding county population, population density, and other factors constant.[20]

INTERSTATE BRANCHING AND COMPETITION

Some opponents of interstate branching have argued that branching restrictions are procompetitive, as they prevent large banks from acquiring smaller banks and turning them into branches. Thus, these restrictions help keep banking markets from becoming too concentrated.[21] This argument is less than convincing, for two reasons. First, many of the mergers or acquisitions that would take place under interstate branching would occur in unconcentrated markets or would be between banks operating in distinct markets or between banks that are subsidiaries of the same holding company. In general, such consolidations would not substantially raise concentration in banking markets. Second, federal bank regulators and the U.S. Department of Justice have the authority to block any acquisition or merger deemed to have anticompetitive effects. Hence, branching restrictions are not needed to prevent excessive market concentration.[22]

On the contrary, economic reasoning suggests that the lifting of interstate branching restrictions would benefit consumers by furthering competition in banking markets. The potential for banks to expand their branch networks across state lines could enhance competition in several ways. First, banks would be able to engage in nonprice competition more efficiently; some banks would be freed from having to provide convenience in forms that are more costly and less satisfactory than branching. The cost-savings would be passed on to consumers through lower prices. Second, for reasons discussed below, a bank establishing an extensive, multimarket branch network might opt to institute uniform pricing (uniform fees and interest rates) across disparate local markets by aligning prices in concentrated markets with those in competitive locales. Thus, branching tends to reduce price differentials between concentrated and competitive mar-

---

[20] Non-MSA counties in states without restrictive branching laws had a mean of 9 branches, while MSA counties in those states had a mean of 58 branches.

[21] Market concentration refers to the number and size distribution of firms in a market. More concentrated banking markets tend to be less competitive (see footnote 3).

[22] Under the Bank Merger Act and the Bank Holding Company Act, federal bank regulators must analyze the competitive effects of proposed mergers and acquisitions of banks and bank holding companies. If a proposed merger is expected to have a substantially adverse effect on competition, the merger application would be denied. In addition, the Justice Department has the authority under antitrust statutes to block anticompetitive mergers or acquisitions.

kets. Third, in many instances banks will choose to branch interstate by establishing de novo branches, thereby reducing concentration in the targeted markets. Let us elaborate on each of these arguments in turn.

Branching and Nonprice Competition. In markets where branching restrictions impose inconveniences on bank customers, banks may be compelled, through competition, to partly "compensate" their customers for these inconveniences. Such nonprice competition could take the form of longer banking hours, more tellers per branch, or other amenities that would mitigate the loss of convenience due to limited branching.

Providing such services drives up bank costs and results in higher fees and lower deposit interest rates for bank customers. Nevertheless, many bank customers will prefer some such nonprice "compensation" for lack of branching, even if they have to pay for it with higher fees. Banks would compete for these customers by providing them with the various amenities.[23]

In this sense, interstate branching restrictions may engender inefficiency in the provision of banking services, at least in markets that straddle state boundaries. Such restrictions may force banks to substitute less suitable and more expensive forms of convenience for their customers, who, in turn, would have to pay higher fees or accept lower deposit interest rates. With the lifting of such restrictions, nonprice competition would become more efficient. Through interstate branching, banks would be able to provide their customers with greater accessibility and convenience, at a lower cost.[24]

Branching and Intermarket Price Differentials. For several reasons, a bank having an extensive, multimarket branch network might opt to institute uniform pricing across disparate local markets by aligning prices in concentrated markets with those in competitive locales. One important motive for a bank to centralize pricing decisions is to economize on managerial or coordination costs. Uniform pricing may also enable the bank to save on advertising costs. In addition, the bank may want to institute uniform pricing across a multimarket area as a benefit to customers who reside in the area's largest banking market (the regional economic center), many of whom may regularly visit and conduct transactions at other localities in the area. A bank may be motivated to do so if the regional economic center is also the area's most competitive banking market.[25]

To the degree that branching motivates uniform pricing across multimarket areas, it tends to reduce price disparities between concentrated and competitive markets. Thus, when banks can branch freely across local markets, deposit interest rates in concentrated markets tend to be higher, and fees and loan rates lower, than they would be in the absence of branching. Through branching, competition is "exported" to concentrated markets. In this way, allowing banks to branch interstate would be procompetitive.

The preceding argument establishes in theory that bank branching furthers competition. But is this effect of branching on competition sig-

---

[23] Of course, there may be some customers for whom limited branching imposes minimal inconvenience. These customers would not require compensation for lost convenience. A bank may choose to specialize in serving these customers by defining itself as a "no-frills" bank, offering lower fees and/or higher rates but few amenities.

[24] I am grateful to Sherrill Shaffer for suggesting the idea that branching restrictions may cause inefficient nonprice competition.

[25] For a formalization of this argument, see Calem and Nakamura (1993).

nificant in practice? Empirical evidence indicates that it is. In particular, comparison of unit banking states to branching states with respect to within-state, cross-market differences in bank deposit interest rates indicates larger differentials in unit banking states. This is precisely what one would expect to find if branching is accompanied by consistency in pricing across local markets.

Table 3 reports statistics pertaining to within-state, cross-market differences in money market deposit account interest rates. The statistics are based on Federal Reserve survey data from 1985.[26] We compute the mean and standard error of these interest rate differentials for randomly selected pairs of banks from states that, in 1985, had severe restrictions on branching (pairs from "unit banking states"), and we do likewise for all other pairs (drawn from "branching states").[27] Paired banks are drawn from distinct markets within the same state. As indicated in the table, cross-market interest rate differentials are larger in unit banking states.[28] This finding is consistent with the view that branching reduces price disparities across local markets.[29]

Additional evidence is found in Mester (1987). Mester's study examines how competition among S&Ls varies across local markets in California. The study presents evidence that competition is "exported" to concentrated markets where rival S&L branch networks meet. Specifically, S&L deposit interest rates are found to be lower in markets (counties or MSAs) that are highly concentrated, but this effect is less pronounced if the market contains local branches of statewide institutions.

Interstate Branching and De Novo Entry. Nationwide interstate branching would further stimulate competition to the extent that it promotes de novo entry. In contrast to entry

---

[26] Data are obtained from the Federal Reserve's 1985 Monthly Survey of Selected Deposits and Other Accounts. We report statistics based on bank MMDA rates averaged over August, September, and October.

[27] As recently as 1985, 13 states had severe restrictions on bank branching: Colorado, Illinois, Iowa, Kansas, Minnesota, Missouri, Montana, Nebraska, North Dakota, Oklahoma, Texas, West Virginia, and Wyoming. In each of these states, more than 97 percent of statewide deposits were in banks with fewer than 10 branches. Since then, each of these states has eliminated or at least relaxed its in-state branching restrictions.

[28] The difference between the two means is statistically significant at the 1 percent level.

[29] Calem and Nakamura (1993) confirm this finding in the more rigorous context of a multivariate analysis and repeat the analysis using 1990 data, obtaining qualitatively the same result.

TABLE 3
MMDA Interest Rate Differentials for Randomly Paired Banks
(Cross-Market Pairs)

	Unit Banking States	Branching States
Mean Rate Differential	.38	.22
No. of Pairs in Sample	48	114
Standard Error	.06	.02

via acquisition of an existing bank or branch, the establishment of a de novo bank or branch has an immediate, direct impact on market concentration, increasing the number of competitors.

Would the elimination of the legal constraints on interstate branching lead to substantial de novo entry into local banking markets? Very likely the answer is yes, assuming that these restrictions are lifted unconditionally or not in a way that would result in legal obstacles to de novo entry. De novo entry via branching can be less costly than entry at the holding company level via the creation of a new bank subsidiary, which, in turn, generally is less costly than the establishment of a new institution directly by investors. Hence, elimination of legal constraints on interstate branching would expand the number of potential de novo entrants into any given banking market.[30]

Recent history provides evidence that easing of geographic constraints on banks is a stimulus to de novo entry. In a carefully executed, empirical study covering the period 1976-1988, Amel and Liang (1993) find a substantial, positive relationship between the number of de novo bank branches established in a state and the lifting of restrictions on in-state branching or on entry by out-of-state bank holding companies.[31]

IMPACT ON CREDIT ALLOCATION

Much of the controversy surrounding interstate branching concerns the impact it may have on the allocation of credit. Opponents of interstate branching fear that large multistate institutions will be less oriented toward small businesses and will siphon funds away from local community needs. Therefore, to the extent that small independent banks are replaced by these large institutions, small businesses will suffer.

There may be some truth to the notion that smaller banks are more oriented toward small-business lending than larger organizations. To some degree, all banks function as "information specialists," uniquely suited to evaluate credit risks and monitor borrowers.[32] Thus, banks in general lend to a more diverse group of borrowers than, for instance, the bond market. Naturally, however, there are differences among individual banks with respect to their informational roles. In general, small banks produce small-business loans more efficiently than large banks, while large banks have a comparative advantage at lending to medium-size or large borrowers.[33] Empirical evidence shows that small businesses depend more heavily on small or medium-size banks.[34]

---

[30] Similarly, repeal of the Douglas Amendment, to allow a bank holding company to establish a de novo subsidiary in any state, would eliminate an additional, important barrier to entry.

[31] Amel and Liang also find that de novo bank entry into local markets declined subsequent to relaxation of statewide branching restrictions, presumably because branch entry is a less costly substitute for bank entry. However, bank entry did not decline in this case as much as branch entry increased.

[32] See Calem and Rizzo (1992) for discussion of (and empirical evidence on) the role of banks as information specialists.

[33] At large banking organizations the lending process tends to be more streamlined, with lenders relying more heavily on standardized underwriting formulas. This favors large and medium-size firms, which are better able to supply information in a standardized form.

In a large multistate banking organization, local branch personnel typically have little discretion in their decision-making, while nonlocal personnel who are less constrained may be less well informed about or less sensitive to the needs of the local economy. Community banks, on the other hand, tend to be more flexible, better able to acquire and respond to specialized information about small local borrowers.

[34] For example, according to Danielson (1992), Barnett Banks (a Florida-based superregional) "claims relationships with 42 percent of Florida companies with annual

But are small institutions in danger of disappearing from the banking scene? Large institutions may, indeed, enjoy a cost advantage relative to small, community banks, in part because lending to small business may be a more costly activity (involving higher expenses per dollar loaned). Also, many small banks may have to pay more for deposits because they do not offer the convenience of a branch network (although others may attract sufficient deposits by offering more personalized service as a substitute for convenience). Large banks also may enjoy economies of scale with respect to advertising and marketing activities. Nevertheless, small banks will continue to coexist with large institutions, even under interstate branching, as long as they have a critical role to play in small-business lending. That is, small banks would remain profitable because small businesses would be willing to pay for their services.

Thus, there is little reason to believe that interstate branching will bring about the demise of independent community banks. To the extent that these banks are particularly responsive to the needs of small businesses and local communities, there will be enduring demand for their services, and they will continue to occupy profitable niches.

Indeed, thus far, fears that unfettered geographic expansion by large banking organizations would lead to the demise of community banks have proven groundless. For example, banks in California have enjoyed unrestricted statewide branching since 1927, and the state has had a regional interstate banking law since 1987; five of the 25 largest banking organizations in the U.S. currently operate subsidiaries there. Nevertheless, California has 442 banking institutions having less than $1 billion in assets, including 343 community banks with less than $200 million in assets, and these banks appear reasonably profitable.[35] Another example is Florida, which has permitted statewide branching for most of the last two decades, and which has had a regional interstate banking law since 1984.[36] As reported by Danielson (1992), "four superregionals now control more than half of the state's deposit base. But these regional giants face stiff competition from more than 300 community banks." Community banks have also held their own vis-a-vis superregionals and other large banks in North Carolina, which, like Florida, has long had statewide branching and has had regional interstate banking since 1984. In North Carolina "roughly 90 banks with assets less than $1 billion registered an average return on assets of 1.05 percent for the first three quarters of last year .... exactly the same as the nine banks with assets of $1 billion or more."[37]

Further, while smaller banks may be somewhat more oriented toward small-business lending than larger organizations, it is certainly not

---

sales exceeding $50 million, and with 30 percent of firms with sales from $5 million to $49 million annually. Its share with smaller companies, however, is only 12 percent, reflecting small bank strengths in this vital market."

Nakamura (1993) argues that smaller banks have a comparative advantage at lending to small borrowers. He summarizes existing empirical evidence and presents new evidence in support of this view.

[35] Only 18 banking organizations in the state have more than $1 billion in assets. These numbers are as of December 31, 1992.

According to Zimmerman (1990), California's community banks earn returns on assets "roughly comparable to those of larger rivals." According to Zimmerman (1992), after 1990, as the recession took hold and earnings at California banks declined across all size categories, larger banks suffered the steepest declines.

[36] Until 1990, Florida permitted statewide branching only through merger.

[37] See Bill Atkinson, "Small Carolina Banks Thrive in a Land of Giants," *American Banker*, February 9, 1993, p. 6. Another state where community banks have held their own, despite statewide branching by large banks, is New York. See King (1985).

the case that large banking organizations have no stake in lending to small businesses. In fact, according to Svare (1992), a number of large interstate banking institutions, such as Albany-based KeyCorp and Minneapolis-based Norwest, have strategically targeted consumers and small to midsize businesses. These institutions have sought to maintain flexibility and a local orientation through decentralized decision-making.

Large banks also engage in small-business lending as a way to meet their responsibilities under the federal Community Reinvestment Act (CRA). The CRA requires that every bank meet the credit needs of its entire community, to a degree consistent with safe and sound banking practices. Large banks' efforts to comply with the CRA generally include lending to small businesses and funding community development projects.[38] These efforts are likely to increase in the future because regulators are placing greater emphasis on banks' CRA obligations. If, however, multistate banks come to dominate some local market and act contrary to the interests of the local community, that case can be addressed through regulatory enforcement of the CRA.

While interstate branching may have the potential to harm local borrowers, it also has the potential to benefit them. In particular, a multistate bank may be in a better position to import funds into a community to finance a major local project. First, the geographically diversified bank can tap into its deposit base outside of the local community as an alternative to the national funds markets. Second, larger banks may have access to larger amounts of funds in the national markets, at lower cost, as compared with small, community banks, holding other factors (such as bank capital ratios) constant.[39] Smaller banks may be perceived as greater credit risks by the funds markets because their asset portfolios tend to be less diversified and because they are less well known.[40]

CONCLUSION

Removal of legal barriers to interstate branching would benefit consumers of banking services. Consumers in multistate areas would gain more convenient access to their accounts and related services. In addition, elimination of these barriers would enhance competition in banking, benefiting consumers through more favorable interest rates and fees. Also, interstate branching may facilitate the importation of funds into areas where credit demand is particularly strong.

Interstate branching raises some concerns regarding domination of local markets by large multistate banks that would be less oriented toward community credit needs. These concerns have been overstated, however. The evidence indicates that as long as there is sufficient demand for the credit services of community banks, there will be a profitable niche for these banks to occupy. And most large interstate organizations will seek to remain responsive to the needs of local customers.

As multistate organizations increase in number, size, and breadth, a few of them may become insensitive to community credit needs.

---

[38] For a detailed discussion of the CRA and related issues, see Calem (1989).

[39] For theory and evidence on the relationship between bank size and access to the federal funds market, see Allen and Saunders (1986) and Allen, Peristiani, and Saunders (1989).

[40] In addition, small-business borrowers, along with other small-bank customers, will obtain the convenience benefits described previously if small banks choose to branch interstate. It seems very likely that some small banks in multistate locales will establish out-of-state branches, just as some small holding companies have chosen to establish out-of-state subsidiaries (recall Table 2).

But through existing regulations governing community reinvestment, regulators have the ability to safeguard community interests. On balance, available evidence indicates that the removal of interstate branching restrictions would be advantageous to consumers.

REFERENCES

Allen, Linda, and Anthony Saunders. "The Large-Small Bank Dichotomy in the Federal Funds Market," *Journal of Banking and Finance* 10 (1986), pp. 219-230.

Allen, Linda, Stavros Peristiani, and Anthony Saunders. "Bank Size, Collateral, and Net Purchase Behavior in the Federal Funds Market: Empirical Evidence," *Journal of Business* 62 (1989), pp. 501-515.

Amel, Dean F., and J. Nellie Liang. "The Relationship between Entry into Banking Markets and Changes in Legal Restrictions on Entry," draft, Board of Governors of the Federal Reserve System (1993).

Calem, Paul S. "The Community Reinvestment Act: Increased Attention and a New Policy Statement," this *Business Review* (July/August 1989), pp. 3-16.

Calem, Paul S., and Gerald A. Carlino. "The Concentration/Conduct Relationship in Bank Deposit Markets," *Review of Economics and Statistics* 73 (May 1991), pp. 268-76.

Calem, Paul S., and Leonard I. Nakamura. "Branching Restrictions and Competition in Banking," draft, Federal Reserve Bank of Philadelphia (1993).

Calem, Paul S., and John A. Rizzo. "Banks as Information Specialists: The Case of Hospital Lending," *Journal of Banking and Finance* 16 (December 1992), pp. 1123-41.

Danielson, Arnold G. "Florida: National Banking's Test-Tube Market," *Bank Management* 68 (September 1992), pp. 30-40.

Evanoff, Douglas D. "Branch Banking and Service Accessibility," *Journal of Money, Credit and Banking* 20 (May 1988), pp. 191-202.

King, B. Frank. "Upstate New York: Tough Markets for City Banks," *Economic Review*, Federal Reserve Bank of Atlanta (June/July 1985), pp. 30-34.

Hannan, Timothy H. "Bank Commercial Loan Markets and the Role of Market Structure: Evidence from Surveys of Commercial Lending," *Journal of Banking and Finance* 15 (February 1991), pp. 133-49.

Mengle, David L. "The Case for Interstate Branch Banking," *Economic Review*, Federal Reserve Bank of Richmond (November/December 1990), pp. 3-17.

REFERENCES (Continued)

Mester, Loretta J. "Multiple Market Contact between Savings and Loans," *Journal of Money, Credit, and Banking* 19 (November 1987), pp. 538-49.

Nakamura, Leonard I. "Commercial Bank Information: Implications for the Structure of Banking," in Michael Klausner and Lawrence J. White, eds., *Structural Change in Banking*. Homewood, Illinois: Business One Irwin, 1993, pp. 131-60.

Svare, J. Christopher. "NationsBank Leads Charge for Interstate Branching," *Bank Management* 68 (June 1992), pp. 36-41.

Trans Data Corporation. "ATMs and Debit Cards: Strategy and Promotion," Wayne, PA (1988).

Trans Data Corporation. "Serving the Small Business Market," Wayne, PA (1989a).

Trans Data Corporation. "Consumer Financial Relationships," Wayne, PA (1989b).

U. S. Congress, "Impact of Bank Reform Proposals on Consumers," Hearing before the Subcommittee on Consumer Affairs and Coinage, Committee on Banking, Finance and Urban Affairs, House of Representatives (April 10, 1991).

Zimmerman, Gary C. "Small California Banks Hold Their Own," *Weekly Letter*, Federal Reserve Bank of San Francisco (January 26, 1990).

Zimmerman, Gary C. "California Banks' Problems Continue," *Weekly Letter*, Federal Reserve Bank of San Francisco (April 24, 1992).

Competitive Forces and Profit Persistence in Banking

Like virtually all industries, banking is subject to regulations that encourage competition. For example, banks cannot merge if doing so would tend to create monopolies in banking markets. However, unlike most other industries, banks are subject to a wide variety of regulations designed to protect the stability of the financial system and meet other objectives. As an unintended side effect, these regulations may dampen the forces of competition. For example, chartering requirements and branching restrictions may impede entry by new competitors and expansion by existing banks. Entry by nonbank financial or nonfinancial firms is limited due to legal restrictions on the activities in which banking firms may engage.

If the opposing influences of bank regulation have the net effect of weakening competitive forces, bank profits should reflect that. When bank profits differ from the "normal" competitive level, adjustment back to that level should take longer in banking than in other industries—that is, profits should be more persistent in banking. In this *Letter*, financial and stock price data are used to estimate the adjustment speed in the banking industry and, hence, to examine the degree to which abnormal bank profits tend to persist in the face of market forces. The results indicate that above-normal profits in banking are fairly long-lived compared to other industries.

Creation and destruction of above-normal profits

In theory, firms in competitive markets should earn normal long-run profits that provide investors with returns identical to those on comparable investments. A bank in a competitive market can earn above-normal profits for some period only by having a product that is perceived as superior in some dimension—successful product differentiation—or by producing the same products as competitors but at lower cost—successful cost leadership. Meaningful cost and product differentials might arise through luck; for example, a bank might happen to be located in a region that experiences a relative decline in labor costs. Or product and cost differences might be created intentionally, through new products and services whose value exceeds their cost to the bank, or innovative ideas for cutting costs without unduly sacrificing current levels of service and product quality. Either good fortune or good ideas can create a "competitive advantage" for a bank, leading to an increase in profits without a corresponding increase in risk.

But if competitive forces are allowed to operate, such an advantage cannot last indefinitely. Competitors will move into a newly profitable market segment—either a product market or a geographic market—as soon as they can, or will imitate successful new practices. Once competitors catch up, the competitive advantage is erased and the bank once again earns only normal profits. Persistent above-normal profits in the face of these market-based adjustments depends in large part on structural characteristics of the markets involved and on the conduct of the players in those markets. The speed of adjustment is an indicator of how competitive the banking industry is; information on bank stock prices can be used to measure that adjustment speed.

The effect of profitability on stock prices

Bank share prices generally reflect expected future profits, with heavier weight given to near-term profitability, but with significant weight also given to long-run profits. In financial terms, the price of a stock reflects the present discounted value of expected future profits. Thus for banks with publicly traded stock, higher profits from a competitive advantage translate into higher share prices. As a very broad generalization, if a bank always earns normal profits, its stock price is equal to the accounting book value per share. Higher profits tend to push the market value above book value.

The relationship between future profits and a bank's current stock price implies that not only the current level, but also the longevity of any above-normal profits is likely to have an important influence on bank stock prices. The longer the above-normal profits are expected to persist, the higher the current market value of the stock will be relative to book value. The relationship between bank stock values and the degree of profit persistence can yield insight into stock market investors' implicit beliefs about the rate of adjustment of profits.

An initial view of the relationship
A necessary first step in analyzing profit persistence is to define what is meant by "profits" and what is meant by "normal" profits. Profits can be measured by the return on equity (ROE), which is net income divided by the book value of the bank's stockholder equity. A normal level for the profit rate could be defined using any of several approaches (the results are relatively insensitive to the method used to establish the normal level). A widely used model from finance, the Capital Asset Pricing Model (CAPM), was adopted for this analysis. The CAPM uses stock returns to provide an estimate of the normal rate of return, taking into account risk and the general level of interest rates. The difference between a bank's actual ROE and the estimated normal return from the CAPM is a measure of the extent to which profits differ from what should be expected given the level of risk taken by the bank. This abnormal profit differential can be termed the "profit spread."

A simple examination of the relationship between stock values and past profit spreads can reveal the existence of bank profit persistence. Expectations of positive profit spreads from competitive advantages should increase bank share prices. Negative spreads from below-normal profits—arising from bad luck or bad decisions —should reduce stock prices. The more persistent the spreads are, the more the stock prices will be raised or depressed relative to book value. But only expected *future* profits have this effect; if *past* profit spreads are systematically related to current market-to-book ratios, the market must believe that bank profits are persistent, with above-normal profits in the recent past signaling the likely continuation of those spreads into the future.

Chart 1 illustrates the relationship between past profit spreads and bank market-to-book ratios, for a sample of 126 banks and bank holding companies (all referred to here as "banks" for convenience). Each point represents one bank. The vertical axis shows the market-to-book ratio as of the end of June 1991. The horizontal axis measures the profit spread for each bank, with profits measured over the year ending in June of 1991. Banks in the right half of Chart 1 earned more than the normal return, while those on the left earned less than they should have for the level of risk taken.

Chart 1: Effect of Profitability on Stock Value

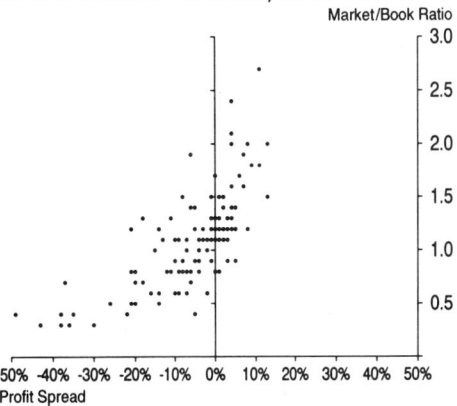

The chart indicates that, as a general rule, firms with higher recent spreads have higher current stock values. Moreover, those with above-normal past profits tend to have market stock prices above book value, while the opposite is true for those with low past profits. The positive relationship suggests that the market takes high profits from the immediate past as an indication of high future profits, and low past profits as an indication of low future profits—that is, profits are persistent. However, more information is needed to determine how great that persistence is.

Quantifying the effects
To look more closely at profit persistence in banking, and to compare it to other industries, a theoretical model was developed describing the linkage between current and future profitability and the market-to-book ratio. The model takes into account the level of interest rates, growth rates of banks, and differences in risk across banks. The unique aspect of the model is that it also incorporates market expectations of profit spread decay over time. The theoretical model was then translated into a statistical model and applied to the same sample of banks used in Chart 1, to examine the empirical relationship between stock prices and profitability, and ultimately to decipher stock market investors' implicit beliefs about the rate of profit decay.

One significant problem was ignored above to simplify the exposition: Reported accounting profits may not accurately reflect banks' true profitability. A variety of well-known peculiarities of accounting practice might lead to accounting profits being imprecise and biased as measures of true economic profitability. Investors in the market probably use accounting information, but also filter the reported numbers to determine a "true" (higher or lower) level of profits. These investor opinions are then reflected in the market price of bank shares. The statistical analysis took this complication into account. (Details are available from the author.)

The statistical results showed that advantages in banking are fairly long lasting. The adjustment speed based on the 1991 sample data is 4.4 percent per year for banks with above-normal profits; that is, 4.4 percent of any positive spread between actual profits and the normal level should disappear each year, all else equal. Comparable evidence for other industries is scarce, but suggests that profit spreads disappear more quickly for other kinds of firms: Other studies have found rates ranging from 30 percent to 70 percent for firms outside of banking.

Interestingly, while above-normal profits last a long time, below-normal profits vanish much more quickly; the estimated speed of adjustment for negative profit spreads was 23.6 percent per year. (Statistically, the adjustment speeds for high and low profit banks are significantly different, and both rates are significantly greater than zero and less than one.) It seems reasonable that negative spreads should be less persistent, since the banks that have the best information about the existence and sources of the losses—the afflicted banks themselves—are also those in the best position to act on that information. In contrast, positive spreads are reduced only when *other* banks notice a competitor with a spread-creating advantage, analyze its sources, and act to copy or eliminate the advantage; in many cases, acquiring the needed information may be expensive and difficult for the other banks.

Chart 2 illustrates the difference in adjustment between positive and negative spreads. The chart shows the time path of the profit spreads implied by the model for a hypothetical bank that begins with normal profits, then develops an advantage (the upper, solid line) or disadvantage (the lower, broken line) producing an initial spread of 10 percentage points either way. For both positive and negative differences, the profit spread adjusts back toward zero (that is, a position of normal profitability) over time, but much more rapidly from below than from above.

Chart 2: Profit Adjustment Paths

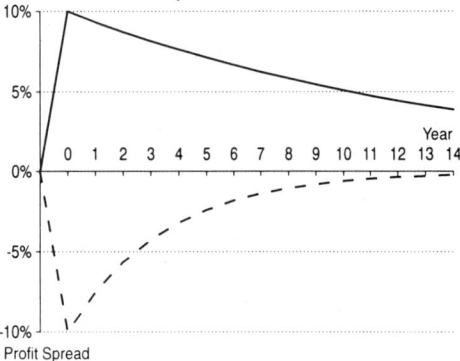

Conclusion

An examination of the relationship between bank profitability and bank share prices shows that once a bank's economic profits rise above or fall below a normal level, the profit spread persists for some time. However, profits do eventually return to normal. The fact that high profits are not infinitely persistent is itself an important point. Despite the fact that banking is a heavily regulated industry, market forces operate to drive high (and low) profits back toward normal levels.

Persistent profits have ambiguous implications for policy. In a sense, above-normal profits mean that bank customers are paying too much. They would be better off obtaining banking products or services at prices closer to cost, with banks earning only normal rates of profit. However, the prospect of persistent high profits may encourage innovation that benefits bank customers, in much the same way that patent protection does in other industries. Moreover, some of the slow adjustment of profits probably results from regulation; the damage from weakened competitive forces must be weighed against the benefits, such as safety and soundness, that banking regulations achieve.

Mark E. Levonian
Research Officer

Article 5

Lenders and environmental policies

Eleanor H. Erdevig

One of the major issues influencing economic development in the nineties is the possible impact of environmental laws and regulations. Many analysts expect the effect to be significant as companies seek to comply with environmental requirements.

Among those increasingly affected by environmental policies are lenders who generally provide the funds to borrowers for business operations and expansion. Lenders have found themselves at risk for environmental compliance both indirectly, when a borrower is faced with the added costs of complying with environmental laws, and directly, when a borrower defaults on a loan.

This article examines the liability of lenders and the nature of the risk exposure for financial institutions as a result of environmental laws and regulations. It reviews the recent court record relating to financial institution lending associated with contaminated properties. It discusses proposed measures to reduce the uncertainty for lenders under current environmental policies. And, given the long history of industrial activity within Seventh District states—Illinois, Indiana, Iowa, Michigan, and Wisconsin—it considers whether this area may be more affected by environmental policies than elsewhere in the United States.

Environmental legislation

On January 1, 1970, President Nixon signed into law the National Environmental Policy Act of 1969 (NEPA) which established environmental protection and preservation of our natural resources as a national policy. The act provided for an Environmental Protection Agency (EPA), the President's Council on Environmental Quality, and an environmental impact review program. With the founding of the EPA in December 1970, the environmental movement entered a new phase.

Other major environmental legislation followed. Most of this legislation was directed primarily toward monitoring and regulating the ongoing activities of individuals and corporations that might contribute to a deterioration in our environment. Among the legislation either enacted or amended was the Clean Air Act, the Solid Waste Disposal Act, amended by the Resource Conservation and Recovery Act (RCRA) of 1976, the Toxic Substances Control Act (TSCA), and the Safe Drinking Water Act.

In 1978, the conditions in the Love Canal community, which had been built over an abandoned hazardous waste dump in upstate New York, prompted Congress to investigate the problems associated with toxic waste sites. The resulting legislation, the Comprehensive Environmental Response, Compensation, and Liability Act of 1980 (CERCLA), commonly known as the Superfund act, was enacted, according to its preamble, "to provide for liability, compensation, cleanup, and emergency response for hazardous substances released into the environment and the cleanup of inactive

---

Eleanor H. Erdevig is a senior economist at the Federal Reserve Bank of Chicago. The author would like to thank David R. Allardice for guidance and help on earlier drafts and the editor for pertinent comments.

hazardous waste disposal sites." The law was subsequently amended by the Superfund Amendments and Reauthorization Act of 1986 (SARA)[1].

The passage of CERCLA ended the disinterested party status of financial institutions. Previously, for the most part, financial institutions were bystanders and not directly affected by environmental legislation. Many were of the opinion that the environmental law developments were a concern only for those enterprises that produced some form of environmental externalities, such as smoke, solid waste, and water discharges.

The intent of CERCLA was to assign the cost of cleanup of contaminated sites to the responsible parties. In addition to the parties responsible for placing the contamination in the ground, the act assigned responsibility to successors in the chain of title, for example, the present property owner. The third parties responsible for the cleanup costs are those "associated" with the title to the contaminated property, for example, a mortgagee. It is in this third grouping that financial institutions have found themselves at risk. This risk exposure has led to and may continue to lead to significant financial losses associated with lending to enterprises responsible for contaminated properties.

CERCLA identifies four broad classes of responsible parties that are liable for the costs of cleaning up hazardous substances when the federal government, state government, or a private party brings suit. The first two classes include any person owning or operating a vessel or an onshore or offshore facility, that is, owners or operators. If the title or control to a facility is conveyed to a unit of state or local government due to bankruptcy, foreclosure, or tax delinquency, the person who owned, operated, or otherwise controlled activities at such a facility immediately before the transfer remains the responsible owner or operator. The third class includes persons who arranged for disposal, treatment, or transportation of hazardous substances. The fourth class includes those who transported any hazardous substances to selected sites.

Persons included in the four classes may be exempt from liability if they can establish that they acquired the contaminated property after the disposal or placement of the hazardous substance at the facility and if they are able to claim the "innocent landowner's" defense. To do so, they must establish that they exercised what is called "environmental due diligence," that is, at the time they acquired the facility, they did not know and had no reason to know that any hazardous substance was disposed of at the facility. To establish that they had no reason to know, the law provides that they must have undertaken, at the time of the acquisition, all appropriate inquiry into the previous ownership and use of the property consistent with good commercial or customary practice.

The definition of "owners or operators" of facilities as potentially liable parties under CERCLA includes an exemption for persons who hold a "security interest" in a facility. According to the law, the owner or operator definition does not include "a person, who, without participating in the management of a vessel or facility, holds indicia [a form] of ownership primarily to protect his security interest in the vessel or facility."

Interpretation of this "security interest" exemption under CERCLA has generated uncertainty within the financial and lending communities, particularly with regard to the extent to which a secured creditor may undertake activities to oversee the affairs of a borrower or debtor, for the purposes of protecting the security interest, without incurring CERCLA liability. Specifically, there is concern over whether certain actions commonly taken by the holder of a security interest—such as monitoring facility operations, requiring compliance activities, refinancing or undertaking loan workouts, providing financial advice, and similar actions that may affect the financial, management, and operational aspects of a business—are properly considered to be evidence that the security holder is "participating in the management of a facility." There is also concern regarding the effect of foreclosure on the security interest exemption of the lender.

Recent major court cases

Court cases have gradually been addressing the issues of lender responsibilities and liabilities. Two types of cases are of particular interest to lenders; those involving the "innocent landowner's" defense and those involving the security interest exemption. Cases involving the innocent landowner's defense are of interest to lenders because of the impact of compliance with environmental law on the borrowers' ability to repay the loan, the consequent default risk, and the risk assumed by the lender if foreclosure is necessary. Cases involving the security interest exemption are of interest because of the uncertainty surrounding the type of activities which might be engaged in by the lender to monitor the loan and the extent of the risk exposure.

In an early 1985 bankruptcy case, *In re T. P. Long Chemical, Inc.*,[2] the EPA applied to be reimbursed by the bankruptcy estate for costs incurred in removing drums of hazardous substances discovered on the property of the debtor, a rubber recycling company. Some of the funds in the estate represented the proceeds from an auction by the trustee of personal property in which a bank held a security interest. The court relied on the security interest exemption to find that the bank as a secured creditor was not liable for costs incurred by the EPA under CERCLA. The court stated that if collateral becomes worthless or poses a risk to the public, the secured creditor is under no obligation to assume possession of the collateral or to insure against the risk. Furthermore, if the bank had repossessed its collateral, it would not be an "owner or operator" as defined under CERCLA because its only "indicia of ownership" was primarily to protect its security interest and it had not participated in the management of the facility.

Subsequently in 1985 a seminal case addressed the protection provided to lenders by the security interest exemption from the liability imposed on owners and operators. In *United States v. Mirabile*,[3] a bank, one of the secured creditors, foreclosed on its mortgage and successfully bid at a sheriff's sale for the property of a defunct business that had created a hazardous waste. Four months later the bank assigned its bid to the Mirabiles. When the EPA sued the Mirabiles to recover its cleanup costs, the Mirabiles joined the bank as third-party defendants. The court held that a lender may be liable as an "owner or operator" of contaminated property if it participates in the day-to-day "operational, production, or waste disposal activities" of its borrower's business on the property. However, facility monitoring, involvement in financial decisions, restrictions on financial decisions contained in loan documents, and general financial advice were permissible. In addition, the court stated that the mere financial ability to control waste disposal practices was not sufficient for the imposition of liability. The court found that the bank was not liable because it had not participated in the management of the business, and its actions after foreclosure were undertaken merely to protect its security interest in the property. Foreclosure and repurchase were considered to be a natural consequence of protecting a security interest.

The following year, in the case of *United States v. Maryland Bank & Trust Company*,[4] a district court adopted a narrower interpretation of a lender's liability after foreclosure. In the *Maryland Bank* case, the EPA sued the bank under CERCLA for reimbursement of the costs of cleanup of a hazardous waste dump after the bank had foreclosed on the property. Maryland Bank, although clearly the owner, claimed that it held title to the property "primarily to protect its security interest in the property," and was, therefore, not an owner as contemplated by the statute. However, the court found that Maryland Bank had "purchased the property at the foreclosure sale not to protect its security interest, but to protect its investment." Only during the life of the mortgage did the Bank "hold indicia of ownership primarily to protect its security interest in the land." Further, the court noted that Maryland Bank had held title for nearly four years after foreclosure and for a full year before the EPA cleanup and that the *Mirabile* decision "pertained to a situation in which the mortgagee-turned-owner promptly assigned the property [after four months]." Consequently, according to the court, current ownership after foreclosure in this case was sufficient to impose liability on the bank, even if the bank was not operating the contaminated facility. As a result, Maryland Bank had to pay more than half a million dollars in cleanup and court costs and was unable to recover its costs or original investment on resale.

Although the court in the *Maryland Bank* case did not address the issue, there is the possibility that a lender, otherwise liable, can take advantage of the "innocent landowner's" defense to liability normally available to a purchaser. For this defense, the purchaser must have "undertaken, at the time of the acquisition, all appropriate inquiry into the previous ownership and uses of the property consistent with good commercial or customary practice"—the so-called "environmental due diligence." On the assumption that the lender may be an owner after foreclosure, he or she may also need to prove that appropriate inquiry was made when the loan was approved and prior to foreclosure.

In *U.S. v. Nicolet, Inc.*,[5] the court also considered the application of the security exemption exclusion to mortgagees. In *Nicolet*, a parent corporation, T&N plc, owned all of the stock of a subsidiary, Keasbey & Mattison Company, the previous owner of Nicolet's contaminated site, and held a mortgage on Keasbey's property. The court denied a motion by T&N plc to dismiss the government's complaint that T&N plc was directly liable because it held a mortgage on the site and actively participated in the management of the facility. Without reaching a final decision on liability, the court stated that "existing case law suggests that a mortgagee can be held liable under CERCLA only if the mortgagee participated in the managerial and operational aspects of the facility in question." In a consent decree, T&N plc subsequently agreed to implement the remedy called for by the EPA.

A subsequent case in 1989, *Guidice v. BFG Electroplating and Manufacturing Co., Inc.*,[6] also addressed bank liability prior to and after foreclosure on contaminated property on which it held a mortgage. In this case, the court relied on the standards stated in *Mirabile* and *Nicolet* in reviewing the bank's activities and concluded that the key question was "whether the bank had passed the point of protecting its security interest and was participating in the management or control" of its borrower. Finding that there was "no evidence suggesting that the bank controlled operational, production, or waste disposal activities" at the facility prior to foreclosure, the court ruled that the bank fell within the security interest exemption for this period. After the foreclosure and the bank's purchase of the property at the sheriff's sale (which it sold after eight months), the court relied on the *Maryland Bank & Trust* decision and the failure of the 1986 CERCLA amendments to specifically exempt mortgagees-turned-landowners to hold the bank liable "to the same extent as any other bidder at the (foreclosure) sale would have been." The court indicated that it viewed lenders as serving an environmental policing function by paying close attention to environmental compliance to protect their financial stake.

A recent decision in the U.S. Court of Appeals for the Eleventh Circuit, *United States v. Fleet Factors Corp.*,[7] however, has introduced additional uncertainty into the meaning of the security interest exemption and the extent of lender liability under CERCLA. In this case, Fleet Factors, a commercial factoring firm, advanced funds to a cloth printing company on the company's accounts receivable, with its facility and its equipment, inventory, and fixtures as collateral. After the textile firm was adjudged bankrupt, Fleet Factors foreclosed on its security interest in inventory and equipment and arranged for its sale and removal, but did not foreclose on its mortgage on the facility. The EPA subsequently found hazardous waste on the property and sued to recover its costs of cleanup. The district court adopted the interpretation of the security interest exclusion previously accepted by other courts, stating that the exclusion permits secured creditors to "provide financial assistance and general, and even isolated instances of specific, management advice to its debtors without risking CERCLA liability if the secured creditor does not participate in the day-to-day management of the business or facility either before or after the business ceases operation." The court denied Fleet Factors' motion to dismiss the government's complaint, but granted Fleet Factors the right to appeal. On appeal, the Eleventh Circuit disagreed with the district court's interpretation of the CERCLA security interest exemption and remanded the case for further analysis consistent with its interpretation. The Eleventh Circuit stated that a secured creditor may be liable under CERCLA "by participating in the financial management of a facility to a degree indicating a *capacity to influence* (emphasis supplied) the corporation's treatment of hazardous wastes. It is not necessary for the secured creditor actually to involve itself in the day-to-day operations of the facility in order to be liable—although such conduct will certainly lead to the loss of the protection of the statutory exemption. Nor is it necessary for the secured creditor to participate in management decisions related to hazardous waste. Rather, a secured creditor will be liable if its involvement with the management of the facility is sufficiently broad to support the inference that it could affect hazardous waste disposal decisions if it so chose." In contrast to previous cases, which permit lenders to exercise general financial controls over a troubled borrower, the appellate court stated that the lender's capacity to influence a debtor facility's treatment of hazardous wastes may be inferred from the extent of its involvement in the financial management of the facility. Thus, according to the court, Fleet Factors could be held liable as the "owner" of the facility because Fleet Factors' mortgage on the property constituted an "indicia of ownership," and its involvement in either the financial management or the operational management of the facility could cause it to lose its security interest exemption.

In support of its interpretation, the Eleventh Circuit reasoned that the lower the threshold of control employed to determine whether the benefit of the exemption had been lost, the greater the incentive would be for lenders to play the role of environmental policeman to keep borrowers in compliance. The court reasoned that its ruling would encourage lenders to investigate the potential borrower's environmental practices and to factor the discovered risks of CERCLA liability into the terms of the loan agreement. The lower threshold would also encourage lenders to monitor borrowers' waste management practices and "insist upon compliance with acceptable treatment standards as a prerequisite to continued and future financial support."

A subsequent decision by the Ninth Circuit Court of Appeals, *In re Bergsoe Metal Corp.*,[8] however, stated that the mere capacity or unexercised right to control facility operations is insufficient to void the security exemption, and stated that "there must be some actual management of the facility before a secured creditor will fall outside the exception." In its discussion of what constitutes management, the court held that "a secured creditor will always have some input at the planning stages of any large-scale project and, by the extension of financing, will perforce encourage those projects it feels will be successful. If this were 'management,' no secured creditor would ever be protected." In addition, the court held that certain rights that a secured creditor reserves to protect its investment, such as the right to inspect the premises and to reenter and take possession upon foreclosure, does not put it in a position of management. According to the court's decision, "what is critical is not what rights the Port (the creditor) had, but what it did. The CERCLA security interest exception uses the active 'participating in management.' Regardless of what rights the Port may have had, it cannot have participated in management if it never exercised them."

The recent *Fleet Factors* and *Bergsoe* decisions have introduced additional uncertainty into the question of the liability of lenders for hazardous wastes produced by the operations of borrowers. Of particular concern are the extent to which lenders may oversee the activities of debtors, particularly troubled borrowers, without being considered to be participating in management, and the effect of foreclosure and subsequent purchase of the collateral by the creditor. The resulting new risks in lending are discussed below.

Traditional risks in lending

Prior to the passage of environmental legislation, particularly CERCLA, during the last two decades, a financial institution's risk associated with lending was generally considered to consist of two elements: default risk and market or interest rate risk. Default risk is related to the probability that the debtor will be unable to perform all of the legal requirements set forth in the loan contract. Most frequently, default is triggered when the borrower fails to meet principal and interest payments in accordance with the terms of the contract. To minimize their exposure to default risk, financial institutions frequently secure loans with collateral. Thus, if the borrower defaults on the loan, the financial institution is able, in theory, to sell the collateral and recover all or a portion of the loan. The maximum possible loss to the financial institution arising from default risk should be no greater than the size of the loan outstanding, plus any legal and administrative costs.

The second type of traditional risk in lending is called market or interest rate risk. For example, as long term interest rates fall, mortgages tend to be refinanced or paid off. The financial institution is then in a position of having to reinvest those funds at the lower market interest rate. Alternatively, as rates rise, the financial institution may be caught holding assets that are yielding a return less than the current market rate.

New risks in lending

Environmental laws and regulations have introduced additional uncertainty and a new dimension to risk for financial institutions in lending. Compliance with environmental legislation in general represents an indirect risk to the lender because of the requirements imposed on the borrower. In reviewing the default risk, the lender must also now consider the borrower's current and potential costs of compliance with environmental laws and regulations. If the compliance imposes an additional financial burden on the borrower, he or she may be less able to pay the interest and principal of a loan. Thus the lender must be assured that the borrower has exercised "due diligence" and is protected by the "innocent landowner's" defense in the acquisition of property which may or may not be used as collateral for the loan. The lender must also be reasonably certain that the borrower is aware of any environmental laws and regulations which might be expected to affect the operation of his or her business.

The new dimension to the risks faced by a lender is that a financial institution may become liable for the costs of cleanup of contaminated property owned by a borrower. The "security interest exemption" was intended to limit the exposure of lenders to such liability, but it requires that lenders not participate in the management of the borrower's business. As discussed in the previous section, recent court decisions have introduced additional uncertainty into what activities are permitted by the lender without losing the security interest exemption. If the security interest exemption is lost and the lender is adjudged to have acted as an owner or operator, the lender may incur environmental cleanup costs which exceed the total amount of the loan.

Much of the uncertainty revolves around whether there should be a low or high threshold for "participation in management" and therefore for lender liability for cleanup. A low threshold means that lenders would be considered to be participating in management even though there was very little oversight of their borrowers' operations. Some advocates of a low threshold believe that lenders would thus be more likely to monitor borrowers' compliance with environmental laws and regulations, rather than risk liability for the costs of cleanup. Lenders would, in effect, serve as environmental auditors. According to the decision in *Fleet Factors*, the ruling was expected to "encourage potential creditors to investigate thoroughly the waste treatment systems and policies of potential debtors. If the treatment systems seem inadequate, the risk of CERCLA liability will be weighed into the terms of the loan agreement. Creditors, therefore, will incur no greater risk than they bargained for and debtors, aware that inadequate hazardous waste treatment will have a significant adverse impact on their loan terms, will have powerful incentives to improve their handling of hazardous wastes.

"Similarly, creditors' awareness that they are potentially liable under CERCLA will encourage them to monitor the hazardous waste treatment systems and policies of their debtors and insist upon compliance with acceptable treatment standards as a prerequisite to continued and future financial support. Once a secured creditor's involvement with a facility becomes sufficiently broad that it can anticipate losing its exemption from CERCLA liability, it will have a strong incentive to address hazardous waste problems at the facility rather than studiously avoiding the investigation and amelioration of the hazard."

Those opposed to a low threshold believe that this would represent additional risks for lenders for which they may not be compensated. Limiting the oversight activities of borrowers' operations to avoid being considered to be "participating in management" would increase the risks to lenders because they would have less information about the operations of borrowers. Lenders are reluctant to make loans where there are additional risks which may be highly uncertain and unquantifiable. In the *Guidice* ruling discussed above, the court stated that "a low liability standard would encourage a lender to terminate its association with a financially troubled debtor and expedite loan payments in an effort to recover the debts."

A high threshold means that a lender would be able to engage in more monitoring of and advising about a borrower's activities without being considered to be "participating in management." In this case, it would be in the interests of the lender to be sure that the borrower is complying with environmental laws and regulations, because failure of the borrower to do so increases his or her liability for cleanup costs and the risk of defaulting on the loan. The decision in the *Guidice* case states, "A goal of CERCLA is safe handling and disposal of hazardous waste. To encourage banks to monitor a debtor's use of security property, a high liability threshold will enhance the dual purposes of protection of the banks' investments and promoting CERCLA's policy goals."

It is important that the appropriate level of threshold for participation in management by lenders be resolved. Although a low threshold may encourage lenders to more carefully assess the risks involved prior to lending with contaminated property as collateral, the inability to carefully monitor the borrower's operations after the loan is made without incurring CERCLA liability will generally restrict the availability of credit for such loans. A high threshold, on the other hand, will enable the lender to more closely monitor a borrower's operations to prevent default and assure compliance with environmental laws and regulations without incurring CERCLA liability.

In either case, lending with possibly contaminated property as collateral involves extra costs for environmental inspections and appraisals. Monitoring the activities of borrowers to ensure compliance with environmental laws and regulations increases the costs of servicing the loan for lenders. Although the terms of the loan can include the recovery of some costs, the extent of the risk assumed by the lender may be difficult to quantify. Consequently, some risk may be uncompensated.

If the borrower defaults on the loan, foreclosure on property serving as collateral presents additional risk and uncertainty. If the lender acquires the property upon foreclosure, he or she may be considered as the owner liable for cleanup of contaminated properties. In addition, the property may not be saleable because it is contaminated.

Proposed clarifications of lender liability

As discussed above, recent court decisions on lender liability under environmental law have increased uncertainty among banks and other lenders and may affect the availability of credit. Currently, both the EPA and Congress are attempting to rectify the situation.

In August 1990, in response to concern regarding the possible effects of lender liability on the availability of credit, the EPA promised a House panel that the agency would issue a rule to clarify the bounds of the "safe harbor" provided by the CERCLA security interest exemption. After a number of reviews and revisions the EPA proposed rule was announced on June 5, 1991.[9] The proposed rule is an interpretation of the existing "security interest exemption" to CERCLA liability of both privately owned financial institutions and governmental loan guarantors or lending entities.

The EPA rule recognizes that security holders that possess an ownership interest in a facility may need to undertake certain activities in the course of protecting their security interest to properly manage their loan portfolios. Such activities may include inspections or monitoring of the borrower's business and collateral, providing financial or other assistance, engaging in loan workout activities, and foreclosing on secured property. In recognition of the need for these activities, the EPA rule describes a range of permissible activities that may be undertaken by a private or governmental lending institution in the course of protecting its security interest in a facility, without being considered to be participating in the facility's management and thereby voiding the exemption. To clarify the *Fleet Factors* decision, it states that participation in management means "actual participation in the management or operational affairs by the holder of the security interest, and does not include the mere capacity, or ability to influence, or the unexercised right to control facility operations."

The EPA regulations also provide a safe harbor allowing the lender either to foreclose on the property or to take a deed in lieu of foreclosure. No time limit is specified for the sale of the property, but the lender is required within 12 months of foreclosure to list the property with a broker and to continue to advertise the property for sale, at least monthly thereafter. At any time more than six months after foreclosure, the lender may not reject or fail to act upon within 90 days a bona fide offer to purchase the property for fair consideration. Fair consideration is defined as outstanding principal plus interest and costs of holding the property.

The EPA rule also encourages, but does not require, the common practice of holders of security interests to undertake or require environmental inspections to minimize the risk that their loans will be secured by contaminated property. Such inspections are considered to be consistent with the security interest exemption and the lender is not considered to be participating in the management of the facility.

Bills were introduced in March 1991 in both the House and in the Senate which were designed to clarify lenders' liability under current environmental laws. The bill submitted by Representative John LaFalce (HR 1450)[10] is a revised version of legislation which he introduced in earlier congressional sessions. In introducing the bill, Mr. LaFalce stated that "testimony [at Small Business Committee hearings during the 101st Congress] from Government agencies, business community representatives, environmentalists, and bankers made clear that banks and other lending institutions are increasingly refusing loans to creditworthy small businesses that either use hazardous materials or are located in areas of possible contamination because of fears regarding potential liability generated by court action." For the most part the revision incorporates the provisions of the rule prepared by the EPA and would amend CERCLA of 1980 and RCRA of 1976. According to Mr. LaFalce, the House bill seeks to clarify the liability under those acts of lending institutions, fiduciaries, trustees, and others holding indicia of ownership primarily to protect a security interest in facilities subject to those environmental laws. At the same time he expects the revised legislation to address concerns of the environmental community by encouraging the conduct of environmental assessments, assuring that lenders and other parties who are directly responsible for environmental damage remain liable, encouraging lenders to take action to remedy environmental damage rather than walk away from their collateral, and requiring lenders foreclosing on property to move diligently to dispose of that property in order to remain within the bounds of the security exemption.

The Senate bill, sponsored by Senator Jake Garn (S 651),[11] is known as the Federal Deposit Insurance Improvement Act of 1991, and is similar to legislation that he introduced a year earlier. It amends the Federal Deposit Insurance Act to cap the liability of insured depository institutions and other mortgage lenders under federal statutes that impose strict liability for the release of hazardous materials, provided that the institution or company involved did not cause or contribute to the contamination. For insured depository institutions, the limitation applies to property acquired through foreclosure, held in a fiduciary capacity, or held as a lessor pursuant to a lease that is the functional equivalent of a loan. If a cleanup is conducted, the liability of the institution is limited to the actual benefit it receives, up to the fair market value of the property. The limitation does not apply if any institution or company, after acquisition of property through foreclosure or the termination of a lease agreement, fails to take reasonable steps to prevent the continued release of a hazardous substance after such release is discovered. To clarify the uncertainty created by the decision in the *Fleet Factors* case, the Senate bill also provides that an insured depository institution or mortgage lender will not be liable under federal law because they have the unexercised capacity to influence operations at or on property in which the institution has a security interest. The Senate bill would also protect federal banking and lending agencies against liability under state and federal laws for contamination on property acquired in connection with receivership or conservatorship activities, in connection with the provisions of a loan, or as a result of a civil or criminal proceeding, as long as they did not cause or contribute to the release of hazardous substances. The Senate bill has been incorporated into the banking reform bill as Title X which is under consideration in the Senate for approval.

The rules and regulations proposed by the EPA have received mixed reviews. Bankers and other lenders have indicated that they still want the level of certainty that only legislation would bring. Lenders fear that courts will not use an EPA rule to block private lawsuits brought by other interested parties against lenders. Environmental groups, on the other hand, claim that the banking industry's contention that it is facing enormous potential liability from hazardous waste sites is exaggerated. They oppose new legislation and assert that the threat of lenders' liability encourages lenders to investigate whether a company has a toxic-waste problem before agreeing to lend to it. Environmentalists expect this to make companies more vigilant about obeying environmental laws.

Contaminated sites in the Seventh District

Seventh District states have a long history of industrial activity and many of the cities in the region have grown into major manufacturing centers. With the activity and the growth have come the need to dispose of wastes that may be contaminated. It is such wastes that may result in liability for remedial action under CERCLA.

Banks in Seventh District states are very concerned with their potential liability under CERCLA. Overall, banks indicate a general unwillingness to lend to borrowers that are involved with hazardous materials. They cite the costs for both legal and investigative reviews which are now included in most commercial lending relationships where real property is taken as collateral. Due to the unsettled state of federal case law concerning the degree of participation in management that will subject a lender to liability for hazardous waste problems, banks are voluntarily absorbing costs for cleanup actions, releasing collateral coverage for existing loans, and not exercising rights as lien holders over real property to avoid claims by the EPA of more extensive liabilities. For existing credits, it is not unusual to have a small- to medium-sized company walk away from its debts, leaving the bank with possession and the problem of disposition of real property. In some cases the banks have refused to foreclose on properties so as to remove the potential determination of "owner or operator." This decision is obviously influenced by the underlying value of properties and the bank's assessment of the cost associated with claims by the EPA. This has not only affected lending relationships, but is increasingly posing problems for bank trust departments in instances where exercising fiduciary responsibilities may pull the institution into the "owner or operator" designation by the EPA.

The following are examples of the types of problems encountered by Seventh District banks.

A bank with a problem mortgage on a scrap yard recovered as much as possible from secondary collateral but walked away from their primary collateral and took a loss rather than take title to the scrap yard.

A 600 acre farm in trust was leased to a horsebreeder. Unfortunately, a relative of the breeder was a wastehauler. Two children found 3,700 barrels of toxic waste in the weeds on the property. At least $400,000 was spent in cleanup. Fortunately, the trust was large enough to cover the cost and no personal assets were attached.

A trust department holds a land contract which is currently in default. The trust officer suspects pollution on the site and is reluctant to take the property back. Likewise he is concerned about his fiduciary responsibility if he doesn't move to make the property income producing.

Some indication of the exposure to environmental risks in the Seventh District is provided in CERCLIS, the CERCLA Information System. CERCLIS is the EPA's comprehensive database and management system that contains the official inventory of CERCLA sites. It supports the EPA's site planning and tracking functions with data from the pre-remedial, remedial, removal, and enforcement sections of the Superfund program. Inclusion of a specific site or area in the CERCLIS data base

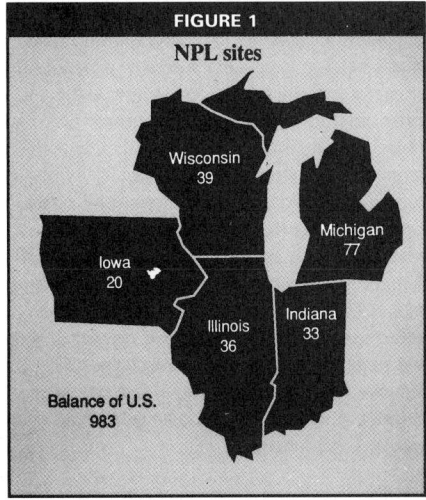

FIGURE 1
NPL sites

Wisconsin 39
Michigan 77
Iowa 20
Illinois 36
Indiana 33
Balance of U.S. 983

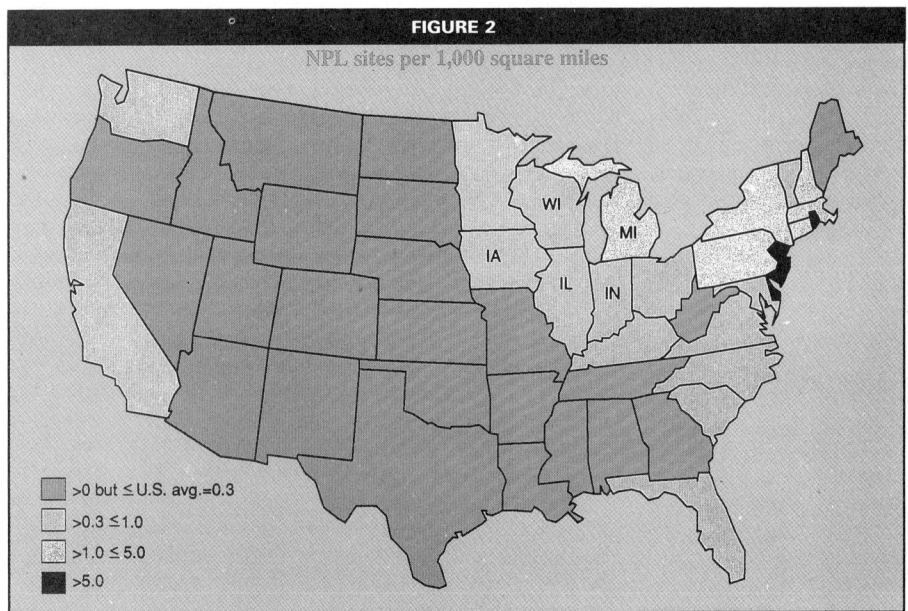

FIGURE 2
NPL sites per 1,000 square miles

- >0 but ≤ U.S. avg.=0.3
- >0.3 ≤1.0
- >1.0 ≤5.0
- >5.0

does not represent a determination of any party's liability, nor does it represent a finding that any response action is necessary. About 50 percent of the CERCLIS sites are eliminated from further consideration at the first step of the evaluation process, the preliminary assessment. Sites that the EPA decides on the basis of available information do not warrant moving further in the site evaluation process are given a "No Further Response Action Planned" (NFRAP) designation in CERCLIS. Sites that the EPA believes pose environmental threats significant enough to warrant detailed evaluation for possible remedial action under Superfund are placed on the National Priorities List (NPL). The EPA uses a Hazard Ranking System (HRS) to identify sites for inclusion on the NPL. Between 2 and 7 percent of the CERCLIS sites evaluated are placed on the NPL.

Currently about 5,200 sites from Seventh District states are listed on CERCLIS. Of this number, 53 percent are designated as requiring no further action. Of the 2,473 remaining, 205 are on the National Priorities List. This represents 17 percent of the total 1,188 NPL sites in the United States. As shown in Figure 1, the number of NPL sites in the individual states ranges from 77 in Michigan to 20 in Iowa. The remaining 2,268 sites may require cleanup but are not considered serious enough to be currently eligible for the Superfund list.

As an indication of the extent of the risk of contaminated sites in individual states, the number of NPL sites per 1,000 square miles of land area is shown in Figure 2. Except for Michigan, the NPL ratio for each of the Seventh District states is moderately above the national average of 0.3. In Michigan there are 1.4 NPL sites per 1,000 square miles. The number of other sites on CERCLIS (not eligible for NPL) per 1,000 square miles is below the U.S. average of 4.4 in Wisconsin and Iowa and moderately above in Michigan, Illinois, and Indiana.

Conclusion

Environmental laws and regulations and recent court cases have introduced additional uncertainty and a new dimension to risk for financial institutions in lending. The apparent attempt to encourage lenders to require borrowers to comply with environmental laws and clean up industrial properties prior to granting a loan and during the life of the loan has introduced additional costs for the lender. In addition, lenders may find themselves liable for cleanup costs if they are adjudged to have participated in the management of a business that has contributed to the contamination of property that serves as collateral for a loan.

The additional uncertainty and costs affect the availability of credit as lenders are reluctant to make loans where the risks are largely unquantifiable. As a result, less funds are available for businesses where the risks of contamination are present either for operations or cleanup.

It is important for both the financial and environmental communities that the uncertainties as to the environmental liabilities associated with lending be clarified. Otherwise there exists a possible reduction in the availability of credit to any industry, area, or borrower that appears to present a risk of liability for hazardous substance removal.

FOOTNOTES

[1] 42 U.S.C.A. §§9601-9657, Public Law 96-510 (Dec. 11, 1980); Public Law 99-499 (Oct. 17, 1986).

[2] 45 B.R. 278 (Bkrtcy. 1985).

[3] 15 *Environmental Law Reporter* 20922 (E.D.Pa. 1985)

[4] 632 F.Supp. 573 (D.Md. 1986).

[5] 712 F.Supp. 1193 (E.D.Pa. 1989); FR 14952 (April 12, 1991).

[6] 732 F.Supp. 556 (W.D.Pa. 1989).

[7] 901 F.2d 1550 (11th Cir. 1990), cert. denied, 111 S.Ct. 752 (1991).

[8] 910 F.2d 668 (9th Cir. 1990). The Ninth Circuit claims to agree with the Eleventh Circuit decision in a footnote: "As did the Eleventh Circuit in *Fleet Factors,* we hold that a creditor must, as a threshold matter, exercise actual management authority before it can be held liable for action or inaction which results in the discharge of hazardous wastes. Merely having the power to get involved in management, but failing to exercise it, is not enough."

[9] FR 28797 (June 24, 1991).

[10] *U.S. Congressional Record*, 102d Congress, 1st Session, House of Representatives, Vol. 137, March 19, 1991, pp. E 987-8.

[11] *U.S. Congressional Record*, 102d Congress, 1st Session, Senate, Vol. 137, March 13, 1991, pp. S 3279-83.

Recent Trends in the Mutual Fund Industry

Phillip R. Mack, of the Division of Research and Statistics, prepared this article. Michael A. Schoenbeck provided research assistance.

Mutual fund assets have grown more than twelvefold from 1980 to mid-1993 and by half in the last two years of that period. Most of this growth has come from net purchases of fund shares by the public, rather than from price appreciation, and it has lately reflected a choice by investors to move funds out of depository institutions. In 1992, the public made net purchases of $206 billion of mutual fund shares, while making net withdrawals from their deposits at banks and thrift institutions. In turn, mutual funds supplied about one-fourth of funds raised by the domestic nonfinancial sectors of the economy last year, while depository institutions provided only about one-tenth. In short, mutual funds are now a significant competitor of depository institutions for household savings and, with more than $1.8 trillion in assets, they are a major source of funds in the capital markets.

Several factors underlie the recent surge in mutual funds. One is the drop in rates on deposits—especially short-term deposits—to relatively low levels at a time when rising stock and bond prices have been generating higher returns. As a result, households seeking to maintain satisfactory returns on their savings have been drawn to capital market instruments, especially mutual funds, whose diversification and liquidity offer advantages over direct investments in securities. In addition, the benefits of economies of scale in the mutual fund industry have been shared with investors through a widening array of services provided by fund families. Finally, many funds have eliminated or substantially reduced the sales commissions, or loads, they charge to investors.

Corporations with access to the capital markets, including firms with lower credit ratings, have benefited from the expanded supply of investment dollars represented by the surge in mutual funds. State and local governments also have benefited, with inflows to tax-exempt mutual funds running at a record pace since the end of 1992. Moreover, in recent years, smaller corporations raising equity through initial public offerings, as well as established firms, have seen mutual funds purchase a significant portion of the new equity they have sold.

In response to the growth of the funds industry, banks have increased their participation in the provision of mutual fund services. For example, many banks sell mutual fund shares to their retail customers and, in some cases, act as an investment adviser to mutual funds and provide other related services. The increased involvement of banks has brought attention to their role in the sale of mutual fund shares, including their responsibility for ensuring that customers are made aware of the differences between mutual fund shares and insured deposits.

The expanding role of mutual funds has had at least two important implications for the performance and structure of the financial markets. By offering households more diversified investment opportunities and corporations a greater market for their financial instruments, mutual funds have improved the efficiency of financial intermediation by reducing transaction costs. And as intermediaries competing with banks and thrift institutions, mutual funds have contributed to the reduction of the role of these depositories as providers of credit in the intermediation process and consequently have affected the relationship between money and economic activity.

TYPES OF MUTUAL FUNDS

A mutual fund is a type of investment company. An investment company sells shares or certificates that represent an interest in a pool of financial assets; a mutual fund (technically an open-end company) is an investment company that continuously issues and redeems its shares. The price of such shares, apart from any brokerage commissions, equals the net asset value of the fund, determined by dividing the market value of the fund's assets, less any liabilities, by the number of outstanding shares. The net asset value is calculated daily as of the close of U.S. securities markets. Open-end funds must redeem their shares on demand at a value equaling the next calculated net asset value and mail proceeds within seven days.

Another type of investment company, the closed-end fund, does not redeem its shares but typically offers a fixed number of nonredeemable shares that are bought and sold on a stock exchange.[1] A third type of investment company is the unit investment trust. Unlike other funds, unit investment trusts hold a relatively fixed portfolio of securities that is not actively managed.

The greater liquidity of open-end funds has helped make them by far the most popular form of investment company. By mid-1993, open-end funds—the focus of this article—held assets of about $1.8 trillion (table 1), as compared with only $90 billion of assets in closed-end funds.

For the most part, the portfolio of a mutual fund consists of marketable securities, both domestic and foreign, such as corporate stocks and bonds, government bonds, municipal bonds, and money market instruments. An individual mutual fund, however, invests in a specific subset of securities defined by its stated investment objective. For example, a money market mutual fund invests in a diversified pool of short-term money market instruments, such as commercial paper, certificates of deposit, and U.S. Treasury bills. Long-term mutual funds are those that invest primarily in stock and bond securities. Because they use certain share valuation techniques based upon historical costs, money funds are allowed to report a constant $1 share value.[2] Stock and bond mutual funds, on the other hand, must report their share values at market prices; hence, investor accounts in these funds may show a gain or a loss on any given day, apart from any distributions.

THE STRUCTURE AND REGULATION OF MUTUAL FUNDS

A mutual fund typically is organized as a business trust or corporation. The board of directors, elected by the shareholders of the fund, is responsible for overseeing the fund's operations. Among the board's duties is the selection, subject to shareholder approval, of an investment adviser to oversee the day-to-day management of the fund.[3]

Responsibilities of the investment adviser include making appropriate investments in line with the fund's investment policies and objectives and conducting economic and financial research. For these services, the adviser receives a fee based on a percentage of the fund's assets. Within certain limits, the adviser's fee income increases with the

---

1. Closed-end funds are well-suited for investment in less liquid securities, which may not be appropriate for the requirements of open-end mutual funds. In recent years, closed-end funds have been important purchasers of foreign stocks and bonds and of municipal bonds.

---

1. Net assets of the mutual fund industry, by fund type, end of period, selected years, 1960–93:H1

Billions of dollars

Period	Stock	Bond	Money market[1]	Total
1960	11.9	5.1	n.a.	17.0
1965	25.2	10.0	n.a.	35.2
1970	38.5	9.1	n.a.	47.6
1975	32.4	9.8	3.7	45.9
1980	41.0	17.4	76.4	134.8
1985	116.9	134.8	243.8	495.5
1990	245.8	322.7	498.4	1,066.9
1991	367.6	440.9	539.6	1,348.1
1992	475.4	580.9	543.6	1,599.9
1993:H1	581.6	673.7	549.8	1,805.1

1. Taxable and tax-exempt.
SOURCE. Investment Company Institute.

---

2. The Securities and Exchange Commission has given money funds the authority to use either of two accounting techniques of share valuation: amortized cost and penny rounding methods. Under the amortized cost method, a money fund values its securities at historical cost, with any interest earned accrued daily over the life of the assets. By declaring these accruals as a daily dividend to its shareholders, the money fund is able to maintain a $1 price per share. Under the penny rounding method, a money fund rounds its net asset value per share to the nearest one cent to compute the current price of its shares. Most money funds use the amortized cost method of share valuation.

3. Under the Investment Company Act of 1940, which establishes the legal and regulatory framework for the mutual funds industry, at least 40 percent of a fund's directors must be unaffiliated with the investment adviser, with any registered broker–dealer, or with any other interested person.

amount of assets under management, an arrangement that gives the adviser an incentive to perform well and to attract new investors. In some cases, the adviser's compensation also varies with the fund's performance relative to some specified benchmark.

The board also retains an independent custodian to hold the fund's assets in trust (except occasionally in the case of a bank-advised fund) and selects a transfer agent to maintain shareholder ownership records and to process orders for sales and redemptions. Governed by the Investment Company Act of 1940, the custodial arrangement is designed to prevent misuse of the fund's assets by the investment adviser. The services provided by the custodian include settling securities transactions, receiving dividends and interest, and making payments for the fund's expenses. Typically, the custodian's compensation varies with the volume of assets under management.

The board also hires an underwriter to sell fund shares either directly to investors or indirectly through brokers.[4] Depository institutions may also sell shares to their customers. Shares in some funds are sold at a premium over the net asset value. This premium, or "front-end load," covers, where applicable, the underwriter's cost, the broker's commission, and other sales and promotional expenses incurred by the fund.[5]

In direct sales or marketing, the underwriter offers shares to investors through the mail, by telephone, or at fund offices. Direct marketers usually do not charge a load; some no-load and low-load funds, however, use annual fees to finance the distribution of their shares to the public.

The Investment Company Act of 1940 is one of several federal statutes governing mutual funds. One of the primary objectives of the act is the protection of investors against abuses, and it contains specific requirements that the mutual fund be operated in the best interests of the fund's shareholders. For example, the statute places restrictions on changing a mutual fund's investment policies without shareholder approval, provides that the adviser's compensation be approved by shareholders and annually approved by the board of directors, prohibits conflict-of-interest transactions between the fund and its affiliates, limits the mutual fund's use of financial leverage, and requires mutual funds to pay redemption proceeds within seven days except under extraordinary circumstances.

Other aspects of mutual fund operations are governed by three other federal statutes: (1) Pursuant to the Securities Act of 1933, mutual funds must provide investors with accurate information about its investment objective, yield, and operating procedures through a prospectus. (2) The Securities Exchange Act of 1934 requires the registration of brokers and dealers with the Securities and Exchange Commission (SEC) and sets certain requirements for the solicitation of shareholder votes and proxies in connection with shareholder meetings. (3) The Investment Advisers Act of 1940 requires the registration of all mutual fund advisers (other than banks or bank holding companies), prohibits fraudulent practices, and gives the SEC enforcement powers.

To determine if the regulatory requirements are met, the SEC reviews disclosure statements and conducts on-site examinations. The SEC reviews fund disclosures about operating plans, management structure, and financial condition. On-site examinations typically probe the funds' valuation techniques, investment activities, management functions, and sales and liquidations of shares.

THE ROLE OF MUTUAL FUNDS IN THE FINANCIAL SYSTEM

Like other financial intermediaries, mutual funds channel savings to different forms of investments. To the saver, mutual funds offer several advantages over the closest, nonintermediary alternative—the direct purchase of stocks and bonds. First, by pooling the savings of many investors, mutual funds can afford to employ professional asset managers and analysts with investment expertise exceeding that of the typical small investor. Second, mutual funds allow small savers to invest in a diversified

---

4. About 59 percent of all sales of stock and bond fund shares in 1992 were brokered.

5. Back-end loads, in contrast, are charges paid by investors only on redemptions that occur within a specified period after purchase, expressed typically as a percentage of redemption proceeds. Such loads, which usually decline over time, are used to recoup advances to brokers and to discourage trading by investors.

portfolio, thus reducing their exposure to certain types of risk. Typically, the higher transactions costs and minimum purchase sizes encountered in direct investment make diversification difficult for the small investor. Finally, mutual funds offer investors a greater degree of liquidity than would be available through direct investments in the capital markets. For example, mutual funds offer a variety of convenient means for purchasing and redeeming shares, such as making fund investments and portfolio adjustments over the phone and (for money market funds and some bond funds) making redemptions by writing checks.

Mutual funds are distinct from other intermediaries, especially depository institutions, in the way they channel savings. In raising funds, mutual funds issue shares that represent an ownership interest. Shareowners assume all the market risk and credit risk of the fund's assets and share proportionally in all the gains and losses of the fund. Consequently, the return on the shareholder's investment fluctuates with general market conditions and the investment performance of the fund. Banks and thrift institutions, in contrast, primarily issue deposit liabilities with a fixed rate of interest. Most depositors are fully protected by deposit insurance and are not subject to any credit risk.

In supplying funds, mutual funds primarily specialize in marketable securities of firms that have access to the capital markets. Funds must confine their investments to marketable securities in order to meet investor redemptions in a timely manner.[6] Although depository institutions purchase marketable securities, their special role is in providing funds to borrowers who, because of their small size or the complexity or monitoring requirements of the debt contract, may lack access to the public securities markets.

Mutual funds actively compete with banks and thrift institutions for the balances of households and in supplying funds to borrowers. Such competition is limited, however, to those households that are willing to take on additional risk for higher expected returns and to those borrowers capable of financing their needs directly through the securities markets.

---

6. SEC guidelines permit a mutual fund to hold up to 15 percent of its net assets in illiquid securities.

THE DEVELOPMENT OF MUTUAL FUNDS

Offered in the mid-1920s, closed-end funds gained acceptance ahead of open-end mutual funds; in 1929 they accounted for 95 percent of industry assets. Open-end mutual funds, however, soon overshadowed them, and between 1940 and 1970 their assets grew more than a hundredfold, to about $48 billion. Throughout this period, they almost exclusively invested in equity, although bond funds also emerged and grew.

In the early 1970s, when volatile stock market conditions along with persistent inflation reduced the attractiveness of bond and equity funds, the industry created money market mutual funds. These funds met the desire of investors to benefit from money market rates, which were then above the level that federal regulation allowed depository institutions to offer on retail accounts, and the success of these funds spurred the development of other funds investing in fixed-income securities: Municipal bond funds were introduced in the mid-1970s, and mortgage-backed and government bond funds were started in the mid-1980s.

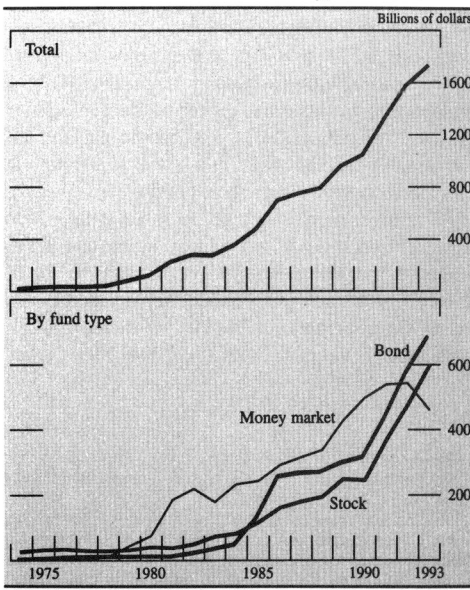

1. Net assets of the mutual fund industry, 1974–93

SOURCE. Investment Company Institute.

Mutual funds have continued to play an active role in equity markets, with holdings of equity funds growing from about $40 billion in 1970 to about $580 billion in the first half of 1993. Bond and money funds grew faster over this period, however (chart 1). As a result, the assets of stock funds declined from about 80 percent of industry assets to 34 percent between year-end 1970 and mid-1993, by which time bond funds accounted for about 40 percent of industry assets and money funds about 26 percent (chart 2).

Money Market Mutual Funds

Money market mutual funds grew rapidly in the late 1970s and early 1980s, when interest rates on money market instruments exceeded regulatory ceilings that applied to depository institutions.[7] Flows from depositories to money funds supported expansion of the commercial paper market, an important alternative to bank loans for businesses. The growth of money funds was interrupted temporarily in 1982, when banks and thrift institutions were permitted to offer money market deposit accounts, which were not subject to interest rate ceilings. Money funds resumed their growth in 1983, partly because they remained important to investors in their broader investment strategies. For example, brokerage houses include them as part of cash management accounts. In addition, mutual fund families offer money funds along with stock and bond funds as part of a menu of products that allows investors to switch between short- and long-term funds.

Stock and Bond Funds

In the 1980s, the growth of assets in stock and bond funds was driven by heavy purchases of fund shares, rising stock prices, and lower interest rates (rising bond prices). During this period, investment companies expanded the number and variety of long-term funds they offered. The development of new financial instruments, such as securities backed by mortgages or other assets, and the increased ease of investing overseas spurred the diversification of fund types. Funds investing in specific industries also became popular. The number of long-term funds increased from about 450 at the end of 1979 to about 3,300 by mid-1993.

Inflows to bond funds surged dramatically during the 1985–86 period (chart 3), with the majority of new money going to municipal, mortgage-backed, and government bond funds. Investors withdrew from bond funds in early 1987, when bond prices fell because of an upward move in

---

7. For a detailed history, see Timothy Q. Cook and J. G. Duffield, "Money Market Mutual Funds and Other Short-Term Investment Pools," in Timothy Q. Cook and R. K. LaRoche, eds., *Instruments of the Money Market*, 7th ed. (Federal Reserve Bank of Richmond, 1993), pp. 156–72.

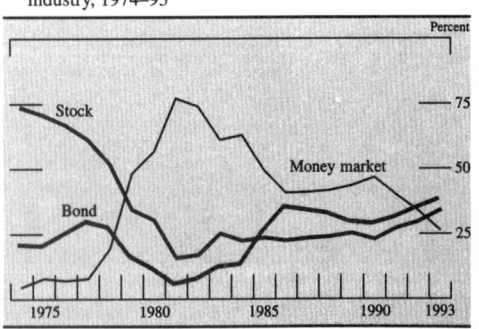

2. Share of fund types in total net assets of the mutual fund industry, 1974–93

SOURCE. Investment Company Institute.

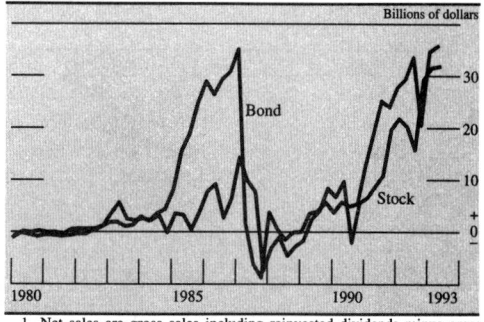

3. Net sales of stock and bond mutual funds, 1980–93[1]

1. Net sales are gross sales including reinvested dividends minus gross redemptions.
SOURCE. Investment Company Institute.

interest rates; as deposit rates fell in relation to bond yields in late 1990, investors began moving aggressively into bond funds again. Stock mutual funds grew during the bull market of the mid-1980s and then shrank in the aftermath of the stock market crash in October 1987. In 1989, with stock funds posting strong investment results, inflows resumed.

Retirement Assets

Some of the growth of mutual funds in the 1980s is attributable to their use as investment vehicles for retirement assets (chart 4). In 1982, U.S. tax laws created incentives for investors to open individual retirement accounts (IRAs) and Keogh accounts, which boosted investments in instruments, including mutual funds, that could be structured in the form of such accounts. The upward trend in the asset size of these retirement-oriented mutual fund accounts was interrupted in 1986, after the Congress enacted the Tax Reform Act of 1986, which reduced the number of households eligible to use IRA and Keogh accounts to defer taxes on current income.

In recent years, the share of mutual fund assets held by institutional retirement plans has increased. In addition, investments in IRA and Keogh mutual fund accounts have once again picked up with their use for lump sum distributions and rollovers from employee pension accounts that are liquidated because of a job change or plan termination.

Sales Loads and Fees

The growth and development of the industry has been associated with a decline in sales loads.[8] Among the mutual funds charging a front-end load, the average load fell from 8.5 percent in 1970 to about 4.5 percent in 1992.[9] Over the same period, the market share of no-load funds increased from 6 percent to about 31 percent of industry assets.

As sales loads have declined, expenses charged to shareholders, as a proportion of assets (the expense ratio), has increased substantially, except in the case of tax-exempt bond funds (table 2). The rise in expense ratios has occurred, however, at the same time that industry assets have been increasing, and insofar as many fund expenses are fixed costs, the growth in industry assets would reduce these ratios. Moreover, mutual funds operate in a

---

8. In the 1970 amendments to the Investment Company Act of 1940, the Congress authorized the National Association of Securities Dealers (NASD) to prescribe sales loads, subject to SEC oversight, and in 1975 the NASD adopted an 8.5 percent maximum on front-end sales loads.

9. Back-end loads or contingent deferred sales loads (CDSL) are sometimes used in junction with 12b-1 fees as an alternative to front-end sales loads (12b-1 fees are those that can be assessed against fund assets to recover distribution expenses of the fund). For example, instead of charging a 6 percent front-end load, a mutual fund could recoup the same amount through a combination of an annual 1 percent 12b-1 fee and a CDSL of 6 percent that declines 1 percentage point per year until reaching zero after the sixth year.

---

4. Retirement assets as a share of total mutual fund assets, by type of plan, 1981–92

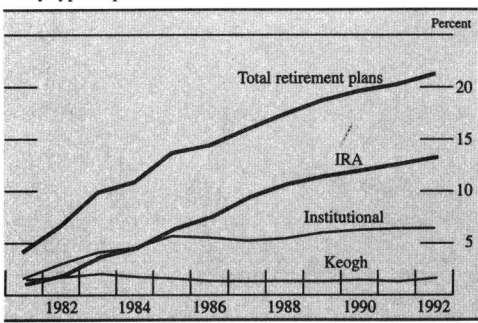

SOURCE. Investment Company Institute.

2. Ratio of mutual fund expenses to fund assets, and 12b-1 component, by selected fund types, 1982 and 1992

Percent

Fund type	Expense ratio[1]		12b-1 fee ratio[2]	
	1982	1992	1982	1992
Equity	1.08	1.49	.08	.42
International and global	1.29	1.83	.06	.41
Bond	.89	.90	.20	.36
Taxable	.94	1.03	.26	.39
Tax-exempt	.81	.74	.13	.31

1. The sum of all expenses and fees, excluding loads (sales commissions), divided by industry assets.
2. For funds imposing such fees, the ratio of 12b-1 fees to assets. See text for definition of 12b-1 fees.

SOURCE. Lipper Analytical Services.

competitive market, which impedes them from charging fees that exceed competitive levels.[10]

Three factors may have contributed to the rise in the industry expense ratio. Before 1980, a mutual fund's investment adviser and underwriter typically incurred the costs of distributing the fund's shares. In 1980, the SEC adopted rule 12b-1, allowing mutual funds to use their assets to pay for sales commissions, sales literature, advertising, and other distribution expenses. Most no-load and low-load funds have adopted 12b-1 fees to finance their distribution expenses, and the fees have grown as a proportion of assets for funds imposing such fees (table 2).[11] Second, the number of small and international funds, which are more costly to operate, has grown. Third, mutual funds have expanded shareholder services that require costly computer, telephone, and shareholder accounting systems. These expenditures may have offset some of the gains achieved with economies of scale resulting from an increase in industry assets.

RECENT GROWTH OF THE INDUSTRY

Net sales of long-term mutual funds were a record $202 billion in 1992, up from $130 billion in 1991 and easily outpacing the previous record of $144 billion set in 1986 (chart 5).[12] During the first half of 1993, net sales amounted to $135 billion and at that rate will set another record.

---

10. According to the antitrust criteria of the Department of Justice, an industry with a Herfindahl index of less than 1,000 is considered unconcentrated. For the mutual fund industry as a whole, the Herfindahl index ranged from 500 in 1984 to 380 in 1992.

The Herfindahl index is calculated as the sum of the squares of market shares of all fund complexes in the market. The larger the index, which can range from zero to 10,000, the more concentrated the market.

11. In a rule that became effective in July 1993, the NASD limits the amount of 12b-1 fees that may be charged. The intent of the rule is to ensure that investors will not pay more than 7.25 percent of the purchase price of a mutual fund share when 12b-1 fees, front-end loads, and back-end loads are combined. Also, under the new rule, no fund that charges 12b-1 fees in excess of 0.25 percent can describe itself as a no-load fund.

12. Net sales are gross sales plus reinvested dividends minus gross redemptions. Net sales of bond funds in 1992 were $115 billion, just under the record of $119 billion set in 1986. Net sales of stock funds were $87 billion in 1992, breaking the previous record of $46 billion set in 1991.

One reason for the surge in net sales has been the drop in deposit rates to low levels by historical standards and the accompanying steepening of the yield curve. Although both short-term and long-term rates have fallen since 1989, the decline in short-term rates has been more pronounced. The rate on the six-month Treasury bill fell from 8.8 percent in the spring of 1989 to 3.2 percent in the summer of 1993, and the yield on the thirty-year Treasury bond fell from 8.7 percent to 6.3 percent over the same period. Thus, the returns on long-term assets, such as stock and bond funds, became increasingly attractive relative to rates on deposits at banks and thrift institutions, which follow short-term market rates. In addition, the heavy inflows in recent years may have been aided by the reduced need of depositories to compete aggressively for funds. For example, weak loan demand may have reduced the need of banks to offer competitive rates on deposits. Moreover, competition for funds may have been further reduced by the resolution of failed thrifts, which typically had paid a premium to attract funds.[13] As a result, deposit rates may have been lower than the given decline in market interest rates would have otherwise produced.

The strong net sales of mutual funds may also reflect the high yields that some mutual funds have

---

13. As the Resolution Trust Corporation closed failed thrifts, it typically paid depositors directly and closed their accounts or sold the deposits to thrift institutions or banks that reset their rates, which in effect pushed average deposit rates down.

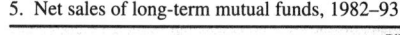
5. Net sales of long-term mutual funds, 1982–93[1]

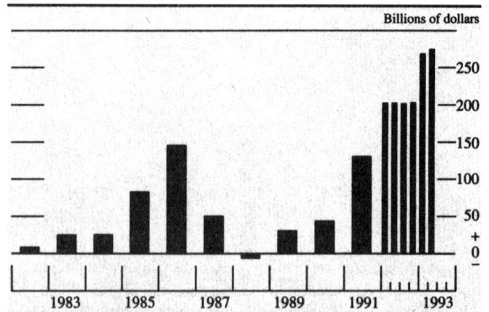

1. Long-term funds exclude money market funds. Sales reported for 1992–93 are quarterly at an annual rate.
SOURCE. Investment Company Institute.

been able to advertise. One way that a mutual fund differentiates itself and attempts to attract potential investors is to publicize its superior investing skills based upon past performance.[14] Advertisements will often highlight holding-period returns, calculated according to SEC guidelines, relative to some benchmark, such as returns on the issues in the S&P 500 index of stock prices or against other funds with similar investment objectives. Although such advertisements include disclaimers that past performance is no guide to future performance, they may still be effective in convincing investors that the fund has superior investment skills and is likely to enjoy superior future returns. Funds that have strong recent performance tend to have strong inflows, even though most research has failed to show that money managers can persistently produce superior returns.[15] Thus, some of the inflows to mutual funds may reflect the actions of investors who base their expectations of a fund's future returns on the fund's past performance.

---

14. See Erik R. Sirri and Peter Tufano, "Buying and Selling Mutual Funds: Flows, Performance, Fees, and Services," Harvard Business School Working Paper 93–017 (1992). They show that the demand for mutual funds is weakly related to fees charged and strongly related to services provided and past performance.

15. See W. Sharpe, "Mutual Fund Performance," *Journal of Business*, vol. 39 (January 1966), pp. 119–38; M.C. Jensen, "The Performance of Mutual Funds in the Period 1945–1964," *Journal of Finance*, vol. 23 (May 1968), pp. 389–416; B. Lehmann and D. Modest, "Mutual fund Performance Evaluation: A Comparison of Benchmarks and Benchmark Comparisons," *Journal of Finance*, vol. 42 (June 1987), pp. 233–56; M. Grinblatt and S. Titman, "Mutual Fund Performance: An Analysis of Quarterly Portfolio Holdings," *Journal of Business*, vol. 62 (July 1989), pp. 393–416.

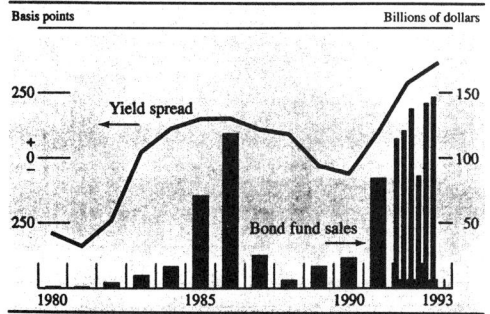

6. Net sales of bond funds and yield spread, 1980–93[1]

1. Yield spread is rate on thirty-year Treasury bond less six-month certificate of deposit. Fund sales reported for 1992–93 are quarterly at an annual rate.
SOURCE. Investment Company Institute.

The surge in purchases of shares in long-term funds is not unprecedented. In 1985 and 1986, investors shifted into bond funds when interest rates fell and the yield curve steepened. In fact, bond funds posted record net sales of $119 billion in 1986, slightly above the $115 billion of net sales in 1992 (chart 6). Inflows came to a halt in April 1987, when interest rates backed up sharply. Also during this period, the demand for bond funds for retirement purposes may have fallen when the Congress placed eligibility limitations on IRA contributions.

HOUSEHOLD OWNERSHIP OF MUTUAL FUNDS

The strong inflows to mutual funds reflect their popularity among households. According to preliminary data from the Federal Reserve Board's Survey of Consumer Finances, households shifted assets from deposits to mutual funds in the 1989–92 period; they held about 13 percent of their financial assets in long-term mutual funds at the end of 1992, up from about 10 percent in 1989, while their holdings of deposits and money funds fell from about 37 percent to 31 percent (table 3). Direct holdings of stocks, bonds, and "other" financial assets (not shown) also slightly increased during this period.[16]

The dispersal of ownership of long-term mutual funds also increased, from about 12 percent of households in 1989 to 15½ percent in 1992. The increase in new ownership was most heavily concentrated among households in which the head was between 55 and 64 years of age. These households apparently shifted assets away from bank deposits and money funds into long-term mutual funds. Their holdings of bank deposits and money fund shares fell from about 40 percent of their financial assets in 1989 to about 22 percent in 1992, while the share of long-term mutual funds in their portfolios rose from about 11 percent to 17 percent over the same period. Somewhat in contrast, the households in the 35–44 age group maintained the share of their financial assets in bank deposits and

---

16. "Other" financial assets include trusts, annuities, managed investment accounts, call accounts, deposits at uninsured institutions, and the cash value of life insurance.

money fund shares, at about 33 percent, over the 1989–92 period; the share of long-term funds in their portfolios did grow, however, from about 9½ percent to about 12½ percent, while the share of other financial assets declined.

MUTUAL FUNDS AS FINANCIAL INTERMEDIARIES

With their rapid growth, mutual funds have become increasingly important suppliers of debt and equity funds. Indeed, corporations with access to the reduced interest rates and elevated share prices of the capital markets have benefited from the surge in mutual fund assets: In recent years, mutual funds as a group have been the largest net purchaser of equities and a major purchaser of corporate bonds (table 4). Companies have repaid shorter-term debt—especially bank loans—and lowered the costs of long-term debt, while reducing overall balance sheet leverage. Such financial restructuring has been a particularly urgent priority for many of the firms that issued high-yield ("junk") bonds in the 1980s.

Mutual funds have been one of the major suppliers of credit in the high-yield bond market, as certain other institutional investors have pulled back from riskier investments. Recent legislation inhibits thrift institutions from investing in below-investment-grade corporate debt. And the public's concern about the financial health of life insurance companies has led most insurers to curtail their purchases of high-yield bonds and concentrate in high-grade securities. Consequently, flows to high-yield bond funds have played a more important role in the high-yield market than in the past, tending to boost bond prices (narrow yield spreads). Industry sources estimate that mutual funds, which purchased roughly 75 percent of new issuance of high-yield bonds in 1992, now hold about one-half of the stock of such bonds, up from about one-third in the 1980s.

Mutual funds also have increased their presence in the market for tax-exempt securities; they are now the largest net purchaser in that market (table 4) and are offsetting the reduced net purchases by households and the runoff at commercial banks. Banks have been net sellers of tax-exempt securities since passage of the Tax Reform Act of 1986, which significantly reduced the tax advantages for banks owning them. Households in the past several years have relied more heavily on mutual funds for their investments in municipal securities.

BANK-RELATED MUTUAL FUNDS

In response to the outflow of deposits, banks are increasingly participating in the mutual fund busi-

3. Proportion of households with selected characteristics that own long-term mutual funds and their allocation of financial assets in long- and short-term fund accounts, 1989 and 1992[1]

Percent

Household characteristic	Proportion of total financial assets				Proportion owning long-term mutual funds	
	Long-term mutual funds		Short-term mutual funds and bank deposits			
	1989	1992	1989	1992	1989	1992
All households	9.8	13.2	36.7	30.7	11.8	15.5
Age of head (years)						
Less than 35	3.6	5.2	37.5	41.3	6.1	8.4
35–44	9.6	12.4	33.5	33.6	14.3	18.7
45–54	10.8	14.0	33.0	23.0	14.6	18.0
55–64	10.9	17.2	41.0	22.1	14.9	22.2
65 or more	9.7	11.9	36.8	36.0	12.3	14.6
Annual income (dollars)						
Less than 30,000	4.1	7.7	60.5	51.4	4.9	5.7
30,000–49,999	8.6	17.0	42.9	35.5	12.5	19.9
50,000–99,999	11.0	13.1	36.9	30.2	26.2	28.4
100,000–199,999	12.2	14.2	33.2	23.0	42.6	41.8
200,000 or more	11.8	14.4	19.2	18.7	51.7	55.5

1. Preliminary data. In this table, long-term funds exclude all money market mutual funds except those in retirement accounts.

SOURCE. Federal Reserve Board, Survey of Consumer Finances.

4. Distribution of net purchases of equities, corporate bonds, and tax-exempt securities, by type of investor, selected years, 1980–93:H1
Billions of dollars

Type of investor	1980	1982	1984	1986	1988	1990	1991	1992	1993:H1[1]	Memo: Level, 1993:H1
Equities										
Mutual funds[2]	−1.8	3.5	5.9	20.2	−16.0	14.4	44.6	67.2	118.6	562.7
Closed-end funds	−1.2	−.7	−.5	3.0	.6	.7	.3	−1.0	−1.2	19.9
Households[3]	−11.5	−31.8	−70.1	−135.2	−101.0	−27.2	−22.8	−15.9	−83.0	3,055.3
Depository institutions	−.6	−.5	−.2	.9	.5	−3.9	1.8	.4	.3	16.6
Insurance companies	3.5	5.1	−4.1	−2.4	.2	−12.6	−5.6	11.6	21.9	251.1
Pension funds	21.8	28.0	2.5	26.7	13.8	2.3	29.0	22.4	17.6	1,503.9
Foreign	4.2	3.7	−3.4	17.9	−2.9	−16.0	10.4	−5.8	8.2	315.1
Broker–dealers	.1	.9	−1.0	1.4	.2	−3.3	2.4	−.6	8.0	19.2
Total	14.5	8.2	−70.9	−67.6	−104.7	−45.7	60.1	78.2	90.4	5,743.8
Bonds										
Mutual funds[2]	1.3	.2	3.6	26.8	14.2	13.6	12.8	28.4	66.7	162.2
Closed-end funds	.0	.4	−.4	1.4	9.4	−1.7	−1.9	1.9	.9	15.1
Households[3]	−13.8	−2.2	−10.6	35.9	−29.9	18.3	26.2	−.5	−67.6	119.4
Depository institutions	7.1	6.1	17.0	30.5	23.9	−14.7	4.7	6.9	18.6	185.1
Insurance companies	8.8	15.7	27.9	54.9	79.3	65.7	36.2	59.6	85.7	798.1
Pension funds	23.3	13.7	28.1	30.4	36.5	26.6	43.5	18.5	31.1	460.0
Foreign	9.2	15.7	15.6	39.1	15.9	5.3	16.2	18.5	24.2	255.5
Broker–dealers	.4	2.5	5.7	.3	9.8	−4.0	12.0	10.0	20.3	61.0
Total	36.3	52.1	86.8	219.4	159.0	109.2	149.6	143.3	179.9	2,056.4
Tax-exempt securities										
Mutual funds[4]	2.0	10.9	12.6	59.3	12.3	29.8	34.2	40.7	53.9	295.8
Closed-end funds	.0	.0	.0	1.1	3.8	1.8	14.1	11.8	10.4	45.1
Households[3]	.8	31.2	31.7	−2.8	50.4	34.1	44.1	11.6	18.1	610.8
Depository institutions	12.7	4.3	12.2	−28.7	−22.5	−16.0	−14.8	−6.0	−1.4	98.9
Insurance companies	8.0	4.9	−3.2	15.6	7.8	5.5	−12.2	8.7	5.8	148.6
Other[5]	.5	1.8	5.4	1.3	2.0	2.2	4.2	−1.1	−25.3	24.8
Total	23.9	53.1	58.7	45.7	53.7	57.4	69.6	65.7	61.4	1,224.0

1. Annual rate.
2. Excludes money market mututal funds.
3. Includes nonprofit organizations and personal trusts administered by banks and nondeposit noninsured trust companies.
4. Includes money market mutual funds.
5. Pension funds, broker–dealers, nonfarm nonfinancial corporate business, and state and local government general funds.

SOURCE. Federal Reserve Board, flow of funds accounts.

ness through the advising of mutual funds and through the brokering of mutual fund shares. Banks and bank holding companies are prohibited from underwriting, distributing, or sponsoring mutual funds, according to interpretations of the Glass–Steagall Act of 1933 by the courts and federal regulatory agencies.[17]

---

17. *Investment Company Institute et al. v. Camp, Comptroller of the Currency, et al.*, 401 U.S. 617 (1971).

Nevertheless, several rule changes have made it possible for banks to increase their participation in the industry.[18] In 1972, the Federal Reserve Board authorized bank holding companies to act as mutual fund investment advisers, transfer agents, and custodians.[19] In an accompanying interpretation, the Board placed several restrictions on the activities of bank holding companies that advise mutual funds. For example, neither a bank holding company nor its bank or nonbank affiliates could promote any mutual fund, or provide investment advice to any customer investing in any mutual fund, for which it acted as an investment adviser. In addition, the Board cautioned bank holding companies from advising a mutual fund, unless the fund was located off the bank's premises. In 1992, the Board relaxed some of these restrictions. Provided that a number of disclosures are made to customers regarding the bank holding company's relationship to the mutual fund and the status of mutual funds as an uninsured investment product, the Board allowed a bank holding company or its subsidiary to provide investment advice and other brokerage services to customers investing in any bank-advised fund. In addition, the Board eliminated the location restriction.

A banking organization can participate in the mutual funds industry in several ways. One is through a proprietary mutual fund (a fund advised by the bank), with the shares brokered by the bank primarily to its customers. An unaffiliated third party, however, organizes the fund and an unaffiliated distributor underwrites the shares. In addition, a bank can sell shares of nonproprietary funds, for which it acts only as broker. Involvement in the brokerage of these funds can range from renting lobby space to an unaffiliated broker to selling fund shares through a brokerage firm affiliated with the bank. Although the bank is providing only brokerage services, it does earn fee income from sales commissions and enters the retail mutual funds market at a low initial expense.

Net assets of bank proprietary mutual funds, including both long-term and money market funds, are estimated to have increased from $31 billion at the end of 1987 to $162 billion at the end of the first quarter of 1993 (table 5). Money market funds account for the majority of bank-related mutual fund assets, but bank-related long-term funds have grown rapidly in the past several years and are about evenly split between stock and bond funds. Between 1987 and early 1993, banks increased their market share of total industry assets from 4 percent to nearly 10 percent (table 5). However, they have had much greater penetration in the money fund sector than in the stock and bond sectors. At the end of the first quarter of 1993, bank money funds accounted for about 20 percent of total money fund assets, whereas bank long-term mutual funds were only about 4 percent of total stock and bond fund assets.

---

18. See Melanie L. Fein, *Securities Activities of Banks* (Prentice–Hall, 1992), for a detailed account of the regulatory changes.
19. The Board's authorization was upheld by the Supreme Court against a challenge by the Investment Company Institute, the trade group for the mutual funds industry (*Board of Governors of the Federal Reserve System v. Investment Company Institute*, 450 U.S. 46 (1981).

IMPLICATIONS FOR THE INTERMEDIATION PROCESS

By providing savers with investment options and by participating in the market for securities, mutual funds compete with other financial intermediaries. Although some intermediaries may have been

5. Net assets of proprietary bank funds, end of period, selected years, 1987–93:Q1
Billions of dollars

Fund type	1987	1989	1991	1992	1993:Q1
Money market	28	45	83	102	113
Long-term	3	7	20	42	49
Total	31	52	103	144	162
MEMO Percentage of all mutual fund assets	4.0	5.3	7.6	9.0	9.5

SOURCE. Calculated from data provided by Lipper Analytical Services.

adversely affected by the rise of such competition, mutual funds have tended to make the financial system more efficient by reducing the transactions costs to households seeking saving alternatives and to borrowers issuing securities.

Clearly, the growth of the mutual funds industry has challenged the traditional role of banks. Mutual funds pose a competitive threat by offering saving instruments that have become more attractive alternative to bank deposits, given their liquidity and other characteristics. Recent experience also suggests that households are quite sensitive to changes in returns on bank deposits relative to those on mutual fund shares. Mutual funds are aggressively attempting to exploit the greater household awareness by offering new types of funds, additional shareholder services, and retirement products.

Mutual funds also challenge banks to the extent that bank borrowers can directly tap the capital markets. As mutual funds grow, they make securities markets accessible to many borrowers that were previously confined to bank loans—medium-sized businesses and individuals, who gain indirect access to the public market through asset securitization.

As investors, mutual funds have played an important role in the development of markets for securitized financial assets. Securitization began with mortgages in the 1970s and has since spread to other types of financial assets, such as automobile loans and credit card receivables.[20] Banks and other nonbank institutions have increasingly securitized such assets and sold them to various investors, including mutual funds. Securitization allows banks and thrift institutions to continue to originate loans by having mutual funds and other investors fund such loans.[21] This form of intermediation thus complements lending by depository institutions but also produces greater competition in the provision of financial services.

Asset quality problems, higher regulatory capital requirements, and cautious lending also have added to the downward trend in the amount of intermediation through banks in recent years. Accompanying this diminished role for depository institutions in the credit markets has been the slow growth in broad measures of the money supply. Such slowness is reflected in the velocity of M2, which is the ratio of gross domestic product to M2. In the past, decreases in short-term interest rates have lowered the opportunity cost of holding deposits, as deposit rates typically lagged the decline in market yields, thus causing the level of M2 to rise relative to output and its velocity to fall. In the past three years, however, the velocity of M2 has risen in the face of the general decline in market interest rates.[22]

OUTLOOK

The mutual fund industry will remain an important investment option for household savings and an important funding source for corporations and state and local governments that can directly tap the capital markets. Growth of the industry may subside as the yield curve flattens and inflows into long-term stock and bond funds slows. However, the introduction of new types of funds and services, the potential for the growth of funds marketed through banks, and the demographic forces that favor retirement products will tend to support industry growth.

---

20. The securitization of loans to small and less creditworthy firms has been rather limited. Thus, banks cannot easily originate and sell such loans into the secondary markets and have accordingly retained the business of these borrowers, who typically cannot directly tap the capital markets to obtain financing. Recent regulatory changes have made it easier for banks and other financial intermediaries to issue securities backed by small business loans in the public markets, but banks still need to evaluate and monitor the creditworthiness of such borrowers

21. By securitizing, banks and thrift institutions save on capital costs, earn fee income from servicing the loans, and earn interest income from the spread between the borrowers' rate and the rate paid to the investors.

22. See Bryon Higgins, "Policy Implications of Recent M2 Behavior," Federal Reserve Bank of Kansas City, *Economic Review*, Third Quarter 1992, pp. 21–36; and John V. Duca, "The Case of the Missing M2," Federal Reserve Bank of Dallas, *Economic Review*, Second Quarter 1992, pp. 1–24.

Article 7

Banks and Mutual Funds

Mutual funds, especially those that invest in stocks and bonds, are attracting ever greater shares of households' financial assets. While it is impossible to trace the flow of money to mutual funds, observers generally agree that bank deposits constitute a major source of those assets. In order to profit from the growing demand for mutual funds, banks themselves have begun to get more deeply involved in mutual funds in various ways. In a recent survey of large banks, the great majority stated that they currently offered mutual funds to retail customers.

In this *Weekly*, I discuss the implications for banks and the economy of banks' involvement with mutual funds. I conclude that, for the most part, banks' mutual fund activities confirm broader trends that have been developing over the past 15 years or so.

What are mutual funds?
A mutual fund is a company that makes investments on behalf of individuals and institutions, who buy shares in the fund. (The term "mutual fund" also may refer to the pool of money that is invested.) Funds differ according to their investment objectives. Objectives may include stability—protecting the original investment (principal) from loss; growth—increasing the value of the principal; or income—generating a continuous flow of income through dividends. Mutual funds also can be categorized into long-term funds and short-term funds. Long-term funds invest mainly in stocks and/or bonds, whereas short-term funds invest in taxable or tax-exempt money market instruments. Money market mutual funds are prohibited from holding any instrument with a maturity greater than 13 months, and the dollar-weighted average maturity of the fund must be no greater than 90 days. Shareholders in both long- and short-term funds have the right to redeem part of all of their holdings at any time.

Mutual funds differ from bank deposits in two important ways. First, a mutual fund share is like a share of stock in that the return on each share is proportional to the return earned by the fund. This means that the mutual fund shareholder will benefit from an unusually high return on the fund's investment. In contrast, a bank deposit is a debt contract; the return, in the form of the interest rate, whether fixed or variable, is independent of bank profitability. Second, mutual fund investments are not insured, whereas bank deposits are. Just as a mutual fund shareholder may reap an unexpectedly high return, she may on the other hand lose part or all of her principal. However, bank deposits are federally insured up to $100,000, and, in practice, depositors have sometimes retrieved even more when banks have failed.

Mutual funds have been growing recently, both in absolute terms and relative to other investments. According to the Federal Reserve's Flow of Funds Accounts, the category "households" (which includes personal trusts and nonprofit organizations) accounts for about 85 percent of all mutual fund assets, and their holdings have grown from $933 billion at the beginning of 1991 to $1.38 trillion in June 1993. Stock and bond funds held by households have shown especially strong growth; around the beginning of 1991, stock and bond funds were 52.9 percent of households' total mutual fund assets, and by the end of June this year, the share had risen to about 68.4 percent.

Banks' involvement
Banks may sell their own "proprietary" and "private label" funds, both of which are sold exclusively through the bank and have names chosen by the bank. The difference between them is simply that proprietary funds also obtain investment advice and portfolio management from the bank. Banks also may sell third party funds, which include many of the nonbank funds that are also sold to investors either directly or through other channels such as brokers. Banks' mutual fund activities do not violate the Glass-Steagall Act, which separates commercial from investment banking, because, in all cases, unaffiliated companies underwrite and distribute the shares.

For the most part, bank involvement in mutual funds is relatively recent. In a survey of large banks, 93 percent stated that they currently offered mutual funds to retail customers. However, of these, 73 percent began marketing mutual funds only within the past seven years, and 50 percent only within the past five years. In addition, the size and availability of banks' mutual fund sales forces have increased over the past three years.

In this relatively short time, banks have become fairly important conduits for mutual funds. For example, in 1991, bank sales accounted for almost 12 percent of all mutual fund industry assets. According to the Investment Company Institute (ICI), about one-third of all mutual funds are available through the bank channel. Bank involvement can also be measured in terms of dollars of new sales. The ICI reports that in the first half of 1992, banks were the channels for about a third of all new sales of money market funds and about 14 percent of all new sales of long-term funds.

Implications
One obvious reason banks benefit from getting involved with mutual funds is that they earn fee income that would otherwise go to nonbanks. This is especially so for banks' proprietary funds, where they typically earn annual custodial and management fees and receive the entire sales commission on each sale.

But there is more to the story. For example, since banks generally are not expanding, they must, to some degree, be shifting productive resources *out of* some other area and into mutual fund activities. Most obviously, banks are doing less lending than even two years ago and, consistent with this, less deposit-taking. In each of the quarters between the fourth quarter of 1990 and the second quarter of 1993, banks actually showed absolute year-over-year declines in commercial loans outstanding, and year-over-year growth in deposits has been negative two of the four quarters ending June this year.

There is some debate as to whether recent sluggish conditions in banking are due mostly to reductions in the supply or demand for loans. It is likely that both play a role. In any case, though, banks' mutual fund activities might be seen as exacerbating and prolonging the recent decline in lending and deposit-taking. By offering an especially convenient method of purchasing mutual funds, banks might be viewed as spurring their depositors into making mutual fund investments that they might not otherwise have made, thereby reducing the funds that banks have available to lend.

Also, even if they preserve their relationships with depositors by being the channel through which depositors invest in mutual funds, this strategy may backfire. For example, as depositors increase in sophistication, they may eventually bypass banks and invest in nonbank mutual funds directly. If banks do lose their relationship with depositors who invest in mutual funds, banks may find it costly to attract depositors once loan demand picks up again (or, depending on your point of view, once banks decide to start supplying loans again). At that point, banks may find that they need to offer unusually high interest rates to attract deposit funds and may therefore decide that deposit-taking and lending are just too costly.

Part of a longer-term trend
While banks' recent mutual fund activities may be viewed as contributing to the current weakness of their lending and deposit-taking activities, they may also be viewed as a *response* to the recent weakness of these activities, an effort to shift into more profitable areas. Both views can be consistent with pictures in which the recent reduction in loan volume is either supply or demand driven. However, an alternative to both of these views is that banks' involvement in mutual funds is not so much a symptom or a cause of recent conditions as it is a symptom of long-established trends in the relative market shares of banks and mutual funds.

The longer-run trends are illustrated in Figures 1 and 2. Figure 1 shows the funding side of the story: Households' bank deposits as a proportion of their total assets have been falling fairly steadily, if slightly erratically, since about 1978 (and especially so since about 1984), while mutual funds' share, including stock and bond funds and money market funds, has been more or less consistently rising. Figure 2 shows the credit side of the story: The share of total credit market assets in the U.S. held by commercial banks (mostly in the form of loans) has been falling at a remarkably steady pace since about 1974, while the share of credit held by mutual funds (which excludes equities held by mutual funds) has been rising since about 1978.

These long-term trends indicate a secular shift in demand away from bank intermediation of funds

Figure 1: Shares of Household Assets

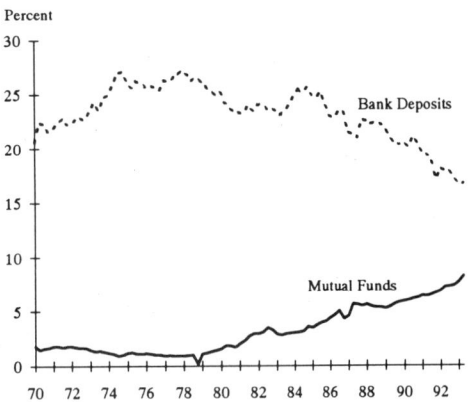

Note: Data are quarterly and are obtained from the Flow of Funds Accounts.

Figure 2: Credit Market Shares

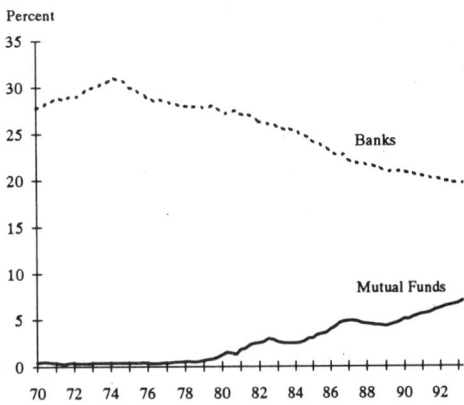

Note: Data are quarterly and are obtained from the Flow of Funds Accounts.

and toward mutual fund intermediation. It is likely that banks' involvement in mutual funds is related more to this shift than to recent reductions in bank lending. The deeper involvement of banks in mutual funds in the past few years has not been accompanied by any appreciable decrease in the rate of growth of deposits or bank loans *relative to* mutual fund growth in the analogous categories. The figures do not show sharp drop-offs in the bank shares or sharp jumps in the mutual fund shares in the last few years; banks' rates of loss and mutual funds' rates of gain have been fairly steady. In addition, there is little doubt that banks have devoted costly productive resources, including training expenses, advertising, and planning, to mutual fund activities. Such costs are more likely to be undertaken in response to well-established conditions than to recently appearing, perhaps temporary, circumstances.

Also, although long-term funds' *share* of mutual funds has increased significantly, mutual funds' overall importance as gatherers of funds and suppliers of funds through the credit markets has grown over the past few years at roughly the same pace as seen over the past fifteen. So, even though banks' recent mutual fund activities have likely drained some resources away from more traditional activities, the secular shift away from bank intermediation and toward mutual funds has been largely independent of this behavior. Finally, the profitability of shifting resources out of traditional banking activities and into mutual fund activities depends more on the rate of growth of mutual funds relative to banks than on the rate of growth of banks relative to their own past growth. Therefore, if and when bank lending resumes growing at rates closer to historical averages, bank mutual fund activity probably will continue to expand.

Conclusion

Although banks' involvement in mutual funds has deepened only in recent years, it is probably largely a reflection of broader changes that have been taking place for a much longer period. Specifically, banks' share of household assets and their share of the credit market began shrinking long before banks became active in mutual funds, yet it is these trends that have likely motivated banks to delve into the mutual fund area. At the same time, the independence of these trends from bank to mutual fund activity indicates that, even if banks were not mutual fund conduits, their relative importance as intermediaries in the economy would continue to shrink. Banks' involvement with mutual funds is best viewed as evidence of banks' recognition of this fact and their attempt to profit from it.

Elizabeth Laderman
Economist

Part Two

Regulation of Banks and Other Financial Institutions

During the 1980s a *deregulation* movement swept through the financial sector of many nations, including the United States, Canada, Great Britain, Australia, Japan, and several other countries, as governments loosened the regulatory restrictions under which financial institutions must operate. Nevertheless, even after a decade or more of deregulation, significant restrictive regulations remain in place as governments strive to protect the public's savings, avoid inflation, and insure a fair and equitable distribution of financial services to all their citizens.

One of the most controversial regulatory issues arising in the 1990s has been the debate over what accounting practices should be followed by banks and other financial institutions. Historically, many financial-service firms have valued their assets, liabilities, and equity at *original cost*—recording the value of these items on the day they are added to their balance sheets and not adjusting that value for subsequent changes in interest rates, in the economy, and in the financial position of borrowers. This long-standing accounting practice makes it difficult for capital-market investors and for depositors to judge the true worth and risk exposure of the financial-service firms with whom they trade.

One proposed solution is to require banks and other financial institutions to employ *market-value accounting* (MVA) to calculate and report the estimated current market prices of their assets and liabilities. Unfortunately, there is no universal agreement on the wisdom of such a move. As Thomas Mondschean of the Federal Reserve Bank of Chicago notes in his article, "Market Value Accounting for Commercial Banks," opponents of MVA contend that switching to such a new accounting system would be costly and potentially misleading to the public. Dr. Mondschean explores such issues as which balance-sheet items would be the most difficult to value at market and whether a compromise can be worked out between opponents and proponents of MVA that would still achieve the goal of better informing the public about the true condition of financial institutions.

Another key regulatory issue of the 1980s and 1990s centers around setting standards for the adequacy of bank capital and enforcing bank capital requirements. Due to massive losses on international loans in the 1970s and 1980s and because of fears that some nations' banks possessed a competitive advantage over other countries' banking firms, bank regulators from the United States, Canada, Japan, and leading nations in Western Europe agreed in 1988 to the Basle Accord, which imposed common capital requirements on banks headquartered in these countries. Under the terms of this landmark international agreement all bank assets are weighted by their credit quality and banks with riskier assets are required to pledge more capital as a cushion of safety.

Unfortunately, the initial Basle Accord based bank capital standards only on the credit (default) risk attached to bank assets. However, in April 1993 the Basle Committee on Banking Supervision proposed a significant revision of international bank capital standards by drafting "market risk" capital requirements. These proposed new capital rules demand that banks exposed to greater loss due to changes in interest rates, stock prices, and currency exchange rates hold greater amounts of capital as a cushion against such risks. In a two-part article entitled "Market Risk and Bank Capital" Mark E. Levonian, Research Officer with the Federal Reserve Bank of San Francisco, reviews these new Basle market-risk proposals, gives examples of how the proposals might work, and explains why he believes these new proposals represent a sensible balance of precision and practical simplicity.,

In a related article, labeled "Interest Rate Risk and Bank Capital Standards," Jonathan A. Neuberger, also an economist with the San Francisco Fed, looks at changes in bank capital standards to deal with market risk that have risen inside the United States as a result of passage of the Federal Deposit Insurance Corporation Improvement Act (1991). This comprehensive law demanded that federal banking agencies develop measures of interest-rate risk to be included in U.S. bank capital requirements. Dr. Neuberger points out that, no matter what new capital requirements are eventually imposed on banks to deal with interest-rate risk exposure, the managers of banks and other financial institutions need to continue working to develop more sophisticated interest-rate risk monitoring tools.

Among the many sweeping reforms included in the landmark FDIC Improvement Act of 1991 (FDICIA) was the adoption of the "prompt corrective action" doctrine. As directed by Congress, federal regulators, in an effort to minimize future deposit insurance losses, can intervene more aggressively in a depository institution's management as its ratio of capital to risk-adjusted assets falls. If a troubled institution's capital-asset ratio falls below 2 percent, the FDICIA law authorizes federal regulators to take over the critically undercapitalized depository and sell it to a healthy firm or liquidate its assets. This strategy of early intervention was designed to allow government authorities to sell a troubled depository institution's assets while some market value still remains in those assets. In his article "The Effects of Legislating Prompt Corrective Action on the Bank Insurance Fund" Dr. R. Alton Gilbert of the Federal Reserve Bank of St. Louis explores the issue of whether prompt regulatory action in dealing with troubled depository institutions will really achieve the goals set for it. He points out that the "prompt corrective action" doctrine is based on the assumption that the longer a depository remains in operation with a low capital-to-asset ratio, the greater the volume of losses it will present to the federal deposit insurance fund. Dr. Gilbert finds *no* relationship, however, between the length of time a troubled bank operates with low capital ratios and the resulting losses to the federal insurance fund when the bank finally collapses.

Another aspect of the 1991 FDICIA law—its assault on the "too-big-to-fail" doctrine in which some banks were judged to be too large (and, therefore, too much of a threat to the stability of the financial system) to be allowed to go bankrupt—is examined in an article entitled "Too-Big-to-Fail After FDICIA." In this interesting study Dr. Larry D. Wall of the Federal Reserve Bank of Atlanta points out that the FDICIA law strictly limits the ability of federal regulators to protect or extend the lives of the largest banks by propping them up with emergency government loans or credit guarantees. FDICIA requires regulators to take the least-cost approach to resolving bank failures and makes the Federal Reserve liable to the Federal Deposit Insurance Corporation (FDIC) if it makes loans over an extended period of time to a critically undercapitalized institution. Dr. Wall explores possible alternative policies to help implement the new rules for dealing with bank failures prescribed by the 1991 FDICIA law.

Another important law affecting depository institutions—the Community Reinvestment Act (CRA), passed by the U.S. Congress in 1977—extended the important concepts of fair treatment and nondiscrimination to the financial-services field. The CRA requires each U.S.-regulated depository institution to mark off on a map the trade territory it plans to serve and to offer its services throughout that designated trade territory without deliberately excluding certain neighborhoods that it deems to be "undesirable." Congress hoped the CRA would stimulate the public to avoid those institutions that practiced geographic discrimination against some neighborhoods. However, as Griffith L. Garwood and Dolores Smith from the Division of Consumer and Community Affairs of the Federal Reserve Board note in their article, "The Community Reinvestment Act: Evolution and Current Issues," the CRA has led to great controversy inside the banking community. Many bankers contend that its real benefits are minimal and the cost of compliance with the terms of CRA are excessively burdensome. On the other hand, several consumer groups believe that the CRA has not been adequately monitored and only weakly enforced. Garwood and Smith detail the problems created by CRA's vagueness and chronicle the law's apparent successes in promoting affordable housing and in supporting the development of small businesses in neighborhoods that are most in need of new capital and new jobs.

Finally, Dr. Christopher L. Holder of the Federal Reserve Bank of Atlanta, in his article entitled "Competitive Considerations in Bank Mergers and Acquisitions: Economy Theory, Legal Foundations, and the Fed," reviews recent Federal Reserve policy regarding the large number of bank mergers and acquisitions that have occurred in the United States in recent years. Dr. Holder evaluates the process by which the Federal Reserve evaluates the competitive effects of proposed bank mergers and acquisitions before giving its approval to these transactions. He finds that regulators increasingly today are taking into account competition from nonbank financial institutions and the issues of bank efficiency and financial condition in assessing how a given bank merger proposal might affect competition and the public interest.

Market value accounting for commercial banks

Thomas Mondschean

One of the repercussions of the savings and loan crisis and recent capital adequacy problems among some commercial banks and insurance companies has been a debate about the system of accounting used by financial institutions. The issue is whether the current method of valuing assets and liabilities conveys information accurate enough to measure the economic net worth of financial institutions. If it does not, then is it possible to design a valuation system for which the benefits of changing exceed the costs? This issue is important to policymakers and taxpayers because better information about the economic net worth of financial institutions could give regulators an opportunity to intervene sooner and potentially reduce the cost of closing insolvent institutions. It is important to shareholders because uncertainty about the actual value of an institution makes it harder to decide whether to invest in its stocks. It is also relevant for creditors since the value of economic net worth affects a bank's ability to absorb future losses and thus is an indication of its ability to bear risk.

One proposal that has been debated in recent years is to require banks to use market value accounting (MVA) to compute the values of their portfolios. MVA would require banks to adjust the values of assets and liabilities periodically for changes in market prices and conditions. This idea is not new in financial circles. For example, futures exchanges require that all futures contracts be marked to market at the end of each trading day. For a variety of reasons, however, marking certain portions of a bank's portfolio to market is more difficult. Opponents of MVA focus on these difficulties and the additional costs a new accounting system would require and contend that such a change is economically impractical. Proponents, on the other hand, emphasize the costs of not changing systems. Under the current historical cost accounting system (HCA), banks record the value of assets and liabilities at the time they are acquired, and these values are not subsequently adjusted until they are sold or written down. Proponents of MVA argue that the current accounting system diminishes the public's confidence in the financial system by not presenting an accurate enough picture of the current economic health of financial firms.

The purpose of this article is to examine the costs and benefits of market value accounting. I focus the discussion on the case of commercial banks; however, much of the analysis presented could be applied to other types of financial intermediaries. Many of the issues discussed here have been examined in greater detail in the chapter on market value accounting in the 1991 U.S. Treasury study on reforming the financial system. After a discussion of the purposes served by an accounting system for banks, I explain how HCA misrepresents the true economic value of financial institu-

---

Thomas Mondschean is a consultant at the Federal Reserve Bank of Chicago and assistant professor of economics at DePaul University. The author thanks David Allardice, Herb Baer, and David Jones for helpful comments, and George Rodriguez and John McElravey for research assistance.

tions. Next, the commercial bank balance sheet is examined in detail both to explain how market value accounting would work and to evaluate the difficulty of marking to market various balance sheet items. Once it is known which balance sheet items are most difficult to value, it is then possible to assess how costly the move to MVA would be and whether the cost-benefit tradeoff for market value accounting is different for large banks than for smaller institutions. I then discuss the major criticisms raised about MVA. The issues raised by both sides imply that there may be some middle ground, so I explore possibilities for improving the system of reporting that does not require a complete move to market value accounting. The article concludes by making suggestions for improving the quality of information provided by commercial banks to both bank regulators and the public.

What should an accounting system for banks achieve?

Any bank accounting system must provide useful information to both bank regulators and the public. According to the recent U.S. Treasury study on financial reform, useful information should be: "(a) relevant, timely, and understandable to users of financial statements; (b) reliable, in the sense of being accurate, objective, and verifiable by outside parties; and (c) reported in a consistent manner to facilitate comparisons over time and across firms."[1] But for what purposes are accounting data useful? One goal is to assist in ensuring financial control. As Benston (1989) points out, the current bank accounting system is "... designed to report on the transactions that occurred between the enterprise and other market participants and among control and decision units within the enterprise and the people responsible."[2] Cost accounting allows banks to trace each dollar as it is acquired or spent, leaving a paper trail that assists both banks and independent auditors in detecting fraud as well as in finding and correcting mistakes. Given the volume of transactions a typical bank handles every day, whatever accounting system is in place must allow banks to monitor accurately all transactions as they take place.

Another purpose of an accounting system is to permit accurate appraisals of the value of bank net worth or capital. Net worth is defined as the difference between the value of assets and the value of liabilities. Shareholders need an accurate measure of accounting net worth in order to make informed investment decisions. To the bank's uninsured creditors, net worth represents the amount a bank could lose and still pay its debts. From their perspective, it is more important that the value of net worth not be overstated than that it be accurate. If net worth is understated, uninsured creditors receive additional protection. Appraisals of net worth should be timely in the sense that valuations of net worth should take into account changing economic conditions, so that, for example, a decline in the value of a bank's assets, other things equal, would result in a decline in the value of its net worth. The information provided should also make it possible for users of these data to compare the relative performance of different banks.

No matter which type of accounting system is in place, a related issue is whether banks should be required to disclose more information to permit the public to reach their own conclusions about a bank's net worth. In particular, should banks be required to release the same information to the public as they do to the regulatory authorities? Some argue that greater disclosure of a bank's loan portfolio might affect the competitive position of a bank or its customers if confidential information valuable to other firms was released. Regulators must balance the public's need to learn about banks with the banks' need to protect confidential or proprietary information. Stockholders and uninsured creditors have a legitimate need to know the economic value of a bank to protect their own interests; however, it may not be in the best interest of bank managers to release such information. Some market participants contend that price-earnings ratios for bank holding company stocks might be higher if banks disclosed more and better information about their portfolios. Thus, the public policy issue is not whether banks should disclose confidential or proprietary information but whether they should be required to release more information than they currently do.[3] It is worth noting that other financial services industries disclose more detailed information about their portfolios to the public than banks do. Mutual funds are required by the Securities and Exchange Commission (SEC) to disclose their complete portfolio holdings every quarter. SEC regulated broker/dealers and futures commissions merchants must report market values.

Insurance companies are required to disclose their complete stock and bond holdings as well as state-by-state breakdowns of their long term mortgage loans to regulators once a year.[4]

Problems with the current accounting system

Under HCA rules, a bank records the nominal value of the asset or liability at the time it is acquired.[5] One justification for HCA is that banks were presumed to acquire assets and liabilities and hold them until maturity. As long as they receive repayment of interest and principal at the contracted periods, changes in market value were presumed to have no effect on the asset's cash flow. However, this motivation for HCA violates basic economic principles. First, an asset's purchase price does not represent the best estimate of what it will be worth in the future because it ignores subsequent information about changes in market interest rates, credit risk, and other variables. Second, the assumption that banks hold all of their assets to maturity is outdated. The development of securitization and other techniques means that many types of loans can be easily sold before maturity. Third, for certain assets, banks can lock in current embedded gains or limit future economic losses by hedging even if the asset is not sold before maturity.

The development and use of generally accepted accounting principles (GAAP), which are based in large part on HCA principles, are designed to give all banks a similar set of rules with which they report the value of their portfolios. However, GAAP allows banks some flexibility in determining the timing of valuation changes. For example, a bank with an unrealized gain on a particular asset may choose a particular time to sell the asset, realize the gain, and use it to offset other losses. Alternatively, a bank may prefer to increase loan loss reserves at discrete intervals rather than taking losses as they become apparent.[6] Thus, the book value of bank capital might understate its economic value if a bank has unrealized gains in its portfolio or overstate its economic value if it has unrealized losses. Because GAAP permits such behavior, meaningful comparisons between banks are more difficult. Proponents of MVA believe the best way to solve this problem is to require banks to report changes in values when they occur, rather than allowing banks to choose when to realize them.

Perhaps the best evidence that the current bank accounting system needs to be improved comes from the stock market itself. Figure 1 compares the ratios of market to book values for a sample of 80 bank holding companies to those of approximately 1,400 nonfinancial

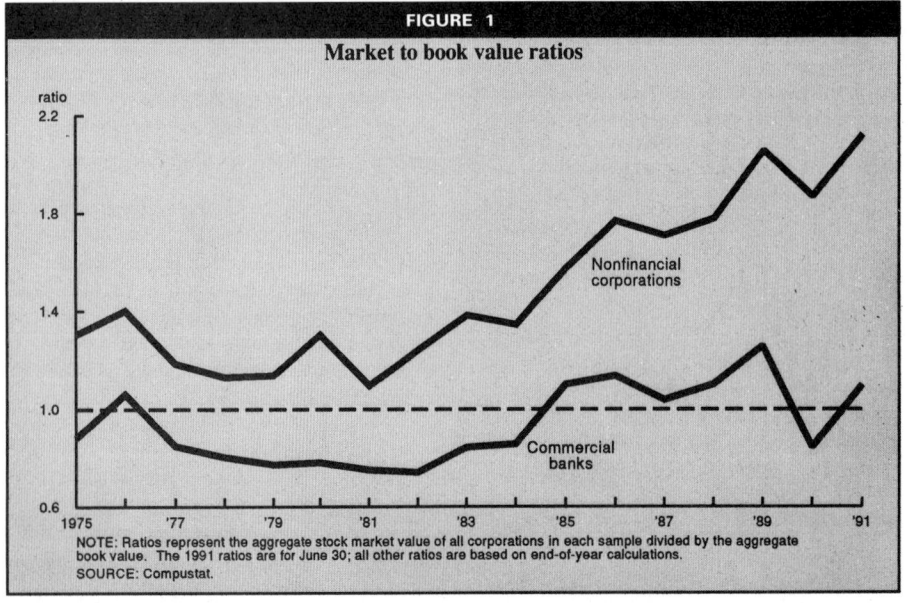

FIGURE 1. Market to book value ratios

NOTE: Ratios represent the aggregate stock market value of all corporations in each sample divided by the aggregate book value. The 1991 ratios are for June 30; all other ratios are based on end-of-year calculations.
SOURCE: Compustat.

corporations from 1975 to 1991. From the perspective of bank creditors, a higher ratio of market to book value is desirable because it indicates a more conservative valuation of accounting net worth, which provides additional protection for the deposit insurer as well as uninsured creditors. Market to book ratios have been consistently higher for nonfinancial corporations than for commercial banks throughout the last fifteen years, and the difference in the ratios has been widening in recent years. This graph also demonstrates that the problems with the system of bank accounting are not a recent phenomenon: market values were below book values in 1975 and from 1977 to 1984. Figure 2 compares the proportion of banks whose market values were less than book value with nonfinancial corporations. In every year, there was a larger proportion of commercial banks than nonfinancial corporations whose market values of net worth did not exceed their accounting values. A system of accounting should produce conservative and relevant assessments of a bank's net worth, but these data show that there were several years when the market did not believe that the book value assessment of bank net worth was low enough.

Changes in market interest rates can cause the market value of bank net worth to differ from its book value. An example of this is illustrated in Figure 3. Market bid prices for mortgage-backed GNMA (Ginnie Mae) securities with 9 and 11 percent coupons are plotted for the last Friday of each month from 1975 to 1991. These securities are backed by federally insured mortgage loans, so that, from the investor's point of view, there is zero default risk. The value of mortgage loans made by a commercial bank would be recorded on its books at the time the loan was made and would not change unless the bank sold the loan. One can observe, however, that the market values of such loans have fluctuated a great deal over the past fifteen years. For example, the market values of GNMA securities with 9 percent coupons were 100.75 percent of their par value at the end of May 1978. By September 1981, these securities were trading at 60 percent of their par value, due to a large increase in long term market interest rates during this period. Because commercial banks held fixed rate mortgage loans during this period, the ratio of market to book value of these loans decreased from 1979 to 1981. In Mondschean (1990), I examined the mortgage portfolios of 75 bank holding companies and found that, on average, the market value of their mortgage loans declined from approximately 90 percent of book value at the beginning of 1979 to approximately 60 percent by the end of 1981. Although banks could have hedged their fixed rate mortgage loans by using futures and options or by

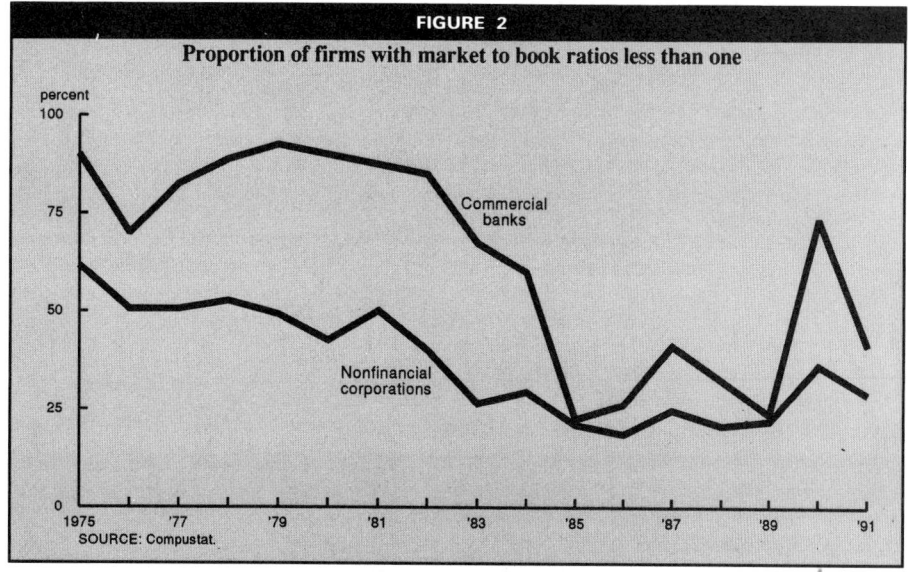

FIGURE 2
Proportion of firms with market to book ratios less than one
SOURCE: Compustat.

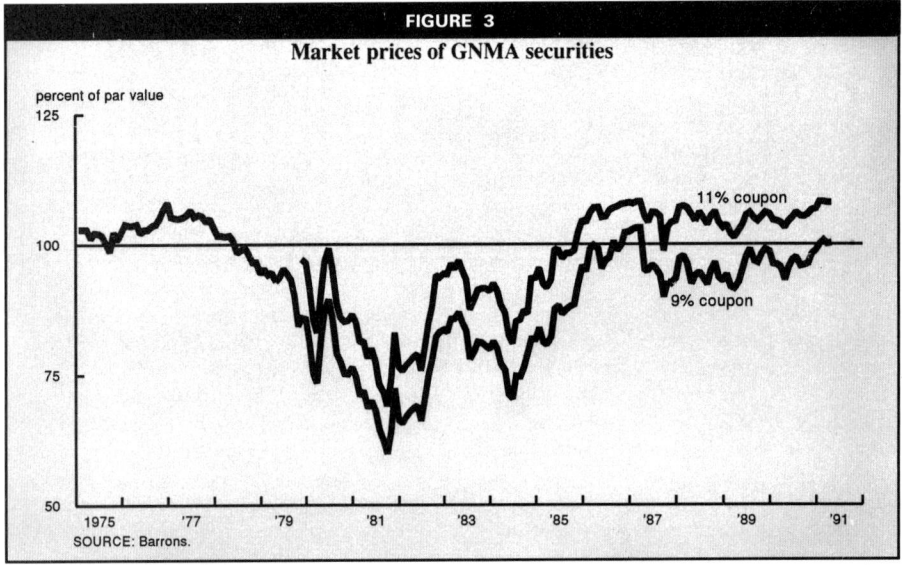

funding the loans with long term deposits, I also found that banks with larger unrealized losses on mortgage loans experienced greater declines in their stock prices than banks with smaller losses. However, the accounting value of their mortgage loans and hence the book value of net worth did not change unless banks were forced to sell or write down these loans.[7]

Besides market interest rates, there are other factors which can affect the market value of bank net worth. The probability of default can increase unexpectedly, adversely affecting a loan's market value. The duration, a measure of the term to maturity of a financial instrument, can decrease unexpectedly, affecting the timing of payments of principal and interest, thereby altering the present value of the loan's cash flow. Changes in the exchange rate value of the U.S. dollar could affect the dollar value of assets and liabilities denominated in foreign currencies. But why should one care if market and book values diverge? Because commercial banks are highly leveraged, small changes in the market values of their assets have a significant effect on their net worth. For example, suppose a bank has a capital-to-asset ratio of 6 percent and the market value of its assets falls by 1 percent with no offsets elsewhere on or off the balance sheet. While a 1 percent decline in total assets may not seem like a large change, it is equivalent to one-sixth of the bank's total capital. Because of this, it is essential for both regulators and investors to know when the market value of a bank's portfolio changes relative to its book value.

When the market value of a firm goes down, other things equal, its stock price should be affected. However, when the value of bank net worth declines without a corresponding change in accounting net worth, both the regulators and the public may believe a bank has more capital than it actually has. Since many investors are aware of the fact that a bank has better information about its true economic value, they must forecast the magnitude of a bank's net unrealized gains or losses. Thus, a bank's debt and equity may be priced differently than it would be if investors had an accurate measure of net worth. For example, a bank with unrealized losses that are larger than the market believes might have a higher stock price than it would if investors had accurate information about market values; consequently, investors would not be adequately compensated for the risk of investing in that bank's stock. On the other hand, if a bank has larger unrealized gains than the market believes, then, other things equal, its stock would be underpriced, raising the cost of issuing new equity for the bank.[8]

The existence of deposit insurance exacerbates the problems that can arise if the market value of bank net worth falls below book value. As its market value gets closer to zero, the bank has a greater incentive to increase its risk exposure. Since shareholders would receive nothing if the institution is closed, a market value insolvent bank acting in the best interest of shareholders has a strong incentive to increase risk in the hope of earning above normal returns. If the institution experiences greater losses, the losses are borne by the deposit insurer and not by the shareholders, thereby placing the deposit insurance fund at greater risk. This moral hazard problem underscores the importance of providing accurate market values of bank net worth to regulators. Because the current accounting system does not guarantee that this will be the case, the probability that taxpayers will be required to absorb part of the cost of future bank failures is increased.[9]

Measurement issues in a market value accounting system

Under a system of market value accounting, banks would be required to adjust all assets and liabilities for changes in the market value of those assets and liabilities. Critics of this approach argue that market value estimates of bank net worth would be unreliable due to the difficulty of measuring the value of various balance sheet items. To evaluate this argument, it is helpful to examine a representative bank's balance sheet in greater detail. In Table 1, bank assets are separated into several categories and asset shares are reported for all banks with total assets of less than $100 million, $100 million to $1 billion, and over $1 billion, respectively, as of the end of 1990. The asset categories are divided into two groups. The first grouping lists assets for which either book and market values are equal or market values can be calculated with little additional cost. The market values of cash assets, representing currency and coin, reserve balances at Federal Reserve Banks, and cash items in the process of collection, are equal to their book values. Assets held in trading accounts are already carried at market value. The market values of overnight federal funds sold and securities purchased under agreement to resell are close to book values because of the short term nature of these financial instruments. The market value of securities held is already reported to regulators.[10]

Deposits due from other banks represent funds one bank may place with another bank. These funds can be interest-bearing or noninter-

TABLE 1
Asset shares of commercial banks
(December 31, 1990)

	Asset size category in millions of dollars		
	Less than 100	100-1,000	Greater than 1,000
	(percent of total assets)		
Easy to mark to market			
Cash and due from deposits	6.86	6.83	10.61
Federal funds sold and reverse RPs	6.70	5.28	3.65
Assets held in trading accounts	0.04	0.21	1.97
Securities (book value)	30.64	23.85	14.40
Premises and fixed assets	1.69	1.64	1.48
Other real estate owned	0.64	0.66	0.63
Subtotal	46.57	38.47	32.74
Difficult to mark to market			
Total loans and leases	51.58	59.47	62.04
Other assets	1.84	2.06	5.23
Total assets	100.00	100.00	100.00
Number of banks	9,144	2,682	363

SOURCE: Federal Reserve Report of Condition.

est-bearing. In general, smaller banks having a correspondent relationship with a larger bank deposit these funds in exchange for services provided by the larger bank. Since there is a great deal of competition for this business among large banks, it is believed that the value of services provided as implicit interest on these balances approximates a market interest rate; hence, the market values of these deposits equal their book values.

Computing market values for other real estate owned (OREO) is somewhat less precise. OREO includes all real estate owned or controlled by the bank excluding bank premises, such as direct and indirect investments in real estate ventures for investment purposes and real estate acquired through foreclosure. Currently, banks report to regulators the book value of these assets less accumulated depreciation, which cannot be greater than fair market value. Fair market values of these assets are generally calculated by independent appraisers. The accuracy of these appraisal reports depends on both the availability of comparable market information as well as the judgment of the appraisers. While they may be imprecise, these estimates would be no less exact under market value accounting than under the current system. Since banks also record bank premises and fixed assets (computers, furniture, etc.) at book value less depreciation, there is no reason why market appraisals could not be used to value these assets as well.[11]

Taken as a group, those assets for which using MVA would entail little or no additional cost to banks represent approximately one-third of total assets for banks with over $1 billion in total assets and just under one-half of total assets for the 9,144 banks with $100 million or less in total assets as of the end of 1990.

Proponents of MVA recognize that certain categories of loans would be difficult to mark to market. While some loans, such as one-to-four family mortgage loans and student loans, are actively bought and sold, most types of loans are not actively traded, and so market values cannot be inferred directly from secondary markets.[12] Although financial institutions must often compute market values of nontraded assets for their own purposes, such calculations are inherently judgmental and could potentially be manipulated. Opponents of MVA point out that the cost of imposing MVA on banks would be high if every bank loan required such a valuation. Proponents counter that banks already use such judgment in determining the appropriate size of their loan loss reserves.

Analyzing the effect of market interest rate changes on loan market values is a primary objective of MVA. Table 2 classifies loans at commercial banks according to the remaining time to repricing or repayment. Floating rate loans are loans whose interest rate is adjusted to reflect market interest rate changes. For banks with over $1 billion in total assets, the majority of loans are made at floating interest rates. The market values of these loans can diverge during the period between repricing dates; however, once the loan interest rate is adjusted, market and book values are equal. Thus, the effect of changes in market interest rates on the market values of bank loans depends on the time period before either the loan is repriced or it is repaid. As Table 2 indicates, for all size classes, the percentage of loans which are repriced or repaid within one year is between 60 and 70 percent.

For loans with longer periods before repricing or repayment, assuming banks revealed accurate cash flow information, market values could be inferred using some form of discounted cash flow analysis. The market value of a loan is equated to the present value of the expected flow of payments accruing from the loan. Assuming, for simplicity, that payments are made at the end of each period, the present value of the flow of payments as of date 0 can be represented by the following:

$$PV_0 = C_0 + C_1/(1 + r_1) + C_2/(1 + r_2)^2 + \ldots + C_n/(1 + r_n)^n$$

where, for example, C_1 represents the expected payment of principal and interest in period 1, r_1 is the discount rate for period 1, and n is the number of years from today to the date of the final payment. The present value of a bank's existing loans can be affected in two ways. First, the timing of interest and principal payments may be altered in the event of a rescheduling of repayments. Second, the interest rate used to discount future payments may change. Using discounted cash flows to derive market values would have several advantages. As long as banks know when expected payments of interest and principal would occur, they could combine loans and report the expected cash flow of the entire loan portfolio. Thus, they need not report the market value of each loan. As banks make new loans

TABLE 2
Loans at commercial banks by remaining time before repricing or repayment
(December 31, 1990)

	Asset size category in millions of dollars		
	Less than 100	100-1,000	Greater than 1,000
	(percent of total loans)		
Floating rate loans with remaining time to repricing			
Within 3 months	26.51	37.25	45.07
3 months - 1 year	6.59	7.56	6.45
1 year - 5 years	1.81	2.65	1.52
Greater than 5 years	0.10	0.16	0.38
Total floating rate loans	35.01	47.62	53.42
Fixed rate loans and leases with remaining maturity			
3 months or less	12.79	8.02	10.07
3 months - 12 months	16.59	8.93	5.43
12 months - 5 years	26.87	24.70	18.66
Over 5 years	8.75	10.73	12.42
Total fixed rate loans and leases	64.99	52.38	46.58
Total loans and leases	100.00	100.00	100.00
Percent of all loans that mature or are repriced within one year	62.48	61.75	67.02

SOURCE: Federal Reserve Report of Condition.

and receive new information about the timing of expected future payments on existing loans, they could update their cash flow projections. Changes in foreign exchange rates which could affect the expected dollar values of future payments can also be incorporated into these estimates. And the present value of the loan portfolio can be adjusted for changes in market interest rates.

However, there are measurement problems inherent in the present value approach. Even for relatively simple fixed rate term loans, valuations depend on assumptions about the expected payments and appropriate discount factors. Borrowers may have trouble servicing the debt according to the terms of the loan contract because of economic difficulties, or they may choose to repay a loan faster than the bank expects. Whatever the reason, the duration of the loan may increase or decrease and the present value would be affected.[13] In addition, many loans with interest rate caps or collars have embedded options which require more sophisticated valuation methods. These issues aside, while adjusting the market values of loans for interest rate risk is relatively straightforward, it is more difficult to determine the effect of changes in credit risk on loan market values. One problem is that since banks possess better information about the borrower than the users of financial statements do, a moral hazard problem exists. It might be optimal for a bank not to reveal its best estimate of a loan's market value. As a bank's net worth decreases, its incentive to overstate the value of its loans increases.[14]

Besides loans, there are other assets for which it may be difficult to compute market values.[15] An example is the value of services provided by the bank in exchange for fees. For example, when a bank sells a mortgage loan to FNMA, it often retains the right to service the loan for a fee. While in principle one could take the present value of the fees net of the bank's own cost, the possibility of prepayment or foreclosure makes such calculations problematic. Evaluating the present value of other services provided by a bank presents similar difficulties.[16]

There are also measurement issues which must be confronted when computing the market values of bank liabilities. When computing the value of bank liabilities, it may be inappropriate to use secondary market prices because they incorporate credit risk. While shareholders would prefer to include the value of the bank's option to default on its liabilities in the market value of net worth, debtholders and regulators would not because they would bear the cost of default. One way of protecting uninsured creditors and the deposit insurance fund would be to discount the contractual cash flows of bank liabilities at the risk free interest rate.[17]

Table 3 shows various liability categories expressed as a percent of total assets. Some liabilities are either easy to mark to market or are already carried at market value. The interest rate on money market deposit accounts is generally indexed to a market interest rate. Borrowed funds, such as federal funds purchased and securities sold under agreement to repurchase, are very short term financial instruments, so market and book values are extremely close. Total time deposits are relatively straightforward to mark to market because they are seldom redeemed before maturity and over three-quarters mature or are repriced within a year. Discounted present values can be calculated for subordinated debentures and other long term bonds.

Demand deposits, savings deposits, and NOW accounts are potentially the most difficult items on bank balance sheets to mark to market.[18] Because of the cost a depositor may incur in transferring accounts from one bank to another, banks often pay below market interest rates on their core deposits; hence, these deposits add market value to a bank's net worth. In theory, the additional value of core deposits can be represented by the present discounted value of future cost savings net of servicing costs over the next best alternative funding source. However, calculating these present values is difficult for two reasons. First, when market interest rates increase, the future cost savings per dollar of deposits may also rise, but the deposit quantities may decrease. Since the value of the cost savings each period equals the cost savings per dollar of deposits times the amount of deposits, there is no precise measure

TABLE 3
Liability and net worth shares of commercial banks
(December 31, 1990)

	Asset size category in millions of dollars		
	Less than 100	100-1,000	Greater than 1,000
	(percent of total assets)		
Easy to mark to market			
Money market deposit accounts	9.71	12.13	11.21
Time deposits	47.95	42.64	27.28
Borrowed funds	0.99	4.78	14.45
Subordinated notes and debentures	0.03	0.12	0.94
Subtotal	**58.69**	**59.67**	**53.89**
Difficult to mark to market			
Total demand deposits	12.34	13.47	14.26
Other transactions deposits	11.40	9.50	5.17
Other savings deposits	7.49	7.97	5.29
Deposits in foreign offices	0.04	0.53	11.45
Other liabilities	1.08	1.20	4.18
Total book value capital	8.96	7.67	5.76
Total liabilities and net worth	**100.00**	**100.00**	**100.00**

SOURCE: Federal Reserve Report of Condition.

of the magnitude of these cost savings over time. Second, because core deposits have no stated maturity, there is no objective method to determine the duration of these deposits. Thus, any calculation using present values must be based on assumptions which are difficult to verify. On the other hand, imprecise though they may be, estimated valuations of core deposits are routinely done by depository institutions interested in purchasing core deposit accounts from insolvent institutions or when analyzing the value of a bank for a prospective merger or acquisition.

Deposits in foreign offices, which fund over 10 percent of total assets for banks with $1 billion or more in total assets, present similar conceptual difficulties for MVA. Time deposits would be relatively easy to mark to market, but other types of foreign deposits may be more difficult. While banks are currently not required to break down their deposits in foreign offices by type of deposit, we do know that over 95 percent of these deposits pay explicit interest. Thus, if foreign deposits were reported in the same detail as domestic deposits are, accurate market valuations could be made for the vast majority of these deposits. Requiring foreign deposit holdings to be reported in greater detail would impose little additional cost since these deposits are concentrated in the largest banks who need these data for internal purposes.

Another set of measurement issues arises when accounting for off balance sheet contingencies under MVA. Examples of such contingencies include interest rate and foreign currency swaps, forward and futures contracts, loan commitments, letters of credit, and guarantees. Since banks are already required to estimate the market value of interest rate and futures positions for regulators, these pose no additional problems under MVA. However, evaluating the market value of loan commitments is complicated by the possibility that they would become loans. The values of loan guarantees depend on the probability that they will be exercised, which implies some estimate of credit risk is necessary.[19]

In summary, while computing accurate market values for some bank balance sheet items is difficult, many proponents of MVA believe the extent of the problems is exaggerated since the majority of bank assets and liabilities can be marked to market with little additional cost. Many of the problems are inherent in any accounting system, but others are the result of assumptions or subjective judgments which must be made in order to provide estimates of market values. Proponents of MVA contend that if banks start valuing their portfolios using MVA, the experience will spur accounting innovations that can improve the quality of information and reduce measurement errors. Also, they argue that the question should not be whether market value accounting is perfectly accurate, but whether MVA is an improvement over historical cost accounting. If MVA can reduce the bias (the difference between economic and accounting values) and the variance of the bias (the tendency for the bias to fluctuate over time) relative to HCA, it would be an improvement over the current accounting system.

Costs imposed by a market value accounting system

The banking industry maintains that the cost of implementing a new system designed to report market values as a basis for GAAP and regulatory reports would be prohibitively expensive. According to this view, MVA requires costly marking to market of all assets, liabilities, and contingent claims it holds using whatever method—observation of secondary market prices, appraisals, or discounted cash flow analysis—is deemed most appropriate. Many depository institutions claim that MVA would require additional developmental and other costs to obtain necessary data, modify or purchase computer software, perform complex calculations, and train personnel. Because many of these costs are fixed, smaller banks would experience even greater burdens on a unit cost basis. Moreover, because many assumptions required to compute market values are subjective, the cost of auditing banks may also rise as verification of a bank's methods would take longer and be more difficult.

Proponents of MVA respond that the incremental cost of adopting MVA is overstated for small banks. Smaller banks hold a larger proportion of assets which are relatively easy to mark to market, partly because they have a higher percentage of their assets in securities but also because of the nature of their loan portfolios. Table 4 shows how the average loan

TABLE 4
Total loans at commercial banks by type of loan
(December 31, 1990)

	Asset size category in millions of dollars		
	Less than 100	100–1,000	Greater than 1,000
	(percent of total loans)		
Loans secured by real estate	50.07	51.10	35.12
Construction and land development	3.50	5.41	6.47
Secured by farmland	4.93	1.26	0.21
Revolving, open-end loans secured by one-to-four family properties	1.55	3.34	3.00
Mortgage loans—one-to-four family dwellings	26.22	3.26	12.72
Mortgage loans—multifamily dwellings	0.94	1.41	0.88
Nonfarm nonresidential real estate loans	12.93	16.41	10.12
Loans to depository institutions	0.25	0.94	3.06
Agricultural loans	9.68	1.81	0.56
Commercial and industrial loans	19.33	22.45	32.53
Consumer loans—credit cards	1.00	3.78	6.76
Consumer loans—other	17.88	17.10	11.33
Loans to foreign governments and official institutions	0.01	0.06	1.65
Other loans	3.61	4.71	10.03
Total loans and leases, net of unearned income	100.00	100.00	100.00

SOURCE: Federal Reserve Report of Condition.

portfolio for smaller banks differs from their larger counterparts. The data show that, for banks with less than $100 million in total assets at the end of 1990, the proportion of relatively easy to value one-to-four family mortgage loans and non-credit-card consumer loans was significantly larger than for banks with over $1 billion in total assets, and small banks held a smaller proportion of commercial and industrial loans They also have a larger proportion of loans secured by farmland, for which there is a great deal of price data. With few exceptions, smaller banks also do not have any foreign deposits. In other words, because smaller banks have portfolios which are easier to value, the costs of adopting MVA per dollar of earnings may actually be less than for larger banks.

Another point is that it is not necessary to mark individual assets and liabilities to market in order to obtain the majority of the benefits of MVA. One could aggregate loans and deposits into pools with similar characteristics and estimate market values for each pool. An advantage of such a method is that idiosyncratic differences among assets within a pool would not have as great an effect on its overall value, so measurement error may be reduced. In addition, while implementation and operating costs may be high initially, they would most likely decline over time. New products would be created and marketed to make it easier to collect and process the additional information required for MVA. Economic incentives to lower these costs would lead to the development of standardized databases and software to compute market values of complex financial instruments. The movement toward standardization would also make it easier for users of bank financial statements to compare relative bank performance.

Even if adopting MVA proves to be costly, proponents believe that any incremental cost of

MVA to the banking industry should be compared with the gains society derives by having better information. Regulators and taxpayers would especially benefit by having better and more timely information about a bank's economic value. Bank managers could use the information derived from MVA to improve their management of risk exposure. Investors would have a better measure of the economic value of banks which would allow investors to make more informed choices about which bank investments to hold. Thus, while it may be in an individual bank's interest to oppose MVA because its cost of implementation may not exceed the benefits for the bank itself, MVA may be worthwhile if the total benefit to society exceeds the total cost to society. Indeed, the difference between private and social net benefits is one of the principal justifications given for imposing regulations in general.

Possible economic effects of market value accounting

In assessing the feasibility of changing the accounting system for banks, it is necessary to evaluate the likely economic effects of such a change. Many researchers have studied the impact of changes in accounting regulations on market values of firms.[20] The general conclusion of these studies is that changes in accounting and reporting rules do affect stock market values. While it seems likely that changes in bank accounting rules may affect market values of bank securities, this is hardly a reason for not making needed reforms since firms must often adjust to changes in accounting methods and standards. Thus, a key question is whether the use of MVA will improve the safety and soundness of the banking system. Also, will banks become more or less competitive relative to other firms under MVA? A third question is how will bank portfolio behavior change under MVA.

Whether market participants perceive banks to be safer under MVA than under current accounting practices depends in part on how serious the measurement problems are. Opponents of market value accounting argue that estimates based on subjective and difficult to verify assumptions will increase uncertainty about the true economic value of banks. This will undermine public confidence in the banks, raising their costs of capital and borrowed funds. Also, MVA opponents argue that current bank earnings will be even more sensitive to fluctuations in interest and exchange rates because they would have to realize capital gains and losses sooner. As a result, investors will demand greater risk premia. Banks may then be induced to focus more on short run profits and avoid long term loans that may be more profitable but also more risky if they must be marked to market.

Proponents of MVA respond that requiring greater disclosure of market values of bank portfolios would allow investors to make better estimates of the economic or true value of bank securities. Thus, MVA comes closer than historical cost accounting to disclosing the true value, and the true risk, of a bank to investors and regulators. In particular, banks' cost of capital will rise under MVA only if banks had been underpaying for capital, deposits, or borrowed funds previously by undercompensating investors or depositors for the risk of investing in or lending to banks. Hence, MVA will benefit investors and lenders because it insures that investors and lenders will be fairly compensated for the risk of investing in or lending to banks. Moreover, since MVA would make it more difficult for banks to overstate their net worth, MVA will benefit regulators by allowing banks that are having capital adequacy problems to be identified more quickly. This would improve the safety and soundness of the banking industry.

The likely consequences of MVA for future bank behavior are difficult to determine. One concern is that banks may reduce credit availability during periods of declining asset prices. Since declining market values would quickly affect capital positions, banks might curtail lending to increase capital-asset ratios. It is also conceivable that if MVA increases the volatility of reported net worth it may also increase the volatility of credit availability. Due to the growth of commercial paper and other types of direct corporate borrowing, the borrowers that would be most adversely affected by increased credit rationing would be those who do not have direct access to capital markets, such as small businesses. Another issue is whether the optimal capital-asset ratio will increase under MVA. If reported earnings under MVA were more volatile and regulators and creditors based their actions on these new earnings estimates, a bank would increase its equilibrium capital ratio and reduce hedgeable risk in order to reassure its customers that it could withstand shocks that reduced its net worth. This behavioral change could mitigate the need to restrict credit availability when market values are falling, and it may also improve safety and soundness.

Alternatives to market value accounting

Acknowledging some of the criticisms of full MVA, some have argued that most of the advantages of MVA can be obtained by modifying rather than overhauling the current accounting framework. One proposal is to require the reporting of values for those instruments for which secondary market prices exist. Such a step would not be very costly to banks because much of this information is already reported to regulators. Proponents believe that this would represent an improvement over the current system and would reduce the degree of measurement error that currently exists by using HCA. Opponents disagree, contending that many institutions use securities to offset positions taken elsewhere in the balance sheet. For example, a bank might decide to purchase some long term Treasury securities to offset long term certificates of deposit. Marking one and not the other to market would reduce the effectiveness of such a hedging position. Moreover, the difficulty of measuring the duration of core deposits implies that it may be not be easy to determine whether some banks have positive or negative gaps (a gap is the difference between the market value of assets and the market value of liabilities of equal times to repricing or repayment). In this case, it becomes unclear whether an increase in interest rates will reduce the market value of net worth. Thus, only marking a portion of the balance sheet to market for changes in interest rates would distort its meaning and lead to greater confusion about bank net worth, according to MVA opponents. Note that this argument would not hold for credit risk since it is difficult to hedge against credit risk.

Another proposal is to require banks to disclose more information about the performance of their portfolios in their financial reports but not necessarily mark their portfolios to market. An advantage of disclosure is that it avoids many of the measurement problems discussed earlier because it would be up to the users of financial data to determine the effect of the additional disclosures on the market value of net worth. As a result, the cost of auditing the bank would be less than it would be under full MVA. Another advantage of disclosure is that investors, depositors, and bank regulators could use the information to make decisions. Investors could respond to disclosure of negative information by selling a bank's securities, thereby imposing greater market discipline on banks.

Disclosure of market value information would be a useful transitional step toward full MVA, because it would give market participants and regulatory bodies time to assess the usefulness of market value information and its likely economic effects. The Financial Accounting Standards Board (FASB) appears to agree. Statement No. 105 requires additional disclosure in financial statements with off balance sheet risk of accounting loss. It also requires greater disclosure of "... all significant concentrations of credit risk of all financial instruments, whether from an individual counterparty or groups of counterparties." A concentration of credit risk exists when the parties have common economic characteristics, such as operating in similar industries or locations, which would cause their ability to meet contractual obligations to be similarly affected by changes in these characteristics. For more details, see FASB (1990) and Carlson and Mooney (1991).

A recent statement, FASB (1991), goes even further. It requires that all entities disclose information about the market value of all financial instruments, both assets and liabilities on and off the balance sheet, for which it is practical to do so. For instruments for which it is impractical to estimate market value, the statement requires descriptive information that would assist users in estimating market values. The proposed date of implementation is for financial statements issued for fiscal years ending after December 15, 1992, for entities with $150 million or more in total assets. For those entities with less than $150 million in total assets, the effective starting date would be three years later.

Conclusion

The savings and loan crisis has focused attention on the accounting system used by financial institutions. Many economists and other researchers believe that the current system of accounting presents a misleading picture of the true economic value of commercial banks. They contend this is both raising the cost of capital for banks and placing the deposit insurance fund at greater risk. Market value accounting has been proposed as a better way to measure the economic value of banks. However, MVA has conceptual and measurement difficulties which need to be addressed. Many of these problems can be mitigated, but it must be recognized that no system of accounting can eliminate the use of judgment in valuations.

Until this debate is resolved, there is still a need for better information to protect the deposit insurance fund and ultimately taxpayers from excessive risk taking by banks with low market values. Because managers of banks may not want to voluntarily improve the quality of information submitted to both regulators and the public, banks should be required to report the expected future cash flows (repayment of principal and interest) on their fixed rate loans and time deposits as a function of the time when repayment is made. Currently, banks are only required to report the value of assets and liabilities which fall into different time periods, as shown in Table 2. To compute present values, one needs the expected future cash flows as a function of time, not what is currently reported.

Disclosing this information would greatly assist regulators in examining interest rate risk of commercial banks. Second, banks should not have as much discretion to choose the time to realize gains or losses as they currently do. In particular, accounting rules for reporting nonperforming loans and for increasing loan loss reserves need to be strengthened, and changes in credit risk must be reported sooner to regulators. Third, deposits held in foreign offices should be reported in the same detail as domestic deposits. Finally, greater public disclosure is necessary to enable investors to estimate bank net worth more accurately. If investors are more accurately informed, market prices of bank stocks and subordinated debentures would better reflect the economic condition of commercial banks. Healthy banks would benefit as reduced uncertainty would raise their stock prices and lower their cost of capital. Less well-capitalized banks would be subject to greater market discipline and thus have a stronger incentive to improve their net worth positions. In the absence of requiring market value accounting, I believe these changes would improve the ability of regulators and investors to monitor the safety and soundness of the banking system and to measure bank performance.

FOOTNOTES

[1] See U.S. Treasury (1991), p. XI-3.

[2] Benston (1989), p. 549.

[3] The total value of bank assets which involve truly proprietary information may be overstated. For example, many business loans are made by groups of banks in which information is shared. Currently, there are approximately $800 billion outstanding in the shared national credits program.

[4] Insurance companies must also report a breakdown of their bond holdings by six quality classes. By contrast, commercial banks only report the aggregate amount of securities for different types (U.S. government, state and local government, corporate, foreign, etc.). They do not report which corporations' securities they are holding nor do they classify their bonds by credit quality.

[5] There are some exceptions. For example, banks report their securities holdings at par value less amortization of discount or plus accretion of premium. Other exceptions are discussed in greater detail in the measurement issues section.

[6] An example of such behavior was Citicorp's decision to increase reserves against its Latin American debt by $3.4 billion in the second quarter of 1989. Many large banks followed Citicorp's lead with substantial increases in their own loan loss reserves.

[7] It is also worth noting that since savings and loan (S&L) associations had over three-quarters of their assets invested in mortgage loans and mortgage-backed securities, the rapid increase in market interest rates from 1978 to 1981 had an even larger negative impact on S&L net worth than it did on commercial banks. It is in part because of this experience that the Office of Thrift Supervision has developed a Market Value Model for adjusting the values of S&L portfolios for changes in market interest rates.

[8] Even if stock prices did accurately reflect unrealized gains or losses, the holders of debt contracts with covenants contingent on accounting values may be arbitrarily penalized.

[9] Since deposit insurance can be viewed as a call option, a market value insolvent bank still open for business can increase its risk exposure and thus the value of its deposit insurance. Since this option is capitalized into the price of the bank's stock, such an action can actually *raise* the stock's value.

[10] Even though market price information may be available for all these financial instruments, one must interpret these data

carefully because of the varying liquidity of the markets in which these instruments trade. For example, the municipal bond market is very heterogeneous, so one might simultaneously receive different price quotations from dealers. A bank could use the highest or lowest price quote depending on whether it is trying to overstate or understate the market value of its net worth.

[11] Requiring banks to carry these assets at lower of cost or market value (LOCOM) reduces the likelihood that a bank could use an overestimated appraisal of its real estate holdings to increase its net worth. On the other hand, reporting real estate using LOCOM makes it more difficult for a bank to realize gains on real estate that may have appreciated in value. In any case, these two asset categories represent less than three percent of total bank assets.

[12] It is possible to get market prices for mortgage loans that conform to the standards set by the Federal Home Loan Mortgage Corporation (FHLMC) and the Federal National Mortgage Association (FNMA). However, it is not possible to get detailed pricing information for nonconforming mortgage loans, and there are problems with using FHLMC and FNMA prices. For more information, see U.S. Treasury (1991), pp. XI-14 and XI-15. In addition to mortgage loans, there are active secondary markets in loans to less developed countries (LDCs) and loans for highly leveraged transactions (HLT). The shared national credit program can be a source of market value information. Also, market values of collateral for some loans may be readily available, such as loans secured by farmland.

[13] Duration is a measure of the effective maturity of a stream of future payments, defined as the weighted average maturity of an instrument's future cash flows, with the present values of the cash flows serving as the weights. A change in the market interest rate can affect the duration of a loan. For example, a decrease in market interest rates may induce borrowers to refinance a loan or pay it off sooner, thereby altering the duration of the loan.

[14] In practice, matrix pricing can be used to reduce the degree of subjectivity involved in determining the risk premia of discount factors employed in the analysis [see U.S. Treasury (1991) for more details]. In addition, auditors provide a check on a bank's use of its information advantage. For a detailed discussion of the incentive problem inherent in a bank valuing its loan portfolio, see Berger, King, and O'Brien (1991). These authors stress the importance of developing some incentive compatible mechanism for getting banks to report truthfully the market values of their loans.

[15] The category "other assets" in Table 1 includes: (1) investments in unconsolidated subsidiaries and associated companies, (2) customers' liability to this bank on acceptances outstanding, (3) intangible assets, which includes loan servicing rights and goodwill, and (4) other assets such as income earned but not collected on loans, net deferred income taxes, and miscellaneous items. Investments in unconsolidated subsidiaries are currently reported to regulators using the equity method of accounting, where the asset is carried at cost and adjusted for earnings and losses of the investee.

[16] Another intangible asset is goodwill, which arises in connection with merger and acquisitions transactions for which the purchase price exceeds the fair value of the identifiable net assets that are acquired. Calculating the market value of goodwill is difficult in any accounting system. One suggestion, contained in U.S. Treasury (1991), is "[b]ecause of the subjective nature of the determination, goodwill under MVA might be handled in much the same way as under current GAAP; that is, goodwill would be recognized only if acquired through arms-length transactions, and its historical cost would be amortized over some appropriate period of time."

[17] For details, see U.S. Treasury (1991), pp. XI-18-XI-19.

[18] The total return on demand deposits and NOW accounts equals the sum of explicit plus implicit interest. Placing noninterest-bearing demand deposit balances with banks represents partial compensation for services provided to the depositor. For corporations and depository institutions with a correspondent relationship, the size of these compensating balances is adjusted for changes in market interest rates.

[19] The current risk-based capital guidelines do require banks to hold additional capital based on the extent of their off balance sheet exposure.

[20] Examples are for mandatory accounting changes in the oil and gas industry [Collins, et. al. (1981)], consolidated reporting requirements [Mian and Smith (1990)], and translation of foreign currency transactions [Salatka (1989)]. The effects of regulatory accounting changes in the savings and loan industry has been studied by Blacconiere (1991).

REFERENCES

American Bankers Association, *Market Value Accounting*, June 1990, monograph.

Benston, George J., "Market value accounting: Benefits, costs, and incentives," *Proceedings of a Conference on Bank Structure and Competition,* Federal Reserve Bank of Chicago, 1989, pp. 547-563.

Berger, Allen N., Kathleen K. King, and James M. O'Brien, "The limitations of market value accounting and a more realistic alternative," *Journal of Banking and Finance*, September 1991, pp. 753-783.

Blacconiere, Walter G., "Market reactions to accounting regulations in the savings and loan industry," *Journal of Accounting and Economics*, March 1991, pp. 91-113.

Carlson, Ronald E., and Kate Mooney, "Implications of FASB Statement No. 105," *Journal of Accountancy*, March 1991, pp. 54-58.

Collins, Daniel W., Michael S. Rozeff, and Dan S. Dhaliwal, "The economic determinants of the market reaction to proposed mandatory accounting changes in the oil and gas industry," *Journal of Accounting and Economics*, March 1981, pp. 37-71.

Financial Accounting Standards Board, "Disclosures of information about financial instruments with off-balance-sheet risk and financial instruments with concentrations of credit risk," Statement No. 105, reprinted in *Journal of Accountancy*, December, 1990, pp. 140-156.

_____, "Disclosures about fair value of financial instruments," Statement No. 107, 1991.

Houpt, James V., and James A. Ebersit, "A method for evaluating interest rate risk in U.S. commercial banks," *Federal Reserve Bulletin*, August 1991, pp. 625-637.

Jones, Jonathan, Robert Nachtmann, and Fred Phillips-Patrick, "Market value accounting and bank income volatility: Some evidence from the investment account," *Proceedings of a Conference on Bank Structure and Competition*, Federal Reserve Bank of Chicago, 1991, pp. 534-550.

Mengle, David L., "Market value accounting and the bank balance sheet," *Contemporary Policy Issues*, April 1990, pp. 82-94.

Mengle, David L., and John R. Walter, "How market value accounting would affect banks," *Proceedings of a Conference on Bank Structure and Competition*, Federal Reserve Bank of Chicago, 1991, pp. 511-533.

Mian, Shehzad L., and Clifford W. Smith, "Incentives associated with changes in consolidated reporting requirements," *Journal of Accounting and Economics*, July 1990, pp. 249-266.

Mondschean, Thomas H., "Market values of mortgage loans at large commercial banks—estimates and applications," DePaul University, unpublished manuscript, March 1990.

Office of Thrift Supervision, *The OTS Market Value Model*, instruction manual, 1990.

Salatka, William K., "The impact of SFAS No. 8 on equity prices of early and late adopting firms," *Journal of Accounting and Economics*, February 1989, pp. 35-69.

U.S. Treasury, *Modernizing the Financial System: Recommendations for Safer, More Competitive Banks*, February 1991.

Article 9

Market Risk and Bank Capital: Part 1

For several years, bank supervisors from major countries have been meeting regularly in Basle, Switzerland, as the Basle Committee on Banking Supervision. There, they discuss and coordinate bank regulatory and supervisory concerns that cut across national boundaries. One major product of this Committee was the 1988 Accord on risk-based capital standards for banks. Although generally successful, a widely recognized defect of those standards is that they reflect only "credit risk," the risk of counterparty default. For example, under the 1988 Basle Accord banks need not hold any capital to protect their investments in long-term government bonds, because such bonds have no default risk. Yet banks may suffer substantial losses on holdings of such bonds if interest rates rise.

In April 1993, the Basle Committee released draft proposals covering so-called "market risks." This broad category of risks encompasses losses that banks suffer due to changes in market-related variables such as interest rates or exchange rates. Currently the proposals are only at a consultative stage. However, with U.S. representatives active on the Basle Committee, it is likely that at least some banks in the United States will be asked to comply with any eventual standards. This *Weekly Letter* is the first of two discussing the new market risk capital proposals. The description of the proposals in this first part highlights the similarities in the key elements. Part 2 discusses whether the proposed standards are likely to work well.

Three types of market risk

Market risk is defined as the possibility of losses due to price changes that are unrelated to changes in the credit standing of any particular counterparty. The Basle Committee's draft proposals cover three sources of such risk.

The first is risk due to changes in interest rates. The proposed capital standards deal with interest rate risk from traded debt securities—things such as notes and bonds that have well-defined market prices. As a result, the proposal covers only part of the interest rate risk that banks face; it ignores the effect of changing interest rates on loans and deposits. (The Basle Committee also has proposed a framework for collecting data on interest rate exposure for the whole bank. At present that framework is for information only, and does not incorporate an explicit risk calculation or capital charge.)

The second source of market risk is changes in stock prices. This might seem irrelevant for U.S. banks, since generally they are not permitted to hold stocks. However, the new standards would apply on a consolidated basis to all components of banking firms. In the U.S. and many other countries, some banks are affiliated (for example, through holding companies) with brokerage or investment banking units, for whom equity exposures, and therefore the new capital standards, might be important. In addition, in some countries (such as Germany) banks are permitted to hold equity directly; affiliates of U.S. banks operating in those countries may have substantial holdings of equity shares and other equity-linked instruments.

The third source is exchange rate risk. Some banks have assets and liabilities denominated in foreign currencies. As the prices of those currencies (the exchange rates) change, banks may gain or lose. As with the other market risks, the Basle Committee proposes that banks hold capital to protect against any such losses. Unlike the debt and equity risk proposals, the exchange rate proposal considers all sources of foreign exchange risk, not just the portion due to traded securities.

Measuring market risk—NAP, GAP, and WAP

For each market risk, the Basle Committee proposes methods for quantifying risk and for calculating the minimum capital to provide adequate protection against any associated losses. The documents describing the proposals are not easy to read; some passages might seem to be written in a kind of "international central bankers' code." However, hidden in their murky depths is a single unified conceptual approach to measuring market risk and assessing capital adequacy. This single approach is easiest to explain using foreign exchange risk as an example.

Exchange rate risk arises from loans, securities, deposits, and so on denominated in foreign currencies. The proposal consolidates these exposures into a single hypothetical portfolio for each bank, with one net position in each foreign currency. This constructed portfolio is what would result if all of a bank's business units transferred their foreign currency exposure to the bank's foreign exchange "desk" through internal transactions. Some banks do precisely that, with the desk then responsible for managing the exposure. However, the same principle applies no matter how the risk is actually handled in a particular bank.

Figure 1 provides an example of the resulting consolidated portfolio, based on figures for an actual U.S. bank as of December 1992. Exposures are either "long" or "short." Long positions are those on which the bank gains if the dollar price of the foreign currency rises (the currency appreciates relative to the dollar); longs generally reflect such things as foreign-denominated assets, on which the bank will receive payment in foreign currency. Short positions are the opposite: the bank gains if currencies fall in value. Shorts reflect amounts that the bank owes to counterparties, and depreciation means that the bank can repay with a currency that is worth less in dollar terms. In the example, the bank has total long positions of $274 million in Swiss Francs, British pounds, Japanese yen, and Australian dollars, and total short positions in German marks and Canadian dollars of $31 million.

Larger foreign exchange portfolios probably are riskier than smaller portfolios. But what is the relevant measure of size? One possibility is the net value, which I call NAP, for "net aggregate position." NAP is simply the difference between longs and shorts. In the example, NAP is $243 million (the difference between 274 and 31). Since short positions can finance long positions, NAP reflects the net investment by the bank in its foreign exchange portfolio. A second possible size measure is the gross position, which I refer to as GAP, for "gross aggregate position." GAP is the sum of longs and shorts; in the example, GAP is $305 million (the sum of 274 and 31).

Regulators in the past have used both GAP and NAP to measure the size—and by implication, the risk—of banks' foreign exchange positions. For example, NAP has been used in Japan, and GAP in Germany. The Basle Committee examined both approaches, and chose yet a third: total long positions or total short positions, whichever is larger. (This method is used by the Bank of England, among others.) Interestingly, the Basle measure of foreign exchange risk is equivalent to a simple fifty-fifty, or equal, weighting of GAP and NAP. This fact can be verified from the example in Figure 1; half the $305 million gross position plus half the $243 million net position is equal to $274 million, which is the total value of the larger long positions.

The result may be called WAP, for "weighted aggregate position." For banks' foreign currency WAP, the Basle Committee implicitly has selected equal 50 percent weights for NAP and GAP, but there is no reason the weights must be equal (and as shown below, other parts of the market risk proposal incorporate different weights). The Basle Committee has proposed a minimum 8 percent ratio of capital to equally weighted WAP for banks' exchange rate risk. In the sequel to this *Letter*, I will explain why this is a sensible approach.

The common threads
The Basle Committee applies roughly similar principles for interest rate and stock price risk.

Figure 1: Typical Bank Foreign Currency Position
(in U.S. $ millions)

Long Positions
Swiss Franc	56
U.K. Pound	151
Japanese Yen	57
Australian Dollar	10
Total Long	274

Short Positions
German Mark	17
Canadian Dollar	14
Total Short	31

NAP = 274 − 31 = 243
GAP = 274 + 31 = 305
WAP = (NAP × 50%) + (GAP × 50%) = 274

Hypothetical portfolios—one for traded debt and one for equity—are constructed to reflect the bank's total exposure. Whereas the individual positions in the foreign exchange example above were in different currencies, for equity the positions are different issuers, and for traded debt the positions are different maturities. As with foreign exchange, NAP and GAP are computed, weighted, and combined into a single weighted aggregate position; this WAP reflects portfolio size, and is presumed to be related to market risk. Minimum capital for each type of risk is set as a ratio to WAP. These common threads unify the approaches to the three market risks: the use of WAP based on a hypothetical portfolio, and assessment of capital adequacy through a capital ratio applied to WAP. However, the relative weightings for each type of risk differ.

In the equity risk proposal, the Basle Committee places 100 percent weights on each of GAP and NAP, unless the bank's equity portfolio is well diversified; in that case, the weights are 100 percent on NAP and 50 percent on GAP. (This contrasts with the implicit 50 percent weight on each in the foreign exchange proposal.) As with foreign exchange risk, the minimum capital to cover equity market risks is 8 percent of the bank's equity WAP.

The treatment of interest rate risk is much more complicated, but it too turns out to be a version of WAP. A portfolio with net positions in 13 different maturity (or repricing) bands is constructed; the positions are multiplied by duration weights to reflect the interest rate sensitivity of each time band. Long and short positions in the 13 time bands are netted within and across the bands, with part of the netting then "disallowed" through the application of varying "disallowance" factors. The way the disallowances are calculated, this turns out to be a WAP calculation, in which the amount of the disallowance is related to the weighting: A smaller disallowance factor gives relatively more weight to NAP versus GAP. The weights on NAP and GAP range from 95 and 5 percent, respectively, to 25 and 75 percent. Instead of multiplying the resulting WAP by a capital ratio, the positions in each maturity band are premultiplied by capital charges ranging from 0 to 12.5 percent that reflect their relative volatilities.

Summary

This brief overview of the Basle Committee's market risk proposals has glossed over the finer and more devilish details. Two unifying themes of the new market risk proposals have been emphasized: gross and net positions are weighted to measure a bank's exposure to market risks, and minimum capital is a percentage of that weighted exposure. Unfortunately, these common threads may not be clear in the consultative documents; the Basle Committee does not present the approaches as simple variations on the WAP theme.

In the sequel to this *Letter*, I argue that the common threads reflect a sensible approach to market risk, balancing precision and practical simplicity. I also present evidence suggesting that the Basle Committee's approach may work well in practice.

Mark E. Levonian
Research Officer

Article 10

Market Risk and Bank Capital: Part 2

In last week's *Weekly Letter* (94-01) I described the problem of market risk in banking and the efforts of the Basle Committee on Banking Supervision to deal with it. The Basle Committee proposes to set bank capital standards to cover losses due to fluctuating exchange rates, interest rates, and stock prices. In this sequel, I evaluate the proposals. I argue that there are good conceptual grounds for the approach taken by the Basle Committee, and that the proposal is an admirable balance of simplicity and precision. I also present evidence that the approach, desirable in principle, may work well in practice.

As explained in the earlier *Letter*, the Basle Committee's approach first consolidates a bank's market exposures into net positions for the bank as a whole. The results are composite portfolios—in different currencies, equities, or maturities in the case of traded debt—that summarize the market risks the bank faces. The bank's position in each of these currencies, equities, or maturities is either long (gaining from an increase in the market) or short (losing from an increase). In each case, the riskiness of a bank's market-sensitive portfolio is assumed to be proportional to the size of the portfolio. The proposals gauge size through a weighted sum of two measures of the aggregate portfolio position: the net aggregate position, or NAP, which is the difference in value between long and short positions, and gross aggregate position, or GAP, which is the sum of the long and short positions. In the earlier *Letter*, I christened the result WAP, for "weighted aggregate position."

WAP versus a theoretical benchmark

It is easy to compute gross and net positions for any portfolio, and from those construct WAP. But does this make sense as an approach to measuring risk? That is, is the actual market risk of a bank's portfolio likely to be proportional to WAP? Finance theory provides a solid benchmark measure of risk against which the Basle Committee proposals can be judged. In finance, risk often is measured by the portfolio variance, or by its square root, which is the portfolio standard deviation. (The standard deviation is related to the average size of unexpected shocks to a bank's capital.) These rigorous measures of risk depend partly on the size of the positions the bank takes; they also depend on the volatility of each exchange rate, stock price, or interest rate, and on the covariances or correlations among these market variables.

Under certain simplifying assumptions about the structure of bank positions, market volatilities, and correlations between different rates or prices, the Basle Committee's WAP-based approach is related to the portfolio standard deviation. Specifically, the portfolio variance is theoretically equal to a weighted sum of the squares of GAP and NAP. (For details, see Levonian 1994.) It follows that WAP, as a simple weighted sum of the same GAP and NAP, plausibly can be viewed as a linear approximation to the portfolio standard deviation; with correctly chosen weights, WAP could be a reasonable measure of the market risk of a bank's portfolio.

Why not just use the portfolio standard deviation itself, instead of something like WAP that is at best an approximation? Calculating a portfolio standard deviation is complicated, at least compared to typical banking regulations. In addition, it requires estimates of market volatilities and correlations, and these would be difficult to codify into capital standards. Such complications tend to increase the costs of implementing and enforcing the standards, and raise the cost to banks of complying. The precision of a risk measure such as the portfolio standard deviation would bring some benefits, but perhaps not enough to outweigh the added costs of complexity. International regulatory bodies consistently have preferred simpler approaches, and WAP represents a happy balance of precision and simplicity.

Choosing the weights

Theoretical modeling shows that WAP *can* be a good proxy for the actual risk, *if* the weights are chosen properly. Theory also has implications for the best weightings of GAP and NAP. Each constructed bank portfolio consists of net positions in its various components: currencies, equity issues, or debt maturities. The model suggests that, ideally, NAP should be weighted more heavily the larger the number of distinct components, or the more highly correlated movements in the prices of the components tend to be, with GAP given correspondingly less weight under those conditions. Together, the number of components and the correlations determine the best *relative* weights on GAP and NAP; the *absolute* level of the weights depends on the overall market volatility of exchange rates, interest rates, or stock prices.

Many elements of the Basle Committee's proposals are roughly in line with the results of the theoretical model. For example, the equity risk proposal places higher absolute weights on NAP and GAP than does the foreign exchange risk proposal; this makes sense, since stocks are generally more volatile than currencies. For diversified equity portfolios, the weight on GAP is reduced to 50 percent; this fits with the theoretical observation that GAP *should* get relatively less weight in diversified portfolios.

The proposal covering the interest rate risk arising from traded debt securities has a more complicated structure, and although similar, it is not exactly the same as the other two segments. However, it too is broadly consistent with the implications of the theoretical model. Longs and shorts are netted in stages, within and then across maturity bands. At each stage some of the netting is disallowed, meaning that some portions of the opposing short and long positions are not permitted to offset. As described in Part 1, the effect of the disallowances is to set relative weights for NAP and GAP at each stage of the calculation, with a smaller disallowance factor implying heavier weight on NAP.

Ideally, NAP should get more weight if correlations are higher, and this is precisely what happens in the proposal: Disallowance factors (and therefore the weights on GAP) are low for debt securities with similar maturities, which are likely to be highly correlated. Within a single maturity band, the weights implied by the disallowance factors are 95 percent on NAP, 5 percent on GAP. Exposures in different maturity or repricing bands tend to be less correlated, and the disallowances shift the weights for netting across adjacent bands to 85 and 15 or 80 and 20 percent. Disallowances are highest for exposures at opposite ends of the maturity spectrum: When netting long term against short term, the weight on NAP is only 25 percent, with 75 percent on GAP. Thus, the system of disallowances is a simple, logical way to incorporate the fact that not all interest rates change in the same way at the same time.

How good?

The results of the formal, abstract model suggest that *in principal* WAP could work as the basis for market risk capital standards. But the Basle Committee has proposed specific variants of WAP, with specific weights, for each of the three types of market risk. Whether the Basle proposals are likely to work well in practice can be judged only by examining how well they track risk in actual bank portfolios.

To develop a feel for the empirical performance of at least one of the three proposals, I examined data that federal banking supervisors have collected on U.S. banks' foreign currency exposures. The data are consolidated foreign currency exposures for each bank at particular reporting dates. Bank portfolios from 1990, 1991, and 1992 were sampled. From these, it is straightforward to compute GAP, NAP, and WAP.

The standard deviation of changes in the value of these bank portfolios is needed as a benchmark for evaluating the performance of the Basle Committee's equally weighted WAP. This requires estimating variances of all of the relevant exchange rates, as well as their correlations. Exchange rate data for these calculations came from the period 1980–1992. The variances are combined with the bank currency portfolios to provide the benchmark measures of actual foreign exchange market risk.

Tests showed that the Basle Committee's foreign exchange proposal works well: equally weighted WAP picked up over 95 percent of the variation in foreign exchange risk as measured by the theoretically correct portfolio standard deviation. WAP was clearly proportional to portfolio risk, and the proportional relationship has been largely stable over time. Such good performance is remarkable from a simple construct like WAP.

Similar empirical analysis of the other two parts of the market risk proposals would be useful. Some testing has been done at central banks in various countries. The bulk of those analyses and their results are confidential; however, they generally support the methods and weightings incorporated in the proposals.

Conclusion

The approach to market risks and bank capital standards taken by the Basle Committee rests on a solid conceptual foundation. A theoretical analysis shows that it might be expected to work well in principle; the specifics as formulated by the Basle Committee seem broadly in accordance with the theory. Empirical tests of one part of the plan, the proposal for foreign exchange risk, suggest that at least this aspect of the framework is likely to work well in practice. The Basle Committee's proposals not only are simple, and therefore practical, but seem reasonably precise in their assessment of the market risks banks face.

The Basle Committee has asked for comments on the draft proposals. Testing and refinement of the framework will continue, probably for some time. As discussed in this pair of *Weekly Letters*, the current version of the market risk capital standards looks promising, and should help correct some of the more obvious deficiencies of the original 1988 risk-based capital standards.

Mark E. Levonian
Research Officer

Reference

Levonian, Mark. 1994. "Bank Capital Standards for Foreign Exchange and Other Market Risks." Federal Reserve Bank of San Francisco *Economic Review* (forthcoming).

Article 11

Interest Rate Risk and Bank Capital Standards

Considerable attention recently has focused on the interest rate risk exposure of U.S. banks. This new-found attention is due in part to a provision in the Federal Deposit Insurance Corporation Improvement Act of 1991 (FDICIA) that requires federal banking regulators to incorporate interest rate risk into bank capital standards by the middle of 1993. In their current form the risk-based capital requirements focus on the credit risk of bank assets, requiring banks to hold more capital against assets assumed to pose a greater risk of default. Although most observers believe that interest rate risk is less important for banks than credit risk, this omission may mean that bank capital levels do not accurately reflect the true risk of bank portfolios.

The Federal Reserve Board has responded to the requirements of FDICIA by proposing a framework for addressing interest risk in bank capital standards. In this *Letter*, I provide some background on the notion of interest rate risk, and describe the general features of the Fed's proposal. I also compare this proposal to an alternative methodology proposed by thrift regulators.

What is interest rate risk?
Interest rate risk refers to the (possibly adverse) effect that changes in interest rates can have on the values of bank assets and liabilities. Financial instruments typically provide a stream of payments that is fixed in nominal terms for a period of time. The fixed-payment period may be relatively short, such as for a Treasury bill or an adjustable-rate mortgage loan, or long, as with a long-term bond or a fixed-rate mortgage loan. When market interest rates change, the value of financial instruments changes as well. An increase in market rates during the fixed-payment period diminishes the value of the fixed stream of payments and thus reduces the market value of the instrument. A decline in rates, in contrast, raises the value of the fixed payment stream.

In general, the longer the period during which the payments are fixed, the greater the relative change in value from a given change in both short- and long-term interest rates. Thus, the market value of a long-term bond or a 30-year fixed-rate mortgage is more sensitive to a parallel shift in interest rates than a short-term debt security or an adjustable-rate mortgage.

The impact of a change in interest rates on the value of a bank depends on the maturity structure of both its assets and its liabilities. If the fixed payments the bank receives from its assets take longer to respond to interest rate changes than the fixed payments it makes on its liabilities, then a rise in interest rates would reduce the value of assets more than the value of liabilities, and the bank's net worth would fall. In practice, most banks have a liability side of the balance sheet that carries a shorter repricing period than the asset side. That is, they typically borrow short and lend long. Thus, a certain amount of interest rate risk appears to be a normal part of the business of banking.

If exposure to interest rate risk is high, then an unfavorable move in interest rates could significantly reduce an institution's net worth and eat into its capital cushion. In extreme cases, an adverse move in interest rates could reduce an institution's capital below the level required by regulators. This is what happened to many thrifts in the late 1970s and early 1980s. Concerns about a repeat of this episode have prompted efforts to identify banks facing significant interest rate risk, and to require them to hold more capital against the possibility of large interest rate-induced declines in value.

How do you measure it?
As the preceding discussion suggests, the interest rate risk associated with any financial instrument is directly related to the length of time over which the instrument makes fixed payments. One commonly used measure of the "length" or effective maturity of a financial instrument is its duration. The duration of a financial asset is the weighted average maturity of its cash flows,

where the present values of the cash flows (as a percent of total present value) serve as the weights. For example, a financial asset that makes a fixed nominal payment every year for ten years has a duration somewhat less than five years. This is because the asset pays more of its present value in the first five years than it does in the second five years; the present discounted value of the fixed payments received far in the future is less than the present value of payments received earlier. In contrast, the duration of a ten-year zero-coupon bond (which makes no payments until maturity) is equal to ten years since 100 percent of the present value of its cash flows are received at maturity. In practice, it is typical to adjust an instrument's duration for noncontinuous compounding of interest, yielding the more commonly used measure known as modified duration.

The duration measure is particularly useful as a gauge of interest rate risk. The longer the duration of an asset or liability, the more its value will change in response to a given percentage point change in both short- and long-term market interest rates. A 30-year fixed-rate mortgage, for example, has a relatively long duration. The value of this asset fluctuates more from a parallel shift in the yield curve than a shorter duration asset, such as a short-term consumer loan. The concept of duration can be applied to both the assets and liabilities of a bank's balance sheet; a weighted average of these individual durations yields a single measure of the exposure of the bank's net worth to changes in interest rates. The measurement system proposed by the Federal Reserve uses this method to assess interest rate risk.

The Fed's proposal
Any system intended to measure the interest rate risk of bank portfolios requires information on the maturity structure of bank assets and liabilities. Thus, the Fed's proposal requires banks to assign their on- and off-balance sheet assets and their liabilities to one of six time bands based either on the maturity of the instrument or (for floating rate instruments) on the length of time until its interest rate adjusts.

In addition to the maturity information, the Fed's proposed system also requires banks to assign their assets to one of three categories: amortizing, nonamortizing, and deep discount. Amortizing assets make periodic payments of both principal and interest, while nonamortizing assets pay interest only, delaying principal repayment until maturity. Deep discount assets make neither interest nor principal payments but instead are sold at a discount from face value and then repay principal at maturity. These differences in cash flow characteristics affect the duration of the different types of assets. For a given maturity, an amortizing asset has a shorter duration than a nonamortizing one, which in turn has a shorter duration than a deep discount asset.

Each bank reports to the regulators its dollar positions in each of the time bands for the three different types of assets and for liabilities. These reported positions are then multiplied by "risk weights" that are derived from the durations of the corresponding assets and liabilities. The risk weights are expressed in percent terms and represent the change in the value of an instrument resulting from a 100 basis point (one percentage point) change in all interest rates. The result of this multiplication is a series of risk-weighted positions that measure the change in the value of the bank's reported holdings that would follow a 100 basis point change in interest rates. For example, multiplying the bank's holdings of long-term fixed rate mortgage loans by the appropriate amortizing risk weight yields a number that represents the change in the value of the bank's mortgage holdings resulting from a 100 basis point change in all rates.

Finally, total risk-weighted liabilities are subtracted from total risk-weighted assets to arrive at the net risk-weighted position of the bank. This number, expressed in dollars, is the change in the net worth of the bank that would occur as a result of a 100 basis point shift in interest rates. Alternatively, this net risk-weighted position can be expressed as a percent of total assets. In this way, the interest rate risk of different banks can be compared easily, just as bank capital ratios are compared.

Normal vs. excessive interest rate risk
One guiding principle of the Fed's proposal is that a certain amount of interest rate risk is inherent in banking. Moreover, credit risk is considered to be significantly more important than interest rate risk in terms of the threat it poses to bank solvency. The Fed's proposal suggests that existing risk-based capital requirements are sufficient to cover "normal" levels of interest rate risk. Banks that have "normal" interest rate risk will not be required under the proposed system

to hold additional capital. Only those institutions that are exposed to "excessive" risk would be required to hold more capital.

The obvious next question is what constitutes excessive risk. To answer this question, Fed researchers look to the historical distribution of banking industry risk exposures. Applying the proposed measurement system to the recent experience of U.S. banks suggests that a net risk-weighted position equal to 1 percent of a bank's assets may be considered "normal." That is, the "normal" change in the net worth of a bank arising from a 100 basis point change in all interest rates is 1 percent of assets. Drawing on this result, the Fed proposal suggests that any bank with a net risk-weighted position equal to 1 percent of assets or less would not be required to hold additional capital over and above the existing risk-based capital requirements. Only exposures in excess of 1 percent would require additional capital, which would be equal to the amount in excess of the 1 percent risk exposure.

Some pros and cons

The Fed's proposal is a relatively streamlined system for measuring interest rate risk. The system balances the need to obtain information to measure interest rate exposures with a desire to minimize the additional reporting burden for banks. While the proposal calls for expanded reporting of asset types and maturity structures, banks are not required to report detailed yield information on individual assets. Ideally, asset-specific yield and coupon information would be required to obtain more accurate duration-based risk factors. Instead, the Fed's proposal uses representative bank assets to derive the risk weights. This approach also neglects asset-specific information like prepayment options and may fail to capture unusual characteristics of new financial instruments. This compromise reduces the accuracy of the final risk measure but also reduces the bank's reporting burden.

The Fed's approach differs somewhat from one proposed last year for thrifts by the Office of Thrift Supervision (OTS). The OTS would require thrifts to report maturity information and cash flow characteristics of assets and liabilities, as well as instrument-specific information on yield, coupon, prepayment options, and so on. This more detailed method would then simulate the impact of a 200 basis point shift in all interest rates, requiring thrifts to hold additional capital equal to a portion of the simulated change in net worth.

How different are these two approaches? The OTS method provides a more accurate measure of the interest rate sensitivity of net worth, and thus of interest rate risk. However, it also imposes a considerable reporting burden on thrifts. Since little work has been done to assess the differences between the two approaches, it is unclear whether the additional reporting requirements of the OTS proposal are worth the cost. Some preliminary work comparing the two methods on a sample of thrifts suggests that the two methodologies largely agree on identifying high interest rate risk institutions. Differences arise between the two approaches when considering institutions with more moderate levels of interest rate risk.

Conclusion

Some measure of interest rate risk will become a reality for the nation's financial intermediaries in the next year, though the exact form of this measure is not yet known. Moreover, this measure will be linked to risk-based capital standards. Some have argued that the failure of the current system to address interest rate risk creates an incentive for banks and thrifts to substitute interest rate risk for credit risk by altering the composition of their portfolios. Recent large increases in bank holdings of Treasury securities, it is claimed, are consistent with this incentive.

Of course, the rather simple systems proposed by regulators should not preclude the use by bank management of more sophisticated interest rate risk monitoring mechanisms. Institutions that take big interest rate risk exposures should already be aware of the nature of their positions and the risks they pose to net worth.

Jonathan A. Neuberger
Economist

Article 12

R. Alton Gilbert

R. Alton Gilbert is an assistant vice president at the Federal Reserve Bank of St. Louis. Richard I. Jako provided research assistance.

The Effects of Legislating Prompt Corrective Action on the Bank Insurance Fund

THE FEDERAL DEPOSIT Insurance Corporation Improvement Act of 1991 (hereafter, FDICIA) authorized more federal government funds for the Federal Deposit Insurance Corporation and made major changes in the supervision and regulation of depository institutions. One section of FDICIA requires supervisors to take prompt corrective action when an institution's capital ratio falls below the required level.[1] Banks that are classified as well-capitalized or adequately capitalized are subject to the fewest constraints on their activities (see table 1). Supervisors are required to impose limits on the activities of banks with relatively low capital ratios and to close them promptly if their capital ratios fall below some critical level. Some examples of the constraints on poorly capitalized banks include limits on their asset growth, dividends and various insider transactions.

As FDICIA states, the purpose of prompt corrective action is "to resolve the problems of insured depository institutions at the least possible long-term loss to the deposit insurance fund." The legislation is based on the assumption that losses to the Bank Insurance Fund (BIF) would have been lower in recent years if supervisors had acted as required by FDICIA. This paper investigates whether the evidence is consistent with the assumptions that underlie the case for this legislation.

THE CASE FOR LEGISLATING PROMPT CORRECTIVE ACTION

A few years ago, as part of a program to reform the supervision and regulation of depository institutions, several economists began promoting proposals for prompt corrective action (PCA) by supervisors.[2] The report on financial reform by the Treasury Department in February 1991 included a version of these early proposals.[3] The General Accounting Office recommended a su-

---

[1] The legislation applies to the supervisors of commercial banks and thrift institutions. This paper refers exclusively to commercial banks and the effects of their failure on the Bank Insurance Fund. The Federal Deposit Insurance Corporation (FDIC) insures the deposits of banks and savings and loan associations but maintains a separate fund for banks. Banks pay their premiums into the Bank Insurance Fund which then covers any losses when a bank fails.

[2] Brookings Institution (1989) and Shadow Financial Regulatory Committee (1989).

[3] Department of the Treasury (1991), pp. 39-41.

Table 1
Supervisory Actions Applicable to Depository Institutions under Provisions of the FDICIA for Prompt Corrective Action[1]

Capital Category	
Well capitalized or adequately capitalized	**Mandatory Actions** May not make any capital distribution or pay a management fee to a controlling person that would leave the institution undercapitalized. **Discretionary Actions** None
Undercapitalized	**Mandatory Actions** Subject to provision applicable to well capitalized and adequately capitalized institutions. Subject to increased monitoring. Must submit an acceptable capital restoration plan within 45 days and implement that plan. Growth of total assets must be restricted. Prior approval from the appropriate agency is required prior to acquisitions, branching, and new lines of business. **Discretionary Actions** Subject to any discretionary actions applicable to significantly undercapitalized institutions if the appropriate agency determines that those actions are necessary to carry out the purposes of PCA.

Significantly undercapitalized	**Mandatory Actions**
	Subject to all provisions applicable to undercapitalized institutions.
	Bonuses and raises to senior executive officers must be restricted.
	Subject to at least one of the discretionary actions for significantly undercapitalized institutions.
	Discretionary Actions
	Actions the institution is presumed subject to unless the appropriate agency determines that such actions would not further the purposes of PCA:
	    Must raise additional capital or arrange to be merged with another institution.
	    Transactions with affiliates must be restricted by requiring compliance with section 23A of the Federal Reserve Act as if exemptions of that section did not apply.
	    Interest rates paid on deposits must be restricted to prevailing rates in the region.
	Other discretionary actions:
	    Severe restriction on asset growth or reduction of total assets may be required.
	    Institution or its subsidiaries may be required to terminate, reduce, or alter any activity determined to pose excessive risk.
	    May be required to hold a new election of its board of directors.

Table 1 (continued)
Supervisory Actions Applicable to Depository Institutions under Provisions of the FDICIA for Prompt Corrective Action[1]

Capital Category	Discretionary Actions
Significantly undercapitalized (continued)	Other discretionary actions (continued)
	Dismissal of any director or senior executive officer and their replacement by new officers subject to agency approval may be required.
	May be prohibited from accepting deposits from correspondent depository institutions.
	Controlling bank holding company may be prohibited from paying dividends without prior Federal Reserve approval.
	May be required to divest or liquidate any subsidiary in danger of becoming insolvent and posing a significant risk to the institution.
	Any controlling company may be required to divest or liquidate any nondepository institution affiliate in danger of becoming insolvent and posing a significant risk to the institution.
	May be required to take any other actions that the appropriate agency determines would better carry out the purposes of PCA.
Critically undercapitalized	**Mandatory Actions**
	Must be placed in receivership within 90 days unless the appropriate agency and the FDIC concur that other action would better achieve the purposes of PCA.
	Must be placed in receivership if it continues to be critically undercapitalized, unless specific statutory requirements are met.
	After 60 days, must be prohibited from paying principal or interest on subordinated debt without prior approval of the FDIC.
	Activities must be restricted. At a minimum, may not do the following without the prior written approval of the FDIC:
	Enter into any material transaction other than in the usual course of business.
	Extend credit for any highly leveraged transaction.
	Make any material change in accounting methods.
	Engage in any "covered transactions" as defined in section 23A of the Federal Reserve Act, which concerns affiliate transactions.
	Pay excessive compensation or bonuses.
	Pay interest on new or renewed liabilities at a rate that would cause the weighted average cost of funds to significantly exceed the prevailing rate in the institution's market area.
	Discretionary Actions
	Additional restrictions (other than those mandated) may be placed on activities.

[1] This description of the mandatory and discretionary supervisory actions under PCA is derived from a proposal by the Board of Governors of the Federal Reserve System in July 1992 to implement the PCA provisions of FDICIA. Other regulations to be adopted by supervisors will make distinctions among institutions based on their capital category, including regulations on brokered deposits and interbank deposits.

pervisory system in which supervisors would be required to act based on certain indicators of the performance and behavior of depository institutions, as well as capital ratios.[4]

Proponents of legislating PCA, including the Treasury and others, have based their case for PCA largely on the *incentive* for banks to assume risk, not on evidence of the behavior of poorly capitalized banks. The recent behavior of savings and loan associations provided most of the evidence that depository institutions assumed greater risk as their capital ratios declined.[5] The following quote illustrates the thinking of PCA advocates:

> As banks approach the point of economic insolvency, they have less and less to lose from pursuing aggressive, high-risk investment strategies in an attempt to return to profitability. The supervisory free rein given undercapitalized thrifts during the 1980s is widely recognized as a leading factor contributing to the cost of resolving insolvent thrifts. Some argue that commercial bank supervision has been far from perfect, too. In this view, banks are allowed to carry assets on their books at unrealistically optimistic values and are not appropriately restrained from high-risk behavior and irresponsible dividend policy.[6]

EVIDENCE ON THE UNDERLYING ASSUMPTIONS

The direct method of determining whether PCA legislation will reduce the BIF's losses is to enact the legislation, then observe BIF losses for several years. Waiting several years to form an opinion about the effectiveness of PCA legislation, however, does not seem the best way. If PCA legislation turns out to be ineffective, we will have wasted valuable time during which more effective reforms could have been doing their job.

This paper takes an indirect approach, specifying the assumptions that underlie PCA legislation and determining whether the behavior of banks before FDICIA's passage supports these assumptions. The case for PCA legislation rests on the assumption that, in recent years, depository institutions assumed greater risk as their capital ratios declined. As poorly capitalized institutions assumed greater risk and failed, they added to the losses of the deposit insurance funds. Advocates of PCA legislation also assume that constraints on bank behavior mandated by PCA legislation will constrain the risk assumed by poorly capitalized institutions.

The evidence that savings and loan associations assumed greater risk as their capital ratios declined, of course, does not necessarily indicate that PCA legislation will reduce the BIF's losses. Commercial bank supervisors may simply have been more effective than the supervisors of savings and loan associations in constraining the risk assumed by poorly capitalized institutions.[7]

Recent studies examine whether poorly capitalized banks have violated the types of constraints that will be imposed under PCA. Gilbert (1991) reported that the behavior of most of the banks with capital ratios below the minimum required level in 1985-89 did not violate such constraints.[8] Large majorities of the banks reduced their assets while undercapitalized, refrained from paying dividends, and restrained loans to insiders. Recent studies of the "capital crunch" report a positive association between the lagged capital ratios of banks and the growth rates of their assets in the current period. These results are consistent with the view that supervisors effectively constrained the asset growth of poorly capitalized banks.[9]

French (1991) found that, through reports by banks and examinations, supervisors were able to detect the weakness of most failed banks several years before failure. In addition, the incidence of paying dividends was lower at poorly capitalized banks than at other banks, and the incidence of capital injections was higher. Horne (1991) presented additional evidence on the association between capital ratios and dividends.

---

[4]U.S. General Accounting Office (1991), pp. 59-71.

[5]Barth, Bartholomew and Labich (1989) and Garcia (1988).

[6]Department of the Treasury (1991), pp. X-1 to X-2.

[7]Several studies examine the incentive for poorly capitalized institutions with deposit insurance to assume risk. See Buser, Chen and Kane (1981), Chirinko and Guill (1991) and Keeley and Furlong (1990).

[8]Gilbert (1991) does not report observations on the banks that reduced their assets while undercapitalized. About 53 percent reduced their assets by more than 10 percent while undercapitalized, and about 22 percent reduced their assets by more than 25 percent.

[9]Bernanke and Lown (1991) and Peek and Rosengren (1992a, b).

Some banks paid dividends while their earnings were negative and capital ratios were below required levels, but the proportion of banks paying dividends is positively related to their capital ratios.[10] These studies are consistent with the view that, in recent years, supervisors of commercial banks influenced the behavior of most undercapitalized banks in ways that will be required under PCA legislation. The exceptional cases may be eliminated by PCA legislation.

One argument for PCA legislation is that the sanctions to be imposed on poorly capitalized banks will induce other banks to maintain their capital ratios above minimum required levels, to reduce the chance that they will be subject to the sanctions. The evidence, however, implies that most poorly capitalized banks were subject to the sanctions prior to PCA legislation. That legislation, therefore, is not incentive for banks to raise their capital ratios.

THE EFFECTS OF CAPITAL RATIOS BEFORE FAILURE ON BIF LOSS RATIOS

Even if PCA legislation has a limited impact on the behavior of banks while undercapitalized, it may achieve its basic objective of reducing BIF losses by reducing the length of time banks *remain* poorly capitalized. The length of time a bank operates with a low capital ratio may influence the risk it assumes because it takes time for some non-marketable bank assets to mature before the proceeds can be reinvested in higher-risk categories. By shortening the time banks are permitted to operate with low capital ratios, supervisors will limit their opportunities to act on incentives to assume greater risk.[11] This argument rests on the assumption that there is a positive association between the length of time banks were poorly capitalized before failure and the BIF losses resulting from their failure.

Measuring Capital Ratios Before Failure

To test the hypothesis that ratios of BIF losses to total assets are positively related to the length of time banks were poorly capitalized prior to their failure, one must specify the following: first, a measure of capital, second, a criterion for classifying banks as poorly capitalized, and third, the lag between changes in capital ratios and changes in risk assumed by poorly capitalized banks.[12]

The paper uses two measures of capital: equity and an alternative measure, which adjusts equity for the market value of securities and for nonperforming loans. The criterion for an adequately capitalized bank is specified initially as a capital-to-asset ratio of 5 percent or more. This level is based on the maximum leverage ratio under the new risk-based capital requirements. For banks with relatively poor asset quality, supervisors may specify a minimum ratio of Tier 1 capital (essentially the same as equity for most banks) to total assets as high as 5 percent. The

---

[10] Horne (1991) reported the results of an equation for predicting the ratio of dividends to assets. In that model, profit rates and capital ratios have positive coefficients.

[11] This paper does not consider all the possible effects of PCA legislation on BIF losses. It is possible that closing banks with low but positive capital ratios will increase BIF losses, for the following reasons: First, some banks eventually would recover with no losses to BIF. It is difficult to estimate the size of this effect with data for periods before FDICIA, since a change in the closure rule may change the behavior of other parties. Shareholders of the banks that ultimately recover may realize that their banks have good prospects and inject capital more quickly than they would have in the past. Second, some theoretical models indicate that an increase in the capital threshold at which banks are closed causes banks with certain characteristics to assume greater risk. See Levonian (1991).

[12] See Bovenzi and Murton (1988) for a description of loss estimates and an analysis of the determinants of FDIC losses from individual bank failures. The sample in this paper excludes savings banks insured by the BIF. Since savings banks hold different types of assets than commercial banks, the determinants of BIF losses for failed savings banks are likely to be different than for failed commercial banks. Thus, the sample includes only failed commercial banks.

A few banks are excluded because they did not report total assets one year before failure and because of other problems with missing data. Sixteen banks are excluded from the sample because they were involved in mergers within two years of their failure dates. Six bank holding companies in Texas had all of their bank subsidiaries closed at the same time, for a total of 88 failed banks. BIF losses attributed to at least some of these banks reflect problems at their affiliates. These 88 banks are excluded from the sample to avoid problems in relating BIF losses to the characteristics of individual failed banks.

Thirty-nine banks were in existence less than three years when they failed. Since new banks tend to have relatively high capital ratios and rapid asset growth, these banks might distort the analysis as outliers in some comparisons. These 39 banks are retained in the sample. Effects of deleting these banks are noted where the difference would affect the description of the data.

analysis in this paper is modified to consider other capital ratios as well.[13]

Advocates of PCA legislation do not specify how quickly they assume poorly capitalized institutions increase their risk after their capital ratios decline. Rather than picking an arbitrary lag, we divide banks into three groups based on the length of time their equity capital ratios were below 5 percent before failure (table 2). Banks in group one had equity capital ratios below 5 percent for five or more consecutive quarters before failure. The choice of this period reflects seasonal patterns in bank accounting practices and capital injections. (Capital injections and accounting entries that recognize loans as losses tend to be clustered in the fourth quarter.) A bank with a relatively low capital ratio for five or more quarters would have a relatively low capital ratio in more than one calendar year, no matter when in the year a bank is declared a failed bank.

Suppose, for instance, that a bank failed in February 1990. If the equity capital ratio of the bank was below 5 percent for five or more consecutive quarters, its ratio would have been below 5 percent at least as early as the fourth quarter of 1988. Thus, as early as then, the shareholders of the bank exhibited their inability or unwillingness to inject the capital necessary to raise the ratio to 5 percent and did not eliminate the capital deficiency in subsequent quarters.

Table 2 also includes an intermediate group of banks that had relatively low equity capital ratios between two and four consecutive quarters before failure (group two). If the groups in table 2 reflect relevant time periods, the arguments for PCA legislation would imply that the BIF loss ratios would be highest for banks in group 1 and lowest for banks in group 3. A comparison of average ratios of BIF losses to total assets at the failure dates does reflect this pattern, but the differences in the mean BIF loss ratios are not statistically significant.

Adjustment for Changes in Assets in the Last Year

The comparisons of the ratios of BIF losses to total assets on the dates of their failure are subject to a bias. The longer capital ratios of banks were below 5 percent before failure, the larger the percentage decline in assets in their last year. Banks with equity capital ratios below 5 percent for five or more consecutive quarters had asset declines, on average, of more than 14.5 percent. The average percentage decline in assets was more than 11 percent for banks with equity capital ratios below 5 percent for two to four consecutive quarters. The other banks, in contrast, had average asset *growth* of about 2.5 percent.

These differences appear to reflect the influence of supervisors, based on the following assumptions. First, supervisors rate the financial strength of banks largely on the basis of capital ratios derived from the report of condition. Second, banks respond to directives from their supervisors to raise capital ratios by reducing assets. And third, the longer a bank is subject to pressure from its supervisor to raise its capital ratio, the larger the percentage decline in its assets.

Data on banks that paid dividends in the year ending on their failure date also appear to reflect the influence of supervisors, adding support to the view that supervisors influenced the asset growth of undercapitalized banks in their last year. Bank regulations restrict dividend payments whenever capital is below the required level.[14] While some undercapitalized banks have violated these regulations, most have foregone dividend payments. Less than 7 percent of the banks with equity capital ratios below 5 percent for five or more consecutive quarters before failure paid dividends in their last year. The proportion of failed banks that paid dividends in their last year is significantly higher for groups of banks with higher capital ratios in their last year.

---

[13] Spong (1990), pp. 64-71, and Keeton (1989) describe the risk-based capital requirements and maximum leverage ratios.

[14] See Spong (1990), pp. 64-71, for a description of the regulation of bank dividends in the years covered by this study. In general, banks were prohibited from withdrawing or impairing their capital through excessive dividend payouts or other means. Member banks (national banks and state-chartered banks that are members of the Federal Reserve System) were required to obtain regulatory approval to pay dividends that exceeded the sum of net profits for a year and retained earnings for the preceding two years. For any banks with federal deposit insurance, dividend payments that could endanger a bank could be restricted under the general enforcement and cease and desist powers of the federal supervisors. See Gilbert (1991), French (1991) and Horne (1991) for additional information on dividend payments by poorly capitalized banks.

Table 2
Distribution of BIF Loss Ratios by the Length of Time Before Failure That Capital Ratios Were Below 5 Percent, 1985-90

Group number	Characteristics of failed banks	Number of banks	Loss to BIF divided by total assets		Percentage change in total assets in the year ending on failure date	Percentage of banks that paid dividends in the year ending on failure date
			Total assets as of failure date	Total assets one year before failure date		
1	Equity capital ratio below 5 percent for five or more consecutive quarters before failure	374	0.2736 (0.1365)	0.2196 (0.1171)	−14.52 (14.40)	6.42%
2	Equity capital ratio below 5 percent in the last two quarters before failure and up to four consecutive quarters before failure	302	0.2693 (0.1184)	0.2145 (0.1022)	−11.15 (14.07)	25.17
3	Failed banks other than those in groups 1 and 2	178	0.2629 (0.1320)	0.2522 (0.1536)	2.45 (23.47)	44.94
4	Alternative capital ratio below 5 percent for five or more consecutive quarters before failure	546	0.2716 (0.1313)	0.2200 (0.1142)	−13.21 (14.54)	11.17
5	Alternative capital ratio below 5 percent in the last two quarters before failure and up to four consecutive quarters before failure	219	0.2752 (0.1226)	0.2247 (0.1078)	−8.09 (15.97)	33.79
6	Failed banks other than those in groups 4 and 5	89	0.2456 (0.1320)	0.2649 (0.1807)	12.26 (28.23)	50.56

NOTE: Standard deviatons are in parentheses under means.

t-statistics, in absolute value, for differences between means for groups:

1 and 2	0.438	0.604	3.064*	6.695*[1]
1 and 3	0.880	2.506*	8.884*	9.782*
2 and 3	0.533	2.916*	7.023*	4.406*
4 and 5	0.360	0.536	4.110*	6.521*
4 and 6	1.724	2.271*	8.333*	7.203*
5 and 6	1.820	1.962*	6.397*	2.046*

[1] t-statistics, in absolute value, for differences in proportions
*Statistically significant at the 5 percent level.

The observations in table 2 are consistent with the view that supervisors forced most banks with persistently low capital ratios before failure to reduce their assets and refrain from paying dividends. Supervisors may have been less aware of the troubles of banks with capital ratios above 5 percent during most or all of their last year, and, therefore, placed less constraint on their behavior.

The higher average BIF loss ratios of the banks undercapitalized for longer periods may reflect sharp declines in assets in their last year, rather than losses on investments in riskier assets. BIF loss ratios can be adjusted for this bias by dividing the losses to BIF by assets one year *before* failure. Average ratios of BIF losses to total assets one year before failure for banks in groups 1 and 2 are significantly *lower* than the average BIF loss ratio of those in group 3. After adjusting for the effects of this bias, the evidence does not indicate a positive association between the length of time banks were undercapitalized before failure and BIF loss ratios.

An Alternative Capital Measure

Advocates of PCA legislation have emphasized the need for improvements in measuring the value of bank capital. Perhaps a positive relationship between BIF loss ratios and the length of time bank capital ratios were low before failure is evident only with an improved measure of bank capital.

Alternative capital measures often are described as "market value" capital, with assets and liabilities marked to market values.[15] Berger, King and O'Brien (1991) indicate the various meanings attached to the term "market value" and the practical difficulties in deriving accurate measures of the market values for some categories of assets and liabilities. The authors suggest, however, the following adjustments to the value of bank assets: adjust marketable assets to market values, and adjust the value of loans for anticipated losses on nonperforming loans.

The following calculations yield an alternative capital measure which reflects these adjustments. The difference between the book and market value of securities is subtracted from equity. Adjustments to equity for anticipated loan losses involve comparisons of allowances for loan and lease losses to the values of nonperforming loans (past due 90 days or longer or nonaccrual). The allowance for loan losses is accumulated earnings of a bank set aside to absorb loan losses.[16] Evidence in Berger, King and O'Brien indicates that a $3 increase in nonperforming loans tends to increase loan losses by $1. If a bank's allowance for loan losses equals or exceeds one-third of its nonperforming loans, there is no adjustment to its equity for anticipated loan losses. The other banks need larger allowances for loan losses to meet this standard. Increases in their allowances would come out of equity. The adjustment to equity involves subtracting one-third of their nonperforming loans and adding their allowance for loan losses.

The results in table 3 add support to use of the three-to-one ratio of nonperforming loans to the allowance for loan losses in deriving the alternative capital measure. Table 3 presents this ratio for banks in various size categories, from one quarter to eight quarters before failure. The ratio is around three for banks of different size and for different lengths of time prior to failure.

Table 3 also has implications for the supervisory treatment of banks as they approach failure. As indicated above, the case for PCA legislation is based on the argument that in recent years supervisors should have done their job differently. For example, supervisors should have forced banks to make their balance sheets reflect more accurately the value of their assets. Supervisors may have allowed troubled banks to show higher equity on their balance sheets than justified by the quality of their assets, by permitting their allowance for loan losses to lag behind the rise in their nonperforming loans as they approached failure. Additions to the allowance for loan losses (called provisions for loan losses) are bank expenses. Thus, additions to the allowance for loan losses reduce earnings and possibly equity, if earnings are negative.

Table 3 shows that, while the ratio of nonperforming loans to total assets rose as banks ap-

---

[15] Mondschean (1992) discusses the issues raised by proposals for market value accounting.

[16] See the appendix for a more thorough discussion of the role of the allowance for loan losses in bank accounting principles.

Table 3
Average Ratios of Nonperforming Loans to the Allowance for Loan and Lease Losses and to Total Assets[1]

Size category of banks (millions of dollars as of failure date)	\multicolumn{8}{c}{Quarters before failure}							
	1	2	3	4	5	6	7	8
Assets < $25								
NPL ÷ ALLL	2.89	3.07	3.26	3.08	2.93	3.09	2.94	2.95
NPL ÷ TA	0.0777	0.0720	0.0677	0.0608	0.0540	0.0504	0.0431	0.0390
$25 ≤ Assets < $50								
NPL ÷ ALLL	2.68	3.19	3.19	3.03	2.83	2.87	2.72	2.82
NPL ÷ TA	0.0892	0.0803	0.0703	0.0618	0.0539	0.0487	0.0443	0.0392
$50 ≤ Assets < $100								
NPL ÷ ALLL	3.40	2.81	3.06	3.14	3.18	3.02	3.16	3.13
NPL ÷ TA	0.0949	0.0789	0.0717	0.0665	0.0587	0.0552	0.0487	0.0438
$100 ≤ Assets								
NPL ÷ ALLL	3.30	3.21	3.72	3.80	3.41	3.58	3.53	3.55
NPL ÷ TA	0.1049	0.0906	0.0808	0.0704	0.0595	0.0526	0.0495	0.0426

NPL — Nonperforming loans (past due 90 days or more plus nonaccrual)
ALLL — Allowance for loan and lease losses
TA — Total assets

[1] In total, 836 banks filed reports of condition for the quarter ending one quarter before failure and for the preceding seven quarters. The ratios are calculated as the sum of the item in the numerator divided by the sum of the item in the denominator for a given group of banks.

proached failure, their allowances for loan losses also rose proportionately. These results are inconsistent with one type of forbearance by supervisors: a general tendency to permit the allowance for loan losses to lag behind the rise in nonperforming loans, to avoid large charges against equity.

Table 2 presents average BIF loss ratios based on this alternative measure of capital. The adjustments to equity reduce the capital ratios for many of the failed banks in their last year. For instance, the number of banks with capital ratios below 5 percent for five or more consecutive quarters before failure rises from 374 with equity as the measure of capital (group 1) to 546 with the alternative measure (group 4).

BIF loss ratios adjusted for changes in assets in the last year (BIF losses divided by total assets one year before failure) are lower for banks with adjusted capital ratios below 5 percent for longer periods. Use of the alternative capital measure *does not* yield a positive association between the length of time banks operated with low capital ratios before failure and BIF loss ratios.

Alternative Levels of Capital Ratios

Perhaps the difficulty in finding an inverse relationship between capital ratios before failure and BIF loss ratios is that all the results in table 2 are based on a 5 percent capital ratio. The relevant ratio for purposes of the hypothesis tested here may be higher or lower than 5 percent. Table 4 examines the relationship between capital ratios and BIF loss ratios, for a fixed lag of one year between the observation of capital ratios and failure dates. The hypothesis that poorly capitalized banks assume relatively high

Table 4
Distribution of BIF Loss Ratios by the Ratio of Capital to Assets One Year Before Failure

		Equity as the measure of capital		Alternative capital measure	
Group number	Range of capital ratio	Number of banks	BIF loss divided by total assets one year before failure	Number of banks	BIF loss divided by total assets one year before failure
1	0.10 < C/A	30	0.2861 (0.2141)	23	0.2898 (0.2364)
2	0.08 < C/A ≤ 0.10	75	0.2306 (0.1346)	40	0.2523 (0.1575)
3	0.06 < C/A ≤ 0.08	211	0.2214 (0.1116)	109	0.2179 (0.1064)
4	0.04 < C/A ≤ 0.06	214	0.2290 (0.1189)	203	0.2281 (0.1112)
5	0.02 < C/A ≤ 0.04	175	0.2177 (0.1181)	178	0.2344 (0.1300)
6	0.00 < C/A ≤ 0.02	109	0.2129 (0.1120)	154	0.2000 (0.1054)
7	−0.01 < C/A ≤ 0.00	15	0.1842 (0.0796)	54	0.2078 (0.1201)
8	C/A ≤ −0.01	25	0.2458 (0.1034)	93	0.2399 (0.1051)

NOTE: Standard deviations are in parentheses under means.

risk, which imposes large losses on BIF if they fail, implies higher BIF loss ratios for banks with capital ratios below some critical level before failure.

Table 4 indicates that the banks with the highest BIF loss ratios are those with the highest and the lowest capital ratios one year before failure. Among other banks, there is no systematic relationship between the capital ratios of banks one year before failure and their BIF loss using either measure of capital. These results do not support the hypothesis that banks with capital ratios below some critical capital ratio have higher BIF loss ratios.[17]

Extreme Cases — A few banks that engaged in extreme behavior may have imposed large losses on BIF. Thus, PCA legislation could contribute to reducing BIF losses by constraining the extreme behavior of a small minority of failed banks. The data are examined for such extreme cases in two ways. The first approach involves determining whether BIF loss ratios

---

[17]Banks in existence less than three years when they failed account for the relatively high average BIF loss ratio for banks with capital ratios in excess of 10 percent one year prior to failure. Eight of the 30 banks with equity capital ratios in excess of 10 percent one year prior to failure were in existence less than three years when they failed. Excluding these eight banks reduces the average BIF loss ratio for the remaining 22 banks to 23.72 percent, which is much closer to the average BIF loss ratios for the banks with capital ratios below 10 percent one year prior to failure. Eliminating the banks in existence less than three years when they failed has a similar effect on the average BIF loss ratio of banks with ratios of the alternative capital measure to total assets in excess of 10 percent one year prior to failure.

Table 5
Characteristics of Banks with Relatively High BIF Loss Ratios

Characteristics	Banks with BIF loss ratios above 50 percent	All banks in the sample
Number of banks	44	854
Mean percentage change in total assets in their last year	−9.13%	−9.79%
Percentage that paid dividends in their last year	20.45	21.08
Percentage with equity capital ratio below 5 percent for five or more consecutive quarters before failure	54.55	43.79
Percentage in the West South Central region	75.00	56.21
Percentage supervised by the Office of the Comptroller of the Currency	56.82	37.70

were relatively high among banks that engaged in extreme behavior. These banks would have the following characteristics: equity capital ratio below 5 percent for five or more consecutive quarters before failure, and asset growth and dividend payments in their last year. No banks in the sample had this combination of characteristics.

The second approach involves examining the characteristics of banks with relatively high BIF loss ratios, to determine whether they exhibited extreme behavior that will be constrained under PCA. Table 5 presents some of the characteristics of 44 banks with BIF loss ratios that exceed 50 percent. Their mean asset growth and the proportion paying dividends in their last year are almost identical to those for the entire sample. The banks with relatively high BIF loss ratios do have a somewhat higher percentage with equity capital ratios below 5 percent for relatively long periods before failure. It is possible, however, to find other ways in which these banks are even more distinct from the entire sample. Their relatively high loss ratios may reflect regional effects: three-fourths were located in the West South Central region of the nation, compared with about 56 percent for the entire sample.[18] A relatively high proportion were supervised by the Comptroller of the Currency. Thus, an examination of extreme cases does not provide clear evidence of the effectiveness of PCA in reducing BIF losses.

REGRESSION ANALYSIS

Loss ratios vary substantially within each of the groups of banks in tables 2 and 4; standard deviations are about half as large as their means. Perhaps an inverse relationship between capital ratios before failure and BIF loss ratios is evident only if other factors are held constant in regression analysis.

A Description of Banks in the Regression Analysis

The 854 banks in the sample failed in the years 1985-90 (table 6). Most banks were relatively small: about 60 percent had total assets

---

[18]States in this region are Arkansas, Louisiana, Oklahoma and Texas.

Table 6
Characteristics of Failed Banks in Regression Analysis

Year of failure	Number of banks	Percentage
1985	112	13.1%
1986	132	15.5
1987	175	20.5
1988	146	17.1
1989	149	17.4
1990	140	16.4
Total	854	100.0
Asset size on failure date (millions of dollars)		
Assets < $25	508	59.5
$25 ≤ Assets < $50	209	24.5
$50 ≤ Assets < $100	90	10.5
$100 ≤ Assets	47	5.5
		100.0
Region		
New England (NE)	5	0.6
Middle Atlantic (MA)	9	1.1
South Atlantic (SA)	19	2.2
East South Central (ESC)	17	2.0
West South Central (WSC)	480	56.2
East North Central (ENC)	16	1.9
West North Central (WNC)	174	20.4
Pacific Northwest (PNW)	34	4.0
Pacific Southwest (PSW)	100	11.7
		100.1
Federal supervisor		
OCC	322	37.7
Federal Reserve	68	8.0
FDIC	464	54.3
		100.0
Method of resolving failure		
Purchase and assumption	667	78.1
Transfer of insured deposits	115	13.5
Liquidation	72	8.4
		100.0

NOTE: States in census regions:
    New England: Connecticut, Maine, Massachusetts, New Hampshire, Rhode Island and Vermont
    Middle Atlantic: New Jersey, New York and Pennsylvania
    South Atlantic: Delaware, Florida, Georgia, Maryland, North Carolina, South Carolina, Virginia and West Virginia
    East South Central: Alabama, Kentucky, Mississippi and Tennessee
    West South Central: Arkansas, Louisiana, Oklahoma and Texas
    East North Central: Illinois, Indiana, Ohio, Michigan and Wisconsin
    West North Central: Iowa, Kansas, Minnesota, Missouri, Nebraska, North Dakota and South Dakota
    Pacific Northwest: Alaska, Idaho, Montana, Oregon, Washington and Wyoming
    Pacific Southwest: Arizona, California, Colorado, Hawaii, Nevada, New Mexico and Utah

less than $25 million, and about 95 percent had total assets less than $100 million. The failed banks were heavily concentrated in certain regions. About 56 percent were in the West South Central region. About 78 percent of the cases were resolved when other banks bought some of the assets of the failed banks and assumed their liabilities. In another 14 percent of the cases, the FDIC transferred the insured deposits of failed banks to other banks. In these cases, the FDIC liquidated the failed banks' assets and made partial payments to uninsured depositors, based on the proceeds of liquidated assets. Failed banks were liquidated in the remaining cases.

Identifying the Variables

The dependent variable is the ratio of BIF loss to total assets as of failure date.[19] Independent variables are described in table 7.

Capital Ratios — The case for applying PCA legislation to the supervisors of commercial banks implies negative, significant coefficients on the capital ratios lagged one year, EC_{-4} and AC_{-4}.

Asset Growth — The coefficient on GROWTH is assumed to have a negative sign: an increase (decrease) in assets in the last year is assumed to increase (decrease) the denominator of the BIF loss ratio, while having little, if any, effect on the size of the BIF loss.

Dividends — Arguments for legislating PCA imply a positive sign for the coefficient on DIV: dividends in the last year, divided by total assets as of failure date. The coefficient on DIV may be positive for two reasons. First, dividends are payments of capital to shareholders, leaving less capital to absorb reductions in the value of assets. Second, dividends may be a signal that the shareholders saw little reason to attempt to prevent failure. Instead, they may have paid out capital in anticipation of failure. These reasons, however, do not account for possible influences of supervisors over which banks paid dividends or the size of their dividend payments.

Quality of Bank Loans — One measure of loan quality is the value of loans that are past due or nonaccrual. A second measure is the value of interest accrued on loans that was not collected. When borrowers fall behind on their scheduled payments, banks continue to accrue the interest due from them as income until their loans are classified as nonaccrual.[20]

These measures of loan quality may help explain the BIF losses from the failure of individual banks. The following two measures of asset quality are included as independent variables:

1. NPL — the ratio of nonperforming loans to total assets.
2. ACCRUED — interest accrued on loans that was not collected, divided by total assets.

The coefficients on these variables will have positive signs under the following assumptions: First, these measures accurately reflect loan quality. Second, the allowance for loan losses is not large enough to cover the gap between the book value of these loans and their value to the FDIC as the receiver of failed banks.[21]

Market Value of Securities — Securities (various types of bonds) are reported on bank balance sheets at book values (purchase prices plus any amortized changes in value), not at their current market values. Thus, the book value of equity reflects the book value of securities. Banks also report information on the market value of their securities on the report of condition. The following independent variable is a measure of the gap between the book and

---

[19]Avery, Hanweck and Kwast (1985) report the results of regressions with the same dependent variable. It is difficult to compare the results in this paper to those, since their objective was to predict FDIC losses from bank failures, not to test hypotheses about coefficients on independent variables. They do not attempt to adjust the specification of equations for possible collinearity. In Bovenzi and Murton (1988) and James (1991), the dependent variable is the loss on assets of failed banks, a concept that is related to BIF loss. Some of the independent variables in Bovenzi and Murton and in James are included, with slight modifications, in this study; the major difference involves measures of asset quality derived from examination reports, which are not included in this study. Barth, Bartholomew and Labich (1989) and Barth, Bartholomew and Bradley (1990) estimate the coefficients of equations designed to explain the cost to the Federal Savings and Loan Insurance Corporation of resolving cases of failed savings and loan associations. Results in Barth, Bartholomew and Bradley are not comparable to those in this study, since they include observations for failed and surviving associations and use a different statistical technique (Tobit regression analysis).

[20]Accrued interest that was not collected may not reflect default by borrowers on scheduled loan payments. In some loan contracts, such as construction loans, the original loan contract specifies a delayed schedule of interest payments.

[21]See the appendix for a discussion of accounting principles which features the role of the allowance for loan losses.

Table 7
Identification of Independent Variables

EC_{-4}	Ratio of equity capital to total assets four quarters before failure.
AC_{-4}	Ratio of the alternative capital measure to total assets four quarters before failure.
GROWTH	Change in total assets of failed bank in its last year, divided by total assets as of failure date.
DIV	Dividends on common stock paid in the year ending in failure, divided by total assets as of failure date.
NPL	Loans and leases past due 90 days or more, plus nonaccrual loans, divided by total assets as of failure date.
ACCRUED	Interest on loans that was accrued but not received on the last report of condition, divided by total assets as of failure date.
MARKET	Book value of securities in the investment account as of the last report of condition, minus the market value of the securities, divided by total assets as of failure date.
IDR	Last observation available on deposits in accounts up to $100,000 each, divided by total assets as of failure date.
P&A	Dummy variable with a value of unity if a failed bank case was resolved through purchase and assumption, zero otherwise.
TID	Dummy variable with a value of unity if a failed bank case was resolved through transfer of insured deposits to another bank, zero otherwise.
OCC	Dummy variable with a value of unity if the bank was a national bank, supervised by the Office of the Comptroller of the Currency, zero otherwise.
FR	Dummy variable with a value of unity if a bank was supervised by the Federal Reserve, zero otherwise.
lnA	Natural log of total assets as of failure date.
1985-1989	Dummy variables for the years in which the banks failed.
NE, MA, SA, ESC, ENC, WNC, PNW, PSW	Dummy variables for the regions in which failed banks were located.

market value of securities: MARKET — the book value minus the market value of securities, divided by total assets.

The expected sign of the coefficient on MARKET depends on the conditions under which supervisors close banks. Suppose they close banks when the book value of equity is zero or negative, without adjustments to the book value of equity for the market value of assets. Under this assumption, the expected sign on MARKET is positive: BIF losses would be related positively to the gap between the book value and the market value of securities.

Methods of Resolving Failed Banks — When a bank fails, the FDIC becomes the receiver. As receiver, the FDIC must dispose of the failed bank's assets and make payments to its creditors. The options chosen to resolve each case may affect the BIF's losses. Those choices, in turn, may reflect additional information about failed banks not captured by the other independent variables, such as characteristics of the customers of failed banks that make them valuable to other banks.[22]

One method of resolving failed bank cases is *liquidation*. Failed banks are closed and depositors are paid off up to the insurance limit per account. The FDIC liquidates the assets and makes payments to uninsured depositors and other creditors of the failed bank. Shareholders generally get nothing.

Resolution methods other than liquidation may be less expensive to BIF. In many cases, a solvent bank purchases some of the assets of a failed bank and assumes its liabilities. The FDIC provides cash to cover the gap between assets purchased and liabilities assumed. This is called a *purchase and assumption* (P&A) transaction. The FDIC solicits bids from solvent banks for the assets and liabilities. Banks bid by offering premiums; the cash payment by the FDIC to the bank with the winning bid is net of the premium. The FDIC generally disposes of failed banks through P&A transactions if its staff estimates that the losses would be lower than under liquidation.[23] As a result, the variable P&A (dummy variable for banks resolved through P&A transactions) is expected to have a negative coefficient.

In some cases, the FDIC liquidates the assets of failed banks but solicits bids from other banks to assume their insured deposits. Bidders may anticipate long-term profits on the accounts of customers who choose to keep their deposits with the winning bidder. This method of disposing of failed banks is called *transfer of insured deposits* (TID). The independent variable TID (dummy variable for bank failure cases resolved through TID) is expected to have a negative coefficient.

Share of Deposits Fully Insured — James (1991) found a positive association between the premiums paid by the winning bidders in P&A cases and the shares of deposits of failed banks that were fully insured (accounts in denominations of $100,000 or less). The smaller accounts tend to be more profitable to banks because banks pay less than market interest rates on them.[24]

The variable IDR (fully insured deposits divided by total assets) is included to reflect the composition of deposits. It is expected to have a negative coefficient because premiums paid to the FDIC by winning bidders are assumed to be positively related to IDR. An increase in the premium reduces the loss to BIF.

Federal Supervisory Agency — The primary supervisor of nationally chartered banks is the Office of the Comptroller of the Currency (OCC). For state-chartered banks that are members of the Federal Reserve System, the Federal Reserve is the primary federal supervisory agency, while, for other state banks, it is the FDIC. Differences in supervisory practices among these agencies may affect BIF losses. Dummy variables (OCC and FR) are used to capture such effects.

Bank Size — BIF loss ratios may be higher for smaller banks for two reasons. First, James (1991) finds that FDIC administrative costs are higher, per dollar of assets, for smaller failed banks.[25] Second, smaller banks may be subject to less frequent examination and less thorough surveillance between examinations than larger banks. When supervisors discover that relatively small banks are bankrupt, the percentage losses on assets may be larger than when larger banks fail. The bank size variable is the natural log of total assets as of failure date.

Location and Year of Failure — The remaining independent variables are dummy variables for the regions of failed banks and the years in which they failed, since BIF loss ratios may vary systematically by region and year of failure.

Regression Results

Table 8 presents the regression results. The equations use different measures of capital in the lagged capital ratio.

Lagged Capital Ratios — The coefficients on capital ratios four quarters before failure are not statistically significant. Other measures yield the same result. In other regressions not reported here, the coefficients on dummy variables

---

[22]The appendix examines in more detail how resolution methods affect BIF losses.

[23]For a discussion of the conditions for disposing of failed banks through P&A transactions, see Federal Deposit Insurance Corporation (1984), pp. 81-108, Bovenzi and Muldoon (1990) and Department of the Treasury (1991), pp. I-30 through I-51.

[24]See Brunner, Duca and McLaughlin (1991) for information on the rates banks pay on various types of deposit accounts.

[25]James (1991), pp. 1234-36.

for banks with capital ratios below 5 percent for various lengths of time before failure also are not statistically significant.[26]

The coefficients on the variables designed to reflect capital ratios before failure may be biased toward zero by including independent variables that reflect the quality and market value of bank assets. To illustrate, suppose the banks with persistently low capital ratios shifted their assets to high-risk categories as they approached failure, resulting in high ratios of nonperforming loans to total assets on their last reports of condition. In addition, suppose these banks sold securities with capital gains and kept securities with capital losses to boost the book value of equity as they approached failure. This selective pattern of securities sales would make values of the variable MARKET relatively high at the banks with persistently low capital ratios. The effects of low capital ratios before failure on BIF loss ratios would be captured to some extent in the coefficients on NPL, ACCRUED and MARKET. To test for this bias, equations 1 and 2 of table 8 were estimated without the variables NPL, ACCRUED and MARKET. In results not reported here, the coefficients on capital ratios before failure were not statistically significant.

Other Independent Variables — The coefficient on GROWTH is negative, as hypothesized. The coefficient on DIV is negative and insignificant; advocates of PCA legislation implied it would have been positive.

The coefficients on NPL and ACCRUED are significant with the positive signs, as hypothesized. The coefficient on MARKET is significant but the sign is opposite of that hypothesized: a wider gap between the book value and market value of securities is associated with a lower BIF loss.

The negative, significant coefficient on IDR indicates that failed banks with higher ratios of fully insured deposits to total assets are more valuable to potential bidders, thus tending to reduce BIF loss ratios. The coefficient on P&A indicates that BIF loss ratios are lower in P&A cases than in liquidation cases, holding other variables constant.[27] BIF loss ratios are not significantly lower in TID cases. The coefficient on OCC is positive and statistically significant. Holding constant the influences of the other independent variables, BIF loss ratios are about 2 percentage points higher for failed banks with national charters.[28] The coefficient on FR indicates that, among state-chartered banks, there is no significant effect of Federal Reserve membership on loss ratios, holding constant the other independent variables.

The coefficient on the natural log of assets is not statistically significant. In other regressions not reported here, dummy variables for banks in various size ranges also were not significant. The results do not support the hypothesis that BIF loss ratios are larger for smaller banks, holding constant other determinants of BIF loss ratios.

---

[26] The most comparable results for S&Ls are in Barth, Bartholomew and Labich (1989). In a regression equation with costs of resolving failed S&Ls as the dependent variable, tangible net worth on the last quarter reported is a highly significant variable. The coefficient is negative unity (a $1 increase in capital reduces resolution costs by $1), with a t-statistic of 13.9. Another significant variable is the number of months an association was insolvent before failure, which has a positive coefficient. The contrast of the results in this paper to those in Barth, Bartholomew and Labich is consistent with the view that the supervisors of commercial banks were more effective in limiting the risk assumed by poorly capitalized institutions than the supervisors of S&Ls.

[27] Bovenzi and Murton (1988) find that, without holding other factors constant, BIF loss ratios were about 7 percentage points lower in P&A cases than in liquidation cases in 1985-86. The coefficient on P&A in table 8 indicates about the same effect.

[28] Gilbert (1991) found differences in the behavior of banks in Texas with national charters and those with state charters that could be interpreted as evidence of differences in practices among the federal supervisory agencies. National banks were allowed to operate with capital ratios below the minimum capital requirement for longer periods than state-chartered banks, and national banks accounted for almost all of the Texas banks that operated at least a year with negative equity. The undercapitalized banks in Texas with rapid assets growth and those with higher insider loans while undercapitalized tended to be national banks. Most of these differences between national and state-chartered banks were not statistically significant outside Texas.

These contrasts might indicate that the positive, significant coefficients on OCC in table 8 reflect differences between national and state-chartered banks in the Southwest. To test for such a regional effect, the regressions in table 8 were estimated separately for banks in the states covered by the Dallas office of the OCC (Arkansas, Louisiana, New Mexico, Oklahoma and Texas) and for banks in other states. In each regression, the coefficient on OCC was positive but not significant at the 5 percent level. The coefficient on OCC was larger, however, in the regressions for banks in states outside the Southwest and significant at the 10 percent level. Thus, the effect on BIF loss ratios of supervision by the OCC is not restricted to the Southwest.

Table 8
Determinants of Bank Insurance Fund Losses Due to Individual Bank Failures

Dependent variable: Bank Insurance Fund loss divided by total assets as of failure date

Independent variables	Regression Number 1	Regression Number 2	Independent variables	Regression Number 1	Regression Number 2
Intercept	0.3539* (5.69)	0.3495* (5.69)	1985	−0.0207 (1.18)	−0.0200 (1.16)
EC_{-4}	−0.0324 (0.22)		1986	−0.0028 (0.18)	−0.0034 (0.22)
AC_{-4}		−0.0021 (0.02)	1987	0.0054 (0.38)	0.0048 (0.33)
GROWTH	−0.0442* (2.64)	−0.0451* (2.73)	1988	0.0214 (1.53)	0.0211 (1.50)
DIV	−1.4038 (1.34)	−1.42 (1.37)	1989	0.0255 (1.87)	0.0255 (1.87)
NPL	0.3554* (4.74)	0.3533* (4.69)	NE	−0.0544 (1.04)	−0.0550 (1.05)
ACCRUED	3.2125* (6.22)	3.2210* (6.24)	MA	−0.0732 (1.86)	−0.0732 (1.86)
MARKET	−1.3307* (2.31)	−1.2988* (2.25)	SA	−0.0693* (2.53)	−0.0689* (2.51)
IDR	−0.0855* (3.50)	−0.0848* (3.46)	ESC	−0.0883* (3.04)	−0.0877* (3.02)
P&A	0.0656* (4.40)	−0.0651* (4.35)	ENC	−0.1069* (3.60)	−0.1066* (3.60)
TID	−0.0024 (0.13)	−0.0021 (0.12)	WNC	−0.0904* (7.29)	−0.0904* (7.30)
OCC	0.0218* (2.39)	0.0222* (2.45)	PNW	−0.0497* (2.36)	−0.0498* (2.37)
FR	0.0179 (1.13)	0.0178 (1.12)	PSW	−0.0659* (4.99)	−0.0662* (5.03)
lnA	−0.0014 (0.29)	−0.0012 (0.25)	$\bar{R}^2$	0.2290	0.2291
			N	854	854

*Statistically significant at the 5 percent level.
NOTE: t-statistics are in parentheses under regression coefficients.

The coefficients on dummy variables for individual years are not statistically significant. Coefficients on several regional dummy variables are negative and significant. The excluded region is the West South Central region. The negative coefficients on some of the regional dummy variables indicate that, holding constant other independent variables, loss ratios are significantly lower for banks in several regions than for banks in the West South Central region.

CONCLUSIONS

The main reason for legislating prompt corrective action (PCA) is to reduce losses to deposit insurance funds. The case for such legislation rests on the following assumptions:

First, depository institutions have an incentive to assume greater risk as their capital ratios decline. Second, the longer an institution operates with a low capital ratio, the greater its opportunity to act on incentives to assume risk. Third, supervisors have been ineffective in limiting the risk assumed by poorly capitalized institutions. Fourth, the insurance fund losses due to the failure of individual institutions reflect, to some extent, the risk assumed by these institutions after they became poorly capitalized. And fifth, the actions mandated for supervisors in the legislation will constrain the risk assumed by poorly capitalized institutions, thereby limiting insurance fund losses if they fail.

This paper considers the likely effects of PCA legislation on BIF losses resulting from the failure of commercial banks. The method involves examining whether the evidence about commercial bank behavior and BIF losses support the assumptions that underlie the case for PCA legislation. The assumptions imply that the longer a bank operates with a low capital ratio before failure, the larger the BIF loss.

The evidence does not support this hypothesis. The evidence, instead, is consistent with the hypothesis that, in recent years, supervisors have been effective in constraining the risk assumed by poorly capitalized banks. These results raise doubts about whether PCA legislation will reduce BIF losses.

REFERENCES

Avery, Robert B., Gerald A. Hanweck, and Myron L. Kwast. "An Analysis of Risk-Based Deposit Insurance for Commercial Banks," *Proceedings of a Conference on Bank Structure and Competition*, May 1-3, 1985 (Federal Reserve Bank of Chicago), pp. 217-50.

Barth, James R., Philip F. Bartholomew, and Carol J. Labich. "Moral Hazard and the Thrift Crisis: An Analysis of 1988 Resolutions," *Proceedings of a Conference on Bank Structure and Competition*, May 3-5, 1989 (Federal Reserve Bank of Chicago), pp. 344-84.

Barth, James R., Philip F. Bartholomew, and Michael G. Bradley. "Determinants of Thrift Institution Resolution Costs," *Journal of Finance* (July 1990), pp. 731-54.

Berger, Allen N., Kathleen Kuester King, and James M. O'Brien. "The Limitations of Market Value Accounting and a More Realistic Alternative," *Journal of Banking and Finance* (September 1991), pp. 753-83.

Bernanke, Ben S., and Cara S. Lown. "The Credit Crunch," *Brookings Papers on Economic Activity*, (2:1991), pp. 205-39.

Bovenzi, John F., and Maureen E. Muldoon. "Failure-Resolution Methods and Policy Considerations," *FDIC Banking Review* (Fall 1990), pp. 1-11.

Bovenzi, John F., and Arthur J. Murton. "Resolution Costs of Bank Failures," *FDIC Banking Review* (Fall 1988), pp. 1-13.

Brookings Institution. *Blueprint for Restructuring America's Financial Institutions—Report of a Task Force* (1989).

Brunner, Allan D., John V. Duca, and Mary M. McLaughlin. "Recent Developments Affecting the Profitability and Practices of Commercial Banks," *Federal Reserve Bulletin* (July 1991), pp. 505-27.

Buser, Stephen A., Andrew H. Chen, and Edward J. Kane. "Federal Deposit Insurance, Regulatory Policy, and Optimal Bank Capital," *Journal of Finance* (March 1981), pp. 51-60.

Chirinko, Robert S., and Gene D. Guill. "A Framework for Assessing Credit Risk in Depository Institutions: Toward Regulatory Reform," *Journal of Banking and Finance* (September 1991), pp. 785-804.

Department of the Treasury. *Modernizing the Financial System* (February 1991).

Federal Deposit Insurance Corporation. *The First Fifty Years: A History of the FDIC, 1933-83* (1984).

French, George E. "Early Corrective Action for Troubled Banks," *FDIC Banking Review* (Fall 1991), pp. 1-12.

Garcia, Gillian. "The FSLIC is 'Broke' in More Ways Than One," *Cato Journal* (Winter 1988), pp. 727-41.

Gilbert, R. Alton. "Supervision of Undercapitalized Banks: Is There a Case for Change?" this *Review* (May/June 1991), pp. 16-30.

Horne, David K. "Bank Dividend Patterns," *FDIC Banking Review* (Fall 1991), pp. 13-24.

James, Christopher. "The Losses Realized in Bank Failures," *Journal of Finance* (September 1991), pp. 1223-42.

Keeley, Michael C., and Frederick T. Furlong. "A Reexamination of Mean-Variance Analysis of Bank Capital Regulation," *Journal of Banking and Finance* (March 1990), pp. 69-84.

Keeton, William R. "The New Risk-Based Capital Plan for Commercial Banks," Federal Reserve Bank of Kansas City *Economic Review* (December 1989), pp. 40-60.

Levonian, Mark E. "What Happens if Banks are Closed 'Early'?" *Proceedings of a Conference on Bank Structure and Competition*, May 1-3, 1991 (Federal Reserve Bank of Chicago), pp. 273-321.

Mondschean, Thomas. "Market Value Accounting for Commercial Banks," Federal Reserve Bank of Chicago *Economic Perspectives* (January/February 1992), pp. 16-31.

Peek, Joe, and Eric Rosengren. "The Capital Crunch: Neither a Borrower Nor a Lender Be," *Proceedings of a Conference on Bank Structure and Competition*, May 6-8, 1992a (Federal Reserve Bank of Chicago).

_____. "The Capital Crunch in New England," Federal Reserve Bank of Boston, *New England Economic Review* (May/June 1992b), pp. 21-31.

Shadow Financial Regulatory Committee. "An Outline of a Program for Deposit Insurance and Regulatory Reform," Statement No. 41, February 13, 1989, in George G. Kaufman, ed., *Restructuring the American Financial System* (Kluwer Academic Publishers, 1990), pp. 163-68.

Spong, Kenneth. *Banking Regulation: Its Purposes, Implementation and Effects*, 3rd. ed. (Federal Reserve Bank of Kansas City, 1990).

U.S. General Accounting Office. *Deposit Insurance: A Strategy for Reform* (March 1991).

Walter, John R. "Loan Loss Reserves," Federal Reserve Bank of Richmond *Economic Review* (July/August 1991), pp. 20-30.

Appendix
An Introduction to Bank Accounting and the FDIC's Practices in Resolving Failed Banks

The text assumes a basic understanding of bank accounting principles and the methods used by the FDIC in resolving failed banks. This appendix provides an introduction to these topics.

The accounting principles can be illustrated by referring to the balance sheets of a hypothetical bank. Items in table A1 reflect book rather than market values. For instance, the book value of loans is the sum of the outstanding balances that borrowers owe the bank, other than the loans that have been declared losses. Values of marketable securities are book values, not current market values.

One of the key balance sheet items for our purposes is the allowance for loan and lease losses, which represents an accumulation of past earnings set aside to absorb anticipated future losses on loans that become uncollectable. In accounting statements filed with bank supervisors, the allowance for loan losses is reported on the asset side of the balance sheet as a deduction from loans. Thus, net loans are net of anticipated losses, as reflected in the allowance.

When a bank cannot collect from a borrower, accounting principles indicate that management is to declare the loan a loss and charge the loss against the allowance for loan losses. The accounting entries involve reductions in both loans and the allowance.[1]

Increases in the allowance for loan losses come out of current earnings. The relevant item in the income statement is called the "provision for loan losses," which is included among bank expenses. If a bank must make a large provision for loan losses in a given period, because of actual or anticipated loan losses, current earnings may be negative. When current earnings are negative, equity is reduced.

The top half of table A1 presents the balance sheet of a solvent bank, based on book value accounting. Securities are recorded at their book value of $40. The allowance for loan losses is one-third of nonperforming loans, which the text indicates is about average for the banks in the study up to two years before their failure. The bank could absorb loan losses up to $2 without reducing equity. The ratio of equity to total assets is above 5 percent.

The financial condition of the bank would look worse if securities were marked to their market value of $35. Net worth actually would be zero.

The bottom half of table A1 is the balance sheet of the same bank after it recognizes some loan losses. All $6 of the nonperforming loans turn out to be uncollectable, and an additional $1 of other loans is charged off as a loss. These losses reduce the allowance and equity to zero. At this point, the bank is closed and the FDIC becomes the receiver. The duties of a receiver of a bankrupt firm are to dispose of its assets and make payments to its creditors from the proceeds.

The FDIC's loss depends on the method used to resolve this case. Under the *liquidation* method, the FDIC would pay the fully insured depositors $70 and liquidate the assets, sharing the proceeds of the assets with the uninsured depositors.[2] Equation A1 indicates the determinants of the loss to BIF under the liquidation method.

(A1) BIF loss = $70 (payment to fully insured depositors)
− (70/(70 + 19)) [$5 (cash)
+ $35 (market value of securities)
+ $33 (liquidation value of loans)]
= $12.58.

The present value of payments to the uninsured depositors, on deposits of $19, would be
(A2)   (19/89)[$73] = $15.58.

Another method of resolving failed banks is called *purchase and assumption*. The FDIC solicits bids from other banks to purchase some of the assets of the failed bank and to assume its liabilities. In this illustration, the bank with the winning bid purchases the $5 of cash and pays $35 for the securities. Whether this bid would result in a lower loss to BIF than under

---

[1] See Walter (1991) for a thorough discussion of the allowance for loan losses.

[2] When the FDIC liquidates a bank, it becomes a creditor of the failed bank for the amount of its payment to the insured depositors. The claim of the FDIC against the assets of the failed bank has equal priority to the claims of the uninsured depositors.

Table A1
Balance Sheet of a Hypothetical Bank

PRIOR TO CHARGE-OFF OF LOAN LOSSES

Assets			Liabilities	
Cash		$ 5	Insured deposits	$70
Securities		40	Uninsured deposits	19
Loans				
Nonperforming	6			
Other	45			
Allowance for loan losses	2	49	Net worth	5
		$94		$94

Memo: Market value of securities is $35

AFTER CHARGE-OFF OF LOAN LOSSES

Assets			Liabilities	
Cash		$ 5	Insured deposits	$70
Securities		40	Uninsured deposits	19
Loans				
Nonperforming	0			
Other	44			
Allowance	0	44	Net worth	0
		$89		$89

Memo: Market value of securities is $35.
The present value of loans in liquidation, net of liquidation costs, is $33.

liquidation depends on the size of the premium paid by the winning bidder, as indicated in the followed equation:

(A3) BIF loss = $49 (payment by the FDIC to cover the gap between $40 of assets purchased and $89 of liabilities assumed
− $33 (liquidation value of loans)
− premium.

The premium would have to exceed $3.42 to make the purchase and assumption transaction less costly to the FDIC than liquidation.

A third resolution method is called *transfer of insured deposits*. The FDIC solicits bids from other banks to assume the insured deposit liabilities of the failed bank, but the FDIC liquidates the assets. The FDIC shares with the uninsured depositors the premium paid by the bank that assumes the insured deposit liabilities of the failed bank. Equation A4 presents the loss to BIF:

(A4) BIF loss = $70 (cash to the bank that assumes the insured deposit liabilities)
− (70/89) [$73 (liquidation value of assets) + premium].

A comparison of equations A1 and A4 indicates that the BIF loss is smaller under the transfer of insured deposits than under liquidation for any positive premium.

Article 13

Too-Big-to-Fail After FDICIA

Larry D. Wall

The author is the research officer in charge of the financial section of the Atlanta Fed's research department. He thanks Robert Eisenbeis, Frank King, Ellis Tallman, Sheila Tschinkel, and Carolyn Takeda for helpful comments.

The special treatment historically accorded large failing banks—judging them "too-big-to-fail"—is an important issue in reforming deposit insurance. All unaffiliated depositors, and in some cases all creditors, at large failing banks have received 100 percent coverage of their funds even though coverage of only the first $100,000 deposited at domestic branches is guaranteed by law.[1] Following this too-big-to-fail policy has been justified in part as necessary for preventing systemic problems that might grow from a larger bank's difficulties. However, the policy itself created problems. It tended to reduce the incentive for large depositors to exercise market discipline, and it tended to increase the cost of resolving large failing banks.[2] Further, operating under a too-big-to-fail policy created a dilemma for bank regulatory agencies, which had to either leave large depositors at small banks uninsured and create an artificial incentive for large deposits to be shifted to too-big-to-fail banks or cover all deposits at all banks, further reducing market discipline at small banks and increasing the cost of resolving small bank failures.

Congress addressed the too-big-to-fail issue as a part of its deposit insurance reform bill, the Federal Deposit Insurance Corporation Improvement Act of 1991 (FDICIA). Section 141 of the act generally requires the resolution of failed banks at the lowest cost to the FDIC, though it provides for an exception that preserves the potential for banks to be considered too-big-to-fail. The exception may be invoked if failure to do so would "have serious adverse effects on economic conditions or financial stability" and providing additional FDIC coverage "would avoid or mitigate such adverse effects." FDICIA allows the exception only with the agreement of a two-thirds majority of the Board of Directors of the Federal Deposit Insurance Corporation, a two-thirds majority of the Board of Governors of the Federal Reserve System, and the Secretary of the Treasury ("in consultation with the President").

Two of the goals of FDICIA are to reduce both the potential for systemic problems and bank regulatory agencies' incentives to follow a too-big-to-fail policy. Having given a mandate to banking agencies to minimize FDIC losses, the act's prompt-corrective-action provisions provide a structured way of addressing a problem bank. A system of automatic review is set in motion whenever a bank failure imposes material costs on the FDIC or when the FDIC treats a bank as too-big-to-fail.[3] Specific changes intended to limit systemic risk include requiring the Federal Reserve to impose limits on interbank liabilities, authorizing the FDIC to provide for a final net settlement to a failed bank's creditors, and establishing statutory backing for net settlement provisions in bilateral and clearinghouse payments agreements.

FDICIA also leaves in place the Federal Reserve's discount window, which is a powerful tool for addressing systemic risk. Indeed, only the Federal Reserve is guaranteed to have the resources to be able to address virtually all conceivable systemic risk situations because only the Fed has the power to create money. However, FDICIA discourages inappropriate uses of the discount window by requiring the Federal Reserve to share in the FDIC's losses if lengthy Fed lending to a failing bank causes an increase in the FDIC's losses.[4]

FDICIA substantially reduces if not eliminates most of the dangers associated with the failure of a large bank. Some systemic risk issues remain, however, and the purpose of this article is to review those concerns as well as FDICIA's provisions designed to reduce such risks. Probably the biggest unresolved issue is what the effects of a large bank's failure would be. According to some preliminary analysis, a too-big-to-fail policy may not be needed to protect financial markets.

Systemic Risk

The concern about systemic risk stems from a fear that a single bank failure could reverberate through the banking system and cause widespread bank failures, adversely affecting bank customers and the real economy in a number of ways. However, not every run on a large bank automatically generates systemic problems. A depositor run on any nonviable bank not 100 percent insured is rational and helps speed closure of an institution that should be closed. Further, the argument that large bank creditors suffer losses in such a closing is not, in and of itself, a legitimate systemic concern.[5]

Systemic risk arises when an institution's failure interferes with financial services consumers' ability to obtain important financial services in a timely manner to such an extent that overall economic activity is reduced.[6] Systemic problems result if the failure of a large bank causes contagious runs on viable banks, thereby diminishing the overall availability of financial services. In addition, failure of a single institution may generate systemic problems if it significantly impairs the payments system or financial markets. This section highlights the channels through which it would be possible for systemic risk concerns to arise. An analysis of the actual magnitude of these risks prior to FDICIA is provided in the box on page 7.

Risks to Other Banks. The failure of one bank poses a potential risk to other banks in a number of ways. For example, other banks could suffer insolvency because of losses on interbank deposits and other forms of credit. They risk illiquidity if access to interbank deposits is delayed or if contagious deposit runs occur. The extent of such risks is usually, but not always, proportional to the size of the failing bank. Larger banks have more interbank deposits likely to be at risk if depositors are not covered, and large bank failures are likely to be noticed by more depositors.

The magnitude of the credit and direct liquidity risks is also a function of whether the collapse of the failed bank occurs over a long period of time or comes as a surprise. If the failure is anticipated, other banks will have had time to implement steps limiting their exposure to the failing organization. In this vein, financially strong banks have recently been limiting their exposure to banks with lower credit ratings in the interest rate and currency swap markets.

Risks to the Nonbank Sector. Nonbank customers and even third parties may also be hurt by a bank's failure. Creditors, including large depositors, directly risk default losses and reduced liquidity when a bank fails. While these risks are analogous to those taken by providers of interbank credit, they differ principally in that nonbank customers, especially small businesses, may have less access to other sources of liquidity.

Nonbank firms can turn to the Federal Reserve discount window under certain situations if a substantial liquidity problem arises, but the central bank has strongly preferred to avoid such lending.[7] Moreover, even if the Federal Reserve chose to lend to nonbank customers, the discount window is not structured to serve as a direct lender to a large number of small businesses.[8]

The ability of bank customers to make payments depends not only on their bank's being solvent and liquid but also on the operation of various payments systems. The failure of a large correspondent bank, which provides check-clearing, ACH, and other ongoing payments services to certain small banks, could directly affect the small banks' access to certain parts of the payments system. Moreover, such a failure could lead to a loss of confidence in bilateral and clearinghouse arrangements that handle a large fraction of the payments transactions. While the Federal Reserve is an important supplier of many payments services and could help sustain confidence in its systems, private arrangements play a critical role in some—especially international—payments systems.

Another problem nonbank customers might face when a bank fails is a temporary reduction in credit availability. Such a reduction might affect local economic conditions adversely.[9] However, implementing a too-big-to-fail policy would protect bank borrowers only to the extent that doing so would prevent contagious runs on viable banks. Borrowers are not necessarily protected by efforts to protect depositors because whoever holds the loans after the bank's failure does not have to extend any prefailure loans. Further, because the postfailure loanholder could demand repayment at the earliest time permitted by the loan contract, protecting a failed bank's depositors would not protect its borrowers.

This list of issues has recently been expanded by increased concern about ways a bank failure would affect financial markets. Banks play an increasing role as market makers in many financial contracts, especially for interest rate and foreign exchange contingent contracts such as options, forward contracts, caps, floors, and swaps. The failure of certain large banks might significantly reduce this market-making capacity for some types of financial contracts. More generally, a bank's failure could result in a loss of confidence in certain markets, with the result that some banks would be unable to maintain adequate hedges for their existing exposure.

Systemic Risk. While certain problems plague a too-big-to-fail policy, it is nonetheless an effective way to limit systemic risk. It prevents one bank's failure from creating any direct solvency or liquidity risk for other banks or nonbank creditors. Its enactment also reduces the risk of contagious runs at other banks by reassuring their depositors. A challenge FDICIA attempts to meet is establishing ways to eliminate the too-big-to-fail doctrine while continuing to minimize systemic risk.

*I*ncentive Changes

FDICIA both provides regulators with various tools for addressing problem banks and suggests changes in regulatory procedures.[10] A simple reading of the act may not disclose its real significance, however. Before FDICIA, regulators already had the power to enforce capital requirements and to stop unsafe or unsound banking practices. Thus, many of the tools the legislation specified were implicit in the agencies' existing authority. Moreover, many of the most important suggested changes in regulatory procedure are simply suggestions (as Richard Scott Carnell 1992 points out). The regulatory agencies retain substantial discretion in their treatment of problem banks, especially large ones.

The act's real significance is that it both provides the banking agencies with a clear goal of minimizing deposit insurance losses and sets up an incentive system to encourage compliance. The most important part of the act in terms of setting the goal and incentive system is section 131, which provides for prompt corrective action. That section begins by giving banking agencies one goal: "to resolve the problems of insured depository institutions at the least possible long-term cost to the deposit insurance fund." Toward that end, regulators are encouraged to strengthen bank capital, to respond to reduced capital levels by taking strong action that will limit risk and encourage recapitalization, and to close failing banks before they exhaust their equity capital. The provisions for prompt corrective action outline a number of steps that bank regulators may take as an institution's capital ratios decline. Although regulators generally retain the authority to tailor their actions to the specific circumstances, FDICIA mandates action in two particular situations: (1) banks that are undercapitalized must submit an acceptable plan to restore their capital to adequate levels, and (2) banking agencies must take action within ninety days of a bank becoming critically undercapitalized, with the act containing a bias toward receivership or conservatorship.[11]

Although the prompt-corrective-action guidelines specify regulatory action, they include a mandatory ex post review of any failure that imposes material costs on the FDIC and thus provide an incentive for regulators to prevent costly bank failures. If a material loss occurs, the inspector general of the appropriate banking agency must determine why and must make recommendations for preventing such a loss in the future. This report must be made available to the Comptroller General of the United States, to any member of Congress upon request, and to the general public through the Freedom of Information Act. Further, the General Accounting Office must provide an annual review of the reports and recommended improvements in supervision. These reporting and review requirements do not force the banking agencies to make any substantive changes in their supervisory practices. However, as discussed, these provisions supply strong political incentives to prevent costly bank failures.

Two sections of FDICIA—sections 141 and 142—change the legislative guidelines for deposit insurance and discount window decisions on banks that might be considered too-big-to-fail. Section 141 generally requires the FDIC to resolve bank failures at the least possible cost to the deposit insurance fund. The agency must document its evaluation of the alternative methods of resolving a failed bank, including the key assumptions on which the evaluation is based.

While section 141 permits a systemic risk exception to least costly resolution, it also provides for increased accountability when this exception is invoked. The FDIC, the Federal Reserve, and the U.S. Treasury must all agree that an institution's ill-health poses a systemic risk. The Secretary of the Treasury is required to document evidence indicating the need to invoke the systemic risk exception. The General Accounting Office must review any actions taken, examining the basis for finding action necessary and analyzing the implications for the actions of other insured depositories and uninsured depositors. The rest of the banking industry, required to pay the cost of a bailout through an emergency assessment to the FDIC that is proportional to each bank's average total tangible assets, is likely to act as a kind of watchdog.[12] The special assessment provides a strong incentive for the industry to question covering uninsured depositors, particularly when there is room for doubt about whether a failure would create systemic risk.

Section 142 limits the Federal Reserve's ability to provide through its discount window de facto too-big-to-fail treatment of a failing bank. Allowing a bank to borrow at the discount window makes it possible for uninsured deposits to be withdrawn prior to the resolution of a failing bank by providing the liquidity needed to cover withdrawals. This section of FDICIA limits such lending to undercapitalized banks to 60 days within any 120-day period unless the bank is certified as viable by the Federal Reserve or its primary federal bank regulator.[13] For banks that are critically undercapitalized the Federal Reserve is instructed to demand repayment no later than at the end of five days. If violation of the five-day limit occurs, the Fed is liable for part of the increased cost to the FDIC, and the Board of Governors of the Federal Reserve must notify Congress of any payments to the FDIC under this provision. Under FDICIA the Federal Reserve discount window retains substantial legal authority to lend to problem banks, but failure to comply with the intent of this portion of the act exposes the Fed to substantial ex post political pressure.

FDICIA clearly provides a mandate to banking agencies and seeks to create a system whereby there is political incentive for the agencies to follow the mandate. The biggest changes to occur as a result of the act will most likely result from the new climate of postfailure reviews and sanctions rather than from formal changes in the agencies' legal powers.

Changes that Mitigate Systemic Risk

Along with supplying a mandate to minimize FDIC losses, FDICIA addresses a number of systemic concerns raised by the banking agencies. The act aims to reduce the systemic risk associated with ending a too-big-to-fail policy by enhancing the overall stability of the banking system, by reducing the losses when a bank fails, and through targeted reforms that address specific potentially systemic problems.[14]

Enhanced Stability and More Timely Closure. A number of reforms in FDICIA call for reducing the likelihood of bank failure. The prompt-corrective-action provisions should result in higher bank capital ratios and are intended to ensure more timely supervisory intervention. The act requires that regulators revise existing credit risk-based capital standards to take account of interest rate risk, concentration of credit risk, and the risks of nontraditional activities. In addition, banks must undergo an annual, full-scope, on-site examination and an independent annual audit. These measures should help prevent significant undetected problems from arising at banks.

The prompt-corrective-action requirements that critically undercapitalized banks be placed in conservatorship or receivership mean that banks may be closed earlier with reduced losses to creditors.[15] Banks may also be closed earlier with higher expected recoveries to the extent that uninsured depositors become more likely to run on failing banks because of FDICIA's provisions virtually eliminating coverage of uninsured depositors.

Limits on Interbank Credit Exposure. The banking system relies heavily on interbank extensions of credit for intraday, overnight, and longer-term purposes, but interbank credit is a potential source of systemic risk. FDICIA directs the Board of Governors of the Federal Reserve to develop a regulation limiting interbank credit exposure. The Board has adopted a new Regulation F on interbank liabilities to satisfy this part of FDICIA.[16] The regulation restricts a bank's total exposure to its correspondent to 25 percent of the respondent's capital unless the correspondent is at least adequately capitalized.[17]

Final Net Settlement. Without immediate access to their funds at a failed bank, both bank and nonbank creditors could face severe liquidity problems. FDICIA addresses this problem by authorizing the FDIC to make a final settlement with creditors when it assumes receivership of a failed bank (section 416). Under these provisions uninsured and unsecured creditors may gain immediate access to their funds. The FDIC pays a sum that is the product of the amount of uninsured and unsecured claims times a final settlement rate. The final settlement rate is to be based on average FDIC receivership recovery experience so that the FDIC receives no more and no less than it would have as a general creditor standing in the place of the insured depositors. The FDIC's exercise of full powers under the final settlement provision should substantially alleviate liquidity problems for bank creditors.

Netting of Interbank Payments. Many payments systems result in banks' experiencing substantial intraday credit exposure to other financial institutions. This exposure may arise both as a result of bilateral agreements and through payments clearing organizations. FDICIA seeks to reduce the risk in these payments systems by explicitly recognizing contractual netting agreements and holding them legally binding if a member financial institution is closed. (Section 403 establishes that bilateral netting agreements are binding, and section 404 applies to clearing organization netting.)

Implications of the Changes. The net effect of FDICIA should be to reduce interbank risk substantially. The prompt-corrective-action provisions and the increase in market discipline are expected to constrain bank risk taking and increase the FDIC's rate of recovery from failed banks. In combination, these factors should almost eliminate the risk that one bank's failure would cause insolvency at other banks.[18]

The final settlement procedure provides the FDIC with a mechanism for resolving potential liquidity problems at creditor banks or nonbanks. The netting procedures under FDICIA further reduce the risk associated with payments systems. Any remaining credit risk is likely to be small as long as banks comply with the limits on interbank credit exposure.[19] The final settlement procedures and payments system netting together should eliminate most of the liquidity risk associated with the payments system. Any remaining liquidity problems could be addressed by the Federal Reserve discount window. Although FDICIA places increased limits on the discount window, as mentioned earlier, the Fed may still lend to adequately capitalized banks and to undercapitalized banks that the Fed (or the bank's primary federal supervisor) certifies as viable.

Unresolved Issues

FDICIA addresses a number of issues associated with large bank failure. However, at least two possible areas of concern remain: the effect of a large bank's failure on financial markets and the effect of sudden massive losses at one or more banks.

Financial Markets. A bank's failure could adversely affect selected financial markets by forcing the immediate unwinding of a large number of hedging transactions, by weakening confidence in derivative products that create credit exposure, and by causing the loss of one market maker.[20] These relatively new issues have received less attention than many others related to systemic risk. Nonetheless, some preliminary analysis is possible.[21]

Knowledge of the implications of large bank failures is most limited in the area of over-the-counter derivative products such as interest rate, foreign exchange, and commodity swaps. Available insight has been derived primarily from the failures of a few large financial institutions, including Drexel, Burnham, Lambert and the Bank of New England. These products seem to have several difficulties, but the biggest ones appear unrelated to systemic risk issues. The problems include (1) contract language in many swap agreements that may yield a windfall profit to counterparties of the failed bank, (2) the occasional inability to unwind derivative contracts at market prices after the institutions' financial problems have become apparent, and (3) increased cost of or inability to maintain adequate hedges at the failed institution while it is unwinding its derivatives book.[22]

The failure of a bank with a large over-the-counter derivatives book poses two risks to its counterparties: credit risk and the risk that the derivatives contract will be closed and the counterparty will lose its hedge. Evaluation of the credit risk is complicated by the nature of most derivatives. Although the size of many markets for over-the-counter derivatives, such as interest rate swaps, is measured by the notional principal of the underlying contracts, this measure generally overstates risks for two reasons. Actual payments on many types of derivatives are a small fraction of the notional principal.[23] Further, at any given time a bank is likely to be winning on some contracts and losing on others. Credit losses to a failed bank's counterparties arise only on those contracts under which the failed bank owes money.[24]

However, the measure that is the obvious alternative to the notional principal, the current credit exposure of the derivatives book (mark-to-market value of those contracts that have positive value to the bank), may understate exposure for many banks affected by systemic risk. The credit exposure on derivative contracts varies with changes in the value of the underlying commodity (interest rates, foreign exchange rates, and so forth). In a systemic risk situation, there may be sharp price movements in the underlying commodity and large changes in the value, and hence credit exposure, of banks' over-the-counter derivatives book. Current U.S. regulatory practice at least partially compensates for the increased risk by requiring banks to maintain capital proportionate to the amount of potential increases in credit exposure.[25] The potential losses to derivative counterparties are limited in two ways: expected credit losses from failed organizations will likely be a small fraction of exposure, and liquidity problems may be addressed by final settlement procedures or the discount window.

A potentially serious problem related to over-the-counter derivatives is the effect of failure on the hedging position of counterparties. These derivatives purchased from large commercial bank dealers are used by corporations and institutions to hedge exposure to interest rate, foreign exchange, and commodity price changes. The failure of the bank dealer may result in early termination of the contracts, raising concerns in two areas. First, the bank's counterparties need to know when the contract will be terminated so that they can arrange for a substitute hedge.[26]

The second consideration is that the counterparties affected by early termination of derivatives contracts will need to reestablish their hedge positions in the over-the-counter derivatives market as quickly as possible to minimize their risk exposure. Most financially strong corporate and institutional users would be unlikely to have problems doing so, given the number of dealers in most markets. However, users whose financial condition had weakened may face greater costs in arranging a hedge.[27]

There may also be systemic implications in the failure of a large bank that results in the immediate termination of all over-the-counter derivatives contracts. Such a failure on the part of a major bank dealer could significantly, if only temporarily, reduce dealer capacity in some derivatives markets. Further, even if remaining dealers have the capacity to service the additional demand, individual dealers may face binding bilateral credit limits that restrict their ability to deal with specific counterparties.[28] Although these limits are most likely to be binding on interdealer hedging trades, that dynamic could reduce dealers' ability to arrange hedges for end-users.[29] Credit limits may also pose a problem in another way: new information that enters the market through a bank failure may cause a reevaluation and possible reduction of selected credit lines by some dealers. There is, therefore, at least the potential for some users to face significant problems reestablishing their hedges in the wake of a major bank dealer's failure.

It is important, however, in evaluating the use of the too-big-to-fail doctrine to protect financial markets, to recognize that whatever problems arise are rooted in a bank's failure, not its treatment of creditors. Providing the protection for uninsured creditors is significant only in that preventing runs may allow more time for the development of new market makers and expanded capacity at existing firms. Even this significance is limited, though, because a bank will come under prompt-corrective-action provisions as its capital position declines, and market participants will be warned about the possible restrictions facing a large market maker. Further, if the loss of market-making capacity through an institution's closing would pose a serious problem, then supervisors should consider encouraging the bank to begin phasing out its market-making activities before it becomes critically undercapitalized so that the market may gradually adjust to the reduced capacity.

Systemic Risk before FDICIA

An important issue in evaluating whether FDICIA is contributing significantly to reducing systemic risk is determining the baseline likelihood of a financial system collapse among generally viable banks before FDICIA. Three commonly expressed concerns about large bank failure need to be considered: The first is the idea that interbank liabilities could generate credit losses leading to widespread insolvency or that delays in access to interbank liabilities could cause widespread illiquidity. The second concern is that the failure of a large bank might spark runs on viable banks. The third, and farther-reaching, fear is that payments systems may collapse in the wake of a large bank's failure.

The analysis below seeks to address two questions central to evaluating FDICIA's merit: (1) What are the odds that one of these three problems would in fact emerge, and (2) how do the banking agencies' pre-FDICIA tools for mitigating a problem at a large bank compare with the tools post-FDICIA?

Interbank Liabilities

The most direct risk a large bank's failure poses for other banks is that they will lose part or all of their investment in that bank. A sudden failure incurring massive losses could threaten the financial stability of respondent banks. However, determining the level of systemic risk should include distinguishing maximum possible losses from expected losses. Expected losses for a bank closed when it first becomes insolvent are likely to be a small fraction of possible losses. For example, total interbank exposure to Continental Illinois greatly overstated other banks' likely losses when Continental was rescued by the FDIC. There were 65 banks with uninsured balances in Continental exceeding 100 percent of their capital, and another 101 banks had uninsured balances equal to between 50 percent and 100 percent of their capital. However, if a recovery rate of 90 percent is assumed for Continental's assets, no banks would have had losses in excess of their capital and only 2 banks would have had losses equal to between 50 percent and 100 percent of their capital.[1] George G. Kaufman (1990) states that the FDIC's estimated recoveries at the time of failure of Continental were 97 percent to 98 percent and that the current estimate is 96 percent.

Even when a failure would not result in substantial credit losses on interbank deposits, theoretically it might still place other banks at risk if they could not obtain immediate access to their funds or if they were to experience a run by depositors fearing insolvency or illiquidity. However, the danger is not as great as it sounds. Even if the FDIC did not provide immediate access to interbank deposits, other banks would not necessarily fail because of illiquidity. A bank widely recognized as viable despite temporary illiquidity could probably borrow from other banks or the Federal Reserve discount window.

Contagious Bank Runs

One bank's failure may lead to withdrawals at other banks if customers lose confidence that their deposits will be fully redeemed. Depositors may also lose confidence because the failure discloses new information on the value of other banks' assets.[2]

The likelihood that financial markets will mistakenly run on solvent banks is important in evaluating the risk of bank runs. Empirical evidence suggests that financial markets generally are able to assess the implications of new information accurately. For example, analysis of the Mexican debt crisis revealed that the stock market responded to individual bank stocks in proportion to each bank's loan exposure even though such information had not been publicly released.[3] Studies of five major domestic failures also found no substantial evidence of contagion risk.[4] Further, when a misleading television story prompted a run on Old Stone, the thrift was able to stop the run within two days by convincing investors it was solvent.[5]

There are also some puzzling examples of possible market mistakes, however. The failure of the Overseas Trust Bank in Hong Kong and that of Penn Square Bank in the United States are two such cases. Gerald D. Gay, Stephen G. Timme, and Kenneth Yung (1991) found evidence that the failure of the Hong Kong bank had a significant negative impact on other banks in the city. This result is surprising because the Overseas Trust Bank's failure resulted from fraud, and such conditions would generally not be expected to provide significant information about other banks. In the case of the Penn Square Bank, Robert E. Lamy and G. Rodney Thompson (1986) and John W. Peavy III and George H. Hempel (1988) discovered that banks with no direct connections to the organization nevertheless suffered significant losses in stock market valuation after that bank failed. Lamy and Thompson suggest that the drop in market value reflected the fact that Penn Square was liquidated with losses to depositors, and this action could have raised doubts about coverage afforded other banks. Another explanation, by Peavy and Hempel, is that the market may have overreacted to the news of Penn Square's failure. Supporting that hypothesis, their findings indicate that losses suffered immediately after the failure by banks not directly connected to Penn Square were subsequently offset by significant positive abnormal returns for institutions.

Another study supplies weak evidence that there may be reason for concern about contagious runs. Randall J. Pozdena (1991) found that similarities in stock returns for firms in the same industry were much greater in banking than in other industries, suggesting that bank values may be more dependent on a common set of factors than those of many other industries. Pozdena also found that similarities in returns were fewer among banks with higher capital ratios.

Thus, there seems to be a risk that the failure of a large bank could spark contagious runs on viable banks if the markets fail to distinguish viable from nonviable banks. Studies of financial market performance generally suggest that markets tend to assess the implications of new information accurately. Some evidence of occasional errors has been found, however. Thus, at least a small potential for contagious runs apparently exists. The risk is minimized, though, by the Federal Reserve's option to provide funding to any viable bank experiencing a run.

Payments Systems

Other banks and the financial system may be exposed to a failed bank through their joint connections to the payments system.[6] The risk may occur through one of several mechanisms—the bilateral provision of services from the failed bank to its respondent, securities positions taken by the failed bank that need to be unwound, or a failure's effect on payments clearinghouses. The discussion that follows focuses on the potential for a bank failure to disrupt the processes by which payments are made in the banking system.[7]

Many small banks are dependent on correspondent banks for services such as check clearing, automated clearinghouse services and access to international payments systems. Loss of access to these services could create significant problems for some respondent banks, especially those that are too small to participate directly in certain payments systems. If a failing bank deteriorates gradually, respondents may reduce their risk by shifting their payments system business to other banks that are still financially strong or by making contingency plans. However, respondents that are still dependent at the time of failure would not necessarily lose access to the payments system. In the case of a troubled institution large enough to be an important supplier of correspondent services, the FDIC, under FDICIA, would likely try to sell the bank and could otherwise be expected to create and operate a bridge bank. Because the FDIC has these powers, invoking a too-big-to-fail policy is not essential for preserving respondent banks' access to the payments system.

Another bilateral issue that can affect payments systems concerns exchanging cash and various securities. The problem is that the exchange of value does not always occur simultaneously. Solvent parties are reluctant to surrender their part of the transaction before receiving value from the bankrupt party for fear that prompt and full payment will not be forthcoming. William S. Haraf (1991) noted that this situation occurred with the failure of the securities firm of Drexel, Burnham, Lambert in 1990 and that third parties were affected by the disruption.[8] Haraf also notes, however, that changes, some of which are being implemented, to the payments and settlement systems designed to shorten or eliminate lags in payments would be more efficient than resorting to declaring certain institutions too-big-to-fail. (He further notes that, despite some delays in winding up Drexel's affairs, their positions were ultimately liquidated.)

Multilateral clearinghouse arrangements may also be strained by the failure of a bank. These arrangements allow their bank members to make payments to each other with a single net payment at the end of each day to cover any net credit balances.[9] Transactions through clearinghouses may generate significant bilateral credit between banks. If the clearinghouse lacks a binding netting agreement and one bank fails to make a required payment, the failed banks are converted to bilateral agreements and the net positions of all other banks are recalculated. The danger is that banks that could have met their net position with the failed bank included may be unable to do so if the failed bank's position is excluded.[10] Thus, the potential exists for a single bank's failure to cascade through a payments system, forcing a number of banks to become illiquid and causing a loss of confidence in the entire netting arrangement.

The Federal Reserve has worked to reduce this risk by requiring banks to monitor and establish caps on their intraday liabilities and credit exposure to other banks. In addition, as a continuation of pre-FDICIA efforts to contain payments system risk, the Federal Reserve is imposing interest charges on banks that run large intraday overdrafts on Fedwire.[11] If a problem arises despite these restrictions the Federal Reserve retains adequate power under FDICIA to provide discount window loans to viable banks that temporarily lack liquidity.

Summary

Two common themes run throughout this review of the risk of systemic problems in the absence of a too-big-to-fail policy prior to FDICIA. First, although some risk of losses on interbank liabilities, contagious runs, and failures in the payments system existed, that risk frequently has been overstated. Second, the Federal Reserve could have contained most systemic risk situations through the discount window.[12] The most likely system risk scenarios would have involved temporary, widespread liquidity problems but limited actual solvency problems. The Federal Reserve's discount window had, as it does now, the resources to resolve temporary liquidity problems. Furthermore, the Federal Reserve has historically had detailed, timely information on banks as a result of its supervision and regulation, and on the payments system as a consequence of its role as a provider of payments services. Thus, the Fed has had both the tools and the knowledge required to effectively address systemic risk situations arising from temporary liquidity problems.

Notes

1. These figures on other banks' exposure to Continental Illinois came from U.S. Congress (1984, 16-18).
2. Finance theory provides a third reason for depositors to lose confidence: they could become concerned about their bank's inability to meet an increase in demand for liquidity by other depositors. Diamond and Dybvig (1983) have developed a model in which banks are solvent at the beginning of the period but are subject to a random amount of withdrawal by depositors. The bank must prematurely liquidate projects at a loss if deposit withdrawals are too high. If too many projects are liquidated, the bank may become insolvent. Empirical examples that correspond exactly to the Diamond and Dybvig model are hard to find. However, the U.S. banking system in the late 1800s and early 1900s was subject to periodic liquidity crises during and shortly after harvest season, and some evidence suggests that the crises were due entirely to liquidity concerns about individual banks. A model of inelastic currency supply developed by Champ, Smith, and Williamson (1991) suggests the potential for periodic liquidity crisis and provides some evidence on the problem. However, Calomiris and Gorton (1991) raise questions about this history of panics in the period prior to the formation of the Fed. In any case, such random withdrawal models are not closely examined here because there is no evidence to suggest that such a problem has occurred since the Fed's creation or that the Fed could not fully resolve any liquidity-based runs with its existing authority. The Federal Reserve can and does provide an elastic supply of currency and liquidity.
3. See Cornell and Shapiro (1986) and Smirlock and Kaufold (1987).
4. Aharony and Swary (1983) found that no significant abnormal bank stock returns occurred around the failures of the United States National Bank of San Diego in 1973 and Hamilton National Bank in 1976. They did find significant negative abnormal returns associated with the failure of Franklin National Bank in 1974, but they suggest that this result could be based on a revaluation of the risks associated with foreign exchange trading. Aharony and Swary further note that some European banks were taking foreign exchange losses around this time. Former FDIC Director Irvine H. Sprague (1986) argued that regulators were concerned about the potential failure of other large banks if Continental Illinois failed in 1984 with losses to depositors. Saunders (1987), Swary (1986), and Wall and Peterson (1990) failed to find clear-cut evidence to support the regulators' concerns. Dickinson, Peterson, and Christiansen (1991) also failed to find evidence of contagion around the time of the failure of the First RepublicBank in 1988.
5. The story of how the run was stopped is provided by Leander (1991).
6. Haraf (1991) has noted that the failure of a nonbank institution can also impose strains on various payments mechanisms. For example, Fedwire and the Clearing House for Interbank Payments (CHIPS) were forced to remain open longer than usual to accommodate problems arising from the failure of Drexel, Burnham, Lambert.
7. See Baer and Evanoff (1990) for a review and analysis of the issues associated with large dollar value payments systems. Roberds (forthcoming, 1993) discusses ways of further controlling the risks of those systems.
8. Moen and Tallman (1992) found that the failure of nonbank firms also disrupted the payments system in the Panic of 1907.
9. For an example of such a system, see the discussion of CHIPS provided by the Group of Experts on Payments Systems (1990, 131-42).
10. Given that the failed bank was presumably financially weak immediately prior to failure, there is a high probability that depositors were, on net, withdrawing substantial amounts of money from the failing bank. These withdrawals would likely be transferred to other banks, with a substantial part of the withdrawals going through clearinghouses. Thus, odds are relatively high that, if a bank fails, it will be a large net payer to various clearinghouses.
11. See Cummins (1992) for a discussion of the Federal Reserve's decision to charge for intraday overdrafts.
12. See Smith and Wall (1992) for a discussion of how discount window and deposit insurance operations could address systemic risk issues without reliance on a too-big-to-fail policy.

Financial markets are also likely to take actions that would reduce their costs associated with the loss of a market maker if the problem bank's financial condition deteriorates gradually. Market participants may shift business to other market makers as a hedge against the institution's possible failure. Moreover, the troubled bank may find that its trading operations are more valuable if sold than if forced to operate as part of a financially weak organization.[30] Alternatively, there may be market adjustment through the individuals whose trading and technical expertise are at the heart of any securities trading operation. These key people may seek to leave the ailing bank or may be bid away by an organization having the resources to support and expand their trading operations.

Overall, there are some risks to financial securities markets when a large bank fails. Although the problems are likely to be temporary, some users may very well have problems arranging substitute hedges in a timely manner. Further research is needed on several issues: (1) the rate at which lost market-making capacity is replaced, (2) the likelihood that credit limits restrict dealers' ability to service users and engage in interdealer hedging, (3) the significance of the costs associated with a temporary reduction in liquidity, and (4) the significance of a large bank's exposure to risk if it lost access to derivative markets for several days.

If policymakers were to conclude that a too-big-to-fail policy is necessary to protect banks that are financial market makers, there would be implications for securities firms that have a similar presence in many financial markets. Securities firms not affiliated with bank holding companies currently have neither insurance like that provided banks by the FDIC or a mandate to comply with safety and soundness regulations like those imposed on banks. Although securities firms are partially regulated by the Securities and Exchange Commission (SEC), the agency regulates only some subsidiaries, and in any case, its historical mandate is consumer protection rather than maintaining financial system stability. If certain banks are considered too-big-to-fail in order to protect the securities markets, logic would suggest that securities firms should receive similar coverage and that the provider of liquidity or solvency guarantees should be able to protect itself via banklike safety and soundness regulations.

Unexpected Massive Losses. The mechanisms that may soften the impact of failure on the financial system are most effective in dealing with slow deterioration of one or more banks. In a variety of ways regulators and markets can gradually disengage troubled banks from the financial system and limit the damage of failure. However, a sudden massive loss at one or more banks could create a situation in which the market's exposure to a failing bank would be at its maximum, and regulators would be in a weak position to implement their full array of crisis management tools.

Fortunately, such economic losses appear to be exceptional. Sudden losses greater than a bank's capital are possible only if a bank has a very large concentration of risk to a single factor such as interest rate risk, foreign exchange rate risk, or having borrowers from a single geographic area that is devastated. Rather than truly being sudden, large losses may only appear to be so because banks and bank regulators have failed to provide for the timely recognition of reductions in asset values. Most often private sector parties will have begun reducing their exposure as soon as economic capital is significantly impaired, even though delays in accounting recognition may have slowed regulatory action.

Notwithstanding the extremely low probability of an unexpected failure of a previously well capitalized large bank that is engaged in a number of complex activities, such a failure would create a big problem for the regulators. The FDIC may be able to avoid invoking the systemic risk exception but only if it and the failed bank were exceptionally prepared for such a contingency. The FDIC would have to identify the bank's insured and uninsured creditors and calculate appropriate payouts for each of them. The Federal Reserve could buy a little time for the FDIC by exercising its discount window power to lend to a critically undercapitalized bank for five days. However, the failed bank would be crippled prior to its closure with a massive outflow of uninsured deposits, severe limits on its access to the payments system, and an inability to function in the over-the-counter derivatives market. Even with the additional time, the FDIC probably would be forced to establish a bridge bank while it evaluated alternative methods of resolving the failure. Further, the FDIC probably would not have time for careful review of the bank's books to determine the amount and type of each of the institution's liabilities (including off-balance-sheet activities). The FDIC could readily evaluate all liabilities only if the bank had organized its financial records in a way that permitted quick access.

Although it might be possible to manage a single bank's unexpected failure, the situation would probably be unmanageable in the even more unlikely case that the viability of a number of large banks became questionable. With several large banks in trouble, depositors would be likely to demand immediate withdrawal of their funds, refraining only if the government were providing 100 percent deposit insurance. Because regulators have limited operational resources (such as people) and may also face financial constraints that restrict the number of bank closings they can handle at one time, they may want to provide 100 percent coverage as a means to avoid closing too many banks in a short period.

The risk of sudden large losses to individual banks or groups of banks is remote and can be further reduced, but it cannot be eliminated. The key to reducing the risk is for institutions to minimize concentrations of exposure to specific events that could cause a sharp drop in their value.

Conclusion

FDICIA has mandated that regulators virtually eliminate deposit insurance losses. The act provides for a systemic exception to its requirement that problem banks must be resolved at the lowest cost to the insurance funds. However, FDICIA also creates some significant political incentives to avoid using the systemic risk exception. Moreover, it is clear from the series of measures to address specific systemic issues that the intent of Congress was virtually to eliminate the practice of the too-big-to-fail doctrine. Congress, having been told that interbank credit created systemic risk, mandated limits on interbank credit. Congress learned that delayed access to funds could pose a systemic problem, so it authorized the FDIC to use final net settlement. In response to reports that the shock waves from a large bank failure could be amplified through the payments system, Congress made contractual netting agreements binding. Indeed, Carnell (1992) has noted that the original bill passed by the House and the bill introduced to the Senate did not allow for a systemic risk exception to least-cost resolution and that the exception was added after regulators and the Bush Administration asked for the change. The earlier versions of FDICIA relied solely on the Federal Reserve's discount window to address any systemic problems.

Although FDICIA does not ban the too-big-to-fail doctrine, it has substantially reduced the likelihood of future large bank bailouts. Bankers and bank depositors should not casually assume that any given bank would be considered too-big-to-fail. Regulators would be well advised to look for ways to close a large failing bank without protecting uninsured creditors. If conditions were such that a large fraction of the banking system was potentially not viable, regulators may have no choice but to protect uninsured depositors.[31] However, for most other systemic risk situations, including financial market risk, the potential still exists for identifying and developing solutions. A careful review of FDICIA's provisions makes it clear that Congress is looking for an end to operating under a too-big-to-fail policy and not for more explanations as to why too-big-to-fail treatment is essential.

Notes

1. "Too-big-to-fail" does not literally mean that a bank cannot fail. The shareholders in large banks have lost their investment, and the managers have been fired. A bank is considered too-big-to-fail when it is thought to be too large to close in a way that imposes losses on uninsured depositors and certain other creditors.
2. Large depositors are not protected when a bank is liquidated, but they have frequently been covered when a failed bank has been sold as a part of a purchase and assumption transaction or when the FDIC assumed ownership of the failed organization and operated it as a bridge bank. The FDIC generally has sought to avoid liquidating a bank in order to preserve any franchise value remaining in the organization. However, the FDIC can preserve the franchise value without providing 100 percent coverage to all depositors by transferring only the insured deposits to the successor organization.
3. The act defines a material loss as one exceeding the greater of $25 million or 2 percent of the institution's total assets, whichever is greater.
4. The exact restrictions on Fed lending are discussed in the section titled "Incentive Changes."
5. Indeed, if a bank is closed by regulatory or market pressure before it wipes out its capital, losses to creditors should be small to nonexistent.
6. Gorton (1988) and Tallman (1988) challenge the view that bank panics caused declines in real economic activity. However, this debate is beyond the scope of this paper. It suffices to note that policymakers in the United States have believed that systemic problems could adversely affect the real economy.
7. One reason for the Federal Reserve to be reluctant to lend to nonbank firms is that, because discount window lending must be fully collateralized, such lending could imperil the

position of the firm's creditors. Thus, if the Fed lends to nonviable nonbank firms it may be transferring wealth away from creditors that cannot or do not withdraw their investment. The Federal Reserve is also not generally in a position to judge the viability of nonbank firms because the agency does not examine and rarely monitors the financial condition of specific nonfinancial firms.

8. For further discussion of the historic operation of the discount window see the Board of Governors of the Federal Reserve System (1985, chap. 4) and Garcia and Plautz (1988).
9. Calomiris, Hubbard, and Stock (1986) and Gilbert and Kochin (1989) have found that the failure of one or more banks may have negative effects on its regional economy. In Gilbert and Kochin's research the effects are largest in two of the three states in their sample if a bank is closed rather than merged with another institution.
10. Many provisions of FDICIA, including the general prompt-corrective-action provisions and the definition of material loss, have delayed effective dates or phase-in clauses. This article focuses on the effects of FDICIA after all parts of the act have taken full effect.
11. FDICIA creates five categories based on capital levels: well-capitalized, adequately capitalized, undercapitalized, significantly undercapitalized, and critically undercapitalized banks. Any bank having a tangible equity-capital-to-total-assets ratio of less than 2 percent is classified as critically undercapitalized. The act also provides that bank regulators may place a bank in receivership or conservatorship on a number of other grounds, including violation of a cease-and-desist order, concealment of records or assets, inability to cover deposit withdrawals, and an undercapitalized bank's failure to develop a plan that would raise its capital or its material noncompliance with a plan to raise capital.
12. Normal FDIC premiums are calculated on the basis of a bank's total domestic deposits. The expanded premium base provided in FDICIA for emergency assessments will tend to increase the relative proposition of costs borne by banks with foreign deposits and substantial nondeposit liabilities. Because banks with foreign deposits and substantial nondeposit liabilities tend to be larger and to affect the financial system more significantly, the effect of FDICIA may be to shift more of the costs to the banks most likely to receive too-big-to-fail treatment.
13. A critically undercapitalized bank is not viable according to the definition in the act.
14. An argument may also be made that the net effect of FDICIA will be to weaken banks. The act will increase the number of regulatory requirements imposed on banks (including some requirements such as Truth in Savings that are unrelated to bank safety) and will also increase bank reporting requirements. It does nothing to enhance banks' ability to compete with nonbank financial firms, which continue to take market share in many of the bank's most profitable markets while remaining free from most of the costly safety and consumer regulations imposed on banks. Moreover, the act was passed in an environment in which deposit insurance premiums had been substantially increased on healthy banks to rebuild the insurance fund.

This argument that FDICIA will weaken banks has some merit but probably misjudges the impact of what is and is not in the act. FDICIA probably will strengthen the financial condition of individual banks and reduce the risk of bank failures that impose significant costs on the banking system. Banks that cannot strengthen their financial position will likely be forced to merge. Instead, the effect of higher regulatory costs will be that banks will continue to concede market share to nonbank firms in markets in which the law has made banks less competitive.

15. No losses need occur if a bank is closed before its losses become too large. However, closing a bank before its capital reaches zero does not guarantee that losses will be avoided unless bank assets are valued at liquidation prices. See Berger, King, and O'Brien (1991) for a discussion of the alternative definitions of "market value" and their limitations.
16. See the press release from the Board of Governors of the Federal Reserve System dated July 14, 1992, Docket No. R-0769.
17. The regulation on interbank liabilities uses a definition of "adequately capitalized" that is similar but not identical to that used to fulfill the prompt-corrective-action sections of FDICIA.
18. The only case in which the failure of one bank could cause insolvency at other banks would be that of a well-capitalized bank failing suddenly and its remaining assets providing creditors with a low recovery rate. These unexpected losses would have to be massive under the currently proposed capital requirements for prompt corrective action because a well-capitalized bank must maintain a total capital-to-risk-assets ratio of at least 10 percent.
19. The limits on interbank credit extension may not be effective at preventing insolvency if a group of related banks fail. For example, if a set of international banks from a foreign country were ordered by its government to stop payments, limits on exposure to any single bank might not be effective.
20. See Holland (1992) for a discussion of some of the risks in the swaps market. That analysis focuses on the credit risks posed by the interbank market for swaps. However, the issues raised by interbank credit exposure to swaps are not fundamentally different from the issues raised by other types of interbank credit exposure.
21. For a general discussion of the risks posed by over-the-counter derivatives to banking organizations see Hansell and Muehring (1992).
22. See Shirreff (1991) and Torres (1991) for discussion of some of the problems encountered in unwinding the derivatives books of some large financial firms. Shirreff (1992) discusses some of the regulators' general concerns about the swap market.
23. For example, consider an interest rate swap with a notional principal of $100 million. One party agrees to pay a fixed rate of 8 percent and the other party agrees to pay the London interbank offered rate (LIBOR) for five years. The $100 million notional principal will never change hands. The party that owes the larger interest payment will pay an amount to the other party equal to the absolute value of LIBOR minus 8 percent.

24. Further, many master derivatives contracts between two parties provide for netting across contracts so that gains on one contract may be offset by losses on other contracts.
25. See Wall, Pringle, and McNulty (1990) for a discussion of the (credit) risk-based capital guidelines as applied to over-the-counter interest rate and foreign exchange derivatives.
26. This issue may require some sensitivity on the part of the FDIC to the needs of the bank's counterparties. For example, the FDIC ordinarily likes to close a bank on a Friday after the U.S. financial markets close. If all over-the-counter derivatives are terminated at this point, those users that lack access to foreign markets may have problems arranging substitute hedges before Monday morning and would therefore be exposed to any changes in market prices during the weekend. A possible solution would be for swap contracts to provide that if a bank should fail at the start of a weekend the contract would be terminated at a fixed time on Monday morning and the remaining obligations of the two parties would be based on market prices at the time of termination. The FDIC may have to agree to this arrangement. The one risk in such an arrangement would be that some dealers may try to manipulate market prices around the termination time, but doing so is likely to be difficult in a market with a large number of users trying to arrange substitute hedges.
27. Many derivatives products involve two-sided credit risk. If a user's credit quality has deteriorated sufficiently, dealers may not be willing to take the credit risk ordinarily involved with products like forward contracts and swaps. Some derivatives contracts contain clauses to protect the parties against material adverse changes in the financial condition of their counterparties, and such contracts would force the parties to recognize deterioration in the user's condition prior to its failure. However, financially weakened users may need to provide additional protection to the dealer in order to reestablish their hedge if the derivatives contract contains no such clause. For example, rather than using an ordinary interest rate swap without collateral to protect against an increase in market interest rates, the user may be required to post collateral with the dealer or buy an interest rate cap.
28. Virtually all dealers impose a limit on their maximum credit to any given counterparty. The limit is established according to the counterparty's size and financial strength. The maximum exposure limits aggregate exposure from all types of credit risk, including any loans. See Arak, Goodman, and Rones (1986) for an example of ways a dealer could calculate its credit exposure on an interest rate swap and Chew (1992) for a recent discussion of a banks' management of derivatives credit risk.
29. The clientele of some dealers tends to be weighted toward one side of the derivatives market. For example, the customer bases of some commercial banks may be weighted toward firms that wish to pay a fixed rate of interest on their interest rate swaps. The bank ends up having a concentration of floating rate contracts. One common way for these commercial banks to hedge their transactions is to arrange offsetting swaps in which the bank pays a fixed rate with a dealer that has a different clientele. If credit lines became exhausted in the interdealer market, dealers could have more problems hedging deals with their natural clientele and, thus, be less willing to offer over-the-counter derivatives to their usual customers.
30. Financially weak banks may handicap trading operations in a number of ways. Their presence may bring the general credibility of the trading operations into question with customers.
31. The policy mistakes, if any, that led to the questionable viability of a large fraction of the banking system would have occurred prior to any decision to exercise the systemic risk exception.

References

Aharony, Joseph, and Itzhak Swary. "Contagion Effects of Bank Failures: Evidence from Capital Markets." *Journal of Business* 56 (July 1983): 305-22.

Arak, Marcelle, Laurie S. Goodman, and Arthur Rones. "Credit Lines for New Instruments: Swaps, Over-the-Counter Options, Forwards, and Floor-Ceiling Agreements." Federal Reserve Bank of Chicago, *Conference on Bank Structure and Competition*, 1986, 437-56.

Baer, Herbert L., and Douglas D. Evanoff. "Payments System Risk Issues in a Global Economy." Federal Reserve Bank of Chicago Working Paper WP-1990-12, August 1990.

Berger, Allen N., Kathleen Kuester King, and James M. O'Brien. "The Limitations of Market Value Accounting and a More Realistic Alternative." *Journal of Banking and Finance* 15 (September 1991): 753-83.

Board of Governors of the Federal Reserve System. *The Federal Reserve System: Purposes and Functions*. 7th ed., 2d printing. Washington, D.C.: Board of Governors of the Federal Reserve System, 1985.

Calomiris, Charles W., and Gary Gorton. "The Origins of Banking Panics: Models, Facts, and Bank Regulation." In *Financial Markets and Financial Crisis*, edited by Glenn R. Hubbard, 109-73. Chicago: University of Chicago Press, 1991.

Calomiris, Charles W., R. Glenn Hubbard, and James H. Stock. "The Farm Debt Crisis and Public Policy." *Brookings Papers on Economic Activity* (1986): 441-79.

Carnell, Richard Scott. "Implementing the FDIC Improvement Act of 1991." Paper presented at a Conference on Rebuilding Public Confidence through Financial Reform, Ohio State University, Columbus, Ohio, June 25, 1992.

Champ, Bruce, Bruce D. Smith, and Stephen D. Williamson. "Currency Elasticity and Banking Panics: Theory and Evidence." The Rochester Center for Economic Research, Working Paper No. 292, August 1991.

Chew, Lillian. "A Bit of a Jam." *Risk* 5 (September 1992): 82ff.

Cornell, Bradford, and Alan C. Shapiro. "The Reaction of Bank Stock Prices to the International Debt Crisis." *Journal of Banking and Finance* 10 (March 1986): 55-73.

Cummins, Claudia. "Fed to Charge Banks for Intraday Overdrafts." *American Banker*, October 1, 1992, 1, 12.

Diamond, Douglas W., and Philip H. Dybvig. "Bank Runs, Liquidity, and Deposit Insurance." *Journal of Political Economy* (June 1983): 401-19.

Dickinson, Amy, David R. Peterson, and William A. Christiansen. "An Empirical Investigation into the Failure of the First Republic Bank: Is There a Contagion Effect?" *Financial Review* 26 (August 1991): 303-18.

Garcia, Gillian, and Elizabeth Plautz. *The Federal Reserve: Lender of Last Resort*. Cambridge, Mass.: Ballinger Publishing Company, 1988.

Gay, Gerald D., Stephen G. Timme, and Kenneth Yung. "Bank Failure and Contagion Effects: Evidence from Hong Kong." *Journal of Financial Research* 14 (Summer 1991): 153-65.

Gilbert, R. Alton, and Levis A. Kochin. "Local Economic Effects on Bank Failures." *Journal of Financial Services Research* 3 (December 1989): 333-45.

Gorton, Gary. "Bank Panics and Business Cycles." *Oxford Economic Papers* 40 (December 1988): 751-81.

Group of Experts on Payments Systems. *Large-Value Funds Transfer Systems in the Group of Ten Countries*. Basle: Bank for International Settlements, May 1990.

Hansell, Saul, and Kevin Muehring. "Why Derivatives Rattle the Regulators." *Institutional Investor* 26 (September 1992): 27-33.

Haraf, William S. "The Collapse of Drexel, Burnham, Lambert: Lessons for the Bank Regulators." *Regulation* 14 (Winter 1991): 22-25.

Holland, Kelley. "Swaps: The Next Debacle for Banking?" *American Banker*, August 4, 1992, 1, 10.

Kaufman, George G. "Are Some Banks Too Large to Fail? Myth and Reality." *Contemporary Policy Issues* 8 (October 1990): 1-14.

Lamy, Robert E., and G. Rodney Thompson. "Penn Square, Problem Loans, and Insolvency Risk." *Journal of Financial Research* 9 (Summer 1986): 103-12.

Leander, Tom. "Old Stone's Theodore Barnes Stopped a Run in Its Tracks." *American Banker*, February 1, 1991, 2.

Moen, Jon, and Ellis Tallman. "The Bank Panic of 1907: The Role of the Trusts." *Journal of Economic History* 52 (September 1992): 611-30.

Peavy, John W., III, and George H. Hempel. "The Penn Square Bank Failure." *Journal of Banking and Finance* 12 (March 1988): 141-50.

Pozdena, Randall J. "Is Banking Really Prone to Panics?" Federal Reserve Bank of San Francisco *Weekly Letter* (October 11, 1991).

Roberds, William. "The Rise of Electronic Payment Networks and the Future Role of the Fed with Regard to Payment Finality." Federal Reserve Bank of Atlanta *Economic Review* 78 (March/April 1993, forthcoming).

Saunders, Anthony. "The Inter-Bank Market, Contagion Effects, and International Financial Crises." In *Threats to International Financial Stability*, edited by Richard Portes and Alexander K. Swoboda, 196-232. New York: Cambridge University Press, 1987.

Shirreff, David. "Dealing with Default." *Risk* 4 (March 1991): 19ff.

_____. "Swap and Think." *Risk* 5 (March 1992): 29ff.

Smirlock, Michael, and Howard Kaufold. "Bank Foreign Lending, Mandatory Disclosure Rules, and the Reaction of Bank Stock Prices to the Mexican Debt Crisis." *Journal of Business* 60 (July 1987): 347-64.

Smith, Stephen D., and Larry D. Wall. "Financial Panics, Bank Failures, and the Role of Regulatory Policy." Federal Reserve Bank of Atlanta *Economic Review* 77 (January/February 1992): 1-11.

Sprague, Irvine H. *Bailout: An Insiders Account of Bank Failures and Rescues*. New York: Basic Books, 1986.

Swary, Itzhak. "Stock Market Reaction to Regulatory Action in the Continental Illinois Crisis." *Journal of Business* (July 1986): 451-73.

Tallman, Ellis. "Some Unanswered Questions about Bank Panics." Federal Reserve Bank of Atlanta *Economic Review* 73 (November/December 1988): 2-21.

Torres, Craig. "Dangerous Deals: How Financial Squeeze Was Narrowly Avoided in 'Derivatives' Trade; Bank of New England's Woes Battle Currency Markets as its Credit Evaporated a Hazard that Could Return." *Wall Street Journal*, June 18, 1991, A1.

U.S. Congress. House. Committee on Banking, Finance, and Urban Affairs. Subcommittee on Financial Institutions, Supervision, Regulation, and Insurance. *Continental Illinois National Bank Failure and Its Potential Impact on Correspondent Banks*. Staff Report. 98th Cong., 2d sess., October 6, 1984.

Wall, Larry D., and David R. Peterson. "The Effect of Continental Illinois' Failure on the Financial Performance of Other Banks." *Journal of Monetary Economics* 26 (August 1990): 77-99.

Wall, Larry D., John J. Pringle, and James E. McNulty. "Capital Requirements for Interest Rate and Foreign-Exchange Hedges." Federal Reserve Bank of Atlanta *Economic Review* 75 (May/June 1990): 14-28.

Article 14

The Community Reinvestment Act: Evolution and Current Issues

Griffith L. Garwood and Dolores S. Smith, of the Division of Consumer and Community Affairs, prepared this article. Jane E. Ahrens, Michael S. Bylsma, and Adrienne D. Hurt provided research assistance.

The Community Reinvestment Act took effect in November 1978. How well is it working? The answer is, probably a lot better than is often recognized. The legislation has had a major influence on reinvestment activity throughout the country and has brought greater attention to local needs, especially in low-income and minority areas. It has also engendered creative strategies and techniques to stimulate lending for community development. In many parts of the country, community groups and financial institutions have moved from adversarial relations to cooperation in pursuit of mutual goals.

Yet many financial institutions complain that complying with the Community Reinvestment Act (CRA) is costly and burdensome. Some criticize the law's requirements as too vague; others say that its implementation amounts, de facto, to credit allocation. Some also are adversely affected by the law's existence when they seek to expand operations, particularly if a public protest is filed. Many community and consumer groups, on the other hand, believe that financial institutions are not doing enough to help meet the credit needs of residents and businesses in low- and moderate-income areas. In part, they blame the supervisory agencies for being too lenient in assessing CRA performance and too generous in assigning grades. Caught in the middle, the agencies over the years have addressed the divergent views and expanded the guidance they offer while seeking to maintain the flexibility called for by the law.

Today the act remains a source of concerns common to regulators, bankers, and community activists—the paperwork burden, the disproportionate effect on small institutions, and a lack of certainty in the law's application. But it also continues to offer each depository institution wide opportunities for meeting its CRA responsibilities creatively, in a manner that best accommodates the institution and the community it serves.

BACKGROUND

In the mid-1970s, a prevalent view among some members of the Congress was that many financial institutions accepted deposits from households and small businesses in inner cities while lending and investing those deposits primarily elsewhere. They believed that, given this disinvestment, or "redlining," credit needs for urban areas in decline were not being met by the private sector; moreover, the problem was worsening because public resources were becoming increasingly scarce.

In January 1977, the original Senate bill on community reinvestment was introduced. In the hearings that followed, opponents of the legislation voiced serious concerns that the bill threatened to allocate credit to geographic areas, according to the volume of deposits coming from those areas, or to specific types of loans, without regard for credit demand or the merits of loan applications. The law would therefore disrupt the normal flow of capital from areas of excess supply to areas of strong demand and undermine the safety and soundness of depository institutions. Proponents of the bill stated that it was meant to ensure only that lenders did not ignore good borrowing prospects in their communities and that they treated creditworthy borrowers evenhandedly. Senator William A. Proxmire, the bill's sponsor, stressed that it would neither force high-risk lending nor substitute the views of regulators for those of banks. He said that safety and soundness should remain the overriding factor when agencies evaluate applications for corporate expansion; meeting the credit needs of the community was only one of the criteria to consider.

Believing that systematic, affirmative programs would encourage lenders to give priority to credit needs in their home areas, the Congress passed the Community Reinvestment Act, and the President signed it into law on October 12, 1977.[1] The CRA reaffirmed the principle that financial institutions must serve "the convenience and needs" of the communities in which they are chartered to do business by extending credit in these communities. This principle is one that federal law governing deposit insurance, bank charters, and bank mergers had embodied long before the enactment of the CRA. Likewise, the Bank Holding Company Act—passed initially in 1956—requires the Board, in acting on acquisitions by banks and bank holding companies, to evaluate how well an institution meets the convenience and needs of its communities within the limits of safety and soundness. Thus, the mandate of the CRA was, in many respects, already in place.

BASIC PROVISIONS

The CRA is directed primarily at the four federal agencies that supervise the institutions covered by the law—the Board of Governors of the Federal Reserve System (the Board), the Office of the Comptroller of the Currency (OCC), the Federal Deposit Insurance Corporation (FDIC), and the Office of Thrift Supervision (OTS, formerly the Federal Home Loan Bank Board). First, the agencies are to use their supervisory authority to encourage financial institutions to help meet local credit needs in a manner consistent with safe and sound operation. Second, as part of their examinations, the agencies are to assess an institution's record of serving its entire community, including low- and moderate-income neighborhoods. Third, they must take that record into account when they assess an institution's application for approval

---

1. In retrospect, the Congress enacted the CRA with surprising ease. In the Senate, a markup of the original bill was reported out of the Banking Committee and adopted as part of the Housing and Community Development Act of 1977. No companion reinvestment bill was introduced in the House; after minimal floor debate, House members adopted the Senate bill as amended by a conference committee of the two houses.

regarding a deposit facility—a charter, a merger, an acquisition, a branch, an office relocation, or deposit insurance.

The act sets no criteria or guidelines for assessing the performance of an institution. It does not explain how an institution's "community" should be selected, how credit needs are to be determined, how to define low- and moderate-income neighborhoods, or what constitutes satisfactory compliance. With little guidance available from the statute, the agencies held hearings in 1978 to elicit the public's suggestions on how the CRA should be interpreted and implemented. Not surprisingly, views differed. Consumer groups favored specific rules—for example, the application of loan-to-deposit ratios for evaluating CRA performance—whereas industry witnesses voiced concerns about credit allocation and focused on the need for flexible standards.

The joint regulations subsequently adopted by the agencies reflected a set of principles that continues to mark the administration of the CRA: Flexibility is important, agency rules should not allocate credit, and institutions in different communities may approach the CRA in various ways. To deal with the lack of standards in the law, the regulations established twelve factors against which the agencies would assess the performance of institutions (see box).

In assessing an institution's CRA record, the supervisory agency examines for technical compliance with a few specific rules and qualitatively evaluates the institution's performance in serving its entire community. The rules call for an institution to do the following:

• Formulate and adopt a public "CRA statement" that delineates the communities it serves, lists the principal types of credit it offers, and indicates where a person should write to comment on the institution's CRA performance
• Maintain a file of comments from the public about its CRA performance (as of 1990, this "public comment file" also must contain the supervisory agency's most recent assessment of the institution's CRA record)
• Publicly display a notice about the availability of the CRA statement and the public comment file.

The agencies also adopted uniform examination procedures. Like the regulations, the procedures

> **Twelve Performance Factors**
>
> The federal supervisory agencies consider the following factors in assessing an institution's record of performance under the Community Reinvestment Act:
>
> • Activities conducted by the institution to ascertain the credit needs of its community, including the extent of the institution's efforts to communicate with members of its community regarding the credit services being provided by the institution
> • The extent of the institution's marketing and special credit-related programs to make members of the community aware of the credit services offered by the institution
> • The extent of participation by the institution's board of directors in formulating the institution's policies and reviewing its performance with respect to the purposes of the Community Reinvestment Act
> • Any practices intended to discourage applications for types of credit set forth in the institution's CRA statement
> • The geographic distribution of the institution's credit extensions, credit applications, and credit denials
> • Evidence of prohibited discriminatory credit practices or other illegal credit practices
> • The institution's record of opening and closing offices and providing services at offices
> • The institution's participation, including investment, in local community development and redevelopment projects or programs
> • The institution's origination of residential mortgage loans, housing rehabilitation loans, home improvement loans, and small business or small farm loans within its community, or the purchase of such loans originated in the community
> • The institution's participation in government insured, guaranteed, or subsidized loan programs for housing, small businesses, or small farms
> • The institution's ability to meet various community credit needs based on its financial condition and size, legal impediments, local economic conditions, and other factors
> • Other factors that, in the supervisory agency's judgment, reasonably bear upon the extent to which an institution is helping to meet the credit needs of its entire community.

stressed that financial institutions could use various means to learn about, and help meet, the financial needs of the surrounding community. The CRA did not establish hard and fast rules or ratios by which to judge an institution's performance. But an institution could expect negative marks if its pattern of loan applications, extensions, and rejections showed a concentration of credit approvals in high-income neighborhoods that was inappropriate given the institution's delineated service area and the presence of qualified applicants in lower-income areas.

In considering an application for a deposit facility, the supervisory agency assesses the applicant's CRA record—including its CRA rating and any actions taken to improve performance following an examination—as part of its decision to approve or deny the application. In the past, the agencies at times approved an application even though CRA performance was unsatisfactory if the applicant offered substantial commitments for future performance. Today, an institution generally is expected to have a satisfactory CRA program in place and working well before its application can receive approval. A poor CRA performance may, however, be outweighed by other factors, such as the need to merge a weak institution into a strong one, in which case the application may still be approved.

Policy Statements of 1980 and 1989

In December 1979 the Federal Reserve Board issued a policy statement on the CRA to guide state member banks; the Board also forwarded the statement to the Federal Financial Institutions Examination Council (FFIEC) for consideration by the three other supervisory agencies responsible for implementing the CRA. In September 1980 the FFIEC adopted a statement similar to the Board's and covering these principal points:

• Although directed toward meeting community credit needs, the CRA does not impose credit allocation.
• Disparities in loan-to-deposit ratios are not, on their face, evidence of discrimination or poor performance under the CRA.

- In the absence of substantial efforts to ascertain credit needs and publicize credit services, a lack of applications is not an adequate explanation for little or no lending in a particular neighborhood.
- Institutions are expected to offer throughout their communities the types of credit listed on their CRA statements.
- Favorable weight will be given to an institution's concerted effort to tailor and adapt programs and services to the needs of low- and moderate-income neighborhoods in its community.
- Commitments for future action will not be viewed as part of the CRA record of performance, but they may receive weight as an indicator of potential for improvement.
- Communication between applicants and protesting parties is encouraged, but the agencies will not approve or enforce agreements.

In subsequent years the CRA attracted increasing public attention. Reduced federal funding for community and housing programs and charges of discriminatory lending patterns intensified interest in bank performance. Community groups grew in number and experience and became more sophisticated in dealing with information about lending patterns. Challenges to applications multiplied, the handling of CRA protests became a significant aspect of the application process, particularly in major acquisitions by bank holding companies, and the volume and complexity of the CRA issues rose as the number of low CRA ratings grew.

The growing pressure on institutions increased their demands for guidance regarding the adequacy of a CRA record and what to expect in the application process. In April 1989 the agencies released a second CRA policy statement based on their decade of experience in evaluating applications, dealing with protests, and conducting examinations. Given the discomfort caused, on the one hand, by any notion of credit allocation and, on the other, by a perceived lack of detailed direction, the 1989 statement attempted to give more guidance to institutions but not hamstring them with rigid requirements. The statement added specificity about the responsibilities of institutions under the CRA, the manner in which the agencies would assess performance, and some of the elements found in effective programs.

A crucial feature of the 1989 policy statement was its emphasis on an institution's management of CRA performance as part of day-to-day activities. The statement reaffirmed the value of an institution's discretion in developing the products best suited to its expertise and the specific needs of its community. It stressed that the CRA requires an ongoing effort by an institution to ascertain the needs of its entire community, develop products in response, and market them throughout the community.

The statement also dealt with the CRA in the context of protested applications. It stressed that an institution's CRA evaluation rating would receive great weight. It encouraged community groups to bring CRA issues to the attention of banks and regulators without delay rather than to wait until an application was pending. Given the desirability of processing cases in a timely manner, the statement made clear that extensions of comment periods would be the exception, not the rule. The agencies also cautioned institutions to address their CRA responsibilities and to have policies in place and working well before they filed an application, signaling a shift away from approving applications on the strength of promised performance. In general, institutions could not hope to use commitments made in the application process to overcome a seriously deficient record.

Guidelines for CRA Evaluations

In August 1989 the Congress amended the CRA to require public release of examination assessments and change the CRA rating scale, effective July 1, 1990. To define the standards, the FFIEC issued "Guidelines for Disclosure of Written Evaluations and Revised Assessment Rating System" in April 1990. The guidelines detailed performance requirements and information about how examiners would evaluate institutions. They placed emphasis on the need for a managed CRA program: Were procedures in place at the institution to promote community dialogue? How did the institution take its assessment of community needs into account in product design and marketing? If it analyzed its geographic distribution of credit on an ongoing basis, what were the institution's own goals for lending distribution, and had they been met?

Although this approach steered clear of any semblance of credit allocation, it created a different problem by appearing to place undue emphasis on documentation. Widely reported statements from some regulators that "if it isn't documented, it didn't happen" contributed to that belief. So did some efforts of trade associations and CRA consultants, who prepared elaborate check lists of the documentation that institutions should provide to examiners. The requirement that public assessments be factually supported by "facts and data"—a provision added to the law in 1991—brought other requests for recorded activities that the examiners could cite.

In 1992, amid rising concerns about excessive reliance on paperwork, the agencies issued new examiner guidelines. These made clear that examiners should base the evaluation of CRA performance primarily on how well an institution was helping to meet credit needs, not on the amount of documentation it maintained. A lack of documentation was not a sufficient basis for assigning a poor rating if satisfactory performance was otherwise demonstrated or apparent. The agencies also emphasized their expectation that documentation would normally be found in a well-managed program and that it would generally be less formal and less extensive in small and rural institutions.

institutions are serving the credit needs of minority populations in their local communities. The provisions of the CRA focus on issues broader than the financing of low- and moderate-income housing, but community activists have always emphasized mortgage lending, in large part because of the combination of unmet needs in low-income areas and the ready availability of mortgage data.[2] As amended in 1989, HMDA calls for lenders to record the race, sex, and income of applicants for all mortgages and home improvement loans, including loans denied and withdrawn; lenders previously reported only loans that they originated or purchased.[3] For both 1990 and 1991, the HMDA data have shown the rate of loan denials to be generally higher for minority and Hispanic loan applicants than for Asian and white applicants. The data also show that the rate of such denials generally increases in neighborhoods as the percentage of nonwhite residents increases.[4]

Other factors have contributed to an intensified focus on the CRA. The financial support of federal programs for low- and moderate-income housing, for example, has dropped significantly over the past decade. In constant dollars, the total budget for low-income housing programs was reduced by more than half between 1980 and 1991, and federal support for rental housing also contracted sharply. These cutbacks have placed yet greater pressure on

PUBLIC FOCUS ON THE CRA

In recent years, interest in CRA activities has increased dramatically, especially since the CRA evaluations became publicly available. Public disclosure in some respects has further empowered community groups and individuals concerned about financial institutions' lending practices. Application activities, marking a movement toward interstate banking and the industry's restructuring, have provided a ready forum in which to raise CRA issues. Those interested in the CRA, moreover, now include not just the traditional groups of community activists but also local government officials, unions, churches, the media, and others.

Coverage of mortgage lending issues by news organizations, particularly of the data produced under the Home Mortgage Disclosure Act (HMDA), has fueled the debate over how well

---

2. Bills to expand HMDA to other types of credit, such as small business loans and personal loans, have been introduced over the years. For example, in 1992 Representative Maxine Waters of California introduced a bill to expand the types of loans for which applicant characteristics are collected under HMDA and to expand the analysis required to evaluate an institution's CRA performance (Community Credit Improvement Act of 1992, H.R. 6206 § 101, 102 Cong. 2 Sess., 1992).

3. To maximize use of the expanded data, the Federal Reserve has developed a system that facilitates access and provides analyses of the data by demographic characteristics, such as race, gender, and income levels, and by geographic boundaries. Examiners are able to compare the HMDA data for a single reporting lender with the HMDA data for others within a defined geographic market. They also can compare the income levels and race of applicants with characteristics of the census tracts where the properties that secure the loans are located.

4. Glenn B. Canner and Dolores S. Smith, "Home Mortgage Disclosure Act: Expanded Data on Residential Lending," *Federal Reserve Bulletin*, vol. 77 (November 1991), pp. 859–84; and Canner and Smith, "Expanded HMDA Data on Residential Lending: One Year Later," *Federal Reserve Bulletin*, vol. 78 (November 1992), pp. 801–24.

financial institutions to support local efforts to create housing.[5]

Some state governments require commitments to community reinvestment before out-of-state institutions can operate in their localities. They premise entry on a standard of net new benefits to the state, such as increased in-state lending and investments. To encourage CRA-related programs, some municipalities, too, condition their placement of deposits upon the institution's making specific types of loans. In Chicago, for example, institutions must file reports on their residential and commercial lending in the Chicago metropolitan area before they can qualify for the city's deposits. Even private organizations may evaluate potential depositories using CRA factors; in 1991, the American Bar Association resolved to place its accounts whenever possible in financial institutions that have shown outstanding or satisfactory performance in helping to meet the credit needs of their communities, including low- and moderate-income neighborhoods.

All this interest has turned the public and congressional spotlight on the agencies' process for examining the CRA performance of institutions and encouraging economic development efforts.

EXAMINATIONS

The CRA relies primarily on the examination process to ensure that depository institutions meet the credit needs of their local communities. The federal agencies have virtually identical CRA regulations, and they work together to promote uniform measures of performance among depository institutions and consistent results within and among agencies.

A major change for the CRA examination process occurred with passage of the Financial Institutions Reform, Recovery and Enforcement Act of 1989 (FIRREA). FIRREA amended the CRA to give the public access to examination assessments and CRA ratings prepared by federal regulators. The disclosure mandated by FIRREA had implications for depository institutions and examiners: Institutions with a negative CRA assessment now had to face the public display of the rating; and examiners preparing CRA reports were under much greater pressure to be precise and to be able to substantiate their findings.

The agencies' written evaluations have two sections: public and confidential. The public section discloses the examiner's conclusions, using the assessment factors developed jointly by the four supervisory agencies, and supporting facts; it gives a rating and explains the basis for it. The amended CRA mandates four possible choices ("outstanding," "satisfactory," "needs to improve," and "substantial noncompliance") from which agencies are to select in assessing the record of depository institutions. The confidential portion includes references to customers, employees, or other members of the community who provided information to the examiner and comments of a supervisory nature that the agencies believe ought not be public.

To implement these rules and promote uniformity in evaluations, the FFIEC published interagency guidelines and a rating system. The guidelines group the regulation's twelve assessment factors into five performance categories:

- What the institution does to ascertain community needs
- How the institution markets products and what types of credit are offered and actually extended
- Where the institution makes loans and where it has placed offices or closed them
- Whether evidence of discrimination or other illegal credit practices exists
- To what extent the institution participates in community development.

The guidelines provide examiners and institutions with sample profiles of CRA records of performance; these profiles correlate the quality and quantity of certain actions and efforts to the ratings for each assessment factor.

The public can influence an agency's evaluation of an institution's CRA record. Examiners review

---

5. For data on HUD's budget for low-income housing, see Cushing N. Dolbeare, "At a Snail's Pace, FY 1993: A Source Book on the Proposed 1993 Budget and How it Compares to Prior Years" (Washington: Low Income Housing Information Service, 1992). See also, Marion A. Cowell, Jr., and Monty D. Hagler, "The Community Reinvestment Act in the Decade of Bank Consolidation," *Wake Forest Law Review,* vol. 27 (1992), p. 90, note 64.

For data on the participation of the Federal Housing Administration in insuring mortgages on multifamily residential projects, see *Report on the Status of the Community Reinvestment Act,* before the Subcommittee on Housing and Urban Affairs of the Senate Committee on Banking, Housing and Urban Affairs, 102 Cong. 2 Sess., p. 21 (Government Printing Office, 1992).

CRA comments from persons in the community placed in the institution's public comment file, and may contact such persons directly. The examiners also seek out local officials, community groups, and others knowledgeable about local credit needs so that they can make an informed judgment about those needs and the institution's responsiveness.

The Federal Reserve uses consumer compliance examinations—as distinct from the commercial examinations for safety and soundness—to assess the CRA records of state member banks and their compliance with fair lending and other consumer statutes. These consumer examinations are conducted, in general, every eighteen months. Banks with a demonstrated need for greater oversight are examined more often; the lowest CRA rating of "substantial noncompliance" can bring a reexamination within six months. Banks with exemplary records may be examined every twenty-four months. The frequency with which other regulators examine their respective institutions may differ somewhat from the Federal Reserve schedule.

The CRA examinations take into account the size, location, and organizational structure of the individual institutions and the nature and needs of the communities they serve. Size and financial strength will affect the expected scope of an institution's efforts to identify and respond to credit needs. For example, examiners would generally expect large institutions to undertake specialized CRA-related activities to a greater extent, given their relative resources and expertise. Institutions that are part of a multibank holding company may be able to draw on the resources of the parent and affiliates.

Expectations also vary about how banks of various sizes demonstrate CRA performance in different settings. For example, CRA recordkeeping and documentation will generally be less formal and extensive in small and rural banks than in large urban institutions. This also holds true for the extent and sophistication of analyses of lending patterns for the CRA and other purposes.

Consistency and Level of Ratings

The agencies have worked to promote uniformity in CRA enforcement—using a common rating scheme, conducting interagency examiner training, adopting jointly developed examination standards and guidelines, and even reviewing examination reports across agencies to identify any lack of comparability in approach. Within the Federal Reserve, staff members at the Board participate regularly in CRA examinations of state member banks in connection with reviews of each Reserve Bank and sample reports from each Reserve Bank District to test for the consistent application of the Board's examination policy.

Nonetheless, institutions and the public alike express concern that, among the regulatory agencies and between different regions, examiners may apply differing standards when they assign ratings for CRA performance. Given the subjective nature of the CRA and the thousands of institutions examined—each with its own business goals and strengths, in communities with different needs and characteristics—some unevenness is probably unavoidable. Even though consistency remains elusive, it is an important goal.

Critics of the agencies' enforcement of the CRA also complain about the current ratings results, which in the aggregate are roughly comparable across agencies (table 1). About 10 percent of examined institutions receive an "outstanding" rating, and another 70 percent to 80 percent receive a "satisfactory." Some community groups see a contradiction between these results and public data indicating that even highly rated institutions have significant racial disparities in their home mortgage lending.

There probably is good reason for the current distribution of CRA ratings. All banks and thrift institutions pledge to meet the "convenience and needs" of their communities when they are chartered; this was so long before the CRA came on the scene. The fact that regulators have been assessing their CRA performance since 1978 also could be expected to have a positive effect. In addition, the "satisfactory" category—into which the vast majority of institutions fall—is quite broad and includes some with good performance and some with marginal but still satisfactory records. Adding a fifth rating has been suggested; doing so might permit a finer distinction in rating activities at the high or low end of a "satisfactory" rating and help produce a wider array of ratings.

The reliability of the rating system takes on special importance in light of legislation proposed

1. Distribution of CRA ratings, by supervisory agency and asset size of institution, January 1–September 30, 1992
Number except as noted

Asset size of institution (dollars)	Federal Deposit Insurance Corporation				Federal Reserve System				Office of the Comptroller of the Currency				Office of Thrift Supervision				All agencies (percent)			
	O	S	N	SN	O	S	N	SN	O	S	N	SN	O	S	N	SN	O	S	N	SN
Less than 100 million	149	969	38	4	37	245	24	4	23	256	65	2	16	248	71	4	10	80	9	1
100–250 million	30	84	3	0	15	37	4	0	21	94	15	0	25	118	28	1	19	70	11	0
250–500 million	9	16	1	0	3	15	1	0	5	29	1	1	8	46	11	0	17	73	10	1
500 million–1 billion	3	4	0	0	3	8	1	0	6	19	1	1	5	27	1	0	22	73	4	1
1–10 billion	2	4	0	0	3	10	0	0	8	49	4	0	9	33	7	0	17	74	9	0
More than 10 billion	0	0	0	0	0	4	0	0	8	9	0	0	2	1	0	0	42	58	0	0
All	193	1,077	42	4	61	319	30	4	71	456	86	4	65	473	118	5	13	77	9	1

O Outstanding.   S Satisfactory.   N Needs to improve.   SN Substantial noncompliance.

in recent years to reward institutions for good CRA ratings. Institutions that have a "satisfactory" or "outstanding" CRA rating—and meet other statutory criteria—could be eligible for expedited approval procedures for opening new branches or could self-certify their compliance with the CRA and avoid routine examination. They could establish branches across state lines, or engage in new expanded powers, or enjoy a "safe harbor" from protests.

Given the current rating distribution, the tying of legislative rewards to CRA ratings does raise certain concerns, however. If the standard for any reward were set at a rating of "satisfactory" or better, almost all institutions would qualify; yet limiting the rewards to the "outstanding" category could be overly restrictive.

Ratings Anomalies

The CRA rating system—one rating per depository institution—may affect similar institutions differently depending on their corporate structure. A bank holding company with ten subsidiary banks will have ten separate CRA ratings because each bank is examined and assigned a rating. A poor rating for even one bank, depending on its size, may cause problems for the holding company. Yet a bank holding company of similar size, but structured as a single bank with multiple branches, will have a single CRA rating, and deficiencies in a few branches might have no major effect on that rating.

If legislation for interstate branching is enacted, the concept of a single CRA rating for a multistate, multibranch depository institution becomes more troublesome. Would the agency simultaneously examine branches in each state for compliance with the CRA? If examinations were not contemporaneous, how would a "moving" rating be determined? One answer would be to change the nature of the focus and of the examination itself from the bank to the areas that it serves. Some legislative proposals, for example, call for separate evaluations for each metropolitan area in which an institution maintains a branch, or separate evaluations for branches in each state, all to be factored into a single rating or used to assign separate ratings for each major locality.

APPLICATIONS

The CRA offers a very big carrot—or stick—for encouraging depository institutions to meet their communities' credit needs. Agencies consider an institution's record when evaluating an application to start a new facility, open or relocate a branch, or merge, consolidate with, or acquire another institution. Thus, depository institutions and holding companies wanting to expand banking operations must assess their CRA performance, as well as financial, managerial, and competitive factors, when gauging their chances for approval.

Because the 1989 policy statement gives guidelines for evaluating the CRA aspects of applications, a common thread runs through the agencies' evaluation procedures, although timing and other processing rules may differ. In the case of the Federal Reserve, Federal Reserve Banks decide most applications under authority delegated by the Board. Often, a prospective applicant may discuss its proposed application with Reserve Bank officials in advance of its submission. Once an application is filed, the depository institution publishes notices in local newspapers and the Federal Reserve publishes a notice in the *Federal Register*. The Board's public comment period is thirty days for most applications, but because the notices in the newspaper and in the *Federal Register* generally are not published concurrently, the public usually has a longer period in which to comment.

Protests of Applications

Protests of applications are received from many sources and on many grounds. Protests from the insurance industry have commonly been made, for example, when bank holding companies seek to engage in insurance activities, on the ground that doing so is unlawful. Disgruntled shareholders may challenge the adequacy of the price offered for shares. Other protestants may raise antitrust issues. Protests of applications are therefore neither new nor restricted to CRA matters. Nonetheless, the linkage between the approval of an application and the evaluation of CRA performance raises the political and economic stakes of the application process both for community groups and for applicants.

The restructuring of the financial industry has involved high-profile expansion moves, and community groups have used protests aggressively to apply leverage on applicants. In private negotiations, protestants may threaten to create regulatory delays—and perhaps impediments to approval—and applicants often complain of "unreasonable demands" for lending commitments, financial contributions, and other concessions. At times, the applicants themselves may want to negotiate, rather than stand on their record.

Few applications filed with the Federal Reserve are protested on CRA grounds—between 1 percent and 2 percent since 1988. If a protest is received, the Federal Reserve stands ready to facilitate private meetings between the applicant and the protestant. These meetings are not required. Their purpose is to collect information and find areas of agreement or misunderstanding, not to force negotiated settlements. Neither the Federal Reserve nor the other agencies will defer action pending negotiation between the parties. Nor will the agencies enforce agreements that may be reached between an institution and a protestant; the agencies' CRA enforcement extends only to commitments made by applicants directly to the agencies.

Agencies may hold public meetings to obtain information not available otherwise or to expedite the application process. For example, the Board in the past two years held public meetings and received testimony from numerous witnesses on the application by Mitsui Taiyo Kobe Bank, Limited, to convert Taiyo Kobe Bank and Trust Company from a nonbank trust company into a bank; on the application by NCNB Corporation to acquire C&S/Sovran Corporation; and on the application by BankAmerica Corporation to acquire Security Pacific Corporation.

The Board is required to consider CRA performance in all applications to acquire or expand a depository institution. Not all applications that raise CRA issues for the agencies involve protests. At the Federal Reserve in the past three years, 63 percent of applications with CRA issues were subjected to an intensive analysis, not because of a protest but because of deficiencies brought to light during the examination process.

In holding company cases, CRA evaluations may especially complicate the application process because of the likely involvement of several agencies. Outdated or incomplete CRA examinations can cause delays. If a protest is filed, the agencies will evaluate the merits and investigate allegations. If a public meeting is held, the volume of information to be considered can be formidable. In BankAmerica's application to acquire Security Pacific, for example, the Board received almost 350 comments and heard the testimony of about 175 witnesses in public hearings held in four cities.[6]

In a contested application, the ability to request and obtain information to conduct an evaluation can be slowed by procedural rules governing communication that includes some parties to the dispute but not others. Once an application is protested, the Federal Reserve generally must notify all parties before discussing issues raised in the protest with any one of them. The agency may communicate with the parties individually about purely procedural matters or matters unrelated to the protest, but isolating issues that are not related in some substantive way to the protest is often difficult. Thus, whereas ordinarily the information needed to complete an application record might readily be obtained from an institution, the process in a contested application is more formal and time-consuming.

In dealings between applicants and protestants, the agencies are sometimes caught in the middle. Their responsibility is to evaluate fairly the entire record on an application, including the issues raised by protestants. Throughout the application process, they attempt to balance the need for a thorough review of the statutory factors with the necessity for an orderly process and a timely decision. In the case of the Federal Reserve, a substantive written protest has the potential to extend the processing period somewhat. In general, however, the worry about delay is exaggerated. Significant delay as the result of a CRA protest or a rating issue is the exception, not, as commonly assumed, the rule. For example, of the cases acted on by the System in 1992 that involved CRA issues, only about 9.5 percent took longer to process than 60 days—the Board's internal deadline.[7]

Commitments

Since 1989 the supervisory agencies have viewed commitments for future action as largely inapplicable to an assessment of the applicant's CRA performance. In February 1989 the Board denied on CRA grounds an application from Continental Bank Corporation and Continental Illinois Bancorp, Inc., to acquire an Arizona bank despite commitments from Continental to improve its CRA performance in specific ways. The Board stated that such commitments could be taken into account only "when there has been a basic level of compliance on which the commitments can be evaluated."[8] In Continental's case, the inadequacy of past CRA performance made it inappropriate to consider such commitments.

More recently, the Board denied an application from Gore–Bronson Bancorp, Inc., to acquire a Chicago bank despite Gore–Bronson's commitment to address CRA deficiencies at two subsidiary banks. The CRA record had been less than satisfactory for two examination cycles for one bank, and for the other bank the CRA record had actually deteriorated under Gore–Bronson's ownership.[9] And in February 1993 the Board denied the application of Farmers & Merchants Bank of Long Beach to establish another branch and make additional investments in bank premises. The denial was based on the bank's prolonged compliance problems in the consumer lending area (which had led to a cease-and-desist order) and a deficient CRA program. Although the bank had begun taking corrective measures during the application process, the Board was unconvinced that the bank's compliance and CRA programs were viable and successful.[10]

Still, the Board may deem commitments appropriate when the proposed acquisition involves a troubled institution whose loss would be a detriment to the convenience and needs of its community. For example, the Board approved the application of First Union Corporation, Charlotte, North Carolina, and First Union Corporation of Florida, Jacksonville, Florida, to acquire Florida National Banks of Florida, Inc., a financially weak institution. The CRA performance of First Union's subsidiary banks showed problems in certain specific areas; but under section 3 of the BHC Act, the

---

6. "Legal Developments," *Federal Reserve Bulletin*, vol. 78 (May 1992), BankAmerica Corporation, pp. 338–69.

7. Some of the cases may have involved proposals that required the applicant to file more than one application.

8. "Legal Developments," *Federal Reserve Bulletin*, vol. 75 (April 1989), Continental Bank Corporation and Continental Illinois Bancorp, Inc., p. 305.

9. "Legal Developments," *Federal Reserve Bulletin*, vol. 78 (October 1992), Gore–Bronson Bancorp, Inc., pp. 784–86.

10. "Legal Developments," *Federal Reserve Bulletin* (this issue), Farmers & Merchants Bank of Long Beach, p. 365.

Board also must consider the convenience and needs of the communities the applicant will serve. The Board reasoned that maintaining services to Florida National's customers—including those in low- to moderate-income neighborhoods—was an overriding factor; the Board also noted that First Union recently had taken significant steps to improve its CRA performance.[11]

The Federal Reserve Board has denied few applications on CRA grounds, but it denies relatively few applications generally. In 1992, only six applications were turned down, one of them because of CRA deficiencies. This record does not, however, fully reflect the influence that the CRA has had. Institutions with poor CRA records often do not file an application with their supervisory agency. Others take concrete steps to address weaknesses in their CRA performance before filing an application. Still other applications are withdrawn if applicants anticipate an adverse finding after the agency's preliminary review.

What happens when some subsidiaries of a bank holding company have less than satisfactory records and the other subsidiaries have adequate, or better, records? In the application of SunTrust Banks, Inc., to acquire shares of Peoples Bank of Lakeland, substantially all of SunTrust's subsidiary banks had ratings that were satisfactory or better. The four subsidiaries identified as having CRA problems represented less than 10 percent of SunTrust's assets, and the problems did not indicate either chronic institutional or CRA deficiencies. The Board approved the application, noting that whenever problems were identified in the CRA performance of its banks, SunTrust had taken immediate steps to correct them and had done so in the case of these four institutions. The Board applied the principle that weight can be given to CRA commitments in addressing specific problems when the institution has an otherwise satisfactory CRA record.[12]

In the case of First Interstate BancSystem of Montana, on the other hand, the Board denied an application for a corporate reorganization based on the CRA record of a quite small banking subsidiary. The deficiencies in that case were serious and substantive; they had continued through successive examinations, and steps taken over a significant period of time had been insufficient to cure the problems.[13]

Over the years, questions have been raised about the bearing of the CRA on various kinds of applications. The obligation to help meet the credit needs of local communities rests with insured depository institutions and their deposit facilities. Thus, the CRA does not apply to applications by bank holding companies to acquire most nonbanking entities under section 4(c)(8) of the BHC Act. The Board had determined, however, that the terms and purposes of the CRA and the BHC Act indicate that the Board has to consider CRA performance in a section 4(c)(8) application by a bank holding company to acquire a savings association. As a depository institution, a savings association is subject to the CRA, and consequently its acquisition as a deposit facility is covered by the CRA.[14]

COMMUNITY AFFAIRS PROGRAM

The CRA mandates that the regulators encourage institutions to help meet local credit needs. In furtherance of this mandate, the Board established a community affairs program more than a decade ago. The community affairs staff of each Reserve Bank routinely assists institutions with information about community development strategies and techniques and other reinvestment issues. They work with financial institutions, banking associations, government, businesses, and community groups to create programs for community development lending that help finance affordable housing, small and

---

11. "Legal Developments," *Federal Reserve Bulletin*, vol. 76 (February 1990), First Union Corporation, p. 88.

12. "Legal Developments," *Federal Reserve Bulletin*, vol. 76 (July 1990), SunTrust Banks, Inc., pp. 542–45.

13. "Legal Developments," *Federal Reserve Bulletin*, vol. 77 (December 1991), First Interstate BancSystem of Montana, Inc., pp. 1007–10.

14. Similarly, regulators consider CRA performance when a bank holding company acquires the assets and liabilities of a thrift institution in a merger that is subject to the so-called Oakar amendment to the Federal Deposit Insurance Act. See "Legal Developments," *Federal Reserve Bulletin*, vol. 79 (February 1993), letter, Jennifer J. Johnson, Associate Secretary of the Board of Governors of the Federal Reserve System, to John H. Huffstutler, Assistant General Counsel, BankAmerica Corporation, pp. 148–52. Conversely, the Board has determined that the CRA does not apply to applications under the Change of Bank Control Act.

minority business, and other community revitalization projects.

Reserve Banks help facilitate the broad-based offering of credit through conferences for bankers on topics such as barriers faced by minority borrowers, steps to ensure that credit is offered on an equitable basis, ways of participating in economic development programs, and credit issues affecting Native Americans. Reserve Banks also provide technical assistance, helping institutions to create community development corporations (CDCs) and multibank lending consortiums and, in the case of institutions with unsatisfactory CRA ratings, helping them to strengthen their CRA program. Reserve Banks publish descriptions of CDCs, limited partnerships, and other community development projects in which bank holding companies have been allowed to invest. They prepare profiles that identify key community and economic development needs and describe resource organizations in major communities.

For example, the Federal Reserve Banks of San Francisco and Philadelphia have produced community profiles used by local financial institutions to address specific issues and projects. The Federal Reserve Bank of Boston has developed a training curriculum on community-development finance for bankers. Reserve Banks also publish a variety of other brochures and manuals that assist lenders in community development activities. Their community affairs newsletters have a combined circulation of more than 40,000.

Other federal banking agencies also have community affairs programs. The OCC's Community Development Division, for instance, oversees CDC and investment programs and approves applications by national banks to invest in CDCs in accordance with the National Bank Act and its interpretations. The FDIC has a community affairs program that, like the Federal Reserve's, has a regional presence.

INDUSTRY INITIATIVES

The CRA has stimulated an abundance of activity by financial institutions and others. For example, in late 1992 the American Bankers Association established a Center for Community Development whose primary mission is to provide information and technical assistance to its members. The center has already published an educational guide, and in 1993 it expects to sponsor workshops and publish a compendium of contacts at community lending agencies and organizations. The center is also involved in credit counseling outreach, offering camera-ready copies of a five-part series of brochures on such issues as home buying and credit rights for member banks to publish and distribute in their communities.

Two recent surveys illustrate the banking industry's efforts. In a survey of banks, thrifts, and holding companies, the Consumer Bankers Association found that roughly 90 percent of its respondents have programs that target purchase-money lending for low- to moderate-income housing. Nearly 95 percent of the programs include mortgage products with flexible requirements for downpayment, loan-to-value ratios, and debt-to-income ratios designed to make home financing more available and affordable.[15] And in late 1992, the OCC announced the results of a survey to which nearly 55 percent of all national banks responded. A majority of the respondents engaged in community development lending and financed low- to moderate-income housing, small businesses, and small farms. The type of lending tended to differ according to their asset size. For instance, among the largest banks (assets of more than $1 billion), 86 percent focused on low- to moderate-income housing, whereas among the smallest banks (assets of less than $100 million), 72 percent reported making small-farm loans.

Depository institutions have access to various forms of assistance to support their CRA activities. For example, the Federal Home Loan Bank System offers two loan programs to its membership of savings banks, savings and loan associations, and banks. It advances funds or subsidizes below-market-rate loans originated for low- to moderate-income families and for businesses in low- to moderate-income neighborhoods. Its Community Investment Program provides home lending funds to projects aimed at individuals with incomes of up to 115 percent of an area's median income; an Affordable Housing Program provides home lend-

---

15. Consumer Bankers Association, *Affordable Mortgage Survey: A Survey of Bank Mortgage Programs as of June 30, 1992* (Washington: CBA, 1992), pp. 2, 4.

ing funds to support housing for people with incomes of 80 percent of an area's median income and rental housing funds where at least 20 percent of the units are occupied by very low income tenants.[16]

Increasingly, attention has turned to the role of the secondary markets in funding loans to low- to moderate-income applicants or in low- to moderate-income neighborhoods. Secondary markets provide liquidity to lenders by purchasing the loans that lenders originate, enabling them to meet additional credit needs. For example, more than half of the "affordable mortgages" reported by the respondents to the Consumer Bankers' survey are sold to the secondary market.

The Federal National Mortgage Association (Fannie Mae) and the Federal Home Loan Mortgage Corporation (Freddie Mac) have both announced initiatives in recent years to purchase loans with underwriting guidelines or payment terms that do not meet their more traditional loan purchase programs. The Congress has spurred these corporations to support low- and moderate-income loans by setting specific volume goals over a two-year period beginning with 1993. For example, for all the loans they purchase, 30 percent of the units financed must be for low- to moderate-income borrowers, 30 percent must be located in central urban areas, and $3.5 billion ($1.5 billion for Freddie Mac, $2 billion for Fannie Mae) must finance loans to low-income and very low income home buyers.[17]

OTHER ISSUES

Throughout its fifteen-year history, the CRA's seemingly simple but vague and imprecise charge has caused much consternation. The act, after all, is not an arcane banking matter of interest only to specialists in finance; in practice, it touches on social issues of great sensitivity and complexity, including issues of race and economic class, and its day-to-day influence on covered institutions has been significant. As a result, questions about the law's administration, including potential conflict with safety and soundness, continue to be raised—as do numerous proposals for better definitions of standards, easing of the regulatory burden, and incentives for superior performance.

Concern with Safety and Soundness

The mandate of the CRA, that institutions are to help meet community credit needs in a manner consistent with safety and soundness, requires lending choices in which some lenders believe they are "damned if they do and damned if they don't." Loans in low- to moderate-income neighborhoods, whether residential or commercial, often require underwriting standards or terms that differ from an institution's more traditional products and from an agency's loan classification standards.

Anecdotal evidence suggests that, by and large, the losses on lending that addresses CRA responsibilities is not significantly different from the losses on other product lines. But lenders express frustration that federal financial regulatory agencies may criticize the very loans the agencies are otherwise encouraging. They argue that the nontraditional loans may satisfy examiners monitoring CRA compliance, but the loans could well be downgraded internally by the bank's loan committee or by commercial examiners unfamiliar with special features—such as "equity substitutes" in the form of government guarantees—that may in fact make them very sound loans.

The agencies have repeatedly emphasized that the CRA does not contemplate the erosion of safety and soundness. To reduce the perception that commercial and CRA examiners work at cross purposes, for example, the Federal Reserve provides training to commercial examiners on the CRA. Nevertheless, there is a widespread impression that institutions are being "whipsawed," and the agencies are having to take special care not to send mixed messages.

Lack of Certainty

Rules that are more precise would, of course, ease the task of examiners, institutions, and the public in

---

16. Federal Home Loan Bank Act, 12 U.S.C. § 1430(i),(j) (Supp. III 1992).

17. Housing and Community Development Act of 1992, P.L. 102–550, 106 Stat. 3672, §§ 1332–34 (1992).

determining the adequacy of CRA performance. Many lenders express frustration at the business of translating the broad mission of the CRA into specific actions. To be sure, most lenders would oppose overt credit allocation and would resist being told what products to offer, or in what volume, or on what terms, or to whom. But many want to know, from the start, exactly what the "right" activities might be for CRA performance and what it takes to get an "outstanding" CRA rating. Examiners who judge performance, and community groups who evaluate institutions, likewise would be more comfortable with greater certainty.

The problem lies in preserving flexibility and providing precision at the same time. The CRA can be criticized for its ambiguities, but that same "flaw" allows for variations by institutions in meeting their responsibilities under the law. Over the years, the regulators have emphasized their position that no single community reinvestment program is perfect for every institution. Financial institutions can design CRA programs that fit their own business orientation and the special needs of their communities. Still, the agencies have offered extensive guidance on the CRA—policy statements, examination procedures, assessment factors considered in evaluations, elements of successful CRA programs, and advice through community affairs programs. Throughout, they have emphasized flexibility, seeking to give detailed guidance without imposing specific mandates.

Initially the industry wanted flexible CRA rules out of concern about regulatory credit allocation. The industry argued that neither the law nor the regulations should set minimums or mandate the types of loans an institution must offer. Increasingly, however, depository institutions and trade groups have asked for more precise rules. Recent interest in community development banks has even brought suggestions that institutions be allowed to meet their CRA obligations by specified investments in such institutions.

The State of New York, which has a community reinvestment law much like the federal law, is considering a proposal that would identify specific activities for which depository institutions covered by the state's statute could earn CRA "credit." The system would require institutions to establish investment targets for the CRA, measure these investments in relation to the institution's assets, and tie CRA ratings to minimum specified amounts of such investments.[18]

Moving toward a cafeteria-style menu of value-weighted, "approved" CRA activities—in a manner similar to what New York has proposed—has some appeal in that it would offer certainty. Potentially it also could increase desirable CRA-related activities in local communities. At the same time, creating such a list would inevitably transfer decisionmaking in some measure from an institution to the government. As it stands, the CRA's broad standard allows each depository institution to be creative in meeting credit needs within its lending community. The incentive to offer innovative service may be lost if institutions find it necessary to choose between engaging in services they know will earn them CRA credit and taking a chance on something that does not quite fit into a preapproved pigeonhole. Also, the CRA is meant to encourage institutions to meet the credit needs of their entire community. Communities could be left with unmet credit needs if institutions were able to fulfill their total CRA responsibilities by a single CRA-related action, such as a passive investment in one community development organization in a sole low- to moderate-income neighborhood.

Paperwork Burden

Among lenders, and even community representatives, one major source of dissatisfaction with the CRA is the paperwork that they believe the agencies require to demonstrate an institution's record of performance. Small institutions, in particular, complain that the documentation provided to agency examiners is costly and unnecessary. Recent studies by trade groups among banks of all sizes point to the CRA as imposing substantial compliance costs. In a June 1992 study by the American Bankers Association on the sources of regulatory burden, the CRA topped the list as the most significant. A study by the Independent Bankers Association of America estimated that compli-

---

18. The state's community reinvestment law is in N.Y. Banking Law § 28-b (McKinney 1990). The proposal for earning CRA credits is in New York State Banking Department, "Proposed Comprehensive Policy Statement Relating to the New York State Community Reinvestment Act: Request for Public Comment" (September 9, 1992).

ance with the CRA cost about $1 billion annually out of a total $3 billion for selected laws.

Some community groups, too, criticize regulators for elevating form over substance. More attention is focused on documenting community outreach, they say, than on whether an institution actually is making loans. While they may have a common complaint with some in the industry, however, their suggested correction for the problem is likely to be more mandated lending—a result most in the industry would oppose.

The technical "hard paper" burden of the CRA is in fact rather small: a CRA statement listing the types of loans the institution is willing to make; a map showing the boundaries of the local communities it serves; evidence (usually a notation in the minutes) that the board of directors has reviewed the statement at least annually; a lobby notice describing how the public can comment on the institution's CRA performance; and a file with its CRA statement, agency assessment, and public comments available for inspection. All are modest requirements, but they do not, of course, reflect the true extent of the documentation actually needed. Other paperwork is unavoidable. The statute calls for the public CRA assessments to contain "facts and data" to support the examiner's conclusions, and as a practical matter most of these "facts and data" can come only from the institution.

One of the twelve assessment factors for CRA performance requires the examiner to evaluate the geographic distribution of the institution's credit extensions, applications, and credit denials. After considerable debate on this point, the FFIEC in December 1991 issued a policy that strongly encourages institutions to analyze the geographic distribution of their major product lines as part of their CRA planning process. Institutions also are encouraged to collect lending data and correlate them with the relevant demographic facts relating to the institution's community. The board of directors and senior management are expected to review the analyses in setting and evaluating the institution's CRA program. Understandably, this geographic tracking also has contributed to complaints about CRA paperwork.

In June 1992 the FFIEC issued examination procedures to address the outcry about unnecessary paperwork burden. The revised procedures emphasize that examiners should focus on performance in meeting credit needs, not on process, and that an institution's size has a bearing on how formal the proof of performance needs to be. Regarding geographic analysis, the FFIEC stated that the extent and sophistication of analyses expected by the agencies will depend on the size and location of the institution. What may be required for a large institution to track its loans, for instance, is not required for a small institution, which could be served by a more informal system.

Any well-conceived, ongoing CRA process will involve normal business documentation. To recognize the credit needs in their communities, as well as to know whether they are meeting those needs, institutions must have a process in place that provides relevant information. This is certainly the case for most large institutions, especially those with widespread branch networks. Smaller institutions, too, need to demonstrate performance, but their documentation may not have to be as sophisticated or extensive.

Despite agency efforts to contain the problem of CRA paperwork, it remains troubling. Through the FFIEC, the federal regulators continue to evaluate the paperwork issue as well as other CRA enforcement matters to see whether clarification or additional change is warranted.

Exempting Small Institutions

The agencies generally have tried to be sensitive to the complaints of small institutions that they are disproportionately affected by the CRA. The institutions say they must serve the needs of their entire community just to exist as viable businesses, and that, therefore, CRA requirements are unnecessary for them. Exemptions for small institutions are not a novel concept. For example, a depository institution's size determines whether it is covered by HMDA and, if it is covered, the data that it must report.

Community groups do not believe that small institutions necessarily meet the credit needs of their communities as a matter of course, and they point to the low loan-to-deposit ratios of some small banks.[19] They say small institutions need to

---
19. FFIEC, *Study on Regulatory Burden* (Washington: FFIEC, 1992), Appendix A, p. 2.

do more, not less, to comply with the CRA, and therefore they strongly oppose proposals for a small-institution exemption and for self-certification.

Apparently, the size of an institution is not a good indicator of CRA performance. Most institutions in all asset-size categories received "outstanding" or "satisfactory" ratings in examinations in the first three quarters of 1992 (table 1).

Some members of the Congress have taken up the proposal to exempt small institutions from the CRA. One bill would exempt an institution from the CRA if it is in a small town, has assets (aggregated with the assets of its holding company) of $75 million or less, and can show that its loans come to 50 percent or more of deposits. Such a proposal would exempt about one-fourth of the 12,000 institutions supervised by the Federal Reserve, the FDIC, and the OCC, but it would maintain CRA coverage of almost all banking assets. Of the total group's $3.6 trillion in assets, the banks that would be exempted account for about 3 percent, or $107 billion.

Another proposal would allow institutions with total assets of $250 million or less to certify their compliance with the CRA—provided, among other things, that they have a "satisfactory" or higher rating and remain in compliance with the Equal Credit Opportunity Act. Self-certification would take the place of agency examinations. The regulators would be required to examine an institution only in response to an allegation that it was not meeting the credit needs of its entire community. If banks with assets of up to $250 million were exempted from the CRA, as many as 87 percent of all financial institutions in the country could be excluded. But again, in terms of total dollars of community lending and investments, the likely effect of the exemption would not be major. Thus, such an exemption might respond to much of the concern about paperwork without undermining the force of the CRA.

Lack of Incentives

Financial institutions complain about the lack of incentives for outstanding performance, noting that even a superior CRA rating offers no protection from a protest. Ideally, of course, good performance should bring its own rewards—new business and enhanced public relations. But after assessing what it might cost to be rated outstanding, some institutions believe the payoff is not worth the extra effort under current law.

Various ideas have been proposed for adding statutory "carrots" to the CRA to increase the incentives, including a "safe harbor." A safe harbor might limit formal protests against applications, for instance, except when the evidence of a CRA performance problem is substantial and specific.

The state of New York is taking public comment on establishing a safe harbor in the application process. A bank with an outstanding rating on its three most recent CRA examinations would be assured that its CRA performance would not bar application approval. The theory is that such a scheme would encourage banks to make the CRA a part of their overall, day-to-day business plans. They would strive for outstanding performance and not view the CRA primarily in the context of applications. The Banking Department acknowledges that a safe harbor might be perceived as reducing community groups' involvement in the CRA. But state officials believe that if public comment were part of CRA examinations and not limited to the application context, its influence could be greatly enhanced.

The Congress has taken a first step in providing incentives. Under the Bank Enterprise Act of 1991, insured depository institutions that do business in economically distressed communities can earn assessment credits for application against their deposit insurance premiums.[20]

CONCLUSION

From modest beginnings and minimal legislative review, the CRA has grown in national importance. At the same time, the vague nature of the act has bedeviled its implementation through the years. In essence, instead of imposing hard and fast rules,

---

20. 12 U.S.C.A. § 1834 (Supp. 1992). The Congress has provided funds for establishing a Community Enterprise Assessment Credit Board, which will create the guidelines for qualifying activities. The program cannot be implemented, however, until additional money is appropriated to fund the assessment credits.

the statute relies on individual institutions and their local communities to define credit needs, with the expectation that the agencies will encourage this process and assess its success. To make up for the lack of precision, the agencies charged with enforcing the CRA have sought to measure CRA performance in a fair and comprehensive manner and to provide increasing guidance while avoiding any appearance of credit allocation.

Through a combination of efforts, the CRA has stimulated loans for home purchase, construction, and rehabilitation and for the development of small business and minority-owned business in low- and moderate-income areas. It has brought increased participation in public–private partnerships in urban and rural communities and has encouraged support for community development corporations and multibank lending consortiums that benefit low- and moderate-income communities. Indeed, many financial institutions have discovered that complying with the CRA helps them to compete for new customers and generate profitable business.

Although progress in community reinvestment marks the evolution of the CRA, unresolved problems remain and frustrations abound for financial institutions, supervisory agencies, and the public. In many cases, the major source of frustration rests on the law's lack of specificity. Yet that very lack also may be the law's most important strength. While providing strong incentives for institutions to reach out to their entire communities, it leaves the question of "how" largely in the hands of the institution and its community. In so doing, it continues to encourage and produce important reinvestment efforts throughout the nation. □

Competitive Considerations in Bank Mergers and Acquisitions: Economic Theory, Legal Foundations, and the Fed

Christopher L. Holder

The author is an analyst in the financial section of the Atlanta Fed's research department. He gratefully acknowledges comments from Dwight Blackwood, Jim Burke, Angela Dirr, Frank King, Al Martin, Bobbie McCrackin, Steve Rhoades, Aruna Srinivasan, Sheila Tschinkel, and Larry Wall.

In the past decade the U.S. banking industry has experienced major structural changes, including a significant reduction in the number of independent banking organizations. This change is partly the result of the increased pace of bank mergers and acquisitions.[1] During the twenty-year period from 1960 to 1979, mergers averaged 170 per year, with an average of $4.9 billion in total bank assets being acquired each year. In contrast, from 1980 to 1989 there was a yearly average of 498 mergers and $64.4 billion in total bank assets acquired.[2] Whatever dynamics underlie this industry consolidation, the overall result at the national level has been the increased concentration of banking resources among fewer banks. At the same time, local market share concentration levels have remained virtually unchanged during the eighties, a particularly important factor because local banking markets are the arena in which banking agencies measure competition between banks in considering antitrust issues.[3]

Consolidation in the banking industry has been a hot media topic in part because one alternative means of exit open to banks—failure—carries such negative force.[4] Ordinarily, stockholders and creditors operating in a market economy accept the risk of failure as a normal part of their investment, but in the banking system the deposit guarantees of the federal government put public funds at risk. Because any funds lost are drawn from insurance premiums paid by the insured institutions, they in fact come only indirectly from taxpayers and consumers of bank products. Nonetheless, the savings and loan crisis has made a direct taxpayer bailout of the banking system all too conceivable. To the extent that consolidation is necessary for the U.S. banking system to remain strong and globally competitive, mergers and acquisitions are clearly preferable, as a means to this end, to large numbers of bank failures.

The Federal Reserve System, created by the Federal Reserve Act in 1913 to provide for a safer and more flexible banking and monetary system, shares responsibility for banking supervision with other federal banking agencies. Part of the Fed's responsibilities includes administration of the laws that regulate bank holding companies and supervision of state-chartered member banks. These institutions are required to obtain approval from the Federal Reserve Board of Governors prior to completing a bank merger or acquisition.[5]

The Fed does not automatically grant approval of applications for merger. Several factors are taken into account—the likely effects of the acquisition on banking competition, financial and managerial resources and prospects for the acquirer's future, the convenience and needs of the community to be served, and any other legal issues related to a particular application. In considering the competitive aspects of a proposed merger, the Fed determines the extent to which existing competition would be adversely affected by the acquisition if an acquiring bank or bank holding company already has one or more banking offices in the market in which it seeks to acquire a bank. The Fed also examines the likely effects of the acquisition on probable future, or potential, competition if the acquirer is not already represented in the markets in which the bank to be acquired operates.

To ensure that safety and soundness criteria are met, the Fed considers the financial and managerial resources and the expected future of both the acquirer and the bank to be acquired. Some of the major factors taken into account include (1) the present and future capital position, asset quality, income, liquidity, and riskiness of the acquirer, (2) the means by which the acquirer intends to finance the merger and its level of debt and ability to service that debt, and (3) the quality of the acquirer's management and any plans for improving it.

The effect of the acquisition on banking products and services in the relevant banking markets is another concern examined by the System. If new or better services or lower prices for bank services are likely to result from an acquisition, the merger is more likely to win approval. The Fed also examines an acquirer's record under the Community Reinvestment Act, such as its performance in meeting the credit needs of its community, including low- and moderate-income areas.

The dynamic nature of the U.S. banking system, the several purposes of bank regulation, and the numerous variables to be considered in each merger transaction—such as different supply and demand conditions and the unique characteristics of different geographic markets—necessitate examining mergers on a case-by-case basis. It is the purpose of this article to focus on one aspect of the Fed's analysis of bank acquisitions over the last decade: the likely effect of mergers on competition.[6] The discussion summarizes the Federal Reserve's general approach to antitrust issues over the last decade. The economic factors and legal precedents that serve as the Fed's foundation for competitive analysis and changes in those criteria over the last decade are also considered.[7] For example, regulators have taken into account that banks have faced increased competition not only from within the banking industry but also from thrifts and other financial institutions as they have experienced deregulation.

Antitrust Issues

Antitrust regulation seeks to fulfill several objectives for bank customers and the general public. One goal is to prevent monopoly prices (excess profits) in the banking industry. Another is maintaining public access to bank products and services, an issue that can be especially problematic in small markets.[8] Antitrust laws seek to avoid static (noninnovating) markets and to allow efficiency-increasing, service-enhancing mergers. In addition, antitrust regulations are connected with safety and soundness issues, including limiting Federal Deposit Insurance Corporation (FDIC) losses.

The Federal Reserve keeps the objectives and concerns of antitrust regulation in mind in analyzing the consequences of bank mergers and acquisitions on market competition. Although few deals are actually denied by regulators on competitive grounds, antitrust issues play an important role in structuring mergers and acquisitions. Many deals are restructured to include divestiture, and an unknown number of banks are deterred from even filing a merger application because of anticipated antitrust concerns.[9]

Economics of Market Structure

One of the main purposes of antitrust regulations in mergers is to prevent acquirers from earning abnormal profits at the expense of consumers within the market where the merger occurred.[10] Defining the relevant market, in terms of both product and geographic area, is crucial for analyzing the economic effects of a proposed merger. Simply defined, a market is a group of buyers and sellers that significantly influence prices, quality, and quantity of specific products and services and the geographic area in which these buyers and sellers interact. A market can also be defined as an area in which the prices of all similar (substitute) goods are dependent on each other but are unaffected by prices for goods outside of the area.

For example, consider the case of two merchants who sell essentially the same product at similar, but not necessarily identical, prices (as banks do). One merchant is located on the north side of town and draws customers entirely from that area while the other merchant, located on the south side of town, draws customers exclusively from the south side. Because these merchants have no common customers, it might seem that they operate in separate markets. That assumption is not necessarily correct, however. To determine whether they are operating in the same market it is necessary to observe buyers' responses to a nontrivial and nontransitory price change in the good being sold. Suppose that one of the merchants—the one on the north side of town—raised the price of the product being offered. If this price change did not affect demand for the comparable good offered by the southside merchant, who did not change prices, the two would be functioning in separate markets. However, if some customers were willing to switch the store from which they buy, the merchants would be in the same market and would be direct competitors, even though they previously had currently drawn their customer base from separate areas.

Besides direct competition, the potential for competition is an important factor in determining markets. A potential competitor is one who would have to make an entry decision, and thus incur entry costs, before competing in a particular market. Because potential competitors help deter the exercise of market power (a single buyer's or seller's ability to influence the price of its product or service) within a market, their presence enhances competition. The degree to which they can forestall anticompetitive behavior is directly related to the proportions of obstacles—the size of entry costs and the existence of legal barriers to entry—standing between the potential competitors and entry. The lower the entry costs, or the fewer the legal restrictions on entry, the more potential competition contributes to sustaining competition within a market. Unfortunately, the importance of potential competition cannot be assessed numerically with the currently available empirical data.

In measuring the effects of either direct or potential competition in markets, it is necessary to determine the degree of substitutability between products—in economic terms, the cross-elasticities of supply and demand. The cross-elasticity of supply indicates the relationship between the produced quantity of one good and a change in the price of another. The cross-elasticity of demand indicates the relationship between the demanded quantity of one product and a change in the price of another. The more responsive the quantity of one product produced or demanded is to a change in price of another product, the higher the cross-elasticities and the more those products are viewed as substitutes (see Frederic M. Scherer 1990 or Jean Tirole 1988).

However, cross-elasticities alone cannot precisely determine markets. For one thing, cross-elasticities are difficult to estimate, and current theory does not define specific numerical levels at which a product becomes an adequate substitute for another product and would be included in the market. Another issue is that of the time frame in which customers and suppliers might switch products—that is, switching products may not be possible in the short term. In addition, the price changes that would induce buyers or sellers to substitute must take into account the relative prices of products and transactions costs. In practice, only those producers that might have a direct and immediate effect on competition are included in the market. The manner in which markets are currently defined by the Fed is discussed later.

Once the relevant market has been determined, competition within the market must be assessed. To do so, federal banking agencies apply theories developed in the field of industrial organization, the area of applied economics that seeks to explain the behavior of firms in a market. In particular, the agencies rely heavily on the concept known as the structure-conduct-performance (SCP) paradigm, which contends that the structure of a market indicates the amount of competition among firms in that market.[11] In this view, market structure is considered to be affected by the basic conditions underlying an industry, such as demand and supply functions and legal constraints. In turn, market

Box 1
Determination of Geographic Markets

The Supreme Court's decision in the 1963 Philadelphia National Bank case—to consider a bank's geographic market to be its local area—remains the foundation of the Fed's delineation of geographic markets. The Fed attempts to define markets in terms of the area in which buyers and sellers can interact without significant transaction costs. Because the market is the basis for calculating the structural effects of a proposed merger, this market definition is often crucial in deciding whether a merger is permissible under antitrust laws.[1]

The job of determining local banking market definitions at the Fed falls to the twelve Federal Reserve Banks, with procedures and guidance from the Board. Recent national studies of consumer and business behavior and local market surveys by various Reserve Banks confirm that the Board's definition of a market as a local banking market is still current (see Gregory E. Elliehausen and John D. Wolken 1990, 1992). The following discussion reviews some of the factors considered by the Reserve Banks in defining banking markets. While their general approach is similar, some Reserve Banks may give greater or less emphasis to certain factors. The Board's staff coordinates general consistency among Reserve Bank definitions. The approach discussed here is that used by the Federal Reserve Bank of Atlanta.

Empirical evidence indicates that convenience is an important determinant in an individual's selection of a financial institution and that many people maintain their primary banking relationships near where they live or work.[2] Commuting patterns are therefore important for identifying an integrated market area. Metropolitan Statistical Areas (MSAs) or Ranally Metro Areas (RMAs) are generally used as a first approximation in delineating urban markets, and county boundaries help define rural markets. MSAs are areas consisting of a central city (or Census Bureau–defined urbanized area) and its dependent fringes. RMAs are similar, made up of areas that contain at least seventy people per square mile and have at least 20 percent of the labor force commuting into the RMA's central city for employment. RMAs are not, however, restricted to following county borders, as are MSAs.[3]

Although RMAs and county boundaries form a good first approximation of market boundaries, other factors also help determine a final market definition. One of the most important is the actual banking patterns of bank customers. This information is obtained partly through interviewing bank and thrift managers, whose detailed knowledge of the customer base can sometimes provide unique insights into market dynamics. In addition, banks often keep detailed records of customer demographics, such as customer addresses analyzed by zip code. Surveys of consumers and small businesses are also conducted to identify actual banking patterns.

Another important question to address in delineating markets is whether there is a continuous chain of development between two areas. For instance, consider three banks, A, B, and C. Bank A does not compete directly with Bank C, but both Bank A and Bank C compete with Bank B. Because Bank A's pricing policies directly influence those of Bank B and indirectly influence those of Bank C, all three banks are considered to be in one market. The fact that prices tend toward equalization within a market makes evidence of pricing discrepancies useful in determining a market's boundaries. Two areas are viewed as becoming more integrated if there are indicators like road construction between the areas and new residential subdivisions and planned commercial development involving both areas. In addition, natural or political barriers that may prohibit integration of two areas are considered in defining markets.

Information regarding the ease with which customers can shift banking relationships is also important for determining markets. U.S. Census Bureau data are used to track commuting between counties. Other items that may be helpful are traffic counts, transportation routes (number, condition, approximate commuting time and distance, existence of controlled access roads, and so forth), major employers in the area and information on where their employees live, and the growth of population compared with employment and public transportation routes.

In addition to examining commuting patterns for what they indicate about customers' ease in shifting banking relationships, it is helpful to consider the extent to which residents and businesses in one area rely on another area for goods, services, and entertainment. This assessment is based on several indicators, including (1) location of major retailers, (2) location of major service providers (hospitals, airports, colleges, and universities), (3) media coverage patterns (newspaper circulation patterns, radio and television coverage patterns) and bank and thrift advertising patterns, (4) mall surveys showing where customers live, and (5) local (toll-free) calling areas.

Market definition in antitrust analysis is not an exact science. Each market has a unique set of economic, legal, and political conditions. In practice, market delineation must rely on secondary and anecdotal evidence. Markets are not static, and changes in demand and supply factors cause the shifting of market boundaries over time.

> **Notes**
>
> 1. For a review of the economic literature on geographic market delineation, see Wolken (1984).
> 2. For a bibliography and further details, see King (1982) or Wolken (1984).
> 3. The Office of Management and Budget (OMB) establishes the official requirements for defining MSAs; see "Revised Standards for Defining Metropolitan Areas in the 1990's," *Federal Register* 55 (March 30, 1990). See also Jerry J. Donovan, "A Primer on MSAs," Federal Reserve Bank of Atlanta *Regional Update* 5 (January-March 1992). RMAs are Rand McNally and Company's definitions of the metropolitan areas of the nation's major cities. For more information see *Rand McNally: 1992 Commercial Atlas and Marketing Guide.*

structure, consisting of the number, size distribution, and market shares of firms, influences the conduct of firms. This conduct—for example, the degree of competition or collusion between firms—determines the firms' performance, measured by profits or prices. The SCP paradigm implies that the fewer the number of firms and the greater their market shares, the more likely it is that those firms have the potential to earn abnormal profits (defined as profits greater than those that would be earned in a perfectly competitive market or as profits exceeding those commensurate to the level of the firm's risk). Banks' abnormal profits imply costs to the public that antitrust regulation seeks to avoid. Estimation of the SCP model for the U.S. banking industry has generally shown that a statistically significant and positive relationship does exist between market concentration and profitability.[12]

Legal Framework

The standards by which the Fed assesses the competitive effects of mergers and acquisitions comes from the Bank Holding Company Act (1956) and the Bank Merger Act (1960) and their amendments in 1966. These acts require federal banking agencies to consider the probable effects on competition of proposed mergers. If a merger is expected to have a substantially adverse impact on competition, the application is to be denied unless the anticompetitive effects of a merger are clearly outweighed by its favorable impact on the convenience and needs of the community. However, neither piece of legislation specifies precise standards for ensuring market competitiveness. In addition, once a merger or acquisition is approved by the appropriate federal banking agency, the Department of Justice has thirty days in which to file suit if it believes the transaction would violate antitrust statutes. If a suit is filed, the merger is automatically stopped pending resolution of legal action.

In a case involving the Philadelphia National Bank in 1963, the Supreme Court clarified the means by which regulators should measure competition.[13] This ruling established three major legal precedents still used by the Federal Reserve. First, the court confirmed that the Sherman and Clayton Antitrust Acts apply to banking, and the court used market structure (as defined above) as an indicator of competition within the market. Secondly, the ruling determined that the "cluster of products (various kinds of credit) and services (such as checking accounts and trust administration) denoted by the term 'commercial banking'... composes a distinct line of commerce" for Clayton Act purposes. Third, the sections of the country affected by an acquisition (the geographic market) must be taken into account. The court opined that "in banking, as in most service industries, convenience of location is essential to effective competition. Individuals and corporations typically confer the bulk of their patronage on banks in their local community; they find it impractical to conduct their banking business at a distance."

Product Market. In determining the relevant product market in which to assess the probable competitive effects of a bank acquisition or merger, the Supreme Court, in the Philadelphia National Bank case, determined that commercial banking is the appropriate line of commerce. The court stated that "the cluster of products ... and services" provided by commercial banks is unique relative to other institutions, including thrifts. This conclusion was based partially on the fact that, by law, only commercial banks could offer demand deposits at the time. In addition, it was recognized that the availability of a package of products and services at a single institution provided a customer convenience and value that surpasses the economic significance of these products and services individually. In measuring this cluster of services, the court used deposits as a proxy for estimating market share.[14]

Geographic Market. Once the appropriate product market has been determined, the relevant geographic market in which competition occurs must be defined.[15]

In the Philadelphia National Bank case the Supreme Court ruled that the market consisted of that area "in which the seller operates, and to which the purchaser can practically turn for supplies."[16] The Court also concluded that convenience factors tended to localize markets in banking. Accepting that at least some consumers and small businesses are limited to their communities for banking services, the standard has been that local markets are the correct area in which to measure the effects of competition between depository institutions.[17]

The Fed

In his 1991 testimony before the Committee on Banking, Finance, and Urban Affairs, John P. LaWare, a member of the Board of Governors of the Federal Reserve System, stated that the "primary objectives of public policy in this area [antitrust] should be to help manage the evolution of the banking industry in ways that preserve the benefits of competition for the consumers of banking services, and to ensure a safe, sound and profitable banking system" (LaWare 1991). With this objective in mind, and given current antitrust laws and judicial precedents, the Federal Reserve analyzes competition, using market structure (concentration) as an important measure of competition and using the concept of a cluster of banking products in a local geographic market.[18]

The Fed's process of analyzing a bank merger's effects on competition begins at one of the twelve Federal Reserve Banks, which are delegated most analysis, data-gathering, and recommendation functions because of the unique information they can access. As a result of their functions, the Reserve Banks are aware of local factors in their districts that might serve to integrate or separate market areas. In addition, the Reserve Banks have, or can acquire from local sources, knowledge of special factors that may reinforce or mitigate public losses through anticompetitive impacts of a proposed merger. For example, information on subtle issues, such as mortgage market concentration, is readily available to the Reserve Banks, which can make use of banker contacts and surveys of local businesses and consumers.[19]

In this process the Reserve Bank first identifies the relevant geographic market and then conducts an initial structural screening, including calculation of market shares and the market's Herfindahl-Hirschman Index (HHI). (See the box on page 26 for a discussion of the factors considered by the Federal Reserve Bank of Atlanta in defining banking markets.) The HHI is calculated by summing the squares of each firm's market shares. (See the box below for a practical example of how the HHI is calculated.) If no serious issues are raised—that is, if the HHI and market shares are within acceptable limits—the Reserve Bank generally approves the application for merger. However, if structural measures exceed benchmark levels, the transaction is deemed to have possible anticompetitive effects. Reserve Bank and Board staff findings and recommendations are then subject to review by the Board of Governors, which makes the final decision based on all factors laid out in the governing laws.[20]

In deciding if a merger potentially involves significant anticompetitive issues and therefore cannot be delegated to the Reserve Bank, the Board uses guidelines similar to those established by the Department of Justice.[21] (See the box on page 32 for a brief discussion of the Department of Justice's activity in recent years.) Although the numerical guidelines the Board uses are admittedly somewhat arbitrary, they do provide a consistent approach to antitrust enforcement, reducing the costs of uncertainty associated with applying antitrust laws.

Box 2
Calculation of the Herfindahl-Hirschman Index

The Fed currently relies extensively on a measure of market concentration—the Herfindahl-Hirschman Index—specified by the Department of Justice in its 1982 merger guidelines.[1] The HHI is calculated by summing the squares of the market share of each firm: HHI = $\Sigma[x(i)/x]^2$, where $x(i)$ is the total deposits of firm i, and x is the total deposits of all firms in the market.

The HHI is generally considered to be better than other concentration measures (such as market-share concentration ratios) because it captures both the number and size distribution of all firms in the market.[2] The calculation of HHIs in practice is illustrated by analyzing two markets in a recently approved Board case in which Barnett Banks, Inc. (Barnett) proposed to acquire First Florida Banks, Inc. (First Florida).[3]

The first market to be considered is the North Lake/Sumter banking market, defined by the Federal Reserve Bank of Atlanta as Sumter County, Florida, plus that portion of Lake County north of the Florida Turnpike. A total of eight banks with $1.58 billion in deposits competed in this market. In addition, there were four thrift institutions holding $405 million in deposits (see Table 1). To compute the HHI, first calculate the market shares of each firm, using bank deposits only (column 4) and bank-plus-thrift deposits at half weight (column 5).[4] For instance, Barnett has a banks-only market share of 24.09 percent and a thrifts-at-half-weight market share of 21.36 percent {381,589/[1,584,019 + (0.5 • 405,215)]}. These market shares squared indicate each firm's contribution to the market's HHI (columns 6 and 7). For example, Barnett Bank adds 580 points (24.09 • 24.09) to the market's banks-only HHI and 456 points (21.36 • 21.36) to the market's thrifts-at-half-weight HHI. To calculate the HHI for the market, sum each firm's contribution to the HHI. In Table 1 the market's banks-only HHI is 1,801 and its thrifts-at-half-weight HHI is 1,468.[5]

To calculate the structural changes that would occur after a merger, add First Florida's $39.7 million in deposits to Barnett's $381.6 million in deposits to get the total amount of deposits for the combined institution. This new deposit total of $421 million represents a new banks-only market share of 26.60 percent [(381,589 + 39,707)/1,584,019] and a new thrifts-at-half-weight market share of 23.58 percent {(381,589 + 39,707)/[1,584,019 + (0.5 • 405,215)]}. Barnett's contribution to the banks-only HHI becomes 708 points (26.60 • 26.60), increasing the market's banks-only HHI by 121 points to 1,922. Barnett's contribution to the thrifts-at-half-weight HHI becomes 556 points (23.58 • 23.58), increasing the market's thrifts-at-half-weight HHI by 95 points to 1,563.

Because the applicable guidelines (the 1,800/200 rule with thrifts at 50 percent weight) were not breached, the Fed would generally conclude that this merger would have no significant anticompetitive effect in the North Lake/Sumter banking market.

To illustrate what happens when competitive guidelines are breached, consider another market in which Barnett and First Florida competed, the Highlands County banking market. Delineated by the county's borders, this market had a total of six banks competing for $691.4 million in total deposits. In addition, five thrifts operated in the market, holding $366.9 million in total deposits (see Table 2). Again calculate the market share of each institution, first with banks-only deposits, then adding thrift deposits at half weight. Then calculate each firm's contribution to the market's HHI, summing to get a total premerger HHI of 2,359 (with thrifts at half weight). Next, add First Florida's deposits to Barnett's and recalculate the market shares and HHIs. This market would have a

Table 1
North Lake/Sumter Banking Market
(Deposits as of June 30, 1991)

Depository Institution	Total Deposits ($000)		Market Share		HHI	
	Banks	Thrifts	Banks Only	Thrifts 50%	Banks Only	Thrifts 50%
Barnett Banks, Inc.	381,589		24.09	21.36	580	456
First Union Corporation	321,203		20.28	17.98	411	323
SunTrust Banks, Inc.	312,120		19.70	17.47	388	305
Citi-Bancshares, Inc.	286,550		18.09	16.04	327	257
First FS&LA of Lake County		205,305		5.75	0	33
First Family FS&LA		154,157		4.31	0	19
UniSouth, Inc.	114,593		7.23	6.41	52	41
First National Bank of Mt. Dora	82,314		5.20	4.61	27	21
BankFirst	45,943		2.90	2.57	8	7
First Florida Banks, Inc.	39,707		2.51	2.22	6	5
Mid-State Federal Savings Bank		24,198		0.68	0	0
Citizens Federal Savings Bank		21,555		0.60	0	0
TOTAL	1,584,019	405,215	100	100		
Premerger HHI					1,801	1,468
Postmerger HHI					1,922	1,563
Change in HHI					121	95

Table 2
Highlands County Banking Market
(Deposits as of June 30, 1991)

Depository Institution	Total Deposits ($000) Banks	Total Deposits ($000) Thrifts	Market Share Banks Only	Market Share Thrifts 50%	HHI Banks Only	HHI Thrifts 50%
Barnett Banks, Inc.	383,714		55.50	43.86	3,080	1,924
Huntington FSB		174,365		9.97		99
First Union Corporation	97,053		14.04	11.09	197	123
SunTrust Banks, Inc.	89,298		12.92	10.21	167	104
BancFlorida, FSB		73,437		4.20		18
Home Savings Bank, FSB		73,385		4.19		18
First Florida Banks, Inc.	57,525		8.32	6.58	69	43
Highlands Independent Bank	32,927		4.76	3.76	23	14
NationsBank Corporation	30,883		4.47	3.53	20	12
Goldome FSB		28,918		1.65		3
Harbor FS&LA		16,777		0.96		1
TOTAL	691,400	366,882	100	100		
Premerger HHI					3,556	2,359
Postmerger HHI					4,479	2,936
Change in HHI					923	577

postmerger thrifts-at-half-weight HHI of 2,936, producing a change in the HHI of 577 points.

This change of 577 points in a highly concentrated market exceeds the applicable 1,800/200 rule with thrifts at half weight, and the Reserve Bank would have had to notify Board staff that applicable guidelines were breached and that the merger was potentially anticompetitive. At this point, both Reserve Bank staff and the Board staff would have conducted an in-depth analysis of the likely effect of the merger within the market.[6] Such an analysis would involve considering a variety of factors such as market attractiveness, potential competition, the financial strength of the target firm, and so forth.

Notes

1. The HHI was developed independently by Orris C. Herfindahl, "Concentration in the U.S. Steel Industry," Ph.D. diss., Columbia University, 1950, and by Albert O. Hirschman, *National Power and the Structure of Foreign Trade* (Berkeley and Los Angeles: University of California Press, 1945).
2. The three- or four-firm concentration ratio, which was used extensively by the Department of Justice and federal banking agencies in the past, ignored the competitive influence of banks not ranked in the top three or four of the market. For an empirical justification of why the HHI might be preferred to firm concentration ratios, see Rhoades (1985b).
3. "Barnett Banks, Inc." *Federal Reserve Bulletin* 79 (1993): 44.
4. The Board's use of thrifts at half weight is discussed on page 31.
5. Notice the substantial difference the inclusion of thrift deposits makes. The market is highly concentrated using bank-only deposits but only moderately concentrated with thrift deposits at 50 percent weight.
6. In the above merger, Barnett committed to divest the only First Florida branch in the market in order to mitigate potentially adverse competitive effects. In light of this divestiture the Board concluded that consummation of the proposed merger would not affect competition in the Highlands County market.

Criteria for Judging Potential Anticompetitive Effects

This article examines all bank merger applications considered by the Federal Reserve System for potentially significant competitive issues during the decade from December 1982 until December 1992. It does not examine applications in which a thrift was to be acquired or merger proposals filed with another federal regulator. In determining whether a particular application entailed potentially significant competitive issues, both Department of Justice merger guidelines and Board rules regarding delegation of authority to the Reserve Banks that were in effect when the application was filed were considered. Consequently, the data were divided into three periods (December 1982-December 1985, January 1986-June 1987, and July 1987-December 1992) in which different benchmarks were used to determine a transaction's potential anticompetitive effects.

In June 1982 the Department of Justice issued new merger guidelines applicable to the enforcement of antitrust laws in all industries. The Board first referred to these guidelines, and specifically to the HHI as a measure of concentration, in a merger decision on November 19, 1982. The Board's publication of this decision in the *Federal Reserve Bulletin* in December 1982 marks the beginning of the data period reviewed in this article.[22]

The Department of Justice guidelines established three postmerger concentration ranges to consider in determining whether a particular transaction is likely to pose a significant anticompetitive threat and thus be subject to in-depth economic analysis and possible challenge by the Justice Department. The Fed continues to make decisions in terms of these three ranges. A market with a postmerger HHI below 1,000 is considered unconcentrated, a market with a postmerger HHI between 1,000 and 1,800 is moderately concentrated, and a market with a postmerger HHI greater than 1,800 is a highly concentrated market. The Department of Justice stated that it was more likely than not to challenge transactions that would result in a change greater than 100 points in a moderately concentrated market and was also likely to challenge mergers producing a change greater than 100 points in a highly concentrated market. Depending on the postmerger concentration of the market, the size of the resulting increase in concentration, and the presence or absence of several other factors relating to the market, the Department of Justice might decide to challenge an approval on the basis of a change between 50 and 100 points in a highly concentrated market.

For the purposes of this article, a merger was flagged as potentially raising competitive issues unless it fell clearly in a category the Department of Justice was unlikely to challenge. For the data sample from December 1982 to December 1985, this set includes mergers in markets that were moderately concentrated (as defined above) and resulted in a change greater than 100 points and mergers in a highly concentrated market effecting a change of at least 50 points.

In February 1985 the Department of Justice informed the Office of the Comptroller of the Currency (OCC) that it would not, ordinarily, challenge a bank merger unless there was an HHI change of at least 200 points in a highly concentrated market.[23] This increase in concentration benchmarks was intended explicitly to recognize competition from nondepository institutions, a factor not captured in deposit market-share data. Although the Board referred to this new rule in six applications in 1985, the new benchmark was not used consistently until 1986, as reflected in the Board's amended "Rules Regarding Delegation of Authority" to the Reserve Banks on December 17, 1985.[24] In examining data from the beginning of January 1986 until December 1992, this so-called 1,800/200 rule is the benchmark that was used to identify applications for mergers that might be significantly anticompetitive.

In the Connecticut National Bank case in 1974, the Supreme Court recognized thrifts as significant competitors for a broad range of consumer services.[25] However, the court concluded that thrifts should not, at that time, be a factor in assessing the competitive effects of bank mergers because thrifts were not competitive in the area of commercial lending. With the passage of the Depository Institutions Deregulation and Monetary Control Act (1980) and the Garn-St Germain Act (1982), which effectively deregulated the thrift industry, thrifts were authorized to compete with banks in providing the cluster of products previously unique to banking. In recognition of this increased competition, the Board began including thrifts as competitors in specific applications. By March 27, 1987, competition from thrifts had grown to such a point that the Board changed its rules regarding delegation of authority to the Reserve Banks to give thrifts a weight of 50 percent when calculating concentration numbers, to reflect both actual and potential competition from thrifts.[26] Beginning with the June 1987 decisions (published in the July 1987 *Federal Reserve Bulletin*), determinations made regarding the competitive effects of mergers were based on this assumption of 50 percent

Box 3
Department of Justice Antitrust Activities in Recent Years

The Department of Justice held a relatively relaxed view of antitrust in banking throughout much of the 1980s. Merger guidelines adopted in 1982, based on permissible market shares, generally were less restrictive than standards used previously and thus enlarged the pool of potentially valid mergers. The 1982 guidelines also established factors that could be used to justify mergers that failed the market concentration test. In 1985, recognizing the increasing importance of nonbank competitors, the Department of Justice established the 1,800/200 rule (with thrifts generally given 20 percent weight), which was quickly adopted by the other federal banking agencies (which generally give thrifts 50 percent weight). Importantly, until 1991 the Department of Justice did not challenge any merger that passed the 1,800/200 rule with thrifts at 50 percent and was approved by one of the federal agencies, even if it failed the 1,800/200 rule with thrifts at the Department of Justice's standard of 20 percent.

In 1989 the Department of Justice began taking a more aggressive approach toward bank mergers. Four large transactions since 1990 demonstrate the changes. In the first of these, late in 1990, the Federal Reserve Board approved First Hawaiian, Inc.'s acquisition of First Interstate of Hawaii, Inc.[1] The Department of Justice sued to block the transaction, citing adverse market effects for small and medium-sized businesses. Then in 1991, the Department of Justice raised strong objections to Fleet/Norstar's acquisition of the failed Bank of New England, citing concentration in three banking markets. In addition, the Department of Justice stated that the "failing firm" defense did not apply to Fleet/Norstar because there were other bidders for the Bank of New England that did not pose any competitive concerns. In a third transaction, on February 13, 1992, the Fed approved the acquisition of Ameritrust Corporation by Society Corporation despite Department of Justice objections that the proposed branches to be divested were weak.[2] The Department of Justice filed suit, citing adverse competitive effects on the availability of loans to small businesses in two counties in Ohio. The agency eventually dropped its opposition to each of these mergers after negotiating divestitures beyond those required by the Fed. In a separate case in 1992, the Department of Justice held talks with BankAmerica Corporation over its proposed acquisition of Security Pacific Corporation. However, after BankAmerica amended its application to include additional divestitures, the Department of Justice did not file to block this merger.

The new merger guidelines published in 1992 spotlight the approach the Department of Justice is now taking with respect to mergers.[3] The guidelines describe the department's five-step process currently conducted with respect to each proposed merger. First, the relevant product and geographical markets are identified, and the structural impacts within these markets are calculated. Second, specific characteristics of the market are then considered to determine whether there are antitrust concerns. Third, the timeliness, likelihood, and sufficiency of entry into the market as it relates to anticompetitive behavior are forecast. Any efficiency gains expected from the merger are calculated, and, as the last step, if the continued existence of either party is doubtful, the expected results of the failure are analyzed.

While this process sounds very similar to the Fed's, there are several important differences. First, in the transactions cited the Department of Justice did not use the cluster of services provided by commercial banks as the relevant product market but instead segregated various financial services into separate product markets.[4] Within these separate product markets, the Department of Justice's emphasis was on the market for commercial loans, especially to small and medium-sized businesses, designated according to various size definitions. Although this case-by-case approach may better reflect market realities, it also increases uncertainty among merging parties concerning the Department of Justice's likely response to a merger proposal.[5] The Department of Justice also indicated that its 1,800/200 rule applied only to the initial screening of a particular merger and that a transaction failing that benchmark was subject to closer investigation using the more restrictive 1,800/50 rule.[6] In addition, although the weighting of thrifts will continue to be determined on a case-by-case basis, the Department of Justice has indicated that it believes thrifts have substantially retreated from business banking and, therefore, deserve no weight in this product market.[7] The Department of Justice has also indicated that divestitures must introduce new and viable competitors into the market. In this regard, the agency has taken a direct hand in choosing which branches are to be divested, as opposed to the Fed's practice of allowing the applicant to select the branches for divestiture.

Notes

1. See "First Hawaiian, Inc.," *Federal Reserve Bulletin* 77 (1991): 52.

2. See "Society Corporation," *Federal Reserve Bulletin* 78 (1992): 302.

3. See "Department of Justice and Federal Trade Commission Horizontal Merger Guidelines," April 2, 1992.
4. This was not the Department of Justice's first attempt at breaking up the "Philadelphia National" cluster. In 1985 the agency appealed a transaction that had been approved by the appropriate federal regulators, arguing that transaction accounts and small business loans were separate product lines. The Court of Appeals held that the District Court did not err when it "concluded that the government failed to factually support its claim that existing circumstances in this case warranted a departure from the definition of the relevant product market as the cluster of banking services traditionally offered in the commercial banking industry adopted by the Supreme Court in U.S. v. Philadelphia National Bank." See U.S. v. Central State Bank, 817 F.2d 22 (6th Cir. 1987).
5. In Society's acquisition of Ameritrust, the Department of Justice concluded that businesses with more than $10 million in annual sales "appear to be able to obtain loans from institutions in Detroit and Pittsburgh as well as locally" (Society Corporation Competitive Factor Report). In First Hawaiian's acquisition of First Interstate of Hawaii, the Department of Justice determined that the "unique geography" of Hawaii limited businesses with less than $50 million in annual sales in obtaining loans from nonlocal institutions (First Hawaiian, Inc., Competitive Factor Report). In BankAmerica's acquisition of Security Pacific, the Department of Justice concluded that businesses with annual sales of less than $100 million were locally limited (BankAmerica Corporation Competitive Factor Report). See Letzler and Mierzewski (1992).
6. See Report of the Department of Justice on the Likely Competitive Effects of the Proposed Acquisition by First Hawaiian, Inc. of First Interstate of Hawaii, Inc. (1990).
7. Letter from James F. Rill, Assistant Attorney General, Antitrust Division, to Hon. Alan Greenspan, Chairman, Board of Governors of the Federal Reserve System, on the application of BankAmerica Corporation to acquire Security Pacific Corporation, March 12, 1992.

weighting for all thrifts, the so-called 1,800/200/50 rule. This rule was the selection criterion used in analyzing the sample data from July 1987 through December 1992.[27]

A total of 155 applications in the sample were identified as mergers that might have significant anticompetitive effects. Of these applications, sixteen involved "prior common control," that is, an attempt to restructure ownership of two or more banks from individuals to a corporation owned by the same individuals.[28] Because none of these mergers were denied and such applications raise issues not relevant to most bank merger transactions, the applications involving prior common control appearing in the sample period were dropped from the data set.

Total Divestiture. The 139 remaining applications for mergers presenting potentially significant anticompetitive problems involved a total of 297 banking markets that exceeded the structural criteria described above. (Many bank mergers involved multiple markets, some but not all of which posed competitive problems.) In eighty-six of these markets, an applicant agreed to divest (sell) all of either its own or its target's branches in the market.

The Board (as well as other federal banking agencies and the Department of Justice) considers divestiture to be an effective way for applicants to address areas of competitive concern to regulators while allowing the nonobjectionable portion of the transaction to proceed. Generally, it is preferred that these divestitures be made to institutions not currently operating in the market, thereby insuring that the competitive structure of the market remains unchanged. However, divestiture to an in-market competitor is permissible, provided that the market's resultant structural changes are not too severe. Because total divestiture usually addresses the competitive issues involved in a market and no further factors are generally considered by the Board, these eighty-six markets were also excluded from the sample studied.

Mitigating Factors. In the remaining 211 markets the Board approved the vast majority of applications for mergers that exceeded the criteria for delegation of authority and were likely to be challenged by the Department of Justice according to its published merger guidelines. The Board cited a number of factors that mitigated the potentially significant anticompetitive effects of these transactions, as indicated by the structural numbers (HHI). Relevant issues included competition from thrifts, market attractiveness, and the financial health of the target firm. As noted earlier, the second part of this discussion, in the next issue of the *Economic Review*, will examine all of the mitigating factors discussed by the Board in applications dating from December 1982 through December 1992.

Conclusion

The increased number and size of bank mergers over the last few years, as well as the larger number of bank failures, has renewed interest in antitrust enforcement by federal authorities. The Fed, considering the public-interest protections of antitrust regulations, has adopted a two-stage approach to competitive issues in bank mergers, first determining whether a competitive problem might exist and then, if so, determining whether the proposed acquisition would have a significantly adverse anticompetitive effect. This article summarizes the Fed's general approach to antitrust analysis over the last decade. It presents the economic theory and legal framework behind the Fed's analysis and cites empirical evidence both for and against the Fed's approach.

Certain elements are essential for each evaluation: specification of the correct geographic and product markets in which competitive effects take place, determination of direct and potential competitors, and analysis of the effects of mergers on the structure of individual markets. While all merger applications are examined in light of the same criteria, the dynamic aspects of the U.S. banking industry and the several objectives of antitrust laws are such that bank merger analysis must be done on a case-by-case basis.

Notes

1. Throughout this article the terms *merger* and *acquisition* are used synonymously.
2. See Rhoades (1985a) and LaWare (1991). Numbers do not include acquisitions of failed banks. Numbers for 1988 and 1989 are estimated.
3. See LaWare (1991), who states that "over the last decade, the average proportion of bank deposits accounted for by the largest three firms in urban markets has increased by only one percentage point, and has remained virtually unchanged in rural markets. These ratios have actually declined in both types of markets since the mid-1970s."
4. Firm shrinkage is an alternative vehicle for consolidation that BankAmerica Corporation has shown can work.
5. The Federal Reserve has jurisdiction over mergers of state member banks and mergers or acquisitions by bank holding companies. The Comptroller of the Currency has primary responsibility for national banks. The Federal Deposit Insurance Corporation oversees insured state nonmember banks. In addition, section 18(c) of the Federal Deposit Insurance Act provides that "before acting on any application for approval of a merger transaction, the responsible agency . . . shall request reports on the competitive factors involved from the Attorney General and the other two banking agencies."
6. A second article, in the next issue of the Atlanta Fed's *Economic Review*, will examine all merger applications filed by state member banks or bank holding companies (applications to acquire another bank or bank holding company) that involved potentially significant competitive issues since the Board first began applying the 1982 Department of Justice merger guidelines to bank mergers in November of that year. The discussion will specifically consider mitigating factors the Board referred to in these applications.
7. The Fed's approach to antitrust issues is not the only accepted view. For instance, the Department of Justice may implement antitrust regulation slightly differently (see Guerin-Calvert and Ordover 1992). Others are critical of the application of antitrust standards to the banking industry, arguing that the current approach of regulators is antiquated and fails to recognize much of the competition currently faced by banks (see, for example, Bove 1991 and Demsetz 1973). A comprehensive analysis of the various approaches concerning antitrust issues is beyond the scope of this paper.
8. See, for example, "SouthTrust Corporation," *Federal Reserve Bulletin* 78 (1992): 769.
9. Federal agencies consider divestiture an acceptable means of reducing the anticompetitive effects of a proposed merger. Reducing the resultant market share of the acquiring bank in turn reduces the ability to exercise anticompetitive behavior in the market. Divestiture as a solution for competitive problems has become increasingly more important over the last decade because of the proliferation of large mergers, in which divestitures are small relative to the size of the entire transaction. For the Federal Reserve Board of Governor's position on the timing of divestitures see "BankAmerica Corporation," *Federal Reserve Bulletin* 78 (1992): 338.
10. For a thorough discussion of the economics of market structure see Scherer (1990) or Tirole (1988).
11. For an overview of the SCP paradigm and a review of the empirical literature, see Rhoades (1977, 1982).
12. See, for example, Hannan (1991), Berger and Hannan (1989), and Rhoades (1982). For alternative explanations of the profit-concentration relationship in banking, such as the efficiency-structure hypothesis, see Smirlock (1985), Berger (1991a, 1991b), and Hasan and Smith (1992).
13. U.S. v. Philadelphia National Bank, 374 U.S. 321 (1963).
14. Recent empirical evidence supports the use of this cluster concept in commercial banking. For instance, studies indicate that businesses and consumers tend to purchase additional products and services from the institution at which they maintain their primary checking account (see Elliehausen and Wolken 1990, 1992).

15. For a review of the economic literature on geographic market definition see Wolken (1984).
16. U.S. v. Philadelphia National Bank, 374 U.S. 321 (1963).
17. Recent empirical evidence supports the idea that banking markets, at least for some consumers and small businesses, are still local in nature (see Elliehausen and Wolken 1990, 1992; Hannan 1991). For another viewpoint see Dunham (1986).
18. While the courts are willing to hear arguments that the appropriate product or geographic markets have changed, it requires that this claim be factually supported, which has not yet been demonstrated in Court. See U.S. v. Central State Bank, 817 F.2d 22 (6th Cir. 1987). In addition, some products offered by banks and bank holding companies have regional, national, or even international markets. Although the Board considers nonbanking activities, only rarely are there any significant anticompetitive effects owing to the large number of competitors within these markets and their small market shares.
19. See "SouthTrust Corporation," *Federal Reserve Bulletin* 78 (1992): 769.
20. The Reserve Banks have been delegated authority to approve transactions that present no significant concerns. If a particular transaction does involve significant competitive, legal, or other issues, the application becomes nondelegated and is subject to Board review. Authority to deny a transaction rests solely with the Board. The Fed's "Rules Regarding Delegation of Authority" spell out the criteria used to determine whether an application is delegated and can be approved by the Reserve Banks or nondelegated and must be acted upon by the Board. The Fed does not structure acceptable deals, such as by adding divestitures to an applicant's original application. However, Fed staff will consult with an applicant on how to structure the application to maximize the chances of approval.
21. See U.S. Department of Justice Merger Guidelines, June 14, 1982. The Department of Justice assumed an important role in bank mergers and acquisitions when the Bank Holding Company Act (1956) and the Bank Merger Act (1960) applied the antitrust provisions of the Clayton Act to the banking industry.
22. "First Bancorp of New Hampshire, Inc.," *Federal Reserve Bulletin* 68 (1982): 769.
23. Letter from Charles F. Rule, Acting Assistant Attorney General, Antitrust Division, to Hon. C. Todd Conover, Comptroller of the Currency, on the application of First National Bank of Jackson, Jackson, Mississippi, to acquire Brookhaven Bank and Trust Company, Brookhaven, Mississippi, February 8, 1985.
24. The six 1985 application decisions in which the Board referred to the new rule were: "United Banks of Colorado, Inc.," *Federal Reserve Bulletin* 71 (1985): 647; "Marshall & Ilsley Corporation," *Federal Reserve Bulletin* 71 (1985): 663; "The Marine Corporation," *Federal Reserve Bulletin* 71 (1985): 795; "Central Wisconsin Bankshares, Inc.," *Federal Reserve Bulletin* 71 (1985): 895; "First Security Corporation of Kentucky," *Federal Reserve Bulletin* 71 (1985): 898; and "First Railroad & Banking Company of Georgia," *Federal Reserve Bulletin* 71 (1985): 963.
25. U.S. v. Connecticut National Bank, 418 U.S. 656 (1974).
26. Letter from Don E. Kline, Associate Director, Board of Governors of the Federal Reserve System, to all officers in charge of supervision at all Federal Reserve Banks, March 27, 1987.
27. The Board continues generally to use 50 percent weight for thrifts in calculating structural numbers. It may give 100 percent weight to thrifts in cases in which thrift behavior suggests that it is appropriate to do so—when thrifts are substantially exercising their banklike powers.
28. In 1978 the Change in Bank Control Act was passed requiring regulators to assess the competitive effects when an individual purchases a bank. In examining such an application, if the common control was established before 1978, the Board considers the competitive effects of the transaction(s) at that time rather than current market conditions. A traditional structural analysis based on deposit data at the time of affiliation is conducted. Other factors considered include the absolute size of the banks at the time of affiliation, the number of years that the institutions have been affiliated, and whether the affiliation existed before antitrust laws were applied to bank mergers. (Prior to the Bank Merger Act of 1960, the banking laws did not refer to competitive effects.) In addition, the Board considers any other issues that would mitigate potential anticompetitive effects of the merger.

In denying approval of a prior common control application, the Board recognizes that any existing anticompetitive effects of the institution's affiliation cannot be reversed. A denial would, however, preserve the possibility of a reversal at some point in the future, whereas approval could perpetuate anticompetitive possibilities.

References

Berger, Allen N. "X-Efficiency and Scale Efficiency in the U.S. Banking Industry." Board of Governors of the Federal Reserve System unpublished paper, 1991a.

———. "The Profit Concentration Relationship in Banking: Tests of Market-Power and Efficient-Structure Hypotheses and Implications for the Consequences of Bank Mergers." Board of Governors of the Federal Reserve System, Finance and Economics Discussion Series 176, November 1991b.

Berger, Allen N., and Timothy H. Hannan. "The Price-Concentration Relationship in Banking." *Review of Economics and Statistics* 71 (May 1989): 291-99.

Bove, Richard X. "Antitrust Action in Hawaii Aimed at Wrong Target." *American Banker*, February 28, 1991, 1, 4.

Demsetz, Harold. "Industry Structure, Market Rivalry, and Public Policy." *Journal of Law and Economics* 16 (April 1973): 1-9.

Dunham, Constance R. "Regional Banking Competition." Federal Reserve Bank of Boston *New England Economic Review* (July/August 1986): 3-19.

Elliehausen, Gregory E., and John D. Wolken. "Banking Markets and the Use of Financial Services by Small and Medium-Sized Businesses." *Federal Reserve Bulletin* 76 (October 1990): 801-17.

_____. "Banking Markets and the Use of Financial Services by Households." *Federal Reserve Bulletin* 78 (March 1992): 169-81.

Guerin-Calvert, Margaret E., and Janusz A. Ordover. "The 1992 Agency Horizontal Merger Guidelines and the Department of Justice's Approach to Bank Merger Analysis." In *Proceedings: Annual Conference on Bank Structure and Competition, 1992*, 545-60. Chicago: Federal Reserve Bank of Chicago, 1992.

Hannan, Timothy H. "Bank Commercial Loan Markets and the Role of Market Structure: Evidence from Surveys of Commercial Lending." *Journal of Banking and Finance* 15 (February 1991): 133-49.

Hasan, Iftekhar, and Stephen D. Smith. "A Note on Competition, Fixed Costs, and the Profitability of Depository Intermediaries." Federal Reserve Bank of Atlanta Working Paper 92-12, October 1992.

King, B. Frank. "Review of Empirical Literature." Federal Reserve Bank of Atlanta *Economic Review* 67 (April 1982): 35-40.

LaWare, John P. Testimony before the Committee on Banking, Finance and Urban Affairs of the U.S. House of Representatives. September 24, 1991. Reprinted in *Federal Reserve Bulletin* 77 (November 1991): 932-48.

Letzler, Kenneth A., and Michael B. Mierzewski. "Antitrust Policy Poses Greater Burdens for Bank Merger and Acquisitions." *Banking Policy Report* 11 (April 20, 1992): 1, 14-18.

Rhoades, Stephen A. "Structure-Performance Studies in Banking: A Summary and Evaluation." Board of Governors of the Federal Reserve System, Staff Economic Study 92, Fall 1977.

_____. "Structure-Performance Studies in Banking: An Updated Summary and Evaluation." Board of Governors of the Federal Reserve System, Staff Study 119, August 1982.

_____. "Mergers and Acquisitions by Commercial Banks, 1960-83." Board of Governors of the Federal Reserve System, Staff Study 142, January 1985a.

_____. "Market Performance and the Nature of a Competitive Fringe." *Journal of Economics and Business* 37 (February 1985b): 141-57.

Scherer, Frederic M. *Industrial Market Structure and Economic Performance*. 3d ed. Chicago: Rand McNally, 1990.

Smirlock, Michael. "Evidence on the (Non)Relationship between Concentration and Profitability in Banking." *Journal of Money, Credit, and Banking* 17 (February 1985): 69-83.

Tirole, Jean. *The Theory of Industrial Organization*. Cambridge, Mass.: MIT Press, 1988.

Wolken, John D. "Geographic Market Delineation: A Review of the Literature." Board of Governors of the Federal Reserve System, Staff Study 140, November 1984.

Part Three

Interest Rates, Financial Instruments, and Financial Markets

The system of financial markets and institutions produces and delivers an incredible array of services and financial instruments. It is also the mechanism through which interest rates and security prices are determined and savings are allocated to those investments carrying the highest expected returns. In this section of the book we examine a portion of the great variety and range of financial instruments and look closely at recent trends in national saving and at the forces that shape interest rates and the yield curve.

This section opens with an article by Dr. Stephen A. Meyer, Vice President and Associate Director of Research at the Federal Reserve Bank of Philadelphia, which compares savings rates in the United States with those of Germany and Japan. In his article entitled "Saving and Demographics: Some International Comparisons," Dr. Meyer finds that the differing age compositions of the populations in the United States, Germany, and Japan help account for differing savings rates among these countries as do the differing sizes of government budget surpluses and deficits in these three nations. The United States has, for example, a much smaller proportion of its population in the peak-earning and high-saving years along with much larger government budget deficits than many other European and Pacific nations. Not too surprisingly, given these differences in population mix and government debt burden, Germany and Japan have reported persistently higher average savings rates than the United States and, consequently, have achieved a greater volume of net investment relative to their GNP. Over time, it seems likely that savings differences among these nations will narrow as the demographic profiles of their populations become more similar to each other.

One of the most familiar concepts in the field of Finance is the *yield curve*—the relationship between yields (rates of return) and the maturities of different securities. An upward-sloping yield curve indicates that long-term interest rates are higher than short-term interest rates. To the extent that the yield curve reflects the expectations of investors, an upward-sloping yield curve is a forecast of higher interest rates expected in the future. Similarly, a downward-sloping yield curve indicates that short-term interest rates are higher than long-term interest rates and suggests that lower interest rates are being forecast for the future.

Timothy Cogley, economist with the Federal Reserve Bank of San Francisco, points out that yield curves also may reflect the market's perception of *risk*, with longer-maturity securities commanding higher risk premiums in their yields due to the greater risk of default over a longer time period and the greater price risk possessed by the longest-term bonds. Dr. Cogley finds that most of the variation in long-term interest rates and most of the changes that occur in the shape of the yield curve over time seem to be related to variations in risk premiums, not to interest-rate expectations. Thus, he finds that conventional yield curve theory, particularly the expectations hypothesis, accounts for a fairly minor share of the changes observed over time in the slope of the yield curve.

In a second article focusing upon the yield curve, economist Steven Russell of the Federal Reserve Bank of St. Louis examines the Expectations Hypothesis—the most popular theoretical explanation for the shape of the yield curve—and gives us a thorough explanation of this theory. Dr. Russell examines some of the conventional notions frequently heard about yield curves, including their tendency to slope upward in most time periods and their tendency to systematically change in shape as interest rates move. He finds that risk plays a significant role in accounting for the shape of the yield curve as risk-averse lenders demand compensation for the greater uncertainties associated with longer-term securities.

Turning to a much broader topic, Federal Reserve Bank of Chicago economists Francesca Eugeni, Steven Strongin, and Paula R. Worthington examine patterns of borrowing and debt accumulation by businesses and households during the current decade compared to the 1980s. They look closely at the evidence for the so-called "portfolio effect" of household and business debt which argues that recent sluggish growth in the U.S. economy is due to sharp cutbacks from the soaring debt growth of the 1980s that allegedly overloaded consumers and businesses with red ink. Chicago economists Eugeni, Strongin, and Worthington point out that this simple explanation of recent linkages between the growth of debt and the growth of the economy may not be completely accurate. They analyze the debt service burdens of American households and corporations and find no convincing evidence that those burdens have been any lighter in the 1990s than they were before. Rather, historically low market interest rates during the early 1990s appear to have given the private sector a substantial interest rebate and allowed businesses and consumers to sustain and even increase their levels of borrowing and spending.

An article by Dr. D. Keith Sill of the Federal Reserve Bank of Philadelphia takes us from the market for loans to the market for stock. In "Predicting Stock-Market Volatility" Dr. Sill explores the various theories about how the volatility of the stock market impacts the economy and people's decisions to spend and save. He asks whether stock-market volatility is predictable and searches for a possible explanation of why the stock market's volatility seems to be different over time. His data on stock returns covering more than 30 years suggests that stock-market volatility can be at least partially explained, though the stock market's behavior in the 1980s appeared to make the volatility of stocks less predictable than in earlier time periods. The author finds that stock price volatility seems to be greater in recessions than in periods of rapid economic growth and that the spread between two money market interest rates—the commercial paper rate and the rate on Treasury bills—appears to be significantly related to stock-price variability.

Staying with the stock market theme, Dr. James Booth, visiting scholar with the Federal Reserve Bank of San Francisco and a Professor of Finance at Arizona State University, researches the strange behavior of the prices of initial public offerings (IPOs) of stock by new publicly-held corporations. In recent decades and in several different countries, investors in those IPOs have frequently experienced a sharp run-up in stock prices the first day a new stock offering is brought out, suggesting that newly offered stock are often underpriced when first sold. Dr. Booth reviews several different explanations that have been offered over the years for the large initial-day returns on public stock offerings and concludes that, frequently, new stock issues are *intentionally underpriced*, perhaps because of a belief that planned underpricing tends to promote the liquidity of stock in the resale market.

The balance of this section of the book is devoted to what are usually called *derivatives*—financial instruments which rely for their value and trading characteristics on an underlying security or loan. Derivatives today include such financial instruments as financial futures contracts, options, forward contracts, swaps, and loan-backed securities. In the first article in this section, entitled "Derivative Markets and Competitiveness," Janet A. Napoli, economist with the Federal Reserve Bank of Chicago, examines the growth of the markets for forward, futures, options, and swaps during the 1980s and early 1990s. Her special interest is the growing number of exchanges on which derivatives are traded and the rapid spread of over-the-counter trading of derivatives in an era of financial deregulation. She believes that competition in derivatives trading has increased, which is contributing to the spreading internationalization of the financial marketplace.

Next, an article by senior economist James T. Moser from the Federal Reserve Bank of Chicago directs us to look closely at the market for financial futures contracts. Dr. Moser explores an issue raised by the Great Stock Market Crash of October 1987 which, some analysts have argued, was caused, in part, by the use of program trading using relatively cheap futures contracts. Financial futures generally carry low cash margins which customers must post in case the value of their investment in futures contracts declines. Some stock analysts believe that excessive futures trading, fueled by cheap required cash margins, causes stock prices to be more volatile than would otherwise be true. Dr. Moser argues that setting higher margins for futures contracts will not necessarily reduce speculative activity and stock price volatility.

An exploration of a different kind of derivative instrument—securities collateralized by residential mortgage loans—is launched by two scholars, James H. Gilkeson and Stephen D. Smith, writing for the Federal Reserve Bank of Atlanta. These securitized loans have unusual cash-flow features and present investors with a new kind of risk called *prepayment risk*, in which borrowers can prepay their loans early, thus affecting the maturity and cash-flow schedule of these loan-based securities. Gilkeson and Smith examine the possible losses that a lending institution can suffer from issuing liabilities of varying maturity to finance a portfolio of mortgage-backed securities and other long-term mortgage instruments. They observe that the asymmetric reactions of customers prepaying their loans in response to changes in interest rates exposes a lending institution to significant risk whether interest rates are high or low. These economists show how greater use of equity capital and selected hedging techniques can deal with this added risk exposure.

Finally, in two interesting articles emanating from the Research Department of the Federal Reserve Bank of New York economists Lisa N. Galaif and Julia D. Fernald look at the characteristics, pricing, and hedging of a relatively new, but popular interest-rate swap contract—the *index amortizing rate (IAR) swap*. IARs are based upon a principal (notional) amount that decreases over time in accordance with the path of future market interest rates and according to a schedule agreed upon by the parties to the swap. IARs are much more complex than conventional swap contracts and require highly technical models in order to price and hedge them properly. They create risks for swap users that investors and dealers should become more fully aware of if they are to achieve their return and risk-hedging goals.

Article 16

Saving and Demographics: Some International Comparisons

*Stephen A. Meyer**

The United States saved only a small share of its aggregate income during the 1980s—a much lower share than most other large, industrial countries saved. As shares of GNP, both household and government saving were smaller in the U.S. The differences in personal saving owe much to demographic factors—especially to differences in the age composition of countries' populations. The differences in government saving around the world reflect budget balances: surpluses in high-saving countries and deficits in low-saving countries.

Differences in saving are important because saving is the source of funds required to finance investment in plant and equipment, structures, and housing. Persistently higher saving shares in both West Germany and Japan, for example, financed greater net investment relative to GNP than in the U.S. Over time, investment has increased the stock of productive capital and contributed to growing labor productivity and a rising standard of living in all three countries. But West Germany and Japan experienced a more rapid increase in labor productivity over

---

*Stephen A. Meyer is Vice President and Associate Director of Research at the Federal Reserve Bank of Philadelphia. He also is an Adjunct Professor of Finance at the Wharton School of the University of Pennsylvania.

the past 40 years because they saved a larger share of their aggregate incomes.[1]

Some analysts argue that the share of personal income saved in the United States will rise strongly during the next 20 years, as more and more of the baby-boom generation enters middle age.[2] These analysts anticipate that saving rates in the U.S. will rise to levels more like those in Germany and Japan. Indeed, recent economic research does suggest that projected demographic changes are likely to narrow the gap in saving rates between the U.S. and Germany or Japan, but this result derives as much from falling saving rates abroad as from a rising saving rate in the U.S.

COMPARING U.S. SAVING IN THE 1980s TO GERMANY AND JAPAN

The net national saving rate in the United States was lower in the 1980s than in many other industrial countries, especially West Germany and Japan (Table 1).[3] The lower saving rate in the U.S. was accompanied by lower net investment relative to GNP. Net national saving in West Germany, when measured as a share of GNP, was more than three times as large as in the U.S. And in Japan the share was six times that in the U.S.[4] Among the components of national saving, household saving was more than twice as big a share of GNP in West Germany as in the U.S., while in Japan it was

TABLE 1
Saving and Investment as a Share of GNP
(Average for 1980s, in percent)

	U.S.	West Germany	Japan
Net National Saving	3.0	10.2	18.1
Household	3.8	7.8	11.0
Business	1.7	1.0	2.8
Government	-2.5	1.3	4.3
Net Fixed Investment	5.1	8.0	15.4

---

[1] From 1950 through 1989, labor productivity grew at an average rate slightly below 6 percent per year in Japan, at an average annual rate somewhat above 4 percent in Germany, and at a rate averaging just 1.75 percent per year in the U.S. For a technical discussion of the relationship between investment and productivity growth, and a careful examination of the data, see Wolff (1991). Productivity growth rates cited here are from Wolff (1991), updated with data for the 1980s from the OECD *Economic Outlook*, July 1991.

[2] See, for example, "Upbeat Generation," *Barron's*, August 1, 1988, pp. 15 and 30.

[3] The saving, investment, and aggregate income data cited in this article are those available as of November 1991. The data are taken from *National Accounts* and from *Quarterly National Accounts*, published regularly by the Organization for Economic Cooperation and Development (OECD) in Paris. These publications draw on each country's official national income and product accounts. Figures for net investment cited here include net fixed investment spending by governments—spending on capital equipment, buildings, and infrastructure such as roads, bridges, dams, water systems, and airports. Government investment is included in the OECD data for Germany and Japan. Investment spending by governments in the U.S. was estimated using other sources.

[4] Part of a country's saving is used to finance the replacement of buildings and capital equipment that wear out or are abandoned each year. To the extent that saving and investment spending exceed replacement investment, they can contribute to growing labor productivity and a rising standard of living. The definition of saving that corresponds to this concept of funds available to finance growth of the capital stock, or net investment, is net national saving.

nearly three times as big. The government sector in the U.S. ran budget deficits throughout the 1980s, thus reducing national saving. In contrast, governments in West Germany and Japan added to national saving by running budget surpluses in most years. Net business saving (mostly retained earnings) differed much less among these countries.[5]

Not only was net national saving a smaller share of GNP in the U.S. than in West Germany and Japan, but the gaps widened during the 1980s. Household saving declined relative to GNP in all three countries as the 1980s progressed. In Germany and Japan, government sector budget surpluses rose relative to GNP, offsetting the drop in personal saving (and in Germany business saving also rose strongly). But in the U.S., the government sector continued to run budget deficits, thus reinforcing the decline in personal saving relative to GNP.

Differences in government saving largely reflect political decisions about government spending and taxes. Differences in household saving rates between the U.S., Germany, and Japan during the 1980s reflect demographic factors, in part. The way in which demographic factors affect household saving can best be understood by looking at some basic economic theory of saving behavior.

THE FORWARD-LOOKING THEORY OF SAVING

Economic theory has focused on five major reasons why people save: (1) to provide for their retirement; (2) to leave a bequest; (3) to bridge temporary declines in their incomes; (4) to finance unanticipated expenditures such as medical bills; and (5) to finance purchases of durable goods such as furniture and automobiles. The theory of saving behavior is complex, and economists' understanding of saving behavior is still evolving. We can avoid many of the complications, but nonetheless gain a good deal of insight into the effect of demographic factors on saving behavior, by focusing on a somewhat simplified description of the basic forward-looking theory of family saving.

Theory. The basic theory of saving begins by recognizing that real earnings usually are relatively low early in people's careers, peak shortly before retirement, and then fall substantially after retirement. The theory proceeds with the idea that people prefer to spread their consumption of goods and services evenly over their lives to the extent they can do so and, in particular, that people would rather not have their consumption fall sharply when they retire.

From these premises, the theory predicts that younger families actually will spend more than their incomes if they have ready access to credit or an inheritance, so their saving will be negative on average. If they do not have ready access to credit or an inheritance, younger families will save at most a small share of their incomes. Middle-aged families typically will save a larger share of their rising earnings as they prepare for retirement and accumulate an estate. Families headed by retired people typically will save little, if any, of their incomes, and in many cases they will dissave. This predicted pattern of changing personal saving rates over one's lifetime is known as *life-cycle saving*.

Evidence. Surveys of consumer spending and finances in the U.S. yield results that are broadly consistent with the life-cycle pattern of earnings and saving discussed above. Average earnings do rise with age, and there is a broad peak in average earnings between ages 50 and

---

[5]Fumio Hayashi of the University of Pennsylvania argues that Japanese national income accounts understate replacement investment, and thus overstate net national saving and investment, so that the gap between Japanese and American saving and investment shares is smaller than indicated here. But Robert Dekle of Boston University and Lawrence Summers of the World Bank present other data suggesting that the gap really is as large as shown by the official statistics. See Hayashi (1989) and Dekle and Summers (1991).

60. Very young families, those headed by people less than 25 years old, do tend to spend more than they earn (their savings are negative, on average), indicating that they are incurring debts or spending gifts and inheritances. Surveys show that average earnings substantially exceed average spending for families in the peak-earning years. And many families do draw down their savings during retirement; families headed by people over 64 save very little of their incomes, on average. During the mid-1980s, the share of income saved by households headed by people between the ages of 45 and 64 averaged 6 to 8 percentage points higher than the share saved by households headed by people over the age of 64.[6] Surveys of saving behavior in Canada and Japan yield similar results.[7] All of these observations are broadly consistent with the predicted life-cycle pattern of saving derived from a simple forward-looking theory.

The simplest version of the life-cycle saving model, described above, does not explain all of what we observe about family saving. Many families in the peak-earning years save an appreciably larger share of their incomes than do families whose heads are between 25 and 44, but some families save a small and relatively constant share of their incomes throughout their working years. Many older families draw down their savings, but others neither save nor dissave, and those with substantial wealth typically continue to save. These observations are broadly consistent with the life-cycle saving pattern predicted by more complex versions of the forward-looking theory, which incorporate precautionary saving, social security, borrowing constraints, uncertainty about lifespans, and saving to accumulate an estate.[8] Even in these more complicated models, age affects saving behavior.

Demographic factors are not the only determinants of household saving. People's saving also is affected by the tax treatment of saving and interest, by the structure of social security and pension systems, by the variability of incomes, by the extent to which people can insure against unanticipated expenditures or income reductions, by unanticipated changes in wealth, and by the strength or weakness of the economy, among other factors.[9] There also is evidence that household saving is affected by the size of government budget surpluses or deficits. Demographic factors do have important influences on household saving, however.

THE EFFECT OF DEMOGRAPHICS ON HOUSEHOLD SAVING

While there is vigorous debate among economists about how much household saving is generated by each of the five major reasons for saving, there is broad agreement that the age composition of a country's population can af-

---

[6]Data cited here are based on Tables 3, 13, and 23 in "Consumer Expenditure Survey: Integrated Survey Data, 1984-86", *BLS Bulletin 2333* (August 1989), published by the Bureau of Labor Statistics of the U.S. Department of Labor. The Survey of Consumer Finances, conducted by the Federal Reserve System, yields broadly similar conclusions; see Kennickell (1990).

[7]Saving behavior in Canada and Japan, as well as in the U.S., is examined in Bosworth, Burtless, and Sabelhaus (1991).

[8]For a brief review of economists' knowledge of saving behavior, see Weil (1991). For a more detailed and extensive treatment of the roles of saving for retirement and for bequests, see Kotlikoff (1989). For a discussion of the role of precautionary saving and evidence of its importance, see Carroll (1991). For a focus on borrowing constraints, see Zeldes (1989).

[9]See Boskin and Lau (1988) for a careful discussion of the roles of these and other factors.

[10]A lively exchange between Franco Modigliani of MIT and Laurence Kotlikoff of Boston University summarizes much of the agreement and disagreement. See Modigliani (1988) and Kotlikoff (1988).

fect the share of income that is saved.[10] The "life-cycle saving" theory suggests that a high share of household income will be saved in a country that has a large fraction of its population in the high-saving years from 45 to 64 and a small fraction in the low-saving or dissaving years up to 20 and beyond 64. Household saving would be a relatively large share of GNP as a result. Conversely, the theory predicts that household saving would be a smaller share of GNP in a country that has a small fraction of its population in the peak-saving years from 45 to 65 and a large fraction of its population in the low-saving or dissaving age groups.

Empirical research largely bears out these expectations. The strongest demographic effect appears to result from an increase in the share of the population that is beyond retirement age, accompanied by a decrease in the working-age share of the population. Researchers estimate that a 1-percentage-point increase in the ratio of the population over the age of 64 to the working-age population, holding constant other factors that affect saving, has been associated with a reduction in the ratio of household saving to GNP by an amount in the range from 0.4 to 1.4 percentage points, for an average estimate of 0.9 percentage point. There also is evidence that an increase in the ratio of the under-20 population to the working-age population reduces household saving relative to GNP, but this effect appears smaller—perhaps half as big.[11]

COMPARING U.S. DEMOGRAPHICS IN THE 1980s TO GERMANY AND JAPAN

The share of the U.S. population in the high-saving age group from age 45 to 64 was appreciably lower than in Germany and Japan in both

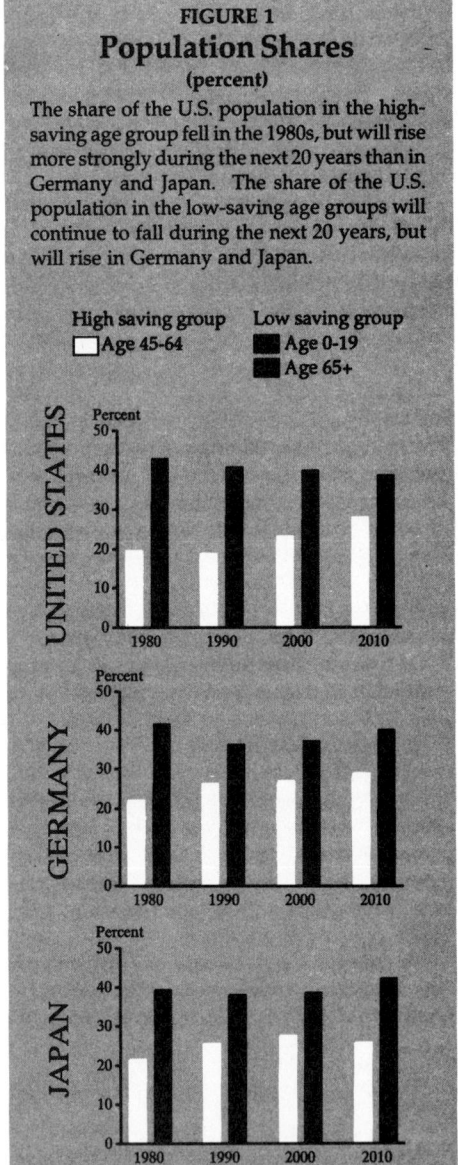

FIGURE 1
Population Shares
(percent)

The share of the U.S. population in the high-saving age group fell in the 1980s, but will rise more strongly during the next 20 years than in Germany and Japan. The share of the U.S. population in the low-saving age groups will continue to fall during the next 20 years, but will rise in Germany and Japan.

---

[11] For a summary of the results of these studies, see Table 9 in Heller (1989). The numbers presented here correspond to those presented by Heller, but here they are presented as shares of GNP rather than as shares of national income.

1980 and 1990 (Figure 1). And the share of the U.S. population in that high-saving age group declined during the 1980s, while it rose strongly in Germany and Japan. In addition, the total share of the U.S. population in the low-saving age groups was larger at both the beginning and the end of the 1980s than was the case in either Germany or Japan.[12]

On average during the 1980s, 19 percent of the U.S. population was in the high-saving group from age 45 to 64—about 4.5 percentage points lower than in Japan and nearly 5.5 percentage points lower than in Germany. The ratio of 65-and-over to working-age populations in the U.S. averaged roughly 4 percentage points lower than in Germany during the 1980s, but 4 percentage points higher than in Japan. The ratio of under-20 to working-age populations also was higher in the U.S., averaging 12 percentage points higher than in Germany and about 4 percentage points higher than in Japan. In total, an average of nearly 42 percent of the U.S. population fell into the two low-saving age groups during the 1980s, about 3 percentage points higher than in Germany and Japan.

On balance, these demographic ratios imply somewhat higher personal saving relative to GNP in Germany than in the U.S. during the 1980s, and much higher household saving relative to GNP in Japan, as we in fact observed. Taken together, the demographic differences can account for roughly one-third of the gap in personal saving relative to GNP between Germany and the U.S. during the 1980s and roughly two-thirds of the gap between Japan and the U.S.[13]

Demographic factors help explain not only why household saving in the U.S. was lower relative to GNP than in Germany and Japan but also why household saving shares declined during the 1980s. As the ratio of the 65-and-over to working-age populations grew in the U.S. from 1980 to 1990, personal saving declined relative to GNP (Table 2). Similarly, the sharp rise in the ratio of 65-and-over to working-age populations in Japan from 1980 to 1990 helps explain why personal saving declined relative to GNP in that country.

Demographic factors, by themselves, do not entirely explain the decline in household saving during the 1980s.[14] Personal saving in Germany did not rise relative to GNP, for example, even though the ratio of 65-and-over to working-age populations declined. Other factors that may have reduced household saving shares include expanded coverage by pension, social security, and medical insurance systems, large capital gains in equity and housing markets, and declining birthrates. While demographic factors are not the sole determinant of household saving behavior, the fact that saving by households was roughly twice as large relative to GNP in Germany as in the U.S. during the 1980s, and roughly three times as large in Japan, does reflect differences in the age composition of these countries' populations.

PROJECTED DEMOGRAPHIC CHANGES AND FUTURE SAVING RATES

Demographers project that the age composition of the U.S., German, and Japanese populations will change markedly during the next 20 years. Those changes have the potential to raise personal saving relative to GNP in the United States and to reduce it in Germany and Japan.

Population Shares Will Change Markedly. Demographers project that the share of the U.S. population in the high-saving years from 45 to 64 will rise by half from 1990 to 2010, to nearly 28 percent from about 18.5 percent, as the baby-

---

[12]Population data and projections cited in this article are taken from United Nations (1982).

[13]Based on the average size of the estimated effects found by the studies cited in Table 9 of Heller (1989).

[14]See Kennickell (1990) and Boskin and Lau (1988) for evidence on this point.

TABLE 2
Ratio of 65-and-Over Population to Working-Age Population and Household Saving

	1980	1985	1990
United States:			
65-and-over/working-age (%)	19.9	20.3	21.4
household saving/GNP (%)	5.0	3.1	3.3
Germany:			
65-and-over/working-age (%)	26.8	23.9	24.1
household saving/GNP (%)	8.3	7.2	8.2
Japan:			
65-and-over/working-age (%)	13.0	16.9	19.0
household saving/GNP (%)	12.7	10.7	9.4*

*This number for Japan is for 1989. Japanese saving data for 1990 were not yet published when this article went to press.

boom generation ages (Figure 1). The working-age share of the population will grow as well. The share of the U.S. population over the age of 64 is projected to be roughly constant during the next 20 years, and the share under the age of 20 is projected to decline.

In Germany and Japan, in contrast, the share of the population in the high-saving age group is projected to change much less during the next 20 years. But demographers project that the share of the population over the age of 64 will rise by one-third in Germany, to nearly 21 percent. In Japan, the share of the population 65 or older will rise by two-thirds, to nearly 20 percent in 2010. While the share of the population under the age of 20 is projected to shrink about as much in each of those countries as in the U.S., the working-age share of the population also is projected to shrink in Germany and Japan, in contrast to the U.S.

People who will be older than 20 during the next two decades have been born already, and major industrial countries have reasonably accurate census data. As a result, demographers' projections of changes in the age composition of those countries' populations over the next 20 years are likely to be fairly accurate. There is uncertainty about future birthrates and about how much average lifespans may increase. Even so, population projections for the next two decades are unlikely to be far off unless birthrates or death rates change dramatically—or unless migration occurs on a larger scale than observed in recent decades. The possibility of larger-than-usual immigration to Germany is quite real, considering ongoing developments in Eastern Europe. Should large-scale migration occur, the working-age population in Germany might not shrink as projected. For the U.S. and Japan, however, larger-than-usual immigration seems unlikely.

If demographic projections prove correct, the ratio of 65-and-over to working-age populations will rise by 6.4 percentage points in Germany and by 9.5 percentage points in Japan during the next 20 years, but will remain essentially unchanged in the U.S. (Figure 2). During the same period, the ratio of under-20 to working-age populations is projected to fall by about 7 percentage points in the U.S., but to rise roughly 1 percentage point in Germany and to reverse course and begin rising in Japan. Clearly, projected changes in the age composition of

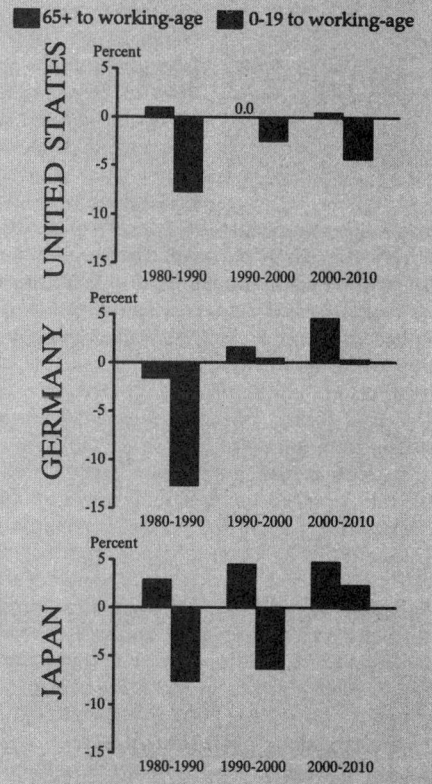

**FIGURE 2
Changes in Ratios of 65-and-over and Under-20 Populations to Working-Age Population**

The ratio of low-saving, 65-and-over population to higher-saving, working-age population in the U.S. will remain essentially unchanged over the next 20 years, but will rise strongly in Germany and Japan. And the ratio of low-saving, under-20 population to higher-saving, working-age population will continue to decline in the U.S., but not in Germany and Japan.

these three countries' populations have the potential to raise household saving in the U.S. and to lower it in Germany and Japan.

Changes in Population Shares Will Affect Household Saving. There is widespread agreement on this point among economists who have studied the issue, but there is disagreement on how large those changes are likely to be. Taking the average of earlier-cited estimates of the effects of changes in population ratios on household saving behavior, and multiplying that average by the projected changes in population ratios, one might conclude that demographic trends, by themselves, have the potential to raise the ratio of household saving to GNP in the U.S. by 3.5 to 4 percentage points by the year 2010, and to reduce the ratio by 6 to 6.5 percentage points in Germany and by 7 to 7.5 percentage points in Japan. Changes in saving shares are unlikely to be so large, however.

Because the U.S. baby-boom generation is so large relative to previous generations, it is difficult to predict just how much baby boomers' incomes and saving will rise as they enter their peak-earning years. Their peak incomes may not exceed the incomes they earned earlier in their lives by as much as was the case for earlier generations simply because so many baby boomers are competing for jobs. Also, if labor productivity in the U.S. continues to grow as slowly as it did during the 1980s, baby boomers' incomes will not rise as rapidly over the remainder of their working lives as was the case for earlier generations. Both of these possibilities suggest that U.S. baby boomers' saving rates may not rise as much when they enter their peak-earning years as was the case for earlier generations. In Germany and Japan, though, the shrinking working-age populations may cause the incomes of those entering their peak-earning years during the next two decades to rise more rapidly than was the case for earlier generations. In addition, if lifespans continue to grow longer, those now at work in all three countries may postpone retirement and may save more as they prepare for a longer retirement. Thus longer lifespans may raise aggregate personal saving.

Although it is difficult to forecast just how much household saving behavior will change as a result of projected demographic changes, some recent economic research provides at least a rough idea. Taking into account projected changes in the ratio of 65-and-over to working-age populations and in the ratio of under-20 to working-age populations, and also taking into account the changes in real wages and in income distribution that seem likely to result, Paul R. Masson of the International Monetary Fund and Ralph W. Tryon of the Federal Reserve estimate that demographic shifts during the next 20 years have the potential to raise the ratio of household saving to GNP in the U.S. by roughly 2 to 2.5 percentage points by the year 2010. In contrast, they estimate that demographic shifts can lower the ratio of household saving to GNP by roughly 1.5 to 2 percentage points in Germany and by roughly 3.5 to 4 points in Japan.[15]

Changes in Population Shares May Affect Government Saving. Changing age distributions may affect government budget balances as well as private saving. As the number of people aged 65 and over in Germany and Japan grows rapidly during the next 20 years, their governments' spending on medical care, pensions, social security systems, retirement housing, and other programs for the elderly is likely to grow rapidly too. On the other hand, spending on education may decline as the number of children shrinks. One careful study undertaken by the OECD estimates that, on balance, projected demographic shifts would increase government spending in Germany by an amount equal to nearly 5.5 percent of GNP by 2010, and in Japan by 9.5 percent of GNP—if there are no changes in government pension or benefit programs.[16] At the same time, the working-age population in those two countries is projected to decline, making it more difficult for governments to raise additional revenues. Thus government saving in Germany and Japan may well shrink relative to GNP during the next two decades and could become negative, although governments are likely to offset at least part of the effect of demographic changes on their budgets.

In the United States, by contrast, the number of people 65 and older is projected to grow slowly during the next 20 years. Over the same period, the working-age share of the population is projected to rise. Thus in the U.S., the demand for government services for the elderly is likely to grow less rapidly during the next two decades than it did during the previous two. The OECD study cited in the preceding paragraph estimates that demographic shifts could reduce government spending in the U.S. by an amount roughly equal to 1.5 percent of GNP over the next 20 years. Over the same period, changing demographics are projected to generate large and growing surpluses in the U.S. Social Security System. Government dissaving in the United States could well shrink as a result.

Over the next two decades, then, projected changes in the age distribution of populations are likely to lower personal saving relative to GNP in Germany and Japan and perhaps re-

---

[15] Masson and Tryon (1990) undertake a careful empirical investigation of the effects of projected demographic changes in these three countries. For studies focusing on the U.S., see Kennickell (1990) and Auerbach and Kotlikoff (1989).

[16] For a discussion of the implications of projected demographic changes for social policy and the demand for government services, see *Ageing Populations: The Social Policy Implications*, published by the OECD (Paris, 1988). Several other estimates of the likely size of changes in demand for government services are summarized in Heller (1989) and in Table 2 of Masson and Tryon (1990).

duce government saving as well. In the United States, by contrast, demographic trends are likely to increase personal saving relative to GNP—and perhaps raise government saving, too.

Beyond 2010, however, the share of the U.S. population over 65 is projected to rise and the share in the high-saving, peak-earning years is projected to gradually decline as the baby-boom generation begins to enter the retirement years. Thus the projected rise in national saving relative to GNP in the U.S. may prove temporary. Demographers project that the ratio of over-65 to working-age populations will continue to rise in Germany and Japan, although more gradually. The projected decline in national saving relative to GNP in those two countries may prove longer lasting.

SUMMARY

From 1980 to 1990, both personal saving and net national saving were much smaller relative to aggregate income in the U.S. than in Germany or Japan. The lower ratio of personal saving to GNP in the U.S. partly reflected the age composition of the three countries' populations: an appreciably smaller share of the U.S. population was in the peak-earning, high-saving years from age 45 to 64 than was the case in Germany and Japan; and the share of the U.S. population in the low saving years before people enter the labor force and after they retire was larger than for the other two countries. In addition, the government sector in the U.S. ran budget deficits throughout the 1980s, thus reducing net national saving, while the government sectors in Germany and Japan ran budget surpluses.

Looking ahead, demographic projections suggest that personal saving will rise relative to GNP in the U.S. during the next 20 years as the share of the U.S. population in the high-saving years rises by half and the share in the low-saving age groups declines. Demographic projections also suggest that personal saving will fall relative to GNP in Germany and Japan during the same period, as the share of their populations that is over the age of 64 rises sharply and the working-age share of their populations shrinks.

The projected changes in the age composition of the German and Japanese populations seem likely to reduce government saving as well as household saving. But in the U.S., demographic changes are likely to contribute to smaller budget deficits—and possibly to budget surpluses.

Overall, projected demographic changes are likely to narrow the gap between high national saving relative to GNP in Germany and Japan and low national saving relative to GNP in the U.S. But demographic trends seem unlikely to raise U.S. saving rates to levels observed in Germany or Japan during the 1980s. The projected narrowing of saving gaps during the next 20 years will result as much from lower saving shares in Germany and Japan as from a higher saving share in the U.S.

REFERENCES

Auerbach, Alan J., and Laurence J. Kotlikoff. "Demographics, Fiscal Policy, and U.S. Saving in the 1980s and Beyond," Working Paper 3150, National Bureau of Economic Research (October 1989).

Boskin, Michael J., and Lawrence J. Lau. "An Analysis of Postwar U.S. Consumption and Savings Behavior, Parts I and II," Working Papers 2605 and 2606, National Bureau of Economic Research (June 1988).

Bosworth, Barry, Gary Burtless, and John Sabelhaus. "The Decline in Saving: Evidence from Household Surveys," *Brookings Papers on Economic Activity* 1 (1991).

Carroll, Christopher D. "Buffer Stock Saving and the Permanent Income Hypothesis," Working Paper 114, Division of Research and Statistics—Economic Activity Section, Board of Governors of the Federal Reserve System (February 1991).

Dekle, Robert, and Lawrence Summers. "Japan's High Saving Rate Reaffirmed," Working Paper 3690, National Bureau of Economic Analysis (April 1991).

Hayashi, Fumio. "Is Japan's Saving Rate High?" Federal Reserve Bank of Minneapolis *Quarterly Review* (Spring 1989).

Heller, Peter S. "Aging, Saving, and Pensions in the Group of Seven Countries: 1980-2025," Working Paper 89/13, International Monetary Fund (January 1989)

Kennickell, Arthur B. "Demographics and Household Savings," Finance and Economics Discussion Series Paper 123, Board of Governors of the Federal Reserve System (May 1990).

Kotlikoff, Laurence J. "Intergenerational Transfers and Saving," *Journal of Economic Perspectives* (Spring 1988).

Kotlikoff, Laurence J., ed. *What Determines Savings?* (MIT Press, 1989).

Masson, Paul R., and Ralph W. Tryon. "Macroeconomic Effects of Projected Population Aging in Industrial Countries," Working Paper 90/5, International Monetary Fund (January 1990).

Modigliani, Franco. "The Role of Intergenerational Transfers and Life Cycle Saving in the Accumulation of Wealth," *Journal of Economic Perspectives* (Spring 1988).

United Nations. *Demographic Indicators of Countries: Estimates and Projections as Assessed in 1980* (New York, 1982).

Weil, David N. "What Determines Saving: A Review Essay," *Journal of Monetary Economics* (August 1991).

Wolff, Edward N. "Capital Formation and Productivity Convergence Over the Long Term," *American Economic Review* (June 1991).

Zeldes, Stephen P. "Consumption and Liquidity Constraints: An Empirical Investigation," *Journal of Political Economy* (April 1989).

Article 17

Interpreting the Term Structure of Interest Rates

This Weekly Letter *is adapted from the discussion at the Conference on Macroeconomic Stabilization Policy held at Stanford University on March 5 and 6, 1993. The conference was jointly sponsored by the Federal Reserve Bank of San Francisco and the Center for Economic Policy Research at Stanford.*

The term structure of interest rates—sometimes called the yield curve—refers to the curve traced out by interest rates on securities as their maturity ranges from short to long-term. Typically, interest rates on long-term securities are higher than rates on short-term securities, so the term structure generally slopes upward. But sometimes, long-term rates are lower than short-term rates; in this case, the yield curve is described as "inverted."

The term structure of interest rates is important because it contains information about the market's forecasts of future inflation and interest rates as well as about its perception of risk. For example, in recent months, long-term interest rates have fallen relative to short-term rates. To some extent, this may reflect beliefs that inflation will be lower in the future, that deficit reduction will reduce future short-term real interest rates, or that risks associated with long-term investments may have diminished. If properly understood, this information can help investors and policymakers formulate long-term plans.

This *Weekly Letter* explains how to interpret the information in the yield curve. It reviews the basic theory of the term structure, discusses the empirical importance of various theoretical factors, provides some insight into the events of the 1980s, and interprets the recent decline in long-term interest rates.

The theory of the term structure

The simplest theory of the term structure is known as the Expectations Hypothesis. According to this theory, the expected return earned by holding long and short-term bonds over the same period of time should be the same. For example, suppose an investor has a choice between two long-term investment strategies, either to buy a long-term bond and hold it until it matures, or to roll over a sequence of short-term bills. If investors were not concerned about risk, they would choose the strategy which pays the higher expected return. Then, in equilibrium, the two strategies would have the same expected return. For example, if the expected return on long-term bonds were greater than the expected return on rolling over short-term bonds, investors would sell short-term bonds and buy long-term bonds. This would increase yields on short-term bonds, while the return on long-term bonds would fall. Investors would continue this operation until expected returns were equalized.

Similarly, suppose an investor has a choice between two short-term investment strategies, either to buy a 3-month bill and hold it until it matures, or to buy a long-term bond, hold it for three months, and then sell it. The Expectations Hypothesis predicts that the interest rate on 3-month bills should be the same as the expected return on holding the long-term bond three months. Therefore, the difference between actual holding returns on long and short bonds, which is called the "excess holding return," should be unpredictable.

According to the expectations theory, the shape of the yield curve is determined by expectations about future changes in short-term interest rates. In particular, the term structure slopes upward when short rates are expected to rise, and it slopes downward when short rates are expected to fall. To see why, suppose that future short-term rates are expected to rise. If the yield curve were flat, investors could make more money by rolling over short-term bills than by holding long-term bonds. To eliminate this arbitrage opportunity, the long-term bond yield must be greater than the current short-term rate. In this case, the yield curve must slope upward.

While the Expectations Hypothesis certainly contains an element of truth, most economists believe that it is oversimplified. In particular, while the Expectations Hypothesis implies that expected holding returns on long and short-term bonds should be the same, empirical studies show that there are predictable differences. This suggests that the expectations theory leaves out an important ingredient. Many economists believe that the missing ingredient is risk. When interest rates change, the value of pre-existing long-term bonds also changes, and the longer the time to maturity the greater is the capital gain or loss. Thus long-term bonds are subject to greater capital risk than short-term bonds. In addition, some bonds are subject to default risk, although this does not apply to Treasury bonds. Since many investors dislike risk, they require a higher expected return—a risk premium—on long-term bonds.

The presence of a risk premium complicates the interpretation of the term structure, since an upward sloping yield curve might indicate that markets expect short-term rates to rise or that there is greater uncertainty about the future. Similarly, if the risk premium is large enough, the yield curve can slope upward even when short-term rates are expected to fall. Thus it is important to account for time-varying risk premia when interpreting the term structure.

Time-varying term premia
To induce risk-averse investors to hold long bonds for one quarter, the expected holding return on long bonds must include a one-quarter risk premium. To induce risk-averse investors to hold long bonds until maturity, long bonds must offer a sequence of quarterly risk premia, covering the period from now until maturity. The yield to maturity on long bonds includes a long-term risk premium which is equal to the present discounted value of the sequence of expected short-term risk premia.

One can interpret the predictable variation in excess holding returns as evidence of variation in short-term risk premia. Thus one can estimate the long-term risk premium by constructing a forecasting model, generating forecasts of excess holding returns over long horizons, and then discounting those forecasts back to the present.

My forecasting model is adapted from Fuhrer and Moore (1993). It predicts future excess holding returns using past observations of short-term bill rates, realized excess holding returns, detrended output, and inflation. The short-term interest rate is the 3-month Treasury bill rate, and the long-term interest rate is the 10-year Treasury bond rate. Output is measured by per capita GDP, and inflation is measured by the percent change in the implicit GDP deflator. I estimated the model using quarterly data over the period 1959 to 1992. The results are shown in the figure, which shows the implied long-term risk premia as well as estimates of the long-term real interest rate. The distance between the two curves is the expected real return earned by rolling over short-term bonds.

Long-Term Real Rates and Risk Premia

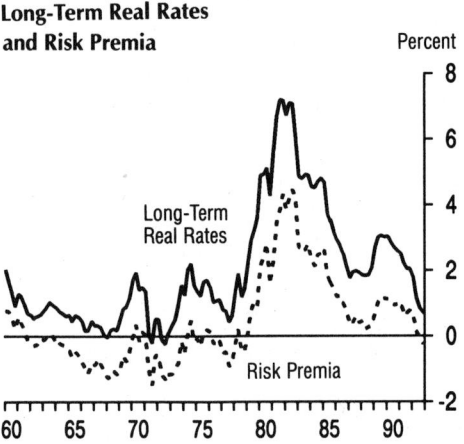

If the Expectations Hypothesis were correct, the long-term risk premium would be zero at all dates in the sample, and variation in the long-term real interest rate would be due entirely to variation in the expected rollover return on bills. In contrast, the figure shows that most of the variation in the long-term interest rate is due to variation in the risk premium. Relatively little is due to the expected rollover return. Thus the shape of the yield curve appears to depend primarily on time-varying risk premia. The factors emphasized by the expectations theory appear to be of secondary importance.

Risk premia vary countercyclically; output tends to be below trend when risk is high. Holding risk constant, the real rollover return varies procyclically. It tends to be higher than average when output is above trend and risk is low. Yield spreads are useful for predicting risk premia, but they do not help to forecast the real rollover return on bills. Thus the ability of yield spreads to forecast output fluctuations (e.g., Huh 1993) appears to be related to uncertainty about future interest rate fluctuations.

Events of the 1980s
During the 1980s there was a substantial increase in long-term interest rates, and most of this was due to an increase in risk premia. For example, during the 1960s and 1970s, the average long-term real interest rate was approximately 1 percent, and risk premia were small, averaging −0.3 percentage points. Negative risk premia may seem anomalous, but they can occur when investors believe that there is a small chance of making a large capital gain on long bonds. During the 1980s, the risk premium averaged 2 percentage points, and average long-term real rates increased to 4.1 percent.

What caused such a large increase in risk? The timing suggests that it might be related to uncertainty about disinflation. Risk premia began to rise around the middle of 1979 and reached a peak in the third quarter of 1982. This roughly coincides with Chairman Volcker's efforts to drive down the inflation rate. At the time, there was a great deal of uncertainty about how long the Federal Reserve would persist in its efforts to reduce inflation. As unemployment began to rise, many people believed that the Federal Reserve might reverse course in order to stabilize employment. Since the commitment to disinflation was in doubt, it became very difficult to predict the path of inflation and thus very risky to hold long-term nominal bonds. Risk premia rose dramatically to compensate investors for the unusually high degree of uncertainty about inflation.

In 1982 the inflation rate fell from roughly 8 percent to around 4 percent, and it remained around 4 percent for the rest of the decade. Risk premia declined more gradually, which suggests that the Federal Reserve's steady inflation policy gained credibility only gradually. After 1986, the risk premium decline to roughly 0.6 percent. Although the likelihood of a return to high inflation was relatively low, unlikely events do sometimes occur. Thus the risk premium on long bonds remained higher than in the 1960s and 1970s. The evidence suggests that our temporary experience with high inflation in the late 1970s and early 1980s had a lasting effect on long-term real interest rates.

Recent events
Over the last few months the term structure of interest rates has become flatter, as long-term yields have fallen while short-term rates were more or less unchanged. In particular, the spread between 10-year Treasury bond rates and 3-month Treasury bill rates fell by roughly 40 basis points. Complete data for the first quarter are not yet available, so one can make only rough guesses about the factors underlying this change. Based on staff estimates of the missing data, my model suggests that this reflects roughly equal declines in risk and expected short-term real rates. For example, in the first quarter of 1993, the expected rollover return on short-term bills fell by 18 basis points, while the risk premium on long bonds declined by 11 basis points. The long-term real interest rate fell to 0.5 percent, a level not seen since 1977.

The timing of the change in the yield curve suggests that it was driven by news about deficit reduction. For example, the biggest drop in long-term rates occurred after President Clinton's economic address, in which he outlined his strategy for reducing the federal budget deficit. This reduces long-term interest rates in two ways. Deficit reduction increases national saving and thus eases pressure on short-term real interest rates. Deficit reduction also reduces the risk of a return to high inflation by slowing the growth of nominal aggregate demand in the intermediate run and by reducing the likelihood that the government will monetize its deficits in the long run.

Timothy Cogley
Economist

References

Fuhrer, Jeffrey, and George Moore. 1993. "Monetary Policy and the Behavior of Long-term Interest Rates." Mimeo. Board of Governors of the Federal Reserve System (February).

Huh, Chan G. 1993. "Interest Rate Spreads as Indicators of Monetary Policy." Federal Reserve Bank of San Francisco *Weekly Letter* 93-12 (March 26).

Understanding the Term Structure of Interest Rates: The Expectations Theory

Steven Russell

Steven Russell is an economist at the Federal Reserve Bank of St. Louis. Lynn Dietrich provided research assistance.

THE INTEREST RATES on loans and securities provide basic summary measures of their attractiveness to lenders. The role played by interest rates in allocating funds across financial markets is very similar to the role played by prices in allocating resources in markets for goods and services. Just as a relatively high price of a particular good tends to draw physical resources into its production, a relatively high interest rate on a particular type of security tends to draw funds into the activities that type of security is issued to finance. And just as identifying the factors that help determine prices is a key area of inquiry among economists who study goods markets, identifying the factors that help determine interest rates is a key area of inquiry for those who study financial markets.

Economic theory suggests that one important factor explaining the differences in the interest rates on different securities may be differences in their *terms*—that is, in the lengths of time before they mature. The relationship between the terms of securities and their market rates of interest is known as the *term structure* of interest rates. To display the term structure of interest rates on securities of a particular type at a particular point in time, economists use a diagram called a *yield curve*. As a result, term structure theory is often described as the theory of the yield curve.

Economists are interested in term structure theory for a number of reasons. One reason is that since the actual term structure of interest rates is easy to observe, the accuracy of the predictions of different term structure theories is relatively easy to evaluate. These theories are usually based on assumptions and principles that have applications in other branches of economic theory. If such principles prove useful in explaining the term structure, they might also prove useful in contexts in which their relevance is less easy to evaluate. One theory of the term structure that will be described here, for example, suggests that a behavioral trait called *risk aversion* may play a major role in determining the shape of the yield curve. If subsequent research lends credence to this theory, economists may give more emphasis to risk aversion in constructing theories of other aspects of financial market operation.[1]

A second reason why economists are interested in term structure theories is that they help explain the ways in which changes in short-term interest

---

[1] Examples include the role of financial intermediaries and the pricing of claims to physical assets (such as stocks).

rates—rates on securities with relatively short terms—affect the levels of long-term interest rates. Economic theory suggests that monetary policy may have a direct effect on short-term interest rates, but little, if any, direct effect on long-term rates. It also suggests that long-term rates play a critical role in a number of important economic decisions, such as firms' decisions about investment, and households' decisions about purchases of homes and other durable goods. Theories of the term structure may help explain the mechanism by which monetary policy affects these decisions.[2]

A third reason economists are interested in the term structure is that it may provide information about the *expectations* of participants in financial markets. These expectations are of considerable interest to forecasters and policymakers. Market participants' beliefs about what may happen in the future influence their current decisions; these decisions, in turn, help determine what actually happens in the future. Thus, knowledge of participants' expectations is critical to forecasting future events or determining the effects of different policies.

Many economists believe that the people best able to forecast events in a market are in fact the participants in that market. If this is true, interest rate forecasting and inferring the nature of financial market participants' expectations amount to the same thing. The term structure theory that will be described in this article, which is called the *expectations theory*, suggests that the observed term structure can indeed be used to infer market participants' expectations about future interest rates—and through them, what actual future rates might be, and how events that tend to influence these rates may unfold. These events could include changes in the rate of economic growth or changes in monetary policy, for example.

The goal of this article is to provide a simple but thorough description of the expectations theory. The first section of the article lays the groundwork by explaining the basic concept and principles of interest rates and securities pricing. The presentation emphasizes issues that are particularly relevant to understanding how the financial market goes about assigning different interest rates to securities with different terms. The second part of the article presents the expectations theory itself. The presentation is oriented around two widely noted observations about the term structure: (1) that yield curves are usually upward-sloping, and (2) that the steepness and/or direction of their slopes tends to change systematically as interest rates rise and fall.

BUILDING BLOCKS OF THE TERM STRUCTURE

Prices, Interest Rates and Time

Since the expectations theory tries to explain certain aspects of the way interest rates are determined, it is impossible to understand the theory without a thorough understanding of the nature and role of interest rates. A good starting point is the analogy we drew earlier between the prices of goods and services and the interest rates on securities. In our economy, purchasers of goods or services almost always pay with money, so the "price" of a given quantity of goods is simply the number of dollars paid for it. In markets where the goods are readily divisible and more or less uniform in quality, such as markets for agricultural commodities, the price is usually thought of as a number of dollars *per unit* of goods. This way of thinking about prices reflects what economists call the Law of One Price: when information is readily available and the number of buyers and sellers is large, each transaction involving a particular good tends to take place at the same unit price, regardless of the quantity of the good exchanged.

Discount and Return Ratios—In the securities market, one can think of lenders as buyers, and of future payments as the items they purchase. People lend to the federal government, for instance, by buying U.S. Treasury securities, which are government promises to repay the loans by making one or more future payments. The direct securities market counterpart of a price in a goods market would be the number

---

[2]Term structure theories are traditionally stated in terms of nominal or money interest rates. Economic theory predicts, however, that it is primarily real interest rates—interest rates net of expected inflation—that influence the decisions of households and firms. It is possible to formulate versions of most term-structure theories, including the theory described in this article, that apply specifically to real interest rates. Since we cannot observe inflation expectations, however, we cannot measure real interest rates directly. This makes it difficult to describe real-interest-rate versions of the theories in terms non-economists are likely to understand.

of dollars lent (paid) today per dollar repaid in the future (future dollar purchased).[3] A security that cost $10,000 and returned $12,500 at a later date, for example, would have a unit price of 0.80. This price might be called a *discount ratio*.[4]

Economists usually conform to financial market practice by thinking about securities in terms of return rather than discount ratios—that is, ratios of amounts repaid to the amounts lent, rather than the reverse. We can define the *return ratio* on a single-payment security as the ratio of its maturity payment to its price (that is, the amount lent). The return ratio on the security just described would be 1.25—the reciprocal of its discount ratio.

Accounting for the Time Dimension—The return ratio, it turns out, is not a very good analogue to the market price: it suffers from a serious problem that is directly connected to the topic of this article. In a competitive market, we think of the unit price as capturing all the price information a prospective buyer needs to allow him to decide whether to buy a particular good. Stated differently, a buyer should be indifferent between two purchases that take place at the same price.[5] This raises the question of whether a lender will actually be indifferent between making two loans (purchasing two securities) that have the same return ratio. Suppose, for instance, that a lender has a choice between making a $10,000 loan that repays $12,500 at the end of two years, and a $10,000 loan that repays $12,500 at the end of five years. Each of these loans has the same return ratio. Which is he likely to choose?

It seems fairly obvious that our hypothetical lender will prefer the former of these loans to the latter: the former loan repays the same amount at an earlier date. The fact that the two loans have identical return ratios is not enough to make this lender indifferent between them.

The return ratio is flawed because it neglects an important aspect of securities transactions that is absent from most goods transactions. This aspect is the *time dimension*. A securities transaction is an exchange that takes place over an interval of time, and the length of the interval is important to the parties in the transaction. Lenders are likely to be less interested in the total amount to be repaid than in the amount to be repaid per unit of time.

How can we adjust the return ratio to take the time dimension into account? If all loans had the same term, no adjustment would be needed. Fortunately, any loan with a term of more than one period can be expressed as a sequence of one-period loans with identical one-period return ratios. A five-year loan, for example, can be expressed as a sequence of five one-year loans with a common annual return ratio. We can use these annual-equivalent return ratios to compare the returns on loans with different terms.

In order to be more concrete about this statement, we need to define some notation. Let's call the current date "date 0" and the maturity date of a given security "date N," so that the term of the security is N periods. From now on we will think of the periods as years; this is convenient, but not essential. Let V_0 represent the amount lent and V_N the amount repaid. The return ratio on the loan is thus V_N/V_0, and the *per-period* (usually annual) *return ratio* is:[6]

$$R \equiv \sqrt[N]{\frac{V_N}{V_0}}$$

We can compute this ratio for any single-payment loan, as long as we know the amount lent, the amount repaid and the term. It provides us with exactly what we are looking for: a numerical yardstick that can be used to

---

[3]For the moment, we will make the (inaccurate) assumption that all loans/securities return a single payment at a fixed maturity date.

[4]Since prospective lenders always have the option of storing their money, the discount ratio should always be less than one. (No lender with this option will make a loan that returns less money than he lent.)

[5]We must assume that the goods do not differ in quality, and that price information is freely available. We must also assume that the goods are readily divisible, so that any quantity can be purchased at the given unit price. These are standard assumptions in the theory of competitive markets.

[6]The symbol "$\equiv$" should be read "is equal, by definition, to."

compare the returns on any two loans, regardless of their terms.[7]

To conform to financial market practice, we must modify the annual return ratio a little further. Market participants like to divide the repayment on loans into two components: one equal to the amount lent, which is called the *principal*, and another representing the remainder, which is called the *interest*.[8] They measure the return on loans as ratios of the interest to the principal. In our notation, market participants think of these returns in terms of *net return ratios*

$$r \equiv \frac{V_N - V_0}{V_0} = \frac{V_N}{V_0} - 1.$$

Unfortunately, the net return ratio suffers from the same problems of term comparison as the return ratio. However, we can define a *net per-period* (again, usually annual) *interest rate* by

$$r \equiv \sqrt[N]{\frac{V_N}{V_0}} - 1 = R - 1,$$

which is a per-period version of r. The annual interest rate serves as the financial market's basic measure of the attractiveness of the returns on securities. Very often it is converted into a percentage by multiplying it by 100.

If the annual interest rate truly serves as the analogue of the market price for securities, we can expect that in a competitive market it will be determined by the interaction of supply and demand. Financial market participants will face a *market interest rate* r^*, which they will view as beyond their power to influence, and will make their borrowing and lending decisions accordingly.[9]

Pricing Securities

The annual interest rate formula can be used to determine the price of a security: the amount a person who comes to the market offering to make a fixed repayment, at a fixed date in the future, will be able to borrow. If we let V_N represent the repayment a borrower promises to make exactly N years in the future, then he will be able to borrow (sell his security for) an amount V_0, where

$$V_0 = \frac{V_N}{(1+r^*)^N}.$$

This is the basic formula for "pricing" (or discounting) securities.

So far, we have assumed that all loans/securities return a single payment at a fixed maturity date. We know that in practice, however, most securities return multiple payments at multiple future dates. As long as the amounts and dates of these payments are known, we can simply price them separately and sum them to obtain the security's total price, or *present value*

$$V_0 = \frac{V_1}{1+r^*} + \frac{V_2}{(1+r^*)^2} + \ldots + \frac{V_N}{(1+r^*)^N} = \sum_{t=1}^{N} \frac{V_t}{(1+r^*)^t}.$$

The present value of a sequence of future payments is the current market value of those payments, where the market value is determined by discounting the future payments back to the present at the market interest rate. Here, V_t represents the payment at the end of any date t (if there is no payment at a particular date $\hat{t}$, we say that $V_{\hat{t}} = 0$) and $1/(1+r^*)^t$ represents the discount factor applied to that payment.

Secondary Market Pricing—We are now ready to confront a pair of questions that are crucial in understanding the term structure. First, suppose the owner of a security wants to sell it before it comes due—that is, in the *secondary* market. How much can he expect to receive for it?

---

[7] Suppose we construct a sequence of one-period loans $\{(V_0, V_1), (V_1, V_2), \ldots, (V_{N-1}, V_N)\}$, where V_j represents the amount lent at date j, and V_{j+1} the amount repaid one period later. This sequence has the properties that (1) the amount lent at date 0 is V_0, (2) the amount repaid at date N is V_N and (3) the amount repaid on the tth loan in the sequence, at any intermediate date t + 1, is identical to the amount lent on the t + 1st loan, which is extended at the same date. (Thus, the loans are "rolled over" from date to date.) Properties (1) through (3) guarantee that, from the lender's point of view, this sequence of one-period loans is identical to the multiperiod loan. It turns out that only one sequence of loans satisfies these three properties and is consistent with our requirement that the return ratios on each loan be identical. This is the sequence produced when each successive one-period loan is extended at a return ratio of R, as defined above.

[8] Part of the reason for this is that, as was noted above, anyone contemplating making a loan has the option of "lending to himself" by simply storing the money. As a result, people are unlikely to make loans unless the dollar repayment exceeds the dollar principal—that is, unless they receive interest.

[9] Hereafter, the "*" superscript signifies that this particular value of the annual interest rate r is the one selected by the market.

The key to answering this question is to recognize that from a lender's point of view, a security purchased in the secondary market is essentially identical to (is a perfect substitute for) a security he might purchase in the *primary* or new issue market. The primary-market substitute would have a term equal to the *remaining term* on the secondary security—the number of years the security has left to run. It would return payments in the same amounts, and at the same dates, as the remaining payments on the secondary security—those that have yet to be made and would consequently be collected by the security's purchaser.

We can use this substitution principle, along with what we have just learned about primary-market pricing, to price a security sold in the secondary market. We will call the date at which the security is sold date T, and the price of the security at that date V_T. The remaining term of the security is then N-T, and its remaining payments are due at dates T+1, T+2, ..., N-1, N.[10] The payments are consequently due 1, 2, ..., N-T-1, N-T periods in the future, relative to date T. (We'll assume that the payment due at date T has already been made.) Continuing our notational convention that subscripts represent dates, we'll let r_T^* denote the market interest rate at date T. We can then write

$$V_T = \frac{V_{T+1}}{1+r_T^*} + \frac{V_{T+2}}{(1+r_T^*)^2} + \cdots + \frac{V_N}{(1+r_T^*)^{N-T}}$$

$$= \sum_{t=1}^{N-T} \frac{V_{T+t}}{(1+r_T^*)^t}.$$

It is important to note that r_T^*, the market rate on the date when the security is sold, may be different from the market rate when the security was issued (which we will call r_0^*). If r_T^* is relatively low then the secondary market price V_T will be relatively high, and vice versa. This dependence of current secondary market prices on current interest rates (and of future secondary market prices on future interest rates) will play a key role in our ultimate explanation for the slope of the yield curve.

Interest Rates and Yields—The securities pricing formula just presented can be used to help us tackle a second important question. Suppose we have a multiple payment security that is selling in the market at a known price. This could be either a newly issued security or a security sold in the secondary market. What is the annual interest rate on the security?

Since this security returns multiple payments, we cannot apply the annual interest rate formula that was presented on page 39. We can, however, exploit the fact that the annual interest rate on this security must be the rate that gives it its current market price—that is, the rate that makes the present value of its stream of future payments equal to its market price. Consequently, the market interest rate r_T^* must solve the equation

$$V_T = \frac{V_{T+1}}{1+r_T} + \frac{V_{T+2}}{(1+r_T)^2} + \cdots + \frac{V_N}{(1+r_T)^{N-T}}.$$

Here, V_T is the price of the security—which we are now assuming that we know—and $V_{T+1}, V_{T+2}, \ldots, V_N$ are the remaining payments on the security.

Since this equation has only the single unknown r_T, we might expect to be able to solve it to obtain r_T^*.[11] This is usually accomplished using numerical methods. These methods proceed by starting with a guess for r_T^*, computing the associated present value, and adjusting the guess according to the sign and size of the difference between this value and the actual market price. An annual interest rate computed in this manner—that is, as the solution to a present value equation—is called a *yield*.[12]

We have now—finally!—learned enough to begin investigating the term structure of interest rates. One way to start is by constructing a *yield curve*: a diagram which, as noted above, displays the relationship between the remaining terms of, and the yields on, different securities.

---

[10] Some of these payments may be zero. In the case of a single-payment security, for example, there is only one remaining payment; it is received at date N.

[11] The fact that this equation is not linear rules out standard algebraic solution methods. If the security in question has only two payments remaining (if N-T = 2), the equation can be transformed into a second-order polynomial equation and solved using the quadratic formula.

[12] For most of the rest of this paper the terms "interest rate" and "yield" will be used interchangeably. Unfortunately, participants in financial markets compute what they call interest rates on securities in a variety of ways, and some of them are significantly different from yields. These differences can be particularly important for securities with terms of less than a year. For details, see Mishkin (1989), pp. 82-92.

A problem we must confront in doing this is that many factors other than different remaining terms can cause differences in the yields on securities. These include differences in credit risk (that is, in the likelihood of default by the borrower) and in tax treatment. To isolate yield differences that are due solely to term differences, we need to compare the yields on securities that do not differ in these other characteristics. One simple way to do this is to compare the yields on securities issued by the U.S. Treasury. Treasury securities are issued with a wide variety of terms and are traded in a large and active secondary market—a fact that makes it possible to obtain a secondary market yield quotation for virtually any term. Treasury securities can also be thought of as essentially riskless, since the federal government is the only organization in the United States that can legally print money to cover its debts. Finally, the interest on all these securities is taxed on the same basis.

THE EXPECTATIONS THEORY

What does economic theory have to say about the term structure? As with most questions in economics, there are a number of differing views. The theory described below, however, is accepted, at least in part, by most economists interested in monetary and financial issues. It is called the expectations theory.[13]

A basic challenge for term structure theory is to explain two empirical regularities, or "stylized facts," of the interest rate term structure. These regularities can be described as facts about the slope or steepness of the yield curve at different points in time. One of them involves the direction the yield curve usually slopes: most of the time, the yield curve is gently upward-sloping. Another involves circumstances that seem to produce curves with unusual slopes: when short-term interest rates are relatively high, the yield curve is often downward-sloping; when short-term rates are relatively low, the curve is often steeply upward-sloping.

Linking Short-Term and Long-Term Interest Rates

A point of departure for the expectations theory is the role of secondary markets in transforming the effective terms of securities. Suppose, for example, that a lender owns a five-year Treasury bond which he purchased in the primary market. The bond is maturing, but the lender now wishes he had lent for 10 years. If he takes the maturity payment on his five-year bond and uses it to purchase a second five-year bond, he will, in effect, have lent for 10 years. The only difference between this and the single 10-year loan is that the rate of return the lender receives over the coming five years will be determined by current market conditions, rather than conditions five years ago.

Suppose, conversely, that this lender owns a 10-year Treasury bond which he purchased five years ago. He has now decided that he needs his money and would have preferred to have lent for five years. If there were no secondary market, he would be stuck: he would not be repaid by the Treasury until the bond matured five years in the future. The secondary market allows him to receive early repayment indirectly, by selling his bond to another lender. If he chooses to sell the bond, he will, in effect, have lent for five rather than 10 years. The only difference between this and a true five-year loan is that the amount of the repayment (the sale price of the bond) will depend on current market conditions, rather than conditions five years ago.

Now suppose (rather unrealistically) that there is no uncertainty about future interest rates, so that lenders today know exactly what market yields on securities with different terms will be five years in the future. Suppose further that they know that the future five-year Treasury yield will be identical to the current five-year yield—say, 7½ percent. How will this affect the current yield on 10-year Treasury securities?

---

[13]Early statements of the expectations theory include various works of Irving Fisher [see the citations listed by Wood (1964), p. 457, footnote 1]. The theory was elaborated by Keynes (1930), Lutz (1940) and Hicks (1946); these authors proposed a variant of the expectations theory that has become known as the liquidity premium theory. This variant will be described at some length below. The most prominent alternative to the expectations theory is the market segmentation theory of Culbertson (1957). Another variant of the expectations theory, which combines elements of both the liquidity premium and market segmentation theories, is the preferred habitat theory of Modigliani and Sutch (1966).

We can answer this question by process of elimination, ruling out possibilities that are clearly wrong until we are left with a single one that must be right. Suppose first that the current yield on 10-year Treasury bonds is higher than 7½ percent. We have seen that if a lender sells such a bond after five years, the yield to maturity its buyer will receive must be exactly the same as the yield on a newly issued five-year bond he might purchase instead. This future five-year yield, we have assumed, will be exactly 7½ percent. Consequently, the (five-year) yield the original lender will receive when he sells the 10-year bond, after holding it for five years, must be higher than 7½ percent: otherwise, the bond's 10-year yield, which is the average of its yields for the first and second five years, could not exceed that figure. But if it is possible to obtain a five-year yield of more than 7½ percent by purchasing a 10-year bond and selling it after five years, why would any current lender buy a newly issued five-year bond, or a secondary bond with five years left to run—each of which, according to our assumptions, will yield exactly 7½ percent? Clearly, if five-year bonds are to survive in the current market, the current yield on 10-year bonds must not in fact be higher than 7½ percent.

Now suppose that the current yield on 10-year bonds is lower than 7½ percent. Then if a lender buys a five-year bond today, he will receive a yield over five years that is higher than the 10-year yield. If he wants to lend for 10 years, he can use the maturity payment on the first five-year bond to purchase a second five-year bond. Since we have assumed that the yield on this second bond will be exactly 7½ percent, the average yield he receives over the 10-year period will also be exactly 7½ percent. This average yield is higher than the 10-year bond yield, however; consequently, no current lender will buy a 10-year bond. If 10-year bonds are to survive in the current market, their yields must not in fact be lower than 7½ percent.

We have just seen that if five- and 10-year bonds are to coexist in the market, the 10-year bond yield can be neither higher nor lower than the five-year bond yield. This means, of course, that it must be equal to the five-year yield. An argument of the same sort could be applied, with equal ease, to any long term, and any pair of short terms that sum to it. Thus, under these assumptions, *if lenders know that short-term rates will remain constant in the future, current long-term rates must be equal to current short-term rates*, so that the yield curve will be perfectly flat.

Now suppose that instead of knowing the five-year rate will remain constant for the next 10 years, we know it will remain constant (at 7½ percent) for five years, and then rise to 10 percent. What must the current rate on a current 10-year security be? Notice that if a lender purchases a five-year bond yielding 7½ percent today, and rolls it over for a second five-year bond yielding 10 percent, he will receive an average annual rate of 8¾ percent over the 10-year period. Under the circumstances, he would be foolish to lend for ten years at any rate lower than 8¾ percent. Conversely, suppose that the U.S. Treasury wishes to borrow for a period of 10 years. If it borrows by issuing a five-year bond and then rolls the loan over for a second five years, it pays an average annual rate of 8¾ percent. Clearly, it would be foolish to offer more than 8¾ percent on its 10-year bonds.

Extending this argument to different long terms and different combinations of short terms that sum to them leads to the following prediction: *if there is no uncertainty about future interest rates, current long-term rates must be an appropriately weighted average of current and future short-term rates.*

Notice that, for the purposes of this prediction, a "long" term does not have to be long by conventional standards. A two-year rate, for instance, must be a weighted average of current and future one-year rates, while a six-month rate must be a weighted average of current and future three-month rates, etc. Clearly, it would be helpful to have a baseline "very short-term" rate to organize these sorts of predictions around. A natural candidate would be the rate on a riskless security with a term of zero.

What kind of security has a zero term? One example would be a security on which you can get your money back at any time. We have securities like this in the form of *demand deposits* or checking accounts. While these deposits are not issued by the U.S. Treasury, the fact that they are insured by the federal government makes them virtually as safe as Treasury securities.[14] We can consequently

---

[14]Strictly speaking, this is true only for personal deposits, and only up to a maximum of $100,000 per deposit.

define the baseline interest rate, r^0, as the rate on a perfectly safe zero-term security and identify it in practice with the market rate on federally insured bank deposits.[15]

We can now state a mathematical rule for determining the rate of interest on a security with a term of N as a function of the base rate r^0. (We must continue to assume that financial market participants know the levels of future rates.) Let r_0^0 represent the current rate of interest on a federally insured demand deposit. Let r_K^0 represent the value of this same rate beginning at date K, when there will be a one-time, permanent change in the rate. Let r_0^N represent the current rate on a security with a term of N. (We will refer to r_0^N as a term-adjusted rate; the rationale for this usage will become clear later in the paper. Notice that we are letting subscripts represent dates, and superscripts terms to maturity.) Then

(*) $\quad r_0^N = r_0^0, \ 0 < N \leq K$, and

$$r_0^N = \frac{r_0^0 K + r_K^0 (N-K)}{N}, \ N > K.$$

The coefficients K of the current base rate r_0^0 and N−K of the future base rate r_K^0, are the appropriate weights referred to in the italicized prediction on page 42. Here, K is the number of years at which the base rate will stay at its original level r_0^0, and N−K is the number of years at which it will stay at its new level r_K^0. While this formula has been stated for the case in which market rates will change only once, it is easy to generalize to cover the case of multiple base rate changes.[16]

A yield curve drawn under the assumption that lenders know that the base rate will fall in the near future (that K is not very large, and that $r_K^0 < r_0^0$) is displayed in figure 1.[17]

The assumption that lenders have complete and perfect knowledge about future interest rates is not very realistic. A more reasonable assumption might be that there is some uncertainty about future rates, but that lenders know their *expected values*—that is, their best forecasts, given the information available. If lenders base their decisions entirely on these best forecasts, then formula (*) is still a valid description of the expectations theory provided that the rate r_K^0 is interpreted as the expected value of the term-zero rate at date K. People who behave like this—those who base their decisions entirely on the forecast provided by the expected value—are said to be *risk neutral*.

Systematic slope changes—We can now explain one of the two empirical regularities identified in the introduction: the fact that yield curves tend to be steeply upward-sloping when when short-term interest rates are low and often slope downward when short-term rates are high. Before we can do this, however, we need to consider what we mean when we say that interest rates are "low" or "high." Is a 20 percent short-term rate high, for example? In the United States, the answer to this question is almost certainly "yes." In Israel, or Argentina, however, the answer to the same question would almost certainly be "no." This is because in recent U.S. history interest rates have rarely risen as high as 20 percent and, when they have done so, have quickly returned to lower levels. In recent Israeli or Argentinian history,

---

[15] A complication arises because demand deposit accounts do not pay interest, while functionally equivalent checkable accounts [negotiated order of withdrawal (NOW) accounts and money market deposit accounts (MMDAs), for example] are interest-bearing. Most economists believe that demand deposits pay interest indirectly, since banks that issue them typically do not charge fees that cover the costs of maintaining the accounts and providing funds transfer (checking, etc.) services. These issues are discussed and the implicit interest rates on demand deposits estimated by Klein (1974) and Dotsey (1983), among others. We will interpret r^0 as this implicit demand deposit rate, or, equivalently, as the explicit interest rate on NOW accounts or MMDAs issued by institutions that do charge cost-covering fees. Under this interpretation, r^0 will be a positive number.

[16] Suppose we know that the base rate will change at future dates $K_1, K_2, \ldots, K_J$, and that the new base rates at these dates will be $r_{K_1}^0, r_{K_2}^0, \ldots, r_{K_J}^0$. For notational convenience, call the current date (heretofore date 0) date K_0. Then the current term-adjusted rate on a security with a term of N (N > K_J) will be given by

$$(**) \quad r_0^N = \frac{\left[\sum_{i=0}^{J-1} r_{K_i}^0 (K_{i+1} - K_i)\right] + r_{K_J}^0 (N - K_J)}{N}.$$

Both formulas (*) and (**) are approximations of the exact formulas. For details, see the shaded insert on the following page.

[17] Along the horizontal axis in figure 1, N represents a particular term longer than K, and r_0^N the term-adjusted rate on a security with that term. Since N is fairly close to K, the weighted average that determines r_0^N is strongly influenced by the K years at which the base rate will remain at its original, high level r_0^0. As the term lengthens, the influence of this period wanes and the term-adjusted rate gets closer and closer to the new, lower base rate r_K^0.

The Exact Formula Linking Short- and Long-Term Rates

Both formula (*) and the generalized version presented in footnote 16 are linearized approximations of the exact formula. The exact version of formula (*) states that, if r_0^0 is the current base rate, and r_K^0 is the base rate at date K, then the current N-period term-adjusted rate r_0^N satisfies the relationship

$$(1 + r_0^N)^N = (1 + r_0^0)^K (1 + r_K^0)^{N-K},$$

which implies

$$r_0^N = \sqrt[N]{(1 + r_0^0)^K (1 + r_K^0)^{N-K}} - 1.$$

If we know the base rate will change at future dates $K_1, K_2, \ldots, K_J$, and that the new base rates at these dates will be $r_{K_1}^0, r_{K_2}^0, \ldots, r_{K_J}^0$ [again, for notational convenience, calling the current date (date 0) date K_0, and the terminal date (date N) date K_{J+1}], then the current term-adjusted rate on a security with a term of N (N > K_J) satisfies the relationship

$$(1 + r_0^N)^N = \prod_{i=1}^{J+1} (1 + r_{K_{i-1}}^0)^{K_i - K_{i-1}}$$

[here $\prod$ is the multiplicative analogue of $\sum$].

This implies

$$r_0^N = \sqrt[N]{\prod_{i=1}^{J+1} (1 + r_{K_{i-1}}^0)^{K_i - K_{i-1}}} - 1.$$

Fortunately, the approximations given by the linearized formulas are adequate for most purposes. In the case described on pp. 42 of the text, for instance, the yield given by the exact formula is 8.743 percent, compared to the linearized figure of 8.750 percent.

The expectations theory can also be shown to imply that, if r_0^N is the current N-period term-adjusted rate, and r_0^K is the current K-period rate, then r_K^{N-K}, the term-adjusted rate on (N−K)-period securities that is expected to prevail at date K, satisfies the relationship

$$(1 + r_K^{N-K})^{N-K} = (1 + r_0^N)^N / (1 + r_0^K)^K,$$

which implies that

$$r_K^{N-K} = \sqrt[N-K]{(1 + r_0^N)^N / (1 + r_0^K)^K} - 1.$$

The rate r_K^{N-K} is often referred to as the "K-period forward rate" on a security with a term of N−K. The expectations theory is often described as a theory that identifies the forward rate with the expected future spot rate.

---

by contrast, rates have rarely fallen as low as 20 percent and, when they have done so, have quickly returned to higher levels.

When we say that interest rates are high or low, what we usually mean is that they are high or low relative to recent historical experience, and that we feel this experience gives us a good deal of guidance about the level of interest rates in the future. Thus, when we say interest rates are high we usually expect them to fall in the future, and vice versa. As we have just seen, the expectations theory predicts that when we expect rates to fall the yield curve will slope downward, and that when we expect them to rise the curve will slope upward.

The simple expectations theory has the virtue of great flexibility: if you are willing to make sufficiently artful assumptions about lenders' expectations about the pattern of future interest rates, you can use this theory to explain the shape of virtually any yield curve. The theory provides an explanation for one basic empirical regularity about yield curves that is rather difficult to believe, however. The regularity in question is that most of the time, during the last century at least, yield curves have been distinctly

Figure 1
Term-adjusted Yield When the Base Rate Will Fall in the Future

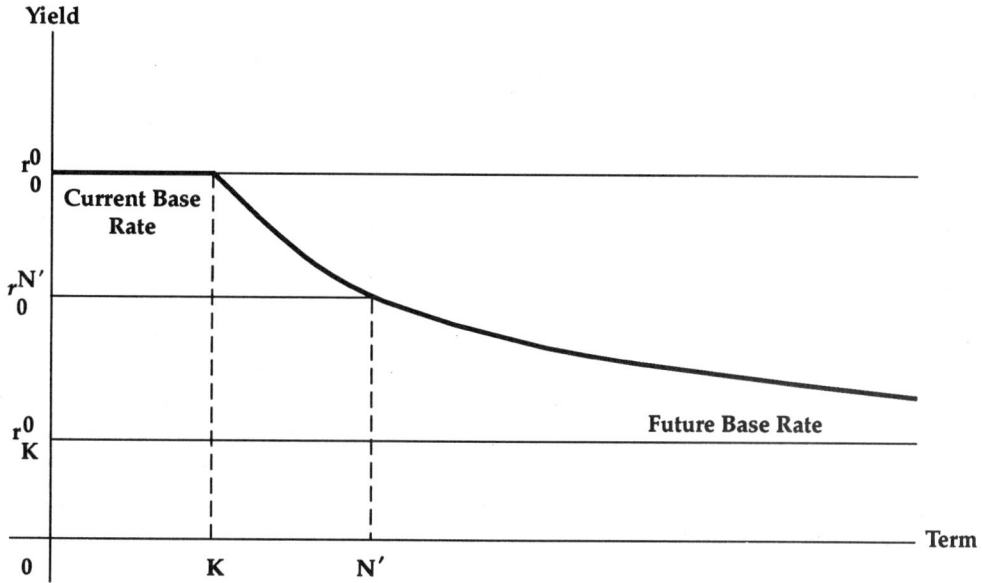

upward-sloping.[18] The simple expectations theory could explain this only by assuming that lenders usually expect rates to rise persistently over time. This assumption does not seem plausible, unless you believe that lenders were extremely poor forecasters. While interest rates have varied considerably during the past century, there is little evidence that they have increased on average, or that market participants had any reason to expect them to do so. Indeed, the evidence suggests that people usually expect future short-term interest rates to remain near current levels.[19] What we need, then, is a modified version of the theory that will predict an upward-sloping yield curve under this assumption.

Interest Risk, Term Premia and the Slope of the Yield Curve

Any alternative explanation for the fact that yield curves are normally upward-sloping must be based on something about long-term securities that makes them systematically less attractive to lenders than short-term securities. As we have just seen, the expectations theory predicts that, if lenders know for certain that short-term interest rates will remain constant, they should

---

[18]See Malkiel (1970), pp. 5-6, 12; Kessel (1965), pp. 17-19; and Shiller (1990), p. 629. It is sometimes asserted that yield curves were usually downward sloping during the late nineteenth and early twentieth centuries: see Meiselman (1962), appendix C, and Homer and Sylla (1991), pp. 317-22, 403-09 for descriptions and explanations of this phenomenon.

[19]The simple statiscal models of interest rate behavior that explain the data best are based on the assumption that rates have a long-run average or mean level and tend to return toward that level, rather slowly, after departing from it. These models imply that, if short-term interest rates are currently near their mean level (where they should be most of the time), they should be expected to stay near the current level in both the short and long run, and that, even if they are far from the mean level, they should be expected to stay near the current level in the short run.

be indifferent between lending by purchasing short-term securities and lending by purchasing long-term ones. Long- and short-term interest rates should consequently be equal, and the yield curve should be flat. This prediction implies that any alternative explanation for the upward slope of the curve must be based on the effects of uncertainty about future interest rates.

Interest Risk and Capital Losses—One reason why uncertainty about interest rates may influence the behavior of lenders is that unanticipated changes in interest rates affect the value of their securities in the secondary market. Suppose, to return to an earlier example, that a lender buys a 10-year security that returns a yield of 7½ percent and sells it in the secondary market after five years. If interest rates have remained unchanged in the interim, the secondary market price of his security will give him a five-year yield of 7½ percent. If they have risen, the price will be lower, and he will receive a lower yield.

As we have already noted, the reason for these price and yield changes is that a security sold in the secondary market must compete with primary market securities with the same term as its remaining term. If the market interest rate on primary securities has risen, the yield on secondary securities must rise to the same level; since the remaining payments on these securities are fixed, this rise can be arranged only through a decline in the securities' market price. A formal way to see this is by inspecting the secondary market pricing formula for a single-payment security:

$$V_T = \frac{V_N}{(1+r_T^*)^{N-T}}.$$

If $r_0^* = r_T^*$, so that interest rates have not changed since this security was issued, its price will be

$$\hat{V}_T = \frac{V_N}{(1+r_0^*)^{N-T}}.$$

It is easy to check, by applying the annual interest rate formula, that both the T-year *ex post* yield on this security (the yield from date 0, when it was issued, to date T, when it is sold) and the N-T year *ex ante* yield (the yield from date T, when it is sold, to date N, when it will mature) are equal to the initial rate r_0^*.

We will call $\hat{V}_T$ the anticipated price of this security. If the actual price V_T exceeds the anticipated price $\hat{V}_T$, we say the original lender has experienced a *capital gain*. The amount of the gain is simply $V_T - \hat{V}_T$. If the anticipated price falls short of the actual price, the lender has experienced a capital loss in the amount $\hat{V}_T - V_T$. It is clear from our pricing formula that capital gains occur if r_T^* falls short of r_0^* (if market interest rates have fallen), and vice versa. This means that lenders' expectations about future capital gains and losses must be tied to their expectations about future interest rates.

What should we assume about expectations regarding future interest rates? As we noted toward the end of the previous section, it seems reasonable to assume that market participants recognize that interest rates may change, but expect them to remain constant on average.[20]

---

[20]The expectations theory offers no explanation for the reasons market participants might expect short-term rates to change. It is a theory that attempts to explain the levels of long-term interest rates relative to the current levels of short-term rates, not one that attempts to explain their absolute levels. Stated differently, the expectations theory is not a true theory of the *determination* of interest rates. Market participants may expect short-term interest rates to change because they expect changes in any of the innumerable factors economic theory predicts might influence them.

Economic theory suggests that interest rates of the sort discussed in this article (money or *nominal* interest rates) are sums of real interest rates (rates expressed in terms of the purchasing power of the dollar amounts lent and repaid) and expected rates of inflation. This is the so-called Fisher equation. As a result, the question of interest rate determination is sometimes thought of as two questions: what determines real interest rates, and what determines inflation expectations. Most economists believe that nominal factors (such as changes in the levels or growth rates of monetary aggregates) play the principal role in driving inflation expectations, while real factors (such as technological changes, changes in the perceived attractiveness of investment opportunities, changes in demographic structure or changes in the nature of financial regulation) play the principal role in real interest rate determination. There is, however, considerable disagreement about the degree of interaction between nominal and real factors, and especially about whether changes in nominal factors can have persistent effects on real interest rates.

Under this assumption, the expected capital gains on future secondary market sales of securities are approximately zero.[21]

It seems conceivable that this situation might not bother lenders. Economists usually assume, however, that the satisfaction a person derives from an extra dollar's worth of expenditures declines as the total value of his expenditures increases. If this is so, he will find the gain in satisfaction provided by the extra goods he can purchase if his returns exceed his expectations to be smaller than the loss in satisfaction from the goods he will have to refrain from purchasing if his returns fall short of his expectations. This should cause actuarially fair (zero expected loss) uncertainty about the future returns on his securities to upset him. A person who behaves like this is said to be *risk averse*.

Since buying term securities exposes lenders to actuarially fair return uncertainty, while buying securities with zero terms (such as demand deposits) does not, risk averse lenders will be reluctant to buy term securities. They will insist on higher expected yields on term securities than on demand deposits to compensate themselves for the uncertainty. The notion that financial decisionmakers are risk averse is widely accepted by economists, and we will adopt it without further discussion.

Interest Risk and the Term Structure—We have just explained why term securities tend to have higher yields than demand deposits when both are default-free: term securities carry interest risk, but demand deposits do not. We have not yet explained why securities with longer terms tend to have higher yields than those with shorter ones. Our discussion certainly suggests a possible explanation, however: longer-term securities may carry more interest risk than shorter-term ones. But why should this be the case?

We will begin our investigation of this question by posing another question that is closely related. Suppose we have two single-payment securities with different terms, but the same original (date 0) prices and yields. If market interest rates remain unchanged, their current (date T) prices will also be identical, even though their maturity payments will not be. But suppose that the market interest rate—specifically, the market "base rate" r^0—rises by a fixed amount from date 0 to date T (so that $r^0_T = r^0_0 + \Delta r$, with $\Delta r > 0$). Which security will fall furthest in price?

Notice that the remaining term of the short-term security will be smaller than that of the long-term security; if we call the short term N_s, and the long term N_l, then the remaining terms of these securities are $N_s - T$ and $N_l - T$, respectively. Since market yields have risen, the short-term secondary security must generate extra interest to compete with newly-issued short-term securities. The amount of extra interest will be approximately $\Delta r V_T (N_s - T)$; this is the rate increase Δr, applied to the (common) secondary market price V_T, for each year of the remaining term $(N_s - T)$. The long-term security must also generate extra interest; in this case, the amount is $\Delta r V_T (N_l - T)$. This is the same rate increase, applied to the same base price, but continued for $N_l - N_s$ additional years.

Of course, neither security can really produce "extra interest" in the conventional sense. The interest is paid indirectly, as part of the maturity payment, and the time and date of that payment are fixed. Instead, the price of each security must decline far enough so that it can increase at the new (and higher) annual rate r^0_T, while still reaching the fixed maturity payment V_N at the maturity date N. Since the price of the long-term security will have to increase at this rate for a much longer time, it will have to fall much further than the price of the short-term security. The relative sizes of the two price declines will be approximately equal to the relative sizes of the securities' remaining terms. A security with four years left to run will suffer a price decline approximately double that of a security with the same secondary market price but only two years left to run, and so on.

The Term Premium—If the risk of capital loss on securities tends to increase in proportion to their remaining terms, lenders who demand interest compensation for bearing this risk will demand more compensation on long-term

---

[21]Since the secondary market price is computed by dividing the maturity payment by the gross interest rate $1 + r$, an increase in the rate by a given percentage causes a fall in the price that is slightly smaller than the rise in the price caused by an equal percentage decrease in the rate. As a result, the expected price change is slightly positive. Although this effect is never very strong, it becomes more pronounced as the remaining term of the secondary security increases.

securities than on short-term securites.[22] This will tend to make the yields on longer-term securities higher than those on securities with shorter terms—that is, it will tend to make the yield curve upward-sloping.[23]

We can define the *term premium* on Treasury securities of a given term as the difference between the yield on those securities and the yield on federally insured demand deposits. That is,

$$\tau^N = r^N - r^0, \text{ or equivalently } r^N = r^0 + \tau^N,$$

where r^N represents the yield on N-term Treasury securities, and τ^N represents their term premium. We now have a theory that predicts that the term premium should increase systematically with the remaining term, and, more specifically, that it should increase *in proportion* to the remaining term. We can formalize this by writing

$$\tau^N = \tau(N) \equiv mN,$$

where m is a positive constant of proportionality. A plot of the sort of yield curve consistent with this prediction is displayed in figure 2.

We might refer to the number m as the *coefficient of risk aversion*. Different values of m can be thought of as indicating different degrees of lenders' risk aversion. If m is relatively high, a small increase in the term and, thus, in the risk of capital loss, will cause lenders to demand a good deal of compensation in the form of a large increase in the term premium. This is the kind of behavior we would expect from very risk-averse lenders. If m is low, on the other hand, it will take a large increase in the term, and, thus, the risk to cause lenders to demand much additional compensation.

This is the kind of behavior we would expect from lenders who are not very risk-averse.[24]

It was pointed out earlier that lenders may not always expect the level of short-term interest rates—in particular, the level of the term-zero rate—to stay constant on average. When they do not, the base rates to which the term premia must be added will also depend on the term. These term-dependent base rates have been referred to as *term-adjusted rates*, and their current values have been denoted r_0^N. The actual yield should be the sum of the term-adjusted rate and the term premium:

$$r_0^N = r_0^N + \tau^N.$$

Abnormal Yield Curves—This latest addition to the expectations theory allows us to consider the role of the term premium in determining the shape of abnormal yield curves—the sort that appear when lenders expect interest rates to change in the future. In this case, the actual yield should be given by the sum of the term-adjusted rate (that is, the weighted-average base rate) and the appropriate term premium. This can produce curves that slope in one direction along one part of their range, but in the opposite direction along another part. If lenders expect interest rates to remain constant for a short period, and then fall sharply, for example, the yield curve will appear humped, sloping upward at very short terms, peaking near the term corresponding to the date at which rates are expected to decline, and sloping downward for a range of terms thereafter (see figure 3).[25] Curves with this shape are frequently observed shortly before economic recessions begin, presumably because interest rates tend to fall sharply during recessions.

---

[22]In reality, the increase in risk is slightly less than proportional to the term, but the deviation from exact proportionality is very small. We are implicitly assuming that the change in the base rate, if any, will occur at a known future date, and that the rate, having changed, will remain at its new level permanently. We are also assuming that T, the date of sale, is fixed and known.

[23]Early statements of the liquidity premium theory include Keynes (1930), Hicks (1946) and Meiselman (1962). The term "liquidity premium" is based on the notion that liquidity—the ability to sell an asset rapidly and without loss—is valuable to lenders, and lenders will charge interest premia on assets that are relatively illiquid. Since the risk of capital loss is the risk that an asset may ultimately be saleable only at a loss, the premium for capital loss risk is in a sense a liquidity premium.

[24]If $m = 0$, lenders do not require any compensation for the risk of capital loss. As noted earlier, lenders who behave in this manner are said to be risk-neutral.

[25]Note that if a normal yield curve (a hypothetical curve observed when interest rates are expected to remain constant, on average) is upward-sloping, the expectations theory does not always interpret an upward-sloping yield curve as an indication that the market expects interest rates to rise. To obtain the right directional signal, the slope of the observed yield curve must be compared to the slope of a normal curve. The theory now interprets an observed yield curve that is upward-sloping, but flatter than normal, as a signal that the market expects interest rates to fall slightly.

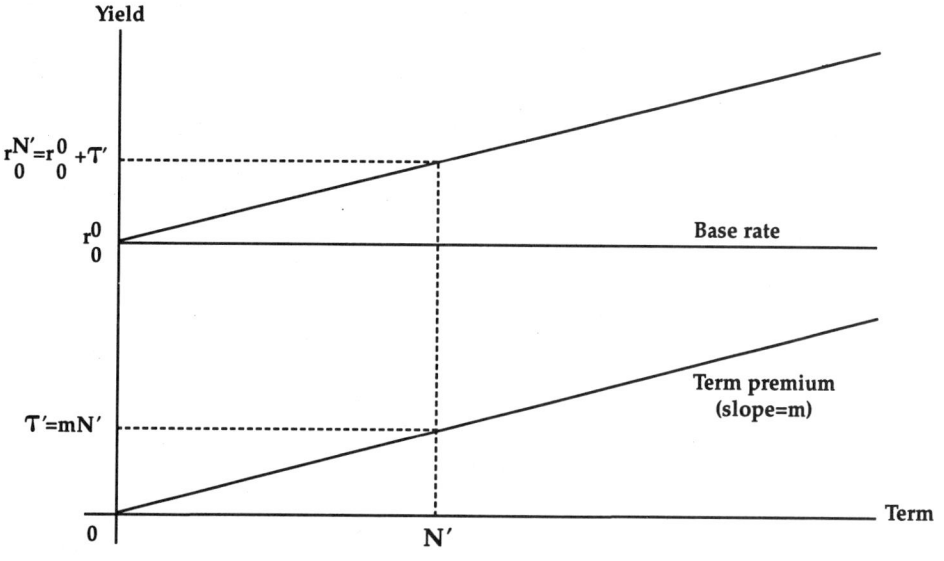

**Figure 2
Yield Curve When the Base Rate Is Constant**

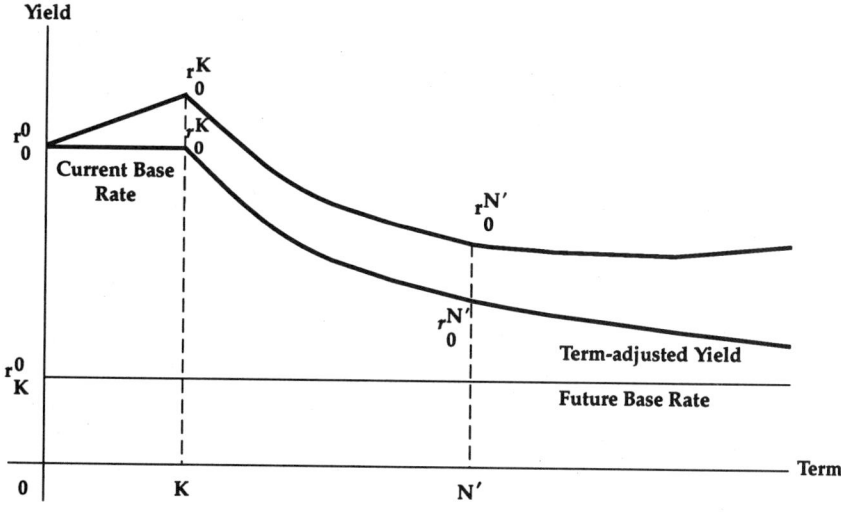

**Figure 3
Yield Curve When the Base Rate Will Fall in the Future**

CONCLUDING REMARKS

This article presents a basic description of the concepts and issues involved in the study of the term structure of interest rates. It has also presented a simple version of the expectations theory of the term structure. This theory predicts that the shape of the yield curve is determined by the expectations of financial market participants about the level of future interest rates and by their uncertainty about the accuracy of their expectations.

The analysis presented here suggests that the expectations theory can help explain two important "stylized facts" about yield curves: the fact that the steepness and direction of their slopes tend to vary systematically with the level of short-term interest rates, and the fact that they are usually upward-sloping. The explanation for the former fact is that forward-looking lenders will refuse to purchase term securities unless long-term interest rates are averages of the short-term interest rates that the lenders expect at various points in the future. The explanation for the latter fact is that the interest risk on securities tends to increase with their terms; this causes risk-averse lenders to demand amounts of interest compensation that also increase with the terms.

REFERENCES

Culbertson, John M. "The Term Structure of Interest Rates," *Quarterly Journal of Economics* (November 1957), pp. 485-517.

Dotsey, Michael. "An Examination of Implicit Interest Rates on Demand Deposits," Federal Reserve Bank of Richmond *Economic Review* (September/October 1983), pp. 3-11.

Hicks, John R. *Value and Capital*, 2d ed. (Oxford University Press, 1946).

Homer, Sidney, and Richard Sylla. *A History of Interest Rates*, 3d ed. (Rutgers University Press, 1991).

Kessel, Reuben A. "The Cyclical Behavior of the Term Structure of Interest Rates," National Bureau of Economic Research Occasional Paper #91 (1965).

Keynes, John M. *A Treatise on Money*, Vol. 1&2 (Harcourt, Brace and Company, 1930).

Klein, Benjamin. "Competitive Interest Payments on Bank Deposits and the Long-Run Demand for Money," *American Economic Review* (December 1974), pp. 931-49.

Lutz, Friedrich A. "The Structure of Interest Rates," *Quarterly Journal of Economics* (November 1940), pp. 36-63.

Malkiel, Burton G. "The Term Structure of Interest Rates: Theory, Empirical Evidence, and Applications," Monograph (General Learning Corporation, Morristown, New Jersey), 1970.

Meiselman, David. *The Term Structure of Interest Rates* (Prentice Hall, Inc., 1962).

Mishkin, Frederic S. *The Economics of Money, Banking, and Financial Markets*, 2d ed. (Scott, Foresman and Company, 1989).

Modigliani, Franco, and Richard Sutch. "Innovations in Interest Rate Policy," *American Economic Review* (May 1966), pp. 178-97.

Russell, Steven H. "Reference Notes on Interest Rates, Securities Pricing, and Related Topics," Unpublished monograph, 1991.

Shiller, Robert J. "The Term Structure of Interest Rates," (with an appendix by J. Huston McCulloch) in Benjamin M. Friedman and Frank H. Hahn, eds., *Handbook of Monetary Economics*, Vol. 1 (North Holland: Elsevier Science Publishing Company, Inc., 1990).

Wood, John H. "The Expectations Hypothesis, the Yield Curve, and Monetary Policy," *Quarterly Journal of Economics* (August 1964), pp. 457-70.

Article 19

Debt in the 1990s

Debt in the 1980s was often pictured as a type of high octane gasoline supercharging the economy by providing investment funds and motivating management. In the 1990s, debt's image is less glamorous, more like sludge in the crankcase than hi-test in the gas tank. Since the stock market crash of 1987, when the debt craze began to falter, GDP growth has only averaged 1.8%. Even if the recession is excluded, GDP averaged only 2.5%, well below the average nonrecession growth rate of 4.4% experienced in the post-war era.

By the late 1980s, firms and individuals had used up more of their capacity to borrow than they could hope to maintain. Precarious financial positions, slow growth, and a new era of enforced frugality were the result. By the end of 1992, the resulting restrictions on activity finally appeared to ease. GDP growth rose to 4.7%, retail sales were up 8% from the previous Christmas, and new claims on unemployment finally began to fall.

Did the economy really clear some magic hurdle in dealing with the debt burden, or was the pick up due to some unrelated improvement in attitudes? At least superficially, the debt story seems plausible. Certainly, newspapers have been full of stories about corporations and consumers finally repairing their balance sheets. Reality is, however, more complicated.

The basic facts are that consumers and businesses recently have paid down certain forms of debt while they have increased other types. No universal trends cut across all parts of the balance sheet. To understand how the size and character of the debt overhang have changed since the onset of the recession in the third quarter of 1990, it is necessary to define exactly what is meant by debt burden and clearly track the complete balance sheet, not just selected subcomponents. It is especially important over this period to distinguish between leverage, which is measured by the ratio of total indebtedness to income, and the debt service burden, which is measured by the ratio of total payments due on debt to income. For instance, if a consumer takes out a home equity loan at a low interest rate to pay off high interest rate credit card debts and to provide a small cash cushion for the future, that consumer's debt service ratio will fall, while the total debt to income ratio will rise.

This *Chicago Fed Letter* analyzes a set of leverage and debt service burden measures for both the household and the corporate sectors. Our basic conclusion is that the debt buildup, to close approximation, has not been eliminated or even significantly reduced. Thus, total leverage is largely the same as it was in 1990. What has changed over this period is that the large reduction in interest rates during the recession has allowed borrowers to reduce their interest expenses to more normal levels, while leaving their debt to income ratios largely untouched.

This suggests that, while interest rate reductions have helped the economy deal with the debt buildup of the 1980s, the economy remains vulnerable to large swings in interest rates. This vulnerability is mitigated to some extent by the fact that much of the recent debt restructuring has been toward longer term instruments, thus reducing the immediate impact of a rise in interest rates.

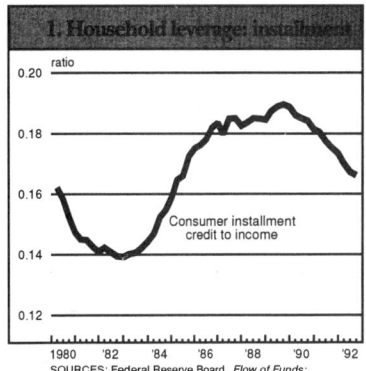

The household sector

When the ratio of consumer installment credit to disposable personal income fell to a seven year low of .167 in the second quarter of 1992, analysts shared a sense of relief, as consumers apparently had begun to reduce their indebtedness to more manageable levels and would be able to increase spending in the near future. As shown in Figure 1, this ratio rose steadily throughout the 1980s, as consumers embarked on a credit card debt binge, and then started to decline steadily in the early 1990s, as consumers paid down some of their outstanding credit card balances, personal loans, and auto loans. However, other components of household debt must be considered in order to assess the true magnitude of the improvement in consumer indebtedness. As Figure 2 shows, total household debt as a share of personal income has not declined very much from its peak in 1991, and still remains at historically high levels in the third quarter of 1992.

The contrast between Figures 1 and 2 is explained by the fact that consumers have been replacing traditional credit card debt and personal loans with less

209

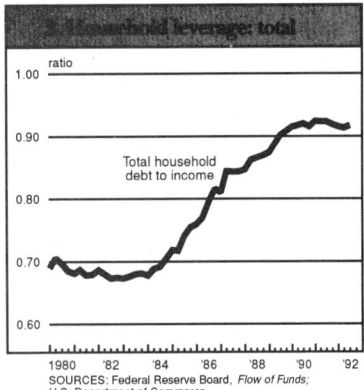

2. Household leverage: total

3. Household debt service burden

expensive home equity loans and lines of credit, which are classified under home mortgage debt.[1] Therefore, while consumer installment credit has declined at an average annual rate of 0.4% since the third quarter of 1990, home mortgage debt has grown at a 5.6% rate, causing total household debt to rise at a 4.4% rate. Thus, even though the accumulation of total household debt slowed down in the early 1990s compared to the 1980s, consumers have not appreciably reduced their debt levels.

Changes in consumer debt service burdens tell a very different story. As shown in Figure 3, debt service payments as a share of personal income increased rapidly throughout the 1980s, stood at historically high levels from 1989 through 1990, and then fell sharply thereafter.[2] The debt service ratio's path over the last eight quarters clearly differs from that of the total leverage ratio depicted in Figure 2. This is because the improvement in the total debt service ratio is due to interest rate reductions and not to a decline in the level of total household debt.

To clearly understand why Figures 2 and 3 tell such sharply different stories, it is necessary to delineate the sources of improvement in debt service burdens. The remainder of this section examines the relative importance of changes in debt levels, income, and interest rates to changes in debt service ratios. Figure 4, panel (a), explains the recent decline in household debt service burdens, calculated as the ratio of estimated interest payments on consumer installment credit, mortgage debt, and total debt to disposable personal income.[3]

Figure 4, panel (a), is divided into four sections. The first section simply reports the actual values of the three ratios in 1990:Q3 and 1992:Q3 and the change over that time period (1990:Q3 values minus 1992:Q3 values). In the other three sections, the 1992:Q3 ratios are analyzed under three alternative assumptions: 1) only the debt level changes, while income and interest rates are held at 1990:Q3 levels; 2) both debt and income levels change, while

4. Debt service ratios*

(a) Household sector

	Installment Credit	Home Mortgages	Total
Ratio in 90:3	0.027	0.064	0.090
Ratio in 92:3	0.022	0.051	0.073
Improvement	0.005	0.013	0.017
Debt at 92:3 levels			
Ratio in 92:3	0.027	0.071	0.098
Improvement	0.000	−0.007	−0.008
$ equivalent (billion)	−1.9	−30.1	−32.1
Debt & income at 92:3 levels			
Ratio in 92:3	0.024	0.065	0.089
Improvement	0.003	−0.001	0.001
$ equivalent (billion)	10.3	−5.7	4.5
Debt, income, & interest rates at 92:3 levels			
Ratio in 92:3	0.022	0.051	0.073
Improvement	0.005	0.013	0.017
$ equivalent (billion)	18.4	51.2	69.6

(b) Nonfinancial corporate sector

	Short term	Long term	Total
Ratio in 90:3	0.098	0.158	0.255
Ratio in 92:3	0.040	0.150	0.190
Improvement	0.058	0.008	0.065
Debt at 92:3 levels			
Ratio in 92:3	0.088	0.172	0.260
Improvement	0.010	−0.014	−0.005
$ equivalent (billion)	7.0	−12.1	−5.1
Debt & cash flow at 92:3 levels			
Ratio in 92:3	0.084	0.164	0.248
Improvement	0.014	−0.006	0.007
$ equivalent (billion)	11.2	−3.8	7.5
Debt, cash flow, & interest rates at 92:3 levels			
Ratio in 92:3	0.040	0.150	0.190
Improvement	0.058	0.008	0.065
$ equivalent (billion)	47.2	15.2	62.5

*See text for data definitions and sources.

interest rates are kept at 1990:Q3 levels; and 3) debt, income, and interest rates are all at 1992:Q3 levels.

The dollar equivalent amounts under each assumption represent either a decline in interest payments, if positive, or an increase in interest payments, if negative. For example, a value of $10 billion means that the decline in the debt service ratio was equivalent to a $10 billion "rebate" on the interest payments.

As shown in the first section of panel (a), all three debt service ratios for the household sector improved in 1992:Q3 compared to 1990:Q3. For example, the total debt service ratio fell from .090 in 1990:Q3 to .073 in 1992:Q3, an improvement of .017. The second section of panel (a) shows that debt level changes alone caused debt service burdens to worsen or at best level off, not decline, between 1990:Q3 and 1992:Q3. The implied increase in the total debt service ratio is equivalent to an increase in interest payments of $32.1 billion. Moreover, although consumer installment credit outstanding declined somewhat over this period, the higher interest rates typically charged on revolving credit offset the decline in debt outstanding, leaving the debt service ratio unchanged. The worsening in the mortgage debt service ratio reflects a substantial increase in mortgage debt outstanding and is equivalent to a $30.1 billion increase in interest payments.

As shown in the third section of panel (a), debt and income changes considered together leave the debt service ratios little changed from their 1990:Q3 values, which indicates that income growth was just about enough to offset the changes in debt levels over this period. The increase in income combined with both a decline in installment credit and an increase in mortgage debt resulted in a total rebate in interest payments of $4.5 billion.

Finally, when the changes in debt levels, income, and interest rates are considered together, all three debt service ratios decline, as shown in the fourth

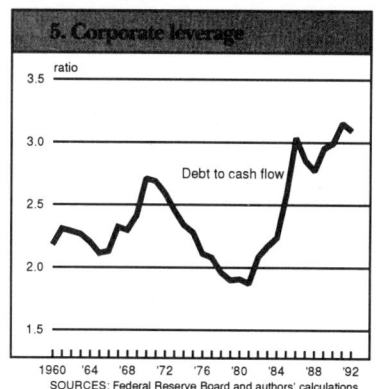

5. Corporate leverage

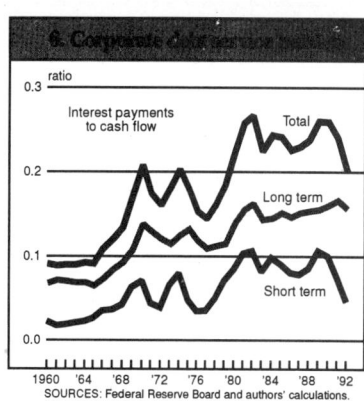

6. Corporate debt service

section of panel (a). The improvement in the total debt service ratio under this last scenario is equivalent to an interest payments rebate of $69.6 billion, compared to a $4.5 billion rebate when only income and debt level changes are considered. This suggests that the interest rate reduction alone was equivalent to $65.1 billion in rebates.

The corporate sector

Developments in the corporate sector bear a strong resemblance to those of the household sector. Debt levels and, to a lesser extent, debt service burdens, rose in the 1980s, and recent quarters show dramatic declines in the debt service ratio with quite modest declines in the leverage ratio.

Figure 5 shows that the leverage ratio, total debt outstanding to cash flow, rose to historically high levels in the 1980s, and has declined very little since its peak in 1991. Figure 6, which plots the ratios of interest payments to cash flow, indicates that the real runup in debt service burdens occurred in the late 1970s and early 1980s, as interest rates reached unprecedented high levels.[4] Debt service burdens remained at or near these high levels until the end of the decade, as rates fell but debt issuance increased. Since 1990, debt service burdens have declined markedly, as interest rates have fallen and debt growth rates have tapered off or even become negative.

Figure 4, panel (b), presents estimates of the relative importance of debt level reduction, cash flow growth, and interest rate reduction in explaining recent declines in corporate debt servicing burdens, and it should be read as panel (a) for the household sector. The first section of panel (b) shows the actual values of three debt service ratios for the corporate sector, and their improvement between 1990:Q3 and 1992:Q3.

As shown in the second section of panel (b), debt level changes alone would have caused a decline in the short term debt service ratio equivalent to an interest payments rebate of $7.0 billion, while they would have increased the long term debt service ratio, equivalent to an increase in interest payments of $12.1 billion. Similar calculations for the total debt service

Karl A. Scheld, Senior Vice President and Director of Research; David R. Allardice, Vice President and Assistant Director of Research; Carolyn McMullen, Editor.

Chicago Fed Letter is published monthly by the Research Department of the Federal Reserve Bank of Chicago. The views expressed are the authors' and are not necessarily those of the Federal Reserve Bank of Chicago or the Federal Reserve System. Articles may be reprinted if the source is credited and the Research Department is provided with copies of the reprints.

Chicago Fed Letter is available without charge from the Public Information Center, Federal Reserve Bank of Chicago, P.O. Box 834, Chicago, Illinois, 60690, (312) 322-5111.

ISSN 0895-0164

burden show a worsening in the total ratio equivalent to a $5.1 billion increase in interest payments.

The third section of panel (b) shows that debt level and cash flow changes together would have improved the short term ratio, since short term debt levels fell and cash flow grew.[5] However, the long term ratio would still have worsened, since cash flow growth was not enough to offset the increase in long term debt. These same factors would have slightly decreased the total servicing burden, equivalent to an interest payments rebate of $7.5 billion.

The fourth section of panel (b) summarizes the actual changes in debt service burdens as debt levels, cash flow, and interest rates have changed. The improvement in the total debt servicing burden is equivalent to a rebate in interest payments of $62.5 billion, compared to $7.5 billion when only debt level and cash flow changes are considered. This implies that the interest rate reduction alone has accounted for $55.0 billion in interest payments rebates.

This *Chicago Fed Letter* suggests that, although both the household and corporate sectors have carried lighter debt burdens in recent quarters, leverage ratios remain near historical highs. Moreover, our calculations show that the marked decline in debt service ratios is due to interest rate reductions, not to debt level declines or income growth. Thus, balance sheet restructurings are likely to remain an important factor for some time.

—Francesca Eugeni, Steven Strongin, and Paula R. Worthington

---

[1] For a discussion of consumer debt and data sources see Francesca Eugeni, "Consumer debt and home equity borrowing," *Economic Perspectives*, Federal Reserve Bank of Chicago, March/April 1993, pp. 2-13.

[2] These are estimates by staff of the Federal Reserve Board of scheduled repayments of principal and interest on total household debt outstanding.

[3] These calculations abstract from principal repayments. Also, total debt service burden is the sum of interest payments on consumer installment credit and mortgage debt.

[4] Cash flow is defined as the sum of before tax profits, depreciation, and interest payments on debt service burden ratios. For data sources and details see Paula Worthington, "Recent trends in corporate leverage," *Economic Perspectives*, Federal Reserve Bank of Chicago, May/June 1993, pp. 24-31.

[5] Here, cash flow growth denotes growth in the sum of pretax profits and depreciation.

Predicting Stock-Market Volatility

D. Keith Sill*

On October 19, 1987, the stock market posted its largest one-day decline ever when the Dow Jones Industrial Average fell 508 points, a drop of over 22 percent in a single day. Prior to the crash of 1987, the largest single-day drop in the stock market occurred on October 29, 1929, when the market fell by about 13 percent. While drops of this magnitude are rare, it is not uncommon for stock prices to rise or fall by 3 percent or more in a single month. Stock prices seem to be very unpredictable. In addition, economists have long recognized that stock prices go through turbulent and tranquil periods. Turbulent periods are times of high uncertainty when stock prices move sharply from month to month; tranquil periods are times when stock price movements are much more subdued.[1] However, only recently have economists begun modeling how stock-market volatility (or stock-price turbulence) changes through time.

---

* Keith Sill is an Economist in the Research Department of the Philadelphia Fed.

[1] This recognition of the changing variability of stock prices goes back to the early 1960s. An early, comprehensive study of the behavior of stock-market prices is that of Fama (1965).

Why does stock-market volatility vary through time? Is stock-market volatility predictable? To address these questions we will need to examine theories about how stock prices are determined. Then we can see whether the behavior of U.S. stock prices over the last 30 years is consistent with the implications of these theories. But first, we would like to know how stock-market volatility affects the economy.

HOW DOES STOCK-MARKET VOLATILITY AFFECT THE ECONOMY?

Economists argue that stock-market volatility can affect the economy in several ways: (1) it influences how much people spend and save; (2) it influences the prices of stocks; and (3) it influences the prices of financial options and thus affects how investors might hedge investment risk.

The Effect on Spending and Saving. How might an increase in stock-market volatility affect people's spending and saving decisions?[2] Consider the case of a hypothetical person named Walter Wealthy who has an uncertain future income because of his investments in the stock market.[3]

Walter's decision about how much to spend today depends on how much income he expects his stocks to produce. If he expects a high return from his investment in stocks, he may want to spend less (and save more) today.[4] Doing this allows Walter to spend more in the future (if the high expected return comes about). This incentive to save more today is called the substitution effect, since future spending is substituted for current spending.

Offsetting this substitution effect is an income effect, which leads Walter to want to spend *more* today. If the expected stock return is high, he feels richer today because he expects to have higher wealth in the future. Feeling richer, Walter may increase current spending. Thus, the income effect works to offset the substitution effect. However, empirical evidence suggests that usually the substitution effect dominates the income effect, so that saving increases with an increase in expected returns.[5]

We have seen that the expected return on stocks affects Walter's spending and saving decisions. His decisions also depend on the degree of uncertainty about the return on stocks. An increase in the degree of uncertainty means that a stock's expected return is unchanged, but there is an increased chance that the actual return will be farther away from the expected return. For example, suppose you buy a stock today for $100 that pays off $105 with a 10 percent chance, pays $110 with an 80 percent chance, and pays $115 with a 10 percent chance. The expected payoff on this asset is then (.10 x $105)+(.80 x $110)+(.10 x $115) = $110. An increase in uncertainty can come about either by an increase in the likelihood of getting a high

---

[2] In the following discussion of the effects of stock-return uncertainty on people's spending and saving decisions, we get the sharpest predictions by assuming that stocks are the only risky assets in which people can invest. Alternatively, we can assume that there are other risky assets but that an increase in stock-return uncertainty reflects an increase in return uncertainty of all risky assets. If the increase in stock-return uncertainty is specific to the stock market, then the primary consequence of the increase may be a portfolio shift away from stocks and into other assets. The overall effect on spending and saving is then more difficult to pin down. For details see the 1989 article by Robert Barsky listed in the References.

[3] In general, part of the income uncertainty that people face is due to their future labor income being uncertain. In the case of Walter Wealthy we will ignore labor income uncertainty in order to focus on the uncertainty associated with holding risky assets such as stocks.

[4] The return from holding stocks includes both the dividends paid to the stockholder plus capital gains that accrue when the price of the stock increases.

[5] For a fuller discussion of the income and substitution effects associated with changes in uncertainty, see the articles by Barsky (1989) and Abel (1988).

or low payoff, for example, a 20 percent chance of $105, a 60 percent chance of $110, and a 20 percent chance of $115 (note that the expected return remains $110); or by a change in the value of the high and low payoffs, for example, a 10 percent chance of $100, an 80 percent chance of $110, and a 10 percent chance of $120. Again, the expected return is $110.

In the case of an increase in uncertainty, as in the case of an increase in the expected return, there are offsetting effects. A precautionary-saving effect induces Walter to cut back on current spending and increase current saving.[6] He increases current saving to guard against the increased likelihood of a bad outcome, which is a low return. On the other hand, a substitution effect leads Walter to spend more today. He spends more today in an effort to sidestep the increase in risk because current spending looks more attractive in the face of increased uncertainty about the future.

Which effect dominates depends on Walter's attitude toward risk. If he has a strong-enough dislike for risk, the precautionary-saving effect dominates, so his current spending will fall, and his saving will rise in response to an increase in the uncertainty of returns.[7] Empirical studies of household preferences toward risk suggest that most people fall into this category.

We can also consider how an increase in uncertainty affects the current prices of stocks. If Walter dislikes risk, an increase in the uncertainty of returns on stocks can lead him to sell some of his stocks and buy other, less risky assets, such as bonds. Since other holders of stock will also behave like Walter, the current prices of the stocks will fall as people sell their shares. Therefore, an increase in the uncertainty of returns can lead to a fall in the current price of stocks.

So, if Walter has a strong-enough dislike for risk, an increase in uncertainty about stock returns may cause him to increase current saving to guard against the possibility of a very low return next period. Thus, increased stock-market volatility can affect how much people spend and save. In addition, increased uncertainty can lead to a fall in the current prices of stocks.

The Effect on Stock Options Prices. An increase in stock-market volatility also affects another variable of economic interest: the price of stock options. A stock option is merely a contract that gives its owner the right to buy or sell a specified number of shares of an underlying stock at a specified price, called the exercise (or strike) price, within a specified period. For example, on July 3, 1992, as reported in the *Wall Street Journal*, one could have purchased a call option on Intel stock that would give the owner the right to buy 100 shares of Intel at a price of $55 per share on or before the third Friday in August 1992. The price to purchase the contract was $350, and Intel stock was selling on the National Association of Securities Dealers Automated Quotation (NASDAQ) system for $55-7/8 per share.

Stock options are like insurance contracts: the owner of a stock option has paid a "premium" to acquire "insurance" that eliminates some of the downside risk associated with holding a share of stock (the chance that the price of the stock will fall dramatically). The writer of the option contract acts like an underwriter, agreeing to "insure" the buyer of the contract against a bad outcome. Options are used by investors, consumers, and producers to hedge against uncertainty.

Investors and producers who use options as part of their financial strategy are of course interested in whether particular options are priced appropriately. In a 1973 article, Fisher Black and Myron Scholes developed a popular and widely used model of option pricing that

---

[6]For more on precautionary savings, see Barsky (1989) and Blanchard and Fisher (1987).

[7]This increased savings will flow partly into assets that are less risky than stocks.

shows how the price of an option can be determined from certain characteristics of the underlying stock. One of these characteristics is the volatility of the stock price. In the Black-Scholes model, the higher the volatility of the stock price, the higher is the price of the option.[8] The intuition behind this result can be understood without going into the complexities of the model. With higher volatility of stock prices, there is a greater chance of receiving both a good outcome (high stock price) and a bad outcome (low stock price). However, the option bears no downside risk. The worst that can happen is that the option will expire worthless at maturity. Referring to our Intel example, suppose that the share price of Intel stock fell to $52 in August. Then the call option would expire worthless, since no one would want to exercise the option and purchase the stock for $55 when it could be bought on the stock market for $52. In that case, the option buyer would lose the $350 spent to purchase the option. However, even if Intel fell to $1 per share, the most that the option owner could lose would be $350, the price of the option contract. Note that the owner of 100 Intel shares would lose over $5400 dollars if the share price fell to $1. On the other hand, if Intel's price rises to $155 in August, the option owner would exercise the contract and buy 100 shares for $55 per share. She could then sell those shares for $155 per share and receive a profit of ($155 - $55)x(100 shares) = $10,000.

---

[8]We should note that in the Black-Scholes derivation of option prices, it is assumed that the volatility of the stock price is constant. Thus, when we compare the effects of higher variance on option prices we are really comparing options written on two different stocks. The arbitrage argument used in the valuation procedure is not sufficient to determine the price of the option when the option depends on variables that are not traded or that cannot be hedged by an existing security, as is the case with stock price volatility. When stock prices have a time-varying variance, more restrictive equilibrium asset-pricing models can be used to derive option prices.

Because the downside risk on a call option is limited and the potential gains on the upside are not, the price of an option should be higher when the volatility of the stock price is high. The higher the volatility, the greater the chance that at the option's expiration date the underlying stock price will exceed the option's exercise price.

There is also an indirect path by which a change in uncertainty might affect the price of a stock option. Recall that an increase in uncertainty can lead to a fall in the price of a share of stock. A fall in the share price will in turn lead to a decrease in the price of a call option written on that stock. Suppose that a stock is trading at a price that is below the exercise price of the call option on that stock. If the share price falls, the option would be less valuable, since the stock price will have to increase by a larger amount in order that, at the expiration date, the selling price of the stock exceeds the exercise price of the option. Thus, a fall in the current price of a share leads to a fall in the price of a call option written on that stock.

We see then that there are offsetting effects on options prices due to a change in the uncertainty of a stock. For a call option, the direct effect of an increase in volatility is to raise the price of the option. The indirect effect is to lower the price of the option through a change in the current price of the share. For a put option, which gives the owner the right to sell shares of the underlying stock at a fixed price, direct and indirect effects of an increase in volatility work in the *same* direction.

We have seen two examples of how stock-market volatility affects behavior. Increased stock-market volatility causes people to spend less and save more, and for a given spread between a stock price and option strike price, it raises the price of the option.

HOW DOES STOCK-MARKET VOLATILITY CHANGE OVER TIME?

We have seen how changes in stock-market

volatility can affect the economy. How has this volatility changed over time? To answer this question, we must first construct a measure of the volatility of the stock market.

A graph (Figure 1) called a histogram illustrates the idea behind volatility. Panel A shows annual returns on common stocks as measured by the Standard & Poor's 500 index (S&P 500), and Panel B shows annual returns on long-term government bonds. The height of the bars in each panel represents the number of times (frequency) a particular return was observed on a yearly basis from 1959 to 1991. A tall bar means that a particular return was observed relatively more often. The horizontal axis measures annual return in percent.

In Figure 1, the three tallest bars in the bond-return distribution account for more than 65 percent of the observations. In the common stock-return distribution, the three tallest bars account for only slightly more than 45 percent of the observations. The distribution of returns for common stocks is more spread out than is the return distribution for long-term bonds, which means that there is a higher likelihood of receiving either a high or a low return when investing in stocks versus investing in long-term bonds. This suggests that common stocks are riskier investments than government bonds, that is, stock returns are more volatile.[9]

One useful way to measure the volatility of an asset is to look at its *variance*. Variance is a measure of dispersion—the larger the variance, the more spread out a distribution is. Another useful concept for measuring volatility is the *standard*

---

[9]Note, however, that an investor is rewarded for taking on the extra risk associated with holding common stocks. The average return on common stocks over this period is about 11 percent per year. The average return on long-term government bonds is 6.6 percent per year.

FIGURE 1
Asset Return Distribution
(1959 - 1990)

Distribution of Annual Returns on Common Stocks

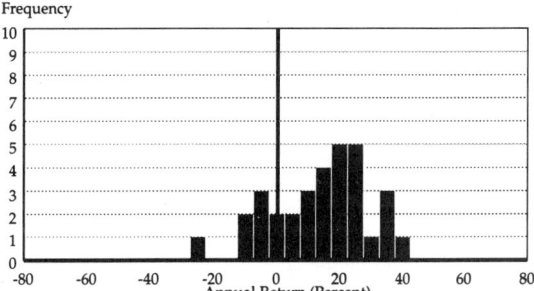

Distribution of Annual Returns on Long-Term Government Bonds

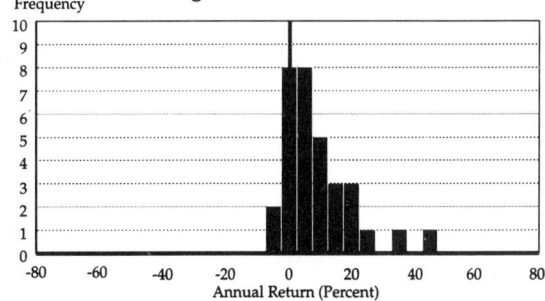

Source: Ibbotson Associates and author's calculations

deviation, which is defined as the square root of the variance (see *Calculating Variances and Standard Deviations* for technical details on variances and standard deviations).[10] In Figure 1 we saw that common stocks are more volatile than long-term government bonds. This is reflected in the statistic for the standard deviation: annual stock returns have a standard deviation of 15.6 percent, which is larger than the standard deviation of annual government bond returns of 10.8 percent.

Forecasting Stock-Market Volatility. People need to forecast how volatile the stock market is so that they can make better decisions about spending and saving and about pricing options. You might think that the best forecast of the volatility of the stock market is simply to calculate the variance of stock returns from a distribution like that shown in Figure 1. That calculation shows that the long-run standard deviation of annual stock returns is 15.6 percent. But this is not the best forecast of the variance at any particular date. Forecasts that use recent information are more efficient than forecasts that do not use recent information. If stock-market volatility is high this month, that may indicate an increased chance that volatility will be high next month. If this is the case, we want to use this information in making forecasts of stock-market volatility.

One method of forecasting the variance of the stock market is to use *time-series models*.[11] A

---

[10] A helpful rule of thumb is that 67 percent of the observations tend to fall within one standard deviation of the mean, and 95 percent of the observations tend to fall within two standard deviations of the mean. This rule of thumb is for symmetric distributions, which means that the tails of the distribution are mirror images of each other.

[11] Alternative methods of deriving and forecasting stock-return volatility are used as well. An estimate of the return variance can be derived using option-pricing theory. In the Black-Scholes model of option pricing, the variables that determine the current price of the option are the current stock price, the time to maturity of the option, the strike

Calculating Variances and Standard Deviations

Variance is a quantitative measure of how spread out a distribution of variables is. The variance is defined as the average value of squared deviations of a variable from its mean. If we have a sample of n observations on a variable x, the general formula for variance is given by:

$$\sigma^2 = \frac{1}{n} \sum_{i=1}^{n} (x_i - \bar{x})^2$$

where $\bar{x}$ is the sample mean:

$$\bar{x} = \frac{1}{n} \sum_{i=1}^{n} x_i$$

We can clarify this formula with a simple example. Suppose a stock yielded 3 percent one month, -2 percent the next month, and 1 percent and 6 percent in the following months. The average return on the stock is, in units of percent:

$$\frac{3 + (-2) + 1 + 6}{4} = 2$$

The variance is given by:

$$\frac{(3-2)^2 + (-2-2)^2 + (1-2)^2 + (6-2)^2}{4} = 8.5$$

The standard deviation of returns is given by the square root of the variance, or 2.92 percent. The standard deviations reported in Figure 1 were calculated this way, using 32 observations on annual returns.

The standard deviation of stock returns exceeds the standard deviation of bond returns in Figure 1 because actual individual stock returns are often quite different from the average value of stock returns. Individual government bond returns are usually much closer to their average value.

time-series model is simply a way to look at the relationship between current and past values of data. In the case of stock-return variance, a time-series model would show how this month's variance is related to the variance of the stock market over the past few months.[12] The best long-run forecast of monthly stock-market variance is the variance calculated from a distribution like that in Figure 1.[13] But the best short-run forecast of variance may be much lower or higher, depending on what the variance has been in recent months.

Economic theory suggests a method for forecasting stock-return variance: calculate the size of past errors in forecasting stock returns,[14] then use the squared values of these forecast errors to estimate the stock-return variance.[15]

This method of forecasting stock-return variance makes intuitive sense as well. In calm times, our forecasting model for stock returns should predict relatively well, and so our forecast error should be relatively small and the predicted variance will be small. In a particularly volatile time, our model will not fit quite as well, so that the forecast error is large and the predicted variance will be large.

We have plotted a measure of stock-market volatility using forecast errors from a time-series model of stock returns (Figure 2). The figure shows the forecast errors from a forecasting model of monthly returns to the S&P 500 stock index from 1959 to 1992.[16] Note that the stock-market volatility measure shows a great deal of variation. Volatility does not appear to be constant. The highest spike corresponds to the month of October 1987. Recall that on October 19, 1987, the stock market experienced its sharpest one-day drop ever. This figure also suggests a correlation through time in return volatility. Visual evidence suggests that sharp upward spikes are bunched together. This pattern indicates that volatility may in part be predictable based on its own past values.

PREDICTING STOCK-MARKET VOLATILITY

Why is it that stock-market volatility changes over time? Are there regular patterns in the time-series behavior of volatility? To help us address these questions it is useful to have an economic model of how stock prices are determined.

---

price, the risk-free interest rate, and the variance of the stock price. Since the current price of the option is observed, the Black-Scholes formula can be inverted to solve for the variance. This method of calculating stock price variance is referred to as the "implied-volatility" method. See, for example, the 1991 book *Option Valuation: Analyzing and Pricing Standardized Option Contracts,* by Rajna Gibson. For a comparison of how well time-series methods and implied-volatility methods characterize stock-return volatility, see Day and Lewis (1992).

[12]Time-series modeling of variances is a very active area of research for economists. See the April/May (1992) issue of the *Journal of Econometrics,* which is devoted entirely to ARCH (autoregressive conditional heteroskedasticity) models of financial market data. In their simplest form, ARCH models assume that the current value of the conditional variance is a linear function of past squared deviations.

[13]We would need to calculate a distribution for monthly stock returns. The distribution in Figure 1 is for annual stock returns.

[14]This method of calculating the variance and standard deviation of stock returns follows Schwert (1989) and Salinger (1989). An alternative method is to calculate the variance of daily stock returns and then use these daily variance observations to calculate a monthly variance. Schwert presents graphical evidence indicating that the two measures are similar.

[15]The forecast errors are the in-sample residuals from the estimated model for returns. The variance that is estimated from these forecast errors is called the conditional variance of returns.

[16]The absolute value of each monthly forecast error is plotted in Figure 2.

FIGURE 2
Stock-Market Volatility

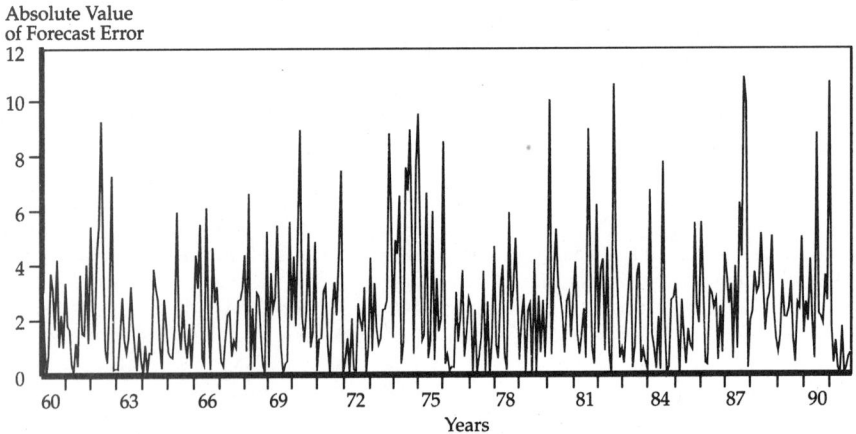

Suppose we take a simple model that expresses the current price of the stock as a positive multiple of current dividend payments.[17] This is certainly an oversimplification, but it will keep the discussion uncomplicated. For a stock portfolio as diversified as the S&P 500, current dividend payments might be proxied by current, economywide output. If the stock price is then represented as a positive fraction of current output, the expected variance of stock returns will be positively related to the expected variance of output *growth*.

In this model, the fundamental factor that drives stock prices is the level of output. We can think of output as indicating the state of the economy. When output growth is high, the state of the economy is good (expansions). When output growth is low, the state of the economy is bad (recessions). Any patterns over time in the volatility of output growth will be reflected in the volatility of stock returns. When we examine output growth (as measured by monthly industrial production), we find that output-growth volatility is correlated over time and that output-growth volatility is higher in recessions than it is in expansions. Our simple model suggests that we should see similar behavior in the time path of stock-market volatility.

Let us first examine whether stock-market volatility is correlated through time. One way to do this is by checking whether past volatility is useful in predicting current volatility. If we take monthly data on the S&P 500 from 1959 to 1992, we find that past volatility does help predict future volatility. However, the model's ability to predict future volatility is rather poor. Only a little over 1 percent of the total variation

---

[17]This result can be derived from an intertemporal model of asset pricing where investors face an uncertain future and have utility that is a logarithmic function of consumption. More general models of stock pricing suggest that the current price of a share of stock is related to the entire future stream of dividends that investors expect to receive. See Sargent (1987) for a technical discussion of these models.

in return volatility is explained by its own past values; over 98 percent of the movement over time in volatility evident in Figure 2 remains unexplained.

To test whether stock-market volatility is higher in recessions than it is in expansions we forecast volatility using data on its own past values and a variable that captures whether the economy is in a recession or an expansion. As suggested by our model, we find that the recession variable does help to explain volatility. Volatility is *higher* in recessions than in expansions. Based on our volatility measure we would forecast that the standard deviation of monthly returns would rise by about 2 percentage points in recessions.[18] By including the recession variable in the volatility forecast equation we can account for about 6 percent of the movement in stock-market volatility over time.

What other things might help us to improve our predictions of volatility? What about the seasons of the year? Is volatility predictably higher in one month than in another? A simple way to test for the presence of seasonal movement in volatility is to form a forecast of volatility using data on its own past values and a set of variables that account for the different months, or seasons, of the year. We can then test whether these seasonal indicators improve the forecast. Some evidence indicates that stock-market volatility is predictably lower in June, but in general, the evidence for a seasonal pattern in stock-market volatility is weak.

What have we learned so far about patterns in the behavior of stock-market volatility? First, stock-market volatility is not constant. It can be predicted, though rather imprecisely, using its own past values. Second, volatility tends to be higher in recessions than in expansions. Third, there is weak evidence of a seasonal movement in volatility.

Prediction Using Macroeconomic Variables. We have seen that there are identifiable patterns in stock-market volatility over time. The observation that stock-market volatility is higher in recessions than in expansions suggests that we might improve forecasts of volatility by using variables that predict recessions. If we can predict recessions, perhaps we can predict stock-market volatility. However, our test will be a little more demanding. Stock-market volatility itself predicts industrial-production volatility and so might predict recessions. Therefore, we will look at how well macroeconomic variables forecast stock-market volatility over and above the forecasting power of past stock-market volatility itself.

I examined a battery of macroeconomic variables to see if they predict future stock-market variability. These variables included inflation, various measures of money-supply growth, industrial production and consumer spending growth, and oil price shocks. Somewhat surprisingly, these macroeconomic variables did not improve forecasts of stock-market volatility over and above forecasts made using past levels of stock-market volatility. However, interest-rate variables did help to improve predictions of volatility because interest rates convey information about the risk of bankruptcy and about the stance of monetary policy.

When a firm borrows money, it might go bankrupt before paying off the loan. Lenders realize this and charge an interest rate on loans that reflects the firm's default risk, which is the likelihood that the firm will not pay off the loan. Strong firms, which are unlikely to go bankrupt, pay low interest rates, while weak firms pay higher interest rates. However, the whole schedule of interest rates changes as the economy changes. During recessions, all firms face an increased risk of bankruptcy, so all firms must pay higher interest rates on loans. Since the chance of bankruptcy is higher in recessions, expected dividend payments are

---

[18] The long-run standard deviation of monthly stock returns, measured by the S&P 500 index, is about 3.1 percent.

lower, and stock prices fall. Thus, there is a correlation between the default risk on corporate borrowing and stock prices.

How can we measure default risk? One way is to look at the interest rates on corporate bonds and compare them with the interest rates on default-free bonds, such as U.S. government bonds. The difference between these two interest rates, called an interest-rate spread, acts as a measure of default risk.

A different interest-rate spread may provide useful information about stock-market volatility in another way: the spread can indicate not just default risk but also changes in monetary policy. We have seen that stock-market volatility is higher in recessions than in expansions. If tighter monetary policy predicts future recessions, it will predict stock-market volatility. If monetary policy tightens, the cost of funds to banks increases. Banks will then have to increase the interest rates they pay on certificates of deposit (CDs). Since CDs and commercial paper are near-perfect substitutes, their interest rates will rise together; but Treasury bills are imperfect substitutes for CDs, so their interest rates won't rise as much. The overall effect is that the spread between interest rates on commercial paper and Treasury bills will increase. Another possibility is that banks may cut back on loans to customers, but again, the spread between commercial-paper interest rates and Treasury-bill interest rates could rise. In this case, firms issue commercial paper rather than borrowing from banks, causing interest rates on commercial paper to rise.[19] If the spread between the commercial-paper rate and the Treasury-bill rate is a measure of the stance of monetary policy, this spread could predict stock-market volatility because it predicts future recessions.

Examining the data, we find that the interest-rate spreads and their volatility help forecast stock-market volatility. In both cases, the default-premium variables have significant explanatory power for stock-market volatility. In fact, including the recession index and the interest-rate spreads, we can account for about 10 percent of the variation in stock-market volatility.

The Time-Series Behavior of Expected Volatility. The data show that stock-market volatility is difficult to predict. However, even though forecasts of volatility might be poor, the economic significance of these forecasts can be large. Forecasts of stock-market volatility are a measure of what people expect future stock-market volatility to be. After all, a forecast is just a best guess of what will happen in the future. Recall from our discussion of people's spending and saving decisions and the discussion of options prices that expected stock-market volatility affects behavior and prices. People act today based in part on their expectation of future events. Therefore, we would like to know if there are large changes over time in expectations of future stock-market volatility.

We have plotted the forecasted, or expected, stock-market volatility (Figure 3), constructed using past values of stock-market volatility and past values of the volatility of the interest-rate-spread variable.[20] Expected stock-market volatility clearly changes through time, though the movement is not as pronounced as the movement in the volatility displayed in Figure 2. (Recall that Figure 2 shows realized values of the forecast errors.) The sharpest upward movement in expected volatility occurs over the period 1973 to 1975, which coincides with

---

[19] See Bernanke (1990) for an in-depth discussion of the predictive power of interest rates and interest-rate spreads for future economic activity.

[20] This measure of expected volatility was constructed by using a bivariate ARCH model for stock returns and the T-bill/commercial paper spread. For details on how the measure of expected stock-market volatility was constructed, see my working paper listed in the References.

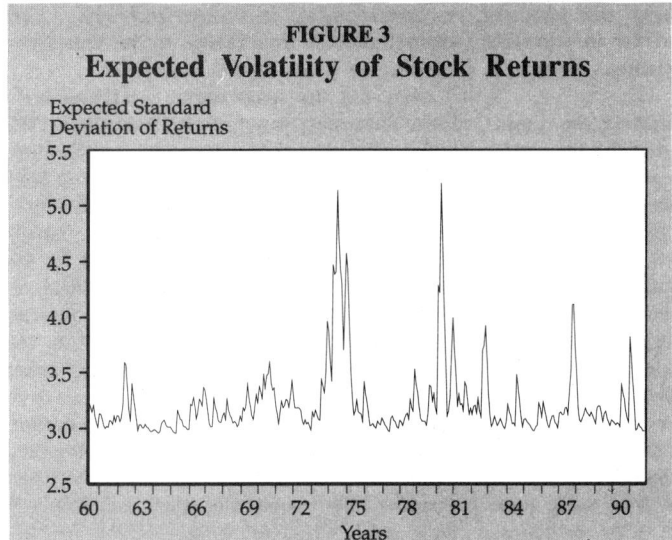

FIGURE 3
Expected Volatility of Stock Returns

the first OPEC oil price shocks and a recession. The next sharpest upward movement in expected volatility occurs in 1980, which also coincides with a recession. In fact, expected stock-market volatility in Figure 3 rises in each of the six recessions since 1959.[21]

How economically significant are these movements in expected volatility? Consider the case of option prices. The Chicago Board Options Exchange trades in call and put options on the S&P 500 index. Suppose that the current level of the S&P 500 index is 426.65, the call option contract has 30 days until maturity, and the strike price of the option is $425. Suppose further that the expected volatility of the index return is 3.1 percent. Under these conditions, the Black-Scholes option pricing formula predicts that the price of the call option is $6.87.[22] Suppose that we keep all parameters the same except for the volatility of returns, which increases by 2 percentage points, the amount that monthly volatility is predicted to increase during recessions. In this case, the Black-Scholes model predicts the call option price will be $10.19. Thus, the option price is quite sensitive to changes in expected volatility. Economic theory suggests that changes in expected volatility can also influence other economic variables such as consumption and investment. Measuring the effects of these changes in volatility is an active area of research for economists.[23]

VOLATILITY IN THE 1980s

The data on stock-market volatility have suggested that: (1) past levels of volatility predict future levels of volatility; (2) interest-rate spreads help to predict volatility; and (3) volatility is higher in recessions than expansions. However, if we test propositions (1) and (2) using data from 1980 through 1991, we find little evidence to support them. That is, in the

---

[21] The recessions occurred April 1960 to February 1961, December 1969 to November 1970, November 1973 to March 1975, January 1980 to July 1980, July 1981 to November 1982, and, most recently, the recession that began in July 1990.

[22] The parameters of the Black-Scholes pricing model include the time to maturity of the contract, the current price of the stock, the strike price of the contract, the volatility of the stock return, and the value of the risk-free interest rate. In the example in the text, the risk-free interest rate was assumed to be 4 percent per year.

[23] For a comprehensive survey of recent empirical work on time-series modeling of expected volatility, see Bollerslev, Chou, and Kroner (1992).

1980s, the forecasting power of past levels of stock-market volatility and the interest-rate spread deteriorated significantly. Why was this the case?

One possibility, suggested by the simple model of stock pricing, is that the time-series behavior of the volatility of output growth changed in the 1980s. However, when the data are examined we find that past values of output-growth volatility still have predictive power for future output-growth volatility in the 1980s. According to the simple model, past levels of stock-market volatility should still have predictive power for future volatility.

The change in the behavior of stock-market volatility may be related to developments in financial markets that occurred over the course of the 1980s. For example, the transaction costs of buying and selling stocks were much lower in the 1980s than in the early 1970s. Institutions, which account for about 80 percent of the trading on the New York Stock Exchange (NYSE), now pay less than 5 cents per share in commissions versus 80 cents per share in the early 1970s. These lower commission charges are reflected in the increased volume of trading on the market. This higher trading volume serves to make the stock market more liquid, thus helping to further reduce the costs associated with executing a trade. With these lower costs of trading, investors are able to react more quickly and more frequently to new information. These developments may have altered the time-series behavior of volatility.

Another possibility is that the time-series behavior of stock-market volatility has been influenced by the trend toward increasing integration of world financial markets. In the 1960s, transactions by foreigners accounted for about 12 percent of the dollar volume of trade on the NYSE.[24] In the 1970s the average had risen to about 16 percent. In the 1980s, the average reached over 19 percent. With the increasing interdependence of world markets, U.S. stock prices are influenced more and more by developments in foreign countries. This could contribute to a change in the time-series behavior of stock-market volatility.[25]

Why did the interest-rate variables have lower forecasting power in the 1980s? In a 1990 article, Ben Bernanke offers two possibilities. First, in the decade of the 1980s there have been changes in the way the Federal Reserve implements its monetary policy. These changes allowed short-term interest rates, such as the federal funds rate, to become more variable, all else equal. As a result, short-term interest rates may have become less tightly linked to the monetary policy actions that ultimately affect the economy.

A second possibility is that financial deregulation and financial innovation in the 1980s may have increased the substitutability between Treasury bills, commercial paper, and CDs. If these assets are closer substitutes, the sensitivity of interest-rate spreads to changes in monetary policy may be reduced. The weaker link between interest-rate spreads and monetary policy might then be reflected in a weaker link between the interest-rate spreads and the economy.

CONCLUSION

The data on stock returns suggest that: (1) stock-market volatility can be predicted based on its own past values; (2) volatility is higher in recessions than in expansions; (3) some variables that theory suggests might help explain

---

[24]The percent of transactions accounted for by foreigners is measured as the sum of sales by foreigners to Americans and sales to foreigners by Americans divided by the dollar volume of trade on the NYSE. These data are taken from various issues of the *New York Stock Exchange Fact Book*.

[25]Another innovation to financial markets in the 1980s has been the introduction of futures and options trading on stock market indexes. These contracts allow investors to buy and sell large baskets of stocks at a fraction of the cost required to execute the same trade in the stock market.

stock-market volatility (such as money-supply variability, inflation variability, and industrial-production variability) are not helpful; and (4) the spread between commercial-paper rates and Treasury-bill rates has predictive power for stock-market volatility. However, the best we can do with these variables is to explain about 10 percent of the variation in stock-market volatility over time. In addition, it appears that volatility became more difficult to predict in the 1980s.

Even though it is difficult to accurately predict stock-market volatility, the forecasts that people make about volatility are important. Economic theory argues that it is these expectations about future volatility that can affect people's decisions to spend and save. Changes in expected volatility can also affect stock prices and investment and the prices of stock options. The evidence suggests that there are substantial movements in expected stock-market volatility relative to the average level of volatility.

REFERENCES

Abel, Andrew. "Stock Prices Under Time-Varying Dividend Risk: An Exact Solution in an Infinite-Horizon General Equilibrium Model," *Journal of Monetary Economics*, 22 (1988), pp. 375-93.

Barsky, Robert. "Why Don't the Prices of Stocks and Bonds Move Together?" *American Economic Review*, 79 (December 1989), pp. 1132-45.

Bernanke, Ben. "On the Predictive Power of Interest Rates and Interest Rate Spreads," *New England Economic Review*, (Nov/Dec 1990), pp. 51-68.

Black, Fisher, and Myron Scholes. "The Pricing of Options and Corporate Liabilities," *Journal of Political Economy*, 81 (May/June 1973), pp. 637-59.

Blanchard, Olivier, and Stanley Fisher. *Lectures on Macroeconomics*. Cambridge: MIT Press, 1987.

Bollerslev, Tim, Ray Chou, and Kenneth Kroner. "ARCH Modeling in Finance: A Review of the Theory and Empirical Evidence," *Journal of Econometrics*, 52 (April/May 1992), pp 5-59.

Day, Theodore, and Craig Lewis. "Stock Market Volatility and the Information Content of Stock Index Options," *Journal of Econometrics*, 52 (April/May 1992), pp. 267-87.

Fama, Eugene. "The Behavior of Stock Market Prices," *Journal of Business*, 38 (January 1965), pp. 34-105.

Gibson, Rajna. *Option Valuation: Analyzing and Pricing Standardized Option Contracts*. New York: McGraw-Hill, 1991.

Salinger, Michael. "Stock Market Margin Requirements and Volatility: Implications for Regulation of Stock Index Futures," *Journal of Financial Services Research*, 3 (1989), pp. 121-38.

Sargent, Thomas. *Dynamic Macroeconomic Theory*. Cambridge: Harvard University Press, 1987.

Schwert, G. William. "Why Does Stock Market Volatility Change Over Time," *Journal of Finance*, 44 (December 1989), pp. 1115-53.

Sill, D. Keith. "Stock-Return Volatility," Federal Reserve Bank of Philadelphia Working Paper (1993).

The IPO Underpricing Puzzle

A large number of initial public offerings (IPOs) have come to market recently, and many have had a substantial run-up in price during early trading. A striking example is the offering by Boston Chicken, in which shares were offered at $20 and appreciated to $48.50 by the end of trading the first day. This level of price appreciation is by no means common, and many initial public offerings are followed by price declines. Nevertheless IPOs in the U.S. have consistently shown substantial initial-day returns averaging 15.3 percent for the 1960 to 1992 period, and similar results have been found for at least 25 other countries (Loughran, Ritter, and Rydqvist 1993).

While several explanations of IPO underpricing have been presented, it remains something of a puzzle to academic researchers who generally support the concept of efficient markets. This *Letter* discusses the structure of the IPO market and presents a summary of the explanations that have ben proffered to account for IPO underpricing. Finally, it looks at the available evidence to distinguish the relative importance of each explanation and briefly discusses some of the questions that remain.

Going public

In the U.S. market, companies going public most frequently issue their equity securities through an investment bank using a "firm commitment" contract, in which the investment bank temporarily purchases the shares before they are allocated to the public. A less popular method is a "best efforts" offering, typically used for small and very young firms. In this case, the investment bank agrees to undertake its best efforts to sell the issue within a designated marketing period (usually 90 days).

In firm commitment contracts, the investment bank and firm agree on a preliminary price range for the shares. Then, during a pre-issue marketing period, indications of interest are collected from potential subscribers. Just before the offer date a final offer price is agreed upon that in the majority of issues is within the initial price range. The investment bank then has discretion to allocate the shares among potential subscribers at this price. Thus, when there is substantial oversubscription, as often happens, some potential subscribers may receive only a fraction of the shares desired or be excluded from the issue.

Outside the U.S., these procedures often differ. For example, new issues on the French *Bourse* require the issuing firm to state a minimum price and then accept sealed bids for price and number of shares. The issuer, investment bank, and exchange agree on a market-clearing price. The most common difference is in the way oversubscription is handled, because not all countries give investment banks discretion to allocate shares. An extreme example is the Singapore IPO market where shares must be allocated by lottery within different classes of order size. Loughran, et al., find that, typically, investment banks use discretionary procedures for allocating shares, unless such procedures are ruled illegal. Regardless of the procedures used, they find initial underpricing in all 25 countries considered.

Theories on IPO underpricing

If markets are efficient, as academic researchers often contend, then the widely documented large initial returns to IPOs are puzzling, because firms appear to be leaving large amounts of money on the table when going public. But analysis suggests that underpricing does not necessarily occur for every issue at every point in time. Ritter (1987) finds that only 54 percent of a large sample of IPOs in the U.S. had positive initial-day returns. Also, evidence indicates that the market for IPOs goes through cycles, with larger amounts of underpricing in "hot" periods, when a lot of issues are coming to market, and smaller amounts of underpricing in "cold" periods, when only a few firms are going public.

This suggests that it is difficult to determine the value of shares in this market. Consistent with this, the rationales for IPO underpricing offered often rely on assumptions that the value of firms cannot be estimated precisely and that there are information asymmetries among groups of market participants.

An early explanation along these lines suggested that the initial underpricing is designed to "leave a good taste in the mouth" of investors. Initial investors, it is argued, remember the firm favorably when it returns to the market later to raise capital. This will increase the demand for shares for the subsequent offerings and allow the firm to recover some or all of the lost proceeds from the initial underpricing. An extension of this argument suggests that large initial underpricing leads to more potential investor interest in the IPO—a lot of "hype," in the jargon—which produces additional information about the firm. That additional information lowers the costs associated with future issues by the firm.

A second explanation focuses on the interests of the investment bank. Investment bankers may use superior information to underprice an issue intentionally to reduce their marketing costs or to create good will with investors. This explanation runs into trouble in terms of the potential damage to their reputation with other firms going public.

Perhaps the most popular explanations of initial underpricing rely on adverse selection associated with receiving an allocation of particular IPOs. Even if values are uncertain, investors with superior information would be less likely to purchase issues that are overpriced. As a result, less informed investors would be allocated more of the shares in the less attractive overpriced issues. As a result, less informed investors would earn lower, even negative, average returns on the issues they are allocated and might choose not to participate in IPOs. Thus to attract these investors to the IPO market, investment bankers must deliberately underprice new shares to overcome this form of the winners' curse problem and permit less informed investors to earn a positive return.

While this explanation has some appeal, it leaves many questions unanswered. Perhaps most important is whether an equilibrium level of underpricing exists that will attract these less informed investors given that the better informed investors will increase demand in response to deliberate underpricing.

An extension of this framework relies on the less informed demand as a lever to extract information from those with superior estimates of the value of the shares. If some potential investors have better estimates of value than the investment bankers, then the investment bankers' threat of allocating to the less informed investors motivates the better informed to reveal their true demand for shares. This information can then be used in setting the final offer price to maximize proceeds. In this framework initial underpricing continues to exist as compensation to those with superior information for truthfully revealing their demand for shares. To make this explanation consistent with equilibrium, investors with superior information must be able to affect the final offer price by understating their demand for shares. Second, this behavior cannot damage their reputation with investment banks who might ration them out of future issues. These interdependent assumptions appear unlikely to hold in equilibrium, particularly if there are several informed bidders.

In a related explanation, investment bankers reduce the adverse selection consequences associated with the issuers' superior information about the value of the firm. If investment bankers develop a reputation for certifying that issues are priced consistent with any superior inside information, they have reason to protect their reputation for this service. Thus investment bankers may underprice to protect their reputation with investors.

A more recent explanation suggests an information framework where the success of an issue depends on getting investors approached early in the IPO process to view it favorably; subsequent investors then base their opinions and demand on the reaction of early potential investors.

Empirical evidence
Each of the explanations for underpricing IPOs has some appeal, but they lack convincing empirical support. Studies that attempt to distinguish between the various explanations for underpricing are rare. Beatty and Ritter (1986) document that investment bankers who underprice more or less than the average for each risk level lose future IPO market share. This suggests that reputation plays an important role in establishing the equilibrium level of underpricing for any particular issue. This evidence is inconsistent with the notion that investment bankers are underpricing to take advantage of less informed issuing firms.

Koh and Walter (1989) provide evidence related to the adverse selection characteristics associated with investing in IPOs. They find in the Singapore IPO market that underpricing is positively related to the level of oversubscription and that the ratio of shares requested by large investors increases with the level of underpricing. Thus small investors are more likely to be allocated shares in less underpriced issues. However, they find that issues are oversubscribed on average by 40 times the number of shares. These results appear, at best, mixed regarding whether initial underpricing is used to attract less informed investors to purchase shares.

More recent evidence for the U.S. market by Weiss-Hanley (1993) relies on data for the preliminary filing range price data relative to the final offer price. With firm commitment issues in the U.S. the preliminary prospectus lists a preliminary price range and then on the offering day the final offer price is set. Evidence shows that if the final offer price is above the midpoint of the filing range then underpricing is higher, because a final offer price above the midpoint of filing range is interpreted as evidence of strong preliminary demand for the issue. These results are consistent with investment bankers adjusting the final offer price to reflect unexpectedly large demand for a particular issue. Why the price is not fully adjusted to reflect the increased demand is not clear.

Perhaps the most interesting evidence related to initial underpricing is found in McDonald and Jacquillat (1974). Using data from the sealed-bid auctions of companies to be listed on the French *Bourse*, they found that even after the issuing firm, bankers, and the exchange know the demand curve for the shares, they attempt to underprice by approximately 3 percent to encourage potential investors to continue to bid for the shares. It is worth noting that the relatively low underpricing they attempt to achieve is for established and well-known firms.

Data presented in these studies, plus the international evidence that initial underpricing is common across different markets, suggest that the bias toward underpricing is intentional. Additionally, it appears that investors' costs of participating in these markets are of concern when attempting to set the level of underpricing. That is, the average underpricing of IPOs may be necessary to compensate potential buyers for the cost of participation.

Conclusions

Large initial-day returns to IPOs on average are well-documented in the U.S. and in other markets. What is less understood is the rationale for this apparent practice of "leaving money on the table" when firms go public. Explanations for this behavior have traditionally relied on some form of informational asymmetry among the issuer, the investment banks, and the different groups of investors. Limited empirical evidence suggests oversubscription and underpricing are positively related and that issues are intentionally underpriced even when the issuer can observe the demand for shares through a sealed-bid auction. A lack of data on discretionary allocation decisions in oversubscribed issues limits research distinguishing between theories presented to date. Virtually ignored in explanations of initial underpricing is the potential benefit to secondary market liquidity from pricing to promote secondary market liquidity.

James Booth
Visiting Scholar, and
Associate Professor of Finance
Arizona State University

References

Beatty, Randolph, and Jay Ritter. 1986. "Investment Banking, Reputation, and the Underpricing of Initial Public Offerings." *Journal of Financial Economics*, pp. 213–232.

Koh, Francis, and Terry Walter. 1989. "A Direct Test of Rock's Model of the Pricing of Unseasoned Issues." *Journal of Financial Economics*, pp. 251–272.

Loughran, Tim, Jay Ritter, and Kristian Rydqvist. 1994. "Initial Public Offering Underpricing: International Insights." *Pacific-Basin Finance Journal* (forthcoming in March).

McDonald, John G., and Bertrand C. Jacquillat. 1974. "Pricing of Initial Equity Issues: The French Sealed-bid Auction." *Journal of Business*, pp. 37–47.

Weiss-Hanley, Kathleen. 1993. "The Underpricing of Initial Public Offerings and the Partial Adjustment Phenomenon." *Journal of Financial Economics*, pp. 231–250.

Correction: Due to a clerical mistake, the example of a nominal income targeting rule in the last issue of the *Weekly Letter* (94-09) contained an error: In the third to last paragraph, trend growth in real GDP should read "2½ percent."

Derivative markets and competitiveness

Janet A. Napoli

"The opening up of new markets, foreign or domestic, and the organizational development...illustrate the same process of industrial mutation—if I may use that biological term—that incessantly revolutionizes the economic structure from within, incessantly destroying the old one, incessantly creating a new one."

Joseph A. Schumpeter

Derivatives are financial instruments, such as forwards, futures, options, and swaps, which are based upon the future value of a good or instrument. Prior to the 1980s, few futures and options exchanges existed outside the U.S. An unprecedented period of growth occurred during the 1980s as existing derivative exchanges continued to expand and as new derivative exchanges opened throughout Europe and the Pacific Rim. The 1980s growth resulted primarily from the increasing importance of financial derivatives. Figure 1 illustrates the dramatic increases in exchange traded financial derivative volume during the 1980s, with the 1990 volume twice the 1985 volume and almost seven times the 1983 volume. An important factor driving the proliferation of new derivative exchanges and new market participants was financial market deregulation. Derivative exchanges opened in countries where the majority of domestic financial markets had already been deregulated as well as in countries undergoing comprehensive programs of credit, capital, and exchange rate deregulation.

Over-the-counter (OTC) financial derivatives also experienced extraordinary growth during the 1980s. Prior to the 1980s, the primary instruments traded on the largest OTC market, the interbank foreign exchange market, were forward, future and, to a lesser extent, option instruments. The 1980s OTC market growth was based upon innovative financial engineering resulting in a number of new instruments: caps, collars, floors, swaps, and swaptions. In many cases, these derivatives are hybrid instruments, combining a conventional financial instrument, like a bond, with a derivative instrument, like an option. The popularity of the new instruments is attributable to the increasing ability of the OTC markets to customize specific risks, notably foreign exposures. The most actively traded of these new OTC derivatives are currency and interest rate swaps. As shown in Figure 2, the 1990 notional principal of these swaps is more than three times the 1987 notional principal.

This article explores the impact of the 1980s expansion on the derivative markets and its participants. In particular, the discussion focuses upon the growing importance of exchange competition and its impact on transaction costs and liquidity. This increase in competition is driving the continuing internationalization of national financial markets. At the

---

Janet A. Napoli is an associate economist at the Federal Reserve Bank of Chicago. The author is especially grateful to Herbert Baer for his insightful comments. The author would also like to thank John Behof, Hesna Genay, Carolyn McMullen, and James Moser for their comments.

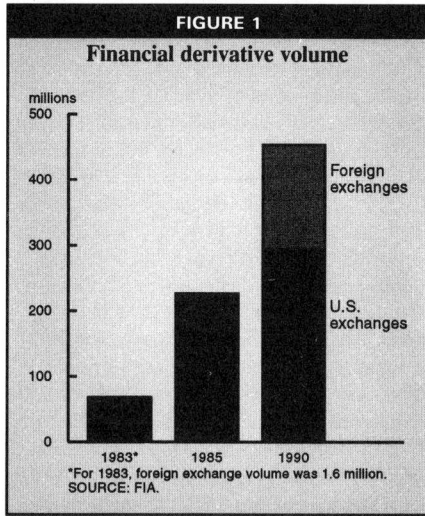

FIGURE 1
Financial derivative volume

*For 1983, foreign exchange volume was 1.6 million.
SOURCE: FIA.

same time, the growth of the exchange and OTC markets is forcing a restructuring of these markets.

Exchange markets and the 1980s expansion

The pervasive deregulation of financial asset markets during the 1980s increased the demand for derivatives based on these assets. The creation of a derivative market largely depends upon features of the underlying asset market. An asset market which is both actively traded and volatile creates investor demand to

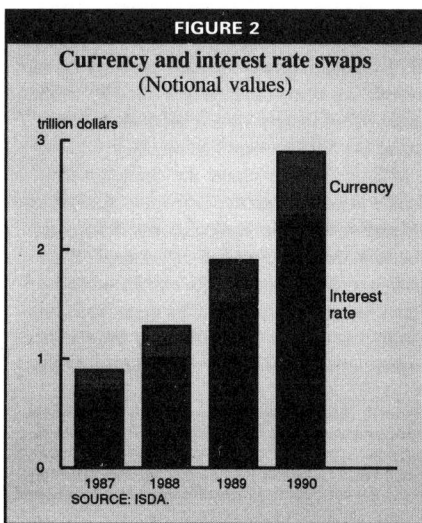

FIGURE 2
Currency and interest rate swaps
(Notional values)

SOURCE: ISDA.

trade on information about future prices and reduce the resulting price risk. The economic role of derivative instruments is to provide these price discovery and risk hedging functions [Black (1986) and Moser (1991)]. As highly regulated asset markets were transformed into open market structures, the liquidity, activity, size, and volatility of these markets increased. The new and expanding exchanges during the 1980s addressed the increased demand for price discovery and risk management instruments by introducing derivatives based on these deregulated assets. Today, more than 100 derivative products trade across different countries in comparison to less than 25 in 1983. These previously unavailable products have made the markets for derivatives an important part of the financial infrastructure in these countries.

Exchange traded derivatives based on financial instruments originated in the U.S. during the 1970s.[1] The currency, interest rate, and stock index futures and options introduced by U.S. exchanges were subsequently emulated by international exchanges throughout the 1980s. Whereas today financial derivative exchanges are an international phenomenon spanning 22 countries, only five exchanges—four U.S. and one non-U.S.—traded financial derivatives in 1980 [Miller (1990)]. Today, the Chicago Board of Trade (CBOT) still trades the most active future contract: the U.S. Treasury bond future; while the Chicago Board Options Exchange (CBOE) trades the most active option contract: the S&P 100 index option. The Chicago Mercantile Exchange (CME) trades the third, seventh, and ninth most active futures: the three month Eurodollar, S&P 500 stock index, and German deutschemark futures. The CME is also one of the more internationally oriented exchanges based upon its foreign currency and interest rate product offerings. In 1990, U.S. derivative exchanges accounted for 65 percent of worldwide volume in exchange traded derivatives (see Table 1 for a list of acronyms used in this article).

One of the largest exchange traded derivative markets arose during the 1980s in Japan, where underlying financial market liberalization, primarily interest rate deregulation, continued to progress from the mid-1970s. Interest rates are now market determined for the money markets, the primary medium and long term government bond markets, as well as the sec-

TABLE 1
Exchange acronyms

Acronym	Exchange
AMEX	American Stock Exchange
CBOE	Chicago Board Options Exchange
CBOT	Chicago Board of Trade
CME	Chicago Mercantile Exchange
DTB	Deutsche Terminbörse
LIFFE	London International Financial Future Exchange
MATIF	Marché à Terme International de France
MIDAM	MidAmerica Commodity Exchange
NYSE	New York Stock Exchange
OM	OM Stockholm
OSE	Osaka Stock Exchange
PBOT	Philadelphia Board of Trade
PHLX	Philadelphia Stock Exchange
PSE	Pacific Stock Exchange
SFE	Sydney Futures Exchange
SIMEX	Singapore International Monetary Exchange, Ltd.
SOFE	Swedish Option and Future Exchange
TIFFE	Tokyo International Financial Futures Exchange
TSE	Tokyo Stock Exchange

ondary bond markets. Financial liberalization in Japan has increased securitization as more financial transactions are explicitly priced, with less reliance on indirect or intermediated finance [Cargill and Royama (1992)]. Secondary market equity trading has correspondingly increased, as trading on the Tokyo Stock Exchange (TSE) increased from 100 billion shares traded in 1980 to almost 220 billion shares traded in 1989. As part of the overall financial liberalization in Japan, derivative trading has also progressed incrementally. In 1985, the Ministry of Finance (MOF) permitted Japanese government bond futures to be traded on the TSE. Beginning in 1987, the MOF permitted a group of financial institutions to trade in foreign derivative markets. Following in 1988, the Japanese Securities and Exchange law was amended to permit Japanese stock exchanges to trade derivative products, notably stock index futures. Simultaneously, the Financial Futures Trading law sanctioned financial derivative exchanges, and the Tokyo International Financial Futures Exchange (TIFFE) opened in 1989 [Japan Securities Research Institute (1990)]. As of 1990, Japanese exchanges traded 13 percent of worldwide volume, constituting the largest derivative market in the Pacific Rim and the second largest worldwide. In the same year, the Nikkei 225 stock index futures contract, traded on the Osaka Stock Exchange (OSE), became the most actively traded stock index futures contract.

In addition to Japan, the Pacific Rim has financial derivative exchanges located in Australia, Hong Kong, New Zealand,[2] the Philippines, and Singapore, with a financial derivative exchange proposed in Malaysia. In 1990, these Pacific Rim exchanges traded 4 percent of worldwide exchange traded volume. The Singapore International Monetary Exchange, Ltd. (SIMEX), the first Asian financial derivative exchange, presently trades only nondomestic financial derivatives. In addition to its international derivative offerings and membership, SIMEX and the CME have effectively offered its members extended trading hours in British pound, German deutschemark, Japanese yen, and three month Eurodollar derivatives since 1984. This is done through a mutual offset system where trading positions established at one exchange can be transferred to or liquidated at the other exchange, providing inter-exchange fungibility for the designated contracts. The remaining exchanges primarily trade domestic financial derivatives.

Numerous financial derivative markets opened in Europe during the 1980s as the European Community (EC) countries modernized financial markets in preparation for Europe 1992. During the 1980s, France was one of the countries which underwent extensive credit, capital, and exchange rate deregulation. The removal of quantitative credit controls and the entry of nonfinancial participants into the money markets created new markets for negotiable rate instruments: commercial paper and certificates of deposit. Capital market reforms were assisted by the Banking Act of 1984 which increased the number of capital market participants by removing the distinction between commercial and investment banking. Throughout the 1980s, exchange rate controls were gradually liberalized [Ducruezet and Papadacci (1992)]. The culmination of France's financial industry liberalization and modernization created the demand for financial derivatives, and the

Marché à Terme International de France (MATIF) opened in 1986. As of 1990, MATIF trades the French *notional* bond future, the third largest government bond future worldwide. In contrast to France's financial market deregulation, Germany was motivated to open a derivative exchange by the successful trading of a German government *bund* future on the nearby London International Financial Future Exchange (LIFFE). Amendments to Germany's gambling law in 1989 permitted retail participation in derivative markets, followed by the opening of Germany's first financial derivative exchange, Deutsche Terminbörse (DTB), in 1990.[3] In addition to France and Germany, European financial derivative exchanges are presently more or less active in Austria, Belgium, Denmark, Finland, Holland, Ireland, the Netherlands, Spain, Sweden, Switzerland, and the United Kingdom, with financial derivative exchanges proposed in Italy, Luxembourg, and Norway. Similar to France, extensive financial market deregulation programs were implemented during the 1980s in Finland, Ireland, and Sweden. In 1990, European exchanges—excluding LIFFE—traded 10 percent of worldwide exchange traded volume.

LIFFE is the oldest and largest European financial futures exchange. Unlike the majority of European exchanges, LIFFE's derivatives and membership are internationally oriented. LIFFE trades EC, German, Italian, Japanese, Swiss, and U.S. financial derivative products. For each country, LIFFE offers a range of products, notably interest rate derivatives with maturities spanning the yield curve. Additionally, LIFFE trades derivatives based upon the four most actively traded government debt markets: German, Japanese, U.K. and U.S. government bond futures. LIFFE is the third largest volume exchange worldwide, following the U.S. and Japanese markets. In 1990, LIFFE traded 8 percent of worldwide exchange traded volume.

The transaction cost difference

The increasing number and growing size of derivative exchanges has increased exchange competition. Derivative exchanges and their members are increasingly competing with other derivative and cash exchanges through product offerings, trading hours, and notably, competitively priced transaction costs. As similar derivative products continue to be listed and traded across multiple exchanges, trading will tend to flow to the market offering the lowest transaction costs. The continuing internationalization of markets finds market participants increasingly trading on exchanges across several countries with different cost structures. Assessing execution costs between markets is a complex exercise because transaction costs vary within an individual market across time. A derivative market's transaction costs vary in accordance with the degree of liquidity and price discovery, the size of the trade, the type of market participant, the activity in the underlying financial asset market, and the legal and regulatory framework over a country's financial markets.

Transaction costs for exchange traded derivatives typically include the bid-ask spread (the difference between the bid price and the asked price), commissions, exchange and clearing fees, and margin requirements. Internationally, the trend has been to reduce these costs. Commissions are generally negotiated in most countries' markets according to the market participant and the size of trade, with the exception of the Japanese markets which still adhere to fixed commission rates.[4] Competitive pressures are reducing negotiated commissions, as shown by a 1991 CBOT survey which reported the majority of CBOT members had reduced average commission rates between 21 percent to 50 percent over the past five years.[5] During 1991, brokers at MATIF dramatically lowered and, in some instances, temporarily waived commission fees to attract market participants.[6] Actively traded markets typically have narrow bid-ask spreads, minimizing this trading cost component. New exchanges, such as DTB and MATIF, have asked dealers to minimize the bid-ask cost in order to attract market participants.

To the extent margin requirements force traders to hold assets in proportions that they would not otherwise hold, these requirements impose indirect transaction costs on the trader. The major exchange clearinghouses generally do not require noninterest bearing (that is, cash) margin, except for the Japanese exchange clearinghouses. This increases Japanese trading costs by the amount of foregone interest which could have been earned on investing the noninterest bearing margin in an interest bearing instrument. Other exchanges are actively seeking to reduce the opportunity costs associated with margin requirements. For instance, a CME proposal currently under review by the Commodity Future Trading Commission (CFTC), the U.S. future exchange regulatory agency, could further reduce margin opportunity costs by extending permissible collateral to include stock and mutual fund shares. Exchanges are also seeking to reduce the burden of margin requirements by recognizing offsetting positions traded on the same exchange. This portfolio approach to margin setting leads to reduced margin requirements because margin is calculated on positions which offset and therefore reduce risk [Behof (1989)]. These intra-exchange cross margin programs have been established by the CBOT, CME, LIFFE, MATIF, SIMEX, and Sydney Futures Exchange (SFE) clearinghouses. Cross margin programs have also been established between exchanges, with an inter-exchange program established in 1989 between the CME clearinghouse and the Options Clearing Corporation (OCC), the clearinghouse for five U.S. exchanges which trade options. As a result of this inter-exchange cross margin program, margin requirements have been reduced by 70 percent for some positions. Similarly, the CBOT clearinghouse and OCC established an inter-exchange cross margin program in 1991.[7]

A country's legislative and regulatory rules may impose additional transaction costs. Although the legislative and regulatory playing field is not yet level, many countries are altering or eliminating laws and regulations which increase trading costs. Between 1990 and 1991, Germany, the Netherlands, Sweden, and the U.K. abolished security transfer taxes on their respective asset markets [White, Kupiec, Duffee (1990)]. Along with the elimination of the taxes on the asset markets, Sweden and the U.K. correspondingly eliminated taxes on derivative trades. Presently, derivative taxes are assessed in Finland, France, Hong Kong, and Japan.[8] Sweden offers an illustration of the impact that transaction taxes can have on an exchange. Sweden doubled its equity transaction tax in 1986, increasing equity trading on Swedish stocks in foreign markets, notably London. In 1989, Sweden extended the tax to futures and options trades, which substantially reduced futures trading on Sweden's OM Stockholm (OM) and closed the Swedish Option and Future exchange (SOFE).[9] Although the derivative tax included option trades, the tax on these trades was considerably lower and did not dramatically reduce option trading on OM. The futures tax effectively eliminated futures trading on OM during 1989 and 1990, in comparison to over 300,000 futures contracts traded at OM in 1988, the year prior to the introduction of the derivative tax. With the abolition of the tax on both the underlying asset and derivative markets in 1990, OM's futures volume for 1991 approached 4 million contracts.

Given the difficulty of making transaction cost generalizations on a "by market" basis, a more feasible comparison can be completed on a "by transaction" basis. A 1991 Salomon Brothers transaction cost study replicated a stock index portfolio transaction specified at a face value of (U.S.) $50 million in the Japan, U.K., and U.S. markets [Gastineau (1991)]. In the futures markets, total transactions costs were lowest in the U.S., followed by Japan and, finally, the U.K. The noninterest bearing margin requirement of Japanese exchanges and the large bid-ask spread on U.K. exchanges were responsible for the relatively lower transaction costs in the U.S. However, since this study was completed, commission and margin requirement increases have substantially increased the total transaction costs of executing this transaction on the Japanese future markets. In the option markets, total transaction costs were lowest in Japan, followed by the U.S. and the U.K. Cost differences between Japan and the U.S. were slight, with the bid-ask spread marginally higher in the U.S. The study highlighted the fact that of all the U.S. cost estimates, the bid-ask spread on options was the most difficult to estimate because this cost varies widely under different market environments. Once again, the relatively large bid-ask spread increased the total costs of executing the option transaction in the U.K.

Competition for liquidity

A primary characteristic of a successful derivative market is liquidity. Liquid markets are actively traded, with small price changes. Prior to the 1980s expansion, trading in a particular type of future or option contract tended to be concentrated on a single exchange, usually the first exchange to introduce the contract. Being first to create a liquid contract market gave an exchange a competitive advantage which typically eliminated any trading for the same contract on a competing exchange [Miller (1990)]. With the industry's expansion, exchanges are aggressively competing for existing liquid contract markets. In some instances, newer exchanges are gaining considerable market share, neutralizing this former "first exchange advantage." Decreasing transaction costs assist in increasing market share and, correspondingly, liquidity. In particular, the exchange growth is challenging the internationally oriented exchanges, such as the CBOT, CME, LIFFE, MATIF, and SIMEX, to retain and expand product offerings. During the 1980s, exchanges opened specifically to recapture trading in domestic financial products that was occurring at foreign exchanges. At the same time, many existing exchanges which trade domestic financial derivatives expanded through foreign product introductions. Exchange markets also faced increasing competition from OTC markets for derivative products. For some financial derivatives, exchanges have had greater difficulty in competing with the older, more established OTC markets.

Prior to 1990, German law prohibited the trading of futures. As a result, trading in the German government *bund* future was launched by a nondomestic exchange, LIFFE in 1988. Since November 1990, DTB has pursued German government *bund* future volume traded on LIFFE. DTB's *bund* futures market has consistently grown to account for 34 percent of total volume and 23 percent of total open interest as of December 1991 (see Figure 3).[10] DTB's growing market share is the result of transaction costs reductions to competitively position its contract against LIFFE's contract (see Table 2). Margin requirements were lowered beginning June 1991[11] and exchange fees were temporarily suspended beginning August 1991. Dealers are increasing market liquidity by trading at least 20 contracts with a maximum spread of no more than 3 ticks—a tick being the minimum allowable price movement—or 75 deutschemarks.[12]

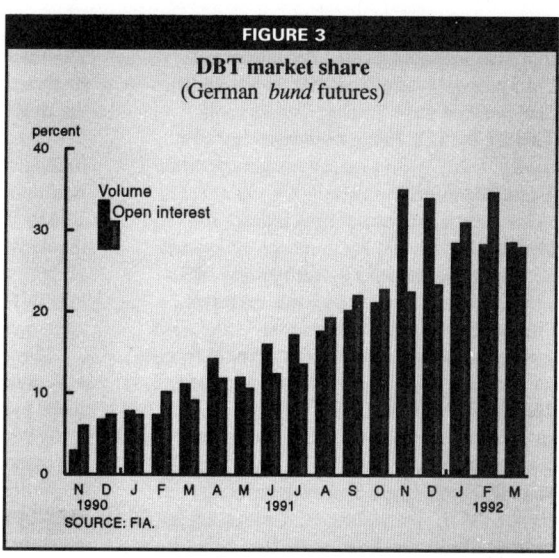

FIGURE 3
DBT market share
(German *bund* futures)
SOURCE: FIA.

Until recently, TIFFE easily dominated trading of its domestic three month Euroyen future, introduced in June 1989. In October of 1989, SIMEX introduced a comparable future, but volume languished. Until the last half of 1991, TIFFE's market share has been 90 percent of total volume and open interest. Since mid-1991, SIMEX trading gains have gradually increased, exceeding 10 percent of total volume and 20 percent of total open interest by December 1991 (see Figure 4).[13] Although the competitive impact cannot yet be assessed, TIFFE has responded to SIMEX's increasing market share by extending trading hours to coincide with SIMEX's longer trading hours. However, competition between the two exchanges is not a straightforward transaction cost issue at present. Although SIMEX's transaction costs are lower than TIFFE's, some observers of the Japanese markets believe SIMEX can compete only for a

TABLE 2		
German *bund* future transaction costs		
	DTB	LIFFE
Commission	Negotiated	Negotiated
Margin	3,000 DM	2,000 DM
B/A spread	50-75 DM (2-3 ticks)	25-50 DM (1-2 ticks)
Exchange fees	None	90 pence

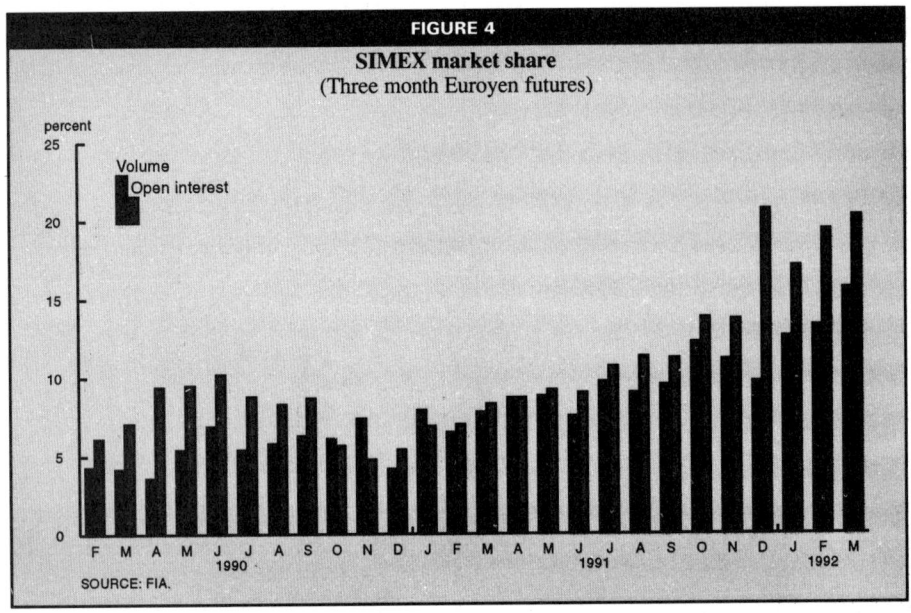

FIGURE 4
SIMEX market share
(Three month Euroyen futures)

SOURCE: FIA.

subset of the total trading volume. These observers indicate Japanese market participants tend to trade through domestic markets, as shown by TIFFE's market share. SIMEX's competitive transaction costs, however, should continue to challenge TIFFE.

Through a series of competitive contract introductions, MATIF is challenging LIFFE's status as the leading international exchange in Europe. The rivalry started in 1989 when MATIF listed its first nondomestic future, the three month Eurodeutschemark future. LIFFE's contract succeeded, in great part attributable to LIFFE's established international product offerings and membership, but MATIF's failed. However, MATIF followed with the successful introduction in October 1990 of an ECU bond futures contract. By December 1991, MATIF traded 99 percent of total volume and 95 percent of total open interest. Competitive transaction costs and a product revision assisted MATIF's success. Increased competition between brokers substantially reduced commission costs, and similar to DTB, dealers committed to competitive position and bid-ask spreads. MATIF revised its contract to broaden the range of deliverable ECU bonds in comparison with LIFFE's contract, ironically extending delivery to include British ECU bonds.[14] Once again both exchanges went head-to-head in the September 1991 launch of Italian bond futures, LIFFE easily dominating trading as London is the largest market for lira denominated debt outside of Italy. However, LIFFE will be challenged by another competing domestic exchange, as Italy is organizing a derivative exchange to trade Italian bond derivatives.[15]

Nikkei 225 stock index derivatives are one of a growing number of derivative products that can be exchange traded almost 24 hours through exchange listings on the OSE, SIMEX, CME, and American Stock Exchange (AMEX).[16] Nikkei 225 stock index futures were introduced on SIMEX in 1986; by the OSE in 1988; and by the CME in 1990. The introduction of OSE's contract after SIMEX's contract did not reduce SIMEX's volume. Rather, contract volume at both exchanges increased, however OSE's volume grew faster than SIMEX's. Although the OSE continues to dominate Nikkei 225 stock index future trading, large increases in transaction costs at the OSE have increased SIMEX and CME Nikkei 225 stock index futures trading. Specifically, OSE commissions have doubled, margin requirements have been successively raised from 9 percent of contract value in 1988 to 30 percent in 1992, and trading has been restricted within a narrow range of the previous trading day's closing price, effectively reducing the price discovery process on the OSE. SIMEX and CME margin requirements are half of the OSE's requirement and, unlike the OSE, do not require noninterest margin collateral [Waltner (1992)]. SIMEX, OSE's regional competitor, has benefitted considerably from OSE's increasing trading costs, increasing market share from only 2 percent of volume in November 1991 to 23 percent in April 1992 (see Figure 5).

Options on the S&P 500 stock index have been traded on nearby rival exchanges (the CME and CBOE) since 1983. The CME option is based on one S&P 500 stock index future contract, also traded at the CME; while the CBOE option is based directly on the S&P 500 stock index.[17] Prior to 1988, the CME option was more actively traded than the CBOE option. As a result of the stock market decline of October 1987, margin requirements on both option contracts were raised, increasing the transaction costs of trading these contracts. CME option trading was more severely impacted than CBOE option trading, possibly due to factors other than the increase in transaction costs. CME option volume declined by 60 percent in 1988, while CBOE option volume declined by only 20 percent. For year-end 1991, the CBOE option traded 57 percent of total option volume. In addition to option competition with the CME, the CBOE now competes with four other U.S exchanges—AMEX, the New York Stock Exchange (NYSE), the Philadelphia Stock Exchange (PHLX), and the Pacific Stock Exchange (PSE)—for option trading. The Securities and Exchange Commission (SEC), the regulatory body of the five exchanges, terminated option exclusivity in October 1991 to foster competition between the five exchanges.

The 1980s exchange expansion did not include growth of exchange traded currency derivatives. For example, LIFFE delisted all currency derivatives in 1990. The majority of currency derivatives have traded and will continue to trade on OTC interbank foreign exchange markets. The largest of these markets is located in London, with New York, and Tokyo

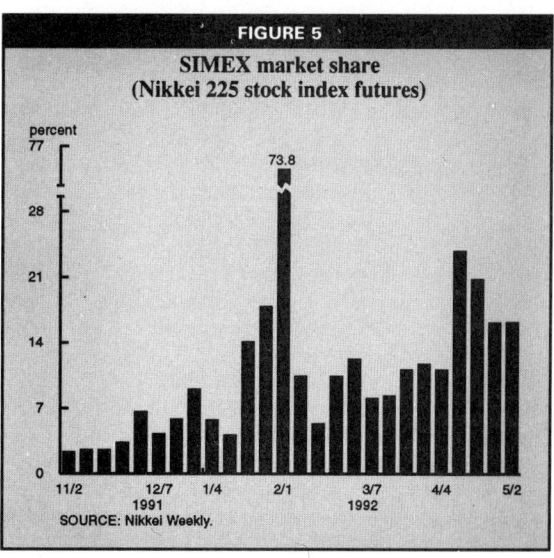

FIGURE 5
SIMEX market share
(Nikkei 225 stock index futures)

SOURCE: Nikkei Weekly.

also major foreign exchange centers. These OTC markets dwarf exchange traded markets because of their large size, product depth, and 24 hour accessibility. The market for yen denominated derivatives illustrates the role of the exchange in this particular product market. Currently, the Japanese yen is the second largest OTC currency traded. Japanese yen derivates are also exchange traded on the CME, and to a much lesser extent on the MidAmerica Commodity Exchange (MIDAM), Philadelphia Board of Trade (PBOT), PHLX, and SIMEX. Similar to LIFFE, TIFFE no longer trades Japanese yen futures due to Tokyo's active foreign exchange market. The gross daily turnover in 1989 of OTC Japanese yen approximated $28 billion [Federal Reserve Bank of New York (1989)], seven times the estimated $4 billion notional principal traded daily on exchanges in 1991.

Exchange versus OTC market structures

The derivative exchange market is a relatively new market organization compared with the OTC market. An exchange market is a highly organized market, specifying rules of trading, contractual terms, market's mode of operation, and conditions of membership. In contrast, an OTC market generally lacks these standardized features [Mulherin, Netter, and Overdahl (1991)]. With growth often a precursor to change, the 1980s expansion foreshadows a change in the structure of derivative markets. Driving these changes is the increasing sophistication of market participants, as institutional participants trade both exchange and OTC markets. Increasingly, many of the new exchanges do not resemble their predecessors, while certain OTC markets increasingly resemble exchanges. Exchange markets are evolving new trading structures, while OTC markets are incorporating exchange clearinghouse features. This restructuring process tends to be more critical for exchanges, because exchange markets are under regulatory jurisdiction.

Many OTC markets span the New York-London-Tokyo trading day. Likewise, exchange traded derivatives are available for an increasing portion of the 24 hour trading day. However, customers are currently required to shift from exchange to exchange as the day proceeds. The financial derivatives which can be traded currently beyond the normal trading day are: the British pound, German deutschemark, three month Eurodollar, Japanese government bond, Japanese yen, Nikkei 225 stock index, and U.S. Treasury bond futures and options.

Developments since the 1980s point to the increasing acceptance of alternative trading methods which bypass the trading pit. Prior to the 1980s, derivative exchanges traded primarily through the open outcry system, where traders physically convey their bids or offers in the trading pit. The majority of new exchanges which opened in the 1980s instead have selected automated forms of trading, ranging from LIFFE's Automated Pit Trading (APT) open outcry trading system to DTB's trade matching system. LIFFE's APT system supplements the trading pit, extending trading hours as well as supporting markets for low volume derivative products during the LIFFE trading day. Other exchanges with after-hour automated trading also operate in Australia and Japan. In contrast, DTB's trade matching system completely replaces the trading pit. Other fully automated exchanges trading financial derivatives also operate in Austria, Belgium, Denmark, Japan, New Zealand, Spain, Sweden, and Switzerland. With the exception of the Japanese exchanges, these exchange markets are small compared to existing open outcry exchange markets.

Automated trading systems are noticeably absent from U.S. derivative exchanges with the CBOT and CME operating several internationally important open outcry markets. In addition, until recently, the only off-exchange trade permitted by the CFTC was an exchange for physicals (EFP), a trade—primarily after-hour—of an asset for a future based on the asset. CFTC records estimate EFP transactions account for between six and eight percent of currency future volume and between four and six percent of bond future volume.[18] However, the CME's forthcoming Global Automated Transaction System for Futures and Options (GLOBEX) represents the first U.S. automated after-hour trading system. Another automated trading system, the CBOT's Project A, will emulate LIFFE'S APT system for facilitating low volume markets, and additionally will provide access to underlying asset markets.[19] Besides automated trading, the CME's Large Order Execution System (LOX) is the first program which permits large, primarily institutional, S&P 500 future trades of 300 or more to be executed outside the trading pit, known as upstairs trades. LOX trades are similar to the crossing trades already permitted on the U.S. stock exchanges.

As trading of exchange products evolves, the exchange clearinghouse remains the critical mainstay of this market structure. The clearinghouse role as guarantor to member trades mitigates counterparty credit risk, permitting exchange members and their customers to focus on price risk. The exchange clearinghouse has various means to monitor members' risk: customer position limits, large customer reporting systems, member capital-based position limits, and sophisticated risk analysis programs. The exchange clearinghouse also reduces the potential for default of a member through mark to market variation settlement, multilateral netting, additional margin requirements, or position reduction requests. If a member defaults, the clearinghouse has various levels of financial recourse. Since clearinghouse positions are marked to market on a daily basis, and can even be updated within the trading day, financial losses are minimized to, at most, a single trading day's price movement. The first level of financial recourse is the member's margin; following is the member's clearing capital; and finally, losses can be divided pro-rata among other clearinghouse members [Baer and Evanoff (1990) and Rutz (1989)]. The extensive exchange clearinghouse guarantee system is a primary, and critical, difference between exchange and OTC markets. Although OTC derivative markets are large, these markets are constrained by the lack of mechanisms to control counterparty credit risk.[20] If an OTC party defaults, counterparties bear the financial losses of the derivative obligations. Lacking the exchange clearinghouse capitalization, the extent of financial losses borne by OTC counterparties may increase financial system risk [Miller (1990)].

The importance of the clearinghouse's guarantor role lessens when the general level of credit quality of its participants is high and comparable to the clearinghouse, while the clearinghouse is a more attractive counterparty as credit quality deteriorates. During the 1980s, pervasive credit quality deterioration increased counterparty risks in international OTC markets. A large number of financial and nonfinancial firms were downgraded by credit rating agencies. For example, only four private sector banks are rated triple-A worldwide. Motivated by the credit deterioration, OTC market participants are incorporating attributes of the exchange clearinghouse above traditional counterparty selection and monitoring systems. Several OTC participants now require collateral or escrow deposits to be marked to market, similar to the clearinghouse margining system.[21] A consortium of banks in North America and Europe, respectively, are planning clearinghouses for foreign currency transactions. Both the North American Clearinghouse Organization (NACHO) and the European Clearinghouse Organization (ECHO) would clear and settle OTC interbank foreign exchange trades. An important precedent for NACHO and ECHO is the Government Securities Clearing Corporation (GSCC). Since 1988, the GSCC has cleared and settled U.S. government securities, which trade on OTC markets like the interbank foreign exchange markets [Woldow (1989)]. The GSCC is the counterparty to every trade, providing the guarantor and multilateral netting functions of the exchange clearinghouse. On a very small scale, clearinghouses of derivative exchanges are already clearing and settling OTC derivative trades. The MATIF clearinghouse clears and settles OTC trades on the *notional* bond future.[22] Beginning in 1992, the clearinghouse for OM Stockholm and its franchise, OM London, will clear and settle OTC trades on a small number of OTC derivatives.[23] By assuming the counterparty risk, the exchange clearinghouse creates fungible exchange traded products.

To the extent OTC markets adopt features of the clearing and settlement systems, such as those employed by exchanges, counterparty credit risk will be more efficiently managed and the safety of the entire financial system will increase [Committee on Interbank Netting Schemes(1990)]. As the OTC market structure increasingly resembles the exchange market structure, regulatory policy will become a central issue. Exchange markets are regulated, while OTC markets are not, although many OTC market participants are regulated. In the U.S., this issue has been raised by the exchanges and is being reviewed by Congress. Currently, the OTC financial swap market, like the OTC forward market, is exempt from the CFTC's regulatory jurisdiction. Forward foreign exchange transactions are exempted under the Commodity Exchange Act (CEA). A 1989 policy statement provided criteria—referred to as the "safe harbor" guidelines—which exempt swap transactions from CFTC regulation [CFTC Policy Statement (1989)]. Several industry analysts argue that the unregulated OTC markets have an unfair competitive advantage compared to the regulated exchange markets [Miller (1990) and Mulherin, Netter, and Overdahl (1991)]. An alternative view would argue that regulated and unregulated markets simply fill different needs. Unlike exchanges, OTC markets facilitate the customization of unique risk management needs and are favored by high credit quality participants who do not require the clearinghouse financial guarantee. Part of the issue is that although the CFTC regulates exchange traded derivatives, there presently is no definition of futurity—what distinguishes a derivative market that is subject to CFTC regulation from a derivative market that is not. Instead, the CFTC has reviewed market issues, like the financial swap market, on a case-by-case basis. The outcome of this issue in the U.S. may serve as a precedent for exchange markets worldwide.

Conclusion

Recent developments indicate that the expansion of the derivative industry will continue. Five countries have opened financial derivative exchanges since 1990 and several other countries are either organizing or proposing financial derivative exchanges. The further application of financial engineering will increase the precision of managing unique risks, expanding the product offerings of the OTC market. Institutional investor preferences with respect to products, transaction costs, and clearing and settlement features will continue to drive competition and changes in both the exchange and OTC markets. As a result, exchanges are increasing their efforts to lower transaction costs and expand their array of products. Competition between exchanges operating under different regulatory regimes is driving regulators to reconsider their approach to regulation. Competition from the OTC markets and the blurring of the OTC and exchange market structures will only add to this pressure.

FOOTNOTES

[1] In 1972, the CME introduced the first financial derivatives: British pound, Canadian dollar, Dutch guilder, German deutschemark, Japanese yen, Mexican peso, and Swiss franc currency futures.

[2] The New Zealand Futures and Options Exchange (NZF&OE) has recently been purchased by Australia's Sydney Futures Exchange (SFE).

[3] Ginger Szala, "Financial walls tumble for German investors," *Futures*, January 1990, pp. 42-44.

[4] "Japan fights big bang," *Futures*, November 1991, pp. 8-9.

[5] Mary Ann Burns, "FCMs today: lean, mean trading machines," *Futures Industry*, September/October 1991, p. 19.

[6] Paul Dickins, "Commissions, commotion, competition trying MATIF," *Futures*, April 1991, p. 48.

[7] "Cross-margining system planned for CBOT trades," *Wall Street Journal*, February 22, 1991.

[8] Thomas R. Donovan, "International taxing matters," *Futures Industry*, May/June 1992, pp. 16-17.

[9] Tony Shale, "Why did SOFE have to die," *Euromoney*, March 1989, pp. 49-52.

[10] LIFFE introduced a German *bund* option in April 1989 and DTB in August 1991. As of December 1991, DTB traded 16 percent of total volume and 12 percent of total open interest.

[11] *DTB Deutsche Terminborse Press Information*, June 12, 1991.

[12] "Global roundup," *Futures*, September 1991, p. 42; Tony McAuley, "Europe's futures markets hotly pursue U.S. leaders," *Wall Street Journal*, December 27, 1991, p. C1.

[13] SIMEX introduced a three month Euroyen option in June 1990 and TIFFE in July 1991. As of December 1991, TIFFE accounted for 80 percent of total volume and 87 percent of total open interest.

[14] "European futures exchanges-street fighters," *The Economist*, December 1, 1990, pp. 96-97.

[15] Paul Dickins, "LIFFE, MATIF meet once again in Eurowars sequel," *Futures*, September 1991, p. 40h.

[16] AMEX trades Painewebber Nikkei put warrants and Japanese index options, similar to the Nikkei 225 stock index.

[17] The CBOE changed the S&P 500 option from an American to a European option beginning in 1986. This contract change also contributed to substantial volume trading of the CBOE option.

[18] Keith Schap, "EFPs: Do regulations ruin their utility," *Futures*, November 1991, pp. 14-16.

[19] Ginger Szala and Kira McCaffrey, "CBOT has A-plan to automate floor," *Futures*, April 1992, p. 46.

[20] Kerry Tremble and Arun Sarwal, "Happiness is a full net," *Euromoney*, April 1991, pp. 34-35.

[21] "Seminar: on-exchange versus off-exchange derivatives," Futures Industry Association's Seventh Annual Futures and Option Conference, Chicago, October 1991.

[22] "Seminar: transnational transaction issues," Futures Industry Association's Seventh Annual Futures and Option Conference, Chicago, October 1991.

[23] *Derivatives Week*, April 13, 1992, p. 13.

REFERENCES

Baer, Herbert L. and Douglas D. Evanoff, "Payment system issues in financial markets that never sleep," Federal Reserve Bank of Chicago, *Economic Perspectives*, November/December 1990, pp. 2-15.

Behof, John P., "Intermarket cross-margining for futures and options," *Issue Summary of the Federal Reserve Bank of Chicago*, May 1989.

Black, Deborah G., "Success and failure of futures contracts: theory and empirical evidence," *Monograph Series in Finance and Economics: Salomon Brothers Center for the Study of Financial Institutions*, 1986, pp. 1-31.

Cargill, Thomas F. and Shoichi Royama, "The evolution of Japanese banking and finance," in George G. Kaufman, ed., *Banking Structures in Major Countries*, 1992, pp. 333-388.

Committee on Interbank Netting Schemes, *Lamfalussy Report*, Bank of International Settlement, Basle, Switzerland, November 1990.

"Commodity futures trading commission: regulation of hybrid instruments; policy statement concerning swap transactions; final rule and notice," *Federal Register*, Volume 54, No. 139, July 21, 1989, pp. 30684-30697.

Ducruezet, L. Beduc F. and P. Papadacci, "The French financial system," in George G. Kaufman, ed., *Banking Structures in Major Countries*, 1992, pp. 245-292.

Euromoney, various issues.

Federal Reserve Bank of New York, "U.S. foreign exchange market survey," April 1989.

Futures, various issues.

Futures Industry, various issues.

Futures Industry Association, *Monthly Volume and Open Interest Reports for Futures and Options*, various issues.

Futures Industry Institute, *Futures and Options Fact Book*, 1992.

Gastineau, Gary L., "A framework for the analysis of portfolio execution costs—stocks versus derivatives," *Portfolio Trading*, Salomon Brothers, October 1991, pp. 1-14.

Japan Securities Research Institute, "Securities futures trading," *Securities Markets In Japan*, 1990, pp. 102-111.

Miller, Merton, "International competitiveness of U.S. futures exchanges," *Journal of Financial Services*, 1990, pp. 129-150.

Moser, James T., "Futures margin and excess volatility," *Chicago Fed Letter*, June 1991.

Mulherin, Harold, Jeffrey M. Netter, and James A. Overdahl, "Prices are property: the organization of exchanges from a transaction cost perspective," Draft, Washington D.C., January 22, 1991, pp. 54-80.

Rutz, Roger D., "Clearance, payment, and settlement systems in the futures, options, and stock markets," Board of Trade Clearing Corporation, February 24, 1989.

The Economist, various issues.

Wall Street Journal, various issues.

Waltner, Nicholas W., "Nikkei 225 futures: Osaka illiquidity and SIMEX boom," *Japanese Equity Research*, Salomon Brothers, Draft, 1992.

White, Pat A., Paul Kupiec, and Gregory Duffee, "A securities transactions tax: beyond the rhetoric, what can we really say?," Finance and Economics Discussion Series, Federal Reserve Board, August 1990, p. 13.

Woldow, Robert, "The Government Securities Clearing Corporation (GSCC)," *Study of International Clearing and Settlement*, Bankers Trust Company, Volume 1, 1989, p. 63.

Article 23

Determining margin for futures contracts: the role of private interests and the relevance of excess volatility

James T. Moser

Margins should be made consistent to control speculation and financial leverage.

—Brady Report

On Monday, October 19, 1987, the Dow Jones Industrial Average declined 508 points. The marketplace on the following day is usually described as melting down. This analogy to a runaway nuclear reaction reflects the fear during the morning hours of October 20, 1987 that overheated trading activity had overwhelmed trading systems. Studies were commissioned to investigate the events of these two days and to propose remedies. One of these studies, the Brady Report, recommends raising margins on stock index futures contracts in order to reduce the chances of a future financial meltdown.[1]

Support for the higher margins proposed by the Brady Report stems from the view that low margins result in greater speculation which, in turn, leads to greater volatility. According to this view, volatility produced by speculative trading can be controlled by regulating margin. I call this view the Excess Volatility Argument. Another explanation of the link between volatility and margin levels is founded on the recognition that stock and futures exchanges face increased risk when stock market volatility increases. According to this view, stock and futures exchanges raise margin levels when volatility increases in order to compensate for the increased risk. I call this view the Prudential Exchange Hypothesis.

This article examines the relation between volatility and margin levels in order to assess the plausibility of the Excess Volatility Argument and the Prudential Exchange Hypothesis. The next section discusses the private interests involved in setting margin levels and their relevance to the justification of the Prudential Exchange Hypothesis. The Excess Volatility Argument is critiqued in the following section. Analysis of the theory underlying the Excess Volatility Argument, a review of existing evidence on the links between margin and volatility, and new tests of the theory all fail to support the proposition that raising margins leads to reductions in volatility. Evidence for the Prudential Exchange Hypothesis is mixed. Tests relating margin changes to previous levels of volatility fail to confirm the hypothesis. A cross-sectional approach to test this hypothesis is introduced and some preliminary results are reported. Conclusions concerning the Prudential Hypothesis and the Excess Volatility Argument are summarized in the last section of the article.

Private interests in determining margin requirements

According to the Prudential Exchange Hypothesis, stock and futures exchanges both have an interest in managing their exposure to

---

James T. Moser is a senior economist at the Federal Reserve Bank of Chicago. The author is indebted to Janet Napoli and Jeff Santelices for research assistance. Comments from Herbert Baer, Ramon P. DeGennaro, Douglas Evanoff, Virginia Grace France, Carolyn McMullen, Janet Napoli, and Steven Strongin have been especially helpful.

risks from trades routed through their exchange. Margins are an important means to this end. However, the nature of the risk in stock and futures markets differs hence, margin requirements play different roles in stock and futures markets. The next two subsections develop this distinction.

The role of private interests in determining stock margin

In stock markets, brokerage firms sometimes lend money to investors for the purchase of stock (see Box 1 for an explanation of how margin lessens the risk of stock brokers). Lending benefits brokerage firms because it increases trading, thus increasing revenues from brokerage fees. The risk inherent in lending is controlled by collateralizing these loans with stock. Brokerage firms further reduce risk by requiring investors to pay a portion of the purchase price in cash. The amount of cash put up by the investor in a leveraged stock transaction is called margin. In particular, the amount of cash required when the position is initiated—the "down payment"—is referred to as the initial margin.[2]

Margin loans expose brokers to the risk that a stock price decline will produce losses in excess of the amount of posted margin. This risk increases both as the degree of leverage in the position increases and as the volatility of stock—the collateral—increases. Prudence motivates brokers to closely examine the ability of investors holding margined positions to cover their debt obligations. Increasing margin reduces the risk taken by the broker's extension of credit. Thus, it is in the broker's interests to require a prudential level of margin.

The interests of the broker also include fees from trades executed on behalf of his or her customers. Lending facilitates trading by increasing the size of positions which can be held given the investor's level of cash. Higher margins result in smaller loans, hence lower trading levels, other things equal. Thus, increasing margins lessens brokerage fee income. Stock brokers set margin by considering both risk and profit, choosing the level of margin which is expected to yield a competitive return for the level of risk.

Stock exchanges take the interests of brokers into account when setting limits on margin lending. Exchanges consistently acting against the interests of their brokers lose business as brokers find more favorable routes for trades. Thus, the Prudential Exchange Hypothesis predicts that a stock exchange sets margin levels which are consistent with the interests of stock brokers affiliated with the exchange. These interests, as previously identified, lead to levels of margin which balance revenues from trading activity with the risk of losses on credit extended to clients.

The role of private interests in determining futures margin

Determination of margin requirements for futures contracts raises concerns which are similar to those of the stock broker. Like stock brokers, futures exchanges, acting on behalf of their members, set futures margins to control their risks. However, the risks faced by the stock broker and the members of the futures exchange are not identical. In this section, I use a hypothetical futures contract on a stock index to develop the role of margin for futures positions.

Futures contracts trade on a variety of assets. Examples are contracts on wheat, frozen pork bellies, foreign exchange, Treasury bonds, and stock indexes. Contracts are distinguished by the price of the asset or commodity used to determine payments to the parties in the contract. As an example, consider the following hypothetical contract. Over the next three months, for every point the Standard and Poor (S&P) 500 rises from its present level, Mr. Short will pay Ms. Long $1,000. For every point it falls from this level, Ms. Long will pay Mr. Short $1,000.[3]

Mr. Short and Ms. Long are referred to as counterparties in the futures contract. The counterparties are further identified as holding the long or short side of the contract. In this contract, Ms. Long holds the long side, which commits her to make payments when the futures price falls and entitles her to receive payments when the price rises. Conversely, Mr. Short holds the short side, which entitles him to receive payments when the futures price falls and commits him to make payments when the price rises. Payments between the counterparties are determined by marking the contract to the current price of other futures contracts on the same underlying basket of commodities or assets. This mark-to-market procedure is conducted daily. Futures contracts feature terms serving two purposes. First, contract terms determine the usefulness of contracts. Second, contract terms enable the exchange to manage customer insolvency problems.

Futures are useful as low cost substitutes for transactions in the underlying asset. To see this, note that by carefully specifying a particular group of assets for determination of the final settlement price, the futures price will move closely with the price of the asset group. Thus, changes in the futures price for the S&P 500 are closely linked with changes in the prices of the 500 stocks used by Standard and Poor in constructing that index. The alignment of these prices is useful to individuals and firms seeking low cost means of altering the sensitivity of their portfolios to price changes.

To see the usefulness of futures contracts, suppose Mr. Short owns a portfolio of stocks, many of which are included in the 500 stocks comprising the S&P Index. This portfolio is called his cash position to distinguish it from the futures contract. When the prices of stocks

---

BOX 1

Leverage, risk, and the role of margin

The relation among leverage, risk, and the role of margin is most easily illustrated in the case of stocks. Borrowing to purchase stocks has leverage implications for both the borrowers (investors) and lenders (brokerage firms). This point can be illustrated with a simple T account.

Market value of shares purchased	$10,000	$6,000	Loan from broker
		$4,000	Equity placed by purchaser

In the example, the initial margin requirement is 40 percent.[1] Stock valued at $100 per share requires the purchaser of 100 shares to pay $4,000 of their purchase price. The broker lends the purchaser $6,000. This combination of funds produces $10,000 paid to the seller of the stock.

To see the consequences of leverage for borrowers and lenders, we examine the effect of stock price changes. First, suppose the stock price rises to $110. After this price change, the T account looks as follows:

Market value of shares purchased	$11,000	$6,000	Loan from broker
		$4,000	Equity placed by purchaser
		$1,000	Gain on stock

Thus, the $4,000 invested has gained $1,000 for a 25 percent return on invested funds. Had the investor not purchased the stock on margin; and paid the full $10,000 for the stock, the rate of return would have been only 10 percent. The margined position earns 2.5 times the percentage change in stock prices (2.5 x 10 percent = 25 percent). These gains can be realized by selling the shares for $11,000, repaying the loan balance of $6,000 from the proceeds, leaving $5,000.

Examining the potential downside from a margined purchase explains why most stock purchases do not use margin. Suppose the stock price declines to $90. Now the T account looks like this:

Market value of shares purchased	$9,000	$6,000	Loan from broker
		$4,000	Equity placed by purchaser
		($1,000)	Loss on stock

The $4,000 invested results in a loss of $1,000 for a 25 percent loss. Had the purchase price been paid in cash, the percentage loss would have been only 10 percent. The alternative way of seeing this is to recognize that the ability to hold 2.5 times more shares implies that any losses will be magnified by 2.5. Further, as shown later, equity balances must be restored when these balances fall below a preset level. Compliance with this rule may require investors to sell other asset holdings to meet the call for additional equity.[2] Thus, from the investor's perspective, margined stock purchases lever up risk. The leverage factor is 1 + Loan/Equity. For the initial position, this is 1 + 6,000/4,000 = 2.5.

Now consider the above transaction from the lender's point of view. The lender will also have an interest in this leverage factor. Suppose the stock price declines to $60, so that the T account is:

in the portfolio decline, the value of Mr. Short's cash position declines. However, his short futures contract position entitles him to receive payments from Ms. Long when stock prices decline. These payments lessen the extent of losses realized from the cash position. Thus, futures contracting can reduce an investor's sensitivity to price changes. This use of futures contracts is called hedging.

Ms. Long finds the contract useful for a different reason. Generally, her cash position consists mostly of low risk bonds. At times she has concluded that stocks are undervalued. Taking the long side of a futures contract allows her to increase the sensitivity of her portfolio to changes in stock prices. In particular, when her assessment that stocks are undervalued proves true, she realizes gains from her futures position. This use of futures contracts is called speculation.

These uses of futures contracts are a cost effective means to the respective ends of Mr. Short and Ms. Long. Both results could be accomplished using transactions in the stocks themselves. Mr. Short could reduce his sensitivity to stock price changes by selling stocks and investing the proceeds in low risk assets such as Treasury bonds. Ms. Long could increase her sensitivity to stock price changes by selling some of her bonds and buying stocks. Each prefers to accomplish his or her respective end at the lowest possible cost. Futures contracts often provide the least costly route to adjusting portfolio sensitivity.

Market value of shares purchased	$6,000	$6,000	Loan from broker
		$4,000	Equity placed by purchaser
		($4,000)	Loss on stock

The broker faces a problem. Liquidating the position at its current market value insures that the outstanding balance of the loan is paid off. Not liquidating the position puts the broker at risk that the stock price will decline further and that the investor will not be able to make up the difference from other sources. If the latter case occurs, the broker suffers a loss. The extent of this loss depends on the additional decline in stock price and the amount the broker can recover from the other resources of the investor. Thus, once the investor has lost the equity in the position, the broker relies on estimates of the extent of these other sources. To avoid the risk inherent in these estimates, the broker establishes a maintenance margin requirement. When the level of equity falls below the maintenance margin requirement, a call for additional margin is made. Receipt of the called-for funds decreases the broker's reliance on estimates of other sources of wealth. Once funds are received, the broker's risk is reduced. An additional decline in stock price will, with certainty, be absorbed by the investor up to the new margin deposit.

However, contracts which are not dependable will not be useful. In the stock index futures contract described above, both Mr. Short and Ms. Long find the contract advantageous in the sense that it represents a low cost means of altering their sensitivities to changes in a broad measure of the stock market. However, Mr. Short might regard such a contract as worthless if he had reason to believe that, should prices fall, Ms. Long would be unable to make the required payment.[4] Similarly, Ms. Long's concerns about Mr. Short's ability to pay lower her assessment of the value of such a contract. Except for this insolvency issue, both find the contract useful. Thus, each party has an interest in resolving the insolvency problem at reasonable cost.

Resolution of the insolvency problem is the role of the exchange. Exchanges fulfill this role by requiring that all contracts clear through members of the clearing association affiliated with the respective exchange. In this process, the clearing association becomes counterparty to each side of all contracts traded on the exchange. Should either the long or short side fail to perform its obligations, the loss is realized by the clearing association rather than the original counterparty. Continuing the above example and introducing the role of the exchange, suppose the stock market rises ten points. Mr. Short owes Ms. Long $10,000. If he has be-

---

[1] Currently initial margin requirements are 50 percent. The example uses 40 percent to clarify which portion is required from the investor (40 percent) and which is lent by the broker (60 percent).

[2] Bankruptcy law prevents access to certain assets to meet financial obligations.

come insolvent, the contract guarantee assures that Ms. Long is paid the $10,000.[5] This performance guarantee removes the respective credit risk concerns and focuses the attentions of the counterparties on contract price. Neither party finds it necessary to expend resources to evaluate the credit risk of the other party. This resolution of the insolvency problem increases the value of futures contracting for both parties. Performance guarantees provided to the counterparties are clearly costly. The exchange, acting to maintain the solvency of its clearing association, attempts to manage its potential for loss. This is accomplished by managing the exchange's exposure to the credit risk stemming from each participant in the contract. Management of the exchange's credit risk uses an overlapping system of solvency requirements, mark-to-market arrangements, and margin requirements. To see the role of the components of this system, I begin with an ideal characterization of the marketplace, then relax various assumptions in order to explain how each of these components is used to manage the credit risk of a futures exchange.

Evidence of solvency is the first level of protection. We can see the role of solvency requirements by imagining an ideal marketplace where monitoring of the wealth of each party is perfect and continuous. With the additional assumptions of immediate access to the wealth of these parties and unlimited liquidity in markets where assets can be immediately and costlessly sold off; no counterparty would be exposed to risk. Under these conditions, at the instant when a party is determined to be insolvent, that party's assets would be immediately attached, their futures positions closed out, and assets sold with the proceeds used to cover shortfalls arising from the futures position. Thus, with this characterization of the marketplace, the exchange avoids all risk of loss by relying on its legal authority to close out futures positions as counterparties become insolvent.

Relaxing the assumption of costless asset liquidation, the exchange incurs transactions costs in liquidating positions. This is readily resolved by applying "haircuts" to asset values when computing net worth for solvency purposes. That is, the value of each asset in the investor's portfolio is reduced—haircut—by the amount of transaction cost incurred on sale.

Thus, solvency requirements are sufficient for the exchange to manage its exposure with this characterization of the marketplace.

If the assumption that assets can be liquidated immediately is dropped, exchanges prefer asset holdings which can be used to settle payment obligations. On determining that a counterparty has become insolvent, the exchange seeks to avoid risk by closing positions and disbursing payments quickly. Delays encountered in the liquidation of assets increase the exchange's risk of realizing further losses. Since futures contracts require that positions realizing gains be paid in cash, exchanges have a strong preference for asset holdings in cash or readily convertible to cash. This enables the exchange to attach assets which can be immediately applied to fulfill its required payments of gains. Thus, margin requirements amend the solvency requirement by stipulating that futures positions be supported by liquid asset holdings. The requirement that margin balances be deposited with the exchange further enhances this liquidity requirement: funds are immediately available to the exchange.

Mark-to-market arrangements augment the arsenal of exchange protections against credit risk by substituting for perfect monitoring of wealth. Frequent marking to market creates a flow of information to the exchange on the solvency of counterparties. To see this, recall that mark-to-market rules require positions incurring losses to cover these losses with cash payments. Cash paid by customers to brokers is forwarded to the clearing member and then to the clearing association. Brokers observing the payments made by their customers can infer their ability to continue to cover losses. Likewise, by observing delays in payments made by clearing members, the clearinghouse can infer their members' abilities to continue to cover losses. Delays in making mark-to-market payments reveal liquidity problems which may develop into solvency problems. The cost of obtaining this information is decidedly less than the cost of direct monitoring systems which might be regarded as nearly ideal.

As the frequency of marking contracts to market increases, the exchange approximates the ideal case of continuous monitoring of counterparty wealth. However, this approach is costly. Reducing the mark-to-market frequency places the exchange at risk that the counterparty has become insolvent since the position was previously marked to market. Thus, futures margin balances are used to collateralize the completion of the obligation to make mark-to-market payments. Margin balances bond the performance of contract holders to make the cash payments required when contracts are marked to market.[6] Failure to complete this obligation creates an exercisable claim on the margin account. By exercising this claim while simultaneously closing out the futures contract, the maximum loss of the exchange is the loss on closing out the futures position netted against the margin balances for the account.[7]

Thus, futures exchanges rely on solvency, mark-to-market arrangements, and margin to control the credit risk inherent in futures contracting. Margin provides the clearinghouse with liquid assets which lowers the cost of making payments to contract holders. Mark-to-market arrangements provide a signal of the level of liquidity available. The combination of mark-to-market arrangements and margin limits the credit risk exposure of the exchange. This combination of lower credit risk, lower costs of transacting, and the presence of an information generating process for customer liquidity lowers the cost of providing guarantees against counterparty risk. This increases the usefulness of futures contracting by increasing its dependability.

Distinctions in margin assessments provide additional support for the idea that futures exchanges rely on multiple avenues to manage their exposure to credit risk. For example, qualified hedgers have long or short cash positions in the asset underlying the futures contract. Because losses and gains on futures positions are offset by changes in the value of the underlying asset, hedgers expose the exchange to less credit risk exposure than do speculative positions. Recognizing their exposure is less, futures exchanges specify lower margin requirements for qualified hedgers than for more speculative positions.[8] Clearing members of the exchange are another category of participants having reduced margin requirements. Clearing associations closely monitor the risk of clearing member insolvency. Having incurred the cost of this additional monitoring activity, the clearing association increases its reliance on these solvency assessments and, consequently, reduces the level of margin required for clearing member positions.

Private interests and the Prudential Exchange Hypothesis

The above discussion shows that private interests motivate both the stock broker and the futures exchange to require margin. Use of margin facilitates trading of stocks and futures contracts, thereby increasing revenues from fees paid to stock brokerage firms and to members of futures exchanges. However, inadequate margin levels for stock positions increase the riskiness of loans made by brokerage firms. Inadequate margin levels for futures contracts increase the cost of contract-performance guarantees. In both cases, the risk of loss encourages the affected parties to reduce these risks by increasing margin levels. Both stock and futures exchanges have incentives to keep margins at an optimal level at which fees from increased trading provide an adequate return for the risks they bear.

Clearly, an increase in stock price volatility increases the potential losses of investors and hence increases the risk of insolvency. Thus, it would make sense for exchanges to respond to increased volatility by increasing margin requirements. This might reduce revenues from trading activity, but will clearly decrease the risk of losses from insolvency. Conversely, a decrease in volatility lessens the threat of insolvency. So, it would make sense for exchanges to respond to decreased volatility by lowering margin requirements in order to increase revenues from trading activity. The Prudential Exchange Hypothesis is the hypothesis that exchanges do indeed act in the way just described, raising margins in response to increased volatility and lowering margins in response to decreased volatility. A positive association between observed changes in volatility and subsequent changes in margin levels would be evidence in favor of the Prudential Exchange Hypothesis. Below I describe the results of research investigating the relation between changes in volatility and changes in margin levels and discuss the implications for the Prudential Exchange Hypothesis.

Margin determination and the Excess Volatility Argument

While the Prudential Exchange Hypothesis suggests that increases in volatility should lead to increases in margin, the Excess Volatility Argument suggests that increases in margin should lead to decreases in volatility. The

Excess Volatility Argument originated as an argument to justify the regulation of margin on stocks.[9] The argument is frequently extended to margins for futures contracts. This section explains the Excess Volatility Argument as it is applied to stocks. I then demonstrate problems with the argument.

Federal regulation of margin requirements on stocks began with the Glass-Steagall Act of 1934. The act empowered the Federal Reserve to specify margin requirements for stock.[10] This portion of the act was motivated by concern that margins prior to the 1929 stock market crash had been too low. Following the 1929 crash, proponents of the Excess Volatility Argument felt that low stock margin requirements encouraged speculation which exacerbated price swings. The claim that there is a direct relationship between speculation and volatility is based on the view that trends in market prices can be identified as they occur and that speculators respond to these trends by taking positions which profit from near term anticipated price changes. This combination produces a bandwagon effect or speculative bubble. For example, according to this view, if speculators perceive markets as rising, they think that easy profits can be had by buying into the market quickly to take advantage of the next round of price increases. The added pressure of these orders to buy elevates prices further. Each round of profits increases interest in "jumping on the bandwagon."[11]

Proponents of the Excess Volatility Argument believe that private brokerage firms cannot be relied on to limit speculation by requiring high margins on stocks because high margins would decrease trading volume and the profits from brokerage fees. The solution to the problem of excessive volatility, according to the Excess Volatility Argument, is to move control of margin from the securities industry to government. By raising the cost of speculative positions, episodes of excessive speculation could be managed by officials who do not benefit from increased trading activity. Further, these officials are answerable to the public for their decisions, making them sensitive to the concerns of the public.

Problems with the Excess Volatility Argument

The Excess Volatility Argument as applied to stocks depends on a number of implicit assumptions. First, investors are assumed to ignore the risk of participating in speculative excesses. Second, brokerage firms are assumed to ignore their risks in facilitating the trades of these investors. Third, investors are assumed to lack opportunities to avoid margin requirements. If any of these implicit assumptions are not plausible, then the argument is less credible.

First, consider the assumption that most investors ignore the risk involved in speculation. According to the above scenario, investors buy in response to price increases produced in previous rounds of buying. They ignore fundamentals, such as the ability of the firm to make expected dividend payments, which determine the fundamental value of stocks. For the scenario to work, investors must ignore the fact that as stock prices rise they become further removed from fundamental values.[12] Investment motivated by this reliance is risky. The larger the distance from the stock price to its fundamental value, the greater the necessary correction. Buy orders which increase upward pressure face the risk of increasingly large losses. Thus, investors placing these orders are ignoring the risk that the price correction will produce a loss. As risk averse investors raise their assessments of risk, they require higher returns. However, in this case, expected returns must decline as the size of the necessary correction increases. It is not plausible to claim that in general, investors ignore the risks of speculation in this way.

The Excess Volatility Argument also neglects the incentive of brokerage firms to set margins prudentially. As previously demonstrated, individual brokerage firms face the risk that margin loans will not be repaid if customer losses exceed available funds. To control this risk, brokerage firms have incentives to raise margin levels. These incentives mitigate the higher revenues from increased trading activity.

The exchanges recognize that brokerage firms near bankruptcy may compete for brokerage fees by lowering margins. These firms will be more willing to require lower margin because lower margin increases the number of orders placed through these firms and increases revenues from brokerage fees. This additional business prevents bankruptcy provided the realized losses from insolvent customers are small relative to the additional revenue from fees. The incentive to take this chance is greatest for firms which have the least to lose; that is, brokerage firms which are nearly bankrupt.

However, this form of competition harms viable brokerage houses in three ways. First, competition for business reduces the immediate revenues from brokerage fees for viable firms. Second, bankruptcy of a brokerage firm lessens industry good will.[13] This intangible asset is the capitalized value of trading activity which stems from confidence that brokers properly represent customer interests. Evidence that brokerage firms are aggressively pursuing their own interests damages this confidence, reducing the value of their good will. Third, brokers must be confident that commitments made with other brokers will be honored. Insufficient margining by individual brokerage firms lessens confidence in the completion of these commitments. This leads to increased costs as brokers replace the surety afforded by adequate margin balances with increased monitoring of the financial well being of the other brokers. To reduce these costs, exchanges, acting in the interests of the industry, set minimum margin requirements. These minimums prevent nearly bankrupt firms from increasing their risks to attract additional brokerage fees at the expense of the remainder of the industry.

Third, for margin regulation to work as proponents of the Excess Volatility Argument suggest, investors must lack alternative sources of funds. Margin requirements specify the amount of collateral which must be deposited for loans which are collateralized by stocks purchased with the funds provided. These requirements can be understood as restrictions on leverage which can be avoided. For example, individuals can avoid margin restrictions by seeking loans on their other sources of wealth, such as funds from a second mortgage or borrowing against the cash value of insurance contracts. These sources can be used to create "homemade" leverage at higher levels than those allowed using credit collateralized with stock holdings. In addition, Fishe and Goldberg (1986) point out that if leverage preferences exceed those available under margin regulations, firms can increase their debt to provide any desired level of leverage. The ability to avoid restrictive margin requirements suggests that the regulation will be relatively ineffective.[14]

The above objections show that the Excess Volatility Argument as applied to stock markets has a number of weaknesses. Consequently, it does not present a strong case for the claim that controlling margin will influence the volatility of stock prices. Proponents extend the Excess Volatility Argument to futures markets.[15] This extension ignores the differing roles of margin in the respective markets. The objections described above also hold for the Excess Volatility Argument as it applies to futures markets. Furthermore, there may be additional difficulties for the case of futures markets since margin plays a different role in futures contracts than in stock transactions. Analysis of the terms of futures contracts reveals no compelling reason to expect margins to control volatility in futures markets.

In this section, I have described some of the conceptual difficulties for the Excess Volatility Argument. In the next section, I consider the empirical evidence concerning the effects of margin changes on the volatility of prices.

Evidence of the effects of margin changes on volatility

A number of empirical findings do not support the claim that margin levels affect volatility. First, in order to have an effect on stock price volatility, equity positions funded by margin loans would have to constitute a sizable portion of investments in the stock market. Figure 1 graphs the dollar value of securities margin loans on equities as a percentage of the market value of corporate equity over the period 1968 to 1988. The dollar value of margined securities positions are a small portion of total stock holdings. Thus, attempt-

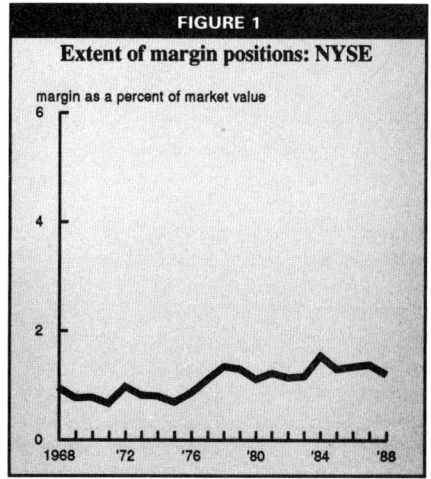

FIGURE 1
Extent of margin positions: NYSE

ing to decrease the number of margined securities positions by raising the cost of holding these positions would influence stock prices only if speculative activity affecting a small portion of stock holdings could have a significant impact on prices for both margined and unmargined stocks. With such a large percentage of equity holdings unaffected by the level of required margin, policies influencing the level of margin required to purchase equities are unlikely to significantly affect volatility.[16]

Considerable empirical research examines the links between margins on securities and the volatility of security prices. This literature is extensive and is not reviewed here.[17] A repeated finding is that changes in equity margins are not related to subsequent changes in stock price volatility.[18]

Similar research for a wide array of futures contracts shows that margins on futures contracts are an ineffective tool for reducing volatility. Previous work by Furbush (1988) compares S&P 500 volatility before and after margin changes on the S&P 500 futures contract, and finds no significant change in volatility. On the other hand, Kupiec (1990) finds a *positive* association between daily volatility estimates for the S&P 500 index and previous initial margin rates (the amount of margin divided by contract value) for that contract. Both results contradict the negative association predicted by the Excess Volatility Argument.

In this section, I present additional evidence that raising futures margins does not lower the volatility of the futures contract price. As with any literature testing for a nonzero effect, econometric difficulties can bias the test toward finding no effect. Recognition of this problem encourages careful researchers to try alternative approaches and repeated testing of a nonzero effect. My evidence improves on the existing literature in several ways. First, I use a new econometric technique to obtain volatility estimates. The procedure uses a method which improves the measurement of volatility and isolates changes in margin from changes in the level of futures price. Second, I test both the Prudential Exchange Hypothesis and the Excess Volatility Argument.

My procedure consists of testing the hypothesis that margin changes are associated with the volatility of two financial futures contracts (see Box 2 for details of this procedure). Using leads and lags of the margin change variables allows a determination of the time ordering of the relationship between margin changes and volatility. That is, using Equation 2 (see Box 2), we can determine whether changes in volatility come before or after changes in margin. The approach utilizes the persistence of volatility to associate margin changes occurring around a volatility shock.[19]

The test employs rates of margin changes which occur before the date of observed volatility (margin change "lags") and rates of margin changes which occur after the date of observed volatility (margin change "leads") in a regression having volatility as the dependent variable. The coefficients on these before and after margin changes are relevant to two quite different hypotheses about the relationship between margin changes and volatility. According to the Prudential Exchange Hypothesis, futures exchanges respond prudentially to higher volatility by increasing margin requirements. If this hypothesis is correct, then margin changes should occur after shocks to volatility. For example, if volatility of a futures price rises due to an oil crisis, margins on affected contracts should rise in response. Thus, there should be positive coefficients on margin changes occurring after observed volatility. That is, positive coefficients on margin changes occurring after observed volatility indicate that futures exchanges, acting to protect their interests, raise margin when exchange officials observe increases in volatility. Thus, positive coefficients on margin changes occurring after observed volatility can be taken as evidence affirming the Prudential Exchange Hypothesis.

Proponents of the Excess Volatility Argument expect margin increases to reduce volatility. Evidence that volatility is persistent implies that volatility will not change unless a subsequent shock produces a change. Proponents of the Excess Volatility Argument argue that margin changes shock volatility by raising the cost of holding speculative positions. Thus, increases in margin lower volatility and decreases in margin raise it, according to proponents of the Excess Volatility Argument. A finding of negative coefficients on margin changes occurring before observed volatility is consistent with this expectation.

A related question concerns the length of time separating futures margin and volatility changes. The low cost of futures trading suggests that responses to a change in margin are likely to be quickly observed. This suggests the time between margin changes and observed volatility need not be long. Alternatively, if margin changes produce purely transitory effects, they would not be a particularly useful policy tool.[20] This motivates examining a longer interval. In order to test the Excess Volatility Argument, I looked at margin changes that occurred up to twelve trading days before observed volatility. Twelve trading days are more than one-half month, so it seems reasonable to expect that any effects from a margin change would be observed during this interval. Also, if margin changes produce effects which persist

---

BOX 2

Procedure to test association of margin changes and volatility

Davidian and Carroll (1987) introduce a method later extended by Schwert (1989) to calculate daily volatility estimates. Schwert and Seguin (1990) show that, assuming normality, this procedure gives unbiased estimates of daily return standard deviations. The procedure iterates between a specification for mean returns and a separate specification for volatility. Equation 1 gives the specification for the mean return from a futures contract as follows:

(1) $r_t = X_t' \beta + \varepsilon_t$;

where r_t is the continuously compounded return for a futures contract at time t. This return is conditional on information available at t such as the month of the year and previous returns. This information set is represented by X_t. The residual, ε_t, captures the effects on returns from unanticipated events occurring at time t. The parameter β summarizes the contribution of information items in the determination of returns. The variance of ε_t summarizes the volatility due to unanticipated events over the sample period. Under certain conditions ε_t is an efficient estimator of the true volatility.[1] One of these conditions is that volatility is unchanging or homoskedastic.

If the error terms are heteroskedastic, then we need to identify the source of heteroskedasticity in order to correct for it in Equation 1. That is, we need a theory which can be tested about the determinants of volatility in futures returns. The Excess Volatility Argument is a testable theory that margin affects volatility. Equation 2 expresses the relevant theory as follows:

(2) $|\varepsilon_t| = Y_t' \alpha + \sum_{\substack{i=-k, \\ i \neq 0}}^{k} \gamma_i \, dm_{t+i} + \mu_t$;

where $|\varepsilon_t|$ is the absolute value of the residual from Equation 1, Y_t are information-set variables which might affect the volatility of returns, and dm_t are percentage changes in margin requirements at time t. The parameters α and γ_i summarize the impact of these variables on volatility. Nonzero values for these parameters imply that volatility is affected by the associated variable. Of primary interest here are the γ_i which summarize the effect of margin changes. A negative coefficient implies that margin increases are related to lower volatility, a positive coefficient implies that margin increases are related to higher volatility.

Variables included in the information set, X_t for Equation 1 and Y_t in Equation 2, require additional explanation. Lags of futures contract returns are included in Equation 1 to capture short term shifts in expected returns. Inclusion of indicator variables for the months of the year incorporates effects on returns from seasonal or contract life-cycle effects. Finally, since returns at time t are dependent on risk assessments, after the first iteration twelve lags of the volatility estimate from Equation 2 are included as a measure of risk. The Y_t variables in Equation 2 include the indicator variables for months of the year and twelve lags of volatility from Equation 1. The motivations for these inclusions differ from those in Equation 1. Including the months of the year is motivated by Samuelson's (1965) theory which implies that the volatility of futures prices changes over the life of the contract. Lags of volatility are included to accommodate the persistence of volatility shocks. French, Schwert, and Stambaugh (1987), Poterba and Summers (1986), and Jain and Joh (1988) provide evidence for this persistence in asset returns.

Finally, it is necessary to iterate the procedure. Iteration is necessary because the hypothesized heteroskedasticity in Equation 1 implies the ε_t are inefficient. The problem can be corrected by using predicted values from Equation 2 as weights in a weighted least squares re-estimation of Equation 1. Each iteration improves the efficiency of the ε_t estimates. Davidian and Carroll (1987), using Monte Carlo experiments, find that two iterations are sufficient to resolve efficiency problems. I found that the earlier iterations often produce some negative predictions. To ensure positive weights are used, I iterate five times to avoid this problem.

---

[1]Efficient in the sense that the information set is being used to the fullest extent possible.

for less than one-half month, they would be relatively useless policy tools. For similar reasons, I looked at margin changes during the 12 days following observed volatility in order to test the Prudential Exchange Hypothesis. It is reasonable to reject the Prudential Exchange Hypothesis if exchange responses to increased volatility occur more than twelve business days after a substantial increase in volatility.

The data consist of daily prices for two financial futures contracts traded at the Chicago Mercantile Exchange: the deutschemark and the S&P 500 futures contract. Sample periods are from June 30, 1974, to December 31, 1989, for the deutschemark contract and from June 30, 1982, to December 31, 1989, for the S&P 500 contract. This sampling interval gives 3,811 observations for the deutschemark contract and 1,842 observations for the S&P 500 contract. On any sample date, futures contracts for several delivery months trade simultaneously. This implies that the prices of any of these contracts might be used to compute returns. Following industry norm, I use prices for contracts which are nearest to delivery. The nearest-to-delivery contract is generally the heaviest traded and, hence, regarded as most representative of that day's trading.[21] As contracts approach expiration, this procedure requires that expiring contracts be replaced by the subsequent contract. Thus, on the last day of the month prior to a delivery month, I roll out of the nearby contract and into the next delivery month. This procedure avoids making inferences which are unique to the delivery month.

Continuously compounded rates of returns from these price series are matched to the effective dates of changes in initial margin requirements for speculative and hedge positions.[22] Over the respective sample periods, there were seventeen changes in initial margin for the deutschemark and nineteen changes of initial margin for the S&P 500. These margin changes are expressed as continuously compounded rates of margin change. This approach produces zeroes where no margin change has occurred and small positive or negative values elsewhere.[23] These data are from the CME clearing association.

Table 1 reports coefficients of margin changes before observed volatility used to test the Excess Volatility Argument. Recall that the Excess Volatility Argument predicts that there should be a negative association between volatility and previous changes in margin. Individual coefficient t statistics for speculative and hedge positions in both contracts do not support the Excess Volatility Argument. For the deutschemark, one speculative margin change coefficient (lag 4) differs reliably from zero at the conventional 5 percent level, but has the wrong sign. Two individual coefficients for the S&P are significant for both speculative positions (lags 1 and 7) and hedge positions (lags 10 and 11), but these are of opposite sign. Coefficient

TABLE 1
Summary of tests for the Excess Volatility Argument

Trading days after a margin change	Coefficient t statistics			
	Deutschemark contract		S&P 500 contract	
	Speculative positions	Hedge positions	Speculative positions	Hedge positions
1	−1.78	−1.08	−2.59	−1.53
2	−0.41	0.68	−1.71	0.59
3	0.82	0.98	1.85	0.49
4	2.02	0.60	0.51	−1.20
5	0.59	−0.17	−0.80	−0.78
6	−0.63	−0.05	1.05	0.11
7	−0.08	−0.40	2.37	0.57
8	1.14	1.33	1.13	−0.16
9	0.42	0.85	0.13	−0.12
10	0.16	−0.44	−0.91	2.44
11	−0.49	−1.75	0.46	−2.74
12	−0.36	−0.33	0.32	−1.22
Coefficient sums	0.0001	0.0001	0.0003	−0.0008
F statistic (hypothesis that coefficient sum equals zero)	0.16	0.06	1.62	1.12
(p value)	(0.69)	(0.80)	(0.20)	(0.29)

sums are examined because the effect of a margin change may be spread across several days, producing a cumulative effect not evident on any one day. Three of the four coefficient sums are positive, indicating that volatility rises following a margin increase. To determine the significance of these coefficient sums, they are tested against 0 with an F test. Asymptotic critical values for this test are: 3.84, at the 5 percent confidence level and 6.63, at the 1 percent confidence level. In each case, the coefficient sums do not differ reliably from 0. Thus, the results do not indicate a negative association between margin changes and volatility realized after these changes, as implied by the Excess Volatility Argument.

An alternative to associating margin changes with the size of price changes is to examine the frequency distribution of price changes. Figure 2 charts the frequency of S&P 500 futures price changes for each level of margin over the sample period. Price changes are categorized as more than 1 percent, more than 2 percent, etc. Thus, horizontal bars in the chart depict the percentage of price changes larger than a given size which were observed for the indicated level of margin. If high volatility is more likely when margin levels are low, then a greater percentage of large price changes should be observed in the low margin regions. Examining each price change row, it appears that large price changes are equally likely to occur at each level of margin observed. Thus, the evidence of this test does not show that low margin levels lead to high volatility.[24]

Table 2 summarizes coefficients on margin changes after observed volatility used to test the Prudential Exchange Hypothesis. Recall that the Prudential Exchange Hypothesis predicts a positive association between volatility and subsequent margin changes. Signs of individual coefficients are mixed and their magnitudes are generally insignificant. No important differences appear to exist between speculative positions and hedge positions, indicating that exchange responses to volatility do not differ between these two classifications. Coefficient sums for the deutschemark contract are positive. This is indicative of a positive association between past volatility and margin changes as predicted by the Prudential Exchange Hypothesis. However, F test results indicate these coefficient sums do not reliably differ from 0. Coefficient sums for the S&P 500 contract are

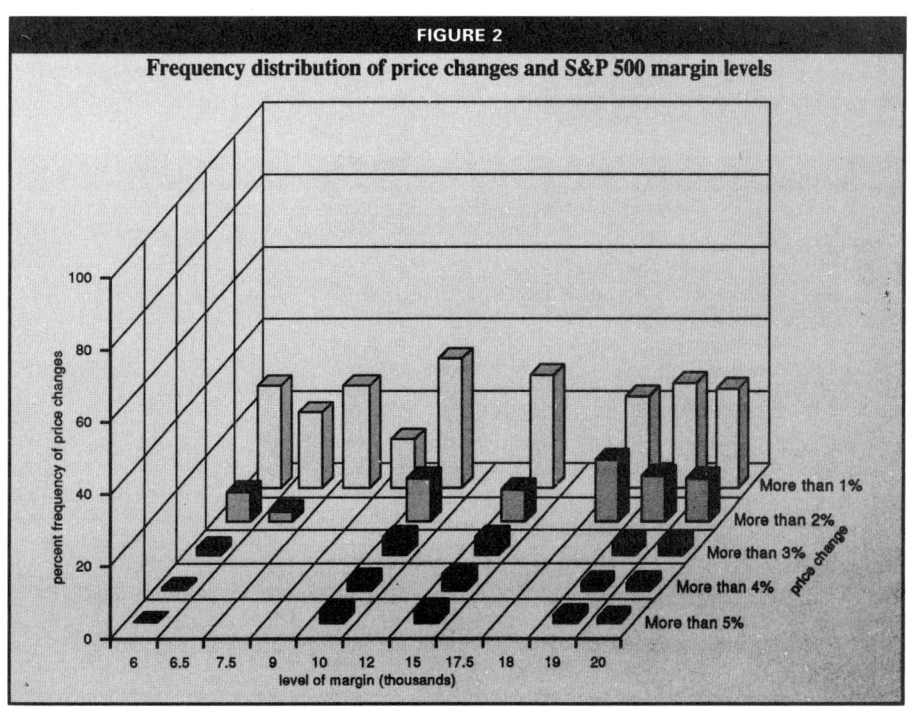

FIGURE 2
Frequency distribution of price changes and S&P 500 margin levels

TABLE 2
Summary of tests for the Prudential Exchange Hypothesis

	Coefficient t statistics			
	Deutschemark contract		S&P 500 contract	
Trading days prior to a margin change	Speculative positions	Hedge positions	Speculative positions	Hedge positions
1	0.62	1.22	0.35	−2.35
2	0.76	0.20	−1.37	−2.44
3	0.38	−1.41	−0.66	2.05
4	2.38	0.63	−0.37	1.10
5	−2.10	−0.47	0.77	0.03
6	−0.33	0.44	−0.26	−1.40
7	−0.24	0.01	0.37	0.58
8	1.34	0.83	0.44	2.43
9	0.39	1.57	−0.96	−0.06
10	−0.07	−0.33	−1.32	−2.67
11	1.24	1.10	0.22	−1.21
12	−0.44	−0.47	−0.67	−0.16
Coefficient sums	0.0004	0.0003	−0.0001	−0.0009
F statistic (hypothesis that coefficient sum equals zero)	1.24	0.89	0.99	1.65
(p value)	(0.27)	(0.34)	(0.32)	(0.20)

negative, but F test results indicate they do not significantly differ from 0. F test results fail to support the Prudential Exchange Hypothesis.

The negative signs for the S&P are opposite those expected. This motivates further examination of volatility and S&P margin levels. Volatilities obtained from the above iterative procedure are restated to obtain the dollar volatility per day of the S&P contract. These volatilities and the level of speculative margin are graphed in Figure 3. The graph shows that the level of required margin has remained high while volatility for most of the period after 1987 fell to 1986 levels. Dividing margin requirements by dollar volatility gives the level of coverage obtained by the exchange. Comparing the pre-1987 period with the post-1987 period, margin levels since October 1987 provide the exchange with 51 percent greater coverage than previously. This greater coverage lessens the need of the ex-

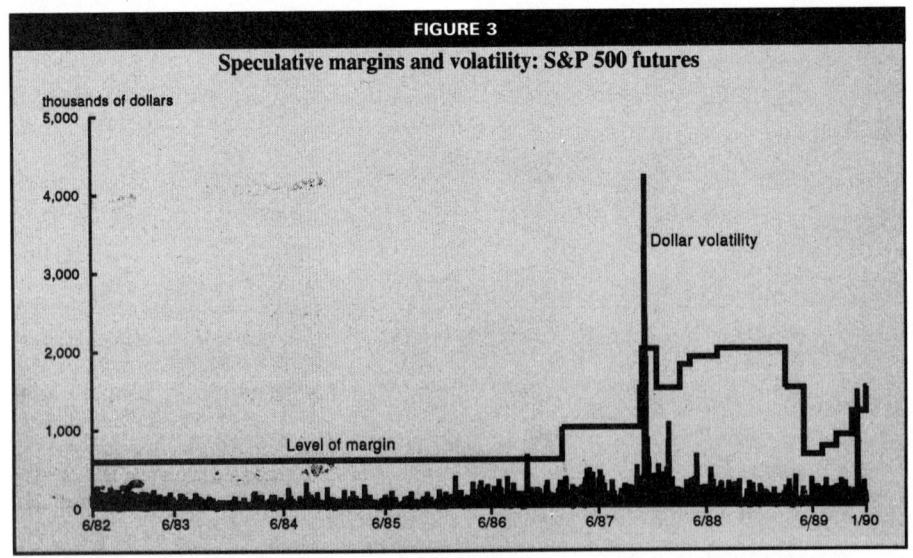

FIGURE 3
Speculative margins and volatility: S&P 500 futures

change to raise margin in response to volatility increases. In other words, the exchange does not need to raise margins in response to higher volatility because margin requirements are already high enough to cover its increased risk. This may explain the lack of evidence for the Prudential Hypothesis.

Another way to test the Prudential Exchange Hypothesis is as follows. Prudential exchanges can be expected to set margin levels for contracts according to the risk of losses from insolvency. Since high price volatility places the exchange at greater risk, levels of margin required for contracts should rise with the anticipated price volatility of these contracts. One way to observe anticipated volatility is to use the volatility implied by observed prices on futures options. Thus, I hypothesize that margin levels will be positively associated with implied volatilities.

To demonstrate this approach, implied volatilities were computed for closing prices on futures options traded on September 9, 1991. The contracts used were: soybean, corn, and Treasury bonds from the Chicago Board of Trade; and S&P 500, live cattle, Swiss franc, deutschemark, and Japanese yen from the Chicago Mercantile Exchange. Volatilities are stated on a per day, dollar basis.[25] This gives, in dollars, the largest up-or-down change which can be expected in a single day with probability .33. Thus, setting margin levels at three times this volatility provides these exchanges with 99 percent confidence that margin balances will be sufficient to cover losses realized in one day by either long or short positions. Figure 4 graphs margin required for these contracts on our volatility estimates. The predicted positive association is demonstrated by the graph. The simple correlation between margin levels and volatility is .92 which does provide some evidence for the claim that margin levels are positively associated with the level of exchange risk. The evidence from a single sample date presented in this article is not sufficient for a test of the Prudential Exchange Hypothesis, however, the positive result suggests that further testing may provide stronger evidence.

Summarizing the evidence, my tests for the link between futures margin and volatility do not support the Prudential Exchange Hypothesis. However, this result may be due to the relatively higher margin requirements after

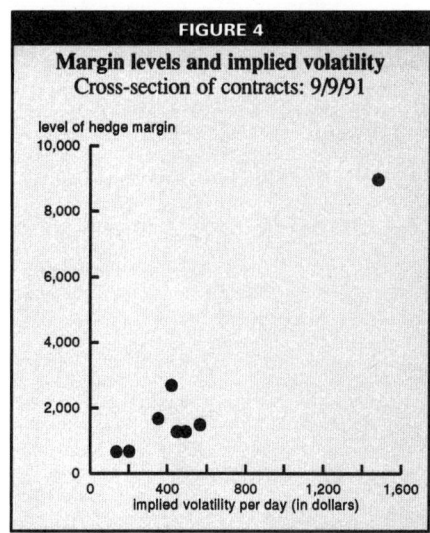

1987. My tests do produce further evidence against the Excess Volatility Argument.

Conclusions

The Excess Volatility Argument implies that higher margin can be used to control speculation resulting from excessive volatility. This article presents several arguments suggesting that this argument is flawed, as well as new evidence indicating that the volatility of futures prices is not reduced by raising futures margin.

The evidence that changes in futures margin do not lead to changes in volatility is quite compelling, consequently, the Excess Volatility Argument should not be a consideration in the government regulation of margins. It is clear that private interests in setting margins do exist. I have described the prudential interests of the futures exchanges. These interests provide some support for the view that exchanges are motivated to set margins at prudential levels.

Effective public oversight of margin setting for futures contracts requires policymakers to identify the interests which are best served by changing margins. Otherwise, financial markets risk being encumbered by unnecessary regulation. Margin regulation is unlikely to reduce the volatility of futures prices. However, other roles for margin, including the public's interest in the safety of futures clearing houses and the payments system, warrant additional research.

FOOTNOTES

[1] The Brady Report is the name generally given to a report prepared by the January 1988 Presidential Task Force on Market Mechanisms headed by Nicholas Brady, Secretary of the Treasurer.

[2] Since 1934, the Federal Reserve Board of Governors has set margins for stock by specifying the initial margin required for stock purchases. Margin regulation is motivated by the Excess Volatility Argument which is explained later. At this point, it is important for the reader to realize that, in addition to this regulatory activity, private interests are also at work in determining margin.

[3] To avoid a technical problem, I oversimplify by assuming the cost of carry for the cash asset is zero. Costs of carry are the financing costs net of returns from holding the cash asset. They determine the difference between futures prices and current prices for the cash asset. For the purposes of this example, they can be ignored.

[4] Further, resources would be expended to make this determination. Thus, the ability of counterparties to avoid this cost will weigh in their assessment of the worth of futures contracting.

[5] This description is somewhat oversimplified. Edwards (1982) goes into more detail. Essentially, the clearing association guarantees payments between the clearing members of the exchange. Were the hypothetical contract made through a single clearing member, Ms. Long would face the risk that the clearing member would be unable to make good on the payment should Mr. Short be insolvent. The clearing association is not obligated to fulfill commitments between a clearing member and any other party.

[6] Fenn and Kupiec (1991) point out that increasing the frequency of marking contracts to market serves as a substitute for raising the level of margin.

[7] This loss may be further reduced by proceeds from the sale of assets going to the exchange.

[8] The Chicago Mercantile Exchange presently determines margin requirements of positions using its Standard Portfolio Analysis of Risk (referred to as "SPAN"). The system evaluates the risk of the individual after netting out positions in several markets and determines the level of margin required for the net position.

[9] See Kindleberger (1989) and Chance (1990).

[10] Federal Reserve Regulations T, U, X, and G state current margin requirements.

[11] Kindleberger's (1989) history provides an excellent description of the events preceding and following the 1929 crash from an Excess Volatility perspective. Similar arguments have also been made regarding the role of margins on stock index futures in the 1987 crash. For an example, see the Brady Report.

[12] Alternatively, it might be argued that these investors all believe they can exit the market prior to the necessary correction. Note that this is an assumption that exit can be perfectly timed. Relaxing the perfect-timing assumption introduces the risk of being late and incurring losses during the correction. Risk averse investors will take on this risk only if it is compensated. Since the risk is costlessly avoided by not participating in the bubble, it is not compensated. Thus, if investors are risk averse, bubbles are not possible.

[13] The presence of performance guarantees offered by the exchange makes these costs more explicit. The membership is contractually obligated to make good on defaults of its nonperforming members.

[14] The effectiveness of regulating margin becomes dependent on the relative costs of leverage obtained through margin loans and leverage obtained from other sources; that is, homemade leverage. If homemade leverage is relatively costly, then raising margin requirements increases the cost of obtaining leverage and may decrease speculative activity.

[15] A clear case of extending the Excess Volatility Argument to futures markets can be found in the Brady Report.

[16] Salinger (1989, Table 1) also makes this point.

[17] Chance (1990) and France (1990) review the literature of the relationship between volatility and stock and futures margin.

[18] Hardouvelis (1988) is a notable exception. Hsieh and Miller (1990) point out that the Hardouvelis procedure is susceptible to problems with persistent variance. Kupiec (1988, Table 5) replicates the Hardouvelis procedure. He finds that much of the effect traces to the last half of the 1930s.

[19] That is, it is assumed that changes in volatility due to shocks are permanent, not temporary. For example, if the volatility of futures prices increases due to an oil crisis, the assumption is that volatility will remain at the new level until another shock occurs. This assumption is important for determining the cause of observed changes in volatility. For example, if volatility responses to shocks were temporary rather than permanent, then an observed change in volatility might be the result of volatility returning to its previous level after a temporary response, rather than a response to a new shock. This assumption is supported by the evidence from Schwert (1989). Additionally, the results from the specifications used in this paper support volatility persistence.

[20] For transitory effects from margin changes to be useful, regulators must be willing to change margin requirements frequently.

[21] France and Monroe (1991) investigate the effects of futures margin on the less heavily traded contracts expiring on later delivery months. This approach investigates the importance of liquidity on the margin-volatility association.

[22] Continuously compounded rates of change are computed as the difference in the log of prices. I am indebted to

Bjorn Flesaker who suggested this approach to obtain symmetry between rates of increase and decrease.

[23]Signed dummy variables were also tried in place of percentage changes of margin. The results were similar to those reported here, however, the level of significance was lower. This suggests that the amount of margin change provides information in addition to the information that margin changed and the direction of that change.

[24]Using margin as a percentage of contract value in place of margin levels does not change this conclusion.

[25]Volatilities were implied using the Black-Scholes option model for options on futures nearest to expiration and at the money. This procedure obtains an annualized volatility for rates of change. Annualized volatilities were restated to dollars per day by dividing them by the square root of 365 and multiplying by the dollar value of the contract.

REFERENCES

Chance, Don M., "The effects of margin on volatility of stocks and derivative markets: a review of the evidence," manuscript, Virginia Polytechnic and State University, 1990.

Davidian, Marie, and Raymond J. Carroll, "Variance function estimation," *Journal of the American Statistical Association* 82, 1987, pp. 1079-1091.

Edwards, Franklin, "The clearing association in futures markets: guarantor and regulator," Conference paper presented at the Industrial Organization of Futures Markets: Structure and Conduct, Columbia University, New York City, November 4-5, 1982.

Fenn, George, and Paul Kupiec, "Prudential margin policy in a futures-style settlement system," Finance and Economics Discussion Series Paper No. 164, Federal Reserve Board, Washington, D.C., 1991.

Fishe, Raymond P. H., and Lawrence G. Goldberg, "The effects of margins on trading in futures markets," *Journal of Futures Markets* 6, 1986, pp. 261-271.

France, Virginia Grace, "The regulation of margin requirements: a survey," University of Illinois at Urbana-Champaign Working Paper No. 90-1670, 1990.

France, Virginia Grace, and Margaret A. Monroe, "The effects of margin requirements on futures trading," mimeograph, University of Illinois at Champaign-Urbana, 1991.

French, K.R., G. W. Schwert, and R. F. Stambaugh, "Expected stock return and volatility," *Journal of Financial Economics* 19, 1987, pp. 3-29.

Furbush, Dean, "The regulation of margin levels in stock index futures markets," working paper, Office of Economic Analysis, United States Securities and Exchange Commission, 1988.

Hardouvelis, Gikas, "Margin requirements and stock market volatility," Federal Reserve Bank of New York, *Quarterly Review*, 1988, pp. 80-89.

Hseih, David, and Merton Miller, "Margin regulation and stock market volatility," *Journal of Finance* 45, 1990, pp. 3-29.

Jain, P., and G. Joh, "The dependence between hourly prices and trading volume," *Journal of Financial and Quantitative Analysis* 23, 1988, pp. 269-283.

Kindleberger, Charles P., *Mania, panics, and crashes: a history of financial crises*, Basic Books, Inc., 1989.

Kupiec, Paul, "Initial margin requirements and stock return volatility: another look," *Journal of Financial Services Research* 3, 1988, pp. 287-301.

_____, "Futures margins and stock price volatility: is there any link?," Finance and Economics Discussion Series, Board of Governors of the Federal Reserve System, 1990.

Moser, James T., "Evidence on the impact of futures margin specifications on the performance of futures and cash markets," Federal Reserve Bank of Chicago Working Paper No. WP-90-20, 1990.

_____, "The implications of futures margin changes for futures contracts: an investigation of their impacts on price volatility, market participation and cash-futures covariances," *Review of Futures Markets*, forthcoming.

Poterba, J. M., and L. H. Summers, "The persistence of volatility and stock market fluctuations," *American Economic Review* 76, 1986, pp. 1142-1151.

Presidential Task Force on Market Mechanisms, "Report of the presidential task force on market mechanisms: January 1988," excerpt reprinted in Robert J. Barro, Robert W. Kamphius, Jr., Roger C. Kormendi, and J. W. Henry Watson, eds., *Black Monday and the Future of Financial Markets*, Homewood, IL, Irwin, 1989, pp. 127-203.

Salinger, Michael A., "Stock market margin requirements and volatility: implications for regulation of stock index futures," *Journal of Financial Services Research* 3, 1989, pp. 121-138.

Samuelson, Paul A., "Proof that properly anticipated prices fluctuate randomly," *Industrial Management Review* 6, 1965, pp. 41-49.

Schwert, G. William, "Business cycles, financial crises and stock volatility," *Carnegie-Rochester Conference Series on Public Policy* 31, 1989, pp. 83-126.

Schwert, G. William, and Paul Seguin, "Heteroskedasticity in stock returns," *Journal of Finance* 45, 1990, pp. 1129-1150.

Telser, Lester G., "Margins and futures contracts," *Journal of Futures Markets* 2, 1981, pp. 225-253.

Article 24

The Convexity Trap: Pitfalls in Financing Mortgage Portfolios and Related Securities

James H. Gilkeson and Stephen D. Smith

Gilkeson is a Ph.D. candidate at Duke University; Smith holds the H. Talmage Dobbs, Jr., Chair of Finance at Georgia State University and is a visiting scholar in the Atlanta Fed's research department. The authors gratefully acknowledge the comments of Peter Abken, Frank King, Bobbie McCrackin, Sheila Tschinkel, and Larry Wall.

The securitization of residential mortgages has been one of the biggest growth areas in credit markets during the last decade. In recent years the supply of new mortgage securities has far exceeded the supply of new corporate bonds (see, for example, Douglas T. Breeden 1991), and these instruments are being purchased in large part by financial institutions. Indeed, the relatively high returns and absence of default risk has made Government National Mortgage Association (GNMA) passthroughs, and their corresponding derivative securities, very attractive investment vehicles for banks in all size categories. Holdings of certificates of participation in residential mortgage pools and collateralized mortgage obligations by U.S. banks increased tenfold between 1985 and 1991 (from around $12 billion to $120 billion).[1] Moreover, these mortgage-related securities now make up about 8 percent of commercial bank assets.

The growing popularity of mortgage credit instruments has caused a tremendous increase in studies analyzing the unconventional cash flow characteristics of mortgage-backed securities. Unlike those of a true fixed-income security (such as a Treasury note or bond), the cash flows to mortgages, and therefore mortgage-backed securities, are influenced by the homeowner's option to prepay the mortgage without penalty. This clause makes traditional yield-to-maturity measures unreliable indicators of return because homeowners are more likely to prepay after rates have fallen. Myriad approaches have been developed to deal with this problem, including the option-adjusted spread and arbitrage-free spread measures of return (see, for example, John D. Finnerty and Michael Rose 1991, Lakhbir S. Hayre 1990, and Stephen D. Smith 1991).

While much work has been devoted to examining the relationship between the value of mortgage-backed securities and interest rates, there has been much less discussion of the interaction between mortgage values and the funding techniques traditionally used by banks. Regulators concerned about bank and thrift solvency should be aware that certain methods of financing mortgage portfolios or securitized mortgage-backed securities may expose institutions to capital losses in both high and low interest rate environments.[2]

In addition, portfolio managers should recognize that traditional methods used to hedge the interest rate risk of fixed-income securities may be counterproductive when applied to mortgage-related products. More generally, managers of financial institutions may lack adequate knowledge of the price/yield relationship associated with mortgage portfolios. It is important to understand that changes in the market values of mortgage-related assets and the liabilities used to fund them can interact in ways that cause unusual swings in the market value of equity positions. Managers need to be aware that the value of such equity (or capital) investments in mortgage portfolios, even those funded by (duration) "matched" liabilities, behaves very differently from the residual ownership claim in more traditional asset/liability combinations. Standard return measures, even those that are "adjusted" for risk, may fail to capture institutions' full exposure to interest rate fluctuations.

Practitioners are well aware that funding long-term assets with variable-rate liabilities produces exposure losses in high-rate environments. This article concerns itself with the potential gains and losses from issuing long-term liabilities to finance a portfolio of mortgages or a mortgage-backed security. It is not simply that prepayments alone cause interest rate risk. Rather, it is the asymmetric response of prepayments to rate changes that exposes the manager to risk in both high- and low-rate environments.

This article reviews the concepts of duration and convexity and ways these measures are influenced by prepayments.[3] The discussion then analyzes how equity values change with rates for alternative financing arrangements. Special attention is paid to a so-called "convexity trap" (equity losses in both low- and high-rate environments) when mortgage-backed securities are financed by fixed-rate liabilities. Finally, some solutions to the risk problem are presented. These include higher initial equity investments and various hedging instruments such as interest rate options, interest rate caps and floors, interest-only and principal-only strip securities, and traded futures contracts.

Prepayments, Mortgage Values, And Negative Convexity

An investment in a fixed-rate mortgage-backed security promises a uniform stream of payments over the life of the contract. For the moment, suppose that the mortgage either disallows prepayments or that prepayments are a fixed proportion of the mortgage pool balance. Chart 1 shows the relationship between the market value of this mortgage-backed security and interest rates. (The box on page 23 provides the example used to construct Charts 1-6 and Tables 1-2.) The absolute value of the slope of this function is often referred to as the security's duration.[4] The duration measure can be viewed as the weighted average maturity of the security, with the weights being the present value of each cash flow divided by the present value of all the cash flows (the price). Unlike maturity, which represents only the timing of the last cash flow, duration recognizes that some cash flows will be received before maturity and that these timing differences influence the security's interest rate sensitivity. Indeed, as noted earlier, the (percentage) change in price as rates change is the duration. Therefore, the slope of the line relating price to interest rates (approximately) equals the security's duration.

Notice, however, that in the case of the fixed prepayment portrayed in Chart 1, the slope (or duration) gets smaller as rates increase. This shape implies that the security's value is decreasing more slowly as market interest rates increase. The change in the duration (or rate of change in the price) is referred to as the convexity of the security, and in this case the convexity is positive. Positive convexity implies that the duration of the security is inversely related to the level of interest rates: when rates are high, later payments get less weight (in a present-value sense) than when rates are low (earlier cash flows are relatively more valuable in high-rate environments).

By way of contrast, Chart 2 shows the market value of a mortgage-backed security whose prepayment rate (realistically) increases as interest rates decline. Notice that the value is still decreasing as rates increase and increasing as rates decline. However, over most of this range of rates, the duration of the mortgage is increasing as rates increase. Similarly, the duration is decreasing as rates decline. This characteristic, called negative convexity, requires that cash flows not only increase as rates decline but that, at least for some time periods, they increase at an increasing rate. (The appendix contains a more mathematically

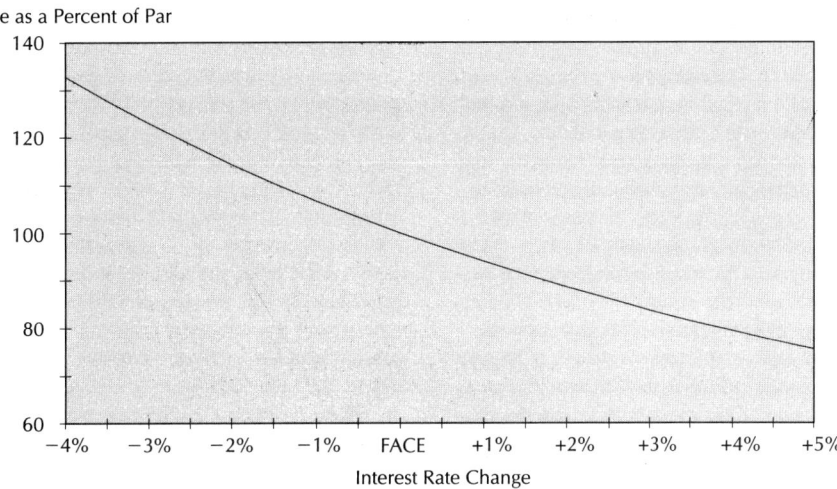

**Chart 1
Constant-Prepayment Mortgage**
(Market Value)

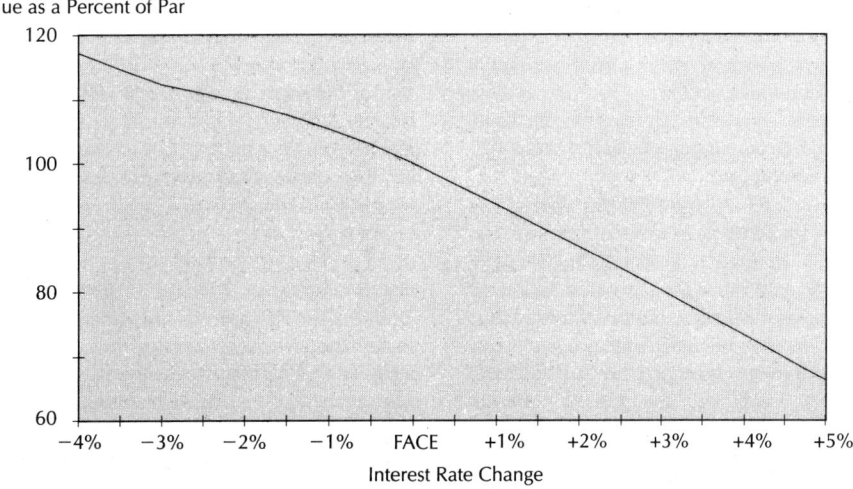

**Chart 2
Variable-Prepayment Mortgage**
(Market Value)

rigorous discussion of this issue.) The intuitive explanation for this unusual value/rate relationship as rates decline is that prepayments are speeding up at exactly the time that these funds must be reinvested at low interest rates. On the other hand, there are few early cash flows in high-rate environments as prepayment rates decline or cease altogether. Therefore, the weighted maturity measure (duration) is increasing as rates rise because less weight is being placed on early cash flows when rates are high. Notice, however, that at a certain low-rate level prepayments (which cannot exceed 100 percent) begin to flatten out, and the value/rate relationship may return to one of positive convexity. In other words, at some (low enough) interest rate, an increase in prepayments is unlikely, and the mortgage portfolio behaves like a fixed-income security.

The following discussion analyzes the ways that three different financing arrangements might influence equity values, depending on whether the funds are placed in a true fixed-income security or a mortgage with varying prepayment rates. The first financing instrument considered is a fixed-term, fixed-rate certificate of deposit (CD). The duration of this instrument is chosen so that liability is initially duration-matched with both assets.[5] Chart 3A shows both the value of a constant prepayment mortgage and the value of the CD as a function of interest rates. The distance between the two curves is the market value of capital. Notice that in this case the value of equity is relatively constant, regardless of the level of rates, because the percentage change in price is the same for both the asset and the liability. The duration is also a measure of the percentage change in price for a 1 percent change in rates, and this depiction is just another way of showing that the durations of the two securities go up and down together as rates change.

Another deposit source commonly used by banks is the fixed-term, fixed-rate deposit that allows the depositor to withdraw funds after paying an early-withdrawal penalty. These deposits typically pay a lower rate than no-withdrawal deposits, allowing a bigger spread (higher equity value) at par. If rates decline, consumers have no incentive to withdraw and, if the liability's initial maturity is chosen to duration-match the asset, the market value of equity remains relatively constant. However, if rates rise significantly, consumers may rationally elect to pay the withdrawal penalty in order to reinvest their funds at the new, higher rates (see, for example, James H. Gilkeson and Craig K. Ruff 1992). At high rates, the market value of the bank's equity position may decline or even become negative unless some hedging activity is undertaken. Chart 3B shows an example of this funding strategy.

Finally, Chart 3C shows how the bank may elect to fund a constant prepayment mortgage security using short-term, floating-rate deposits, such as money market deposit accounts (MMDAs). These accounts typically pay the lowest rates, offering the highest equity value at par.[6] If interest rates fall, the rates on these deposits fall as well and the market value of the bank's equity increases. However, if interest rates rise, the deposit rates will also rise (leaving the market-value line for deposits flat) and the market value of equity will decrease quickly. Under this funding strategy, the bank will have to hedge against rising rates. While the market value changes shown in Chart 3 (and throughout the other graphs) will not immediately show up on an institution's balance sheet (which is in book-value terms), the lower net cash flows will eventually dilute earnings and, therefore, capital.

Charts 4A-C consider the same three financing alternatives for variable-prepayment mortgages that Charts 3A-C considered for fixed-prepayment mortgages. In Chart 3A, a fixed-term, no-withdrawal deposit was shown to "lock in" a positive equity value through duration matching. Chart 4A shows that, for a mortgage that exhibits negative convexity (as discussed previously), this kind of asset-liability management is not, by itself, feasible. If rates rise, the market value of the mortgage security falls more quickly than the cost of the deposits, implying a decrease in equity value. As rates decline, the market value of the mortgage security increases more slowly than the cost of deposits, again implying a decrease in equity value.

For fixed-rate, fixed-term deposits with a withdrawal option, the upside-rate risk is similar to that associated with fixed-prepayment mortgages. However, there is also the risk that, if rates fall far enough, the slower increase in mortgage value will be overwhelmed by the faster increase in the cost of the deposit, entailing a loss of equity value. Chart 4B represents this risk.[7]

If mortgages are financed by short-term, floating-rate deposits, as shown in Chart 4C, the interest rate risks are much the same as for financing fixed-prepayment instruments. Equity value grows as interest rates decrease and falls as they rise. However, a close comparison of Charts 3C and 4C will show that, in this case, the increase in equity value is smaller and the decrease in equity value is larger for mortgages with variable prepayments. However, Chart 4C shows that the institution still has only a one-sided hedging problem when using the floating-rate funding strategy.

Chart 3
Mortgage with Constant Prepayments

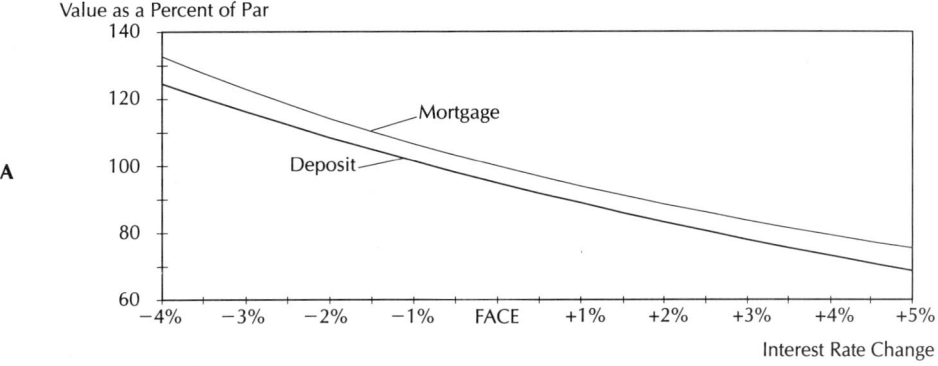

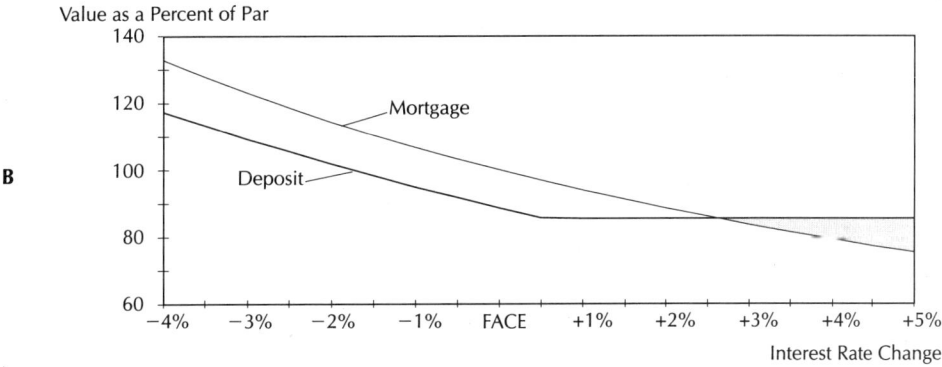

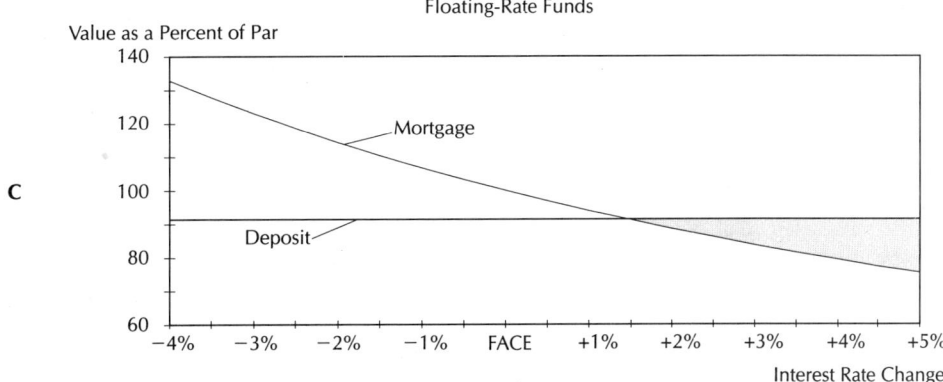

Note: Shaded areas represent negative equity.

Chart 4
Mortgage with Varying Prepayments

Fixed-Rate Funds
(no withdrawal option)

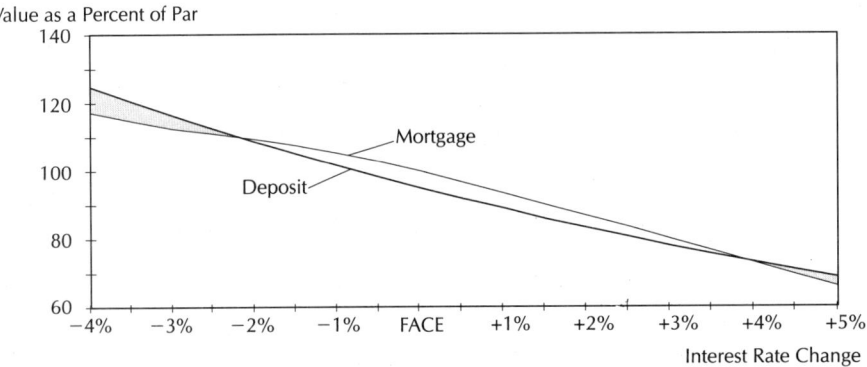

A

Fixed-Rate Funds
(withdrawal option)

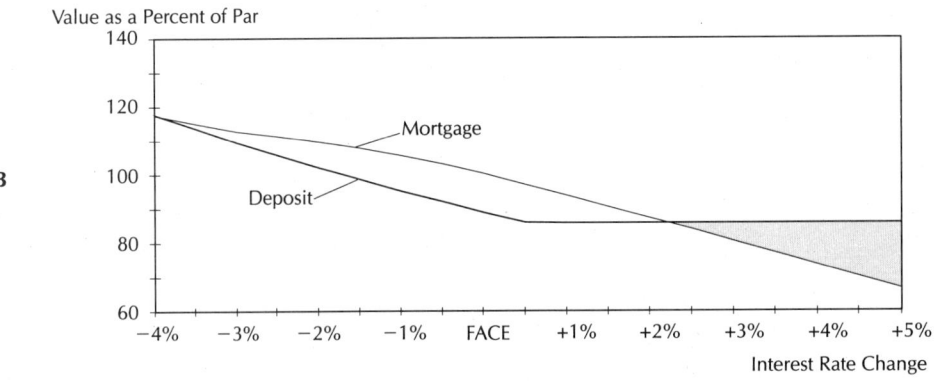

B

Floating-Rate Funds

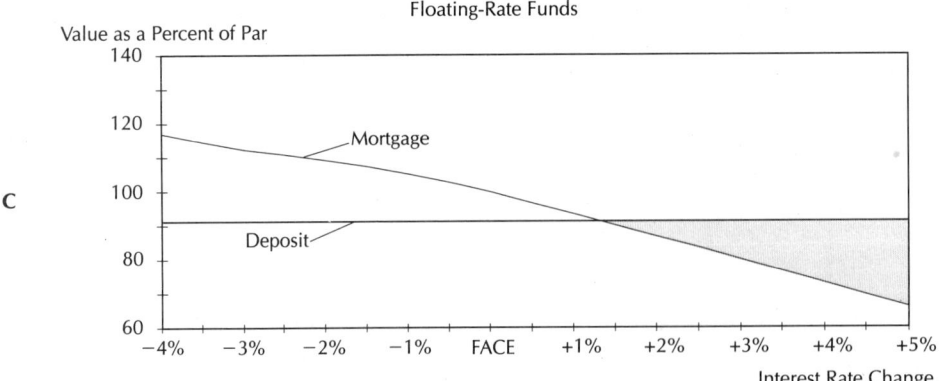

C

Note: Shaded areas represent negative equity.

The Convexity Trap

It is worthwhile to take a closer look at the implications of Chart 4A, which demonstrates financing variable-prepayment mortgages with fixed-term deposits. By traditional asset-liability techniques, the asset and liability pictured are duration-matched. The market value of equity should not change as interest rates rise or fall, yet the figure clearly shows that equity decreases under any sizable interest rate movement, up or down.

This seeming paradox can be called a "convexity trap," to coin a phrase.[8] The duration-matching strategy ignores the effects of varying prepayments or, equivalently, of negative convexity. Although the duration of the mortgage and the deposit are initially matched (at the face interest rate), the convexities are of opposite signs (the mortgage is negatively convex, and the deposit is positively convex). As rates fall, the deposit curve becomes steeper as the mortgage curve gets flatter. Similarly, when rates rise, the mortgage curve gets steeper and the deposit curve flattens. The durations are no longer matched at rates other than par, implying that equity cannot be held constant except by using hedging instruments, which protect equity from large swings in interest rates, either up or down. Of course, the magnitude of potential losses in low-rate environments is limited (because nominal interest rates generally do not fall below zero). (See the box on page 23.)

Equity Cushions and Off-Balance-Sheet Hedging Instruments

Purchasers of mortgage-backed securities can try to protect themselves from losses associated with large interest rate swings in a variety of ways. The most straightforward involves reducing the leverage ratio used to fund the security. In this case, the initial equity cushion is a higher percentage of par value. Charts 5A-C compare three initial equity positions: 10 percent, 5 percent, and 3 percent of the purchase price, respectively. The liability used is the fixed-rate deposit with a no-withdrawal clause, but the same idea would apply with early withdrawal as well. The extreme cases can be seen by comparing Chart 5A with Chart 5C. With a 10 percent initial investment, the bank can withstand rate movements over a 9 percent range and still retain a positive market value of equity. Alternatively, Chart 5C shows that with a 3 percent initial in-

vestment the equity value of the position will turn negative if rates either decline by roughly 1.5 percent or increase by 3 percent. Moreover, as noted earlier, this relatively small rate window would persist even if the original par interest rate were 9 percent or 10 percent. For example, purchasers of 9 percent mortgage-backed securities who fund with 3 percent equity capital, with the remainder being funded by 7 percent fixed-rate liabilities, could encounter a negative equity position (in market-value terms) if rates should fall to around 7.5 percent. Keep in mind that the prepayment assumptions used here are relatively conservative, so the potential problem could be more severe than that shown in Chart 5C.

Other alternatives for hedging the convexity trap involve the use of off-balance-sheet instruments. For example, the portfolio manager could purchase interest rate caps and floors. An interest rate cap is an agreement whereby one party agrees, for an up-front fee, to pay a counterparty the difference between market interest rates and some base rate, in the event that future market rates should rise above the cap rate. Conversely, an interest rate floor can be purchased that pays off the difference between a base rate and market rates should future interest rates fall below the floor. Such instruments are not costless. However, the simultaneous purchase of an interest rate cap and floor at the ends of the interest rate range would provide some insurance against large rate swings and, therefore, the negative convexity of the mortgage. In this case, the net hedged position (the market value of the mortgage plus the caps and floors minus the cost of the deposit) would remain positive. Peter A. Abken (1989) and Keith C. Brown and Donald J. Smith (1988) provide good introductions to the mechanics of interest rate caps and floors.

A less esoteric, but potentially useful, approach to hedging these convexity-induced swings in value involves the purchase of put and call options on Treasury bonds. Chart 6 shows the hedged and unhedged value of equity as a function of interest rates for the duration-matched funding strategy. The unhedged curve is simply the difference between the asset and liability value curves in Chart 5B. The initial equity position is 5 percent of assets. The options are puts and calls on a thirty-year, 8 percent coupon-rate Treasury bond. The strike prices are 90 (for the put) and 110 (for the call). The hedged market value of equity function shows that purchasing such puts and calls can be used to lock in the market value of equity. The assumption used in Chart 6 is that the up-front cost of purchasing the options is 1 percent of the mortgage's par value. Therefore, the net market

Chart 5
The Convexity Trap under Varying Initial Equity Positions

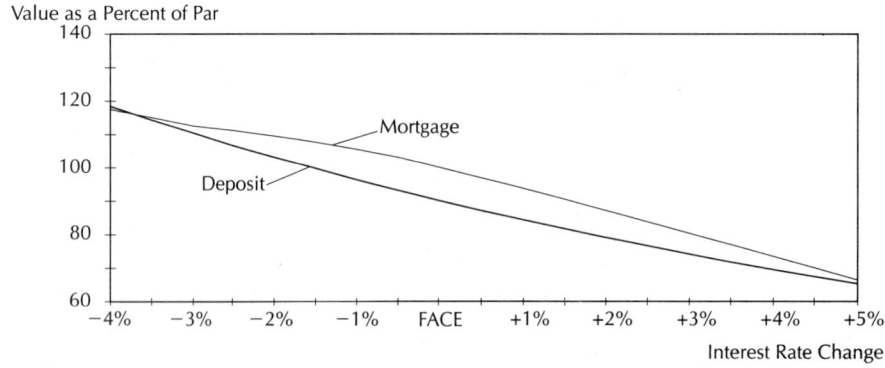

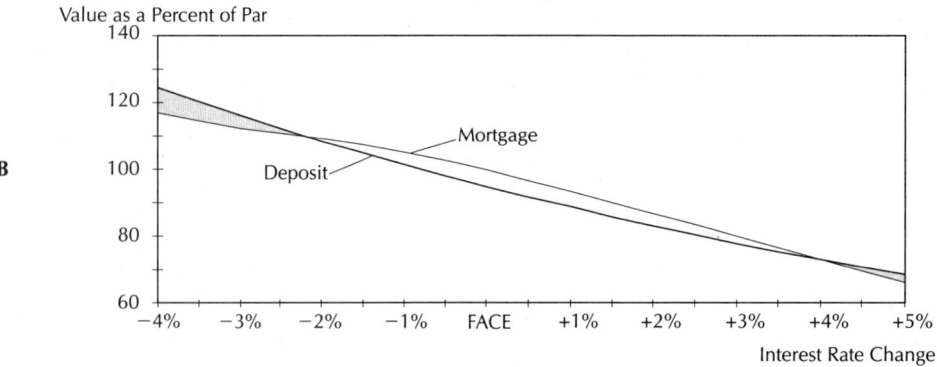

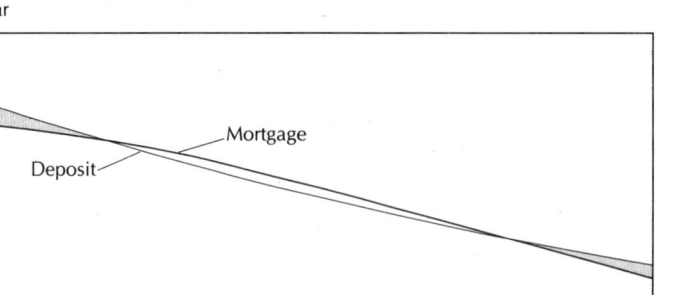

Note: Shaded areas represent negative equity.

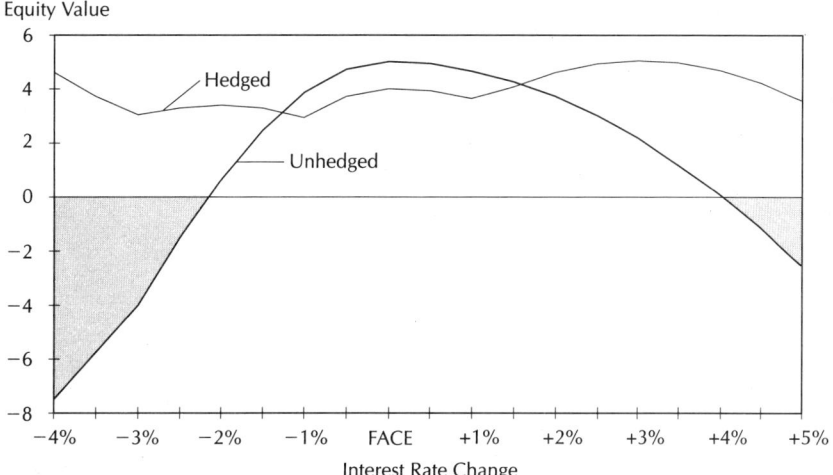

**Chart 6
Market Value of Equity**
(*Hedged versus Unhedged*)

Note: Shaded areas represent negative equity.

value of equity is lower than 5 percent (5% − 1% = 4%) but still roughly constant.

A third off-balance-sheet hedge involves principal-only and interest-only securities. As their names imply, these contracts pay off only as a function of principal and interest payments on the mortgage pool, respectively. When properly priced, the market value of an interest-only security plus that of a principal-only security must equal the value of the mortgage-backed security when purchased alone. Not surprisingly, the value of interest-only securities tend to move directly with interest rates because in high-rate environments prepayments tend to slow down and more interest income is received during the life of the contract. On the other hand, the value of principal-only securities tends to move inversely with rates. When rates fall, the values tend to rise as principal repayments speed up and the discount rate factor falls. Thomas J. O'Brien (1992) provides a discussion of the valuation of interest-only securities, principal-only securities, and whole mortgages.

A final off-balance-sheet hedging alternative would be to create a short position in the Treasury bond futures market. For small interest rate changes it is possible to estimate the change in the mortgage portfolio value (including the effect of changing prepayment rates) with some precision. As stated earlier, the value of the mortgage portfolio will increase as rates fall and decrease as rates increase. Conversely, the short futures position will increase in value as rates rise and decrease as rates fall. Because futures are not subject to prepayment risks, the change in value given a particular rate movement is known. The proper strategy is to short (sell) a specific number of contracts so that, if rates rise, the loss in value to the mortgage portfolio is approximately offset by the gain in value to the futures contracts and vice versa if rates fall.

Each of these strategies has some advantages and disadvantages. The use of higher capital ratios is the most straightforward, but it involves the opportunity cost of allocating capital for this purpose. Purchasing interest rate caps and floors or T-bond puts and calls is much like purchasing an insurance policy.[9] For a fixed fee, paid up-front, the risks from both upward and downward rate movements are covered. However, these insurance-type contracts present three potential problems. First, because options tend to be short-term (at most nine months), the "insurance contract" must be rewritten in no more than nine months at an unknown future "premium." Second, options can often be the

An Example

The graphs presented in this article are constructed using representative mortgage asset and deposit liability pools and a set of conservative mortgage prepayment and deposit withdrawal assumptions. On the asset side, it is assumed that the bank holds a $1 million pool of 8 percent mortgages, all currently at par. For Charts 1 and 3A-C, a constant annual prepayment rate of 6 percent is used. This rate is equivalent to 100 percent of the Public Securities Association rate, a prepayment rate standard developed in the 1970s. Although a constant level of prepayments will cause the mortgage pool to mature faster, the convexity characteristics, as shown in these four graphs, are similar to those of a coupon-paying annuity (that is, they exhibit positive convexity).

Charts 2 and 4A-C incorporate a prepayment schedule in which prepayment rates rise as mortgage rates fall (see, for example, Smith 1991) and vice versa. Table 1 shows mortgage values, as a percentage of par, for various market rate changes. The first column shows the alternative market rates for mortgage-backed securities. Prepayments are assumed to be 6 percent at par. The second and third columns provide the constant prepayment rate and the corresponding market value of the mortgage-backed security (shown in Chart 1). The fourth column shows moderate changes in prepayment rates as interest rates change, and the fifth column provides the corresponding market value. The fifth column is represented in Chart 2. Finally, the sixth and seventh columns show "fast" prepayments and corresponding market values, respectively. If charted, the last column would look similar to Chart 2, differing in that would display more negative convexity.

The convexity trap displayed here is not dependent on mortgage rates falling to 4 percent. Table 1 could be reconstructed using a 10 percent coupon rate and the risk of negative equity would still exist for rate declines of 2 percent to 3 percent (that is, market rates of 7 percent to 8 percent). It is the market rate relative to the coupon rate, rather than the absolute level of rates, that causes the relationship between prices and rates to be negatively convex.

On the liability side, Charts 3A-C and 4A-C compare the effect on equity of three funding alternatives. In each of the three cases, the market value of the cash flows is calculated using a discount rate equal to the current mortgage rate minus 2 percent (200 basis points). In Charts 3A and 4A, a pool of eight-and-a-half-year, 6 percent interest bank notes, making monthly coupon payments, is considered. These deposits may not be withdrawn under any circumstances. This maturity was chosen because it is duration-matched (when variable prepayment effects are ignored) with the thirty-year, 8 percent mortgage. In Charts 3B and 4B, another pool of eight-and-a-half-year, 5 percent interest bank notes making monthly coupon payments is utilized for funding purposes. These deposits may be withdrawn upon payment of a penalty equal to two years' interest (or 10 percent). Note that the market value of the deposit flattens out at 90 percent of par (which is 100 percent minus the 10 percent penalty for early withdrawal).

Finally, in Charts 3C and 4C, a pool of floating-rate deposits is used. The deposit rate is equal to the fixed-term deposit rate minus 3 percent. Note that the market values of these floating-rate deposits remain constant, at less than par, over all interest rates. These are a cheap source of funds, but they always cost the same relative to the current mortgage rate. In summary, Charts 1, 2, 3A-C, and 4A-C were not constructed using extreme data assumptions. The convexity effects of actual mortgage and deposit prices should be the same or greater than those seen here. For completeness, Table 2 shows the market value of the alternative funding sources as a function of market rates.

most expensive method of hedging interest rate risk. An option, by nature, can never be worth less than zero. The price of the option reflects this limited liability. Finally, as these instruments are based on Treasury rates, their values reflect positive convexity while, as stated earlier, mortgage portfolios often exhibit negative convexity. As can be seen in Chart 6, option-hedged equity values continue to show some volatility. The remaining convexity mismatch can, however, be corrected by purchasing a series of options at different strike prices.

It is often argued that interest-only securities and principal-only securities provide the best protection for prepayment risks because these instruments are subject to the same prepayment effects as mortgage portfolios. Further, as the interest-only securities and principal-only securities are based on thirty-year mortgage pools, the hedge positions do not have to be frequently rewritten (in contrast to option-based strategies). However, this approach is subject to a somewhat subtle, though quite important, risk. When hedging with options or futures contracts, the only prepayment risk comes from the mortgage portfolio being hedged. While prepayment rates can be estimated for alternative future interest rates, they cannot be exactly predicted. If hedging is undertaken using interest-only securities and principal-only securities, three prepayment rate schedules must be estimated, one each for the mortgage portfolio, the mortgage

Table 1
Discounted Present Value of Thirty-Year Mortgage-Backed Security (MBS) Cash Flows for Alternative Prepayment Rates
(8 percent coupon rate)

Current Mortgage Rate	Constant Prepayment		Moderate Prepayment		Fast Prepayment	
	Rate	MBS Value	Rate	MBS Value	Rate	MBS Value
4%	0.06	132.82	0.18	117.18	0.42	108.52
	0.06	127.74	0.18	114.72	0.42	107.38
5%	0.06	122.98	0.18	112.37	0.42	106.26
	0.06	118.53	0.16	110.96	0.36	105.88
6%	0.06	114.35	0.14	109.36	0.30	105.40
	0.06	110.43	0.12	107.52	0.24	104.75
7%	0.06	106.74	0.10	105.40	0.18	103.82
	0.06	103.27	0.08	102.92	0.12	102.39
8%	0.06	100.00	0.06	100.00	0.06	100.00
	0.06	96.91	0.054	96.81	0.054	96.81
9%	0.06	94.00	0.048	93.58	0.048	93.58
	0.06	91.24	0.042	90.31	0.042	90.31
10%	0.06	88.63	0.036	87.00	0.036	87.00
	0.06	86.18	0.030	83.66	0.030	83.66
11%	0.06	83.81	0.024	80.27	0.024	80.27
	0.06	81.58	0.018	76.85	0.018	76.85
12%	0.06	79.46	0.012	73.38	0.012	73.38
	0.06	77.44	0.006	69.88	0.006	69.88
13%	0.06	75.52	0.000	66.33	0.000	66.33

pool on which the interest-only security is based, and the mortgage pool on which the principal-only security is based. If actual prepayments vary widely across groups of mortgages the hedge may, on net, be much less effective in practice than alternative strategies.

The principal advantage of hedging with futures contracts is the low up-front cost. Futures positions are always entered into at the current market price so that the only initial cost is the exchange transaction fee. Further, as the risk of upward and downward rate movements is retained, no "insurance" fee is paid. However, futures contracts are marked to market, with the gains or losses paid each day. With options, daily gains and losses are experienced only on paper until the instrument is exercised or sold. A further problem with futures-based hedging, as with options-based hedging, is that the underlying instrument is a Treasury bond, which exhibits positive convexity. As rates change, it is necessary to adjust the hedge ratio (change the number of futures contracts held). Specifically, as rates rise (and T-bond prices fall) it is necessary to short (sell) additional contracts. Conversely, as rates fall (and T-bond prices rise) the short hedge position must be decreased, requiring that some contracts be bought. Futures-based hedging is often referred to as a dynamic hedging strategy because of the need for continual adjustment of the hedge position. This point brings out a final concern with futures-based or dynamic hedging. What if rates move up and then move back down? According to the strategy, a manager would first short additional contracts (at the low price) and then buy back those contracts (at the high price). Buy high and sell low is not generally a profitable business strategy. A manager must, however, weigh these potential losses against the higher up-front cost of purchasing options.

In summary, there is no clear-cut best hedging strategy. Users must weigh the fixed costs of each choice against the risks of differing prepayments or high interest rate volatility. Finally, transactions and monitoring costs of frequent adjustments to the hedge ratio must be considered.

Table 2
Discounted Present Value of Potential Funding Sources

Current Mortgage Rate	Deposit Discount Rate[a]	Eight-and-a-Half Year Banknote[b]	Eight-and-a-Half Year Banknote with Withdrawal Provision[c]	Money Market Deposit Account[d]
4%	0.020	131.24	123.42	96.20
	0.025	126.78	119.13	96.20
5%	0.030	122.48	114.99	96.20
	0.035	118.36	111.01	96.20
6%	0.040	114.39	107.20	96.20
	0.045	110.58	103.53	96.20
7%	0.050	106.91	100.00	96.20
	0.055	103.39	96.61	96.20
8%	0.060	100.00	93.35	96.20
	0.065	96.74	90.22	96.20
9%	0.070	93.61	90.00	96.20
	0.075	90.59	90.00	96.20
10%	0.080	87.69	90.00	96.20
	0.085	84.91	90.00	96.20
11%	0.090	82.22	90.00	96.20
	0.095	79.64	90.00	96.20
12%	0.100	77.16	90.00	96.20
	0.105	74.77	90.00	96.20
13%	0.110	72.47	90.00	96.20

[a] It is assumed that the proper discount rate for all liabilities is the eight-and-a-half-year optionless certificate-of-deposit rate.
[b] This is a fixed-term (eight-and-a-half years), fixed-rate (6.0 percent) certificate that cannot be withdrawn.
[c] This is a fixed-term (eight-and-a-half years), fixed rate (5.0 percent) certificate that can be withdrawn. The withdrawal penalty is two years' interest (2 • 5% = 10%). The assumption used is that the balance **will be withdrawn and reinvested** whenever the discounted present value falls below 90 percent of par.
[d] This is a demand deposit paying the current eight-and-a-half-year rate minus 3 percent (300 basis points).

Conclusion

Mortgage-backed securities have become popular investment vehicles for managers of financial institutions. Much has been written about prepayment options and how to adjust return measures to reflect this variable. This article has provided an introduction to the interactions between variable prepayments and the choice of liabilities used to fund investments in mortgage securities. The discussion highlights the fact that variable prepayments often cause mortgage durations to react to interest rate changes in a fashion opposite that of a true fixed-income asset. The negative convexity of the mortgage creates a situation in which an institution that funds mortgage purchases with duration-matched liabilities may expose itself to capital losses should rates either increase or decrease dramatically. This convexity trap is contrasted with the alternative strategy, which uses floating-rate securities to fund the purchase of the mortgage-backed security. In the latter case the institution faces losses only if interest rates should increase. The examples presented show the possibility of negative equity values for rate decreases as small as 150 basis points below the face, or par, interest rate. Methods for hedging convexity risks are discussed, and it is shown that increasing capital ratios or off-balance-sheet instruments can offset much of the risk of negative net worth positions in mortgage-related investments.

Managers should be aware that the interest rate risk of funding mortgage-backed securities with fixed-rate liabilities is more, rather than less, complex than using floating-rate securities to fund the same mortgage purchase. This fact does not mean that mortgage-backed securities should be funded short-term and the net position left unhedged, however. Rather, managers should realize that they are carrying up- and downside risk should they fund the same mortgage-backed security with duration-matched liabilities.

In conclusion, asset/liability decisions should be made jointly. Relative value measures of mortgage-backed securities (such as the option-adjusted-spread measure) assume that the mortgage is duration-matched with some base security. This article shows that, unfortunately, for anything more than very small rate changes, such matching does not lock in the market value of capital for purchasers of variable prepayment mortgage portfolios or mortgage-backed securities. Indeed, in this case the actual return on invested capital in the mortgage-backed security may fall below the expected return in both high- and low-rate environments. Managers should be sensitive to the convexities of alternative mortgage-backed security pools and how much of the reported excess return is compensation for this risk. Likewise, regulators should be aware that a duration-matched investment in mortgage-backed securities does not necessarily reflect the same interest rate risk as, say, a matched position in Treasury bonds.

Appendix

This appendix contains a simple presentation of the condition necessary for variable-prepayment mortgages to have the negative convexity property discussed in the text. For simplicity, let the term structure be flat and let the expected cash flow per period from the mortgage portfolio be C_t. O'Brien (1992), for example, shows what C_t would be in terms of a constant-prepayment rate and a fixed-coupon rate on the mortgage pool. Notice that if the prepayment rate is a function of market interest rates (not a constant), then C_t will vary as market rates change. If the term structure is flat, the mortgage price is just

$$P = \sum_{t=1}^{t=N} \frac{C_t}{(1+r)^t}, \quad (1)$$

where r is the market yield to maturity, Σ is the sum operator, N is the maturity, and P is the price.

Because the analysis of duration and convexity are in percentage terms, it is convenient to use the continuously compounded rate i, $i = \ln(1+r)$, where $\ln(\cdot)$ is the natural log function. Taking the derivative of $\ln(P)$ with respect to i yields a measure of duration,

$$\frac{d \ln P}{di} = -D = \sum_{t=1}^{t=N} \left[\left(\frac{d \ln C_t}{di} - t \right) w_t \right], \quad (2)$$

where D is the duration and w_t is the present value of period t's cash flow divided by the sum of the present value of the cash flows (the price). If $(d\ln C_t)/(di) = 0$ for all periods t, as would be the case with either no prepayments ($C_t = C$) or a constant prepayment rate, equation (2) is just the standard measure of duration,

$$D = \sum_{t=1}^{t=N} (t w_t).$$

In any case, it is the change in duration with respect to interest rates that is of interest here.[1]

Taking the derivative of equation (2) with respect to i and doing some algebra results in

$$\frac{d^2 \ln P}{di^2} = \sum_{t=1}^{t=N} \left[\left(\frac{d \ln C_t}{di} - t \right)^2 w_t \right] + \sum_{t=1}^{t=N} \left[\frac{d^2 \ln C_t}{di^2} w_t \right]. \quad (3)$$

Notice that the first term on the right-hand side is the sum of squared terms multiplied by positive numbers (the w_t's). Therefore, it is always positive. So, unless

$$\sum_{t=1}^{t=N} \{[(d^2 \ln C_t)/(di^2)] w_t\} < 0,$$

the mortgage will display positive convexity (similar to a fixed-income security). In order to get negative convexity, the percentage change in the cash flows must, on average (with weights w_t) decrease at an increasing rate as interest rates rise. Put another way, the variable-prepayment function must be such that on average the cash flows are increasing at an increasing rate as interest rates fall. This property alone is not enough, of course, because the first term is always positive.

Finally, the fact that the price, P, is a monotone increasing function of $\ln P$ and r is monotone increasing in i establishes that the price itself will have the same qualitative properties with respect to i that $\ln P$ does. These facts establish the link between the pictures in the text (relating P and r) and equation (3) in this appendix.

Note

1. Note that the standard duration measure will, however, differ for the zero-prepayment and constant-prepayment rate scenarios because for $C_t = C$ (a constant),

$$w_t = [1/(1+r)^t]/\{\sum_{t=1}^{t=N} [1/(1+r)^t]\},$$

while for $C_t \neq C$,

$$w_t = [C_t/(1+r)^t]/\{\sum_{t=1}^{t=N} [C_t/(1+r)^t]\}.$$

Notes

1. Because of their tax advantages (as qualifying real estate assets for thrifts) and flexibility, one of the largest growth rates in holdings has come from a particular type of collateralized mortgage obligation—namely, real estate mortgage investment conduits, or REMICS.
2. The terms mortgage portfolio and mortgage-backed security will be used interchangeably when there is no ambiguity.
3. Bartlett (1991, chap. 7), provides an alternative introduction to these concepts in the context of mortgage-related securities.
4. Technically, the slope of the function displayed in the figures is minus the duration multiplied by the price. Duration measures percentage changes.
5. More specifically, a deposit is chosen such that the resulting duration of equity is zero. It can be shown that $D_E = D_A - (L/A)D_L$, where L/A is the liability (L) to asset (A) ratio in market value terms, D_E, D_A, and D_L are the duration of equity, assets, and liabilities, respectively. Choosing $D_E = 0$ is consistent with the idea that investors have a very short-term horizon. See, for example, Smith and Spudeck (1993, chap. 8) for a discussion of this point. As an example, consider a fifteen-year, 8 percent coupon mortgage. If prepayments are fixed at 6 percent annually, this asset has a duration of four and three-fourths years, or fifty-seven months. If the initial equity investment is 5 percent, then L/A equals .95. Setting $D_E = 0$ implies that D_L is equal to sixty months or five years. Therefore, a five-year, pure-discount CD will roughly "duration-match" a fifteen-year mortgage. The result should be a steady equity value, assuming these fixed prepayments of 6 percent annually (similar to that portrayed in Chart 3A). Keep in mind, however, that the durations of amortizing instruments (like mortgages) and nonamortizing instruments (like CDs) change at different rates through time. Therefore, hedges must be periodically adjusted. This scenario is discussed in more detail in a later section.
6. The implicit assumption is that the liquidity preference theory of the term structure is true (see, for example, Abken 1990), indicating that, on average, funding short-term is cheaper than funding long-term.
7. The withdrawal option given to depositors in this case allows the bank to offer a lower rate when compared with the case portrayed in Chart 4A. This provision allows an equity cushion vis-à-vis the no-withdrawal case.
8. The term is used because it seems representative of the price behavior associated with large changes in interest rates.
9. These strategies are almost identical, though the instruments trade on different exchanges.

References

Abken, Peter A. "Interest-Rate Caps, Collars, and Floors." Federal Reserve Bank of Atlanta *Economic Review* 74 (November/December 1989): 2-24.

———. "Innovations in Modeling the Term Structure of Interest Rates." Federal Reserve Bank of Atlanta *Economic Review* 75 (July/August 1990): 2-27.

Bartlett, William W. *Mortgage-Backed Securities: Products, Analysis, Trading*. New York: New York Institute of Finance, 1991.

Breeden, Douglas T. "Risk, Return, and Hedging of Fixed Rate Mortgages." *Journal of Fixed Income* 1 (September 1991): 85-107.

Brown, Keith C., and Donald J. Smith. "Recent Innovations in Interest Rate Risk Management and the Reintermediation of Commercial Banking." *Financial Management* 17 (Winter 1988): 45-58.

Finnerty, John D., and Michael Rose. "Arbitrage-Free Spread: A Consistent Measure of Relative Value." *Journal of Portfolio Management* 17 (Spring 1991): 65-77.

Gilkeson, James H., and Craig K. Ruff. "The Valuation of Retail CD Portfolios." Paper presented at the Financial Management Association Meetings, San Francisco, California, 1992.

Hayre, Lakhbir S. "Understanding Option-Adjusted Spreads and Their Use." *Journal of Portfolio Management* 16 (Summer 1990): 68-69.

O'Brien, Thomas J. "Elementary Growth Model Valuation Expressions for Fixed-Rate Mortgage Pools and Derivatives." *Journal of Fixed Income* 2 (June 1992): 68-79.

Smith, Stephen D. "Analyzing Risk and Return for Mortgage-Backed Securities." Federal Reserve Bank of Atlanta *Economic Review* (January/February 1991): 2-11.

———, and Raymond E. Spudeck. *Interest Rates: Principles and Applications*. Fort Worth, Tex.: Dryden Press, forthcoming, 1993.

Article 25

Index Amortizing Rate Swaps

by Lisa N. Galaif

As short-term interest rates have declined over the past several years, investors have increasingly sought higher yielding investment vehicles. The index amortizing rate (IAR) swap is one of several new instruments that have been developed in response to this investor demand for yield enhancement. An IAR swap is an interest rate swap based on a notional principal amount that may decrease over time in accordance with the path of future interest rates.[1]

The IAR swap market has grown rapidly since its inception in 1990, achieving a market size in late 1993 estimated at $100 billion to $150 billion notional principal. IAR swaps should continue to be popular because they can be an attractive investment under certain interest rate scenarios and a good hedging vehicle for dealers' written options exposures.

This article explains the structure and pricing of IAR swaps, the risks associated with the product, and the uses as well as the growth prospects for the market. We find that while the product has advantages for dealers and investors, its complexity may be a drawback. To price and hedge IAR swaps, dealers must use highly technical models with parameters whose values are difficult to forecast. Investors may have trouble comparing the risk-return tradeoffs of an IAR swap with those of more liquid and traditional instruments.

The structure of IAR swaps

An IAR swap is an over-the-counter contract between two parties to exchange interest payments—one based on a fixed rate and the other on a floating rate—on an amortizing notional principal amount. Like the so-called plain vanilla interest rate swap, the IAR swap involves no exchange of principal. But unlike the plain vanilla swap, whose net interest payments are made on a fixed notional amount, the IAR swap calls for net interest payments made on a notional principal balance that may decrease over the life of the swap. The rate at which the notional principal amount decreases will vary with a specified short-term interest rate according to a schedule predetermined by the two parties. In general, however, notional principal amortizes more quickly when short rates fall and more slowly when short rates rise.[2]

In a typical IAR swap, an end-user[3] (or fixed rate receiver) receives interest payments based on the fixed rate while paying the dealer (or fixed rate payer) floating interest indexed to three-month LIBOR. The amortizing notional amount on which both interest payments are based is typically $100 million at origination. Net interest payments are most often made quarterly throughout the life of the swap, just as they are in a plain vanilla swap.

The standard contractual maturity for an IAR swap is five years with a two-year "lockout" period, meaning that the swap does not start amortizing until the beginning of the third year. The amortization schedule is usually designed so that if short-term interest rates remain unchanged, the IAR swap will have a life of about three years. However, if the floating rate index falls sufficiently, the swap could fully amortize at the end of the lockout period. Alternatively, if rates rise, the swap would amortize at a slower rate and

---

[1] The IAR swap is also known as an index principal swap (IPS) or an index amortizing swap (IAS).

[2] Despite the use of the term "amortization" by market participants, the amortization of notional principal does not imply payment of principal; it refers to the declining notional principal amount on which interest payments are based.

[3] An end-user or customer is typically an institutional investor such as an insurance company, bank, or mutual fund.

273

have a longer than expected maturity, perhaps reaching its five-year maximum life. The variable maturity of an IAR swap is another feature distinguishing it from a plain vanilla swap, which has a fixed maturity date.

Table 1 presents a typical IAR swap amortization schedule. If LIBOR remains at 4.50 percent, the swap amortizes by 80 percent per year after the lockout period; if LIBOR rises to 5.50 percent, the swap amortizes at 30 percent per year. Alternatively, if LIBOR drops to 3.50 percent, the swap amortizes at 100 percent in year 3. This particular schedule assumes yearly amortization, although quarterly amortization is also common in IAR swap schedules.

Changes in future short-term interest rates affect the swap in three ways: they 1) directly affect future net interest payments, 2) indirectly affect future net interest payments by changing the principal amount on which interest calculations are based, and 3) alter the maturity of the swap.

The interest rate scenarios presented in Table 2 illustrate how the notional principal of an IAR swap amortizes given the schedule set forth in Table 1. If future interest rates follow LIBOR path 2 (case 2), then, in year 3, $800 of the notional principal amortizes, reducing the remaining notional principal to $200.[4]

An IAR swap's maturity is usually described in terms of a weighted average life because the instrument's maturity and notional principal may vary. First, the date of the swap's last payment will vary with the path followed by short-term interest rates. Second, the date of the last payment can be a misleading representation of the swap's maturity because the remaining notional principal is also variable. Consider, for example, two IAR swaps that originate with the same notional principal of $100. While both may end after three years, one may end with a notional principal amount of $60 while the other may end with a notional amount of $30. The weighted average life of an IAR swap is calculated by summing the percentage of the remaining notional principal amounts over each interest rate path. These amounts are then averaged across the possible paths. Note that the weighted average life is simply used to describe the instrument's maturity. It is not used for pricing and hedging because it does not describe the actual cash flows with sufficient precision.

Table 1
Amortization Schedule of Typical IAR Swap

LIBOR[†] (Percent)	Change in Basis Points	Amortization Rate (Percent)
3.50	−100	100
4.50	0	80
5.50	+100	30
6.50	+200	10

Notes: The amortization rate in the table is based on annual changes in LIBOR. The terms and conditions of the IAR swap illustrated here are as follows:

Notional amount:	$1,000
Fixed rate:	4.745 percent
Lockout period:	2 years
Final maturity:	5 years
Payment frequency:	Annual
Amortization:	After the lockout period, yearly amortization of remaining notional principal balance based on changes of yearly LIBOR.

[†] The initial spot rate is 4.50 percent.

[4] Given an interest rate of 4.50 in year 3 (case 2), the amortization schedule specifies that $800 of the notional principal will amortize. This amortization leaves $200 in remaining notional principal at the end of year 3. In this example, the amortization rate applies to the current outstanding notional principal.

Table 2
IAR Swap Notional Principal Balance
Notional Principal Given Various LIBOR Paths

Paths	Year:	0-1[†]	1-2[†]	2-3	3-4	4-5
Case 1: declining rates						
LIBOR		4.50	4.00	3.50	3.25	3.00
Notional principal		1,000	1,000	0	0	0
Case 2: stable rates						
LIBOR		4.50	4.50	4.50	4.50	4.50
Notional principal		1,000	1,000	200	40	8
Case 3: rising rates						
LIBOR		4.50	5.01	5.53	5.82	6.13
Notional principal		1,000	1,000	705	539	445

Notes: Amortization is applied to the remaining notional principal balance of the previous period and is based on the schedule in Table 1. Amortization for rates not given in Table 1 is computed through linear interpolation.

[†] No notional principal amortization during two-year lockout period.

Optionality of an IAR swap

The amortizing feature of an IAR swap is an implicit call option that essentially gives the fixed rate payer the right to "call" or cancel a portion of the swap (according to the predetermined schedule) if interest rates decline substantially. The fixed rate payer in an IAR swap thus owns an implicit option analogous (but not identical) to the prepayment option in a callable bond or mortgage security. For this right, the fixed rate payer pays a yield premium for the implicit option. However, in contrast to the embedded options on long-term rates in callable bonds and mortgage securities, the implicit options in an IAR swap are usually options on short-term interest rates.[5]

Because an IAR swap's behavior is dependent on the path of interest rates, the exact set of interest rate options embedded in an IAR swap are difficult to determine directly from the amortization schedule. Instead, these implicit options must be determined indirectly from interest rate models that estimate the IAR swap's exposure profile in different interest rate scenarios. For example, in Table 2, the amount of notional principal remaining in case 2, year 4, depends not only on the short-term rate that will prevail in year 4, but also on the rate that will prevail in year 3. Hence, it is not always possible to purchase the correct number of options or futures contracts in year 1 to hedge the cash flow risk in year 4, since the exposure in year 4 depends on the intermediate path of future interest rates. Specifically, dynamic hedging is required as the exposures to be hedged change with each period.

Behavior of IAR swaps when interest rates change

Like a plain vanilla interest rate swap, an IAR swap has a present value for the fixed rate receiver that will fall when interest rates rise and increase when interest rates fall. However, the magnitude of these changes for an IAR swap and a plain vanilla swap differs because of the option-like behavior of the IAR swap. Specifically, when rates fall, the gain in an IAR swap's value is smaller than the gain in a plain vanilla swap's value; when rates rise, the loss in value of an IAR swap exceeds that of a plain vanilla swap.

The chart illustrates the performance difference between an IAR swap and a plain vanilla interest rate swap (of the same maturity as the expected maturity of the IAR swap) from the perspective of the fixed rate receiver. When long and short rates move together (producing parallel shifts of the yield curve), the IAR swap outperforms the plain vanilla interest rate swap in a **stable** interest rate environment and underperforms it in a **volatile** environment. In other words, if interest rates do not **change** by a large amount, an IAR swap offers the **investor** a more favorable fixed rate of return than the plain vanilla swap because of the option premium embedded in the IAR swap's fixed rate.

[5] Thus, IAR swaps are not ideal hedges for mortgage securities unless perfect correlation exists between long-term and short-term rates.

However, for large parallel shifts in the yield curve, the IAR swap will provide a lower return than the plain vanilla swap. If both short and long rates fall, the IAR swap will amortize rapidly after the lockout period, subjecting the IAR swap's fixed receiver to reinvestment losses at the lower rates. If both short and long rates rise, the amortization rate will slow, lengthening the maturity. In this scenario the fixed rate receiver is paid a below-market fixed rate for a longer period than would be the case in the plain vanilla swap.

As the chart shows, if the net present value of the plain vanilla swap is subtracted from the net present value of the IAR swap, the difference is similar, but not identical, to the exposure profile of a short straddle.[6] In other words, an IAR swap can be thought of as a plain vanilla swap (of the same maturity as the expected maturity of the IAR swap) combined with a collection of interest rate options written by the fixed rate receiver that replicate the "straddle-like" exposure in the chart. For the fixed rate receiver, the option premium

[6] A short straddle is a collection of written interest rate options. Some pay off when rates rise, while others pay off when rates fall.
Our chart is modeled loosely on a chart that appeared in *Derivatives Week*, vol. 2, no. 3 (January 25, 1993).

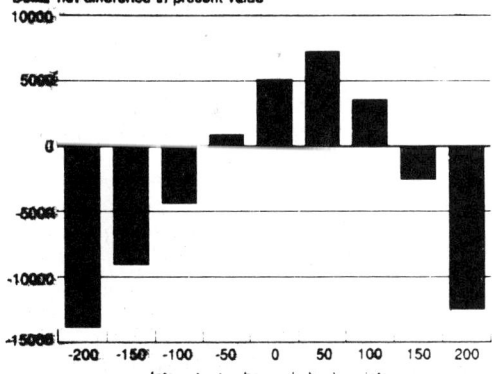

Net Difference between an Index Amortizing Rate Swap and an Interest Rate Swap from the Perspective of a Fixed Rate Receiver

Dollar net difference in present value

Interest rate change in basis points

Notes: The net difference equals the present value of the cash flows of the IAR swap along the given interest rate path minus the present value of the cash flows of the interest rate swap along the same interest rate path. The interest rate changes are based on parallel shifts in the yield curve. The weighted average life for the IAR swap is three years, with a contractual maturity of five years and a two-year lockout period. The maturity of the interest rate swap is three years. The original notional principal for both the IAR swap and the interest rate swap is $1,000,000. The fixed rate on the IAR swap is 4.745 percent and the fixed rate on the interest rate swap is 4.50 percent.

embedded in the fixed rate of the IAR swap causes the IAR swap returns to exceed the plain vanilla swap returns when interest rates stay within a narrow range (because the option is not exercised). But when rates either fall or rise by a large amount, some of the embedded options will be exercised against the fixed rate receiver, thus causing the returns from the IAR swap to fall short of the returns from the plain vanilla swap.

Nonparallel shifts in the yield curve

The embedded options in an IAR swap have complex features that become apparent as soon as nonparallel yield curve changes are considered. If long rates rise and short rates fall, an IAR swap outperforms a plain vanilla swap from the perspective of the fixed rate receiver.[7] As short rates decline, an IAR swap amortizes faster, allowing the fixed rate receiver to enter into another swap at a higher long-term fixed rate, whereas the owner of a plain vanilla swap will continue to hold an instrument that now pays a below-market fixed rate.

Similarly, if long rates fall and short rates rise, the IAR swap will also outperform the plain vanilla swap for the fixed rate receiver. As short rates rise, the IAR swap amortizes at a slower pace, enabling the fixed rate receiver to continue receiving an above-market fixed rate for a longer period. In contrast, the owner of a plain vanilla swap experiences reinvestment losses at the now lower long-term fixed rate when the plain vanilla swap matures.

Pricing of IAR swaps

In principle, the fixed rate of an IAR swap is set at the level that gives the swap an expected net present value of zero at origination. That is, the IAR swap is priced by taking the swap's net cash flows over each of the possible paths of LIBOR rates (in Table 3, three equally likely paths) and solving for the fixed rate that makes the average present value of the net cash flows equal to zero. In practice, all pricing models apply weights to the possible paths. To maintain the internal consistency of the pricing model, these paths and their weights are chosen so that arbitrage possibilities are eliminated.

Table 3 illustrates the difference in pricing between an IAR swap and a plain vanilla swap. Consider an IAR swap with a $1,000 initial notional principal and the amortization schedule presented in Table 1. The cash flows calculated in the example are from the perspective of the fixed rate receiver. For simplicity, assume that the possible future paths of LIBOR rates are the three paths indicated by cases 1, 2, and 3. Case 2 is the path of LIBOR rates implied by forward rates derived from the initial yield curve, and the other two paths are possible alternative interest rate paths.

The price (or the fixed rate) of the plain vanilla swap is the fixed rate that causes the present value of the fixed payments to equal the present value of floating payments as forecast by the initial forward rates.[8] The fixed rate of the IAR swap is 4.745 percent, while the fixed rate of the plain vanilla interest rate swap is 4.50 percent. In effect, the 24.5 basis point difference between the two rates represents the value of the implicit options in the IAR swap.

The complexity of the IAR swap's valuation process is itself a source of uncertainty. Market participants will use different assumptions about volatilities, future interest rate paths, and the correlations between long and short rates in their IAR swap interest rate models. These different assumptions can create larger price variations between different market participants' pricing models for IAR swaps than is the case with plain vanilla interest rate instruments, which are priced using the observable yield curve.

Risk issues
Price risk

The greatest risk for an investor (that is, fixed rate receiver) in an IAR swap is the opportunity cost of holding an IAR swap in the event of a significant interest rate move up or down. If short rates rise sufficiently, the net payout for the fixed rate receiver (end-user) can become negative if the amount of the floating rate payment exceeds the amount of the fixed rate receipt. This interest rate risk is amplified in an IAR swap because as rates rise, the swap's amortization slows and the fixed rate receiver may have a negative cash flow for a longer period.

Since the birth of the IAR swap market in 1990, short-term rates have declined. Thus, most IAR swaps initiated to date have ended immediately after the lockout period, and the behavior of IAR swaps in a rising rate environment has not yet been tested.[9]

Many end-users may find it difficult to determine precisely the risk-return tradeoff provided by IAR swaps. The exact set of interest rate options embedded in an IAR swap is not easily identified because of the IAR swap's path-dependent nature. Hence, buyers cannot go to an exchange and price a specific set of options equivalent to those embedded in the IAR swap. As a result, fixed rate receivers will have a difficult time judging whether or not they have received the appropriate premium for the implicit options

---

[7] In reality, medium-term rates of under five years are relevant for IAR swaps because the contractual maturity in most IAR swaps is five years or less.

[8] Alternatively, the plain vanilla swap can be priced over the same set of possible interest rate paths used in pricing the IAR swap. If these interest rate paths satisfy a consistency condition known as the "arbitrage-free" condition—a requirement that profitable, riskless strategies be ruled out—then the two pricing methods for the plain vanilla swap will produce the same price.

[9] Recently, barrier-type options called "knock-outs" have been offered on some IAR swap contracts. A knock-out clause typically states that if interest rates rise above a certain level (the knock-out rate), the swap will terminate automatically. This feature effectively eliminates the extension risk for the end-user. However, these contracts are expensive and thus tend to defeat the yield-enhancement feature of the IAR swap.

they have sold, because they lack readily apparent and equivalent market prices for the set of options embedded in an IAR swap.

Hedging risk

To hedge IAR swaps, dealers use interest rate term structure models that incorporate several assumptions about the volatility of rates and the correlation of movements in short and long rates. As a first step, the dealers estimate the IAR swap's exposures with an interest rate model.[10] Next, they take into account the offsetting exposures already in their portfolios to determine a residual exposure. These residual exposures (both to changes in interest rate levels and changes in interest rate volatilities) are then hedged, usually using Eurodollar futures and interest rate options.

An interest rate model is required for hedging because, as mentioned previously, the exact structure of the interest rate options embedded in an IAR swap cannot be easily determined from the swap's amortization schedule. The path-dependent nature of the IAR swap requires dealers to use interest rate models to "reveal" and then dynamically hedge the swap's embedded options because the path-dependency of these options cannot be replicated by any simple buy-and-hold options portfolio. Moreover, dealers must use sensitivity analysis or simulations of both the IAR swap and the rest of their portfolios to determine the degree to which the IAR swaps and other exposures in the portfolio offset each other. Hence, hedging the IAR swap's exposures depends on the reliability of the interest rate model used in the simulations.

Model risk

Estimating the true profitability over time of an IAR swap can be difficult. Because of the IAR swap's path-dependent behavior, the instrument cannot be easily broken down into

[10] See Julia Fernald, "The Pricing and Hedging of Index Amortizing Rate Swaps," in this issue of the Quarterly Review.

Table 3
Comparison of the Pricing of an IAR Swap and a Plain Vanilla Swap

Year	Forward Rate (Percent)	Notional Principal	Fixed Payment†	Floating Payment‡	Net§	Present Value of Net
IAR swap pricing						
Case 1						
0-1	4.50	1,000	47.45	45.00	2.45	2.35
1-2	4.00	1,000	47.45	40.00	7.45	6.85
2-3	3.50	0	0.00	0.00	0.00	0.00
3-4	3.25	0	0.00	0.00	0.00	0.00
4-5	3.00	0	0.00	0.00	0.00	0.00
					Sum	9.20
Case 2						
0-1	4.500	1,000	47.45	45.00	2.45	2.35
1-2	4.500	1,000	47.45	45.00	2.45	2.24
2-3	4.500	200	9.49	9.00	0.49	0.43
3-4	4.500	40	1.90	1.80	0.10	0.08
4-5	4.500	8	0.38	0.36	0.02	0.02
					Sum	5.12
Case 3						
0-1	4.50	1,000	47.45	45.00	2.45	2.35
1-2	5.01	1,000	47.45	50.10	-2.65	-2.41
2-3	5.53	705	33.45	38.99	-5.54	-4.79
3-4	5.82	539	25.58	31.37	-5.79	-4.73
4-5	6.13	445	21.12	27.28	-6.16	-4.74
					Sum	-14.32
Average¶	= (9.20)	+	5.12	+ -14.32	÷3 =	0.00
Plain vanilla swap pricing††						
1	4.50	1,000	45.00	45.00	0.00	0.00
2	4.50	1,000	45.00	45.00	0.00	0.00
3	4.50	1,000	45.00	45.00	0.00	0.00

† Fixed payments are calculated by multiplying notional principal by 4.745 percent.
‡ Floating payments are calculated by multiplying notional principal by LIBOR.
§ Net is the difference between the fixed and floating payments.
¶ The average is calculated under the assumption that the three possible LIBOR paths are equally likely.
†† Since the average life of this IAR swap is approximately three years, the comparable swap is the three-year plain vanilla swap.

pieces that look exactly like other instruments whose prices are known. Hence, the product's valuation depends critically on interest rate models. This dependence on interest rate models and the possibility of mispricing is known as "model risk."

The set of possible interest rate paths over which an IAR swap is priced and valued is usually generated using one or two factor interest rate models. One factor interest rate models implicitly assume perfect correlation between changes in short and long rates. Two factor interest rate models, by contrast, can simulate imperfectly correlated short- and long-term rates. In this respect, two factor models would appear to provide better representations of the term structure than one factor models. Two factor models, however, require their users to make explicit assumptions about the correlation between separately varying short- and long-term rates. If inappropriate assumptions are made, then a two factor model's results can be less accurate.

The pricing models must also rely on assumptions about the volatility of short- and long-term rates. Assumptions about volatility, like those concerning the correlation of short and long rates, make IAR swaps difficult to "mark to market" and to hedge. The correlation of rates, however, is an especially difficult parameter to forecast, and problems can arise because pricing model results are particularly sensitive to the assumed magnitude of the correlation. For example, the assumptions about correlations can have a substantial impact on the level of the fixed rate determined by the model.

Closely related to model risk is "personnel risk." When the IAR swap market was first formed, finding personnel familiar with the instrument's pricing and hedging demands was difficult. In some cases, only one trader at an institution may have been familiar with IAR swap pricing models. If that trader left the firm, a knowledge gap could arise, making the risk management of outstanding IAR swap positions more difficult. Fortunately, personnel risk tends to diminish as a product matures and market participants become more familiar with the instrument's behavior in a variety of market conditions.

Liquidity risk
For end-users, significant illiquidity exists in the IAR swap market because of the difficulties of hedging and the customized nature of the instrument. Because only dealers with sizable interest rate option exposures can successfully compete in the IAR swap market, only a handful actively trade this product. Smaller dealers, who generally lack sizable interest rate options positions, find it more difficult to hedge IAR swaps in a cost-effective way and typically execute these swap deals only if they can earn a substantial margin up front. Without a sizable interest rate options book, small dealers would have to sell options in the market to offset their IAR swap positions.

Dealers have expressed their willingness to make a secondary market in this product for customers, but as of yet an active secondary market has not developed.[11] Normal industry practice is for the initiating dealer to make a bid to the customer who wants to liquidate an existing contract. But if the dealer chooses not to buy back the swap from an end-user and the end-user is unable to find another dealer to assume the swap, the end-user cannot easily liquidate or offset the position. Hedging, instead of unwinding, would be difficult for most end-users because the precise nature of the exposure to be hedged can be discovered only with an interest rate model, which IAR swap end-users normally do not possess.

Credit risk
Principal risk is not present in an IAR swap because there is no principal investment (as there is in mortgage securities). Hence, potential credit losses are limited to the net exchange of interest payments over the remaining life of the swap. Like plain vanilla interest rate swaps, IAR swaps are priced with a zero net present value at inception. As short-term interest rates change, the net interest payments will acquire a net positive or negative present value. This present value is the credit exposure between the two counterparties and is usually only a small fraction of the notional principal. Thus, IAR swaps pose no additional or fundamentally different credit or settlement risks than those already present in the plain vanilla interest rate swap.

The market for IAR swaps
The number of dealers currently active in the IAR swap market is small but growing. While major U.S. securities firms dominate the market, U.S. money center banks and foreign bank subsidiaries also participate in the market. New York is the market center for IAR swaps, and most IAR swaps are denominated in U.S. dollars. The low short-term interest rate environment in the United States has no doubt been more conducive to the development of the IAR swap market than have other countries' interest rate environments. If the yield curves of other countries begin to steepen, however, investors may begin to use IAR swaps pegged to non-U.S. rates.

Initially, regional banks were the primary end-users of IAR swaps. Much of the recent growth in demand, however, has come from mutual funds, insurance companies, and other institutional investors.

Uses of IAR swaps
For dealers with sophisticated risk management systems, IAR swaps provide offsets to the exposures arising from

---

[11] Secondary market liquidity has yet to be tested in the swaps initiated before or during 1991 because these swaps ended immediately after the lockout period owing to a dramatic drop in rates over the past two years.

their over-the-counter interest rate options business. As fixed rate payers, the dealers own the options embedded in the IAR swap. Hence they can use these options to hedge their written interest rate option positions as well as other exposures in their interest rate swap book.

From the viewpoint of investors such as mutual funds, insurance companies, and regional banks, IAR swaps provide enhanced yields in a low interest rate environment. These investors, as writers of the options embedded in IAR swaps, are essentially speculating that interest rate changes will be less volatile than buyers of the embedded options expect. In other words, these investors are betting that short- and medium-term rates will remain unchanged or will rise more slowly than predicted by the forward curve. If this scenario does in fact occur, investors will receive an above-market fixed return over the life of the swap from the premiums on the unexercised implicit options that they sold in the swap.

Investors also find IAR swaps to be a useful substitute for mortgage-related securities such as collateralized mortgage obligations (CMOs) and pass-throughs. IAR swaps offer mortgage-bond-type yields and a similar risk profile, but remove the idiosyncratic portion of prepayment risk associated with mortgage securities. Idiosyncratic prepayment risk refers to risk not directly related to changes in interest rates. For example, the need to relocate or a death in the family may prompt a homeowner to prepay a mortgage in what would otherwise seem to be an unfavorable interest rate environment. IAR swaps eliminate risks of this kind, leaving only the interest-rate-sensitive portion of prepayment risk.

For many end-users, the IAR swap combined with a position in Treasury securities provides additional advantages over owning CMOs and other types of cash mortgage instruments. IAR swaps offer a less uncertain absolute final maturity than do CMOs, and as a result, they have a more predictable weighted-average-life profile than CMOs and other mortgage assets. IAR swaps also have fewer operational complexities than mortgage securities. For example, the IAR swaps' typical quarterly pay structure is easier to track than the pay structure of mortgage-backed securities, whose principal and interest payments must be recalculated monthly as prepayment rates change.

By entering into an IAR swap while holding Treasury securities, a regional bank can increase its liquidity while receiving yields similar to those of a CMO and maintaining an interest rate exposure comparable to a mortgage product's. Dealers' marketing materials for IAR swaps also emphasize "capital efficiency," suggesting that some regional bank end-users use IAR swaps to reduce capital requirements. A position combining government securities and an IAR swap has low capital requirements that can offer advantages over the purchase of similar short-dated CMO securities. Note, however, that this difference in capital requirements is justified by the lack of any principal risk in the IAR swaps.

Size and growth prospects

The IAR swap market has been expanding rapidly for the past two years, showing particularly fast growth through the first half of 1993. An estimated $100 billion to $150 billion in notional principal has been originated since 1990. It is unlikely that this expansion will slow markedly unless the yield curve flattens dramatically.

The market for IAR swaps to date is almost completely one-way in nature. Dealers are almost exclusively the fixed rate payers (buyers of the embedded options), and end-users are almost exclusively the fixed rate receivers (writers of the embedded options). Recently, however, a small interdealer market has developed and a modest number of transactions have been completed through interdealer brokers.

Although the market seems to be expanding and maturing, growth could ultimately be limited by dealers' inability to sell the embedded options they have purchased by paying the fixed rate. Dealers must manage their options risk and thus do not want a large net long or net short options position. Dealers may be forced to cease writing IAR swaps if they cannot use the purchased options to hedge other written option risk or if they cannot resell the long options exposures. The cost of hedging the residual exposures created by unmatched positions can become prohibitive, especially as the IAR swap market becomes more competitive and the cost of the embedded options begins to increase.[12] In fact, some dealers have shown reluctance to originate new transactions because the difficulties of hedging and evaluating the prospective profitability of these instruments become more critical as spreads narrow.[13]

Conclusions

IAR swaps have proved useful to both investors and dealers. Investors in this instrument can acquire a position that pays off if rates rise more slowly than predicted by the forward curve. Investors in the swaps have also earned enhanced yields comparable to those on mortgage bond securities while remaining exempt from the idiosyncratic portion of the prepayment risk embedded in mortgage securities. Through IAR swaps, investors have been able to earn short-dated mortgage-type yields for at least two

---

[12] If dealers were able to sell all of the IAR swaps' embedded options, they would not be forced to go to the Eurodollar futures market to hedge residual risk not offset within their portfolio of other options. Alternatively, if a two-way market for IAR swaps existed, dealers would be able to receive the fixed rate and create a natural hedge for those existing IAR swap positions where they are the fixed rate payer.

[13] The rating agencies have prohibited dealers from placing IAR swaps in their special-purpose AAA-rated swap subsidiaries. The agencies cite concerns that the one-way nature of the IAR swap market would make it more difficult to unwind such a swap book in a timely manner.

years, while many cash mortgage securities have prepaid. Dealers with large interest rate options books have found IAR swaps attractive as an alternative instrument for hedging the exposures arising from their over-the-counter options business. In other words, IAR swaps have created a natural offset for most dealers' net short positions in options, thereby helping dealers to meet the market's demand for interest rate options.

Most of the risks associated with IAR swaps are similar to those of other instruments. The IAR swap poses the same threat of negative cash flows as plain vanilla interest rate swaps or equity-index swaps, along with prepayment and reinvestment risks similar to those of mortgage securities. Nevertheless, while IAR swaps pose few unique risks for most market participants, significant problems may materialize in a portfolio with a high concentration of IAR swaps.

Certainly, model risk figures more prominently in IAR swaps than in other kinds of instruments. Pricing and hedging IAR swaps require highly technical interest rate models, and the absence of benchmark market prices and the instrument's relatively long life mean that pricing model inaccuracies may not become immediately apparent. A dealer who enters the market without strong technical expertise may encounter problems arising from mispricing and mishedging. Risk management systems in place for plain vanilla interest rate swaps and options may not be sufficient to handle the complexity of IAR swaps. A firm's internal risk control unit must be capable of accurately monitoring the trading desk's pricing and hedging models for IAR swaps. In sum, dealers who are active in the IAR swap market need considerable technical knowledge as well as strong risk management systems.

The variable maturity feature of IAR swaps requires that an institution's risk management system take proper account of longer term exposures embodied in these instruments. For example, excessive emphasis by management on short-term trading results may create incentives to enter into IAR swaps strictly for short-term yield enhancement or trading gains, without consideration of the long-term performance results of the instrument. Note, however, that this problem exists for all instruments with medium- to long-term option-like exposure, not only IAR swaps.

This problem highlights potential weaknesses in current methods of recognizing trading gains in accounting systems. For example, the fixed rate return of an IAR swap contains an option premium for future option-like liabilities or exposures. This feature leads one to ask how much of an IAR swap's yield premium should be incorporated in current income. From a broader perspective, the proliferation of IAR swaps and similarly complex financial transactions underscores the need for accounting and disclosure practices suited to such instruments.

Appendix: Reverse Index Amortizing Rate Swaps

Instrument structure
Anticipating a possible rise in short-term interest rates, investors are seeking to limit potential losses on their floating rate exposures. In response to this demand, dealers are currently marketing a variation of the IAR swap called the reverse index amortizing rate swap or RIAR swap. Like an IAR swap, an RIAR swap is an interest rate swap whose notional principal amortizes at a rate that varies with the level of market interest rates according to a predetermined schedule. In a typical RIAR swap, as in an IAR swap, an end-user receives the fixed rate while paying the dealer a floating rate. An RIAR swap's amortization schedule differs from that of an IAR swap, however, in calling for the notional principal to amortize more quickly as market interest rates rise. For example, if the floating rate index rises sufficiently, the swap could fully amortize at the end of the lockout period. Alternatively, if rates decrease, the predetermined structure of the RIAR swap could cause the swap to amortize more slowly or, in some cases, not at all.

The amortizing feature of an RIAR swap can be viewed as an implicit put option, giving the floating rate payer the right to "put" or reduce a floating rate liability if rates increase. For this right, the floating rate payer receives a somewhat lower fixed rate than would be paid on a plain vanilla interest rate swap.

At the present time a small number of U.S. securities firms and money center banks are developing this product. Only a handful of trades are believed to have taken place in the market to date.

RIAR swaps are being marketed to corporate end-users, banks, mutual funds, insurance companies, and other institutional investors.

Risks
The RIAR market is presently one-sided. To date, only dealers have written the embedded put option in the RIAR swap, and in their normal course of business, they are typically net sellers (writers) of options. Thus, for dealers with net short option positions, writing put options embedded in RIAR swaps may increase their overall portfolio's residual exposure and raise hedging costs.

Like IAR swaps, RIAR swaps involve no principal risk. The greatest risk to an investor would be the opportunity cost of holding an instrument paying a below-market rate of interest if rates were to remain stable.

Article 26

The Pricing and Hedging of Index Amortizing Rate Swaps

by Julia D. Fernald

Index amortizing rate (IAR) swaps have been popular yield enhancement instruments over the past few years.[1] The enhanced yields associated with these instruments result from premiums earned on options embedded in the swaps. Because these options depend on the path of interest rates, the pricing of IAR swaps requires a model of interest rate movements.[2]

This article presents a simple example of an interest rate model, outlines IAR swap pricing derived from the model, and develops a hedging strategy to offset the uncertain cash flows from the swap. Finally, the article discusses the complications that arise in more realistic pricing and hedging situations.

Interest rate model
In this example, we assume that one-year interest rates are well represented by a model with the binomial tree structure illustrated in the figure.[3] The tree is consistent with initial two- and three-year interest rates of 9.995 percent and 9.988 percent, respectively, if the probabilities of rates rising or falling equal one-half.[4]

Description of the swap
Although the interest rate tree has only two periods of uncertainty, the IAR swap in our example has three cash flow payments. If we assume an IAR swap with a one-year lockout period, the first cash flow at time 0 is based on an original notional amount of $100 and the current one-year rate. The two subsequent payments depend on the realization of the one-year rates at time 1 and time 2 and on the amortization schedule in Table 1.

---

[1] See Lisa Galaif, "Index Amortizing Rate Swaps," in this issue of the *Quarterly Review*.

[2] Models used to value path-dependent interest rate options must be free from arbitrage in the sense that they price fixed-income instruments consistently with the current term structure of interest rates. The models can be represented by interest rate trees or lattices that give possible outcomes of future short-term interest rates. These representations are used to calculate both the initial price of the IAR swap and the dynamic hedges that swap dealers would enter over time.

[3] Our example assumes that future short-term rates are determined by one factor. The example is consistent with one-year rates that are normally distributed with a constant annual volatility of 1.0 percentage point.

[4] The price of a two-period zero coupon bond with an interest rate of 9.995 percent equals the price of a two-year zero coupon bond derived from the tree:

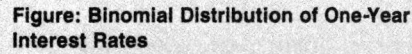

In the pricing and hedging of IAR swaps, the relevant probabilities are those that make the binomial tree consistent with the current term structure of interest rates.

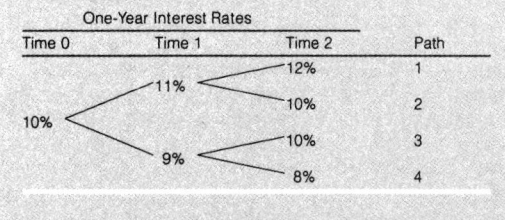

Figure: Binomial Distribution of One-Year Interest Rates

Because the swap's notional principal amortizes on the basis of the short rate, the swap cash flows at each period depend not only on the rate that period but also on the path of previous rates. Table 2 shows the four possible cash flow paths (from the perspective of the fixed rate payer) that arise from our interest rate model. In this example, F is the fixed rate paid on the IAR swap.

Pricing

As with any swap, the fixed rate on a IAR swap is determined such that the initial present value of the swap's cash flows is zero. The present value of the cash flows from an IAR swap is more difficult to calculate than the corresponding value for a plain vanilla swap, however, and depends on the assumed arbitrage-free interest rate model. In pricing our IAR swap, we find the fixed rate consistent with the predetermined amortization schedule, the assumed distribution of one-year interest rates, and our binomial representation of the model. The cash flows are functions of the fixed rate F, the current rate, and the path of previous rates. Because we have only four possible cash flow paths, we can solve explicitly for the fixed rate, F, that makes the average present value over these possible cash flow paths equal to zero. In this way, we obtain a fixed rate of 10.26 percent.[5]

In this example, with its virtually flat 10 percent term structure, the fixed rate on a plain vanilla swap is approximately 10 percent. The 26 basis point premium in the IAR swap fixed rate is the value of the embedded options that the fixed rate payer implicitly purchases.

Table 3 shows the fixed rate payer's cash flows over the four paths and the three time steps, given the 10.26 percent fixed rate. Notice that when the interest rate is 10 percent at time 2 (paths 2 and 3), the cash flows depend on the interest rate at time 1. This difference illustrates the path-dependent nature of the IAR swap.

[5] Let $R_{p,t}$ be the one-year interest rates and let $CF_{p,t}$ be the cash flows for the four possible paths, p, and the three time periods, t. We solve for the fixed rate that sets the present value of the cash flows, or

$$\frac{1}{4} * \sum_{p=1}^{4} \sum_{t=0}^{2} \frac{CF_{p,t}}{\prod_{q=0}^{t}(1+R_{p,q})}$$

equal to zero.

Hedging

Fixed rate payers (usually swap dealers) may wish to hedge their highly variable payments. For example, if rates rise in the first period, dealers receive $.663, but if rates fall, the dealer pays $.631. In the second period, dealers face a similarly variable outcome that depends on the path of interest rates. We show that if fixed rate payers hedge the uncertain cash flows every period, they will earn exactly the additional 26 basis points that they pay as option premium.

Although there are many ways to implement hedges, all methods involve calculating changes in the swap's value given small changes in the underlying interest rates. Because our interest rate model involves only one factor, we need only one instrument to hedge the swap. For simplicity of exposition, we choose to replicate the IAR swap's payoffs using forward contracts instead of the more typically used futures contracts. In our example, the forward rate implied by the initial term structure is 9.991 percent on one-year contracts maturing at time 1.

We choose the first hedge at time 0 to offset the two possible time 1 swap values. The time 1 swap values are composed of two elements: the actual cash flows paid or received on the swap and the expected value of the time 2 payments or receipts. The actual cash flows from the swap are the value of the time 0 payment (-$.263) at time 1 plus the time 1 amount (+$.663 in the up-state, or -$.631 in the

Table 1
Amortization Schedule

Interest Rate (Percent)	Notional Amortization (Percent)
12	0
11	10
10	20
9	50
8	100

Table 2
Fixed Rate Payer's Cash Flows from the IAR Swap

	Cash Flows		
Path	Time 0	Time 1	Time 2
1	$100*(10%-F)	$90*(11%-F)	$90*(12%-F)
2	100*(10%-F)	90*(11%-F)	72*(10%-F)
3	100*(10%-F)	50*(9%-F)	40*(10%-F)
4	100*(10%-F)	50*(9%-F)	0*(8%-F)

Table 3
Fixed Rate Payer's Cash Flows from the IAR Swap with a Fixed Rate of 10.26 Percent

	Cash Flows		
Path	Time 0	Time 1	Time 2
1	$-0.263	$0.663	$1.563
2	-0.263	0.663	-0.189
3	-0.263	-0.631	-0.105
4	-0.263	-0.631	0.0

down-state).[6] The expected remaining value of the swap is $.612 in the up-state, and -$.048 in the down-state.

If the dealer combines the $100 swap with -$97.5 of the forward contract, the portfolio's value will be equal to zero at time 1 whether rates rise to 11 percent or fall to 9 percent.[7] At time 1, the dealer follows the same type of calculation, keeping track of the time 2 values of the swap and the previous hedge. The new hedge amounts are -$87.0 if we are in the up-state or +$5.2 if we are in the down-state. The process of readjusting hedges through time is known as "dynamic hedging."

If we adopt these hedge amounts, the outcome from hedging the swap along each path offsets the payoffs from the swap along that path. Table 4 illustrates the calculations of the hedged swap's value along the first path. The hedged swap's value along the other three paths will also equal zero at time 2.

Another hedging method computes the change in the swap's value for changes in each forward rate. This "bucket" hedge method involves (1) the initial purchase of a series of forward contracts in amounts that offset the recomputed swap's value and (2) the dynamic adjustment of the hedge through purchases or sales of additional forward contracts in the future.[8] Because bucket hedging allows for nonparallel shifts in the yield curve, it implicitly assumes multiple sources of risk; it thus requires multiple hedging instruments. Bucket hedging is useful if interest rate dynamics are more complicated than the single factor model assumes.

Issues

In this example, the hedges perfectly offset the swap if any of the four modeled interest rate paths is realized. Although it is simplistic to assume that interest rates will follow one of these four paths, the example illustrates potential issues that can arise when valuing and hedging interest-rate-dependent derivatives. In particular, the pricing and hedging of any interest rate derivative security depend on decisions at several levels concerning:

- the interest rate model: How many factors are relevant? What type of process do they follow—for example, normal, lognormal?
- the parameters of the model: What are the volatilities? If the model includes more than one factor, what are the correlations?
- the implementation of the model: How small are the time steps? Is it a binomial or trinomial tree? How many simulations are used?

If assumptions about the model and the parameters of the model are incorrect, the hedging cannot offset realized gains and losses. In our example, hedging depends on the forward rates implied by our interest rate tree. If these rates are not realized, the cash flows from the hedges cannot perfectly offset the cash flows from the swap. These rates can be wrong because the short rate process is in fact not well represented by a single factor normal distribution with constant volatility. Valuing the swap using other interest rate models—for example, a two factor lognormal interest

---

[6] The total cash flow from the swap in the up-state is therefore $.372, which equals -$.263*(1.11) + $.663.

[7] The hedge amounts are essentially (the negative of) the derivative of the swap's value with respect to interest rates. In our example, the first hedge amount, $97.5, equals $.983 (the swap's value in the up-state) less $-.966 (the value in the down-state), divided by .02 (the difference in the interest rates).

[8] In our example, we would initially sell $80.1 of the forward contract maturing at time 1 and $19.1 of the contract maturing at time 2. If rates rise to 11 percent, we would sell $68.1 of the contracts maturing at time 2 at the new forward rate; if rates fall to 9 percent, we would buy $24.5 of the time 2 forward contracts.

Table 4
Payment Stream for the First Path

	Cash Flows				Future Value
	Time 0	Time 1	Time 2		
Swap at time 0	-.263	-.263(1.11)	-.263(1.11)(1.12)	=	-.327
Swap at time 1		.663	.663(1.12)	=	-.743
Swap at time 2			1.563	=	1.563
Hedge entered at time 0		-97.5(.11-.0999)	-97.5(.11-.0999)(1.12)	=	-1.102
Hedge entered after up-jump at time 1			-87.0(.12-.1099)	=	-.878
Value of the hedged swap at the end of time 2					0.0

rate model—can give a different fixed rate and different hedges.

Different assumptions about the parameter values also affect the fixed rate. In our example, if the volatility is 1.5 percentage points instead of 1.0, the fixed rate will increase from 10.26 percent to 10.60 percent. The differences across models and parameter values can be considerable, and careful judgment should be used when testing the sensitivity of the results to different assumptions.

The fixed rate and the subsequent hedging also depend on how the model (with its assumptions) is implemented. The goal in implementing the model is to approximate numerically a stochastic process. If we shorten the time steps, we will find a different fixed rate than we find with annual time steps. The appropriate time step for valuation is the one in which the fixed rates have converged on a value. In our example, the hedge ratios at time 1 are significantly different when the rates rise to 11 percent than they are when the rates fall to 9 percent. If we shorten the time steps and update the hedge ratios more often, the hedging will change more gradually than is illustrated by our example.

Actual models are more complex than our example at all levels: volatilities are not necessarily constant, the initial term structure is not conveniently flat, and models are implemented with higher frequencies. Adjustments need to be incorporated for nonparallel shifts in the yield curve because nonparallel shifts will affect the swap's value. Making errors at any of these levels will potentially result in a misvalued instrument.

Part Four

Monetary and Fiscal Policy

Central banks around the world pursue *monetary policy*—manipulating money and credit conditions in an effort to stabilize the financial system and achieve broad economic goals, such as full employment, sustainable economic growth, and the avoidance of inflation. Their pursuit of monetary policy must take place, however, within an environment of changing market conditions and changing government rules. These forces of change are particularly evident in the articles in this section of the book which address primarily the new monetary policy issues of the 1990s.

One of the most widely debated and important monetary policy issues of this decade is the question of *central bank independence*. Are central banks really free enough from government control to pursue those policies they believe are best for the economy and the financial markets? In many countries central banking activities are closely monitored and controlled or influenced by government and have little independent authority to act in the public interest. In a fascinating article by Patricia Pollard, economist with the St. Louis Federal Reserve Bank, we get a glimpse of a worldwide trend toward greater political independence for central banks, which many governments have pursued in hopes of subduing inflation and stabilizing their financial markets. Dr. Pollard reviews several recent studies and concludes that an independent central bank, by itself, does *not* guarantee improved economic performance for a nation. She believes that more studies are needed to see if variations in central bank powers might actually be associated with how well an economy performs in serving businesses and consumers.

Staying with this same theme of central bank independence, Dr. Carl E. Walsh, Visiting Scholar at the San Francisco Federal Reserve Bank, examines the statistical evidence in favor of having a more independent central bank. He finds only mixed evidence that having a more independent central bank really affects a nation's real economic performance. However, his review of recent studies suggests that greater political and governmental influence over the conduct of monetary policy appears to be associated with higher average inflation rates without apparent gains in real economic performance. Clearly, this is an important area which very much needs more detailed research.

Inside the United States the Federal Reserve System (the Fed) has enjoyed relative freedom from federal government control, largely because the members of its governing board are appointed to long terms of office and the Fed does not depend on the government for its income. Thus, the Federal Reserve has been able to shape its own policies and procedures with a significant degree of freedom. One of those policy procedures is *interest rate smoothing*—

acting daily in the financial markets to keep interest rates relatively stable and avoid too many sudden and sharp turns in monetary policy. Research Officer and Senior Economist William Roberds of the Federal Reserve Bank of Atlanta in his article, "What Hath the Fed Wrought? Interest Rate Smoothing in Theory and Practice" explains both why and how the Fed as central bank smooths out interest-rate movements and evaluates the possible consequences of this daily market activity. He finds that the Fed has a long history, from its beginnings in 1914, of attempting to smooth out the "bumps" in interest-rate movements and that recent research reaches mixed conclusions about the benefits and costs of interest-rate smoothing. Central bank smoothing *may* help to avoid some bank failures and reduce the incidence of financial panics, but it may also limit a central bank's ability to manage the economy successfully.

There is a worldwide trend today toward eliminating *reserve requirements* as a monetary policy tool due to their inflexibility and potentially uncontrollable impact. Indeed, the central banks of Australia, Canada, New Zealand, and Switzerland have recently eliminated reserve requirements on bank sources of funds and the United States seems to be gradually phasing out this potent credit-control weapon. Dr. Stuart E. Weiner of the Federal Reserve Bank of Kansas City, in an article entitled, "The Changing Role of Reserve Requirements in Monetary Policy," examines the reasons behind this trend. He finds that many leading central banks have turned away from attempts at controlling the money stock in favor of interest-rate targeting and reserve requirements seem to play a much different role when interest rates, not money, are the central bank's principal policy target. Reserve requirements can play a helpful role in stabilizing bank demand for reserves, but central banks must decide if this traditional monetary tool has shortcomings that are so serious that they offset its possible benefits.

This part of the book swings in its last section from monetary policy to *fiscal policy*—the taxing and spending activities of the government. In the first of three articles devoted to fiscal policy, entitled "The Federal Budget Deficit, Saving and Investment, and Growth," Research Officer Adrian W. Throop from the Federal Reserve Bank of San Francisco examines the possibly damaging effects of government budget deficits on the public's savings and investment activity. Dr. Throop begins by exploring the most popular belief regarding budget deficits and the economy—that government borrowing absorbs the private sector's savings and, thereby, reduces national investment, setting the stage for lower productivity and lower consumption by future generations. The author points out that not everyone agrees with this conventional view regarding the linkages between government budget deficits and the economy. However, he concludes that recent increases in U.S. federal budget deficits have been significant contributors to lower saving and investment rates and slower economic growth in the United States.

Andrew B. Abel, a Visiting Scholar at the Federal Reserve Bank of Philadelphia, also tackles the subject of federal budget deficits in his article "Can The Government Roll Over Its Debt Forever?" Examining the findings of recent research he concludes that much of the information we require to decide if the federal government's debt can be rolled over indefinitely is missing. However, there is at least some evidence that current U.S. taxing and spending policies are sustainable in the long run because the government's deficits tend to decline as the nation's debt-to-GNP ratio rises. Nevertheless, Dr. Abel observes that the United States cannot be complacent about its current budget deficits because the nation's debt-to-GNP ratio has been rising in recent years and this trend is likely to require increased taxes or a cut in government spending.

This section concludes with an article by economists E. J. Stevens and Diana Dumitru from the Federal Reserve Bank of Cleveland, entitled "Auctioning Treasury Securities." The authors explore in detail current U.S. Treasury auction techniques and conclude that these techniques contain both incentive and opportunity for private bidders to manipulate and "corner" the government securities market. They argue that the Treasury needs to give serious consideration to adopting *new* auction techniques. One potentially beneficial approach is to use a single-price auction in which all successful bidders pay the *same price* for their securities. Economists Stevens and Dumitru also recommend using recent advances in electronic communications technology to conduct Treasury auctions with all bidders for Treasury securities filing their bids simultaneously.

Article 27

Patricia S. Pollard

Patricia S. Pollard is an economist at the Federal Reserve Bank of St. Louis. Heather Deaton and Richard D. Taylor provided research assistance.

Central Bank Independence and Economic Performance

IN RECENT YEARS MANY countries have adopted or made progress toward adopting legislative proposals removing their central banks from government control, that is, making them independent. Between 1989 and 1991, New Zealand, Chile and Canada enacted legislation that increased the independence of their central banks. The 1992 Treaty on European Union (Maastricht Treaty) requires European Community (EC) members to give their central banks independence as part of establishing the European Monetary Union. As a result, EC countries that do not yet have strongly independent central banks have introduced legislation or announced their commitment to make their central banks more independent.[1] Furthermore, in recent months the governments of Brazil and Mexico have announced their intentions to introduce legislation to create more independent central banks.

In view of these developments, it might seem reasonable to conclude that unambiguous links had been established between economic performance and the degree of central bank independence. Interestingly, however, the two post–World War II star performers among the industrialized economies—Germany and Japan—have different levels of central bank independence. The German Bundesbank is viewed as one of the most independent central banks in the world, whereas the Bank of Japan is seen as more subject to government control. Thus the contrast between the movement to grant central banks more independence and widely different degrees of independence across the major economies raises several questions. Among these are: Why is the idea of an independent central bank popular? Are there economic benefits of having an independent central bank?

This paper examines empirical and theoretical studies of central bank independence to address these questions. Empirical researchers have devised measures of independence to focus on the relationship between central bank independence and a country's economic performance. Theoretical studies have modeled the strategic be-

---

[1] To meet the level of independence prescribed by the Maastricht Treaty, a central bank must be prohibited from taking instructions from the government. The term for central bank governors must be set at a minimum of five years, although it can be renewed. In addition, the central bank must be prohibited from purchasing debt instruments directly from the government (that is, in the primary market) and from providing credit facilities to the government. Both Denmark and the United Kingdom have reserved the right to decline membership in the European Monetary Union. Thus neither country has introduced legislation to ensure conformity of their central banks with the Maastricht provisions.

For a detailed analysis of the institutional status of the central banks of the EC countries, see the Committee of Governors of the Central Banks of the Member States of the European Economic Community (1993).

havior of monetary and fiscal policymakers to be able to compare an economy's performance when policymakers cooperate in setting policies with its performance when they do not cooperate.

The next section of this paper presents a survey and evaluation of empirical studies. Next, theoretical studies are presented and evaluated. The final section examines the extent to which these studies either explain the current movement toward greater central bank independence or highlight unresolved questions in this debate.

EMPIRICAL STUDIES: CENTRAL BANK INDEPENDENCE AND ECONOMIC PERFORMANCE

Inflation and Central Bank Independence

As a broad generalization, interest in central bank independence was motivated by the belief that, if a central bank was free of direct political pressure, it would achieve lower and more stable inflation.[2] Bade and Parkin (1985) conducted one of the first empirical studies of this link. The authors used data for 12 Organization for Economic Cooperation and Development (OECD) countries in the post-Bretton Woods era and measured the degree of central bank independence according to the extent of government influence over the finances and policies of the central bank.[3] The degree of financial influence on the central bank was determined by the government's ability to set salary levels for members of the governing board of the central bank, to control the central bank's budget and to allocate its profits. The degree of policy influence was determined by the government's ability to appoint the members of the central bank governing board, government representation on this board, and whether the government or the central bank was the final policy authority. Countries were given a rank of one through four in each category, with four being the highest level of central bank independence.

Bade and Parkin concluded that the degree of financial independence of the central bank was not a significant determinant of inflation in the post-Bretton Woods period. Policy independence, however, was seen as an important determinant of inflation because the two countries with the highest degree of policy independence (Germany and Switzerland) had inflation rates significantly below those of all other countries in the sample. They found no significant differences in inflation performance among countries with lower rankings of independence in the post-Bretton Woods era.

Alesina (1988) used the Bade and Parkin (1985) index but added the following four countries: Denmark, New Zealand, Norway and Spain. He found, as hypothesized, that there was generally an inverse relationship between average inflation rates and the level of central bank independence.

Grilli, Masciandaro and Tabellini (1991) created two indexes of central bank independence—one based on economic measures of independence (with a scale ranging from zero to eight), and the other based on political measures of independence (with a scale ranging from zero to seven).[4] The political factors were similar to those identified by Bade and Parkin. The economic factors considered were the ability of the government to determine the conditions under which it can borrow from the central bank and the monetary instruments under the control of the central bank. The data set comprised 18 OECD countries over the period 1950-89.[5] For the period as a whole, Grilli, Masciandaro and Tabellini found that economic independence was negatively related to inflation. Political independence also had a negative correlation with inflation, but the relationship was not statistically significant. Breaking the data into four decade-long subperiods, they found that neither measure of independence had a significant effect on inflation in the first two decades. In the 1970s both measures of independence were significant, whereas in the 1980s only the economic independence measure was significant.

Alesina and Summers (1993) calculated a measure of central bank independence by averaging the indexes created by Bade and Parkin,

---

[2]Buchanan and Wagner (1977) point out that even an independent central bank may not be immune from political pressures and thus exhibit an inflationary bias.

[3]The 12 OECD countries are Australia, Belgium, Canada, France, Germany, Italy, Japan, Netherlands, Sweden, Switzerland, United Kingdom, and United States.

[4]In both measures the scale is increasing in the level of independence.

[5]Grilli, Masciandaro and Tabellini add Austria, Denmark, Greece, New Zealand and Portugal to Bade and Parkin's group of countries and eliminate Sweden.

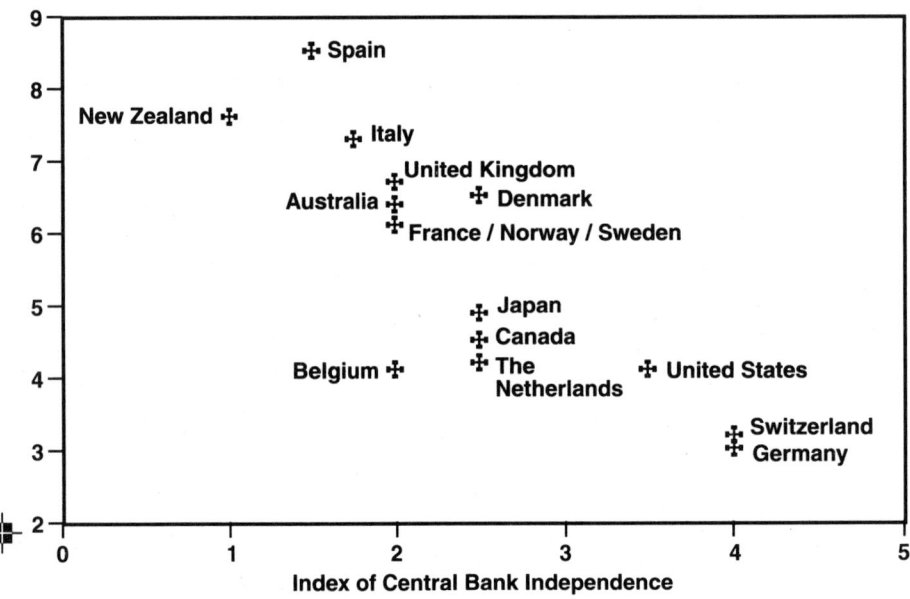

Figure 1
Average Inflation: 1955-1988

Source: Alesina and Summers (1993).

and Grilli, Masciandaro and Tabellini.[6] The countries included were the same as in Bade and Parkin with the addition of Denmark, New Zealand, Norway and Spain. The sample period was 1955-88.[7] As in the previous studies, they found a negative correlation between the level of central bank independence and the rate of inflation (figure 1). They also found that the more dependent a central bank was, the greater the variability in inflation (figure 2). This, they argued, was a result of a correlation between the level and variability of inflation.

Cukierman (1992) provided an extensive analysis of central bank independence and its relationship to inflation performance using data for 1950-89. Unlike previous studies, he used not only legal measures of central bank independence, but also practical measures of the level of independence. One such measure was the frequency of turnover of the central bank governors. Another measure of practical independence was based on answers from a questionnaire completed by qualified individuals at the central banks.[8] Cukierman's analysis is the most comprehensive to date, not only because it incorporates information about the actual level of independence a central bank enjoys in practice, but also because it includes a sample of 70 countries.[9] Cukierman concluded that "central

---

[6]See Bade and Parkin (1985) and Grilli, Masciandaro and Tabellini (1991).

[7]See Alesina (1988). Alesina and Summers report that the results of their study are the same if the data period is restricted to 1973-1988, the post-Bretton Woods era.

[8]The sample period for the questionnaire data was 1980-89.

[9]The questionnaire data were available for only 24 countries.

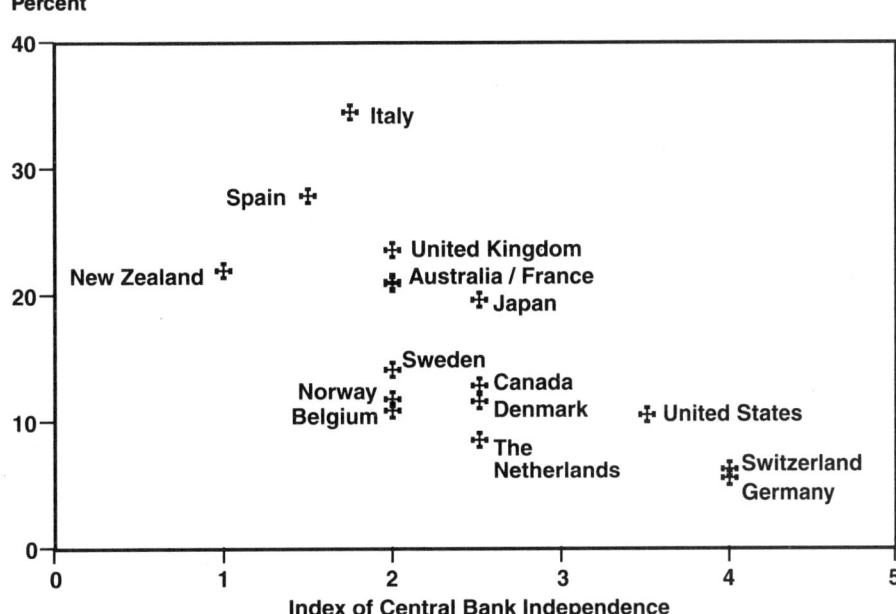

Figure 2
Variance of Inflation: 1955-1988

Source: Alesina and Summers (1993).

bank independence affects the rate of inflation in the expected direction."[10] This result was also found by Cukierman, Webb and Neyapti (1992).[11]

Central Bank Independence and the Real Economy

Although most of the empirical work focused on the relationship between central bank independence and the rate of inflation, some studies examined the link between independence and economic output. If an independent central bank can produce lower inflation than a dependent central bank, does this come at the cost of lower output? Conversely, are dependent central banks attempting to exploit a short-run Phillips Curve relationship, accepting higher inflation in order to achieve higher output?

Grilli, Masciandaro and Tabellini (1991) found no systematic effect of central bank independence (using either of their two indicators) on the growth rate of real output. Alesina and

---

[10]Cukierman did not actually use the rate of inflation, but the rate of depreciation of the real value of money, defined by the following formula:

$$d_t = \frac{\pi_t}{1 + \pi_t},$$

where π_t is the inflation rate in period t. The use of d, as noted by Cukierman, moderates the effects of hyperinflation on the results.

[11]Capie, Mills and Wood (1992) also studied the link between inflation and central bank independence. Their data set consisted of 12 countries, with the data series beginning between 1871 and 1916 and ending in 1987. Central banks were classified as either dependent or independent according to the extent of their control over monetary policy. The authors examined the relationship between the status of the central bank and inflation over the entire sample period and four subsample periods—pre-World War I, the Interwar Years, Bretton Woods and post-Bretton Woods. Periods of hyperinflation, however, were excluded from the data. In all sample periods, the countries with independent central banks were in the low inflation group. Nevertheless, some of the dependent central banks were also in this group. The authors concluded that independence may be a sufficient condition for low inflation but not a necessary one.

Figure 3
Average Real GNP Growth: 1955-1987

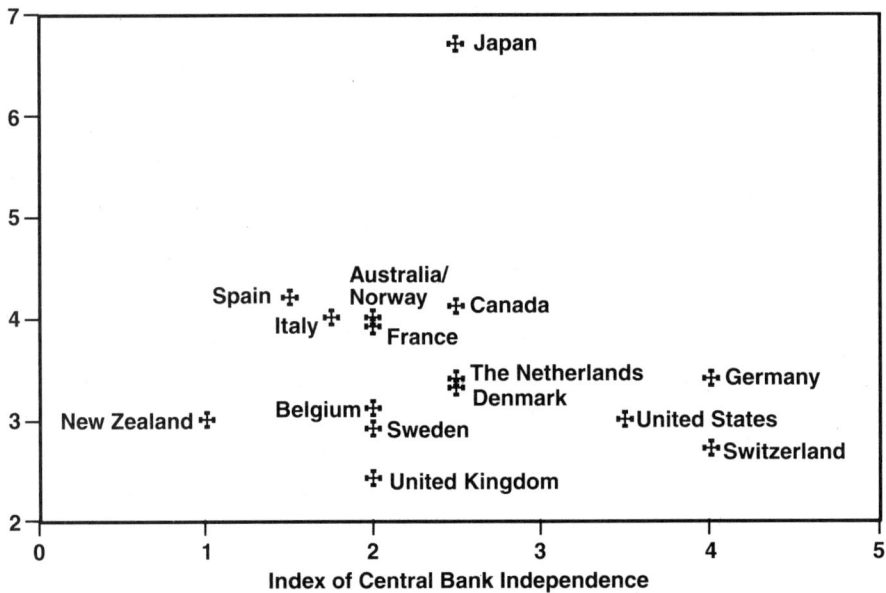

Source: Alesina and Summers (1993).

Summers (1993) likewise found no correlation between average economic growth or the variability of growth and the level of central bank independence (figures 3 and 4).[12]

De Long and Summers (1992) looked at the relationship between central bank independence and output per worker while trying to eliminate differences between countries that were due solely to convergence effects.[13] To do this, they examined the growth rate of real gross domestic product (GDP) per worker during 1955–90, controlling for the level of GDP per worker in 1955.[14] This procedure showed a positive relationship between central bank independence and economic growth.[15] More precisely, they found that holding constant the 1955 level of real output per worker, a unit increase in their index of central bank independence was associated with a 0.4 percentage point increase in growth per year.[16]

In contrast, Cukierman, Kalaitzidakis, Summers and Webb (1993) found that output growth in industrialized countries was unrelated to central bank independence even after controlling for structural factors that might influence growth. The factors they considered were the initial level

---

[12] The results are the same if per capita gross national product (GNP) is used rather than GNP.

[13] Standard neoclassical growth models suggest that growth rates of economies tend to converge over time. Thus given two countries, the one with the lower per capita output will have a higher growth rate than the other until their levels of real output per capita converge.

[14] GDP per worker levels are based on the Summers and Heston (1991) estimates, which use purchasing power parity conversions.

[15] This study does not take into account that the degree of independence of the central bank of New Zealand changed dramatically in 1989. Furthermore, all of the studies, with the exception of Alesina (1988), do not take into account that there was an institutional change in the structure of the Bank of Italy in 1981 that increased its independence. The latter change, however, was not as substantial as the former.

[16] De Long and Summers regress the average growth rate of GDP per worker over the period 1955-90 on GDP per worker in 1955 and the central bank independence index.

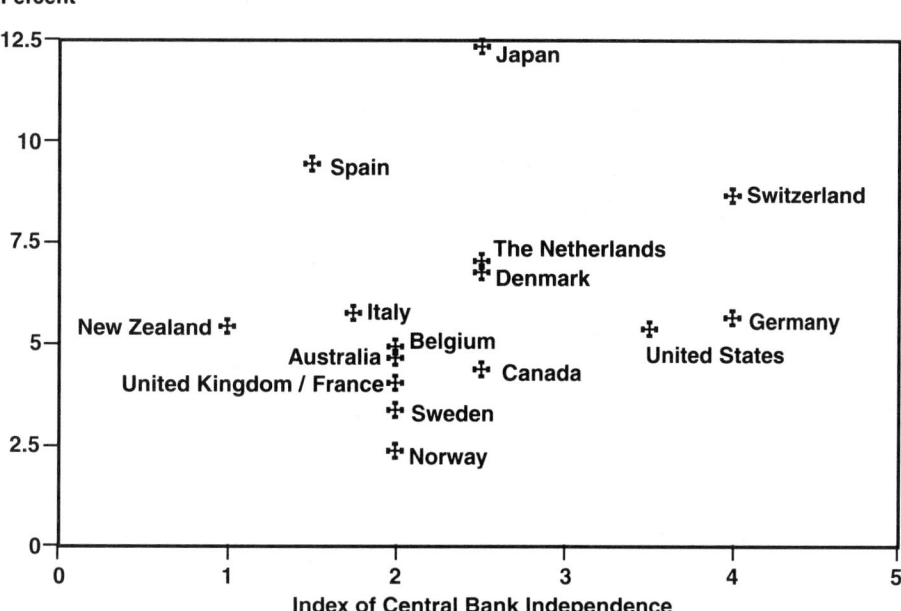

Figure 4
Variance of Real GNP Growth: 1955-1987

Source: Alesina and Summers (1993).

of a country's GDP, its initial enrollment rates for primary and secondary education, and changes in its terms of trade. The authors did find, however, using the turnover rate of central bank governors as a proxy for independence, that central bank independence did have a positive effect on growth in developing countries.

The difference in the results for industrialized countries versus developing countries, they argue, may imply that "dependence on political authorities is bad for growth only when the level of independence is sufficiently high."[17] Central bank independence is higher in all the industrialized countries than in most of the developing countries.

Central Bank Independence and Fiscal Deficits

Another area of empirical study has been the relationship between central bank independence and fiscal deficits. The motivation for these studies is the belief that independent central banks should be better able to resist government efforts to have them monetize deficits. Thus governments realizing that there may be some limit on their ability to issue bonds continuously to finance deficits may decide to limit deficit spending.

Parkin (1987) investigated this question for the same 12 countries as Bade and Parkin for the period 1955–83.[18] He found that there was some evidence of a negative relationship between central bank independence and the long-run behavior of government deficits as a percent of gross national product (GNP). The deficits of Switzerland and Germany, the countries with the highest levels of central bank independence, had long-run equilibrium values near zero with little variance. However, other countries, notably France, that had low levels of central bank in-

---

[17]See Cukierman, Kalaitzidakis, Summers and Webb (1993), p. 42.

[18]See Bade and Parkin (1985).

dependence also had small long-run deficits as a percent of GNP.

Masciandaro and Tabellini (1988) looked at fiscal deficits as a percent of GDP in Australia, Canada, Japan, New Zealand and the United States during the period 1970-85.[19] They found that New Zealand, which had the lowest level of central bank independence of the five countries during this period, had the highest fiscal deficit as a percent of GDP. The United States, however, with the highest level of central bank independence among this group of countries, had a deficit/GDP ratio similar to those of the other countries.

Grilli, Masciandaro and Tabellini (1991) found that there was generally a negative correlation between the deficit/GNP ratio and the degree of central bank independence. However, if political factors, as well as central bank independence, were included in their regression, the latter variable was insignificant.[20] Thus they conclude that an independent monetary authority apparently does not discourage the government from running fiscal deficits.

A further examination of the relationship between fiscal deficits and central bank independence, which is consistent with the work done by Alesina and Summers and De Long and Summers, is presented here.[21] Using the same index of central bank independence and the same 16 countries as these previous papers, there is some evidence of a negative correlation between average deficits as a percent of GDP and central bank independence for the period 1973-89, as shown in figure 5.[22] The degree of independence, however, is not a statistically significant (at $\alpha = .05$) determinant of the deficit/GDP ratio. The variability of deficits as a percent of GDP is also negatively correlated with central bank independence (figure 6) and this relationship is statistically significant.

EVALUATION OF THE EMPIRICAL STUDIES

At first glance, these studies seem to indicate that a country that wants to lower its inflation rate and do so without hurting growth should create an independent central bank. Such a central bank apparently could also help reduce fiscal deficits and increase output. These benefits would explain the recent popularity of independent central banks. Thus Grilli, Masciandaro and Tabellini commented:

> Having an independent central bank is almost like having a free lunch; there are benefits but no apparent costs in terms of macroeconomic performance.[23]

Alesina and Summers (1993) went a step further in concluding their findings: "Most obviously they suggest the economic performance merits of central bank independence."[24]

A more careful analysis of these studies, however, indicates weaknesses that highlight the need for further evidence before one should believe that creating an independent central bank will improve a country's economic performance. The following four weaknesses are considered: 1) the difficulty in measuring central bank independence; 2) the possibility of a spurious relationship between independence and economic performance; 3) the possible endogeneity of central bank independence; and 4) the inclusion of the fixed exchange rate period in the sample data of some of the studies.

The measures of central bank independence used in empirical studies have been determined by establishing a set of factors thought to be relevant for independence and then analyzing central bank charters and laws for compliance with these factors. With the exception of the in-

---

[19] The deficits are as a percent of GNP for Japan.

[20] These political factors include the frequency of government changes, significant changes in the government and the percent of governments in a given period supported by a single majority party.

[21] See Alesina and Summers (1993) and De Long and Summers (1992).

[22] The 1989 ending date was chosen because of the change in the status of the Bank of New Zealand, which occurred in 1989. All data are from the International Monetary Fund, *International Financial Statistics*.

[23] See Grilli, Masciandaro and Tabellini (1991), p. 375.

[24] See Alesina and Summers (1993), p. 159. Even the press has picked up the banner of central bank independence. A recent headline in *The Washington Post* proclaimed: "More Independence Means Lower Inflation, Studies Show." See Berry (1993).

Figure 5
Average Deficit as a Percent of GDP: 1973-1989

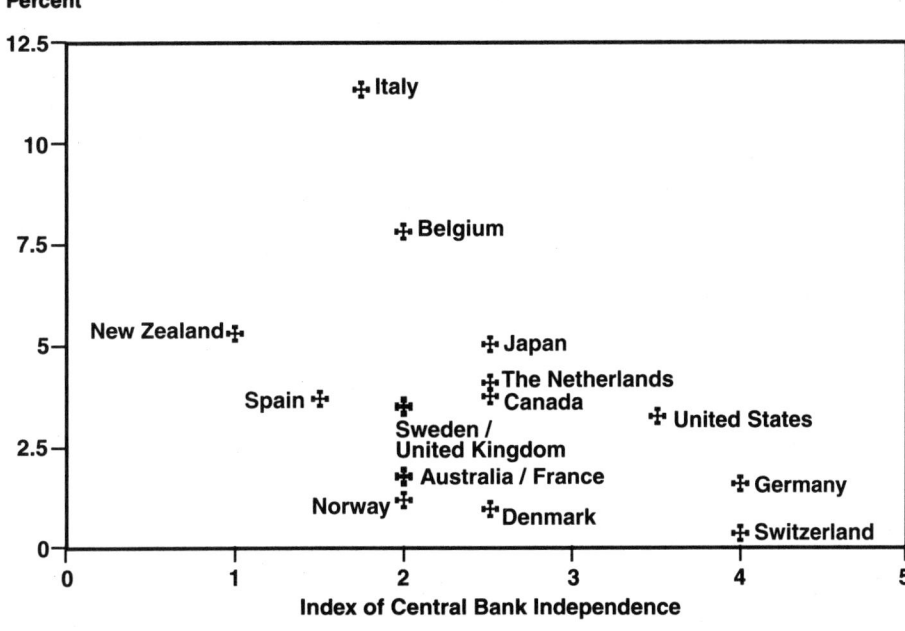

Figure 6
Variance of Deficit as a Percent of GDP: 1973-1989

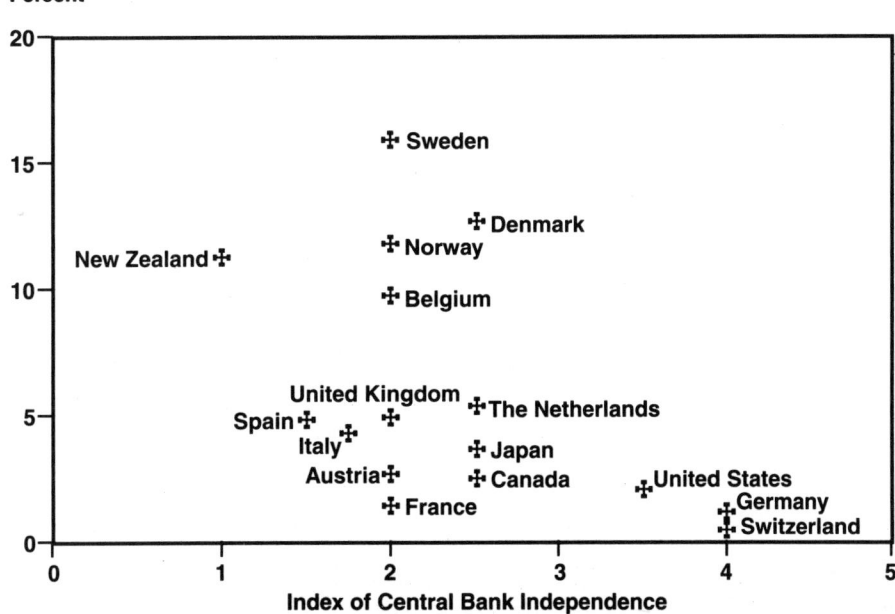

dex created by Cukierman, all of the indexes of independence apply equal weight to each factor. For instance, the Grilli, Masciandaro and Tabellini index based on political measures of independence gives a country one point if no one on the central bank board is appointed by the government and one point if the policy formulated by the central bank does not require approval by the government. Although the latter certainly places a greater constraint on the actions of the central bank than the former, the two are treated the same empirically.

Another concern is that the studies are based on a legal measure of independence that may not reflect a bank's *de facto* level of independence. If there is a difference between legal and practical independence, studies based on the former type of measures may provide misleading results. Cukierman (1992), in an attempt to address this possibility, uses central bankers' responses to a questionnaire to determine the actual degree of independence in the 1980s. He finds that the correlation between the legal index and this practical index of independence is 0.33 for developed countries, 0.06 for developing countries and 0.04 overall.[25] This finding indicates, as Cukierman notes, that a legal index of independence is not useful for studying developing countries. It also indicates that a legal index may be a weak measure of actual independence for the developed countries.

There also may be bias in the factors selected to measure independence. For example, Grilli, Masciandaro and Tabellini include: "statutory requirements that central bank pursues monetary stability amongst its goals" in their index.[26] Likewise, a central bank is more independent under Cukierman's system if price stability is its only objective than if price stability is one of a number of objectives or not an objective at all. Using the goal of price stability as a measure of central bank independence may result in a bias between the measure of independence and the inflation rate.

The problems in developing precise measures of central bank independence are less important, however, if there is a consensus in ranking central banks within broad levels of independence. Table 1 lists 16 OECD countries along with their relative rankings as given by Alesina, Cukierman, and Alesina and Summers.[27] All agree that Switzerland and Germany have the most independent central banks of the countries studied. There are, however, a few countries which are ranked quite differently by the authors. For example, Japan has the second lowest level of independence of all 16 countries, according to Cukierman, whereas Alesina, and Alesina and Summers give it a much higher level of independence.

This discrepancy over the degree of independence of the Bank of Japan is not due solely to differences in factors considered in measuring independence. The index used by Alesina is based on the criteria of independence created by Bade and Parkin (1985). The index used by Alesina and Summers is constructed by averaging the indexes created by Alesina, and Grilli, Masciandaro and Tabellini. Bade and Parkin claim that the Bank of Japan is independent from the government in formulating and implementing monetary policy, and Grilli, Masciandaro and Tabellini claim that there are no provisions for handling policy conflicts between the Bank of Japan and the government. In contrast, Cukierman claims that the Bank of Japan and the government formulate policy jointly and

Table 1
Comparison of Relative Rankings of Central Bank Independence

	Alesina	Alesina and Summers	Cukierman
Australia	14	8	7
Belgium	5	8	14
Canada	5	4	5
Denmark	5	4	4
France	5	8	9
Germany	1	1	2
Italy	13	14	12
Japan	3	4	15
Netherlands	5	4	6
New Zealand	14	16	10
Norway	5	8	16
Spain	14	15	13
Sweden	5	8	10
Switzerland	1	1	1
United Kingdom	5	8	7
United States	3	3	3

---

[25] The correlations are based on the weighted indexes. Giving each factor related to independence an equal weight in the indexes results in a correlation of 0.01 for developed countries and 0.00 for developing countries.

[26] See Grilli, Masciandaro and Tabellini (1991), p. 368.

[27] The measure of independence developed by Cukierman is based on more factors than the measure used by Alesina, and Alesina and Summers. Thus Cukierman's rankings are more delineated than the other two.

further notes that in the case of a policy conflict, the executive branch of the government has final authority.[28]

Since most of the empirical studies consider only central bank independence as a determinant of economic performance, it is possible that if other factors are accounted for, these results could be spurious. Grilli, Masciandaro and Tabellini attempt to account for other factors that could affect the rate of inflation by including political variables. They find that after accounting for political factors, central bank independence was still negatively related to inflation in the countries studied over the period 1950-89. The incorporation of political variables is a step in the right direction, but other factors also should be considered. As noted by Cukierman, "monetary policy is generally sensitive to shocks to government revenues and expenditures, employment, and the balance of payments."[29] The types of shocks that a country experienced over the sample period and the reaction of the central bank to these shocks can affect its economic performance. A study by Johnson and Siklos (1992) found that the reactions of central banks (as measured by changes in interest rates) to shocks to unemployment, inflation and world interest rates were not closely related to standard measures of central bank independence.

Empirical use of these indexes may be problematic if central bank independence is an endogenous variable in the sense that countries with a commitment to price stability may have a greater propensity for independent central banks. If this is true, the mere establishment of an independent bank without a commitment to price stability will not bring inflation benefits to a country. In fact, a public aversion to inflation predates the establishment of many independent central banks. This was true for the creation of the Bundesbank and more recently with respect to central banks in Chile and New Zealand. New Zealand had one of the highest inflation rates of all industrialized countries in the 1980s. In 1989 legislation was passed to increase the independence of its central bank substantially. This change is often credited with bringing inflation down to near zero. Though the legislation certainly formalized the country's commitment to price stability, New Zealand had succeeded in reducing its inflation rate from nearly 16 percent in 1987 to 6 percent before the creation of an independent central bank.

In theory, the degree of independence of a central bank should not be a determinant of a country's inflation performance under a fixed exchange rate system because monetary policy cannot be set exogenously.[30] During the Bretton-Woods era, it is not clear that any central bank (with the possible exception of the U.S. Federal Reserve) could be considered independent in the sense of an ability to pursue an independent monetary policy.[31] Thus the empirical finding of a negative relationship between independence and inflation when the sample period extends over both the Bretton Woods and post-Bretton Woods eras may indicate a flaw in these studies. To assess the effect of central bank independence on inflation, the data used in these studies could be divided into two periods. If no evidence of a relationship between independence and inflation is found in the Bretton Woods period, this would strengthen the underlying argument of these studies that central bank independence is a primary determinant of a country's inflation performance.[32] If, however, evidence is found of a relationship between central bank independence and inflation in the Bretton Woods period, this would conflict with theory and could indicate that the empirical findings are spurious.

THEORETICAL MODELS OF FISCAL AND MONETARY POLICY INTERACTIONS

In contrast to the empirical studies, the theoretical studies of central bank independence and economic performance concentrate on the conflicts that can arise when monetary and fiscal policy are delegated to independent institutions. In this literature an independent central bank is one that does not cooperate with the fiscal au-

---

[28] Aufricht (1961) reproduces the Bank of Japan charter and subsequent changes in its governing regulations, which support the conclusion reached by Cukierman.

[29] See Cukierman (1992), p. 438.

[30] See McCallum (1989), pp. 285-88, for an explanation of the limitations on monetary policy under a fixed exchange rate system.

[31] Indeed, the primary argument in favor of a flexible exchange rate system was that such a system would permit individual countries to pursue independent monetary policies. See, for example, Friedman (1953) and Johnson (1969).

[32] This is Grilli, Masciandaro and Tabellini's finding (1991).

thorities in setting economic policy. A dependent central bank is one that cooperates with the fiscal authority in setting policy.

In examining the theoretical implications of central bank independence, this paper focuses on models in which the policymaking process is decentralized.[33] The basic framework of these models is as follows. The government controls fiscal policy, and the central bank controls monetary policy. Both parties set goals for the economy (generally inflation and output targets) and assign priority to these goals. The goals and priorities may differ across the policymakers. Each institution uses the instruments available to it in an attempt to reach its goals. In most models the central bank controls the growth rate of the monetary base and the government controls fiscal spending. There is an underlying model of the economy that indicates how fiscal and monetary policy will affect the relevant economic variables. All of the models assume that there are no stochastic shocks to the economy.

The government and the central bank can either cooperate in implementing their policies or choose not to cooperate. If they do not cooperate, they either can set policies simultaneously, or one party can set its policies first and the other then adopts its policies in reaction to these.

Consider Andersen and Schneider's (1986) simple model in which the government and the central bank establish targets for inflation and output.[34] The further the actual level of output and rate of inflation are from their respective targets, the more disutility each authority receives. Thus, using the following equations, each authority can be modeled as setting policy to minimize its respective loss functions:[35]

(1) $L_f = a_f(y-y_f)^2 + b_f(\pi-\pi_f)^2 \qquad a_f \geq b_f$

(2) $L_m = a_m(y-y_m)^2 + b_m(\pi-\pi_m)^2 \qquad b_m \geq a_m$

(3) $\pi_f \geq \pi_m, \; y_f \geq y_m$

where:

L_f is the fiscal authority's loss function
L_m is the monetary authority's loss function
y is output
π is inflation
y_f is the fiscal authority's output target
y_m is the monetary authority's output target
π_f is the fiscal authority's inflation target
π_m is the monetary authority's inflation target
a is the weight placed on the output target
b is the weight placed on the inflation target

Andersen and Schneider compare the economic outcomes under cooperation vs. noncooperation given three different models of the economy. The first model is Keynesian in nature. This is a short-run model with price sluggishness so that even anticipated changes in policy affect aggregate demand. The level of output and the rate of inflation prevailing in the economy are affected by both fiscal and monetary policies, which can be shown in a simple reduced form model with the following equations:
where f is the fiscal policy instrument and m is the monetary policy instrument.[36]

(4) $y = \gamma_0 f + \gamma_1 m \qquad 0 < \gamma_1 < \gamma_0$

(5) $\pi = \theta_0 f + \theta_1 m \qquad 0 < \theta_0 < \theta_1$

In the second model, which Andersen and Schneider refer to as Keynesian-New Classical, anticipated monetary policy is neutral; it can affect only inflation. Thus in a world of certainty, equation (4) becomes the following:

(6) $y = \gamma_0 f$

In the third model, the economy is New Classical in nature, characterized by perfect price flexibility and rational expectations. Anticipated policy, both fiscal and monetary, affects only inflation, not output. The economy is modeled by the following equations:

(7) $\pi = \eta_0 f + \eta_1 m$

---

[33] There have been studies concentrating solely on monetary policy that have shown that better economic outcomes result from the policymaker placing a greater weight on inflation than society as a whole. Rogoff (1985) argues that these results indicate the economic benefits of central bank independence. These studies ignore the interaction of fiscal and monetary policy in determining economic outcomes and thus are not discussed here.

[34] Generally it is assumed that the government places more weight on meeting its output target than its inflation target, whereas the opposite holds for the central bank. Further-

more, it is generally assumed that the inflation and output targets set by the government are greater than or equal to the targets set by the central bank.

[35] The quadratic nature of the loss functions, which is standard in the macroeconomic game theory literature, implies that deviations on either side of the targets produce an equal loss to the policymaker.

[36] The restrictions in equations (4) and (5) imply that fiscal policy has a greater (lesser) effect on output (inflation) than does monetary policy.

$(8)\ y = \pi - \pi^e$

$(9)\ \pi - \pi^e = \eta_0(f - f^e) + \eta_1(m - m^e),$

where y now refers to output relative to capacity and the superscript e refers to the expectation of the variable. Output can be increased above capacity only through unanticipated inflation, and unanticipated inflation can occur only through unanticipated changes in fiscal policy, monetary policy or both.

The relevant issue for policy is the size of the loss to each policymaker under cooperation and noncooperation. Cooperation in the determination of monetary and fiscal policies is modeled by the government and the central bank choosing the policy variables (f and m) to minimize a weighted average of their loss functions:

$(10)\ \min_{f,m} L_c = \rho L_f + (1-\rho) L_m \qquad 0 \leq \rho \leq 1$

$\qquad = \rho [a_f(y - y_f)^2 + b_f(\pi - \pi_f)^2]$
$\qquad + (1-\rho)[a_m(y - y_m)^2 + b_m(\pi - \pi_m)^2],$

where the weight placed on each loss function is determined by the relative bargaining strength of the two parties. Solving this minimization problem yields the equilibrium values for output and inflation, which can be substituted into the loss functions for the government, equation (1), and the central bank, equation (2), to determine the loss to each.

As noted above, noncooperation can be modeled in two ways. In the first, fiscal and monetary policies are chosen simultaneously; that is, the government selects a level of spending to minimize its loss function, equation (1), taking as given the actions of the central bank. At the same time, the central bank chooses the growth rate of the monetary base to minimize its loss function, equation (2), taking as given the actions of the government. This structure is referred to as a Nash game and the resulting equilibrium is called a Nash equilibrium. In a Nash equilibrium, neither authority, taking the actions of the other as given, can decrease its loss by unilaterally changing its policy.

In the second model of noncooperation, one policy is set before the other is determined. This process is known as a Stackelberg game, and the policymaker who moves first is known as the Stackelberg leader, whereas the other policymaker is known as the Stackelberg follower. The leader chooses its policy, and the follower sets its policy in reaction. Furthermore, the leader, in choosing its policy, knows how the follower will react.

Although the equilibrium level of output and the rate of inflation vary depending on which model of the economy is used, in all three models the cooperative solution is Pareto superior to the noncooperative solution. This result is invariant to the structure of noncooperation—Nash or Stackelberg. The performance of the economy is better under cooperation in the sense that the losses to the government and the central bank are each lower than they are under noncooperation. This result holds even if the government and the central bank each place the same weight on meeting their inflation targets relative to their output targets ($a_f = a_m$ and $b_f = b_m$) but maintain different targets.

Andersen and Schneider summarize these results by noting the following:

> When we have two independent authorities who act in their own selfish interest, then we quite often observe a conflict over the "right" policy direction. This result should be kept in mind when quite often the argument is put forward that an independent monetary authority should be created. ... Two independent policymakers do not automatically guarantee a policy outcome which is preferred to other outcomes under different institutional solutions.[37]

Alesina and Tabellini (1987) show that adding one more target to the loss functions of the government and the central bank also does not change the nature of the results. Noncooperation is once again suboptimal.

Adding a time dimension to the model also does not change the basic result that cooperation can improve the outcome from the perspective of both policymakers. Pindyck (1976) presents one of the first dynamic models analyzing the strategic interaction of monetary and fiscal policy. He argues that the

> separation of monetary and fiscal control may considerably limit the ability of *either* authority to stabilize the economy, particularly when the conflict over objectives is at all significant.[38]

Petit (1989) examines the issue of policy coordination in a continuous time model. The

---

[37]See Andersen and Schneider (1986), p. 188.

[38]See Pindyck (1976), p. 239.

government sets targets for output and inflation, giving higher priority to output. The central bank targets inflation and the level of international reserves, giving higher priority to inflation.[39] As is standard, the government sets the level of public expenditures to minimize its loss function, whereas the central bank sets the growth of the monetary base to minimize its loss function.

In this model, policies are set at the beginning and are unchanged over the period considered. Once again, cooperation is Pareto superior to the Nash and the Stackelberg equilibriums. Furthermore, cooperation in this dynamic system leads to a decrease in the variability of the targets (particularly prices and international reserves), and raises the speed of adjustment of the system. The latter indicates that, given a shock to the system, the economy will return more quickly to its long-run values of output and inflation if the government and the central bank are coordinating their policies. Thus Petit concludes that policymakers should coordinate their policies.[40]

Other studies concentrate on the interaction of the government and the central bank in financing fiscal deficits where the deficit must be financed through bonds, seignorage or both.[41] Under the assumption that there is some limit on the ability of a government to continually issue bonds to finance its deficit, the need for inflation revenues becomes important.[42] Sargent and Wallace (1981) conducted the seminal research on this question and showed that if the government embarks on a path of unsustainable deficits, the central bank might eventually be forced to inflate to fund the deficits. If the public realizes that the government debt is on such a path, it will expect inflation to increase, which may cause inflation to increase well before the debt limit has been reached.[43] This outcome is a result of the government being able to set its policies and the central bank having to react to those policies (a Stackelberg game).[44]

In general, a conflict over the public debt can arise at any time when the government and the central bank are allowed to adopt independent policies. Tabellini (1986) develops a dynamic model in which the central bank sets targets for changes in the monetary base and the stock of outstanding public debt while the government sets targets for the fiscal deficit net of interest payments and the stock of outstanding public debt. The target value of public debt is the same for both authorities. In choosing the level of the monetary base and the fiscal deficits, the two authorities are constrained by the government's dynamic budget constraint.[45] The stock of public debt as a proportion of income is considered too high by both the fiscal and monetary authorities. In the noncooperative setting, however, each authority ignores the benefit to the other of its own actions to reduce the level of debt. In the cooperative setting these benefits are internalized, resulting in a lower level of debt.

Tabellini (1987) and Loewy (1988) provide two more examples of models examining the conflict between central banks and governments over fiscal policy. Both show that such a conflict can lead to an increase in government debt. As noted by Blackburn and Christensen (1989), a conflict will always arise between a central bank whose goal is to maintain price stability and a government whose objective is to increase output and is pursuing this goal by running a stream of large deficits. Such a macroeconomic program is infeasible; one party will have to revise its strategy (give in). The conflict creates

---

[39]The target for international reserves reflects a balance of payments objective.

[40]Hughes Hallett and Petit (1990) also model the interaction of fiscal and monetary policy in a dynamic setting, reaching this same conclusion.

[41]Seignorage is the revenue received from the creation of money. It occurs because base money costs only a fraction of its face value to produce.

[42]As the public debt grows, there may be increasing concern among bondholders that the government will be unable to repay the bonds.

[43]As Sargent and Wallace note, if money demand today depends on inflationary expectations, then the price level today is a function of not only the current money supply, but also expectations of the future levels of the money supply.

[44]The concern that undisciplined fiscal policies could result in inflation was recognized by the EC in drafting the Treaty on European Monetary Union. In the regulations concerning the proposed European Central Bank, the bank is prohibited from financing fiscal deficits of the member countries.

As pointed out by Sargent and Wallace, and expounded on by Darby (1984), the need for the central bank to monetize government debt through an inflationary policy is based on the assumption that the rate of growth of the real economy is less than the real rate of interest.

[45]Note that monetary base and fiscal deficits in this model are both instruments and targets.

problems for the economy because of the uncertainty over the future course of policy: the public can expect higher inflation or higher taxes, depending on which policymaker gives in.[46]

EVALUATION OF THE THEORETICAL LITERATURE

The theoretical studies indicate that noncoordination of fiscal and monetary policies will result in a suboptimal economic performance from the perspective of both the government and the central bank. Policy targets are more closely met when coordination occurs. Thus an independent central bank is not conducive to achieving better policy outcomes.

However, the theoretical work, like the empirical studies, has its weaknesses. One criticism is that the models are too simplistic. Neither the preference structures of the two authorities, nor the models of the economy, are completely specified. Furthermore, most of the models operate in a world of certainty. Policy, however, is not made in a world of certainty. Extrinsic uncertainty—shocks to the economy—can drive a wedge between the implementation of policy and its outcome. Intrinsic uncertainty—lack of knowledge of the preferences of a policymaker—is incorporated only in Tabellini and Loewy's models.[47] As these two models illustrate, adding uncertainty can increase the policy conflict between an independent central bank and fiscal authority.

In addition to assuming certainty, the models also omit one important player in these policy games—the public. Public perception of the credibility of a macroeconomic program is important to its results because the public can limit the ability of policymakers to take advantage of an inflation/output tradeoff. If an independent central bank can increase the public perception of the credibility of policy, this in turn should produce better economic results.[48]

Another deficiency of this literature is its failure to address the feasibility of the policymakers' goals. The output goals set by the government, for example, may not be sustainable without accelerating inflation. Tax and expenditures plans, which lead to a stream of deficits, may also raise questions about the sustainability of fiscal policy. In this environment, an independent central bank could be useful if its credible commitment to price stability forced the government to evaluate the sustainability of its policy goals. In contrast, centralization of policies might reduce the long-run economic performance of a country when the government's focus is short-run performance.

CENTRAL BANK INDEPENDENCE AND THE ECONOMY—WHAT DO WE KNOW?

This paper began with two questions: Why is the idea of an independent central bank as popular as it is? Are there economic benefits to be gained from having an independent central bank? Unfortunately, the empirical and theoretical studies surveyed do not provide clear answers. The empirical studies find that there is a negative correlation between central bank independence and long-run average inflation. They also show a negative correlation between independence and long-run average government deficits as a percent of GDP. In general, they find no evidence of a positive correlation between output growth and central bank independence. These results all point in the same direction yet do not provide unequivocal evidence that an independent central bank will lower inflation and government deficits and raise a country's output.

In sum, these empirical studies provide evidence of a negative correlation between central bank independence and inflation and central bank independence and fiscal deficits, but they do not provide evidence of causality. Countries with an aversion to inflation may formalize this aversion through the creation of an independent central bank. If this is true, it is the inflation aversion, not the independence of the central bank, that is the primary causal factor behind the low inflation result. The empirical measures themselves are biased toward the finding that

---

[46] A government may adopt a strategy of running deficits, through decreasing taxes, to force future governments to cut expenditures. Under this strategy, the government would prefer an independent central bank, which will refuse to monetize the deficits and thereby increase the likelihood that fiscal spending will be reduced. See Sargent (1985) for a discussion of this type of strategy.

[47] See Tabellini (1987) and Loewy (1988). In Tabellini's model the government is initially unaware of the preferences of the central bank. In Loewy's model both parties are initially unaware of the preferences of the other.

[48] This issue has been studied in the literature that focuses only on monetary policy. See Blackburn and Christensen (1989) for a survey of this literature.

independence promotes low inflation. This is because the measures place much weight on legal requirements that a central bank pursue price stability and place this goal above all others. Cukierman is explicit in stating that his measure of independence:

> is not the independence to do anything that the central bank pleases. It is rather the ability of the bank to stick to the price stability objective even at the cost of other short-term real objectives.[49]

Given such a definition of independence, it is not surprising that independence is equated with low inflation.

Theoretical studies indicate that an independent central bank can increase policy conflicts with the government whenever the preferences of the two differ and, in so doing, worsen the economic performance of a country. These studies, however, do not provide overwhelming support for the idea that countries should place monetary policy in the hands of the executive or legislative branches of government. The simple structure of these models ignores some factors that affect the outcome of policy decisions—for example, the role of the public and the overall credibility of policy. Central bank independence may enhance credibility and thus the overall effectiveness of a policy program.

In sum then, in the empirical studies, emphasis on price stability and freedom to pursue this goal are primary determinants of independence. In the theoretical studies independence is equated with noncooperation between the fiscal and monetary authorities in policy implementation. These different definitions of independence may partly explain the different results. Furthermore, countries that may be classified as independent using the empirical definition may be classified as dependent using the theoretical definition. New Zealand is one such example. The 1989 Reserve Bank of New Zealand Act made price stability the *only* goal of the central bank, and the central bank is free to adopt policies to achieve that goal. Thus according to the empirical definition of independence, the 1989 act created an independent central bank in New Zealand. The central bank's inflation target, however, is established by the government for a multi-year period. The governor of the central bank signs an agreement pledging the bank to adopt policies to meet this target. Such cooperation between the monetary and fiscal policymakers is consistent with a dependent central bank in the theoretical models.

Altogether these studies indicate that we are far from fully understanding the role of central bank independence in producing favorable economic outcomes.

REFERENCES

Alesina, Alberto. "Macroeconomics and Politics," in Stanley Fischer, ed. *NBER Macroeconomics Annual* (MIT Press, 1988), pp. 13–52.

_____, and Lawrence H. Summers. "Central Bank Independence and Macroeconomic Performance: Some Comparative Evidence," *Journal of Money, Credit and Banking* (May 1993), pp. 151–62.

_____, and Guido Tabellini. "Rules and Discretion with Noncoordinated Monetary and Fiscal Policies," *Economic Inquiry* (October 1987), pp. 619–30.

Andersen, Torben M., and Friedrich Schneider. "Coordination of Fiscal and Monetary Policy Under Different Institutional Arrangements," *European Journal of Political Economy* (February 1986), pp. 169–91.

Aufricht, Hans. *Central Banking Legislation* (International Monetary Fund, 1961).

Bade, Robert, and Michael Parkin. "Central Bank Laws and Monetary Policy," unpublished manuscript, University of Western Ontario, 1985.

Berry, John M. "More Independence Means Lower Inflation, Studies Show," *The Washington Post* (February 17, 1993).

Blackburn, Keith, and Michael Christensen. "Monetary Policy and Policy Credibility: Theories and Evidence," *Journal of Economic Literature* (March 1989), pp. 1–45.

Buchanan, James M., and Richard E. Wagner. *Democracy in Deficit* (Academic Press, 1977).

Capie, Forrest H., Terence C. Mills, and Geoffrey E. Wood. "Central Bank Dependence and Inflation Performance: An Exploratory Data Analysis," Centre for the Study of Monetary History, City University Business School, Discussion Paper No. 34 (March 1992).

Committee of Governors of the Central Banks of the Member States of the European Economic Community. *Annual Report 1992* (April 1993).

Cukierman, Alex. *Central Bank Strategy, Credibility, and Independence: Theory and Evidence* (MIT Press, 1992).

_____, Steven B. Webb, and Bilin Neyapti. "Measuring the Independence of Central Banks and Its Effect on Policy Outcomes," *The World Bank Economic Review* (September 1992), pp. 353–98.

_____, Pantelis Kalaitzidakis, Lawrence H. Summers, and Steven B. Webb. "Central Bank Independence, Growth, Investment, and Real Rate," *Carnegie-Rochester Conference Series on Public Policy* (autumn 1993).

Darby, Michael R. "Some Pleasant Monetarist Arithmetic," Federal Reserve Bank of Minneapolis *Quarterly Review* (spring 1984), pp. 15–20.

De Long, J. Bradford, and Lawrence H. Summers. "Macroeconomic Policy and Long-Run Growth," Federal Reserve Bank of Kansas City, *Economic Review* (fourth quarter 1992), pp. 5–30.

---

[49]See Cukierman (1992), p. 370.

Friedman, Milton. "The Case for Flexible Exchange Rates," in Milton Friedman, ed. *Essays in Positive Economics* (University of Chicago Press, 1953), pp. 157–203.

Grilli, Vittorio, Donato Masciandaro, and Guido Tabellini. "Political and Monetary Institutions and Public Financial Policies in the Industrial Countries," *Economic Policy 13* (October 1991), pp. 341–92.

Hughes Hallett, Andrew and Maria Luisa Petit. "Cohabitation or Forced Marriage? A Study of the Costs of Failing to Coordinate Fiscal and Monetary Policies," *Weltwirtschaftliches Archiv* (1990), pp. 662–89.

Johnson, David R., and Pierre L. Siklos. "Empirical Evidence on the Independence of Central Banks," unpublished manuscript, Wilfrid Laurier University (March 1992).

Johnson, Harry G. "The Case for Flexible Exchange Rates, 1969," this *Review* (June 1969), pp. 12–24.

Loewy, Michael B. "Reaganomics and Reputation Revisited," *Economic Inquiry* (April 1988), pp. 253–63.

Masciandaro, Donato and Guido Tabellini. "Monetary Regimes and Fiscal Deficits: A Comparative Analysis," in H. Cheng, ed. *Monetary Policy in the Pacific Basin Countries* (Kluwer Academic Publishers, 1988), pp. 125–52.

McCallum, Bennett T. *Monetary Economics: Theory and Policy* (MacMillan, 1989).

Parkin, Michael. "Domestic Monetary Institutions and Deficits," in J. M. Buchanan et al., eds. *Deficits* (Basil Blackwell, 1987), pp. 310–37.

Petit, Maria Luisa. "Fiscal and Monetary Policy Co-ordination: A Differential Game Approach," *Journal of Applied Econometrics* (April-June 1989), pp. 161–79.

Pindyck, Robert S. "The Cost of Conflicting Objectives in Policy Formulation," *Annals of Economic and Social Measurement* (May 1976), pp. 239–48.

Rogoff, Kenneth. "The Optimal Degree of Commitment to an Intermediate Monetary Target," *Quarterly Journal of Economics* (November 1985), pp. 1169–90.

Sargent, Thomas J. "Reaganomics and Credibility," in Alberto Ando et al., eds., *Monetary Policy in Our Times* (MIT Press, 1985), pp. 235–52.

Sargent, Thomas J., and Neil Wallace. "Some Unpleasant Monetarist Arithmetic," Federal Reserve Bank of Minneapolis, *Quarterly Review* (fall 1981), pp. 1–17.

Summers, Robert, and Alan Heston. "The Penn World Table (Mark 5): An Expanded Set of International Comparisons, 1950–88," *Quarterly Journal of Economics* (May 1991), pp. 327–68.

Tabellini, Guido. "Money, Debt and Deficits in a Dynamic Game," *Journal of Economic Dynamics and Control* (July 1986), pp. 427–42.

_____. "Central Bank Reputation and the Monetization of Deficits: The 1981 Italian Monetary Reform," *Economic Inquiry* (April 1987), pp. 185–200.

Article 28

Is There a Cost to Having an Independent Central Bank?

In recent years, many economists have argued that average inflation can be kept low if central banks are insulated from political pressures. Politically independent central banks, it is argued, will be less likely to give in to pressures to adopt expansionary monetary policies for political purposes, and, therefore, will be able to deliver lower average inflation. Indeed, using a variety of measures of independence, a number of researchers have documented empirically the association between greater central bank independence and lower average inflation (for a survey, see Cukierman 1992).

But are there costs associated with keeping inflation down? This *Weekly Letter* examines recent evidence on the relationship between measures of real economic performance, such as output growth, and measures of central bank independence. The evidence suggests that central bank independence, while associated with low inflation, is not associated with either slower of more volatile economic growth. Moreover, given that low inflation helps to reduce arbitrary wealth transfers and economic uncertainty, an independent central bank is likely to enhance economic welfare.

Independence and the conduct of monetary policy

The usual reason cited to explain the correlation between independent central banks and lower average inflation is that independent central banks are often viewed as more concerned with achieving and maintaining low inflation than politicians are. Thus, independent central banks are similar to other systems of "checks and balances" in a democratic society: An independent central bank would tend to offset a bias towards excessive inflation that is commonly thought to characterize monetary policy that is not guided by a specific mandate or rule on inflation. While society benefits from lower average inflation as a result, it also gets a less activist monetary policy. By placing greater weight on its inflation goals, the central bank might be willing to tolerate greater fluctuations in real economic activity and unemployment.

A recent study of 16 major industrial economies by Alesina and Summers (1993) attempts to determine if central bank independence is associated with either slower real growth or greater economic fluctuations. Perhaps somewhat surprisingly, they find that the degree of central bank independence is not related to average real GDP growth or average unemployment, nor to measures of the volatility of economic growth or unemployment, nor to the average level of real interest rates. These are important findings, since they would seem to indicate that central bank independence yields lower and less volatile inflation at no cost in terms of slower average real growth, higher average unemployment, or increased economic fluctuations.

Before drawing very strong policy conclusions from this work, however, it is important to determine whether these findings hold for a larger set of countries. And since economists have disagreed over how to measure central bank independence, it is also of interest to determine if these results still hold when using different indexes to measure central bank independence.

What is central bank independence?

Most research has focused on two dimensions of central bank independence. One, usually called political independence, represents the degree to which a country's central bank has policy objectives that are insulated from political pressures to expand aggregate demand rapidly. Political independence is influenced by institutional structure, such as the process for appointing the bank's policymaking board, and the existence of explicit policy goals, such as price stability. For example, a central bank with government representatives and political appointees with short terms of office on its policymaking committee would be classified as having a low degree of independence.

The second dimension of independence, called economic independence, is the degree to which the central bank is free to use its policy instruments to pursue its objectives. In some countries, the central bank must finance government deficits; such a central bank lacks economic independence, since it cannot control the extent to which government deficits are monetized.

Alesina and Summers employ as their measure of central bank independence an index that is an average of measures of political and economic independence. Among the 16 countries examined, Germany and Switzerland are ranked as having the most independent central banks, with New Zealand having the least (prior to the 1989 reform of the Reserve Bank of New Zealand). The U.S. is ranked just below Germany and Switzerland.

Formal institutional independence may bear no relationship to the actual degree of independence enjoyed by a central bank. For example, Cukierman, Webb, and Neypati (1992) constructed a measure of independence based on the legal description of the bank's structure and a measure based on surveys of experts in each country who were asked to assess the independence the central bank had *in practice*. The analysis covered 24 countries and found no correlation. That is, a central bank ranked as highly independent by one measure was no more likely to be highly ranked than lowly ranked on the other index (see Walsh 1993).

The Bank of Japan (BOJ) provides an interesting case in point. The BOJ is legally subordinate to the Ministry of Finance. For this reason, Cukierman, Webb, and Neypati (CWN) rank it as having little formal independence. In fact, they rank it below even the pre-reform Reserve Bank of New Zealand, the Bank of Italy and the Bank of Spain. In contrast, Alesina and Summers rank the BOJ as having a degree of independence slightly above the average in their sample, because, over the past 20 years, it has operated much like the most independent central banks in keeping inflation at low levels. Part of the explanation may lie in the connection found by Cukierman, Edwards, and Tabellini (1992) between inflation and political instability. Countries with unstable political cultures, with frequent changes in office by competing political parties, are more likely to generate pressures on the central bank to follow inflationary policies. Until the elections of 1993, Japan had been governed by a single party for nearly 40 years. Cargill and Hutchison (1990) argue that, with the LDP party holding a monopoly on power, it was unnecessary to exploit the government's control over the Bank of Japan to engage in expansionary policies. It will be interesting to see if more competition for electoral control also leads to greater political pressure on the Bank of Japan.

Independence and economic activity
Converting a description of a central bank's institutional and policymaking structure into an index of independence of necessity involves judgment calls. Therefore it is useful to see if measures of central bank independence other than the one employed by Alesina and Summers display any relationship to average real growth or measures of economic fluctuations. To investigate this, I used the CWN index of legal independence which covers 68 countries, compared to the 16 analyzed by Alesina and Summers. Data on real per capita GDP were obtained from the Penn World Table (Summers and Heston 1991). Focusing on the period from 1971 to 1985 yielded a sample of 60 countries for which both the CWN index and real per capita GDP data were available.

To explore the effects of using an alternative measure of central bank independence the average growth rate of real per capita GDP and its standard deviation (a measure of its volatility) can be compared to the CWN index of independence for the same countries used by Alesina and Summers. Such an analysis shows a slight negative relationship between central bank independence and average GDP growth. However, this is the result of one data point—Japan— which had the highest average growth rate over this period and has the least independent central bank according to CWN. If Japan is dropped from the sample, or if the BOJ is reclassified according to Alesina and Summers' ranking, any relationship between growth and central bank independence disappears.

Using the CWN index of central bank independence in place of the Alesina-Summers measure, therefore, provides some further evidence in support of their finding that, for the industrialized countries, the degree of central bank independence is unrelated to average real economic growth or its fluctuations. This result, however, is based on a small group of countries. Since the CWN index is available for a large number of countries, one can examine the robustness of the finding when the number of countries in the sample is greatly expanded. Figure 1 shows the average growth rate of real per capita GDP and its standard deviation for 60 countries for 1971 to 1985.

Figure 1 shows no apparent relationship between central bank independence and either average income growth or its volatility. More formal statistical analysis is consistent with the absence of

Figure 1
GDP Growth and its Standard Deviation 1971–1985: CWN-Based Sample

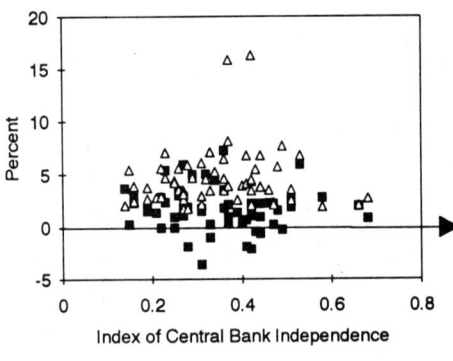

any relationship. This holds even if the two outliers with extreme output fluctuations (Nicaragua and Uganda) are excluded.

Conclusions

Using an alternative measure of central bank independence and examining a larger sample of countries serves to confirm the findings of Alesina and Summers: There appears to be no association between a country's real economic performance, as measured by average growth or its volatility, and the degree of political and economic independence enjoyed by its central bank. Many researchers, however, have documented a negative association between average inflation and central bank independence. While both the degree of independence granted the central bank and the average inflation rate reflect fundamental attitudes of the population, countries that insulate their central banks from direct political pressure do not seem to suffer adverse effects on real incomes.

Inflation imposes significant costs on an economy, particularly by causing arbitrary wealth redistributions and heightened economic uncertainty. These costs clearly lower the level of real income and overall economic welfare, and there is some evidence that inflation may even lower long-term average real growth (see Motley 1993).

Consequently, a policy of price stability is seen by many as the most important contribution monetary policy can make to ensuring desirable real economic performance. While there certainly may be important transitional costs to eliminating existing inflation, greater political control over the conduct of monetary policy seems to result in higher average rates of inflation with no apparent gain in average real economic performance.

Carl E. Walsh
Visiting Scholar, FRBSF
Professor of Economics, U.C. Santa Cruz

References

Alesina, A., and L. Summers. 1993. "Central Bank Independence and Macroeconomic Performance." *Journal of Money, Credit and Banking,* 25 (May) pp. 151–162.

Cargill, T.F., and M. Hutchison. 1990. "Monetary Policy and Political Economy: the Federal Reserve and the Bank of Japan." In *The Political Economy of American Monetary Policy,* ed. T. Mayer, pp. 165–180. Cambridge University Press.

Cukierman, A. 1992. *Central Bank Strategy, Credibility and Independence.* Cambridge: MIT Press.

_____, S. Edwards, and G. Tabellini. 1993. "Seigniorage and Political Instability." *American Economic Review* 82, pp. 537–555.

_____, S. Webb, and B. Neypati. 1992. "The Measurement of Central Bank Independence and its Effect on Policy Outcomes." *The World Bank Economic Review* 6, pp. 353–398.

Motley, B. 1993. "Growth and Inflation: A Cross-Country Study." Federal Reserve Bank of San Francisco Working Paper 93-11.

Summers, R., and A. Heston. 1991. "The Penn World Tables (Mark 5): An Expanded Set of International Comparisons, 1950–1988." *Quarterly Journal of Economics* 106 (May) pp. 327–368.

Walsh, C.E. 1993. "Central Bank Strategy, Credibility and Independence: A Review Essay." *Journal of Monetary Economics* 32 (October).

What Hath the Fed Wrought? Interest Rate Smoothing in Theory and Practice

William Roberds

The study of monetary policy has traditionally been hobbled by a yawning gap between theory and practice. Research economists who study monetary policy are usually concerned with the behavior of one or more aggregate measures of money—M1, M2, and so forth. Participants in financial markets, on the other hand, view monetary policy as primarily affecting interest rates, especially at the short end of the term structure. Financial market press and wire accounts of monetary policy emphasize its role in reducing short-term interest rate fluctuations. This aspect of monetary policy, often referred to as interest rate "smoothing," has traditionally been either ignored or criticized by academic economists. Despite being unpopular in academic circles, interest rate smoothing is nonetheless practiced to a greater or lesser extent by the monetary authorities of every major industrialized nation and has been practiced by the Federal Reserve System since its inception.[1]

The continued and widespread use of interest rate smoothing as a proximate goal for monetary policy poses a number of questions for economic research. Three of the most important questions are as follows. The first and most obvious question is, Why smooth interest rates in the first place, in spite of all academic advice to the contrary? Second, What are the long-term consequences of interest rate smoothing for the economy? And the third question is, Provided that interest rate smoothing is a desirable objective, to what extent should interest rate smoothing take precedence over other goals of monetary policy?

These questions are difficult ones, but they are obviously crucial to the management of the nation's monetary policy. They remain by and large unanswered. Still, researchers have made a considerable amount of progress on these questions in recent years. The following discussion reviews some

The author is a research officer and senior economist in the macropolicy section of the Atlanta Fed's research department.

of the most important contributions by economists to the understanding of these complex issues. Because so much of the discussion of interest rate smoothing involves historical comparisons, it is appropriate to begin with a brief history of the Federal Reserve System's approaches to open market policy, with particular emphasis on the impact of Fed policy on short-term fluctuations in interest rates.

Interest Rate Smoothing and Federal Reserve Policy: Historical Summary[2]

For the purposes of this article, it is assumed that the principal instrument of Federal Reserve policy has been and will continue to be a short-term interest rate such as the federal funds rate.[3] The term policy "instrument" refers to the Federal Reserve System's practice of attempting to influence some economic variable, such as the fed funds rate, in an attempt to achieve its policy goals. The Federal Reserve's use of the fed funds rate as a policy instrument is well known and without controversy. What has been less well understood by academic economists, until recently, is the extent to which Fed policies have traditionally worked to smooth fluctuations in short-term rates. In the 1980s, however, a number of studies pointed out that 1914, the year the Federal Reserve System was founded, represents something of a watershed in the financial history of the United States, if not the world.[4] A number of changes in the patterns of financial market data are evident after that point. Chief among these are the disappearance of seasonal fluctuations in most short-term interest rates, an increase in seasonal fluctuations in the money supply, and the general increase in the tendency of rates to persist at or near their current levels over time.

How many of the changes in financial markets after 1914 can be attributed to the policies of the Fed and how many are owing to other circumstances is a matter of continuing debate. It is undeniable, however, that Fed policies did substantially contribute to changes in U.S. and world financial markets. A plausible explanation for the impact of the Fed's monetary policies is clearly laid out by Marvin Goodfriend (1988), expanding on the earlier analysis of Milton Friedman and Anna J. Schwartz (1963). In the early years of its existence, the Fed found itself in a historically unique position because of its statutory role as a public agency charged with managing the nation's money supply and also because a large domestic stock of gold reserves had built up following the outbreak of World War I in Europe. The fact that the United States was on the gold standard at the time meant that monetary policy actions had to be backed by a sufficient gold reserve to maintain the gold standard. Such reserves were readily available to the United States as the warring European nations abandoned the gold standard and started using their own gold reserves to pay for their military operations. Also contributing to the efficacy of the Fed's actions was its statutory role as a stabilizing influence on the banking system rather than as a profit-maximizing entity. Fed officials had a greater degree of latitude in their attempts to stabilize financial markets than "central banks" had enjoyed before 1914, when policy-making was often constrained by the need to safeguard the banks' (private) shareholders' profits or by an insufficient gold reserve.[5]

In the 1920s the primary focus of the Fed's monetary policy changed from the discount window to open market operations, where it has remained ever since.[6] The historical record suggests that this structural change in monetary policy did not result in any lessening of the Fed's taste for interest rate smoothing. There was little need for the Fed to smooth interest rates during the years immediately following the banking crisis of 1933, as rates on short-term government securities remained at extremely low levels. From April 1942 until March 1951, Federal Reserve open market policy was very tightly constrained by the need to finance wartime expenditures. Over this period, interest rates on short-term government securities were "pegged" at levels agreed to by the Treasury Department.

With the signing of the Treasury–Federal Reserve Accord in March 1951 the Fed regained the ability to initiate monetary policy. The data records of the 1950s and 1960s again suggest that interest rate smoothing continued to be an important goal of monetary policy. In the meantime, the development of the Federal Funds Market led to an ever greater amount of emphasis being placed on the fed funds rate as a measure of credit market conditions. By the late 1960s movements in the fed funds rate were frequently mentioned in the minutes of the Federal Open Market Committee (FOMC). As open market operations were increasingly concentrated in the fed funds market, stabilization of day-to-day movements in the funds rate became an important short-term goal of open market policy. In the mid-1970s relatively narrow ranges for the funds rate were given in the FOMC directive. Over the latter part of the 1970s the width of the "intermeeting" (between FOMC meetings) range for the fed funds rate shrank from around 1 percentage point to as little as

1/4 percentage point. As emphasized by Ann-Marie Meulendyke (1990), this extreme concern with short-term fluctuations in the funds rate developed gradually over time, not as a result of an active decision to target the funds rate tightly.

The period from October 1979 through October 1982 is officially known as the "nonborrowed reserves-targeting" (NBR) period and unofficially as "the Fed's monetarist experiment." During this time, nonborrowed reserves officially replaced the fed funds rate as the short-run target for open market operations. Whether this move was monetarist or not, its effect was to allow much more variation in the fed funds rate than had occurred under the funds rate-targeting regime. The variability of reserves during the NBR-targeting period did not change much from the funds rate-targeting period, confounding some predictions that loosening the peg on fed funds would reduce the average magnitude of fluctuations in bank reserves. (See Charts 1A and 1B and 2A and 2B.) The continued volatility in reserves during the NBR period reflects at least in part the turbulent economic conditions in that era. However, at least some portion of the fluctuations in reserves during the NBR period can be attributed to the continued use of the funds rate as an operating target. A recent study by Timothy Cook (1989) found that despite the nominal adoption of NBR targeting, two-thirds of the variation in the funds rate during the October 1979 through October 1982 period can be attributed to direct policy actions on the part of the Fed; that is, these movements in the funds rate were not necessary to meet the reserves target. If this estimate is even approximately correct, then the distinction between the open market policies in the NBR and fed funds rate-targeting periods is perhaps best characterized as quantitative rather than qualitative.

The borrowed-reserve operating procedure that has been in place since October 1982 has been seen by many academic observers and financial market participants as a retreat toward the funds rate-targeting procedure of the 1970s. Although the current operating procedure incorporates some important reforms, it is difficult to find fault with this generalization. Comparing the time series data on the fed funds rate and bank reserves since 1982 (Chart 3) with the data record of the 1976-82 period (Charts 1 and 2) shows that the current operating procedure falls somewhere between the two earlier operating procedures in terms of the variability of interest rates. In particular, Chart 3A indicates that except for an occasional well-publicized miss, the funds rate has tended to move within fairly close bounds since October 1982, particularly since 1986.

Why Smooth Interest Rates?

In discussing the desirability of interest rate smoothing, it is necessary to specify carefully the horizon over which the relevant interest rate is to be smoothed. There is widespread (though not universal) agreement among economists that a monetary authority cannot successfully influence the real or inflation-adjusted rate of interest over the long run.[7] In other words, according to the mainstream view, the Fed does not have the option of simply pegging the interest rate at some level deemed to be desirable. At the other extreme, most economists would agree that it is feasible for the Fed to exercise considerable influence over at least nominal interest rates on a day-to-day or week-to-week basis. During the late 1970s, for example, short-term movements in the fed funds rate were virtually eliminated by Fed interventions. Consequently, the debate over the "short-run" smoothing of interest rates is centered to some extent on what should be designated as the short run.

The Fed's very strict smoothing of day-to-day movements in the funds rate in the late 1970s generated an unprecedented amount of attention to Fed operating procedures by the economics profession, much of it critical in tone. The logical basis for a good deal of this criticism was laid in an article by William Poole (1970). Analyzing open market operations from an informational perspective, Poole showed that strict targeting of interest rates, even in the very short run, would result in what economists call an "identification" problem. That is, strict targeting of interest rates necessarily entails some loss of information. This loss of information occurs because successful open market operations require some knowledge of the banking industry's demand schedule for reserves: specifically, what quantity of reserves would be demanded at various rates of interest. By keeping interest rates constant, even over some short interval, some knowledge of banks' demand schedule will necessarily be forgone. Thus, to smooth interest rates effectively, some variation in interest rates is desirable, even in the short run. In everyday terms, Poole's argument would say that it is easier to steer a car by making a series of small probes and corrections than to keep the same vehicle headed arrow-straight into the great unknown.

Poole's theoretical observations were borne out in practice. In the late 1970s very narrow targeting of the funds rate in the short run led to a general hesitancy to move the funds target. Moves in the funds target were generally anticipated by financial markets and were

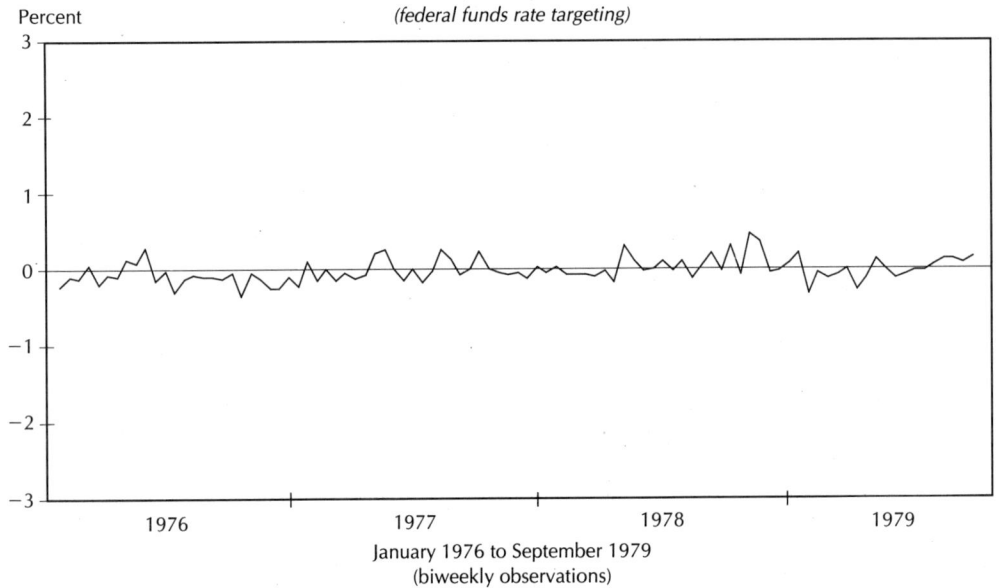

Chart 1A
Variability of Fed Funds Rate
(federal funds rate targeting)

January 1976 to September 1979
(biweekly observations)

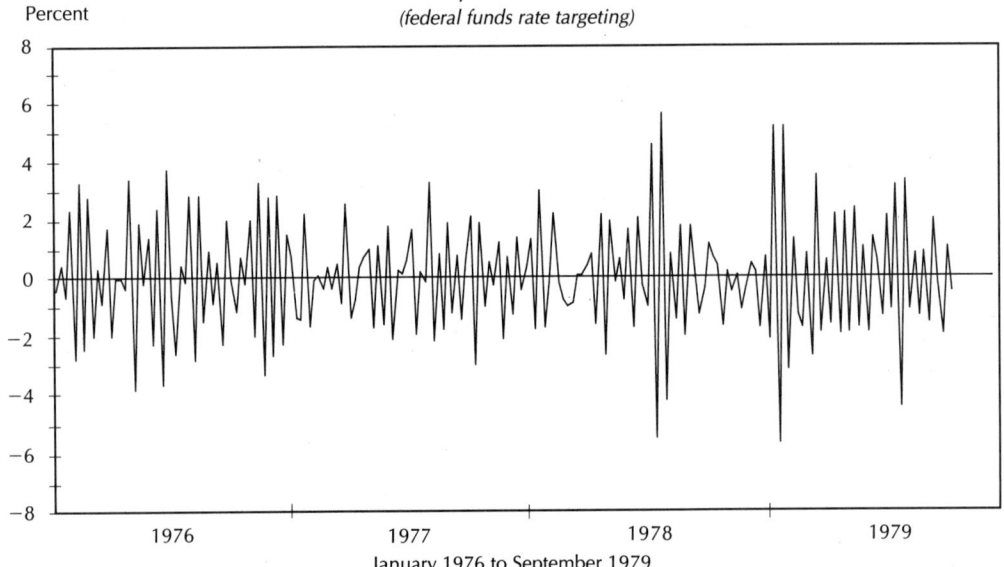

Chart 1B
Variability in Reserves Growth
(federal funds rate targeting)

January 1976 to September 1979
(weekly observations)

Source: All charts calculated by the author using data from the Board of Governors of the Federal Reserve System.

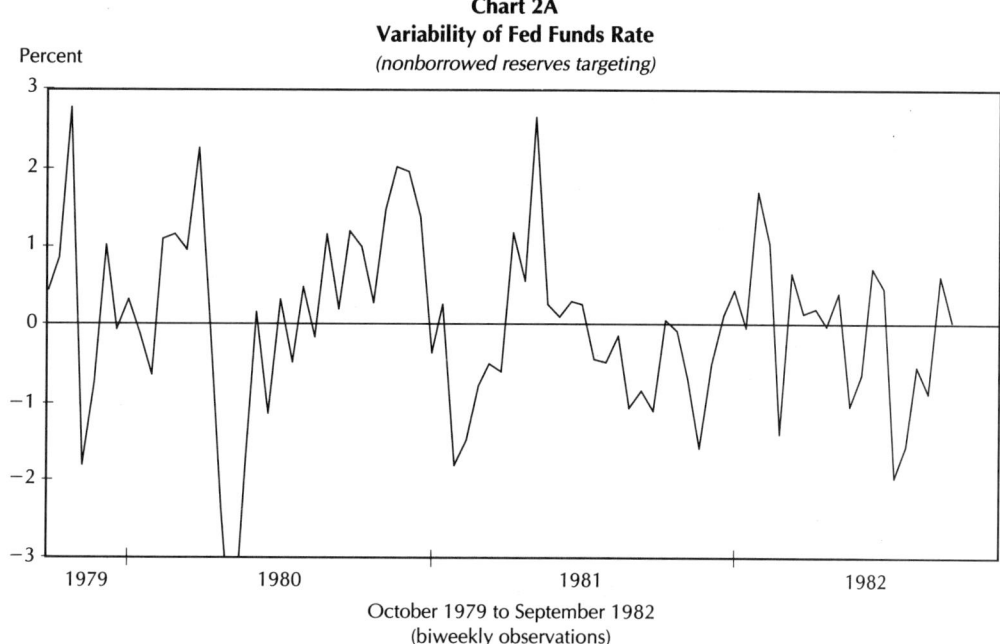

Chart 2A
Variability of Fed Funds Rate
(nonborrowed reserves targeting)

October 1979 to September 1982
(biweekly observations)

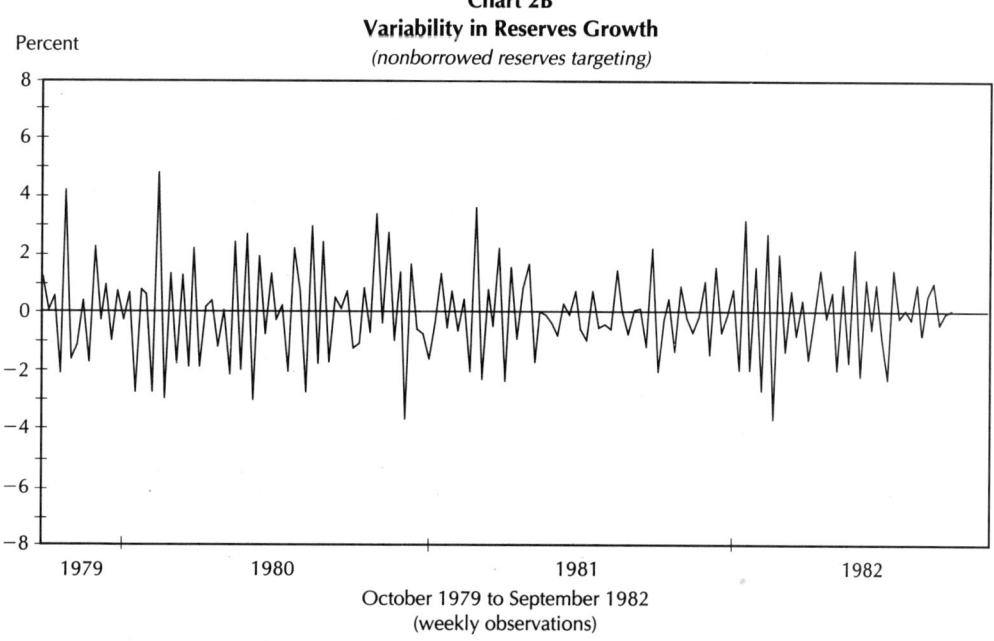

Chart 2B
Variability in Reserves Growth
(nonborrowed reserves targeting)

October 1979 to September 1982
(weekly observations)

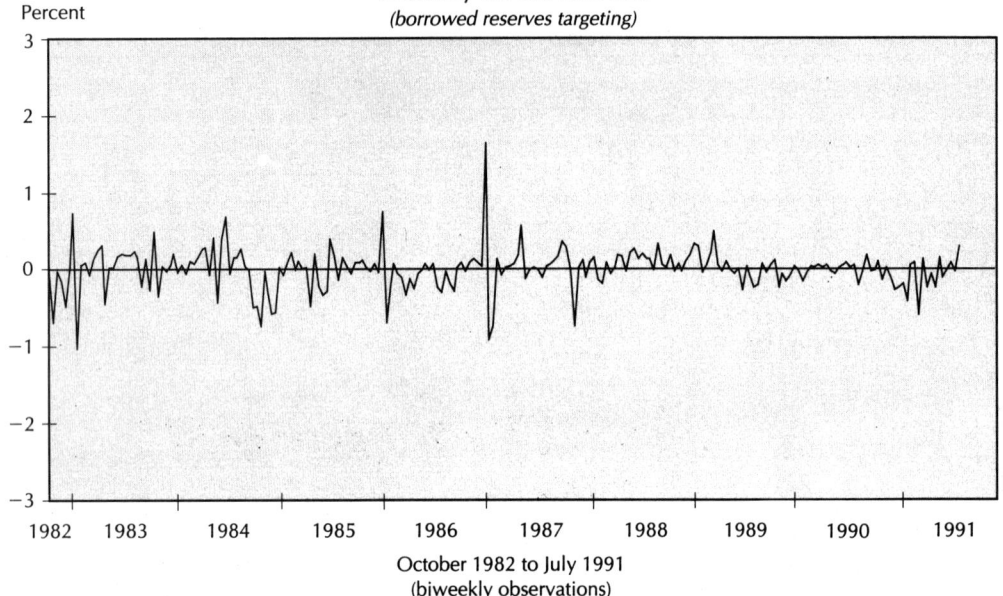

**Chart 3A
Variability of Fed Funds Rate**
(borrowed reserves targeting)

October 1982 to July 1991
(biweekly observations)

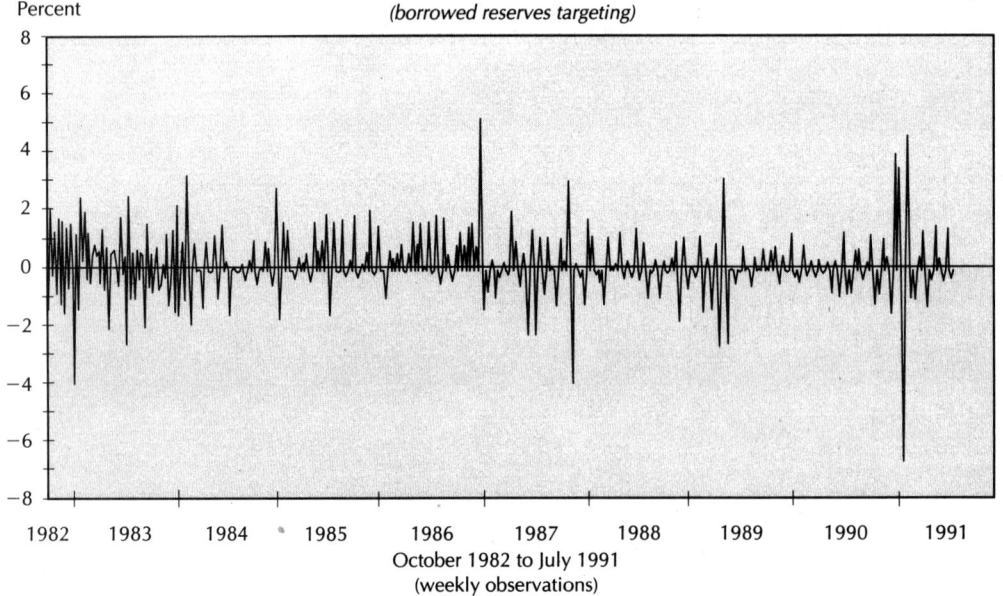

**Chart 3B
Variability in Reserves Growth**
(borrowed reserves targeting)

October 1982 to July 1991
(weekly observations)

often seen both by market participants and academic observers as too little, too late. The consensus view of the funds rate targeting of the late 1970s is aptly summarized by Meulendyke (1990), who observed that during this period the "[fed funds] rate moves during the week were so limited that they provided little or no information about reserve availability or market forces."

Following the interest rate volatility associated with the nonborrowed reserves targeting, Fed policy since 1982 has emphasized the stabilization of the fed funds rate in the short run. This renewed attention to short-term interest rate stabilization continues to be a subject of academic controversy.[8] However, potentially important differences exist between the current operating procedure and that followed in the late 1970s. The first difference is that the nominal short-run target is borrowed reserves rather than the funds rate per se. The second is that interventions by the Fed in the funds market are limited to one per day. The third important difference is that since early 1984 bank reserves have to be maintained with a two-day rather than a two-week lag. The net effect of these changes has been to introduce a somewhat greater amount of day-to-day variation in the funds rate, particularly on alternate Wednesdays when reserve balances are settled.

To date, researchers have not fully resolved the extent to which these changes have helped avoid some of the difficulties associated with 1970s operating procedures. Bennett T. McCallum and James G. Hoehn (1983) provide a theoretical analysis of targeting interest rates versus total reserves under lagged and contemporaneous reserve accounting environments. They find that under contemporaneous reserve accounting, targets on total reserves perform better than interest rate targets in terms of hitting an overall monetary target. More elaborate versions of McCallum and Hoehn's model, which are capable of distinguishing between borrowed and nonborrowed reserves, are presented by Michael Dotsey (1989) and David D. Van Hoose (1988). Dotsey also presents simulations suggesting that there is little quantitative distinction between interest rate and borrowed reserves targeting. This conclusion is consistent with the econometric analysis of Daniel P. Thornton (1988).

A number of recent studies have chosen to ignore the question of what the Fed does or does not do on a day-to-day basis, focusing instead on the effects of interest rate smoothing over the seasonal horizon. Jeffrey A. Miron (1986), in particular, calls attention to the changes in seasonal behavior of interest rates and the monetary aggregates after the founding of the Fed.

Miron notes that late nineteenth- and early twentieth-century money crises almost always occurred during the fall harvest season. According to Miron, in the years immediately following its founding the Fed was able to prevent the recurrence of such crises by lessening seasonal movements in interest rates and seasonally expanding the monetary base. Miron's work is extended in N. Gregory Mankiw and Miron (1986) and Mankiw, Miron, and David N. Weil (1987).[9]

Historical accounts such as that found in Friedman and Schwartz (1963) indicate that the lessening of seasonal strains in the money market was one of the most important, and perhaps the overriding, goal of early Fed policy. There seems to be widespread professional agreement, both then and now, that in the early twentieth century some amount of seasonal accommodation was needed to offset the strains put on the financial system by the seasonal cycle of agriculture. In recent years the pace of the U.S. macroeconomy has retained its seasonal character, but the available evidence suggests that the primary source of this seasonality is now the Christmas shopping season, not the agricultural cycle.[10] In other words, instead of seasonality induced by a shock to aggregate supply (that is, the fall harvest), seasonality in the macroeconomy is now driven by a seasonal shock to aggregate demand (Christmas shopping). The absence of seasonal movements in interest rates, together with seasonal movements in various monetary aggregates, indicates that smoothing of seasonal fluctuations continues to be an important focus of Fed policy.

Given the demand-driven nature of seasonal fluctuations in the U.S. economy, a natural question to ask is whether the smoothing of seasonal shocks to output should be an important focus of U.S. monetary policy. A recent study by Mankiw and Miron (1991) argues that the answer to this question would be yes if the economy behaves in a sufficiently "Keynesian" fashion—that is, if real quantities such as output and employment are sensitive enough to changes in purely nominal quantities. Mankiw and Miron estimate that nonaccommodation of seasonal demands for money could result in relatively large welfare losses, arising from seasonal movements in interest rates. Taking the opposite point of view, McCallum (1991) argues that stabilization of the economy over the year might not be inherently desirable, citing the examples of Christmas shopping and the seasonal construction cycle as two "rational" causes for seasonality. McCallum concludes that the welfare gains to the seasonal smoothing of interest rates are probably less than $1 per U.S. resident per year.

In summary, a search of the literature on the possible rationales for interest rate smoothing raises more questions than it answers. The bulk of the studies appear to weigh in against very strict short-term smoothing of interest rates in favor of some sort of reserve-based operating procedure, but it would be a mistake to characterize this issue as settled. Nor is there anything approaching a professional consensus concerning the issue of the degree to which the Fed should accommodate seasonal pressures in the money market.

What Are the Long-Term Consequences of Interest Rate Smoothing?

The classic criticism of interest rate pegging was advanced by Knut Wicksell in 1898. Wicksell reasoned that if a central bank attempted to peg interest rates below their natural equilibrium level, over the long run larger and larger infusions of cash and reserves would be needed to satisfy the resulting excess demands for money. Any such attempt to peg rates below their natural equilibrium was therefore destabilizing and ultimately doomed to failure.

Wicksell's argument against interest rate pegging (which is still found in economics textbooks) was concerned with the long-run consequences of a sustained policy. Partly as a consequence of the Fed's increased attention to interest rate objectives during the 1970s, numerous articles appeared in professional journals that explored the long-term consequences of smoothing interest rates, even when the smoothing is done over the very short run.

One of the most influential studies was a theoretical analysis by Thomas J. Sargent and Neil Wallace (1975). Sargent and Wallace were able to breathe new life into Wicksell's argument by introducing the idea of rational expectations into a model similar to that used by Poole (1970). Specifically, Sargent and Wallace demonstrated that the potentially destabilizing indeterminacy arises when a monetary authority such as the Fed attempts to stabilize interest rates, even over the very short term. For an interest rate target to be credible, it has to be backed by the willingness to defend this target via open market operations. The degree of intervention necessary to maintain the interest rate target, however, will depend, among other things, on the rate of inflation anticipated by the public over the interval that the interest rate is to be stabilized. The indeterminacy arises from the fact that essentially any expected rate of inflation is consistent with an interest rate target, given a sufficient willingness on the part of the Fed to defend the targeted rate of interest.

McCallum (1981) reconsiders the Sargent-Wallace indeterminacy and finds that it can be resolved by the use of a "nominal anchor"—for example, a monetary target—on the part of the Fed. That is, if policy is adjusted not only to smooth interest rates but also in response to changes in some other nominal target variable, then this type of policy does a better job of signaling the Fed's intentions. This result occurs because the response to movements in a nominal anchor gives the public a more definite idea concerning how staunchly a given interest rate target will be defended. To return momentarily to the automotive analogy, the use of a nominal anchor might be compared to a driver's adherence to the rules of the road. By driving on the right side of the road, stopping at stop signs, and so forth, individual drivers reduce the potential scope of their own actions. Yet this reduced freedom of action produces the desirable outcome of fewer collisions because better information about each individual driver's likely behavior is available to other drivers.

McCallum's results provide some intellectual backing for the combination of short-term interest rate smoothing and longer-term monetary targeting now in use by the Fed. In practical terms, however, the usefulness of monetary targeting schemes has been limited by uncertainty about which measured monetary aggregate is the appropriate measure of "the" money supply.[11] Despite these practical difficulties, and despite the usual amount of initial academic skepticism, the policy conclusions of the Sargent-Wallace-McCallum approach have come to be viewed as orthodoxy by a broad cross section of the economics profession, even as their theoretical analyses have become seen as somewhat dated.

Numerous refinements have been suggested for the basic approach used by Sargent and Wallace (1975) and McCallum (1981). While these refinements have offered some useful insights into the possible long-term consequences of various approaches to monetary policy, no single point of view on this subject has been widely accepted within the economics profession. The waters around this issue have been further muddied by the publication of another controversial article by Sargent and Wallace in 1982. In the context of a theoretical model Sargent and Wallace were able to show that under certain assumptions, the "best" interest rate smoothing policy was not adjusted with reference to a nominal anchor such as a monetary aggregate but according to the needs of people in the model who are engaged in trade.[12] This conclusion, though widely discussed within the economics profession, has not been as widely accepted. Dissenting viewpoints can be found, for example, in articles by David Laidler (1984) and McCallum (1986), who view the Sargent and Wallace (1982) result as lacking in sufficient generality to be applicable to the problems of real-world monetary policy.[13]

Despite the apparent divergence of professional opinion on the subject, the literature on the long-term stability of interest rate smoothing policies has made substantial progress over recent decades. The seminal article by Sargent and Wallace (1975) provided a useful insight into the possibility that even short-term interest rate smoothing, without reference to some other policy guidelines, could be destabilizing over the long term. The recent literature in this area has tended to focus not on whether such guidelines (or "nominal anchors") are needed but on which anchor would provide for the smoothest sailing.

To What Extent Should Interest Rate Smoothing Take Precedence over Other Goals of Monetary Policy?

Certainly, monetary authorities such as the Fed were not created for the sole purpose of smoothing interest rates. This fact is recognized by researchers in this area, in that the objective of the Fed is traditionally modeled as incorporating "stable" prices and economic growth. Stability means different things to different researchers, but it is traditionally taken to mean "as close as possible to some desired path."

According to the various models that follow in the tradition of Sargent and Wallace (1975) (for example, McCallum 1981; Dotsey 1989; and Goodfriend 1987), monetary policy actions that smooth interest rates are essentially in direct conflict with the goals of price and output stability. In these models, interest rate smoothing leads to increased confusion over real versus nominal quantities and hence to greater uncertainty in both real output and prices. Thus, the analysis in these articles suggests that the practice of interest rate smoothing will eventually be at odds with other traditional stabilization objectives.

An alternative perspective on the long-term effects of interest rate smoothing is presented in an article by Wallace (1984). Wallace argues that debates over monetary policy should not be centered on questions of stability per se but rather on questions of who benefits and who loses, and by how much, as a result of monetary actions. For example, if open market operations by the Fed are able to lower the real rate of interest permanently, as occurs in Sargent and Wallace's (1982) model, then holders of nominally denominated assets (that is, fixed-rate debt) are made worse off, and people who are borrowing money are better off than they would be without this open market intervention. In an example Wallace (1984) uses, it is impossible to say that the economy as a whole is better off, either with or without the presence of monetary policies designed to influence interest rates. Under each policy scenario, some people are adversely affected while others are better off.

For many researchers it would be difficult to evaluate the real-world significance of this argument. If monetary policy can substantially influence real interest rates over time, as Wallace (1984) argues it can, then such an argument is almost surely correct. However, as noted above, many economists do not believe that real interest rates can be influenced by monetary policy, especially over the long run. For this reason, those economists would probably dispute the direct applicability of Wallace's argument. However, it is a useful exercise to apply a similar line of reasoning to what is known about the dynamics of financial markets before and after the founding of the Fed.

From the end of the Civil War to 1914 movements in interest rates were characterized by sudden, large, and relatively short-lived swings, as compared with movements in interest rates since 1914. Movements in the very short end of the term structure, as typified by the rate on overnight call money, were particularly subject to large fluctuations. Goodfriend (1991) notes that on a monthly average basis overnight money rates jumped by more than 5 percentage points on twenty-six occasions and changed by more than 10 percentage points eight times during this forty-nine-year period.[14] There were clearly winners (lenders) and losers (borrowers) who gained and lost money during these brief episodes of high interest rates, but high levels of interest rates were hardly seen by contemporary observers as the most negative aspect of these "money panics." More generally, such episodes were associated (most often in a causal fashion) with bank runs, contractions in credit, and a reduction in the overall level of real economic activity. A potentially strong argument in favor of interest rate smoothing as a goal of monetary policy would be that smoothing prevents the occurrence of such crises, given that such crises are, after the fact, in no one's best interest. Thus, if one accepts the idea that interest rate smoothing leads to an avoidance of money panics, with few other serious long-term consequences on the economy, then the argument advanced by Wallace (1984) would lose much of its force.

The importance of central bank liquidity provision in preventing financial panics is an accepted part of central banking doctrine, dating back to at least Walter Bagehot (1873). As was noted above, the elimination of money panics associated with the harvest season has been viewed by many observers as an important accomplishment of early Fed policy. More recently, however, economists have been revising traditional views on the causes and remedies of money panics. In the recent literature the tendency has been to view pre-Fed money panics as well as the Great Depression of the 1930s not as exercises in pure mass hysteria but as being caused by the markets' rational responses to a poorly designed regulatory structure.[15] In a widely cited paper, Douglas W. Diamond and Philip H. Dybvig (1983) use such an argument to rationalize deposit insurance as a means of avoiding panics. In a related paper V.V. Chari (1989) argues that under certain conditions monetary policy may be superior to deposit insurance for this purpose because deposit insurance carries with it the potential for skewing banks' incentives toward risky investments. On the other side of the question Wallace (1988, 1990) argues, in effect, that temporary suspensions of convertibility such as occurred often during the money panics could be desirable as a means of eliciting otherwise unavailable information about the economy's demand for liquid assets.

An unfortunate aspect of the new literature on panics is that it has generally yielded only limited insights into the appropriate role of monetary policy in the prevention of panics. Overall there has been a tendency to focus on the consequences of various regulatory constraints (for example, restrictions on banks' assets, liabilities, reserves, and so forth), with relatively little attention being paid to the interaction between direct regulation, emergency credit provision, and open market policies. The implicit message (occasionally made more explicit in papers such as Ben S. Bernanke's 1983 analysis of the Great Depression in the United States) has been that the role of monetary policy in preventing the recurrence of such crises must be subordinate to that of regulation. Whether or not this last view is correct remains a matter of dispute (see, for example, James D. Hamilton 1987 for a somewhat contrary view of the Great Depression). Still, the burgeoning literature that seeks to link the structures of financial intermediation to aggregate consequences suggests that a good understanding of the potential effects of monetary policy depends on a deeper understanding of the workings of financial intermediaries. A number of recent papers—for example, John H. Boyd and Edward C. Prescott (1986), Bernanke and Mark Gertler (1987), and Sudipto Bhattacharya and Douglas Gale (1987)—have suggested that banks may represent a particularly efficient solution to the problem of how to evaluate the creditworthiness of potential borrowers. If this conclusion is accepted, it is fairly easy to rationalize the expenditure of public funds to protect the banking system in moments of illiquidity. What is lacking is a precisely defined role for open market policy in this protective mission, especially open market policies that incorporate interest rate smoothing.

Conclusion

Real-world objectives of monetary policy have historically incorporated some degree of interest rate smoothing. Traditional economic analyses suggest that, at best, very strict smoothing of interest rates through open market operations leads to some loss of information about the demand for funds provided by the central bank through such operations. Since 1975 various branches of academic economics have brought a number of different approaches to this problem.

One branch of the macroeconomics literature has had very little good to say about interest rate smoothing. This research has offered no rational basis for the practice of interest rate smoothing and has often concluded that strict smoothing of interest rates would be destabilizing in the absence of other observable policy guidelines ("nominal anchors"). Another common conclusion of these studies is that interest rate smoothing is inherently in conflict with other stabilization objectives.

Another branch of the recent macroeconomics literature has a much more benign view of interest rate smoothing. According to these studies, in some cases it may be possible for even a sustained interest rate peg to result in better monetary policy than if policy were adjusted according to movements in a monetary target. Interest rate smoothing is seen as inherently neither good nor bad, but as beneficial to some people and injurious to others. Although this branch of the literature has been influential, it is fair to say that its conclusions have not been widely accepted by the mainstream of the profession.

Yet another stream of research has focused on the changes in seasonal patterns that accompanied the founding of the Federal Reserve System in 1914.

These studies have provided interesting comparative analyses of the "smooth" financial markets characteristic of the post-1914 world versus the "noisy" pre-1914 markets. The theme underpinning much of this research seems to be that post-1914 seasonal smoothing of interest rates by the Fed could be justified because of the association of pre-1914 money panics with the agricultural production cycle. However, to date these studies have not provided an entirely satisfactory explanation of the pre-1914 panics. Nor has this branch of the literature built up much of a case as to why seasonal interest rate smoothing is needed when seasonal fluctuations are driven by shocks to demand rather than supply.

A noteworthy counterpoint to the literature mentioned above has been provided by new research in the general area of banking, and particularly in the area of modeling "runs" or "panics." While not directly focusing on the issue of interest rate smoothing, this research has the potential to provide a more complete understanding of the monetary policy's interaction with the regulatory and institutional structure of the financial system. By providing a stable operating environment for the financial sector, monetary policy actions such as interest rate smoothing may serve as a useful complement to more direct regulation. No doubt this idea will be explored in greater detail as the literature on financial intermediation develops.

As with many such debates in economics, the controversy over interest rate smoothing is a long way from being resolved. It would be a mistake, however, to say that research in this area has made no contribution to knowledge about the issue. To the contrary, the research has brought forth a number of insightful arguments both for and against this aspect of monetary policy. No doubt there is some degree of truth in all of these arguments, and each deserves careful consideration by policymakers.

Notes

1. On the prevalence of interest rate smoothing in the major industrialized countries, see Batten et al. (1990), Kneeshaw and Van den Bergh (1989), and Beaulieu and Miron (1990). For information about the Federal Reserve System's practice of interest rate smoothing, see the historical summary below, Goodfriend (1991), or Meulendyke (1989).
2. Much of the summary below is drawn from Goodfriend (1991), Meulendyke (1990), and Friedman and Schwartz (1963).
3. The fed funds rate is the rate paid by banks on funds needed to meet the banks' reserve requirements. Transactions in the fed funds market are generally limited to very short maturities, and many agreements only last a single night. On the workings of the Federal Funds Market see Goodfriend and Whelpley (1986).
4. These studies include papers by Barro (1989); Canova (1988, 1991); Clark (1986); Mankiw and Miron (1986); Miron (1986); and Mankiw, Miron, and Weil (1987).
5. The quasi-private nature of the major European central banks prior to 1914 is recounted in the various essays in Toniolo (1988). Earlier attempts at activist monetary policies by the U.S. Treasury were hindered by inadequate reserves, according to Timberlake (1978).
6. A helpful summary of the changeover from discount to open market operations can be found in Chapter 2 of Meulendyke (1989). For a more extensive discussion of this topic, see Wicker (1966). Both of these sources emphasize that this change took place gradually during the 1920s and not as a result of a single decisive change in policy. Evidently, the idea that bank reserves could be managed through open market operations was not widely understood at this time, even within the Federal Reserve System. Consequently, many Federal Reserve policymakers in the 1920s viewed open market policy as being subordinate to discount window operations.
7. At the heart of this belief is the idea that money is just an accounting device for recording the values of goods and service, and it is only the relative value between any two goods that should matter in people's economic decisions. For example, if next week the United States were to start phasing in a new currency, the "shmoo," with two of the new shmoos equal to a dollar, no one would seriously expect such a change to have any real effects. The belief that monetary policy does not affect real rates over the long run amounts to a belief that over the long run an increase in the supply of money amounts to a sort of backhanded dollar-shmoo substitution.
8. See, for example, Benjamin Friedman's (1988) comments on current Fed operating procedures; also see Spindt and Tarhan (1987).
9. Other important articles in this area differ somewhat in their interpretation of the historical record. Clark (1986) disputes the notion that the Fed was responsible for the disappearance of interest rate seasonals. Arguing on the basis of a number of statistical tests, Clark concludes that the international scope of the 1914 changes in the financial markets requires a more careful explanation than, say, that advanced in Miron (1986). Two plausible explanations are offered in Barsky et al. (1988) and Canova (1991).
10. See Barsky and Miron (1989), Beaulieu and Miron (1990), and Braun and Evans (1991).

11. See Roberds (1989) for a survey of the difficulties associated with measuring the money supply.
12. The latter point of view is generally associated with a concept known as the "real bills doctrine." The debate over the validity of the real bills doctrine goes back well into the nineteenth century, and even a cursory summary of this debate would go beyond the scope of the present article. The interested reader should consult *The New Palgrave* (Eatwell, Milgate, and Newman 1987).
13. While a full recounting of the academic disagreements about Sargent and Wallace (1982) goes beyond the scope of the present article, the essence of the debate has to do with how to best characterize money in an abstract setting. It turns out that money is something that is extremely easy to spend but difficult to characterize in an abstract sense. As a result, various branches of monetary theory have tended to emphasize differing aspects of "moneyness." The approach used by Sargent and Wallace (1982) emphasizes money's role as a store of value, so that buying and selling need not happen simultaneously. Other researchers, particularly McCallum (1986), have found this characterization of money inappropriate. These researchers have tended to emphasize the role of money as a medium of exchange—that is, its acceptability in transactions among parties not well known to each other.
14. By way of contrast, under current operating procedures, a month-to-month movement of 1 percentage point in the fed funds rate would be considered a large move. As pointed out in Miron (1986) and other papers summarized above, interest rates prior to 1914 showed as distinctly seasonal in the fall of the year, suggesting that even such large interest rate movements as described above were predictable to some extent.
15. See Tallman (1988) for a nontechnical introduction to the recent "bank panic" literature. Williamson (1987) and Gertler (1988) also present useful surveys of this literature.

References

Bagehot, Walter. *Lombard Street*. London: H.S. King and Company, 1873.

Barro, Robert. "Interest Rate Targeting." *Journal of Monetary Economics* 23 (January 1989): 3-30.

Barsky, Robert B., N. Gregory Mankiw, Jeffrey A. Miron, and David N. Weill. "The Worldwide Change in the Behavior of Interest Rates in 1914." *European Economic Review* (June 1988): 1123-54.

Barsky, Robert B., and Jeffrey A. Miron. "The Seasonal Cycle and the Business Cycle." *Journal of Political Economy* 97 (June 1989): 503-34.

Batten, Dallas S., Michael P. Blackwell, In-Su Kim, Simon E. Nocera, and Yuzuru Ozeki. "The Conduct of Monetary Policy in the Major Industrial Countries: Instruments and Operating Procedures." International Monetary Fund Occasional Paper 170, July 1990.

Beaulieu, J. Joseph, and Jeffrey A. Miron. "A Cross-Country Comparison of Seasonal Cycles and Business Cycles." National Bureau of Economic Research Working Paper 3459, October 1990.

Bernanke, Ben S. "Nonmonetary Effects of the Financial Crisis in the Propagation of the Great Depression." *American Economic Review* 73 (June 1983): 257-76.

———, and Mark Gertler. "Banking and Macroeconomic Equilibrium." In *New Approaches to Monetary Economics*, edited by William A. Barnett and Kenneth J. Singleton, 89-111. Cambridge, U.K.: Cambridge University Press, 1987.

Bhattacharya, Sudipto, and Douglas Gale. "Preference Shocks, Liquidity, and Central Bank Policy." Chap. 4 in *New Approaches to Monetary Economics*, edited by William A. Barnett and Kenneth J. Singleton. Cambridge, U.K.: Cambridge University Press, 1987.

Boyd, John H., and Edward C. Prescott. "Financial Intermediary Coalitions." *Journal of Economic Theory* 38 (April 1986): 211-32.

Braun, R. Anton, and Charles L. Evans. "Seasonal Solow Residuals and Christmas: A Case for Labor Hoarding and Increasing Returns." Federal Reserve Bank of Chicago Working Paper 91-20, October 1991.

Canova, Fabio. "An Econometric Analysis of the Disappearance of Interest Rates Seasonals: Real Factors or the Fed?" Brown University Working Paper 88-9, January 1988.

———. "The Sources of Financial Crises: Pre- and Post-Fed Evidence." *International Economic Review* 32 (August 1991): 689-714.

Chari, V.V. "Banking without Deposit Insurance or Bank Panics: Lessons from a Model of the U.S. National Bank System." Federal Reserve Bank of Minneapolis *Quarterly Review* 13 (Summer 1989): 3-19.

Clark, Truman A. "Interest Rate Seasonals and the Federal Reserve." *Journal of Political Economy* 94 (February 1986): 76-125.

Cook, Timothy. "Determinants of the Federal Funds Rate: 1979-82." Federal Reserve Bank of Richmond *Economic Review* 75 (January/February 1989): 3-19.

Diamond, Douglas W., and Philip H. Dybvig. "Bank Runs, Deposit Insurance, and Liquidity." *Journal of Political Economy* 91 (June 1983): 401-19.

Dotsey, Michael. "Monetary Control under Alternative Operating Procedures." *Journal of Money, Credit, and Banking* 21 (August 1989): 273-90.

Eatwell, John, Murray Milgate, and Peter Newman, eds. *The New Palgrave: A Dictionary of Economics*. 4 vols. New York: The Stockton Press, 1987.

Friedman, Benjamin. "Lessons on Monetary Policy from the 1980s." *Journal of Economic Perspectives* 2 (Summer 1988): 51-72.

Friedman, Milton, and Anna J. Schwartz. *A Monetary History of the United States: 1867-1960*. Princeton, N.J.: Princeton University Press, 1963.

Gertler, Mark. "Financial Structure and Aggregate Economic Activity: An Overview." *Journal of Money, Credit, and Banking* 20 (August 1988): 559-88.

Goodfriend, Marvin. "Interest Rate Smoothing and Price Level Trend-Stationarity." *Journal of Monetary Economics* 19 (May 1987): 335-48.

_____. "Central Banking under the Gold Standard." *Carnegie-Rochester Conference Series on Public Policy* 29 (1988): 85-128.

_____. "Interest Rates and the Conduct of Monetary Policy." *Carnegie-Rochester Series on Public Policy* 34 (Spring 1991): 7-30.

_____, and William Whelpley. "Federal Funds." Chap. 2 in *Instruments of the Money Market*, 6th ed., edited by Timothy Q. Cook and Timothy D. Rowe. Richmond, Va.: Federal Reserve Bank of Richmond, 1986.

Hamilton, James D. "Monetary Factors in the Great Depression." *Journal of Monetary Economics* 19 (March 1987): 145-69.

Heller, H. Robert. "Implementing Monetary Policy." *Federal Reserve Bulletin* 74 (July 1988): 419-29.

Kneeshaw, J.T., and P. Van den Bergh. "Changes in Central Bank Money Market Operating Procedures in the 1980s." Bank for International Settlements Economic Paper 23, January 1989.

Laidler, David. "Misconceptions about the Real Bills Doctrine: A Comment." *Journal of Political Economy* 92 (February 1984): 149-55.

Mankiw, N. Gregory, and Jeffrey A. Miron. "The Changing Behavior of the Term Structure of Interest Rates." *Quarterly Journal of Economics* 101 (May 1986): 211-28.

_____. "Should the Fed Smooth Interest Rates? The Case of Seasonal Monetary Policy." *Carnegie-Rochester Series on Public Policy* 34 (Spring 1991): 41-70.

_____, and David N. Weil. "The Adjustment of Expectations to a Change in Regime: A Study of the Founding of the Federal Reserve." *American Economic Review* 77 (June 1987): 358-74.

McCallum, Bennett T. "Price Level Determinacy with an Interest Rate Policy Rule and Rational Expectations." *Journal of Monetary Economics* 8 (1981): 319-29.

_____. "Some Issues Concerning Interest Rate Pegging, Price Level Determinacy, and the Real Bills Doctrine." *Journal of Monetary Economics* 17 (1986): 135-60.

_____. "Seasonality and Monetary Policy: A Comment." *Carnegie-Rochester Series on Public Policy* 34 (Spring 1991): 71-76.

_____, and James G. Hoehn. "Instrument Choice for Money Stock Control with Contemporaneous and Lagged Reserve Requirements: A Note." *Journal of Money, Credit, and Banking* 15 (February 1983): 96-101.

Meulendyke, Ann-Marie. *U.S. Monetary Policy and Financial Markets.* New York: Federal Reserve Bank of New York, 1989.

_____. "A Review of Federal Reserve Policy Targets and Operating Guides in Recent Decades." In *Intermediate Targets and Indicators for Monetary Policy: A Critical Survey.* New York: Federal Reserve Bank of New York, 1990.

Miron, Jeffrey A. "Financial Panics, the Seasonality of the Nominal Interest Rate, and the Founding of the Fed. *American Economic Review* 76 (March 1986): 125-40.

Poole, William. "Optimal Choice of Monetary Policy Instruments in a Simple Stochastic Macro Model. *Quarterly Journal of Economics* 84 (May 1970): 197-216.

Roberds, William. "Money and the Economy: Puzzles from the 1980s' Experience." Federal Reserve Bank of Atlanta *Economic Review* 74 (September/October 1989): 20-35.

Sargent, Thomas J., and Neil Wallace. "Rational Expectations, the Optimal Instrument, and the Optimal Money Supply Rule." *Journal of Political Economy* 83 (April 1975): 241-54.

_____. "The Real-Bills Doctrine versus the Quantity Theory: A Reconsideration." *Journal of Political Economy* 90 (December 1982): 1212-36.

Spindt, Paul A., and Vefa Tarhan. "The Federal Reserve's New Operating Procedures: A Postmortem." *Journal of Monetary Economics* 19 (January 1987): 107-23.

Tallman, Ellis. "Some Unanswered Questions about Bank Panics." Federal Reserve Bank of Atlanta *Economic Review* 73 (November/December 1988): 2-21.

Thornton, Daniel P. "The Borrowed-Reserves Operating Procedure: Theory and Evidence." Federal Reserve Bank of St. Louis *Review* 70 (January/February 1988): 30-54.

Timberlake, Richard H. *The Origins of Central Banking in the United States.* Cambridge, Mass.: Harvard University Press, 1978.

Toniolo, Gianni, ed. *Central Banks' Independence in Historical Perspective.* Berlin: Walter de Gruyter, 1988.

Van Hoose, David D. "Discount Rate Policy and Alternative Federal Reserve Operating Procedures in a Rational Expectations Setting." *Journal of Economics and Business* 40 (November 1988): 285-94.

Wallace, Neil. "Some of the Choices for Monetary Policy." Federal Reserve Bank of Minneapolis *Quarterly Review* 8 (Winter 1984): 15-24.

_____. "Another Attempt to Explain an Illiquid Banking System: The Diamond and Dybvig Model with Sequential Service Taken Seriously." Federal Reserve Bank of Minneapolis *Quarterly Review* 12 (Fall 1988): 3-16.

_____. "A Banking Model in Which Partial Suspension is Best." Federal Reserve Bank of Minneapolis *Quarterly Review* 14 (Fall 1990): 11-23.

Wicker, Elmus R. *Federal Reserve Monetary Policy, 1917-1933.* New York: Random House, 1966.

Wicksell, Knut. *Geldzins und Güterpreise bestimmenden Ursachen.* Jena: G. Fischer, 1898. Translated by R.F. Kahn as *Interest and Prices: A Study of the Causes Regulating the Value of Money.* London: Macmillan, 1936.

Williamson, Stephen D. "Recent Developments in Modelling Financial Intermediation." Federal Reserve Bank of Minneapolis *Quarterly Review* 11 (Summer 1987): 19-29.

Article 30

The Changing Role of Reserve Requirements in Monetary Policy

By Stuart E. Weiner

Reserve requirements have traditionally been viewed as an integral part of the monetary control process. In conjunction with central bank control over the supply of reserves, reserve requirements have been seen as placing an upper limit on deposit creation, helping central banks directly control the growth of money and credit.

Yet, reserve requirements are on the wane worldwide. Central banks have been reducing or eliminating them in an effort to make banks and other subjected depository institutions more competitive. In the past two years, for example, the Federal Reserve has lowered requirements on transactions deposits and eliminated requirements on time deposits. The central banks of Switzerland, New Zealand, Australia, and Canada have eliminated their requirements. And the German Bundesbank reportedly has considered lowering its requirements. How does one reconcile these actions with the traditional view of reserve requirements and monetary control?

The answer is, in many countries the traditional view no longer holds. Reserve requirements

Stuart E. Weiner is an assistant vice president and economist at the Federal Reserve Bank of Kansas City. Carrie Ross, an assistant economist, and Michael Kim, an intern at the bank, helped prepare the article. The author thanks Kevin Clinton, Heinz Herrmann, and David Longworth for helpful comments.

are no longer seen as a vehicle to directly control the money stock but rather as a vehicle to facilitate control over short-term interest rates. As such, depending on a country's institutional framework, there may be scope for reducing or even eliminating reserve requirements.

This article examines the monetary policy implications of lower reserve requirements. The article focuses on the United States, Canada, and Germany. The first section outlines the traditional "multiplier" view of reserve requirements, showing that in this context the recent reductions in requirements would be cause for concern. The second section shows, however, that in a broader context, one in which most central banks now operate, the recent reductions are not necessarily cause for concern. Indeed, one can view the reductions as secondary to more fundamental policy decisions made much earlier. The third section provides a more detailed analysis of current operating procedures, stressing that reserve requirements may still have an important, albeit different, role to play in the monetary policy process.

RESERVE REQUIREMENTS IN A MULTIPLIER FRAMEWORK

Discussions of reserve requirements and monetary policy have typically taken place in the context of the multiplier model of the money supply. This model has come to provide the basic textbook framework for examining many monetary control issues. In this framework, reserve requirements play a crucial role.

The multiplier model

The multiplier model emphasizes the direct link between reserve requirements and monetary control. The simplest version of the model assumes that all money, M, is held in the form of bank demand deposits, D, that is,

(1) $M = D$.

Banks are required to hold a fraction of their assets as required reserves, RR, against these deposits,

(2) $RR = rrr*D$.

The central bank sets the required reserve ratio, rrr, at a value between 0 and 100 percent and also supplies the reserves. Rewriting (2) yields

(3) $D = (1/rrr)*RR$.

And, substituting (1) into (3) implies

(4) $M = (1/rrr)*RR$.

Thus, the money supply is a multiple of reserves. If the central bank wishes to expand the money supply, it adds reserves; if it wishes to contract the money supply, it drains reserves. The "multiplier," $1/rrr$ provides the link between changes in reserves and changes in the money supply. The multiplier, in turn, is determined by the level of reserve requirements. The higher the required reserve ratio, the smaller the multiplier, and vice versa.[1]

Reserve requirements clearly play an important role in this model. First, for a given level of reserves, they impose an upper limit on the money supply. Algebraically, the money supply can be no higher than $(1/rrr)$ times RR. In practical terms, what this is saying is that banks face a limit on the amount of deposits they can create for a given amount of reserves.

Second, reserve requirements are a crucial factor in determining the size of money supply "misses." Suppose, for example, the central bank seeks to attain a certain level of the money supply but finds out too late that reserves are too plentiful. The unexpected surplus in reserves will lead to an undesired surplus in money. The size of the money supply overshoot will depend critically on the level of reserve requirements—the higher the required reserve ratio, the smaller the multiplier, hence, the smaller the overshoot. The reverse is also true, of course—the lower the required reserve ratio, the greater the overshoot.

This key result, that lower reserve requirements imply less monetary control in the presence of reserve disturbances, carries over into more complex versions of the multiplier model. Introducing currency into the model, for example, changes the form of the multiplier but not the basic result.[2] Nor does incorporating more than one type of deposit.[3] The message remains the same: monetary control suffers the lower are reserve requirements.

The decline in reserve requirements

Notwithstanding the above discussion, reserve requirements are on the decline worldwide. Several central banks have reduced or eliminated statutory requirements in recent years. At the same time, deregulation and innovation have allowed a growing portion of deposits to escape reserve requirements. Consequently, many countries have experienced steady declines in effective required reserve ratios, that is, in the ratio of required reserves to the money supply.

Table 1 shows the decline in statutory reserve requirements in the United States, Canada, and Germany over the past 20 years. The most dramatic decline has occurred in Canada. A key provision of comprehensive financial market legislation proclaimed in June 1992 sets the marginal reserve requirement to zero and eliminates all reserve requirements over a two-year phaseout

Table 1

Statutory Reserve Requirements, Selected Years

(Percent)

	1974	1989	1992
Transactions deposits			
United States	18[a]	12	10[b]
Canada	12	10	0[c]
Germany	19.1[d]	12.1	12.1
Term deposits			
United States	8[a]	3	0
Canada	4	3	0[c]
Germany	13.25[d]	4.95	4.95

[a] Effective January 1 through December 11, 1974.
[b] Effective April 2, 1992.
[c] The marginal reserve requirement is zero. Overall reserve requirements are being phased out over a two-year period that began in mid-1992.
[d] Effective January 1 through August 30, 1974.

Note: Figures shown are highest marginal ratios; in some cases, applicable marginal ratios may vary according to specific type of deposit, location of depository institution, or level of deposit liabilities.

Sources: Federal Reserve System; Bank of Canada; Deutsche Bundesbank.

---

period.[4] The United States also has seen recent declines. In December 1990, the Federal Reserve eliminated reserve requirements on term deposits. In April 1992, it lowered requirements on transactions deposits. German reserve requirements also are markedly lower today than 20 years ago, and German officials reportedly have considered lowering them further (Evans).

The principal reason central banks have been reducing reserve requirements is to ease the burden on subjected depository institutions and thereby allow them to become more competitive. Reserve requirements impose a cost on depository institutions and their customers. Because reserves typically do not earn interest—and in the United States, Canada, and Germany they do not—reserve requirements force depository institutions to forego interest income. Some reserves would be held in the absence of reserve requirements but a portion would not. The interest that is foregone on involuntarily held reserves is in effect a tax that is either borne directly by the institutions and their shareholders or passed on to customers via lower deposit rates, higher borrowing rates, or reduced services. Like any other selective tax, the reserve tax distorts the allocative process. It makes banks and other subjected institutions less competitive, channeling financial resources away from them and toward potentially less productive uses at institutions not subject to reserve requirements.[5]

Central banks are very aware of the burden of reserve requirements. In announcing its December 1990 reserve requirement reduction, for example, the Federal Reserve noted that "lower reserve requirements . . . will reduce costs to depository institutions" (Board of Governors 1990). In announcing its April 1992 reduction, the Federal Reserve stressed that "the reduction . . . will reduce funding costs for depositories and strengthen their balance sheets. Over time, it is expected that most of these cost savings will be passed on to depositors and borrowers" (Board of Governors 1992).[6] Similarly, the Bank of Canada has emphasized that the recent financial market legislation "will result in increased competition" (Bank of Canada 1991a), and the German Bundesbank has acknowledged that reserve requirements "create a certain competitive bias" against German banks vis-a-vis Euromarket competitors (Pohl). Hence, the move toward lower reserve requirements.[7]

Reductions in statutory requirements, however, are not the only reason for a decline in effective reserve ratios. Deregulation and innovation have also played important roles. Precisely because reserve requirements are a tax, financial institutions have a strong incentive to avoid them,

Chart 1
Effective Required Reserve Ratios

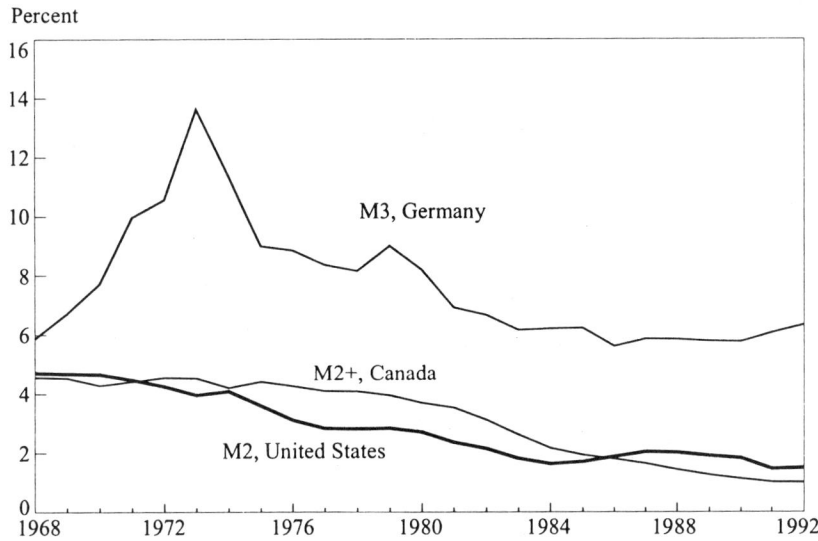

Note: Calculated as required reserves divided by monetary aggregate, based on nonseasonally adjusted, nonbreak adjusted average annual data. Figures for 1992 computed as average of January-May for Germany and Canada, as average of January-June for the United States.
Source: Federal Reserve *Bulletin;* Bank of Canada *Review;* Monthly Report of Deutsche Bundesbank.

either by taking advantage of changes in rules or by innovating around existing rules. Much of the decline in the Canadian effective reserve ratio in the 1980s, for example, was attributable to strong growth in nonreservable deposits at trust and mortgage loan companies, including mortgage loan subsidiaries of chartered banks. This growth was made possible by earlier deregulation.[8] Much of the decline in the U.S. ratio in the 1970s was attributable to banks leaving the Federal Reserve system, a very blunt form of innovation. And there are numerous other examples.[9] Acting in tandem with the reductions in statutory requirements, deregulation and innovation have contributed to the steady decline in effective reserve ratios.

The extent of the decline in effective reserve ratios is shown in Chart 1. From a high of 13.6 percent in 1973, the German effective reserve ratio has declined to 6.3 percent in 1992. Likewise, the Canadian ratio has fallen from 4.5 percent to 1.0 percent over the same period, while the U.S. ratio has fallen from 4.0 percent to 1.5 percent. And as effective reserve ratios have declined, effective money multipliers—defined as the ratio of the money supply to required reserves, that is, the reciprocal of the reserve ratio—have risen (Chart 2).[10] In the context of the multiplier model discussed above, the decline in reserve ratios (increase in money multipliers) would appear to be cause for concern from a monetary control standpoint. Feldstein, for example, has argued that it is. The next section takes up this issue.

Chart 2
Required Reserve Money Multipliers

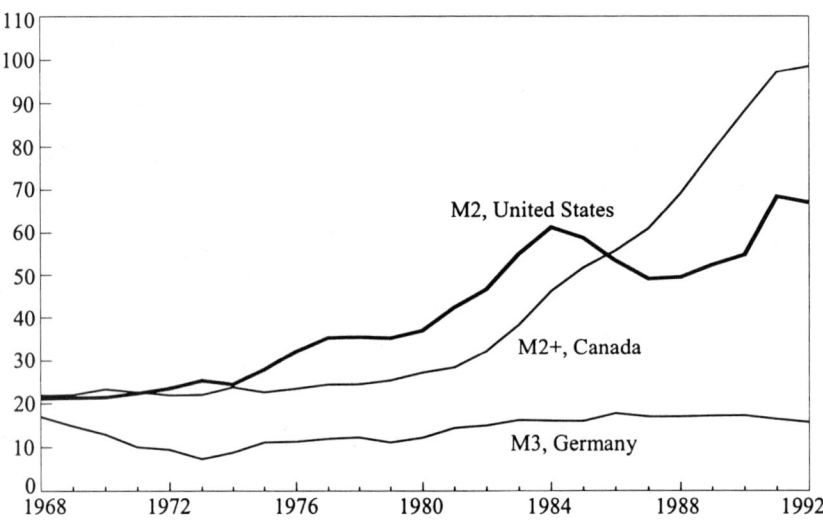

Note: Calculated as required reserves divided by monetary aggregate, based on nonseasonally adjusted, nonbreak adjusted average annual data. Figures for 1992 computed as average of January-May for Germany and Canada, as average of January-June for the United States.
Source: Federal Reserve *Bulletin;* Bank of Canada *Review;* Monthly Report of Deutsche Bundesbank.

RESERVE REQUIREMENTS IN A BROADER FRAMEWORK

Should the decline in reserve requirements alarm monetary policymakers? The multiplier model of the previous section suggests yes. A richer model developed in the first part of this section also initially suggests yes. But by enriching that model even further and incorporating central banks' current focus on interest rates, the answer becomes no.

Money supply and demand

The multiplier model of the preceding section indicates that the decline in reserve requirements could impair monetary control. One might suspect, however, that a richer model, a model that explicitly considers money demand as well as money supply and allows both money demand and money supply to be sensitive to interest rates, would yield different results. In fact, the results of the much simpler model continue to hold. As long as the central bank continues to operate in a way that relies on the direct link between reserves and the money supply, monetary control suffers when reserve requirements decline.

In examining this issue, it is useful to adopt a money supply and demand framework like that depicted in Figure 1. Money stock levels are measured on the horizontal axis and market interest rates are measured on the vertical axis. The equilibrium levels of the money stock and interest rate, $M*$ and $i*$, respectively, are determined where money supply equals money demand, that is, at the intersection

Figure 1
Supply of and Demand for Money

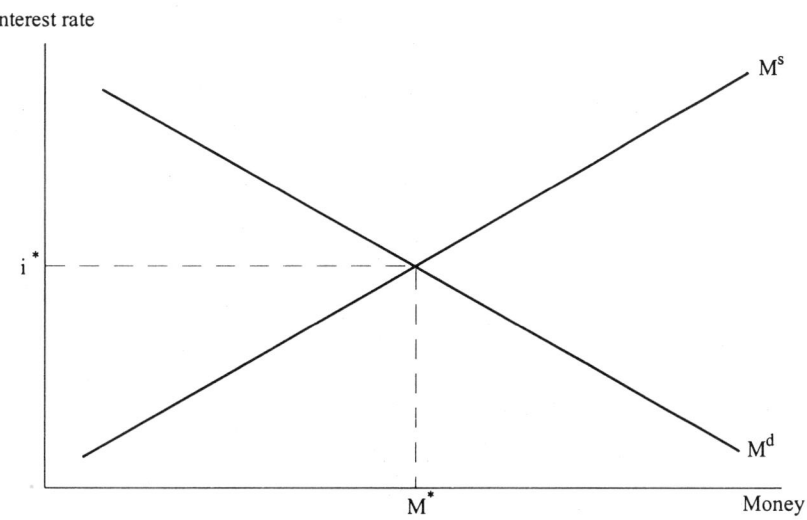

of the money supply and money demand curves.

The money supply curve is derived from a series of equations similar to those underlying the multiplier model. For simplicity, it is again assumed that all money is held in the form of demand deposits, that is,

(5) $M = D$.

Also as before, banks are required to hold a fraction of their assets as reserves against these deposits,

(6) $RR = rrr*D$.

However, banks are now permitted to hold excess reserves as well, so that total reserves are the sum of required reserves and excess reserves,

(7) $TR = RR + ER$.

By assumption, excess reserves do not earn interest. As a result, excess reserves are negatively related to the market interest rate. An increase in the market interest rate, for example, will lead banks to hold fewer excess reserves because excess reserves become more costly in terms of the interest foregone.

As in the multiplier model, the central bank sets the required reserve ratio, rrr, and supplies the reserves, TR. However, a distinction is now made between two types of reserves provided: nonborrowed reserves, which the central bank supplies via open market operations, and borrowed reserves, which the central bank supplies via direct lending at an administered interest rate. Thus, total reserves can also be expressed as the sum of nonborrowed and borrowed reserves,

(8) $TR = NBR + BR$.

Like excess reserves, borrowed reserves are assumed to be sensitive to interest rates. Specifically, borrowed reserves are positively related to the market interest rate. An increase in the market interest rate, for example, will lead banks to borrow more from the central bank as alternative sources of funds become relatively more expensive.

Equations (5) through (8) can now be combined to derive the money supply curve. Rewriting (6) yields

(9) $D = (1/rr)*RR$.

Substituting (5) into (9) implies

(10) $M = (1/rr)*RR$.

From (7) and (8),

(11) $RR + ER = NBR + BR$,

or, rearranging terms,

(12) $RR = NBR + BR - ER$.

Finally, substituting (12) into (10) yields

(13) $M^s = (1/rr)(NBR + BR - ER)$.

Thus, the money supply is determined by the required reserve ratio and the levels of nonborrowed reserves, borrowed reserves, and excess reserves. The money supply curve slopes upward because increases in the market interest rate encourage borrowings and discourage excess reserves, boosting the money supply.

The money demand curve, in contrast, slopes downward on the assumption that money assets do not pay a market rate of return. When the market interest rate declines, the opportunity cost of holding money also declines, reducing the incentive for households and businesses to economize on their money holdings. Hence, the demand for money increases. Conversely, when the market interest rate rises, the demand for money falls.

Lower reserve requirements reduce monetary control in this framework. Disturbances in either money demand or money supply will cause greater movement away from the desired money stock.

Figure 2 shows the effect of a disturbance in money demand. Suppose M^* is the central bank's target level of the money stock, M^d and M^s are the money demand and money supply curves, and the economy initially is in equilibrium at point A. Now suppose the money demand curve shifts to $M^{d'}$. This shift could arise either because of an increase in the transactions demand for money due, say, to higher income growth, or because of an increase in the demand for money vis-a-vis other assets in the public's investment portfolio. Whatever the reason, the economy moves to the new equilibrium point B, and the money stock increases to M'. The central bank finds that its target has been exceeded.

The overshoot would be even greater, however, with lower reserve requirements. Manipulation of equation (13) reveals that a lower required reserve ratio implies a flatter money supply curve. Analytically, at a given interest rate, banks have more free reserves with which to make loans and create deposits.[11] The flatter money supply curve M^s_{lrr} reflects such a decline in reserve requirements. Note that the same money demand disturbance now leads to equilibrium point C, and the money stock now increases to M'_{lrr}, a larger deviation from M^*. Thus, monetary control is worsened.

The same result holds in the case of a money supply disturbance. This point is illustrated in Figure 3. M^s is assumed to be the initial money supply curve, and M^s_{lrr} is assumed to be the money supply curve after reserve requirements have been lowered. Suppose the initial money supply curve shifts rightward to $M^{s'}$, a result, say, of banks unexpectedly deciding to increase borrowings or lower excess reserves. The economy moves to equilibrium point B, and the money stock increases

Figure 2
Money Demand Shock in Presence of Lower Reserve Requirements

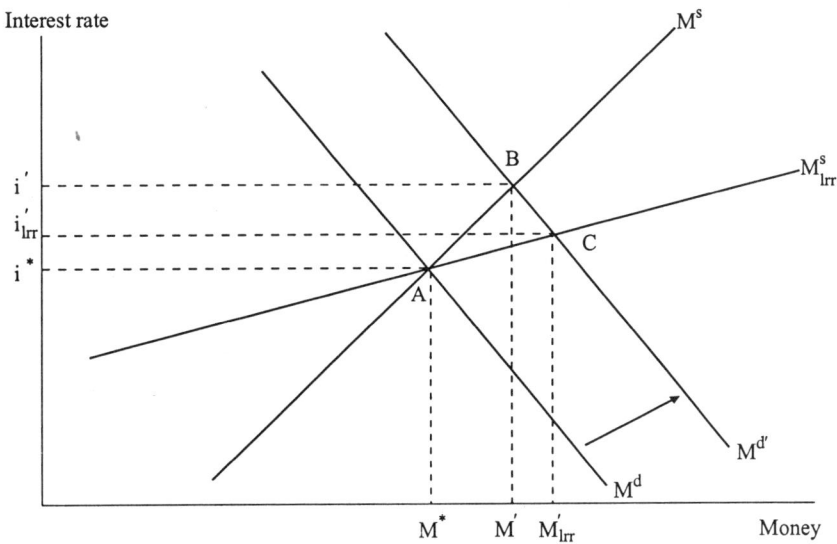

to M'. An identical shift in M^s_{lrr}, in contrast, moves the economy to equilibrium point C and increases the money stock to M'_{lrr}, a level exceeding M'. So again, monetary control is worsened.

Operating procedures and intermediate targets

The results discussed so far all seem to indicate that lower reserve requirements impede monetary control. But a crucial underlying assumption has been that central banks seek to achieve monetary control by exploiting the direct link between reserves and the money supply. This approach to policy, referred to as a "reserves operating procedure," is not the only approach available to central banks. Central banks may instead seek to control the money stock by controlling short-term interest rates, that is, by following an "interest rate operating procedure." Or, central banks may choose to deemphasize monetary control altogether and focus on interest rates as their principal "intermediate target." In such situations, it may be possible to reduce or even eliminate reserve requirements without deleterious effect. The money supply and demand framework developed above again proves useful in examining these issues.

First, however, it is necessary to carefully define some terms. The distinctions among "ultimate goal variables," "intermediate targets," "operating procedures," and "instruments" are very important in discussing the monetary policy implications of lower reserve requirements. Ultimate goal variables are the long-run objectives of the central

Figure 3
Money Supply Shock in Presence of Lower Reserve Requirements

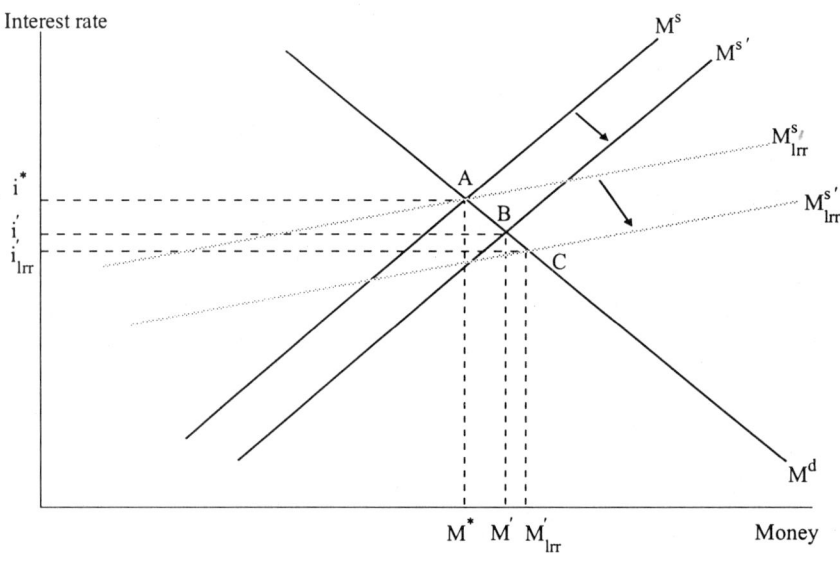

bank. In most countries, these objectives are price stability and sustainable real growth. Central banks cannot directly control ultimate goal variables, however, so they seek instead to control some intermediate target that is thought to be closely related to the ultimate goal variables. Candidates for intermediate targets may include the money stock, medium or long-term interest rates, the exchange rate, or a credit aggregate. Even intermediate targets are difficult to control over a short period of time, however, so central banks establish an operating procedure to guide them in their day-to-day policy actions. Central banks may elect to target reserves, for example, or alternatively may attempt to keep short-term interest rates at a certain level. Finally, in implementing policy on a day-to-day basis, central banks have two primary instruments at their disposal, open market operations and direct lending to depository institutions.[12]

Lower reserve requirements impede monetary control only in the case where the central bank has adopted a reserves operating procedure to achieve its money stock intermediate target. This policy pairing was implicit in the discussion of the preceding subsection. There it was assumed the central bank sought a certain level of the money stock, $M*$, and provided an amount of reserves it thought consistent with that money stock. Disturbances in either money demand or money supply then led to deviations from the targeted money stock, deviations made worse by lower reserve requirements.

But as an alternative the central bank could have attempted to achieve its money target by

Figure 4
Interest Rate Operating Procedure

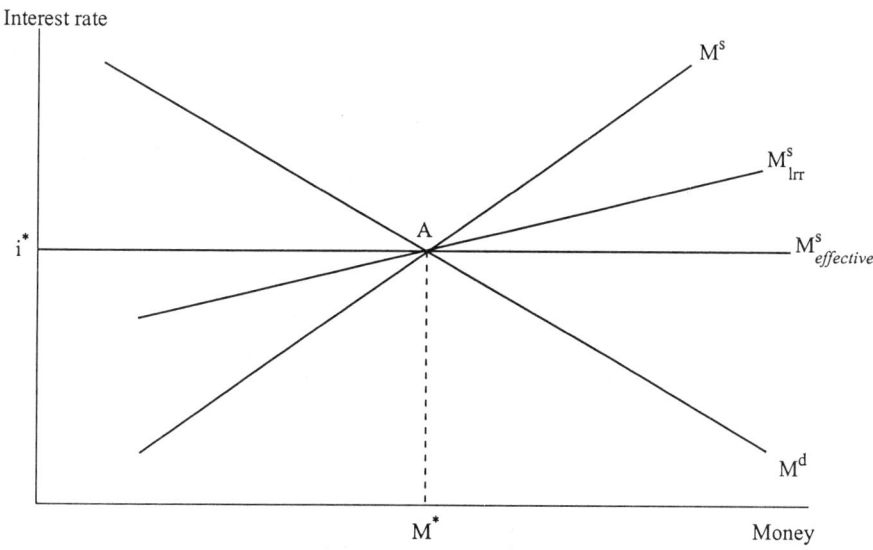

controlling short-term interest rates. That is, it could have adopted an interest rate operating procedure. Under such a procedure, reserve requirements become irrelevant from a direct monetary control standpoint.

The money supply and demand diagram in Figure 4 illustrates this point. Its basic features are identical to those of earlier diagrams. As before, $M*$ is assumed to be the central bank's target level of the money stock, and M^s and M^s_{lrr} are the money supply curves before and after a reduction in reserve requirements. What is different in Figure 4 is the mechanism for achieving $M*$. Rather than providing a predetermined level of reserves and relying on the direct link between reserves and the money supply to achieve $M*$, the central bank focuses instead on achieving the market interest rate $i*$ associated with equilibrium point A—and $M*$. That is, it provides whatever reserves are required to achieve $i*$ and, hopefully, $M*$. In effect, the central bank continuously shifts the upward sloping M^s or M^s_{lrr} curve to the right and left, adding and draining reserves, the intent being to hold the effective money supply curve horizontal at the chosen interest rate in the hope it will cross the money demand curve at the targeted money stock. This horizontal effective supply curve is shown as $M^s_{effective}$ in Figure 4.[13]

A crucial implication is that the level of reserve requirements is now irrelevant. The fact that lower reserve requirements lower the slope of the money supply curve is unimportant—the effective money supply curve is $M^s_{effective}$ in either case. Thus, reserve requirements no longer play a direct role in monetary control.[14]

Going one step further, there is no inherent reason why a central bank need target the money stock. It could be the case that another intermediate target, say, a medium-term interest rate, is deemed to be more closely related to the ultimate goal variables. If so, monetary control can be deemphasized or even abandoned, in which case reserve requirements again become irrelevant as a vehicle for directly controlling the money stock.

Thus, if a central bank chooses to target the money stock via an interest rate operating procedure, or chooses to target some intermediate target other than the money stock, reserve requirements lose their traditional monetary control function. Many central banks, including the Federal Reserve, the Bank of Canada, and the German Bundesbank, have made such choices.

Policy choices

Observers both inside and outside the respective institutions agree the Federal Reserve, the Bank of Canada, and the German Bundesbank are currently following interest rate operating procedures paired with varying degrees of adherence to a money stock intermediate target.[15] Although the three banks have different techniques for implementing policy, their overriding policy orientations are quite similar.

The Federal Reserve's current operating procedure is to target the federal funds rate, the interest rate banks charge each other for overnight loans. The federal funds rate, in turn, strongly influences other short-term market interest rates.

The Federal Reserve's current intermediate target can best be described as a hybrid. The Federal Reserve continues to set annual target ranges for M2 and M3, the broadest measures of the money stock. But the Federal Reserve also carefully monitors medium and long-term interest rates, credit availability, the exchange rate, and incoming data on real growth and inflation. Monetary aggregates' status as intermediate targets has slipped in recent years. As Chairman Greenspan recently explained in discussing the current operating procedure, "policy tactics have evolved away from according top priority to short-run control of any monetary aggregate and hence also away from an operating procedure that targets on a reserve aggregate" (Greenspan 1992a).

The Bank of Canada has adopted a comparable policy approach. It too focuses on short-term interest rates in its day-to-day policy, and it too has reevaluated its intermediate targets. In his most recent annual report, for example, Governor Crow noted that "In putting its policy into effect, the Bank operates at the short end of the financial market.... This involves influencing the rate on overnight financing in the money market" (Bank of Canada 1991a). Regarding intermediate targets, the Bank of Canada no longer establishes formal monetary targets but instead monitors an array of economic variables much like that of the Federal Reserve.[16] Indeed, an alternative characterization of both the Bank of Canada's and the Federal Reserve's current approach is that neither has an intermediate target per se but rather a collection of "information variables," variables that help guide policy decisions but are not targets themselves. For example, Charles Freedman, Deputy Governor of the Bank of Canada, recently described the Bank of Canada's policy structure as one without a formal intermediate target.

German monetary policy has a similar orientation, although geared somewhat more toward traditional monetary control considerations. Like the Federal Reserve and the Bank of Canada, the Bundesbank follows an interest rate operating procedure. Bundesbank officials have described the procedure as one in which, to varying degrees, "key interbank rates are normally kept within narrowly conceived tolerance ranges" (Dudler).[17] Unlike the Federal Reserve and the Bank of Canada, however, the Bundesbank has not deemphasized the money stock as an intermediate target. The Bundesbank continues to set an annual target for M3, the broadest measure of the German money supply, and M3 remains its principal intermediate target. However, the Bundesbank is flexible when deemed necessary. For example, exchange rate considerations have forced the money target to be compromised on occasion.[18]

What are the relative merits of one intermediate target over another or one operating procedure over another? It is beyond the scope of this article to go into much detail, but it is useful to sketch some of the relevant issues.

Most analyses of intermediate target choice focus on the types of disturbances hitting an economy.[19] An economy subject to frequent shocks in money demand emanating from portfolio shifts, for example, is best served by an interest rate intermediate target. Such an approach insulates the real economy from unwanted fluctuations, and while the money stock may increase or decrease unexpectedly, such movements have no effect on the inflation rate. An economy subject to frequent shocks in money demand emanating from unexpected changes in consumer or business spending, on the other hand, is best served by a money stock intermediate target. By allowing interest rates to adjust, a money stock target prevents large fluctuations in real growth and at the same time keeps inflation close to its desired level.[20] Money supply disturbances, such as unintended overprovision or underprovision of non-borrowed reserves or unexpected changes in borrowed or excess reserves, can be accommodated under either an interest rate or a money stock intermediate target.

Most analyses of operating procedure choice proceed along similar lines. A reserves operating procedure is more effective in dealing with spending disturbances, while an interest rate operating procedure is more effective in dealing with portfolio disturbances. An interest rate operating procedure is also superior in the case of money supply shocks.

Thus, according to these studies, a central bank will presumably choose its intermediate target and operating procedure on the basis of the types and relative frequency of disturbances impacting an economy. Mention should be made as well of another group of studies that seeks to explain central banks' policy choices in terms of certain non-disturbance factors, for example, financial market concerns or credibility considerations.[21] Whether the choices made by the Federal Reserve, the Bank of Canada, and the Bundesbank are consistent with these frameworks is left for others to study.

What is relevant here is the implication of the operating procedure/intermediate target choice for the role of reserve requirements. To restate: if a central bank chooses to target the money stock via an interest rate operating procedure (the Bundesbank), or chooses to target some intermediate target other than the money stock (the Federal Reserve and the Bank of Canada, both of which use an interest rate operating procedure in any case), reserve requirements lose their traditional monetary control function. That is, reserve requirements no longer serve as a vehicle for directly controlling the money stock. Nevertheless, reserve requirements may still have a role in monetary policy, that of facilitating control over short-term interest rates. This issue is taken up in the final section.

CURRENT ROLE OF RESERVE REQUIREMENTS

The previous section stressed that many central banks, including the Federal Reserve, the Bank of Canada, and the German Bundesbank, are currently following interest rate operating procedures. In such an environment, reserve requirements are unnecessary from a direct monetary control standpoint. However, depending on the institutional structure within a country, reserve requirements may still have an important monetary policy role to play. By definition, an interest rate operating procedure requires close control over short-term interest rates. Reserve requirements may prove useful, or even necessary, in facilitating this control. It has been argued, in particular, that reserve requirements are needed on these grounds in the United States and Germany but are not needed in Canada.

The interbank market

Most central banks following interest rate operating procedures do so by targeting interbank interest rates. These are the rates banks and other depository institutions charge one another for short-term, typically overnight, loans. Interbank rates, in turn, strongly influence other short-term interest rates. As noted previously, for example, the Federal Reserve targets the federal funds rate, which has an important effect on other short-term private rates as well as on U.S. Treasury bill rates. Similarly, the Bank of Canada focuses on the overnight money market rate, while the Bundesbank pays close attention to the overnight call money rate, also referred to as the day-to-day money rate.[22]

Like any other market interest rate, an interbank rate is determined through the interaction of the supply of and the demand for funds. In this case, the supply ultimately comes from the central bank, while the demand comes from depository institutions.[23]

Depository institutions have two reasons for desiring interbank funds.[24] One, they may want to use interbank funds to help meet their reserve requirements. A depository institution short on reserves can raise funds in several ways. It can call in loans or sell securities out of its portfolio, for example. Alternatively, it can borrow funds in the interbank market.

The second reason depository institutions may want to use interbank funds is to help meet their clearing needs. Although payments systems vary widely across countries, one common feature is the maintenance of accounts at the central bank or elsewhere through which depository institutions settle their payments with one another. To replenish or augment an account used for check clearing or wire transfers, for example, a depository institution may wish to turn to the interbank market to raise funds.

Two conditions are necessary for an interest rate operating procedure to be effective. First, the central bank must have close control over the supply of interbank funds on a weekly or even daily basis. Second, the demand for interbank funds must be reasonably predictable. If these two conditions are met, the central bank will be able to anticipate and offset unwanted movements in the target interbank rate. If the conditions are not met, the interbank rate will fluctuate undesirably. To the extent reserve requirements help stabilize the demand for interbank funds, they facilitate an interest rate operating procedure.[25] It is in this context that the Federal Reserve, the Bank of Canada, and the Bundesbank now discuss the monetary policy merits of reserve requirements.

Current practices

The Federal Reserve operates in what might be considered a traditional institutional framework. Banks and other depository institutions are subject to reserve requirements. Depository institutions can meet their reserve requirements either through their holdings of vault cash or by maintaining reserve balances at the Federal Reserve. For many institutions, vault cash holdings are adequate. For others, reserve balances must also be held. Reserve balances are not idle funds, however, but rather can be used to clear transactions with other depository institutions. Many institutions use their reserve balances to clear and settle checks, for example. Reserve requirements are said to be binding if an institution is forced to hold more reserve balances than it would want to hold solely for clearing purposes.

The Federal Reserve is able to exercise very close control over the supply of interbank funds. To be sure, control is not perfect—on any given day, unanticipated supply factors (for example, currency drains or float increases) can generate an underprovision or overprovision of reserves. But in general the Federal Reserve has a very good idea of the level of funds in the interbank market and can take steps via open market operations to adjust that level when necessary.[26] Thus, the first condition for a successful interest rate operating procedure is met.

The second condition, a predictable demand for interbank funds, is also reasonably well met. Again, surprises are not uncommon. Banks will often hold fewer or greater excess reserves than expected or borrow more or less at the discount window than anticipated. But on average such surprises are manageable. It has been argued that binding reserve requirements facilitate this relatively stable demand by ensuring that a given level of reserve balances will be held.[27]

The potential importance of reserve requirements in this context was illustrated following the December 1990 elimination of reserve requirements on nontransactions deposits. Many depository institutions found that reserve requirements were no longer binding, implying that their holdings of reserve balances were dictated by clearing needs alone. Such needs were often difficult to forecast. Other institutions were still bound by the requirements, but because the overall requirements were now lower, institutions were less willing to hold excess reserves early in the reserve-averaging period for fear of not being able to run sufficient offsetting deficits later in the period. These and other considerations led depository institutions to act less predictably in the interbank market. The result: the federal funds rate showed considerable volatility for many weeks thereafter.[28]

The April 1992 reduction in reserve requirements on transactions deposits, in contrast, was not nearly as disruptive. For one thing, depository institutions had gained valuable experience in managing lower reserve balances. Second, they were given more time to prepare for the change. And third, and probably most important, the level of reservable deposits was sufficiently high to generate a relatively high level of required reserves even after implementation of the reduction. As a result, the Federal Reserve was able to maintain close control over the federal funds rate.[29]

Are further reductions in reserve requirements possible? The potential tradeoffs are clear. Further reductions would further lower the reserve tax, benefiting U.S. depository institutions and their customers. But further reductions might also bring greater interest rate volatility, diminishing the efficacy of current Federal Reserve procedures.[30]

The Bank of Canada operates in a very different institutional framework. Within two years, reserve requirements will be completely eliminated. But because of the unique structure of the Canadian payments system and the framework it has instituted, the Bank of Canada is confident its interest rate operating procedure will not be adversely affected.

The Canadian financial system is highly concentrated. A dozen or so banks, trust and mortgage loan companies, and credit unions account for the lion's share of assets held by Canada's roughly 800 depository institutions. Within the banking sector, for example, the six largest banks controlled 90 percent of all bank assets at the end of 1991.[31]

The payments system in Canada is also highly centralized. Canada has a national payments system operated by the Canadian Payments Association but settling on the books of the Bank of Canada. Thirteen large depository institutions, including eight banks, have "Direct Clearer" status. Direct Clearers are required to hold clearing balances at the Bank of Canada. While these balances do not earn interest, they can be maintained at low levels—the "requirement" is that they not be negative at the end of the day. Through these accounts, daily net clearing gains and losses vis-a-vis other Direct Clearers are settled. Direct Clearers represent not only themselves but may also act as clearing agents for other depository institutions (that is, indirectly clearing members of the Canadian Payments Association). Thus, in effect, all payment items are settled on the books of the Bank of Canada.[32]

The Bank of Canada puts these arrangements to good use in implementing its interest rate operating procedure. On the supply side, the Bank is able to exercise close daily control over the supply of interbank funds by transferring federal government deposits into and out of the settlement accounts of the Direct Clearers. This technique, the "drawdown/redeposit mechanism," is the Bank of Canada's principal operating tool. On the demand side, the framework ensures that the direct clearers have a more or less determinate target each day. As well, the Bank closely monitors and gauges the demand for settlement balances by contacting the large direct clearers.[33]

Thus, in a manner very different from the Federal Reserve, the Bank of Canada meets the two conditions necessary for an effective interest rate operating procedure. Notably, reserve requirements play no role.

The Bundesbank operates in an environment much closer to that of the Federal Reserve. The German banking system is relatively diffuse, with the payments system not inextricably linked to the central bank.[34] Like its two counterparts, the Bundesbank is successful in maintaining close control over the supply of interbank funds.[35] Like the Federal Reserve, it sees reserve requirements as an important factor helping to stabilize the demand for interbank funds.

Helmut Schlesinger, President of the Bundesbank, recently declared reserve requirements "an indispensable targeting instrument... unmistakingly enhance[ing] the efficiency of monetary policy" (Schlesinger). His predecessor, Karl Otto Pohl, held similar views, explaining that "If there were no reserve requirements, the banks would attempt to minimize their balances at the Bundesbank to the greatest extent possible... something which could lead to extreme interest rate responses on the money market" (Pohl).[36] German banks, like U.S. banks, would prefer not to pay a reserve tax. But their doing so in effect helps the Bundesbank control short-term interest rates.

SUMMARY

It remains an open question whether the Federal Reserve and the Bundesbank will follow the Bank of Canada and further reduce reserve requirements. It is clear, though, that monetary policy discussions will turn on interest rate considerations, not on direct monetary control considerations. While to varying degrees central banks still seek to target the money stock over longer periods of time, in the short run most use an interest rate operating procedure. Under such a procedure, reserve requirements play a different monetary policy role than that traditionally espoused. Reserve requirements are seen not as an instrument for directly controlling the money stock but rather as a tool for facilitating control over short-term interest rates. It is in this context that future debates over reserve requirements will take place.

ENDNOTES

[1] Early multiplier studies include Brunner, and Brunner and Meltzer. More recent treatments include Garfinkel and Thornton, Cacy and Winningham, and virtually any money and banking or intermediate macroeconomics textbook. Many multiplier models choose to emphasize the monetary base (reserves plus currency) rather than reserves; that is, the "multiplier" is calculated as the money stock divided by the base. In such models, it is still the case that a decrease in reserve requirements leads to a larger multiplier, implying a reduction in monetary control.

[2] By introducing currency into the model, where c equals the public's desired currency-to-deposit ratio, the multiplier becomes $(1+c)/rr$. Note that, as in the simpler case, a decrease in the required reserve ratio increases the multiplier, implying less monetary control.

[3] It is straightforward, for example, to accommodate nonreservable time deposits. It is also straightforward to accommodate interest-insensitive excess reserves (interest-sensitive excess reserves are modeled explicitly in the money supply and demand framework of the next section). For an example of a fully developed multiplier model, see Mishkin, pp. 356-58.

[4] Strictly speaking, then, it is not the Bank of Canada per se but the Canadian federal government that has eliminated reserve requirements. Included in the legislation are a number of other provisions designed to enhance competition among financial institutions. Of course, it has been left to the Bank of Canada to implement the elimination of reserve requirements, a process the Bank began on November 18, 1991

(Bank of Canada 1991a, p. 30). The marginal reserve requirement is zero during the two-year phaseout period.

[5] It has been argued that a portion of the reserve tax is offset by benefits. Prior to the 1980 Monetary Control Act, for example, member banks of the Federal Reserve received free services such as check clearing and collection. In Germany, banks are permitted to borrow a large amount of funds at the below-market discount rate. In Canada, banks until recently had more lending powers than competitors. Nevertheless, virtually all analysts agree the reserve tax is still burdensome on net.

[6] See also Greenspan 1992a and 1992b.

[7] An alternative way of reducing the reserve tax would be to pay interest on reserves, an idea supported by the Board of Governors of the Federal Reserve System (Greenspan 1992a and 1991). But in the United States, at least, such a policy has always been resisted by the Congress because of the resulting revenue loss for the government. For discussion, see Weiner; Meulendyke; and Goodfriend and Hargraves.

[8] See Kryzanowski and Roberts; Clinton.

[9] An important example in the United States is the growth of money market mutual funds in the late 1970s and early 1980s. The argument that reserve requirements induce innovations has been advanced by several authors (Greenbaum).

[10] U.S. M2 includes currency, demand deposits, other checkable deposits, savings deposits (including money market deposit accounts), small time deposits, overnight repurchase agreements and overnight Eurodollars, and general-purpose and broker-dealer money market funds. Canada M2+ includes currency, demand deposits less private sector float, personal savings deposits, nonpersonal notice deposits, deposits at trust and mortgage loan companies and savings banks, deposits and shares at credit unions, and holdings of money market mutual funds and annuities issued to individuals. German M3 includes currency, sight deposits, time deposits, and savings deposits. For the United States, it would be preferable to calculate the effective required reserve ratio as required reserves *behind M2 deposits* divided by M2 (the approach followed in the Canadian and German cases). Unfortunately, complete U.S. data are not available, so in early years some of the reserves in the numerator were actually held against non-M2 M3 deposits, causing the measured effective ratio, and hence the decline, to be somewhat overstated. However, by calculating reserves against transaction deposits as a fraction of M2, thus establishing a lower bound for the true effective reserve ratio, one can safely infer that the true effective reserve ratio has indeed declined sharply.

[11] Let FR = free reserves = $ER - BR = \alpha - \beta i$ where i = market interest rate and $\beta > 0$. Then rewriting equation (13),

$$M^s = \frac{1}{rrr}(NBR-FR) = \frac{1}{rrr}(NBR) - \frac{1}{rrr}(\alpha - \beta i).$$

$$\frac{dM^s}{di} = \frac{-1}{rrr}(-\beta) = \frac{\beta}{rrr}, \text{ implying}$$

as rrr decreases, $\frac{dM^s}{di}$ increases, that is, the M^s curve becomes flatter.

[12] For discussions of the target hierarchy, see Sellon and Teigen (1982a and 1982b), Freedman, Friedman, and Sellon.

[13] In the absence of disturbances to money demand and money supply, an interest rate operating procedure and a reserves operating procedure yield equivalent outcomes. In terms of Figure 4, for example, an absence of shocks implies equilibrium point A, with a money stock $M*$ and interest rate $i*$. But if money demand and money supply are subject to shocks, the alternative operating procedures imply very different outcomes. By its very nature, an interest rate operating procedure strives, at least initially, to keep the interest rate at its current level, so that any shock translates fully into a deviation in the money stock. A reserves operating procedure, in contrast, accommodates movements in the interest rate, with the result that shocks translate into both money stock and interest rate deviations.

[14] For formal derivations of this key result, see Kaminow, Laufenberg, and Horrigan.

[15] Surveys of current operating procedures in several countries include Kneeshaw and Van den Bergh; Batten and others; Bernanke and Mishkin; Kasman; and Morton and Wood. Country-specific analyses include Greenspan (1992a) and Meulendyke (United States); Clinton; Freedman; Freedman and Dingle (Canada); and Dudler; Neumann (Germany).

[16] The Bank of Canada abandoned monetary targets in 1982.

[17] In the same citation, Dudler characterizes the Bundesbank as not following a "pure 'interest rate' strategy," but stresses as well that short-run procedures neither are based on a "rigorous 'money multiplier' approach." Analysts outside the Bundesbank typically characterize the Bundesbank's approach as an interest rate operating procedure (Neumann; Kasman). An interest rate operating procedure also appears implicit in recent statements by Bundesbank presidents Schlesinger and Pohl.

[18] See Issing (1992a and 1992b) for a description of the importance currently accorded money stock targeting. See Kahn and Jacobson for a discussion of foreign exchange considerations.

[19] A seminal work is Poole. A particularly useful, comprehensive treatment is provided by Sellon and Teigen (1982a and 1982b).

[20] Of course, an interest rate intermediate target can be equally effective to the extent the central bank (i) can identify a shock as emanating from a change in spending, and (ii) can immediately adjust its intermediate interest rate target to the appropriate level.

[21] For discussion, see Goodfriend (1991 and 1992).

[22] The Bank of Canada and the Bundesbank seek to closely

influence longer term money market rates as well. As a signal, the Bank Rate, which is tied to the 90-day Treasury bill rate at Thursday tender, is important in Canada. The one and two-month repurchase agreement rates are important in Germany. For detailed discussion, see citations in note 15.

23 Some depository institutions may be "suppliers" in the sense they lend funds in the interbank market; however, the funds available to the financial system as a whole are ultimately provided by the central bank.

24 The term "interbank funds" is used broadly. In some countries, funds are rarely lent and borrowed directly between banks, in which case a more descriptive term for "interbank funds" might be "clearing balances" or "settlement balances."

25 This is a point made by several authors, including Freedman and Kasman. The two conditions for an effective interest rate operating procedure can be stated in terms of the money supply curve, equation (13): the first, the central bank must have close control over the (net) supply of interbank funds corresponds to close control over NBR; the second, the (net) demand for interbank funds must be reasonably predictable, corresponds to predictable movements in BR and ER. It is also worth noting that reserve requirements, by inducing innovations (see note 9), could induce more portfolio-related money demand shocks than would otherwise be the case, making attainment of an intermediate target (money stock or interest rate) more difficult. But within the context of an interest rate operating procedure, and, specifically, the day-to-day control of an interbank interest rate, reserve requirements are a stabilizing factor.

26 For a discussion of Federal Reserve open market operations and factors affecting the supply of reserves, see Roth.

27 Chairman Greenspan in a recent letter stressed the role played by reserve requirements in stabilizing reserve demand: The most important current advantage [of reserve requirements] is that reserve requirements provide for a reasonably predictable demand for overall reserve balances. They do so by keeping required operating balances at a relatively stable level above the quite variable amount needed to clear volatile payments. Such a predictable demand is essential for the effective implementation of open market operations in avoiding unnecessary fluctuations in the federal funds rate (1992a).

28 For a discussion of some the problems associated with the December 1990 episode, see Meulendyke; and Dumitru and Stevens.

29 For discussion, see Gilbert.

30 Within the Federal Reserve there are different views on the desirability or practicality of further reductions. For example, Greenspan (1992a and 1991) and Muelendyke take cautious positions; Stevens endorses further reductions at this time. In considering further reductions, the Federal Reserve might also wish to consider changes in discount window operation, a point made by Muelendyke. Under current law, the reserve requirement on transactions deposits cannot be lowered below 8 percent.

31 For a discussion of the Canadian banking system, see Kryzanowski and Roberts.

32 For a description of the Canadian payments system, see Bank for International Settlements and Crow. It should be noted that U.S. depository institutions, in addition to holding reserve accounts, also have the option of holding separate "clearing balance accounts" at the Federal Reserve. However, this is an optional program and very different from the Canadian case. For a description of the U.S. payments system, see Bank for International Settlements. For a brief discussion of Federal Reserve clearing balance accounts, see Stevens.

33 For a detailed description of the Bank of Canada's planned operating procedure without reserve requirements, see Bank of Canada 1991b and 1987; Clinton; Longworth; and Sufrin and Amsden.

34 For a discussion of the German banking system, see Pozdena and Alexander. For a discussion of the German payments system, see Bank for International Settlements.

35 For description of Bundesbank policy instruments, see Deutsche Bundesbank 1989 as well as the relevant citations in note 15.

36 See also Deutsche Bundesbank 1990 for Bundesbank perspectives on reserve requirements.

REFERENCES

Bank of Canada. 1991a. *Annual Report of the Governor to the Minister of Finance and Statement of Accounts for the Year.*

———. 1991b. "The Implementation of Monetary Policy in a System with Zero Reserve Requirements," Discussion Paper No. 3, May 1 (revised September 6, 1991).

———. 1987. "Discussion Paper on the Implementation of Monetary Policy in the Absence of Reserve Requirements," September 29.

Bank for International Settlements. 1989. *Payment Systems in Eleven Developed Countries*, Bank Administration Institute, May.

Batten, Dallas S., and others. 1990. "The Conduct of Monetary Policy in the Major Industrial Countries: Instruments and Operating Procedures," Occasional Paper No. 70, International Monetary Fund, July.

Bernanke, Ben, and Frederic Mishkin. 1992. "Central Bank Behavior and the Strategy of Monetary Policy: Observations from Six Industrialized Countries," National Bureau of Economic Research, Working Paper No. 4082, May.

Board of Governors of the Federal Reserve System. 1992. Press Release, February 18.

_____. 1990. Press Release, December 4.

Brunner, Karl. 1961. "A Schema for the Supply Theory of Money," *International Economic Review*, January, pp. 79-109.

_____, and Allan H. Meltzer. 1964. "Some Further Investigations of Demand and Supply Functions for Money," *Journal of Finance*, May, pp. 240-83.

Cacy, J. A., and Scott Winningham. 1982. "Reserve Requirements Under the Depository Institutions Deregulation and Monetary Control Act of 1980," Federal Reserve Bank of Kansas City, *Issues in Monetary Policy: II*, March, pp. 68-81.

Clinton, Kevin. 1991. "Bank of Canada Cash Management: The Main Technique for Implementing Monetary Policy," *Bank of Canada Review*, January, pp. 3-25.

Crow, John W. 1992. "What Makes A Good Payments System?" Third Annual Conference of the Canadian Bankers' Association, Montreal, Quebec, June 18.

Deutsche Bundesbank. 1990. "Minimum Reserve Arrangements Abroad," *Monthly Report of the Deutsche Bundesbank*, March, pp. 21-28.

_____. 1989. *The Deutsche Bundesbank: Its Monetary Policy Instruments and Functions*, 3d ed., Deutsche Bundesbank Special Series, no. 7, July.

Dudler, Hermann-Josef. 1986. "Changes in Money-Market Instruments and Procedures in Germany," *Changes in Money-Market Instruments and Procedures: Objectives and Implications*, Bank for International Settlements, March, pp. 53-73.

Dumitru, Diana, and E. J. Stevens. 1991. "Federal Funds Rate Volatility," Federal Reserve Bank of Cleveland, *Economic Commentary*, August 15.

Evans, Garry. 1992. "Bundesbank Clings to Power," *Euromoney*, April, pp. 55-58.

Feldstein, Martin. 1991. "Reasserting Monetary Control at the Fed," *The Wall Street Journal*, June 10, p. A10.

Freedman, Charles. 1990. "Implementation of Monetary Policy," *Monetary Policy and Market Operations*, Reserve Bank of Australia, pp. 27-49.

_____, and J. F. Dingle. 1986. "Monetary Policy Implementation in Canada: Traditional Structure and Recent Developments," *Changes in Money-Market Instruments and Procedures: Objectives and Implications*, Bank for International Settlements, March, pp. 23-40.

Friedman, Benjamin. 1975. "Targets, Instruments, and Indicators of Monetary Policy," *Journal of Monetary Economics*, October, pp. 443-73.

Garfinkel, Michelle R., and Daniel L. Thornton. 1991. "The Multiplier Approach to the Money Supply Process: A Precautionary Note," Federal Reserve Bank of St. Louis *Review*, July/August, pp. 47-62.

Gilbert, R. Alton. 1992. "The Federal Funds Rate's Limited Response to Lower Reserve Requirements," Federal Reserve Bank of St. Louis, *Monetary Trends*, May.

Goodfriend, Marvin. 1992. "Interest Rate Policy and the Inflation Scare Problem: 1979-1992," mimeo, Federal Reserve Bank of Richmond, June.

_____. 1991. "Interest Rates and the Conduct of Monetary Policy," Carnegie-Rochester Conference Series on Public Policy 34, Spring, pp. 7-30.

_____, and Monica Hargraves. 1983. "A Historical Assessment of the Rationales and Functions of Reserve Requirements," Federal Reserve Bank of Richmond, *Economic Review*, March/April, pp. 3-21.

Greenbaum, Stuart. 1983. "Legal Reserve Requirements: A Case Study in Bank Regulation," *Journal of Bank Research*, Spring, pp. 59-74.

Greenspan, Alan. 1992a. Letter written to the Honorable Stephen L. Neal, House of Representatives, March 6.

_____. 1992b. Testimony Before House Committee on Banking, Finance and Urban Affairs, February 19.

_____. 1991. Letter written to the Honorable David Dreier, House of Representatives, January 11.

Horrigan, Brian R. 1988. "Are Reserve Requirements Relevant for Economic Stabilization?" *Journal of Monetary Economics*, January, pp. 97-105.

Issing, Otmar. 1992a. Lecture at the Paolo Baffi Centre for Monetary and Financial Economics, Bocconi University, Milan, June 5, 1992, reprinted in *Bank for International Settlements Review*, no. 121, June 24, pp. 5-8.

_____. 1992b. Address Before the Verband Deutscher Geldhandler, Frankfurt, April 5, 1992, reprinted in *Bank for International Settlements*, no. 104, May 29, pp. 9-13.

Kahn, George A., and Kristina Jacobson. 1989. "Lessons from West German Monetary Policy," Federal Reserve Bank of Kansas City, *Economic Review*, April, pp. 18-35.

Kaminow, Ira. 1977. "Required Reserve Ratios, Policy Instruments, and Money Stock Control," *Journal of Monetary Economics*, pp. 389-408.

Kasman, Bruce. 1992. "A Comparison of Monetary Policy Operating Procedures in Six Industrial Countries," Federal Reserve Bank of New York, *Quarterly Review*, Summer, pp. 5-24.

Kneeshaw, J. T., and P. Van den Bergh. 1989. *Changes in Central Bank Money Market Operating Procedures in the 1980s*, Bank for International Settlements, Economic Papers no. 23, January.

Kryzanowski, Lawrence, and Gordon S. Roberts. 1992. "Bank Structure in Canada," *Banking Structures in Major Countries*. Norwell, Mass.: Kluwer Academic Publishers, pp. 1-57.

Laufenberg, Daniel. 1979. "Optimal Reserve Requirements Ratios Against Bank Deposits for Short-Run Monetary

Control," *Journal of Money, Credit and Banking*, February, pp. 99-105.

Longworth, David. 1989. "Optimal Behaviour of Direct Clearers in a World with Zero Reserve Requirements," mimeo, Bank of Canada, May.

Meulendyke, Ann-Marie. 1992. "Federal Reserve Tools in the Monetary Policy Process in Recent Decades," mimeo, Federal Reserve Bank of New York, May.

Mishkin, Frederic S. 1992. *The Economics of Money, Banking, and Financial Markets*, 3d ed., New York: Harper Collins Publishers.

Morton, John, and Paul Wood. 1992. "Interest Rate Operating Procedures of Foreign Central Banks," mimeo, Division of International Finance, Board of Governors of the Federal Reserve System.

Neumann, Manfred J.M. 1990. "Implementing Monetary Policy in Germany," *Financial Sectors in Open Economies: Empirical Analysis and Policy Issues*, Board of Governors of the Federal Reserve System, pp. 499-528.

Pohl, Karl Otto. 1991. Speech, Frankfurt, March 3, reprinted in *Bank for International Settlements Review*, no. 66, April 5, pp. 1-9.

Poole, William. 1970. "Optimal Choice of Monetary Policy Instruments in a Simple Stochastic Macro Model," *Quarterly Journal of Economics*, May, pp. 197-216.

Pozdena, Randall Johnston, and Volbert Alexander. 1992. "Bank Structure in West Germany," *Banking Structures in Major Countries*. Norwell, Mass.: Kluwer Academic Publishers, pp. 555-90.

Roth, Howard L. 1986. "Federal Reserve Open Market Techniques, Federal Reserve Bank of Kansas City, *Economic Review*, March, pp. 3-15.

Schlesinger, Helmut. 1992. Address at the Conference of the Assoziation für die Europaische Wahrungsunion, Frankfurt, May 26, 1992, reprinted in *Bank for International Settlements*, no. 117, June 18, pp. 1-7.

Sellon, Gordon H. 1984. "The Instruments of Monetary Policy," Federal Reserve Bank of Kansas City, *Economic Review*, May, pp. 3-20.

_____, and Ronald L. Teigen. 1982a. "The Choice of Short-Run Targets for Monetary Policy, Part I: A Theoretical Analysis," Federal Reserve Bank of Kansas City, *Issues in Monetary Policy: II*, March, pp. 27-40.

_____, and Ronald L. Teigen.. 1982b. "The Choice of Short-Run Targets for Monetary Policy, Part II: An Historical Analysis," *Issues in Monetary Policy: II*, Federal Reserve Bank of Kansas City, March, pp. 41-50.

Stevens, E. J. 1991. "Is There Any Rationale for Reserve Requirements?" Federal Reserve Bank of Cleveland, *Economic Review*, no. 3, pp. 2-17.

Sufrin, Kerry, and Barbara Amsden. 1992. "The Real Meaning of Reserve Reform," *Canadian Banker*, January/February, pp. 14-18.

Weiner, Stuart E. 1985. "Payment of Interest on Reserves," Federal Reserve Bank of Kansas City, *Economic Review*, January, pp. 16-31.

Article 31

The Federal Budget Deficit, Saving and Investment, and Growth

In the last decade and a half the federal budget deficit has mushroomed. Some analysts would argue that this sets the stage for lower rates of U.S. consumption in the future. The rationale is that government borrowing absorbs private sector saving and thereby reduces the rate of capital formation. This view underlies the current deficit reduction program of the Clinton Administration. Other analysts, however, question whether the linkage between the deficit and investment is as close as this.

This *Weekly Letter* first discusses the sources of the growing federal budget deficit. It then summarizes the evidence in support of the view that there is a strong linkage between high federal budget deficits and low national investment, as well as the possible criticisms of that view.

Sources of the budget deficit
From World War II to about 1970, federal expenditures grew faster than the net national product (NNP), but on average, the expenditures were balanced by growing receipts. Between 1970 and 1992, however, federal expenditures rose from 22 percent to 27½ percent of NNP, while receipts remained at around 22 percent.

On the expenditure side, entitlement payments (primarily Social Security, Medicare, and Medicaid), which rose from 6 to 11½ percent of NNP, accounted for all of that increase. Defense spending fell from 8 to 6 percent of NNP, despite temporary increases during the Reagan years, while net interest on the federal debt rose by an equal amount. All other federal spending has been quite constant as a share of NNP since 1970, running at about 6 percent.

On the revenue side, contributions to social insurance rose from 5 percent of NNP in the late 1960s to 9 percent in 1992, covering about three quarters of the increase in entitlement expenditures. But other taxes were reduced by an equal amount, leaving total receipts as a percent of NNP unchanged throughout the past two decades. The biggest offsetting changes in other receipts were in corporate and personal income taxes, which fell by 2 and 1½ percentage points of NNP, respectively. In addition, federal excise taxes on such things as alcohol, tobacco, and gasoline dropped by ½ percentage point of NNP.

In summary, the entire increase in the federal budget deficit was accounted for by higher entitlement payments, while taxes remained constant as a fraction of national income. But the composition of taxes changed: Taxes for social insurance rose, while taxes on personal income, corporate profits, and some commodities fell.

Effect on national investment
Concerns that the large federal budget deficit will hamper long-term growth revolve around the deficit's effect on national saving and hence investment. The amount of investment in capital goods per worker plus improvements in technology and workers' skills ultimately determines long-term growth in real per capita incomes.

In the national income accounts, net private investment (both domestic and foreign) equals net private saving less the government's dissaving (represented by its budget deficit). Net private saving has trended downward in the last two decades from about 8½ percent of the net national product (NNP) to about 6½ percent in 1992. (Net private saving here includes a fairly steady and small amount of surpluses of state and local governments, which are mainly due to employee pension funds and are therefore analogous to private saving.) Net private *investment*, however, has fallen from about 8½ percent of NNP to a record low of only about 1½ percent; most of this decline took place in the 1980s when the increase in the federal budget deficit was the greatest.

The view that a budget deficit diminishes investment assumes that the higher government expenditures or increased private incomes from tax reductions associated with the deficit are at least partly spent on current consumption. The borrowing to finance a government budget deficit tends to absorb private saving that would otherwise go into private investment. If the proceeds of the borrowing are at least partly spent on consumption goods, then the overall level of investment in the economy is reduced. If private *domestic* investment gets crowded out by the budget deficit and the government's borrowing is not spent on investment goods, then future productivity and hence future consumption in the economy suffers. Alternatively, if private *foreign* investment gets crowded out, then future incomes that U.S. residents would receive from their investments abroad, and therefore also their future consumption, are lowered. Either way, the benefits of higher consumption today are counterbalanced by lower consumption in the future.

Conversely, reducing the budget deficit would result in a reduction of consumption today, and an increase in consumption in the future. Determining whether this delayed benefit is worthwhile requires an estimate of the actual trade-off in the economy between present and future consumption, as well as some measurement of the public's time preference, or the rate of interest that equates the utility of current and future consumption. A reasonable measure of the public's time preference would lie somewhere between the current real after-tax yield on long-term bonds of about 1½ percent and that on common stocks of around 3 to 4 percent. Standard growth models can be used to estimate the actual trade-off between present and future consumption; and they show that the future gains in consumption from a policy of higher saving and investment would outweigh the current losses in consumption at any real interest rate below 10 percent. (See, for example, Harris and Steindel (1991).)

Possible criticisms
Several criticisms have been made of the view that the federal budget deficit has contributed significantly to the collapse in national saving and investment and that the surest way to raise saving and investment is by moving toward budget balance. First, the national income accounts treat all government spending as consumption. So theoretically, a rise in the federal budget deficit could have been accompanied by an increase in the rate of public investment, with no necessary effect on the true rate of national investment.

Unfortunately, the empirical evidence does not suggest that this happened. As discussed earlier, the overall increase in federal spending can be traced to higher entitlement payments, which tend to be spent on consumption. Nor has the composition of federal expenditures on goods and services shifted toward investment. Net federal investment in nonmilitary physical capital is relatively small, currently running at only about $7 billion a year. Moreover, according to the Congressional Budget Office (1990), net federal investment in nonmilitary physical capital has not increased relative to the size of the economy in the last two decades; and a broader measure of net federal investment that includes research and development and investment in human capital has actually declined.

Military assets yield returns over an extended period also, and net federal investment in such assets increased by about 0.5 percent of NNP in the 1980s. But there is an offsetting trend in net investment by state and local governments, which has declined rather significantly since the 1970s. All in all, a proper accounting for the trend in government investment probably would accentuate the decline in net national investment seen in the national income accounts, rather than reduce it.

A second criticism argues that the size of the budget deficit's contribution to reducing national saving and investment, is overstated because of inflation. Payments of interest on government debt contain an inflation premium to compensate wealthholders for losses in the real value of their holdings of government debt. But since wealthholders should tend to reinvest the inflation premiums in financial markets in order to maintain their real wealth, any government borrowing undertaken to pay for these premiums would tend to be matched by a heightened flow of private saving and therefore would not tend to crowd out private investment. It is therefore argued that the measured federal budget deficit overstates the claim of the government on private saving by the amount of the inflation premiums.

However, while the argument that both the federal budget deficit and private saving are overstated because of inflation is correct, the inflation adjustment has changed remarkably little over time relative to NNP because changes in inflation have tended to be offset by opposite movements in the debt-to-NNP ratio. Thus, the debt-to-NNP ratio fell through the 1970s as inflation rose, but then rose in the 1980s as inflation fell. So the inflation-adjusted deficit increased in relation to NNP by about as much as the unadjusted deficit did (Congressional Budget Office (1990)). As a result, the measured contribution of the federal budget deficit to the collapse in national saving and investment is about the same, whether this adjustment is made or not.

A final criticism is that households make farsighted adjustments to government deficits. In this case, any increase in the federal budget deficit would be perceived to imply equally large tax increases (plus interest payments on the accumulated debt) to be paid in the future either by themselves or their heirs. Therefore, households would save an equal amount and use it to pay future taxes. As a result, the increase in government dissaving due to the emergence of the deficit would be exactly offset by a rise in private saving, leaving total saving and investment unaffected by the budget deficit.

This point, known as "Ricardian Equivalence," is currently disputed among economists. On the surface, at least, this view appears to be grossly contradicted by the events of the last two decades: The increase in the federal budget deficit was accompanied by a decrease, not an increase, in private saving. Proponents argue, however, that other factors were working to reduce the saving rate at the same time that the budget deficit was acting to increase it. The most likely candidate is an unanticipated increase in wealth, due first to price increases in houses and later in equities, which reduced the incentive to save. However, by the end of the 1980s the Federal Reserve Board's comprehensive measure of real national net worth, at market value, was somewhat below trend rather than above it.

In practical terms, would balancing the budget be more likely to return the economy's saving and investment back toward historical norms or leave them unchanged? According to the Ricardian Equivalence view, private saving would fall by about as much as the reduction in the budget deficit. But that would lower private saving to levels far below the range of historical experience. Specifically, the 4 percentage point reduction in the high-employment budget (relative to NNP) required to move it to a balanced position would push the private saving rate down from its current level of about 6½ percent of NNP to only 2½ percent, compared with a historical range of 6½ to 11 percent during other periods of balanced budgets, which seems unlikely.

Conclusion

The basic source of the growing federal budget deficit since the late 1960s has been rising entitlement payments relative to income. Taxes to pay for social insurance have risen by almost as much, but offsetting this on the revenue side have been falling corporate, personal income, and excise taxes relative to income. Although net private saving has declined somewhat in this period, the rising federal budget deficit appears to have been the largest contributor to the collapse in national saving and investment. All else equal, moving toward a federal budget balance likely would contribute to bringing the rate of national saving and investment back to normal. Absent a correction in the rate of saving and investment, the economy likely would continue on a lower long-term path of growth, in which losses from lower future consumption would outweigh the gains from higher current consumption.

Closing the budget deficit requires restoring some taxes, as well as cutting entitlement and nonentitlement spending. However, high marginal tax rates that tend to yield little revenue and discourage private saving and investment and cuts in government investment that would be counterproductive should be avoided. In this connection, the Clinton Program does increase tax revenues and reduce spending growth; however, it remains to be seen whether its relatively high marginal tax rates will yield as much revenue as projected, or encourage investment as much as hoped.

Adrian W. Throop
Research Officer

References

Congressional Budget Office. 1990. "The Federal Deficit: Does It Measure the Government's Effect on National Saving?"

Harris, E., and C. Steindel. 1991. "The Decline in U.S. Saving and Its Implications for Economic Growth." Federal Reserve Bank of New York *Quarterly Review* (Winter).

Article 32

Can the Government Roll Over Its Debt Forever?

*Andrew B. Abel**

In the past dozen years, the federal government has regularly run large deficits, usually well in excess of $100 billion per year. The amount of federal government debt outstanding has quadrupled during this time, from a value of $908 billion at the end of fiscal year 1980 to a value of $3,665 billion at the end of fiscal year 1991. Even after correcting for inflation, the amount of government debt has grown by a factor of 2.5 over this period. This apparent explosion in the amount of government debt has led to spirited and protracted public debate about federal tax policy and federal expenditures. Despite the widely professed desire to reduce the federal deficit and to limit the growth of federal government debt, a consensus about how to achieve these alleged goals has not yet emerged. Faced with continuing deficits, the

---

*Andrew B. Abel is Robert Morris Professor of Banking, Department of Finance, Wharton School, University of Pennsylvania, and a Visiting Scholar, Research Department, Federal Reserve Bank of Philadelphia. Andy thanks Thomas Stark for extremely capable research assistance. He also thanks Henning Bohn, Satyajit Chatterjee, Dean Croushore, Jamie McAndrews, Steve Meyer, and Stephen Zeldes for helpful discussions, and Sally Burke for valuable editorial advice.

government has resorted to rolling over its debt—that is, issuing new debt to pay the interest on existing debt and to pay off holders of maturing debt.

Is rolling over the debt the solution that we have been looking for? Can the government simply roll over its debt forever without having to take the politically costly steps of raising taxes or cutting expenditures in the future? This article discusses the feasibility of rolling over government debt forever. As we will see, this question is related to another important question about the future of the economy: Is the economy as a whole saving an appropriate amount for the future? In addition, both of these questions are related to the question of whether an entity can run a Ponzi game.

THE SIMPLE ARITHMETIC OF GOVERNMENT DEBT ACCUMULATION

To address the question of whether the government can roll over its debt forever, we need to quantify the factors that contribute to the growth of government debt over time. We begin by specifying the relationship between government deficits and the growth rate of government debt. Then we examine whether the public would be willing to hold ever-increasing amounts of government debt, thereby permitting the government to roll over its debt forever.

Primary and Total Deficits. Although it is tempting to think of both "debt" and "deficits" as representing the "D word," there is an important distinction between debt and deficits. Government debt is the liability of the government owed to holders of government bonds at any particular moment; it is measured in dollars as of a particular date, such as $3,665 billion as of September 30, 1991. A government deficit is the excess of government expenditures over government receipts during a particular period. The government deficit equals the increase in the amount of government debt during a particular interval; it is measured in terms of dollars per unit of time, such as $320.9 billion per year during fiscal year 1991 (October 1, 1990 - September 30, 1991). In terms of familiar accounting concepts, government debt is a balance sheet concept, whereas the government deficit is an income statement concept.

Although the definition of the government deficit as the excess of government expenditures over government receipts during a particular period seems fairly unambiguous, actually two different deficit concepts are widely used. The difference between these two deficit concepts lies in whether interest payments on government debt are included as part of government expenditure. One deficit concept, known as the primary deficit, does not include interest payments on the government debt as part of government expenditure. Thus, the primary government deficit is calculated as all noninterest expenditure by the government minus government receipts. The primary government deficit was "only" $34.9 billion in fiscal 1991 (Table 1).

The other deficit concept, known as the total deficit or simply the deficit, includes interest payments by the government as part of government expenditure. Thus the total deficit equals total government expenditure, including interest payments, minus government receipts. In fiscal 1991, interest payments by the government amounted to $286.0 billion, so that the total government deficit of $320.9 billion exceeded the primary government deficit by $286.0 billion.

Why are there two different deficit concepts? The reason economists and policymakers look at both of these deficit concepts is that each concept provides the answer to a different question. Specifically, the primary deficit answers the question: Are current taxes sufficient to pay for spending on current government programs? More precisely, the primary deficit measures the extent to which spending on current programs exceeds the taxes currently collected. The total deficit answers a different

TABLE 1
Government Deficit
Fiscal Year 1991
(October 1, 1990 - September 30, 1991)

Government Expenditures

Noninterest expenditures[a]	$795.3 billion
Interest payments by government[b]	$286.0 billion
Total expenditures[c]	$1,081.3 billion
Government Receipts[c]	$760.4 billion

Primary Deficit = $795.3 billion - $760.4 billion = $34.9 billion
Total Deficit   = $1,081.3 billion - $760.4 billion = $320.9 billion

[a] Source: calculated as total expenditures minus interest payments by government.

[b] Source: Treasury Bulletin, March 1992.

[c] Source: Economic Report of the President, 1992, Table B-75.

question: How much will the government have to borrow to pay for its expenditures? The total deficit during a year measures the increase in government debt during that year.

The Debt-GNP Ratio. How do we gauge whether a government's debt is too large? One way to gauge the size of a government's debt is by the government's ability to repay the debt. Governments that have access to larger tax bases would be able to support larger amounts of debt than governments with smaller tax bases. For the federal government, we can gauge the size of the tax base by some measure of national income, such as Gross National Product (GNP) or Gross Domestic Product (GDP). In this article, we will use GNP as the measure of national income, and thus we will use the ratio of government debt to GNP—known as the debt-GNP ratio—to gauge the size of government debt.

The historical behavior of the debt-GNP ratio over the last century in the United States is shown in Figure 1. Notice that the debt-GNP ratio rose sharply during World War I and World War II, and then fell gradually after these wars (and also fell gradually for about a half century after the Civil War). In addition to the increases in the debt-GNP ratio during wars, the debt-GNP ratio also rose sharply during the Great Depression of the 1930s and during the 1980s.

What causes the debt-GNP ratio to increase from one year to the next? Just as a matter of simple arithmetic, the debt-GNP ratio will rise whenever the growth rate of the numerator, i.e., the growth rate of government debt, is higher than the growth rate of the denominator, i.e., the growth rate of GNP. As we have discussed earlier, the increase in government debt during a year equals the total deficit, which in turn equals the primary deficit plus interest payments by the government. Thus, the debt-GNP ratio tends to increase when (1) the primary government deficit is large; (2) interest payments by the government are large; and (3) the growth rate of GNP is small. The following equation, which is an approximation derived in Appendix A, captures the simple arithmetic of government debt accumulation:

(1) growth rate of debt-GNP ratio =
  primary deficit/debt
  + interest rate
  - growth rate of GNP

Note that when the growth rate of the debt-

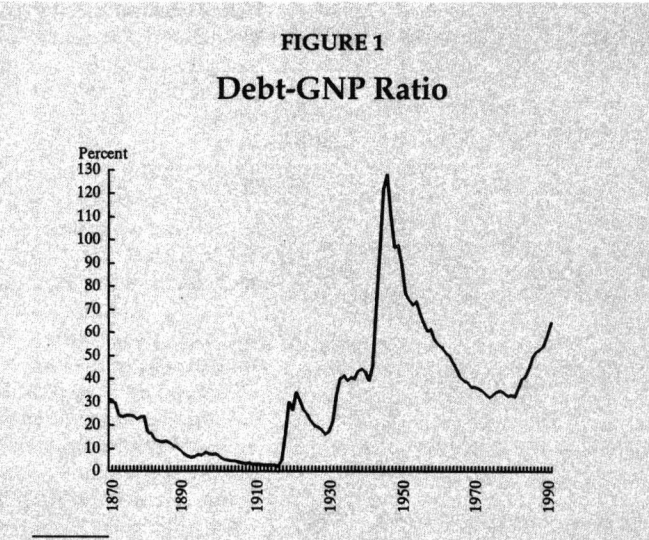

FIGURE 1

Debt-GNP Ratio

Sources: Ratio of government debt to GNP. Source of government debt (end of fiscal year): 1869-1939 from Historical Statistics of the United States, series y338; 1940-1969 from Banking and Monetary Statistics, 1941-1970, Table 13.1, C; 1970-1979 from Federal Reserve Board Annual Statistical Digest, 1970-1979, Table 27; 1980-1989 from Federal Reserve Board Annual Statistical Digest, 1980-1989, Table 26; 1990-1991 from Treasury Bulletin, March 1992, Table FD-1. Source of GNP: 1869-1958, Balke, Nathan S. and Robert J. Gordon, Appendix B Historical Data, in The American Business Cycle: Continuity and Change, Robert J. Gordon (ed.), Chicago and London: The University of Chicago Press, 1986; 1959-1991 from Data Resources Incorporated (1960 GNP is 2 percent higher in DRI than in Balke and Gordon).

GNP ratio is positive, this ratio is growing, and when the growth rate of the debt-GNP ratio is negative, the debt-GNP ratio is falling.

The three components of the growth rate of the debt-GNP ratio on the right-hand side of equation (1) explain, in an arithmetic sense at least, the historical behavior of the debt-GNP ratio shown in Figure 1. The sharp increase in the debt-GNP ratio during both world wars resulted from sharp increases in the primary deficit (Figure 2). Of course, the increase in the primary deficit reflects the large increase in military expenditure during wartime. The rise in the debt-GNP ratio during the Great Depression resulted from large declines in GNP during the early 1930s and from large primary deficits beginning in 1932. The decline in the debt-GNP ratio during the three-and-a-half decades following World War II resulted from a combination of factors: (1) a small—indeed usually negative—primary deficit; and (2) an interest rate that was usually smaller than the growth rate of GNP. However, during the 1980s the debt-GNP ratio departed from its typical pattern of peacetime behavior and began to rise. Arithmetically, the positive growth rate of the debt-GNP ratio was accounted for by a relatively large ratio of the primary deficit to government debt in the early 1980s and by the fact that the interest rate exceeded the growth rate of GNP for most of the 1980s.

Rolling Over Government Debt. Our discussion of the debt-GNP ratio was motivated by the desire to gauge the size of government debt relative to the government's ability to repay that debt. What problems might be associated with a high value of the debt-GNP ratio? If the debt-GNP ratio were to become too large, the public might begin to suspect that one day the government would default on its debt, and this suspicion might make the public unwilling to buy additional government debt.

There are many ways the government could default on its debt. The government could simply renounce its liabilities and refuse to pay holders of government bonds. Alternatively, the government could heavily tax the principal and/or interest on government bonds, effectively defaulting on at least a fraction of its liabilities. More subtly, the government could print money and create inflation, which reduces the real purchasing power of its dollar liabilities represented by government bonds. Another problem with a very high debt-GNP ratio is that the interest payments on government debt become a very large fraction of GNP. If the debt-GNP ratio becomes extremely large, the increase in government debt needed to pay the interest on the outstanding government debt could become larger than all of GNP,[1] and the public would not be able to buy this debt.

The willingness or unwillingness of the public to buy additional government debt when the debt-GNP ratio gets large determines whether the government can roll over its debt forever. If a policy of rolling over government debt forever would cause the debt-GNP ratio to grow forever without bound, the public would become unwilling to buy the government debt offered for sale and the rollover policy would have to terminate. However, if the debt-GNP ratio falls forever when the government is pursuing a rollover policy, it would be possible to roll over government debt forever.

But how could the debt-GNP ratio fall forever while the government is rolling over its debt? To answer this question, we will first precisely define a policy of rolling over the debt in terms of the primary deficit, and then we will use equation (1) to see how the debt-GNP ratio changes over time under a policy of debt rollover.

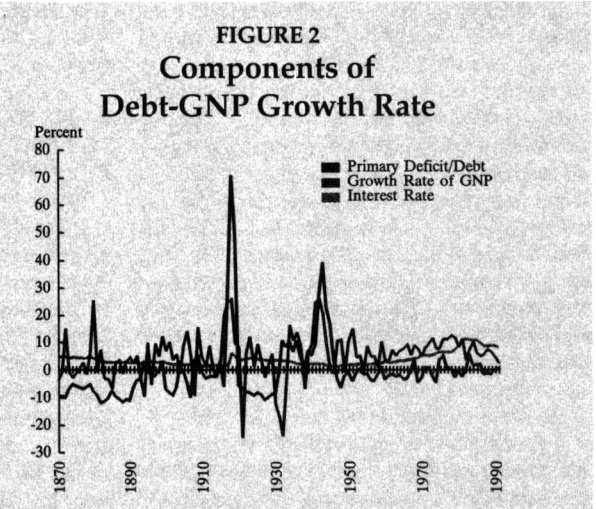

FIGURE 2
Components of Debt-GNP Growth Rate

Sources: Primary deficit calculated as total deficit minus interest payments by the government. Source of total deficit: 1869-1939 from Historical Statistics of the United States, series y337; 1940-1991 from Economic Report of the President, February 1992, Table B-74, on-budget. Source of interest payments: 1869-1969: from Historical Statistics of the United States, series y461; 1970-1991 from Treasury Bulletin, various issues, Table FFO-3. Interest rate calculated as interest payments in current fiscal year divided by government debt at end of previous fiscal year (see note to Figure 1 for source of data on government debt). Growth rate of GNP calculated from GNP data described in note to Figure 1.

---

[1] If the debt-GNP ratio exceeds the reciprocal of the interest rate on government bonds, interest payments on government debt would exceed GNP.

Quite simply, a government is rolling over its debt if its primary deficit is zero, so that its total deficit equals its interest payments on government debt. In this case, the government sells additional government bonds (debt) to pay the interest on government debt and to pay off holders of maturing government debt. If the government can run a zero primary deficit forever, selling bonds to cover the total deficit, then it can roll over its debt forever. Whether the government is able to run a zero primary deficit forever depends on whether the debt-GNP ratio eventually becomes too large when the government runs a zero primary deficit year after year.

To see if a government can run a zero primary deficit forever, we simply set the primary deficit in equation (1) equal to zero and observe that in this case the growth rate of the debt-GNP ratio equals the interest rate minus the growth rate of GNP. If the interest rate is higher than the growth rate, the debt-GNP ratio grows forever without bound, and eventually the government would lose its ability to roll over its debt. However, if the interest rate is smaller than the growth rate of GNP, the growth rate of the debt-GNP ratio would be negative, and the government could roll over its debt forever. For instance, if the interest rate is 3 percent per year and the growth rate of GNP is 4 percent per year, interest payments amount to 3 percent of government debt. If the government sells new bonds to pay these interest payments, the supply of government debt will increase by 3 percent per year, which is less than the 4 percent annual growth rate of GNP. Thus, the debt-GNP ratio would decline.

For most of the last century in the United States, the interest rate on government debt has been lower than the growth rate of GNP (Figure 2). In fact, the average interest rate on government debt was 4.12 percent per year, and the average growth rate of GNP was 5.86 percent per year over the period 1869-1991. If this pattern with the average interest rate below the average growth rate were to continue to hold forever, it would appear that the U.S. government could roll over its debt forever.

WHAT HAPPENS WHEN THE INTEREST RATE IS LESS THAN THE GROWTH RATE OF GNP?

We have seen that over the last century the average interest rate on government debt was lower than the average growth rate of GNP. One important implication of having an interest rate lower than the growth rate of GNP is that the government can roll over its debt forever. In this section, we discuss two other important—and surprising—implications of having an interest rate lower than the economy's growth rate.

The Economy Has Too Much Capital. The most important factor determining the standard of living of future generations is the long-run rate of economic growth. One of the primary ways that an economy can help promote economic growth is to save for the future by increasing the capital stock of productive equipment and structures. This process of capital accumulation combines a present sacrifice in the form of reduced present consumption with a future benefit in the form of increased future output and consumption. At various times in recent history, policymakers have made the judgment that the future gain is worth the present sacrifice, and national economic policy focused directly on stimulating capital formation by providing tax incentives in the form of accelerated depreciation allowances and the investment tax credit.

Is it possible for an economy to overdo it? More precisely, is it possible for an economy to accumulate and maintain a level of capital that is unambiguously too high? Surprisingly, the answer is yes. An economy can accumulate so much capital that the current sacrifice associated with current investment actually leads to a future sacrifice in the form of reduced future consumption. In this situation, the present sacrifice associated with capital formation is clearly not worth undertaking. An interest rate smaller than the growth rate of the economy signals that such a situation exists.

To see how it would be possible to have too much capital, suppose a piece of capital requires $5 worth of resources every year to maintain it in working order, but the capital contributes additional output worth only $4 per year. The economy would be suffering a net loss of $1 per year and would be better off without the capital.[2] At the level of the national economy, we can say that an economy has too much capital if in every year the amount of resources devoted to creating new capital and maintaining old capital is greater than the contribution to total output of the total capital stock. To put this condition in the language of national income accounting, an economy has too much capital if in every year gross investment (the amount of resources devoted to new capital formation and replacement of depreciated capital) exceeds gross capital income (which measures the contribution of capital to total output). We write this condition as:

(2) too much capital if:
gross investment > gross capital income
in every year.

Now we can relate the condition for too much capital to the relationship between the interest rate and the growth rate. This relationship is clearest for an economy growing at a constant rate year after year, so let's suppose that the economy is growing at constant rate g every year. Thus, for example, GNP is growing at the rate g and the total capital stock, K, is also growing at the rate g. With the capital stock growing at the rate g per year, the amount of net capital formation during a year is gK. In addition, some resources are devoted to replacing capital that depreciates during the year. Letting d be the fraction of the capital stock that depreciates during a year, the total amount of depreciation during a year that must be offset by capital formation is dK. Gross investment is the sum of net capital formation and depreciation:

(3) gross investment = gK + dK = (g + d)K

The contribution of capital to total output is measured by gross capital income. Letting R denote the gross rate of return on capital, we have:

(4) gross capital income = R K

Comparing gross investment in equation (3) with gross capital income in equation (4), we see that the economy has too much capital if $(g + d)K > R K$ in every year, or equivalently:

(5) too much capital if:
g + d > R
in every year

To see the role of the interest rate in this condition, we observe that in an economy in which there is no uncertainty, the interest rate r would equal the net rate of return on capital, which is the gross rate of return R minus the rate of depreciation. In symbols we have:

(6)   r   =   R - d
(interest rate) (net rate of return on capital)

Finally, we obtain the condition for too much capital in terms of the interest rate and the growth rate by subtracting the depreciation rate d from both sides of equation (5) and using the fact that r = R - d to obtain:

---

[2] In this numerical example, net investment is zero, but the same principle applies when there is positive net investment. For example, consider a firm that operates a factory with a work force that grows by 2 percent per year. If the firm maintains a constant ratio of capital to labor, the firm's capital stock would grow by 2 percent per year. However, if the contribution to total output of each unit of capital is only 1 percent of the value of the capital stock, then the firm would be pouring more resources into the factory than it gets out of the factory, and it would be better off closing that factory.

(7) too much capital if: g > r
                         in every year.

Thus, we can see that in the absence of uncertainty, an economy growing at a constant rate has too much capital if the interest rate is less than the growth rate. An economy in this situation could realize both a present gain and a future gain by permanently reducing the amount of investment. Present consumption would increase as the economy's current resources shifted from investment to consumption. Future consumption would increase as fewer resources were, on net, poured into the formation and maintenance of capital. As a result of the reduction in investment, the capital stock would fall, and as capital became less abundant, the rate of return on capital would increase. When the rate of investment has fallen enough, the net rate of return on capital and the interest rate will rise above the growth rate of the economy, so that the symptom of too much capital will disappear.

Recall that during the period 1869-1991 the average interest rate in the United States was smaller than the average growth rate. Thus, equation (7) would seem to suggest that the United States has too much capital. We will take another look at this provocative implication later in this article.

Ponzi Games. In the early 20th century, Charles Ponzi promised investors the opportunity to double their money in 90 days by investing in international postal coupons. Over the course of eight months, Ponzi acquired about $15,000,000 from 40,000 investors. Not surprisingly, Ponzi's promises proved to be too good to be true, and Ponzi was arrested in August 1920.[3] Economists now use the term "Ponzi game" to describe a situation in which an entity (a person, business, or government) sells securities to investors and never uses any of its own money to pay dividends or interest or to repay the principal. Any subsequent payments (such as dividends, interest, or return of principal) to holders of these securities are financed by selling additional securities. Our discussion will focus on rational Ponzi games, which are Ponzi games in which there is no fraud or deceit on the part of the seller of securities and no lack of understanding or foresight on the part of buyers of these securities.

As a simple example of a rational Ponzi game, consider an entity that sells $100 million of long-term bonds, promising to pay an interest rate of 4 percent per year. At the end of one year, when it is time to pay investors $4 million in interest, the entity sells an additional $4 million of bonds to investors, bringing total bonds outstanding to $104 million. Then at the end of two years, when $4.16 million of interest (4 percent of $104 million) is due, the entity sells an additional $4.16 million of bonds, and so on. The amount of bonds outstanding grows at the rate of interest, which is 4 percent per year in this example. For this Ponzi game to be feasible, the public must be willing to hold the ever-increasing amount of bonds issued. If investors' wealth is growing at, say, 5 percent per year, there would be sufficient demand by the public for newly issued bonds, and thus the entity would be able to sell additional bonds to pay the interest on its debt without having to use any of its own resources.

In the Ponzi game described above, suppose that the entity selling the bonds is the government. Then the Ponzi game amounts to rolling over government debt forever. The Ponzi game will be feasible, that is, the government will be able to roll over its debt forever, provided that the growth rate of aggregate wealth exceeds the interest rate. The growth rate of aggregate wealth is not readily measured, but in the absence of a trend in the ratio of wealth to GNP, the growth rate of aggregate wealth can be proxied by the growth rate of GNP. Thus, the government will be able to roll over its debt

---

[3] See O'Connell and Zeldes (1992).

forever if the growth rate of GNP exceeds the interest rate.[4]

To summarize, if the interest rate is lower than the growth rate of GNP, (1) the economy has too much capital; (2) entities can run rational Ponzi games; and (3) in particular, the government can roll over its debt forever. As we have seen, over the last century in the United States, the average interest rate has been lower than the average growth rate of GNP. Thus, it might seem that the United States has too much capital, that entities can run rational Ponzi games, and that the government can roll over its debt forever. However, these three results do not strike most observers as plausible descriptions of the U.S. economy. The implausibility of these results stimulated new research into these questions in the past several years. A point of departure for much of this research is the fact that the results presented above were derived under the assumption of a constant interest rate and a constant growth rate, but, as is evident in Figure 2, the interest rate, and especially the growth rate, have displayed substantial variability in the United States. Recent research has focused on uncertainty as the source of variation in the interest rate and the growth rate and has found that the results summarized above need to be substantially altered when uncertainty is incorporated into the analysis.

---

[4] The discussion in this article ignores distortions arising from taxes or from externalities. In a recent paper, Ian King (1992) has argued that with endogenous growth arising from externalities in the stock of knowledge, it is possible for Ponzi games to be feasible even though the economy does not suffer from overaccumulation of capital. This result arises because the private and social returns to capital differ in the presence of externalities. Capital overaccumulation occurs if the social rate of return to capital is lower than the growth rate of the economy, and Ponzi games are feasible if the private rate of return to capital is lower than the growth rate of the economy. In King's model, the social rate of return can be higher than the growth rate, which can be higher than the private rate of return.

THE IMPORTANCE OF UNCERTAINTY

Recent research into the questions of whether an economy has too much capital and whether a government can roll over its debt forever has shown that simply comparing the average interest rate and the average growth rate of the economy can produce misleading answers to these questions. Much of this research is ongoing and many important questions remain unanswered, but this research has yielded some important insights.

Another Look at Whether an Economy Has Too Much Capital. In a world without uncertainty, we can compare the interest rate and the growth rate of the economy to determine whether the economy has too much capital. In deriving equation (7) we used the fact [equation (6)] that in the absence of uncertainty, the net rate of return on capital, R - d, equals the interest rate, r, on government debt. However, in the presence of uncertainty, the rates of return on different assets, in particular the rates of return on capital and on government bonds, can in general differ. Thus, the comparison of the interest rate and the growth rate in equation (7) is no longer appropriate for assessing whether an economy has too much capital.

In the presence of uncertainty, the appropriate criterion for determining whether an economy has too much capital is equation (2): If gross investment exceeds gross capital income in every year, the economy has too much capital. If gross investment is less than gross capital income in every year, we conclude that the economy is not plagued by too much capital. A recent study[5] has examined gross investment and gross capital income in the United States for the period 1929-1985 and found that

---

[5] Andrew B. Abel, N. Gregory Mankiw, Lawrence H. Summers, and Richard J. Zeckhauser, "Assessing Dynamic Efficiency: Theory and Evidence," *Review of Economic Studies*, 56 (January 1989), pp. 1-20.

in every year, including the Great Depression of the 1930s, gross investment was less than gross capital income. Thus, despite the fact that the average interest rate was less than the average growth rate of the economy, we can conclude that the United States was not afflicted with too much capital.[6] This study also examined six other countries, including Japan, which is often cited as a country with high rates of saving and investment. For all of these countries, including high-investing Japan, gross investment was always less than gross capital income, and hence, none of these countries had too much capital.

Debt Rollover When the Average Interest Rate Is Lower Than the Average Growth Rate. We have just seen that the introduction of uncertainty invalidates the comparison of the average interest rate and the average growth rate for the purpose of determining whether an economy has too much capital. Now we will see that the introduction of uncertainty also invalidates the comparison of the average interest rate and the average growth rate for the purpose of determining whether a Ponzi game is feasible. We focus this discussion on a particular Ponzi game, namely rolling over government debt forever. This section presents a numerical example with the following surprising feature: despite the fact that the interest rate on government debt is lower than the average growth rate of GNP, the expected value of the debt-GNP ratio grows without bound. Eventually, the government would become unable to roll over its debt.

Before presenting this example it is useful to calculate an exact expression for the growth rate of the debt-GNP ratio when the government is following a rollover policy. (Equation (1) is an approximate expression.) Remember that a rollover policy means that the primary deficit is zero in every year. If the current amount of government debt is B and if the government has a zero primary deficit, its total deficit is rB, where r is the interest rate. Thus, the government must sell an additional rB bonds, and the amount of bonds next year rises to $(1+r)B$. If the current level of GNP is Y and if the growth rate of GNP over the next year is g, the level of GNP next year is $(1+g)Y$. Thus, the value of the debt-GNP ratio next year is $[(1+r)/(1+g)][B/Y]$, which is $(1+r)/(1+g)$ times as large as the current debt-GNP ratio, B/Y. Thus, if r is larger than g, so that $(1+r)/(1+g)$ is larger than one, the debt-GNP ratio grows between this year and next year. Alternatively, if r is smaller than g, so that $(1+r)/(1+g)$ is smaller than one, the debt-GNP ratio falls between this year and next year. These results are consistent with the approximation in equation (1).[7]

Now we can discuss the numerical example presented in Table 2, which has the following features: the interest rate r is constant and is smaller than the average value of g, the growth rate of GNP. However, g varies in such a way that the average value of $(1+r)/(1+g)$ is greater than 1, so that the expected value of the debt-GNP ratio in the next period is always greater than the current value of the debt-GNP ratio. In this example, the uncertainty comes from the fact that GNP growth is unpredictable from one period to the next. To make the example simple, suppose that GNP growth is determined by the flip of a fair coin each period. If the coin comes up heads, GNP grows by 60 percent during the next period, and if the coin

---

[6] This conclusion is based on the implicit assumption that the fact that gross investment has always been smaller than gross capital income will continue forever.

[7] The approximation involved in equation (1) is that the growth rate of a ratio is approximately equal to the growth rate of the numerator minus the growth rate of the denominator. (See Appendix A, Derivation of the Growth Rate of the Debt-GNP Ratio.)

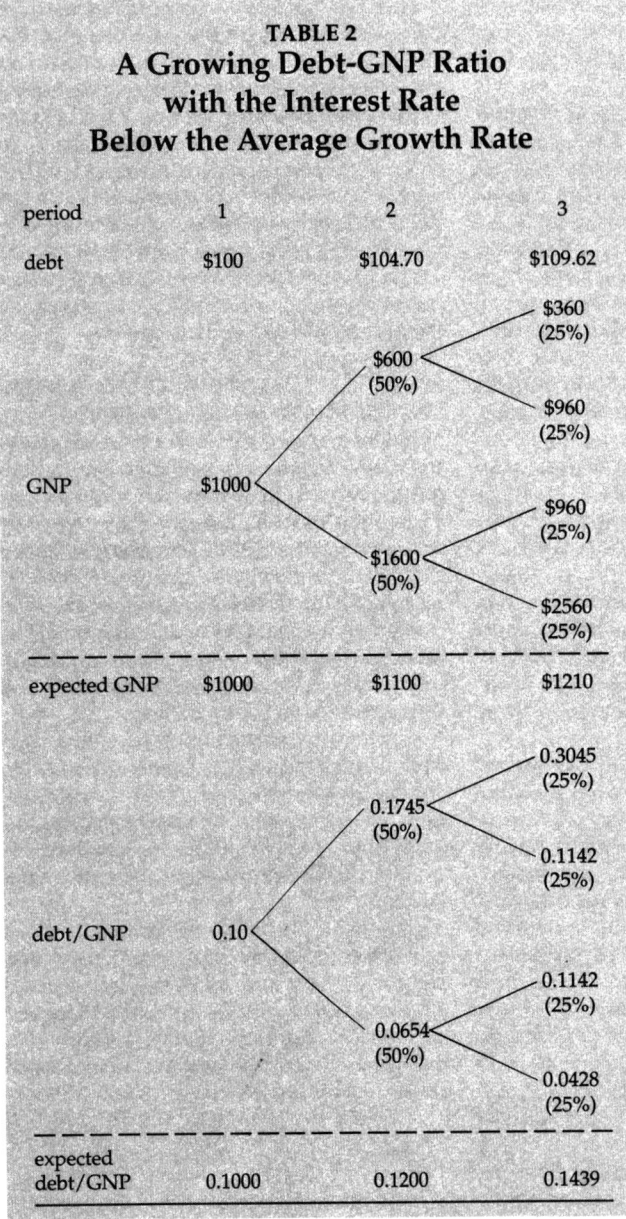

**TABLE 2
A Growing Debt-GNP Ratio
with the Interest Rate
Below the Average Growth Rate**

comes up tails, GNP falls by 40 percent.[8] Thus, if GNP is currently $1000, there is a 50 percent chance that next period's GNP will be $1600 and a 50 percent chance that next period's GNP will be $600. Thus, the average, or expected, value of next period's GNP is $1100 (($1600+$600)/2), which represents a 10 percent expected growth rate.

Now suppose that the interest rate on government debt is always 4.7 percent per period, which is less than the average growth rate of the economy, and let's see how the debt-GNP ratio behaves in this economy. Suppose that in period 1 the amount of government debt is $100. Thus, the debt-GNP ratio is $100/$1000 = 0.10.

The first panel of numbers in Table 2 shows the evolution of government debt over time. With a 4.7 percent interest rate, the

---

[8] These large changes in GNP in this example were chosen to make the effects very apparent. To make the example seem more realistic, think of a period as being a decade rather than a year. Notice that between 1929 and 1933 in the United States real GNP fell by 30 percent and nominal GNP fell by 46 percent, so a 40 percent drop in GNP during a decade is not inconceivable. However, the probability of such a bad decade is almost surely much less than the value of 50 percent assumed in this example.

amount of government debt grows at the rate of 4.7 percent per period. Thus, government debt equals $104.70 in period 2 and $109.62 in period 3.

The second panel of numbers in Table 2, which shows GNP, requires a little additional explanation. As shown in the first column, GNP is $1000 in period 1. The second column shows that there is a 50 percent chance that GNP in period 2 will be $600 and a 50 percent chance that GNP in period 2 will be $1600, so that the expected value of GNP in period 2 is ($600 + $1600)/2 = $1100. The third column of numbers shows the possible values of GNP in period 3. If GNP in period 2 is $600, there is a 50 percent chance it will fall by 40 percent, to $360, in period 3, and a 50 percent chance it will rise by 60 percent, to $960, in period 3. Alternatively, if GNP in period 2 is $1600, there is a 50 percent chance it will fall by 40 percent, to $960, in period 3, and a 50 percent chance it will rise by 60 percent, to $2560, in period 3. Taking account of all of these possibilities for the value of GNP in period 3, there is a 25 percent chance it will be $360, a 50 percent chance it will be $960, and a 25 percent chance it will be $2560. The average, or expected, value of GNP in period 3 is $1210.

The third panel of numbers in Table 2 shows the possible values of the debt-GNP in each of the three periods. These numbers are calculated by dividing the value of debt in the first panel by the value of GNP in the second panel. For example, in period 2, debt will equal $104.70. There is a 50 percent chance GNP will equal $600, in which case the debt/GNP ratio will be $104.70/$600 = 0.1745, as reported in the third panel; there is a 50 percent chance GNP will equal $1600, in which case the debt/GNP ratio will be $104.70/$1600 = 0.0654. The average, or expected, value of the debt-GNP ratio in period 2 is (0.1745 + 0.0654)/2 = 0.1200, which is higher than the debt-GNP ratio in period 1. Despite the fact that the interest rate is smaller than the average growth rate of GNP, the risk of a sharp drop in GNP makes the expected value of the debt-GNP ratio in period 2 higher than the value of the debt-GNP ratio in period 1. As shown in the third column, the expected value of the debt-GNP ratio in period 3 is 0.1439. In fact, the expected value of the debt-GNP ratio will grow at a rate of approximately 20 percent per period forever. Eventually, the expected value of the debt-GNP ratio would become so large that the government would be unable to roll over its debt despite the fact that the interest rate on government debt is lower than the average growth rate of the economy.

WHAT CAN WE CONCLUDE ABOUT UNITED STATES FISCAL POLICY?

We have shown that in the presence of uncertainty it may be impossible for the government to roll over its debt forever, even though the average interest rate is lower than the average growth rate of GNP. So, how then do we empirically assess whether the government can roll over its debt forever? This question is at the frontier of economic research and has not yet been fully resolved. Nevertheless, recent research has yielded some insights and some speculation about future findings.

One important insight is that if an economy has too much capital, Ponzi games are possible and the government can roll over its debt forever. However, a recent study cited earlier[9] found that none of the countries studied, including the United States, is afflicted by too much capital.

Does the finding that an economy does not have too much capital imply that Ponzi games are not possible and, in particular, that the government cannot roll over its debt forever? In a world without uncertainty, the answer to this question would be "yes," as we illustrated earlier. Unfortunately, the answer is ambigu-

___

[9] Abel, Mankiw, Summers, and Zeckhauser (1989).

ous in the presence of uncertainty: in some economies that do not have too much capital, it is possible for the government to roll over its debt forever, while in other economies that do not have too much capital, it is impossible for the government to roll over its debt forever.[10]

The current state of economic research suggests that the crucial issue for determining whether a government can roll over its debt forever is whether there is a rich enough set of existing securities in the economy. If the set of existing securities is not rich enough in the relevant sense, government debt might be such a sufficiently different and attractive security that investors would welcome the opportunity to hold it in their portfolios and would allow the government to roll over its debt forever. However, if the set of existing securities is sufficiently rich, government debt may not be sufficiently different or attractive for investors to allow the government to roll its debt over forever.[11] Unfortunately, the current state of economic research does not allow a convincing empirical test to distinguish between these two cases, so we cannot yet test whether an actual government can roll over its debt forever.[12]

Although we cannot yet empirically test whether an economy can roll over its debt forever, we are not left entirely in the dark about the future course of U.S. fiscal policy. Recently, Henning Bohn (1991a) has developed and implemented a test of whether a government is following a sustainable policy. This is not a test of whether a zero primary deficit accompanied by rolling over the debt is permanently sustainable. Rather it is a test of whether the historical tax and expenditure policies of the government can be permanently maintained without a major shift in the conduct of policy. Applying this test to data on U.S. fiscal policy, Bohn finds that this policy is sustainable. An important component of this conclusion is the finding that, on average, U.S. fiscal policy produces a smaller primary deficit (or a larger primary surplus) when the debt-GNP ratio becomes larger. This tendency of the government to run smaller (or even negative) primary deficits as the debt-GNP ratio gets larger is a means of keeping the debt-GNP ratio from growing too large.

While Bohn's result that U.S. fiscal policy is sustainable may appear comforting, this finding focuses attention on potentially painful choices. If the United States is to follow its historical pattern of reducing primary deficits when the debt-GNP ratio rises, the increase in the debt-GNP ratio over the past dozen years would seem to require a reduction in the primary deficit. Such a reduction in the primary deficit would require an increase in tax revenues and/or a cut in government expenditure, neither of which will be universally popular.

---

[10] Technically, under certainty, capital overaccumulation is a necessary and sufficient condition for Ponzi games and for rolling over government debt forever. Under uncertainty, capital overaccumulation is a sufficient, but not necessary, condition for Ponzi games and for rolling over government debt forever.

[11] Blanchard and Weil (1992) present examples of economies that do not have too much capital. In some of these examples, the set of securities is not sufficiently rich, and the government can roll over its debt forever. In other examples, the set of securities is sufficiently rich, and the government cannot roll over its debt forever.

[12] A related—and also unresolved—question is why the average interest rate on government debt is so much lower than the average rate of return on capital. One potential explanation is that there is a very rich set of securities available but investors are very risk averse and essentially pay a large premium for the opportunity to hold safe government debt. In this case, the government would not be able to roll over its debt forever. Another potential explanation is that the set of securities is not sufficiently rich and that investors find government debt sufficiently different and attractive that they willingly hold it at a low interest rate. In this case, the government might be able to roll over its debt forever. See Bohn (1991b).

APPENDIX A

Derivation of the Growth Rate of the Debt-GNP Ratio

Let B be the amount of government bonds outstanding, and let Y be the measure of national income, such as GNP. Thus the debt-GNP ratio is B/Y. The growth rate of any ratio is approximately equal to the growth rate of the numerator minus the growth rate of the denominator so that

$$\text{(A1)} \quad \frac{\Delta(B/Y)}{B/Y} = \frac{\Delta B}{B} - \frac{\Delta Y}{Y}$$

where the symbol Δ denotes the change from one period to the next. The change in government bonds, ΔB, equals the total deficit, which equals the primary deficit plus interest payments:

$$\text{(A2)} \quad \Delta B = \text{primary deficit} + rB$$

where r is the interest rate on government bonds, so that rB is the amount of interest payments by the government. Now divide both sides of (A2) by the amount of government bonds B to obtain

$$\text{(A3)} \quad \Delta B/B = \text{primary deficit}/B + r$$

Now let g denote the growth rate of income so that

$$\text{(A4)} \quad \Delta Y/Y = g$$

Substituting (A3) and (A4) into (A1) yields

$$\text{(A5)} \quad \frac{\Delta(B/Y)}{B/Y} = \text{primary deficit}/B + r - g$$

which is equation (1) in the text of the article.

APPENDIX B

An Economic Model of the Interest Rate and the Growth Rate

This appendix presents a general equilibrium model underlying the example presented in Table 2. Suppose that consumption equals output in every period as in the widely used Lucas (1978) asset pricing model. The standard condition determining the riskless interest rate r in a representative consumer economy is

(B1) $(1 + r)\beta E_t\{u'(c_{t+1})/u'(c_t)\} = 1$

where $E_t\{\ \}$ is the expectation conditional on information at time t, c_t is consumption per capita at time t, $u'(c_t)$ is the marginal utility of consumption at time t, and $\beta > 0$ is the time preference discount factor (so that $\beta^{-1}-1$ is the rate of time preference). Assume that the utility function is logarithmic so that $u'(c_t) = 1/c_t$. In this case, equation (B1) becomes

(B2) $1 + r = [\beta E_t\{(c_t/c_{t+1})\}]^{-1}$

Now let $g_{t+1} = (c_{t+1}/c_t) - 1$ be the growth rate of consumption and output between time t and time t+1, and assume that g_{t+1} is i.i.d. over time. Under this assumption we have

(B3) $1 + r = [\beta E\{1/(1+g_{t+1})\}]^{-1}$

The ratio of the debt-GNP ratio in period t+1 to the debt-GNP ratio in period t is $(1+r)/(1+g_{t+1})$ and the expected value of this ratio is

(B4) $E\{(1+r)/(1+g_{t+1})\} = E\{1/(1+g_{t+1})\} [\beta E\{1/(1+g_{t+1})\}]^{-1} = 1/\beta$

Notice that if $\beta < 1$, then $1/\beta > 1$ and the expected value of the debt-GNP ratio grows over time. The example in Table 2 is based on the following assumptions: $\beta = 0.8333$; and $\Pr\{1+g_{t+1} = 0.6\} = \Pr\{1+g_{t+1} = 1.6\} = 0.5$. These assumptions imply that $1+r = 1.0473$, $E\{1+g_{t+1}\} = 1.1$, and $E\{(1+r)/(1+g_{t+1})\} = 1/\beta = 1.2$.

REFERENCES

Abel, Andrew B., N. Gregory Mankiw, Lawrence H. Summers, and Richard J. Zeckhauser. "Assessing Dynamic Efficiency: Theory and Evidence," *Review of Economic Studies*, 56 (January 1989), pp. 1-20.

Blanchard, Olivier J., and Philippe Weil. "Dynamic Efficiency, the Riskless Rate and Debt Ponzi Games Under Uncertainty," National Bureau of Economic Research Working Paper No. 3992, February 1992.

Bohn, Henning. "On Testing the Sustainability of Government Deficits in a Stochastic Environment," Rodney L. White Center for Financial Research Working Paper No. 19-91, August 1991(a).

Bohn, Henning. "Fiscal Policy and the Mehra-Prescott Puzzle: On the Welfare Implications of High Budget Deficits with Low Interest Rates," Wharton School of the University of Pennsylvania, April 1991(b).

King, Ian. "Ponzi Games, Dynamic Efficiency and Endogenous Growth," Department of Economics, University of Victoria, British Columbia, mimeo, 1992.

Lucas, Robert E. Jr. "Asset Prices in an Exchange Economy," *Econometrica*, 46 (November 1978), pp. 1429-45.

O'Connell, Stephen A., and Stephen P. Zeldes, "Ponzi Games," in *The New Palgrave Dictionary of Money and Finance*, 1992 (forthcoming).

Article 33

Auctioning Treasury Securities

by E. J. Stevens and Diana Dumitru

The U.S. Treasury expects to sell about a trillion dollars of new securities this fiscal year to finance a projected $400 billion budget deficit and to refinance maturing debt. Most of the securities will be issued through public auctions, where competition among bidders might be expected to minimize interest payments on the debt.

The competitiveness of Treasury auctions was called into question last August, however, when Salomon Brothers, a large securities dealer, admitted to having placed unauthorized bids in the names of customers during eight auctions. For example, in the May 22, 1991 note auction, the firm controlled more than 90 percent of the issue, far exceeding the 35 percent limit set by the Treasury. Rumors of a market "squeeze" had surfaced even before the notes were issued on May 31.[1] Disappointed bidders, with contracts to deliver the security after it was issued, had to pay an unexpectedly high price for the issue in the secondary market, where Salomon controlled most of the supply.

Two causes for concern emerge from this incident. First, of course, is simply that the market is not fair when auction rules are broken. Some investors might shun the Treasury securities market rather than be exposed to losses resulting from market manipulation. Thus, any short-term gain to the Treasury from an artificially high price at a single auction could be outweighed by lower demand and prices in all auctions. Second, as suggested here, is the possibility that the auction process itself may be at fault. Perhaps a different system of selling new issues of Treasury debt would reduce incentives for manipulation.

Following Salomon's admissions and other reported irregularities, the Treasury Department, the Board of Governors of the Federal Reserve System, and the Securities and Exchange Commission conducted a study in 1991 leading to a joint report on the government securities market. The report reaffirms that public auctions are the best means of issuing new Treasury debt and recommends some minor adjustments that have already been adopted to ensure public access to the existing auction process. It also recommends a more thorough exploration of alternative methods of conducting public auctions. This *Economic Commentary* examines the rationales for adopting a different system for determining the price paid by a winning bidder and a new technology for bidding.[2] Both of these changes could make public auctions of Treasury securities less susceptible to manipulation.

■ **Today's Auctions:
Multiple-Price, Sealed-Bid**
The Treasury maintains a regular schedule of auctions in which it sells bonds, notes, and bills. Bonds and notes are sold in $1,000 denominations and pay interest every six months until maturity, which ranges from 10 to 30 years for bonds and from one to 10 years for notes. The recent schedule has included monthly auctions of two- and five-year notes and quarterly

The current method of auctioning Treasury securities contains both incentives and opportunities for market manipulation. Two suggested changes in the auctions might eliminate these problems and thus reduce the need to police arbitrary auction rules.

auctions of three-, seven-, and 10-year notes and 30-year bonds.

Treasury bills, in $10,000 denominations, have no coupon. An investor's return comes from the difference between the maturity value and the price paid — the "discount." Bills maturing in 13 weeks and 26 weeks are auctioned every Monday. Bills maturing in 52 weeks are offered every four weeks.

About a week before each auction, the Treasury announces the auction day, size, maturity, and the settlement day when successful bidders must make payment. From this announcement until settlement, the impending security actually trades in the market on a "when-issued" basis, with the promise of delivery on settlement day. When-issued trading thus may provide potential bidders with information about the likely price in the auction.

By 1:00 p.m. on auction day, bidders must submit tenders (written, sealed bids) at Federal Reserve Banks or their branches. Two kinds of tenders can be used: Competitive tenders state the amount of securities desired (as much as several billion dollars) and either a

358

yield bid (for bonds and notes) in one-basis-point increments or a price bid (for bills) on the basis of 100 (for example, 98.995). Noncompetitive tenders can be placed only for smaller amounts (up to $5 million for notes and bonds, or $1 million for bills), with the yield or price determined by the average of awards in competitive bidding.

At 1:00 p.m. on the day of an auction, bids are tabulated and transmitted to the Treasury. Securities are awarded to all noncompetitive bidders; the remainder of the issue is awarded to competitive bidders in descending order of price bid (increasing yield bid).[3] A bidder may submit tenders up to a maximum of 35 percent of the amount being auctioned, with bids at various prices. The exception is that if too many bids are received at the lowest accepted "stop-out" price, these awards are made in proportion to the total of all bids received at that price.

The process can be summarized as a sealed-bid auction, open to anyone, with awards at multiple prices. Modifications already adopted address the openness of the process, to ensure that any financially responsible party can participate in a Treasury auction. Some drawbacks are nevertheless associated with multiple prices and sealed bidding.

■ **The Winner's Curse**
Making auction awards at multiple prices means that the highest bidders must follow through, actually paying the prices they offered even though others are paying less for the identical security. This may seem only fair. After all, if the high bidders didn't think the securities were worth so much, they shouldn't have bid so much. This view assumes that the item's value to the winner may be largely independent of the lower value placed on the item by unsuccessful bidders.

In the case of Treasury auctions, however, the value of a security is not independent of the market. A dealer wants the security being auctioned only in order to sell it, but must compete with other dealers who may have paid less in the auction; an investor wants the securities for portfolio purposes and could wait to buy in the post-auction market. No matter how fair it may seem, paying a high price for an award of securities that others have bought more cheaply truly involves a "winner's curse."

The winner's curse has serious implications for Treasury auctions. While a high bid will increase the chances of an award, it also raises the possibility of paying more than the post-auction market value of the security. The auction process might reveal something about that value, but only the smallest-volume bidders can benefit by submitting noncompetitive tenders; competitive bidders cannot take advantage of the information revealed in the auction. The winner's curse dampens the aggressiveness of their bidding, resulting in a lower auction price received by the Treasury. Bids may be lowered to cover the costs of gathering information about what others are likely to bid. Alternatively, customers may submit their bids through a small number of well-informed dealers, where bidding might tend to become concentrated. Thus, a winner's curse may dampen all competitive bidding and lower multiple auction prices relative to market values.

Sealed bidding, on the other hand, when coupled with multiple prices, enables a single bidder to corner the post-auction market, transforming the auction-winner's curse into a post-auction blessing. A well-informed and well-financed bidder or group of bidders could deliberately submit a high bid to ensure receiving a dominant share of auction awards. Because of the substantial volume of when-issued trading, controlling the post-auction supply of a Treasury security places the high bidder in a position to squeeze unsuccessful bidders who had contracted to deliver the security after the auction. While not a necessary outcome, the current auction setup does contain the seeds of market manipulation that can discourage demand. The winner's curse places a premium on discovering how others will bid, creating the basis for a bid that will corner an auction and squeeze the post-auction market.

■ **Safeguards against Manipulation**
Treasury auctions contain an important safeguard against cornering the supply of a new issue: A single bidder is prohibited from acquiring more than 35 percent of an issue. As the Salomon example attests, enforcing this rule is not easy. For example, winning bidders must be contacted to ensure that customers' names are not used improperly by a dealer trying to control more than his share of an issue. Moreover, 35 percent is an arbitrary limit that may restrict demand and unnecessarily lower auction prices when there is no threat of manipulation.

One alternative to this rule is to reopen the issue whose supply has been cornered. Augmenting supply would drive down an artificially high price and eliminate profits expected by the perpetrators of the squeeze. Knowing that the Treasury would respond in this way would eliminate the incentive to manipulate the market. Of course, this approach is simply the price equivalent of the 35 percent rule, reducing the high bidder's market share by increasing total supply. It would involve an equally arbitrary judgment about the permissible range within which the post-auction price could vary without triggering a reopening, as well as arbitrary judgments about whether prices reflected manipulation or a change in market fundamentals.

■ **A Single-Price Auction**
Changing to a single-price auction has been proposed as an alternative to enforcing arbitrary rules on the current auction process.[4] This procedure would be identical to the current one, except that all competitive awards would be made at the stop-out price, which is the price that clears the market. The winner's curse would disappear because winning bidders would receive their awards at the stop-out, even if they bid higher.

Resistance to a single-price auction centers around its implication for the

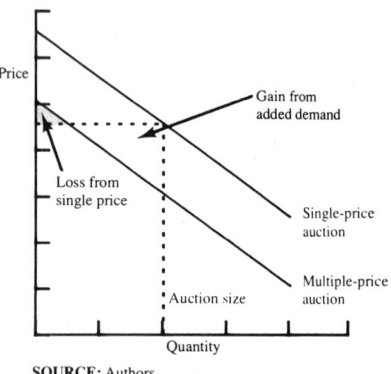

FIGURE 1 SINGLE-PRICE AUCTIONS: GAINS AND LOSSES

SOURCE: Authors.

cost of servicing government debt. With a single-price auction, the Treasury would forgo revenue now received from the difference between successful price bids and the stop-out price. Actually, however, Treasury auction revenues might increase, although auction theory is ambivalent on this matter.[5] Revenue forgone by shifting from a multiple- to a single-price auction might be more than offset by an increase in demand as participants bid more aggressively in the absence of a winner's curse, as illustrated in figure 1. Whether the gain would actually exceed forgone revenues, though, depends in part on the *size* of the increase in demand. It could be slight if most participants are already so averse to the risk of not getting an award that they bid aggressively in multiple-price auctions, despite the winner's curse. So, a single-price auction will increase demand, but might not reduce the interest cost of financing the debt.

More to the point, a single-price auction also might or might not produce a less fertile environment for market manipulation. A high bid could garner a dominant market position without requiring the successful bidder to pay any more than the stop-out price. But other incentives to corner the market might be weaker, because bidders would no longer conduct as intensive a pre-auction search for information about others' bids. Thus, a bidder would have to make special efforts to gather information; cornering the market would become more costly. Chances of pre-auction detection by other bidders, who might raise their own bids by enough to defeat an attempted corner, would also increase.

■ **An Auction by Open Outcry**

Perhaps the most intriguing alternative presented in the joint report is that of conducting Treasury auctions by open outcry, rather than by sealed bid. The disadvantage of sealed bidding is that participants cannot be certain of the distribution of all other bids. In the multiple-price auction, winning with a bid higher than the stop-out implies that your estimate was too high, and the risk of this winner's curse leads to conservative bidding. In a single-price auction, your winning bid is lowered to the stop-out, based on the auctioneer's information about the actual distribution of bids, all of which will be less conservative than in a multiple-price auction. In an open-outcry auction, which is typically used to sell antiques or works of art, information about the distribution of bids is revealed gradually to all bidders before the auction closes. As the auction process drives the bidding higher and higher, low prices become irrelevant.

An attempt to gain a dominant share of Treasury auction awards seems unlikely to succeed with this system, because the auction process reveals more information about the actual distribution of bids. If the distribution of bids initially contains an unusually large bid at a high price, the ascending price reveals that a large number of bidders underestimated the value of the security and therefore can raise their bids. While the final auction price may be unusually high, the individual who attempted to corner will not gain a large share of awards.

In the past, formidable obstacles have stood in the way of conducting Treasury auctions by open outcry, obstacles mostly absent from the typical auction of a unique art object. At one time, it might have been difficult even to assemble all bidding in a single place, but today, open communication lines to Federal Reserve offices and to individual bidders could overcome that geographic problem, just as telephone bidding does in major art auctions.

More difficult, and unlike an auction of a single work of art, bidders must cry out not just a price, but a *quantity* at each price. Bidding must ascend from low prices, where the demand for securities exceeds the supply, to the market-clearing price, where demand exactly equals supply. As envisioned in the joint report, bidding would have to proceed in discreet "rounds," starting from a low price and rising by small increments. As the results of each round were announced, participants could drop out, resubmit the same quantity, or adjust the quantity in light of information gained from the previous round.

Auctioning Treasury securities by open outcry would consume too much time to be feasible with current auction technology. Each round of bidding probably would take more than an hour using today's paper tenders, manual tabulation, verification of payment status, transmission to the Treasury, and final compilation. Each open-outcry auction might consume most of a day, during which unfolding world events might be moving market fundamentals enough to change bidding decisions and to prevent the process from moving smoothly toward an equilibrium market-clearing price.

The Treasury expects to automate the current sealed-bid, multiple-price auction process this year, allowing telecommunication of tenders and computerized compilation of bids. Going any further toward auctions by electronic open outcry would require substantial investments, both in hardware and software and, before that, in design. One critical design question would involve the information feedback provided at the end of each round of bidding. Simply announcing the amount of excess demand might not be sufficient for bidders to detect an aggressive effort to dominate the awards. On the other hand, a complete (anonymous) list of all bid quantities received might prove too cumbersome for rapid rounds of bidding. Another design question involves the computer and telecommunications capacity required to receive large numbers of bids virtually simultaneously. Too little is known at this time, but automation could conceivably reduce the turnaround time between successive rounds of bidding to a matter of minutes, with an entire auction lasting perhaps less than an hour.[6] Given the information benefits of open outcry, serious further exploration seems warranted.

■ Conclusion

The U.S. Treasury securities market is the largest and most efficient market in the world today. Nonetheless, the events of 1991 demonstrated that concerted strong bidding in the primary market for an issue could result in a squeeze in the secondary market. More aggressive policing of the current rule against control of more than 35 percent of a new issue promises to reduce chances of similar episodes in the future.

Embedded in the current sealed-bid, multiple-price auction process are both incentives and opportunities for a bidder to seek a dominant share of awards. New methods of conducting auctions are worth serious consideration if they would reduce the need for arbitrary policing of the market. A single-price, sealed-bid auction would reduce the current incentive of each bidder to discover the price at which other bidders will make tenders. With less of their activity focused on discovering one another's intentions, bidders would have less opportunity and incentive to corner an issue. Perhaps more promising would be to enlist telecommunications and computer technology in conducting auctions by electronic open outcry, relying on competition among the bidders themselves to limit the share of auction awards controlled by any single bidder.

■ Footnotes

1. A squeeze occurs when there is an unexpected restriction of supply relative to demand for a particular security, manifested by an unusually high price of that security relative to prices of comparable securities.

2. See *Joint Report on the Government Securities Market*. Washington, D.C.: Department of the Treasury, Securities and Exchange Commission, and Board of Governors of the Federal Reserve System, January 1992. A somewhat more technical examination of these matters appeared recently in Vincent Reinhart, "Theory and Evidence on Reform of the Treasury's Auction Procedures," Federal Reserve Board, Finance and Economics Discussion Series No. 190, March 1992.

3. Federal Reserve Bank and government tenders are also awarded in full at the price established for noncompetitive bidders, but the amount of these awards is added to the amount being auctioned.

4. Milton Friedman has been a long-time proponent of this procedure. For references, see *Joint Report on the Government Securities Market*, p. B-22.

5. See Robert J. Weber, "Multiple-Object Auctions," in Richard Engelbrecht-Wiggins, Martin Shubik, and Robert M. Stark, eds., *Auctions, Bidding, and Contracting: Uses and Theory*. New York: New York University Press, 1983.

6. An alternative to rounds of bidding might be to conduct auctions on an interactive, open-screen basis: Qualified bidders would have access directly (or at a Federal Reserve Bank) to a telecommunications terminal. Beginning hours (or days) before the close of an auction, a screen would display an instantaneously updated list of all (anonymous) bids received and their implied auction stop-out price. Bidders would have the right to alter their bids up until the close of the auction, when the final stop-out price would be determined, with awards made to all who bid at or above that price.

E. J. Stevens is an assistant vice president and economist and Diana Dumitru is a senior research assistant at the Federal Reserve Bank of Cleveland. The authors thank Charles Carlstrom for helpful comments.

The views stated herein are those of the authors and not necessarily those of the Federal Reserve Bank of Cleveland or of the Board of Governors of the Federal Reserve System.

Part Five

International Finance

Rapid advances in communications technology have recently drawn the world's many markets and institutions closer together. Certainly the financial markets are no exception to this global trend. New securities exchanges have proliferated in Europe, Asia, and North and South America and many financial instruments—particularly government securities and stocks and bonds of the largest corporations—now trade worldwide in markets that never sleep. In this section of the book we try to capture the flavor of the internationalization movement now sweeping through the financial marketplace.

In the first article in this section Peter A. Abken, senior economist in the Federal Reserve Bank of Atlanta's Research Department, focuses upon new electronic systems that are stimulating the spread of around-the-clock trading throughout the world. The author reviews some of the globe's largest organized exchanges for common stock, financial futures contracts, and options as well as key over-the-counter markets for the stock issued by some of the world's largest corporations. Dr. Abken also addresses the controversial issue of whether recent advances in electronic communications have increased the volatility of security prices.

As investors have expanded their holdings of securities issued worldwide many questions have arisen about the supposed benefits of *international diversification*. In a short, but interesting article entitled "Measuring the Gains from International Portfolio Diversification," Kenneth Kasa, economist with the Federal Reserve Bank of San Francisco, looks at the evidence concerning the impact of holding a globally diversified stock portfolio upon investor returns. Dr. Kasa finds that the gains from international diversification appear to be quite large, yet most investors seem to be strongly biased in favor of *domestic* assets in place of foreign assets. One possible explanation offered by the author is that offsetting movements in the terms of trade between nations may significantly reduce the potential gains from international portfolio diversification.

One of the most rapidly growing economies in the world since World War II has been the economy of Japan, though the Japanese have suffered a serious recession in recent years. Michael M. Hutchison, a Visiting Scholar with the Federal Reserve Bank of San Francisco, explores the issue of whether Japan's long-run economic gains have increased the interdependence of U.S. and Japanese real interest rates. He finds that the answer is a strong "yes"—U.S. real interest rates appear to exert a substantial impact upon Japan's interest rates and economic developments in Japan seem to significantly influence U.S. real interest rates. Any differences in real rates between the two nations appear to close up quickly, a not-too-surprising result given Japan's current importance in world trade and in the field of technological innovation.

One of the most dramatic structural changes in the global economy of recent years is the movement toward greater political and economic union among Western Europe's leading countries. After centuries of war and divisional hatreds, Europe has committed itself to move toward a unified political and economic trade area which eventually is supposed to have a single financial system, single currency, and a single central bank. In her article "The Path to European Monetary Union," Paula Hildebrandt of the Federal Reserve Bank of Kansas City discusses the history and prospects of Europe's move toward a homogenous money and credit system. Unfortunately, as the tumultuous events in the currency markets of the early 1990s suggest, the steps needed to forge a truly integrated European financial system will *not* be easy to take. One key stumbling block is the hesitancy of some member nations to transfer some of their political and economic power to the European community as a whole.

One of the most important steps in Europe's drive toward political and economic unity will be the creation of a common market for financial services that allows banks and other financial-service providers to have free access to local markets throughout the European Community (EC). Drs. K. Alec Chrystal and Cletus C. Coughlin of the Federal Reserve Bank of St. Louis, in their article, "How the 1992 Legislation Will Affect European Financial Services," explore the progress that has been made toward uniform regulation of financial-service institutions throughout Europe. In particular, the sweeping reforms of 1992 are reviewed by these authors who see definite forward strides toward a uniform market for wholesale financial services, but the market for retail financial services for households and smaller businesses seems to be lagging behind. For many retail services each European nation still appears to have a relatively isolated financial marketplace. These Federal Reserve economists believe that the movement towards a single European currency will aid greatly in the development of a homogenous European financial system.

This section of the book closes with an exploration of the effects of the adoption of NAFTA—The North American Free Trade Agreement. Federal Reserve Bank of Dallas economists William C. Gruben, John H. Welch, and Jeffrey W. Gunther look at NAFTA's structure and probable effects in an article entitled "U.S. Banks, Competition, and the Mexican Banking System: How Much Will NAFTA Matter?" They see NAFTA as furthering Mexico's announced goal of improving efficiency and competition in that nation's financial-service markets. Moreover, Drs. Gruben, Welch, and Gunther believe that nonbank financial services, such as security brokerage, insurance, and access to stock and bond markets, are likely to experience more of a favorable impact from NAFTA than banking services will because Mexico has taken special steps to protect its banks from foreign competition, at least until NAFTA is fully phased in early in the next century.

Article 34

Globalization of Stock, Futures, and Options Markets

Peter A. Abken

The author is a senior economist in the financial section of the Atlanta Fed's research department. He would especially like to thank Jim Shapiro of the New York Stock Exchange and Bruce Phelps of the Chicago Board of Trade for helpful comments. However, any errors are the author's responsibility.

Of the trendy buzzwords to emerge from the 1980s, "globalization" surely ranks high on the list of overused words in the business lexicon, but not without good reason. The word has become associated with financial markets' growing interconnections, facilitated largely by advances in communications and computer technology. Capital moves across national borders primarily as investment flows and secondarily as international trade financing. In dollar terms, global financial transactions today stand at a historically high multiple of world trade volume (John G. Heimann 1989). Record trade imbalances, however, have also contributed to financial interdependence, the most prominent example being the net current account surplus of Japan, leading to large overseas investments of the surplus, and the net deficit of the United States, necessitating borrowing from abroad.

Financial transactions' increasing volume and their decreasing costs have put strong competitive pressures on financial institutions to change the ways in which they intermediate credit and other financial flows. The financial industry has turned to automated securities trading, which is transforming and displacing the face-to-face and mouth-to-telephone methods of making financial transactions and strengthening the globalization or internationalization of securities markets in the process. Automation of trading encompasses a number of innovations that have improved the efficiency of making financial transactions. The technologies range from quotation and communications systems that facilitate traditional trading methods to so-called screen trading systems that supplant them. Their operation can be confined to one organized financial exchange, as the New York Stock Exchange's SuperDot system is, or can link many organized exchanges, as the Chicago Mercantile Exchange's Globex system does. For convenience in this discussion of the gradual automation of securities trading, these innovations will be referred to generically as automated trading systems.

This article examines currently running and proposed automated systems for many of the world's principal organized exchanges for common stock, futures, and option contracts. These exchanges are voluntary associations of members who come together to trade securities in auction markets, paying for the right to trade on an exchange—they buy a "seat" on the exchange. They generally trade for their own accounts and for outside customers. In contrast, participants in over-the-counter (OTC) markets, who are geographically dispersed, are brought together by telephone and computer lines. Over-the-counter trades go through dealers, who quote prices to buy and sell. The National Association of Securities Dealers (NASD) is one of several important OTC markets for common stocks in the United States that will be discussed below.

The article concludes with a section on market performance and regulation that takes a broader perspective on globalization. The perceived impact of globalization is closely tied to one's view of market efficiency. Integrating markets through electronic trading may reduce the magnitude of certain kinds of price shocks that propagate across markets because of a lack of information about the sources of such shocks. If markets are efficient, twenty-four-hour trading has the potential to reduce such market volatility. On the other hand, some market observers and participants, believing that markets are inefficient and excessively volatile, have proposed measures to curb speculative activity and the volatility they believe it engenders. The continuing reduction in transactions costs through technological innovation may only exacerbate market volatility. The final section considers this debate.

The Growth of International Securities Trading

Since the 1980s, securities markets of all kinds have been developing rapidly around the world. The volume of equity and bond market transactions has grown steadily, and both American purchases and sales of foreign securities and foreign purchases and sales of U.S. securities have been expanding, as Table 1 shows. A useful indicator of market activity, the growth in transactions volume coincided with increases in volatility of most financial markets, which has been attributed to causes ranging from deregulation of financial markets, fiscal and trade imbalances, and so forth, to out-and-out irrationality and a gambling-casino mentality among traders. Some economists have recommended taxing securities transactions to alleviate the apparently unnecessary volatility.[1] On the other hand, there are substantive reasons for expecting that transactions volume will increase as uncertainty about "fundamentals" rises. For one thing, trading securities is necessary to adjust portfolios optimally in response to changing expected securities' payoffs.[2] In addition, volatility is a prime factor motivating financial risk management, which has spawned a variety of derivative instrument markets. Options and futures markets, for example, deal in contracts that are valued on the basis of stock, bond, and other primary securities prices. A discussion of the growth of primary and derivative securities markets follows.

Equities. Table 1 shows international equity market transactions, comparing activity for selected countries and regions in 1980 with 1990. The sum of purchases and sales, referred to here as transactions volume, measures the total transactions in equity markets by foreigners in U.S. stock markets and by Americans in foreign stock markets.[3] The dollar volume of transactions in 1980 and in 1990 was greater for foreigners transacting in U.S. markets than for Americans dealing in foreign markets. However, the overall margin of foreign volume over domestic volume diminished from 321 percent in 1980 to 43 percent in 1990.[4] The absolute levels of dollar purchases and sales have increased markedly, well in excess of the dollar's inflation rate and twice as fast as the growth of transactions volume on domestic exchanges during this period (Joseph A. Grundfest 1990, 349).

The compound annual growth rate for foreign transactions volume in U.S. securities was 17 percent, while the growth rate for U.S. transactions volume in foreign securities was 30 percent. Japanese transactions in U.S. stock markets grew at a 41 percent compound annual rate, faster than those of all other countries or regions. Japan's percentage share of the international transactions volume has correspondingly risen from 2.5 percent to 16 percent over the decade. The United Kingdom accounts for nearly half the 1990 European volume, up substantially from 1980. Much of its transactions volume probably stems from Middle Eastern and other non-United Kingdom buying and selling of U.S. stocks that occurs through London's markets, which are the preeminent financial

Table 1
Transactions Volume in Stocks

	Foreign Transactions in U.S. Securities				U.S. Transactions in Foreign Securities			
	Purchases[a]	Sales[a]	Aggregate Purchases and Sales[a]	Percentage Share of Market	Purchases[a]	Sales[a]	Aggregate Purchases and Sales[a]	Percentage Share of Market
1990								
France	5.82	7.01	12.83	3.55	6.05	5.90	11.95	4.72
Germany	5.90	6.27	12.17	3.37	6.69	7.45	14.14	5.58
United Kingdom	44.94	48.07	93.01	25.74	44.80	45.52	90.32	35.64
Total Europe	84.95	93.53	178.47	49.39	74.53	78.40	152.94	60.36
Japan	27.47	30.38	57.85	16.01	30.89	31.52	62.41	24.63
Canada	19.52	18.63	38.14	10.56	4.78	4.92	9.70	3.83
Total Worldwide	173.04	188.34	361.37	100.00	122.49	130.89	253.38	100.00
1980								
France	2.73	2.24	4.97	6.60	0.47	0.67	1.14	6.36
Germany	2.75	2.56	5.30	7.05	0.24	0.22	0.46	2.57
United Kingdom	7.44	4.94	12.38	16.44	1.38	1.36	2.75	15.38
Total Europe	24.62	21.55	46.16	61.32	3.16	3.62	6.78	37.97
Japan	0.87	1.03	1.90	2.52	0.93	1.77	2.70	15.10
Canada	6.35	5.48	11.83	15.71	3.02	3.66	6.68	37.43
Total Worldwide	40.32	34.96	75.28	100.00	7.89	9.97	17.85	100.00

Compound Annual Growth Rate, 1980-90
(percent)

	Foreign	U.S.
France	9.95	26.53
Germany	8.66	40.88
United Kingdom	22.35	41.81
Total Europe	14.48	36.56
Japan	40.73	36.92
Canada	12.42	3.80
Total Worldwide	16.98	30.38

[a] *In billions of U.S. dollars.*
Source: Derived by the Federal Reserve Bank of Atlanta from U.S. Department of the Treasury, *U.S. Treasury Bulletin* (Winter 1991), Table CM-V-5; (Winter 1981), Table CM-VI-10.

markets in Europe. From 1980 to 1990, both the United Kingdom and Japan were responsible for net inflows (cumulative excess of purchases over sales) into U.S. equity markets of about 17 billion dollars each.

U.S. transactions volume in foreign equities also grew markedly during the decade, almost twice as fast as foreign volume. This growth rate reflects the low 1980 level of U.S. purchases and sales of foreign stocks relative to foreign participation in U.S. markets. The transactions volume shares in the United Kingdom and Japan realized significant increases from 1980 to 1990, as did the corresponding compound annual growth rates. Though the share of overall volume was still relatively low in 1990, the growth rate for German stock market participation by U.S. investors was about as rapid as the rates for the United Kingdom and Japan.

Chart 1 gives another view of world equity trading, showing the dollar trading volume in major world equity markets. Clearly, the New York and Tokyo markets surpass other world markets. Each of these will be discussed further in connection with automated trading systems.

Bonds. The dollar transactions volume for bonds was approximately ten times as large as that for stocks in 1990; they were roughly comparable a decade earlier. The domestic and foreign bonds included in Table 2 exclude short-term bonds with remaining times to maturity of less than one year. Although there is considerable trading in these short-term securities, much of that trading includes government intervention in foreign exchange markets, leading in turn to sizable purchases and sales of short-term government securities such as U.S. Treasury bills. Long-term securities better gauge the growth in private cross-border capital movements. The securities included in U.S. market transactions are marketable Treasury and federally sponsored agency bonds as well as corporate bonds.

Almost all bonds are traded over-the-counter, though some are traded on organized exchanges. Somewhat less than 10 percent of all U.S. corporate bonds are traded on organized exchanges (Jack Clark Francis 1991, 87). As seen in Table 2, most foreign transactions in U.S. bond markets are in government bonds. Although the bond market is primarily

Chart 1
Dollar Trading Volume in Major World Equity Markets in 1990[a]

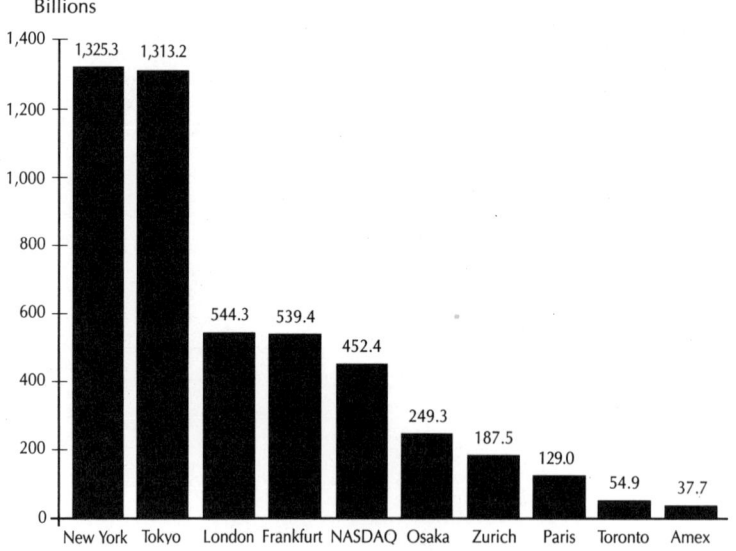

[a] Annual trading volume is the sum of each issue's daily share volume multiplied by its closing price and aggregated over all issues and trading days in the year.
Source: NASDAQ (1991).

Table 2
Transactions Volume in Long-Term Bonds[a]

	Foreign Transactions in U.S. Securities				U.S. Transactions in Foreign Securities			
	Purchases[b]	Sales[b]	Aggregate Purchases and Sales[b]	Percentage Share of Market	Purchases[b]	Sales[b]	Aggregate Purchases and Sales[b]	Percentage Share of Market
1990								
France	13.47	12.78	26.24	0.68	14.67	15.50	30.17	4.65
Germany	45.31	39.87	85.18	2.21	15.91	18.23	34.14	5.26
United Kingdom	564.62	555.67	1,120.29	29.08	113.95	114.16	228.10	35.12
Total Europe	804.32	773.85	1,578.17	40.97	185.46	189.78	375.25	57.77
Japan	731.08	744.96	1,476.04	38.32	36.71	43.50	80.21	12.35
Canada	66.81	69.46	136.26	3.54	54.48	56.91	111.39	17.15
Total Worldwide	1,945.19	1,906.80	3,851.99	100.00	313.58	335.93	649.50	100.00
1980								
France	0.71	0.45	1.16	0.94	0.66	0.62	1.28	3.64
Germany	2.54	5.21	7.75	6.31	0.45	0.43	0.88	2.50
United Kingdom	22.36	20.15	42.51	34.60	6.07	6.16	12.23	34.97
Total Europe	30.29	30.37	60.65	49.37	9.09	9.59	18.68	53.39
Japan	2.59	4.21	6.81	5.54	1.35	2.65	4.00	11.44
Canada	0.96	2.39	3.35	2.73	2.20	2.42	4.63	13.22
Total Worldwide	66.61	56.25	122.86	100.00	17.07	17.92	34.98	100.00

Compound Annual Growth Rate, 1980-90
(percent)

	Foreign	U.S.
France	36.66	37.22
Germany	27.09	44.24
United Kingdom	38.70	33.99
Total Europe	38.53	34.99
Japan	71.24	34.96
Canada	44.86	37.46
Total Worldwide	41.13	33.93

[a] Bonds having maturities of one year or greater.
[b] In billions of U.S. dollars.
Source: Derived by the Federal Reserve Bank of Atlanta from U.S. Department of the Treasury, *U.S. Treasury Bulletin* (Winter 1991), Table CM-V-5; (Winter 1981), Table CM-VI-10.

over-the-counter (and thus not the point of interest in this discussion), the growing number of international transactions in bonds has stimulated derivative securities markets worldwide. Increasingly, derivative securities trade in one country on underlying securities originating in another. Several examples—including the futures contracts on U.S. Treasury bonds that trade on the Tokyo Stock Exchange (TSE) and the German government bond futures that trade at the London International Financial Futures Exchange (LIFFE, pronounced "life")—will be discussed below.

The picture of globalization that emerged from the earlier consideration of equities trading comes into even sharper relief when cross-border bond trading is examined. Aside from the greater magnitude of dollar transactions volume mentioned earlier, the most striking feature is the uniformly high growth rates across countries and regions from 1980 to 1990. Equity market growth rates, particularly for French and German involvement in U.S. markets, do not show this evenness. All but one compound annual growth rate exceeds 30 percent. The transactions volume of Japanese investors in U.S. markets increased 71 percent annually! Similar to the equity data, the Japanese share in transactions volume rose over the decade from 5.5 percent to 38 percent, while the European share declined from 49 percent to 41 percent. U.S. investor participation in foreign bond markets mirrored the increased foreign activity in U.S. markets.

Futures and Options. Exchange-traded futures contracts have a long and—to some—notorious history. Commodity futures originated at the Chicago Board of Trade (CBOT) in the 1860s (see Chicago Board of Trade 1985, 1-4). Not until 1972 were the first financial futures introduced at the Chicago Mercantile Exchange (CME, or the "Merc"). The development of these currency futures reflected the anticipated hedging needs stemming from the decision allowing the dollar and other major currencies to float against one another rather than to be maintained at fixed parities. At the time agricultural contracts accounted for 97 percent of the CME's volume (William J. Brodsky 1990). Many new financial futures and options soon followed. The CBOT established the Chicago Board Options Exchange (CBOE) in 1973 to trade options on listed stocks; they created the Ginnie Mae futures contract in 1975.[5] The CME countered with its Treasury bill futures contract in 1976; the CBOT, with its Treasury bond futures contract in 1977. The latter is the most heavily traded futures contract in the world today.

In the early 1980s, these exchanges developed futures and options contracts on equity indexes, such as the Standard and Poor's (S&P) 500 futures (CME) and S&P 100 options contracts (CBOE). At the time of the market crash of October 1987, the S&P 500 futures achieved a notoriety in the minds of many investors and stock exchange members that lingers to this day. While a number of factors had contributed to the crash, the use of index futures in conjunction with so-called program trading, which uses the automated order-routing system at the New York Stock Exchange, was widely blamed. (This subject will be considered further in a later section.) In any case, many exchanges, including the New York Stock Exchange, greatly expanded capacity through automation to handle future surges in volume.

While volume in other futures contracts has remained generally flat during the 1980s, financial futures volume has grown steadily (see Robert W. Kolb 1991, 23). For example, by 1989 financial futures volume made up 91 percent of the CME's volume, with only the remaining 9 percent accounted for by commodity futures. At all U.S. futures exchanges in 1972, the total annual volume of futures trading measured by the number of contracts traded was 18.3 million. In 1990 this volume had risen to 276.5 million contracts, a compound annual growth rate of 16.3 percent. Though the U.S. exchanges are the world's most established, foreign futures markets are rapidly making inroads in the share of trading volume. For instance, since the opening of the London International Financial Futures Exchange in 1982, thirty options and futures exchanges have opened outside the United States (Brodsky 1991).

The U.S. exchanges are still dominant in the world, but, as Table 3 shows, foreign options and futures markets that emerged in the 1980s are also well represented in the top-twenty ranks. In particular, the Osaka Securities Exchange's Nikkei 225 index futures contract and Tokyo International Financial Futures Exchange's Euroyen contract surged in volume during 1990.

Automation of Equity Markets

Individual stock exchanges everywhere have adopted some degree of automation, reflecting the exigencies of competitive pressures from domestic as well as foreign exchanges. Derivative securities markets have aggressively employed the new technologies to

Table 3
Most Heavily Traded Futures and Options Contracts

Rank 1990	Rank 1989	Contract[a]	Exchanges[b]	Contract Volume 1990	Contract Volume 1989
1	1	T-bond (f)	CBOT	75,499,000	70,303,000
2	2	S&P 100 (o)	CBOE	58,845,000	58,371,000
3	3	Eurodollar (f)	CME	34,694,000	40,818,000
4	4	T-bond (o)	CBOT	27,315,000	20,784,000
5	5	Crude oil (f)	Nymex	23,687,000	20,535,000
6	6	Japanese government bond (f)	TSE	16,307,000	18,942,000
7	7	Notionnel government bond (f)	MATIF	15,996,000	15,005,000
8	30	Euroyen (f)	TIFFE	14,414,000	4,495,000
9	25	Nikkei 225 (f)	Osaka	13,589,000	5,443,000
10	8	S&P 500 (f)	CME	12,139,000	10,560,000
11	18	S&P 500 (o)	CBOE	12,089,000	6,274,000
12	11	Corn (f)	CBOT	11,423,000	9,271,000
13	10	Soybeans (f)	CBOT	10,302,000	9,635,000
14	9	Gold (f)	Comex	9,730,000	9,999,000
15	26	German bond (f)	LIFFE	9,582,000	5,330,000
16	17	Nikkei 225 (o)	Osaka	9,186,000	6,610,000
17	12	Deutsche Mark (f)	CME	9,169,000	8,186,000
18	16	Short Sterling (f)	LIFFE	8,355,000	7,131,000
19	13	Yen (f)	CME	7,437,000	7,824,000
20	15	Notionnel government bond (o)	MATIF	7,410,000	7,177,000

[a] (f) = futures contract; (o) = options contract.
[b] Nymex is the New York Mercantile Exchange; Comex is the Commodities Exchange (New York); other exchanges are described in the text.
Source: *Futures and Options World: 1991 Annual Worldwide Directory and Review* (Surrey, England. Metal Bulletin Journals Ltd., 1991), 9. Data used by permission of the publisher.

link exchanges. The discussion below considers the movement toward automated trading in equity markets and derivative markets.

New York Stock Exchange. U.S. equity markets are the largest and most liquid in the world. The biggest domestic exchange, the New York Stock Exchange (NYSE), is facing mounting competitive pressures from regional domestic exchanges and from foreign stock exchanges. The heart of the New York Stock Exchange is its specialists, charged by the exchange to maintain "fair and orderly" markets in the individual listed stocks assigned to them. The New York Stock Exchange is organized as a continuous two-sided auction market, with the specialist acting as auctioneer for incoming orders to buy or sell a particular stock. The specialist conducts an auction in the sense that he or she continually adjusts a stock's price to balance supply and demand throughout the trading day. She at times may also need to take the buy or sell side to keep prices from fluctuating too greatly. Overall about 10 percent of share purchases and 10 percent of sales on the NYSE result in specialists' staking their own capital in the trade (New York Stock Exchange 1991a, 17). This role is part of their obligation to the exchange in performing the specialist's function.

Also, the specialist has access to the computerized limit-order book, which displays orders to buy or sell if the market price reaches a specified level. Because of their knowledge, specialists have an informational advantage over traders off the exchange floor.[6] Although they may profit from their inventory position, exchange rules constrain trading for their own accounts. On every trade the specialist also receives the difference between the sale price (the ask) and the purchase price (the bid). Other market participants are willing to incur these costs in order to gain the liquidity specialists provide. However, the specialist's role is being questioned with increasing frequency: How important is it? Is the provision of liquidity worth the price?

Since the rise of institutional trading in the 1960s, the so-called upstairs market has developed, partly insulating the specialists from having to take positions in large blocks of 10,000 or more shares. Such blocks sent directly to the specialists may cause too much price fluctuation and be too risky for them to handle. Instead, block positioners match buyers and sellers and may also take positions in blocks themselves. Blocks are then sent to the specialist post for execution. Because of economies of scale, low commission rates are charged for block transactions. During the latter half of the 1980s, about half the NYSE's volume was accounted for by institutional block trading (NASDAQ 1991, 39). Preferring new, automated mechanisms that are even cheaper, institutional investors are beginning to dispense altogether with using the exchange.

More efficient handling of trading volume led to the development of the NYSE's automated routing system in 1976 called the Super Designated Order Turnaround System (SuperDot). SuperDot routes market orders of less than 2,099 shares to the specialist (or to a floor broker) for rapid execution, usually in less than a minute.[7] The system can also route large orders to the specialist. SuperDot is frequently used by program traders dealing in whole portfolios of stocks; they route lists of stocks through the system to appropriate specialists. The system handles market orders of as many as 30,099 shares and limit orders of as many as 99,999 shares of individual stocks, although the specialists are not obligated to execute these orders as rapidly as the New York Stock Exchange requires for smaller ones. Odd-lot orders of less than 100 shares are executed automatically by SuperDot at the prevailing price quote. About 75 percent of daily NYSE orders are processed through the system (New York Stock Exchange 1991a, 21).

Regionals. Regional exchanges have developed their own versions of automated order-routing and execution systems for small trades. The Midwest Stock Exchange (MSE), Pacific Stock Exchange (PSE), Philadelphia Stock Exchange (PHLX), and Boston Stock Exchange (BSE) use systems named MAX, SCOREX, PACE, and BEACON, respectively.[8] The Cincinnati Stock Exchange (CSE) is in fact an over-the-counter market with competing market makers. All trades on the CSE pass through the National Securities Trading System (NSTS), which is an order-matching system akin to the NASDAQ system to be discussed shortly (U.S. Securities and Exchange Commission 1991, 23-26).

The Securities Act amendments of 1975 mandated the Securities and Exchange Commission (SEC) to establish a national market system with the objectives of increasing competition among market makers at different exchanges and strengthening links among different exchanges (see Francis 1991, 132-33). One major change was that negotiated commissions replaced fixed commissions on securities sales and purchases. Another consequence of the act was the establishment of the "Consolidated Tape," which continuously lists the trades at seven stock exchanges and two over-the-counter markets (NASD and Instinet). Since 1978 the regional exchanges, the American Stock Exchange (Amex), NASD, and NYSE have been linked by the Intermarket Trading System (ITS), which enables a broker or specialist at one exchange to send orders to buy or sell at another exchange showing a better price.

Most of the stocks traded via the ITS communication system are NYSE-listed stocks, and a much smaller number traded are Amex-listed and regionally listed stocks. At the broker's or specialist's discretion, orders are routed to the exchange showing the best bid or offer. Once a small order is received, the BEACON, MAX, and SCOREX systems "expose" it to the specialist for fifteen seconds during which he or she may better the bid or offer price; otherwise, the order is automatically executed at the specialist's quoted bid or offer. (PACE automatically executes all small orders.) The Amex has an order-routing system called Post Execution Reporting (PER) that is very similar to the NYSE's SuperDot. Amex members can send orders for as many as 2,000 shares directly to the specialist using the system and receive an execution report for the trades (U.S. Congress 1990b, 49-50).

The regional exchanges and Amex have only a small slice of the trading-volume pie. Table 4 shows where they stand in relation to the NYSE and NASD, viewed both in terms of share volume and in terms of dollar volumes.

NASDAQ. National Association of Securities Dealers runs a telecommunications network called NASDAQ, for NASD Automated Quotations. In this over-the-counter market NASD dealers compete with one another in making bids and offers on stocks.[9] These OTC securities tend to be smaller capitalization stocks that do not meet exchange listing requirements; only a subset of them are also listed on organized exchanges.[10] To buy or sell a stock, an investor

Table 4
U.S. Equity Markets: 1990 Share and Dollar Volumes

	Share Volume		Dollar Volume	
	Millions	Percent	Millions	Percent
NASDAQ	33,380	39.2	$ 452,430	21.8
NASDAQ/OTC Trading in Listed Securities	2,589	3.0	86,494	4.2
Amex	3,329	3.9	37,715	1.8
Regionals (BSE, CSE, MSE, PSE, and PHLX)	6,208	7.3	178,139	8.5
NYSE	39,665	46.6	1,325,332	63.7
Totals	85,171	100.0	$2,080,110	100.0

Source: NASDAQ (1991).

calls a dealer, who checks NASDAQ to find the best quotation from competing dealers in a particular stock at the lowest cost (that is, lowest bid-ask spread and commission). Unlike stock exchange specialists, dealers are not obligated to provide liquidity through their own position-taking. The OTC market instead relies on interdealer competition.

About 13 percent of OTC transactions are handled by NASD's Small Order Execution System (SOES), in operation since 1985. Public buy or sell orders of as many as 1,000 shares go through SOES to the dealer offering the best price quote. However, if there are currently better price quotes on NASDAQ outside SOES, that dealer is required to fill the order at the better price.[11] In 1990 SOES added the capacity to automatically execute matching limit orders entered into the system.

Another NASDAQ system is SelectNet, which allows NASDAQ members to send buy or sell securities orders to other system members' terminals. SelectNet enables market makers to accept and execute orders partially or fully as well as to conduct price and quantity negotiations. System users are therefore not anonymous. NASDAQ securities orders must be for more than 1,000 shares.[12]

NASDAQ leads other domestic exchanges, most notably the New York Stock Exchange, in the indirect trading of foreign equities. This indirect trading is through American Depository Receipts (ADRs). Foreign corporations have American commercial or investment banks buy their equity shares and place them in a trust account, against which ADR certificates are issued. These certificates are negotiable and can be traded on exchanges and through NASDAQ. Investors find ADRs convenient because their purchase and sale and the distribution of dividend payments are entirely in dollars, not foreign currency. Foreign-currency denominated cash dividends are converted into dollars by the trustee, usually a commercial bank, and are passed on to the American Depository Receipts holders. The foreign corporation benefits by not having to comply with the SEC's disclosure requirements and other regulations enforced for domestic corporations (see Francis 1991, 62, 806-7).

In 1990 NASDAQ reached new records in ADR trading with a trading volume of 2.2 billion shares of eighty-seven ADR issues. In comparison, the NYSE had a 1.4 billion share volume for sixty-two ADR issues. NASDAQ dollar volume was 21 billion, while the dollar volume in foreign securities directly listed on NASDAQ was 7 billion.[13] NASDAQ is expanding in 1991 to offer an international quotation network based in the United Kingdom called NASDAQ International.

Instinet. NASDAQ dealers earn their livelihood from the difference in price between what they will pay for stock and their selling price, the bid-ask spread.

That spread has come under pressure to narrow because of an electronic order-execution system called Instinet, owned by Reuters Holdings PLC. Instinet is a screen trading system in that it enables subscribers to trade anonymously. These participants include not only OTC broker-dealers but also institutional investors. For example, NASDAQ dealers can trade with other NASDAQ dealers on Instinet to adjust their inventory of stocks. These trades can be accomplished within the bid-ask spread quoted on NASDAQ so that NASDAQ quotes would be unaffected. Institutional investors have also been trading actively on Instinet at much lower spreads than through NASDAQ dealers or exchange specialists. To stay competitive, dealers have had to cut their spreads.[14]

Most Instinet trades involve OTC and listed U.S. stocks, but an increasing number are in British, French, German, and other European stocks as well. The system, on-line an average of fourteen hours per day, can remain operational almost around-the-clock during periods of heavy trading.[15]

Anonymity is important to traders because a trader's identity can reveal how often and how much he or she is buying or selling, information that could move prices against the trader. For example, traders usually avoid selling large orders at once because doing so may prompt a stock's price to be bid down rapidly in the process of making the trade, on the assumption that some bad news is behind the sale. In that scenario, known as adverse selection risk, large orders will be put on the market in smaller blocks. Instinet allows traders to poll each other almost instantaneously on a prospective trade. They can send anonymous messages over the system to particular traders to negotiate quantity or price. They can see all of the bids and offers on particular stocks at a given time on the Instinet "book."

Madoff Investment Securities. This firm has set itself up in direct competition with NYSE specialists. Madoff makes a market in 350 of the S&P 500 stocks by attracting mainly retail trades from brokers, paying them a penny per share for orders. These orders are executed at prices that match the best quoted on any exchange, as reported through ITS. Madoff operates through the Cincinnati Stock Exchange's National Securities Trading System, which is essentially an over-the-counter market. Because of low overhead costs, his commission costs are much lower than for trades carried out on an exchange floor. According to a recent estimate, this firm alone generates 2 percent of the daily trading volume in NYSE listed stocks (Barbara Howard 1991, 16; William E. Sheeline 1990, 122).

Crossing Networks. To reduce transactions costs, many institutional investors have turned to so-called crossing networks, such as Instinet's The Crossing Network and Posit (Portfolio System for Institutional Trading) of Jefferies & Company, a registered broker-dealer. Many institutional investors deal in indexed equity portfolios—for example, a portfolio mimicking the S&P 500 index. These "passive" portfolio managers are not concerned about the precise timing of trade executions for individual stocks making up an index. For institutional investors seeking to trade in whole portfolios of stocks, crossing networks offer a low-cost alternative to transactions on organized stock exchanges.

The Crossing Network allows whole portfolios of stock to be bought or sold at primary markets' closing prices (for example, NYSE closing prices) and the mean of the bid-ask OTC prices. Because the trades are based on the closing price, and hence passive, there is no "market impact" on the trades themselves—that is, large buy and sell orders are matched or crossed at that price, unaffected by the unfavorable price movement such a trade might ordinarily produce. The price does not adjust to balance supply and demand, so some orders will go unmatched in a single after-hours session.

Posit is a crossing network that operates during trading hours as well as off-hours. Portfolio trades can be executed at the primary markets' opening, at prespecified times of day after the opening, or at closing prices. This system has many options that users can select; their choices affect the cost of their trades. For example, trades not matched through Posit's computer can be canceled, held for matching at a later time, sent to the primary markets for execution, or "price-guaranteed" by Jefferies (that is, Jefferies takes the other side of the trade). These alternatives entail different commission costs. The amount of information about a prospective trade, like the size of the order or identity of the investor, may be revealed or hidden from other system users (U.S. Securities and Exchange Commission 1991, 83-86).

Overseas Trading. The NYSE is also affected by the movement of institutional program trades overseas, particularly to London's over-the-counter market. A common transaction involves a stock-index futures purchase or sale on a U.S. futures exchange with a subsequent exchange-for-physicals (EFP) transaction to unwind the futures position.[16] For example, a portfolio manager who wishes to buy an S&P 500-

indexed portfolio could buy the underlying stocks on the New York Stock Exchange or alternatively buy S&P 500 contracts on the Chicago Mercantile Exchange. In the latter case, the long futures position could then be offset through an EFP over the counter in London by finding a trader (or traders) short the S&P 500 futures who holds the underlying stock portfolio. The cash prices and futures price for the EFP transaction would be determined by negotiation but typically reflect the underlying stocks' closing prices on the New York Stock Exchange, Amex, and OTC markets as well as the futures on the transaction date. The parties have traded stocks outside of the NYSE and have closed out their futures positions off the Chicago Mercantile Exchange exchange floor, saving commissions and market impact costs.[17] Similar over-the-counter program transactions also occur that do not involve index futures.

About 10 to 15 million NYSE shares currently trade after-hours in London every day (Kevin G. Salwen and Craig Torres 1991, C1). This exodus from the exchange floor was spurred in part by a postcrash NYSE rule requiring immediate display of program trades' price and volume.

SPAworks. A new system operated by R. Steven Wunsch takes after-hours trading a step further. He has designed a system, SPAworks, to trade stocks in an after-hours call market, which involves a single-price auction. This institutional arrangement was actually prevalent in the nineteenth century before the advent of continuous auction markets, and many relatively illiquid international exchanges still rely on it (see below). SPAworks has been operational since April 1991.

The system works by allowing buy and sell orders to accumulate after the NYSE closes at 4:00 P.M. (U.S. Securities and Exchange Commission 1991, 73-77; Wunsch 1991). At a predetermined time before the next day's opening, a single computerized auction of each individual stock would be held, whereby trades would be consummated at the price resulting in the largest volume of trade. Participants entering bids above or below the auction price are able to execute their trades at the auction price. Other orders go unmatched. This system saves the cost of paying for the immediate liquidity provided on the exchange floor.

Off-Hours Trading. In response to the inroads these outside trading systems have made, the NYSE announced in May 1991 that it would institute two after-hours sessions. "Crossing Session I" runs from 4:15 until 5:00 P.M. and allows investors to buy and sell at the 4:00 P.M. closing price. Once submitted by NYSE members through SuperDot, single-sided orders are matched against others based on the times they were submitted. Matched single-sided orders and paired (prearranged) orders are then executed through SuperDot at 5:00 P.M. "Crossing Session II," which operates from 4:00 to 5:15 P.M., specifically accommodates program traders. After the close New York Stock Exchange member firms place paired orders for programs that contain at least fifteen NYSE-listed stocks having a one-million-dollar market value or more. These coupled orders are executed as soon as they are received by the system. To make the new sessions attractive to program traders, the NYSE has granted a

Physical marketplaces (the trading floors) are becoming obsolete, while "virtual" marketplaces—networks of computers and computer terminals—are emerging as the "site" for transactions.

nine-month exemption from being required to report price and volume information for individual program trades Only the aggregate volume and dollar value of program trades are disseminated at 5:15 P.M. Single-sided and coupled order volume are each reported separately for Crossing Session I, beginning at 5:00 P.M. (Salwen and Torres 1991, C1; U.S. Securities and Exchange Commission 1991, 36-39; New York Stock Exchange 1991b, 1-5).

Foreign Equity Markets. Many foreign stock markets are considerably less liquid than U.S. stock markets, and their institutional arrangements reflect this fact. The Austrian and Norwegian stock markets simply hold a single daily call auction. Others use a mixed system of call auctions at some times of day and continuous trading at other times. Mixed auctions are prevalent in Belgium, Denmark, France, Italy, Spain, Sweden, and Switzerland.[18] The Australian, British, Canadian, French, and Japanese markets have automated trading systems. Four of the major automated exchanges are relatively well developed.

The Toronto Stock Exchange uses the Computer Assisted Trading System (CATS), which functions as an electronic auction for less actively traded stocks and is being updated to handle more active stocks. Broker-dealers using the system can choose to have their trades executed by either a specialist or computer. CATS currently handles about 75 percent of trades on the exchange, a small volume compared with that of major American exchanges (Hansell 1989, 93; U.S. Congress 1990b, 63; Howard 1991, 15). CATS also displays the best five buy and sell limit orders along with the name of the broker making the order (Hansell 1989, 93; Howard 1991, 15).

The Paris Bourse (stock exchange) relies on a licensed version of CATS, which is also under consideration for use at exchanges in Madrid, Brussels, and Sao Paulo (Hansell 1989, 93, 98; Ian Domowitz 1990, 170). The system used by the French exchange is named CAC, for Cotation Assistée Continu. This exchange, overshadowed by the London market, is much less liquid. In fact, exchange member firms hold a single daily auction in stocks complemented by forward trading in listed stocks using both continuous trading and call auctions in forward contracts (Richard Roll 1988, 29).

The London International Stock Exchange is a dealer market very similar in operation to NASDAQ. The ISE is the most active world market in foreign (non-United Kingdom) stock trading, which makes up slightly more than half of the exchange's volume. The average daily foreign issue volume was 1.3 billion pounds sterling per day in 1990. ISE members have benefited from the migration of some U.S. program trading. The ISE's analog to the NASDAQ quote-display system is the Stock Exchange Automated Quotation System (SEAQ); small orders of fewer than 5,000 shares are automatically executed on the Stock Automated Exchange Facility (SAEF).

The Tokyo Stock Exchange (TSE) has a system similar to Toronto's CATS. Its Computer Assisted Order Routing and Execution System (CORES) now handles all but 150 of the exchange's most actively traded issues; however, the TSE is moving toward a fully automated system. Instead of specialists, the exchange has a group of overseers, called *saitori*, who use computer screens to monitor the trades arranged by the computer and by floor traders and to approve the prices. The saitori can also allow CORES to generate trades automatically within a specified price range. In addition, they act as human circuit breakers on the exchange floor when trading becomes too volatile; they have the authority to suspend trading briefly (Hansell 1989, 97).

Futures and Options Markets

Like prices of exchange-traded stocks, futures prices are established through an auction system, but one with no counterpart to the single individual, the specialist, making a market in a stock. Instead, futures prices are determined by an auction known as the open-outcry system. Exchange members—floor traders—congregate at designated trading pits and shout bids and offers at each other or use hand signals to indicate trading intentions. Exchange officials record the price and amount of each transaction. Effective in providing liquidity, this system is also subject to error and even abuse.[19]

As discussed above, international competition is forcing efficiency-enhancing automation. Many new overseas exchanges are fully or partially automated and trade many of the same contracts as American exchanges, although their volume levels are usually much lower. Systems emerging on futures and options markets harbinger the internationalization soon to come. In particular, the Chicago Mercantile Exchange's Globex (Global Exchange) system is being designed to handle volumes that exceed current open-outcry volume levels at peak trading times.

Globex. Globex, expected to be operable in early 1992, will automate *and link* participating exchanges. To date, the Chicago Board of Trade and Marché à Terme des Instruments Financiers (MATIF), the French financial futures market, are members of Globex. Other exchanges in the Far East are considering joining Globex, including Australia's Sydney Futures Exchange (SFE) and possibly Japan's Osaka Securities Exchange, or OSE (Ginger Szala and Amy Rosenbaum 1990, 44). Globex will operate after-hours, beginning at 6 P.M. Chicago time, when Japanese markets open.

The genesis of Globex lay in efforts to extend the futures trading day. In 1984 the CME established a relationship with the newly founded Singapore International Monetary Exchange (SIMEX), a relationship based mainly on mutual advantages gained from trading compatible Eurodollar and foreign currency futures contracts. The two exchanges set up a mutual offset permitting contracts opened on one exchange to be closed on the other and vice versa. This link effectively lengthened the trading day almost to twenty-four hours, helping the Chicago exchange to secure a foothold in booming East Asian financial markets. SIMEX enjoyed the benefits of the additional liquidity generated by the infusion of Chicago-based trades. Also catering to growing interest from abroad, the Merc's Chicago rival, the Chicago Board of Trade, instituted nighttime trading of its Treasury bond futures contracts in April 1987. However, this insomniac trading, as one observer termed it, and the CME's mutual offset arrangement were regarded as stopgap measures ("Futures Markets" 1988). More efficient and less error-prone electronic trading seems inevitable; the Chicago Board of Trade joined with the Chicago Mercantile Exchange as a Globex partner in 1990. Up to that point the CBOT had been developing its own after-hours system, called Aurora, that would electronically emulate open-outcry trading. (See the discussion below of LIFFE's Automated Pit Trading for a similar system).

The mechanical heart of Globex is a network of computer screens. The system is a joint venture of the "partner exchanges" (CME, CBOT, and MATIF) and Reuters Holdings PLC, which already has a large presence in over-the-counter spot foreign exchange markets. The Reuters network of computer terminals in banks and brokerage firms numbers about 180,000 worldwide. The CME emphasizes that trading via Globex is an alternate method of placing an order on its exchange or on partner exchanges (Brodsky 1990, 621). Because the exchanges do not view Globex as a new kind of futures exchange, they argue that regulatory approval of the system (particularly in Japan) should be straightforward.

Globex automatically matches and executes orders entered into the system. The system first checks the credit standing of the member firm initiating a transaction and then matches orders based on the time an order was submitted and its price. Unlike standard open-outcry trading, Globex does not allow for orders to be executed at the prevailing market price (that is, there can be no market orders); all orders must be good-until-canceled limit orders (the order stays on the book until it is executed or canceled).[20]

Trades are confirmed at participants' screens, prices and quantities are reported through the system, trades are cleared, and buyers' and sellers' accounts are adjusted. Traders on Globex deal anonymously with one another, an important consideration for most participants, as mentioned earlier. However, Globex, like other automated systems, does produce a so-called electronic audit trail, which is regarded as an improvement over the open-outcry system's less accurate recording procedures. Electronic monitoring is expected to give traders more confidence in the trading process and makes the regulator's job easier.

Although trading has not yet begun on Globex, its relative performance compared with the open-outcry auction has been assessed by Domowitz (1991). Using simulated trading experiments, he finds that Globex is the more efficient trading mechanism according to a number of measures. Globex tends to result in lower price volatility and greater market liquidity, and the differences become more pronounced as the size of the market increases.

In contrast, Merton H. Miller (1990) argues that screen trading systems, especially of the order-matching type like Globex, put traders (market makers) at a disadvantage because they cannot observe the order flow on a screen as they can from the trading pit. Traders with more current information can take advantage of previously posted traders' price quotes. For this reason Miller does not believe that electronic systems will ever attract sufficient competing market-maker participation to match the liquidity of the most active trading pits. To date, most screen trading systems have been used at low-volume exchanges or for low-volume contracts. Validation of Miller's or Domowitz's predictions will have to await actual trading through Globex as well as more extensive deployment of other screen trading systems.

Domestic Options Markets. A number of automated trading systems have been introduced to facilitate options trading. The most significant of these is the Chicago Board Options Exchange's Retail Automatic Execution System (RAES), which has been in operation since 1985. The system now handles both index options, including the heavily traded S&P 100 index option, and all CBOE equity options (on individual stocks). About 3.5 percent of contract volume is currently executed through RAES (U.S. Securities and Exchange Commission 1991, 19). The Amex uses a system called AUTO-EX for market and limit orders of as many as twenty equity contracts. The system is designed for use of Amex member firms and exchange specialists. In addition, the Amex has a mutual-offset link with the European Options Exchange in Amsterdam for the stock index options contract on the Amex's Major Market Index, or MMI (U.S. Congress 1990b, 96). The Pacific Stock Exchange has a similar system for equity options called POETS (Pacific Options Exchange Trading System). The Philadelphia Stock Exchange uses AUTOM (Automated Options Market System) for equity options. The NYSE's SuperDot also routes orders for trades on its equity and equity-index options.

Delta Government Securities, a screen-based system for trading options on U.S. Treasury bills, notes, and bonds, is operated jointly by RMJ Securities and RMJ Options, which are a registered clearing agency and registered broker-dealer, respectively. Delta always stands as the intermediary between buyer and seller using the system. It effectively operates like an electronic options exchange, issuing any options traded through the system (U.S. Securities and Exchange Commission 1991, 89).

Foreign Derivatives Markets. There is stiff competition among European futures exchanges. Marché à Terme des Instruments Financiers vies with the London International Financial Futures Exchange primarily over the three-month Euro-deutsche mark futures (a futures on the three-month rate on interbank deutsche mark-denominated deposits). MATIF, Europe's most active futures exchange, joined Globex in November 1989 and plans to list its government bond future (the Notionnel) and its short-term interest-rate future (on PIBOR—Paris Interbank Offered Rate) on the system. Part of the motivation behind MATIF's Globex membership was to boost foreign participation on the exchange and lessen London's advantage of having the offices of almost 600 international banks and brokerage firms (Janet Lewis 1990, 130).

The fact that LIFFE also offers a futures contract on the long-term German government bond, the Bund, in part spurred the creation of the first German futures market, the Deutsche Terminbörse (DTB) in 1990. A consortium of fifty-three institutions, mostly large banks, belong to the DTB. The exchange offers futures contracts to compete with LIFFE's as well as stock options on German firms (Lewis 1990, 130).

The Frankfurt-based exchange is organized as a computer network that matches and processes all trades electronically. The automated trading system employed is based on a similar system used by the Swiss Options and Financial Futures Exchange (SOFFEX), also an entirely automated order-matching system that allows member firms to be market makers, quoting bids and offers. Trades are entered anonymously, so large trades can be anonymously negotiated over the system (Hansell 1989, 93). Five fully automated futures and options exchanges now operate worldwide, as seen in Table 5.

LIFFE has a partially automated system, called Automated Pit Trading (APT), that mimics actual pit-trading (London International Financial Futures Exchange 1991). The after-hours system operates from 4:30 to 6:00 P.M. local time, with access restricted to LIFFE members. APT is not driven by quote-making dealers but by traders who post bids and offers for specified quantities. By the touch of a computer key, any trader can instantaneously accept bids and offers that appear on the screen. This system is the analog of the open-outcry method, in which bids and offers of floor traders are valid for "as long as the breath is warm." Because the futures exchanges deal in a limited set of futures contracts, liquidity is concentrated and rapid interactions between traders can be emulated on a screen. LIFFE expanded the system in 1990 to include a central limit-order book that enables purchases and sales of futures contracts if the market price reaches the posted limit price.

In Japan financial futures were banned until 1985. Regulators and legislators have gradually been deregulating and expanding their financial and derivative markets, and the Japanese have become very active in developing futures exchanges. Japanese firms are eager to use the new contracts. They may now deal directly in securities on foreign exchanges, and foreign brokerage firms may be members of Japanese futures exchanges (see Szala and Rosenbaum 1990, 42).

The first Japanese contracts were ten- and twenty-year yen bond futures, introduced on the Tokyo Stock Exchange in 1985. As of December 1989 the TSE offered U.S. Treasury bond futures equivalent to those of the CBOT. The Japanese Ministry of Finance, however, requires higher margins to be posted against Tokyo Stock Exchange futures contracts than does the Chicago Board of Trade for comparable positions. The higher margin levels apply even for Japanese firms taking positions in CBOT contracts, so these firms have little incentive to look abroad (Szala and Rosenbaum 1990, 42).

The TSE bond contracts, now the sixth most heavily traded future in the world (see Table 3), can all be traded through CORES. The TSE stock-index future on TOPIX (Tokyo Stock Price Index) is fully automated on CORES. Fully automated trading of a three-month Euroyen contract is conducted on the new Tokyo International Financial Futures Exchange (TIFFE), which competes against SIMEX in Singapore. SIMEX is still dominant in a number of contracts, including yen-U.S. dollar futures and Eurodollar futures, but it lags in Euroyen. Unlike TIFFE, SIMEX is a traditional open-outcry exchange.

The Nikkei 225 futures, the highest-volume Japanese index futures contract, trades at the Osaka Securities Exchange (OSE). The CME has acquired the rights to offer a Nikkei 225 contract on its exchange, though it would prefer to link up with the OSE through Globex (Szala and Rosenbaum 1990,

Table 5
Automated Trading Systems

System Operator	System
Equities	
American Stock Exchange	Post Execution Reporting
Amsterdam Stock Exchange	System based on MSE's MAX
Australian Association of Stock Exchanges	Stock Exchange Automated Trading (SEAT)
Boston Stock Exchange	BSE Automated Communication and Order Routing Network (BEACON)
Cincinnati Stock Exchange	National Securities Trading System (NSTS)
Instinet Corporation	Instinet The Crossing Network
Jefferies & Company, Inc.	Portfolio System for Institutional Trading (Posit)
London International Stock Exchange	Stock Automated Exchange Facility (SAEF)
Midwest Stock Exchange	Midwest Automated Execution (MAX)
National Association of Securities Dealers	Small Order Execution Service (SOES) SelectNet Private Offerings, Resales, and Trading through Automated Linkages (PORTAL)
New York Stock Exchange	Designated Order Turnaround system (SuperDot) Crossing Sessions I and II
Pacific Stock Exchange	Securities Communication Order Routing and Execution System (SCOREX)
Paris Bourse	Cotation Assistée en Continu (CAC)
Philadelphia Stock Exchange	Philadelphia Automated Communication and Execution System (PACE)
Tokyo Stock Exchange	Computer Assisted Order Routing and Execution System (CORES)
Toronto Stock Exchange	Computer Assisted Trading System (CATS)
Wunsch Auction Systems, Inc.	SPAworks
Futures and Options	
American Stock Exchange (equity options)	AUTO-EX
Chicago Board Options Exchange	Retail Automated Exchange System (RAES)
Chicago Board of Trade	Globex
Chicago Mercantile Exchange	Globex
Deutsche Terminbörse	Fully automated, integrated clearing
Irish Futures and Options Exchange	Fully automated, ATS-2
London International Financial Futures Exchange	Automated Pit Trading (APT)

(table continues)

Table 5 (continued)

System Operator	System
Futures and Options	
London Traded Options Market	Associated with LIFFE
Marché à Terme des Instruments Financiers	Globex
New York Stock Exchange	SuperDot
New Zealand Futures and Options Exchange	Fully automated ATS system
Pacific Stock Exchange	Pacific Options Exchange Trading System (POETS)
Philadelphia Stock Exchange	Automated Options Market System (AUTOM)
Stockholm Option Market	Integrated clearing facilities based on electronic trading and telephone brokering
Sydney Futures Exchange	Sydney Computerized Overnight Market (SYCOM)
Swiss Options and Financial Futures Exchange	Fully automated; integrated clearing
Tokyo Stock Exchange	Derivative markets fully automated CORES-F

Sources: U.S. Securities and Exchange Commission (1991); Angrist (1991); U.S. Congress (1990b); Kang and Lawton (1990); Rosenbaum (1990); Hansell (1989).

44). The CME's first overtures to the Ministry of Finance, one of the chief regulators of Japanese exchanges, were made in August 1988 and are still ongoing. The CBOT now lists a Japanese stock-index futures on the TOPIX and several Japanese government bond futures and options.

Market Performance and Regulatory Issues

Regulation of securities markets in the United States is generally intended to ensure that securities trading is conducted openly and based on publicly available information. The Securities Act of 1933 and Securities Exchange Act of 1934 mandated extensive registration and disclosure requirements for firms issuing securities to the public. However, recent policy discussions have shifted regulators' sights to safeguarding the performance and stability of financial markets.

The Brady Commission's recommendations in the wake of the 1987 crash stand out as the most sweeping proposals for changing the ways financial markets operate and for reorganizing their regulators' responsibilities.[21] To the Brady Commission and to a large number of market observers, the crash was prima facie evidence that private financial markets can fail—spectacularly. Concerns about the flow of information and the ability of participants to act on it superseded traditional questions about fairness and honesty in the marketplace.[22] The crash underscored the potential systemic risk of market failure as trading disruptions spread from one market to another. The problems can engulf the banking system as credit demands mount, for example, because of timing differences between the receipt and disbursement of funds by clearinghouses, straining liquidity and threatening widespread defaults.[23]

An important policy challenge is determining the appropriate mix of government and private-market actions to lessen the risk of securities market failure. It is feared that the electronic globalization of financial exchanges might contribute to systemic risks. The 1987 crash broadened the concerns, touching off a debate about whether a crash in one country's markets can trigger shocks beyond domestic boundaries to other countries' markets. The desirability and feasibility of international regulatory cooperation to contain such potential problems is an open question just beginning to be addressed (see Grundfest 1990; Paul Guy 1990; and U.S. Congress 1990a).

A survey of international regulatory issues is beyond the scope of this article. Rather, the following discussion focuses on the interconnections between markets and proposals to manage the international transmission of volatility. The basic issue to be considered has to do with the source of volatility and arguments for and against counteracting it. Since the stock market crash of October 1987, and even earlier in the decade, regulators and other market observers have become concerned about market volatility and cross-market spillovers.

The increasing prevalence of cross-border trading as well as the opening of new exchanges and deepening of existing ones would seem to imply that world financial markets are becoming unified. However, the evidence of such merging is not clear-cut. In fact, the Brady Commission concluded that through 1987 correlations of price movements from different world markets provide no evidence of closer links: "The correlations between the market in the U.S. and the markets in Germany and Japan appear to form totally random series.... [T]here is no evidence to suggest that the association is any closer today than it was a decade ago" (Nicolas F. Brady et al. 1988, II-6). Roll (1988) has observed that the only month in the 1980s in which all major world markets moved together was October 1987.

A number of recent academic papers address the question of world financial market integration. Using a sophisticated model of global equity market equilibrium (an international capital asset pricing model with time-varying moments), Campbell R. Harvey (1991) found evidence of a lack of integration, particularly for Japanese markets with the rest of the world. The basic object of study is the reward-to-risk ratio on equities required by investors. In a world of integrated markets, the reward-to-risk ratio would be the same in every equity market. In fact, this ratio turned out to be twice as large in Japanese markets as in U.S. markets.

In other words, Japanese investors require expected returns on stocks to be double the magnitude expected by U.S. investors. Complete integration across markets would equalize differences in the reward-to-risk ratio across countries because otherwise, for example, U.S. investors would skew their portfolios toward Japanese equities offering better trade-offs between return and risk than domestic equities. Increased U.S. purchases of Japanese stocks would bid up their prices and bid down U.S. stock prices, driving Japanese expected returns down and U.S. expected returns up. There are many subtleties and qualifications in this analysis, but the preponderance of evidence is against the simple hypothesis that world markets have become integrated.

The empirical work of David Neumark, P.A. Tinsley, and Suzanne Tosini reveals that price movements for U.S. stocks listed on New York, Tokyo, and London exchanges are more highly correlated during periods of high volatility than during times of low volatility because "only larger price changes pierce the transaction cost barriers between markets" (1991, 160). These authors noted that ordinarily the stock price volatility for this group of U.S. stocks (which are contained in the Dow Jones Industrial Average) is three times greater during New York trading hours than during London or Tokyo trading hours. In their view, this phenomenon occurs because the largest share of news relevant to the determination of the stock prices is disseminated during New York trading hours. This pattern was disrupted in the aftermath of the October 1987 crash when, in the authors' judgment, news was more globally dispersed and had mostly to do with "the volatile behavior of other investors" (176).

Yasushi Hamao, Ronald W. Masulis, and Victor Ng (1990) conducted another detailed study of intermarket linkages focusing on what they term price "volatility spillovers" among the New York, London, and Tokyo stock markets. For a subperiod that excludes the 1987 crash, they found that, while there was no significant transmission of volatility from Tokyo to either London or New York, the latter two cities' volatility did spill over to trading in Tokyo. When the post-1987 period is included, evidence indicates that all three markets were shocked by "volatility surprises," although Tokyo markets still did not affect New York's.

Mervyn A. King and Sushil Wadhwani (1990) have examined the market events surrounding October 1987 and offer a hypothesis about the worldwide scope of the market crash. To investigate the conundrum of what change in market fundamentals could explain a 23 percent drop in the Dow and similar gigantic declines in other markets around the globe, the authors developed a model in which rational traders in one market have less information about stocks than traders in the home market and must infer information partly from stock price movements abroad. This situation leads to the possibility of price movement "contagion" from one market to another, which will be particularly severe during periods of high market volatility. A sharp decline in a foreign price index is a (noisy) signal of bad news, some of which home market traders may not know from other sources. While the authors' hypothesis does not shed light on the "news" that triggered the October 1987 crash, it does explain why the crash was so uniform around the world despite important differences in markets and economic circumstances.

Gerard Gennotte and Hayne Leland (1990) have also developed a model in which rational traders' lack of information can precipitate a crash. Their concern is with informationless trading associated with hedging strategies like portfolio insurance. Formal portfolio insurance techniques systematically increase exposure to the market as stock prices rise and reduce it as stock prices fall (by shifting a portfolio's mix between index stocks and bonds or by adjusting the size of a short index futures hedge against a stock index portfolio). Although portfolio insurance-related selling is strictly passive, responding to declining stock prices, it could be mistaken for selling based on adverse information, and other traders look to prices and price changes as a way to glean information that they may lack. If nonpassive traders knew that they were taking the buy side of an informationless trade, they would more likely be willing to do so and would thereby supply liquidity to the market.

Gennotte and Leland's model shows how unobserved hedging programs, though only a small proportion of total trading, can destabilize a market. The disturbance may then propagate to other world markets. Their recommendation is that informationless trades should be preannounced and that "[e]lectronic 'open books' should be a seriously considered reform [to show the buy and sell order flow], and other forms of market organization (such as single-price auctions) should be examined" (1990, 1016). Some recent institutional developments are consistent with the authors' recommendations. Toronto's Computer Assisted Trading System displays limit orders to system users, and Wunsch's after-hours single-price auctions help concentrate market liquidity.

The King and Wadhwani and Gennotte and Leland models explain how trading itself can generate intermarket volatility. Joseph E. Stiglitz (1989) and Lawrence H. Summers and Victoria P. Summers (1989), go further by asserting that financial markets are excessively volatile because of irrational traders' speculative activity. Decreasing transactions costs owing to technological innovation and derivative markets promotes this speculation. These authors recommend a transactions tax to "throw sand into the gears" of financial markets (Tobin 1984, cited in Summers and Summers 1989, 263). Each securities purchase or sale would be subject to a "small" tax—for example, 0.5 percent of the stock price. In fact, many governments around the world impose stock transaction taxes, although the trend abroad is toward eliminating such taxes (see Roll 1989, table 4).

The gradual unification of world financial markets and continuing improvement in information flows will probably reduce the information asymmetry that produces contagion effects. However, in the view of those advocating transactions taxes these developments would just exacerbate irrational trading. At the core of their argument is the belief that financial markets are inefficient—that is, asset prices do not reflect "fundamentals." A growing list of so-called market anomalies seems to contradict efficient-markets theory. The apparent excess volatility analyzed by Robert J. Shiller (1989) stands as a challenge to efficient-markets proponents. Nevertheless, the theory is only being challenged, not overturned. Transactions taxes and other remedies for supposed excess trading and excess volatility have been proposed and sometimes implemented with little regard for their efficacy or possible adverse consequences.

Trading halts or circuit breakers, margin requirements, and price limits are also suggested as means of controlling trading. Of all these devices, margin requirements have been the most extensively studied and debated. In essence this work concludes that adjustments to margin requirements have no significant impact on stock market volatility (see David A. Hsieh and Miller 1990). Using data from twenty-three stock markets, Roll (1989) undertook a cross-market study of the effects of transactions taxes, margin requirements, and price limits on market volatility and found that none effectively reduce volatility.

Circuit breakers shut down an entire market temporarily to give participants a "time-out," mainly to avoid a panic selling spree. Both the New York Stock Exchange and Chicago Mercantile Exchange have instituted such circuit breakers (see Franklin R. Edwards 1988, 1989), although evidence is lacking concerning their usefulness. As Gennotte and Leland (1990) point out, the weekend of October 17-18, 1987, was an extended trading halt for the market declines of the previous week, but participants were not inclined to stage a market reversal the following Monday. It is not at all obvious that circuit breakers stabilize prices. To the contrary, they could induce traders to sell earlier and in larger quantities, fearing that a trading-halt price limit will soon be reached. This movement could destabilize prices. Sanford J. Grossman (1990) has argued persuasively that market equilibrium would be restored more quickly without halting trading. Rather than attempting to suppress mispricings, Grossman concludes that the market would be better served by being informed of them, whether they arise from panic or any other source, because better-informed traders would recognize such occurrences as profit opportunities and thus reverse the price movements.

Conclusion

The globalization of financial markets simultaneously fragments traditional financial transactions marketplaces and integrates them via electronic means. Physical marketplaces (the trading floors) are becoming obsolete, while "virtual" marketplaces—networks of computers and computer terminals—are emerging as the "site" for transactions. The new technology is diminishing the role for human participants in the market mechanism. Stock-exchange specialists are being displaced by the new systems, which by and large are designed to handle the demands of institutional investors, who increasingly dominate transactions. Futures and options floor traders also face having their jobs coded into computer algorithms, which automatically match orders and clear trades or emulate open-outcry trading itself.

International capital flows and the trading volume associated with them have been expanding over time. The internationalization of financial markets implies that investment portfolios are becoming more homogenized and creates a demand for worldwide twenty-four-hour trading. Derivative markets also benefit from this trend as multinational corporations need financial services around the clock for hedging and other reasons.

The competitive forces propelling changes in financial markets also compel changes in regulatory oversight of these markets.[24] Technology helps minimize some problems—for example, by making it possible to establish accurate audit trails of trades and thereby discouraging certain kinds of trading abuses—while it creates others, such as business being drawn to markets with the most lenient regulatory standards. Nevertheless, financial marketplaces are perhaps closest to the textbook paradigm of voluntary exchanges for mutual benefit of transacting parties. Competition among the world's financial exchanges as well as among their regulators is likely to be the most efficient way to elicit the best mechanisms for conducting and regulating transactions.

More problematic is the nature of trading and volatility associated with it. Does trading itself generate volatility that interferes with consumption, investment, and other economic decisions, in turn lowering social welfare? This article has given an overview of new automated trading systems and communications networks that are integrating markets. The technology discussed improves market mechanisms and information flows, but it may have the negative side effect of promoting "excess" trading. If markets are efficient, volatility per se is generally regarded as a neutral characteristic of markets. Derivative markets will continue developing to allow any desired degree of hedging against volatility. Only if markets are inefficient can a case can be made for curtailing volatility, but the evidence is ambiguous regarding market inefficiency. Even less clear is the efficacy of measures proposed to safeguard markets against volatility.

Notes

1. See Summers and Summers (1989) and the discussion of their proposal below.
2. Frequent trading will be necessary when the number of securities available to "complete markets" is smaller than the number of future "states." See Huang and Litzenberger (1988, chapter 7). This situation will be all the more likely if financial markets are incomplete. However, theory does not give an indication of how much trading is appropriate to allocate wealth over time efficiently.
3. The difference between purchases and sales represents the net capital flow, which is less relevant in considering the growth of securities trading and market liquidity.
4. $321\% = [(75.28/17.85) - 1] * 100$ and $43\% = [(361.37/253.38) - 1] * 100$.
5. See Smith (1991). Ginnie Mae stands for Government National Mortgage Association, a government-chartered agency that makes a secondary market in home mortgages and enhances the liquidity of that market by securitizing individual mortgages into "pass-through" certificates. The futures was on this underlying security.
6. The NYSE is in the process of instituting "A Look at the Book" program that permits public subscribers to the service to view the limit orders for 50 of the 2,370 NYSE-listed stocks. This service will be available through vendors and will show the limit-order book at three fixed times during the trading day. Currently, only the specialists and other NYSE members, such as floor brokers, on the exchange floor have access to the specialists' books.
7. Market orders specify quantity for trade at the current price. Limit orders specify price and quantity.
8. The meanings of the acronyms are given in Table 5.
9. The bid price is the price for which a dealer is willing to buy a stock, and the offer is the price for which he or she is willing to sell the stock.
10. See Bodie, Kane, and Marcus (1989) or Francis (1991) for further institutional details about organized exchanges and OTC markets and such details as listing requirements.
11. This account of SOES is based on Domowitz (1990).
12. See U.S. Securities and Exchange Commission (1991, 69); another NASDAQ system described in this source is PORTAL (Private Offerings, Resales, and Trading through Automated Linkages), which is used in the secondary market for privately placed equity and debt. See note 24 below for further description.
13. See NASDAQ (1991, 14-15). Because of differences in accounting conventions, the NASDAQ figures are inflated compared with the NYSE figures.
14. See Hansell (1989, 102). The amount of institutional participation in NASDAQ stocks as measured by the volume of block trading has been about 43 percent in recent years. See NASDAQ (1991).
15. Instinet-sponsored section in *Institutional Investor* (January 1991).
16. See Kolb (1991, 17-18) for a general discussion of EFP transactions and Miller (1990) for EFPs in connection with the CME's S&P 500 stock-index futures contract.
17. The futures exchange, however, would collect an additional fee for allowing the off-exchange or ex-pit EFP. The Commodity Exchange Act prohibits noncompetitive and prearranged transactions in futures, with the exception of EFPs. See Behof (1990, 2).
18. See Roll (1988, 29). Roll notes that the Spanish market trades groups of stocks continuously for ten minutes at a time. This article contains much interesting information about foreign stock markets.
19. See Kolb (1991, 59-61) for a succinct account of the FBI undercover sting operation at the CME and CBOT, which began in early 1987 and resulted in indictments against forty-seven traders in January 1989.
20. Information on Globex came from 1991 CME promotional literature. Domowitz (1990) provides a detailed description and analysis of the Globex trading algorithm as well as those for two other trading systems.
21. The Brady Commission's basic recommendations were: (1) to have one agency be the overarching regulator of U.S. financial markets; (2) to have a unification of clearing systems of financial exchanges and OTC markets; (3) to have "consistent" margin requirements across different exchanges; (4) to institute coordinated "circuit breakers" across exchanges; and (5) to improve information systems to monitor trading activity in related markets.
22. The Securities and Exchange Act of 1934 authorized the Federal Reserve Board to established initial and maintenance margins to prevent excessive leveraging of securities purchases on securities exchanges. (In practice, the Board has set only minimum initial margin levels.) Part of the rationale for control over margins was to limit massive selling off of leveraged positions during market downturns.
23. See Brady et al. (1988, especially 51-52). Despite the potential dangers, no defaults occurred in the clearinghouse system during October 1987.
24. The SEC's April 1990 approval of Rule 144A is an instance of a change in regulatory standards that reflect changes in the nature of financial transactions. This rule simplifies the SEC's disclosure requirements for private placement issuers (see Chu 1991). Foreign corporations are now able to raise capital in U.S. markets without having to meet the SEC's stringent financial disclosure requirements as long as transactions are limited to large institutional investors. British financial authorities have instituted a similar relaxation of regulations for institutional investors (see Grundfest 1990).

NASDAQ's new PORTAL system is used for communicating bids and offers on privately placed securities traded under the provisions of Rule 144A.

References

Angrist, Stanley W. "Futures Trade on Screens—Except in U.S." *Wall Street Journal*, May 21, 1991, C1, C14.

Behof, John P. "Globex: A Global Automated Transaction System for Futures and Options." Study by the Federal Reserve Bank of Chicago, June 1990.

Bodie, Zvi, Alex Kane, and Alan J. Marcus. *Investments*. Homewood, Ill.: Irwin, 1989.

Brady, Nicholas F., James C. Cotting, Robert G. Kirby, John R. Opel, and Howard M. Stein. *Report of the Presidential Task Force on Market Mechanisms*. Submitted to the President of the United States, the Secretary of the Treasury, and the Chairman of the Federal Reserve Board, January 1988.

Brodsky, William J. "Futures in the Nineties: Confronting Globalization." In *Proceedings from a Conference on Bank Structure and Competition*, 615-23. Federal Reserve Bank of Chicago, 1990.

———. "The Future Is Now." *Institutional Investor* 25 (January 1991): 7.

Chicago Board of Trade. *Commodity Trading Manual*. CBOT, 1985.

Chu, Franklin J. "The U.S. Private Market for Foreign Securities." *The Bankers Magazine* 174 (January/February 1991): 55-60.

Domowitz, Ian. "The Mechanics of Automated Trade Execution Systems." *Journal of Financial Intermediation* 1 (1990): 167-94.

———. "Equally Open and Competitive: Regulatory Approval of Automated Trade Execution in the Futures Markets." Center for the Study of Futures Markets Working Paper #214, forthcoming 1991.

Edwards, Franklin R. "Studies of the 1987 Stock Market Crash: Review and Appraisal." *Journal of Financial Services Research* 1 (1988): 231-51.

———. "Regulatory Reform of Securities and Futures Markets: Two Years after the Crash." Center for the Study of Futures Markets Working Paper #189, June 1989.

Francis, Jack Clark. *Investments: Analysis and Management*. 5th ed. New York: McGraw-Hill, Inc., 1991.

"Futures Markets Will Let Their Fingers Do the Dealing." *The Economist*, March 19, 1988, 77-78.

Gennotte, Gerard, and Hayne Leland. "Market Liquidity, Hedging, and Crashes." *American Economic Review* 80 (1990): 999-1021.

Grossman, Sanford J. "Institutional Investing and New Trading Technologies." In *Market Volatility and Investor Confidence: Report to the Board of Directors of the New York Stock Exchange, Inc.*, G2-1-17. June 7, 1990.

Grundfest, Joseph A. "Internationalization of the World's Securities Markets: Economic Causes and Regulatory Consequences." *Journal of Financial Services Research* 4 (1990): 349-78.

Guy, Paul. "IOSCO Moves Ahead." *FIA Review* (May/June 1990): 8-10.

Hamao, Yasushi, Ronald W. Masulis, and Victor Ng. "Correlations in Price Changes and Volatility across International Stock Markets." *Review of Financial Studies* 3 (1990): 281-307.

Hansell, Saul. "The Wild, Wired World of Electronic Exchanges." *Institutional Investor* (September 1989): 91ff.

Harvey, Campbell R. "The World Price of Covariance Risk." *Journal of Finance* 46 (1991): 111-57.

Heimann, John G. *Globalization of the Securities Markets*. Statement in hearings before the Senate Subcommittee on Securities of the Committee on Banking, Housing, and Urban Affairs. June 14, 1989, 76.

Howard, Barbara. "The Trade: Technology Aims to Take the Final Step." *Institutional Investor* 25 (January 1991): 15-16.

Hsieh, David A., and Merton H. Miller. "Margin Regulation and Stock Market Volatility." *Journal of Finance* 45 (1990): 3-29.

Huang, Chi-fu, and Robert H. Litzenberger. *Foundations for Financial Economics*. New York: North-Holland, 1988.

Kang, Jane C., and John C. Lawton. "Automated Futures Trading Systems." *FIA Review* (May/June 1990): 6-7.

King, Mervyn A., and Sushil Wadhwani. "Transmission of Volatility between Stock Markets." *Review of Financial Studies* 3 (1990): 5-33.

Kolb, Robert W. *Understanding Futures Markets*. 3d ed. Miami: Kolb Publishing Company, 1991.

Lewis, Janet. "The Euro-Futures War." *Institutional Investor* 24 (March 1990): 129ff.

London International Financial Futures Exchange. *APT Information Package*. 1991.

Miller, Merton H. "International Competitiveness of U.S. Futures Exchanges." *Journal of Financial Services Research* 4 (1990): 387-408.

NASDAQ. *Fact Book 1991*. 1991.

Neumark, David, P.A. Tinsley, and Suzanne Tosini. "After-Hours Stock Prices and Post-Crash Hangovers." *Journal of Finance* 46 (1991): 159-78.

New York Stock Exchange. *Fact Book 1991*. 1991a.

New York Stock Exchange. *Off-Hours Trading*. Brochure. 1991b.

Roll, Richard. "The International Crash of October 1987." *Financial Analysts Journal* 44 (September/October 1988): 19-35.

———. "Price Volatility, International Market Links, and Their Implications for Regulatory Policies." *Journal of Financial Services Research* 3 (1989): 211-46.

Rosenbaum, Amy. "Scouting Automation: What's the Competition Like?" *Futures* 19 (April 1990): 52-54.

Salwen, Kevin G., and Craig Torres. "Big Board After-Hours Trading May Lead to a Two-Tiered Market." *Wall Street Journal*, June 13, 1991, C1, C17.

Sheeline, William E. "Who Needs the Stock Exchange?" *Fortune*, November 19, 1990, 119ff.

Shiller, Robert J. *Market Volatility*. Cambridge, Mass.: MIT Press, 1989.

Smith, Stephen D. "Analyzing Risk and Return for Mortgage-Backed Securities." Federal Reserve Bank of Atlanta *Economic Review* 76 (January/February 1991): 2-11.

Stiglitz, Joseph E. "Using Tax Policy to Curb Speculative Short-Term Trading." *Journal of Financial Services Research* 3 (1989): 101-15.

Summers, Lawrence H., and Victoria P. Summers. "When Financial Markets Work Too Well: A Cautious Case for a Securities Transactions Tax." *Journal of Financial Services Research* 3 (1989): 261-86.

Szala, Ginger, and Amy Rosenbaum. "Deregulation in Japan May Have Different Meaning." *Futures* 19 (February 1990): 42-44.

Tobin, James. "On the Efficiency of the Financial System." *Lloyds Bank Review*, no. 153 (July 1984): 1-15.

U.S. Congress. Office of Technology Assessment. *Trading Around the Clock: Global Securities Markets and Information Technology—Background Paper*. OTA-BP-CIT-66. Washington, D.C.: U.S. Government Printing Office, July 1990a.

_____. *Electronic Bulls and Bears: U.S. Securities Markets and Information Technology*. OTA-CIT-469. Washington, D.C.: U.S. Government Printing Office, September 1990b.

U.S. Securities and Exchange Commission. *Questionnaire of the Working Party on Regulation of Secondary Markets*. May 29, 1991.

Wunsch, R. Steven. "Single-Price Auctions." *Institutional Investor* 25 (January 1991): 20.

Measuring the Gains from International Portfolio Diversification

A remarkable feature of the world economy during the past several years has been the explosive growth in international flows of equities and bonds. For example, during the period 1984 to 1990, gross cross-border equity flows increased from approximately $300 billion per year to about $1.7 trillion, an annual rate increase of over 30 percent. Moreover, currently one out of seven equity trades worldwide involves a foreign party, while one out of ten U.S. equity trades takes place outside the United States. The numbers associated with the growth of the emerging markets of Southeast Asia are even more dramatic. During the period 1988 to 1993, it is estimated that capitalization of the Malaysian stock market increased from $15 billion to $76 billion, Thailand's market grew from $6 billion to $27 billion, and capitalization of the Indonesian stock market soared from $100 million to $10 billion, with most of the money flowing into these markets coming from foreigners.

On the face of it, these trends suggest that there must be large gains from international diversification. Before jumping to conclusions, though, it is important to realize that despite the recent surge in international equity *flows*, when cross-border equity holdings are expressed as a share of total wealth or income they remain quite modest; in particular, they are much smaller than most theories of optimal asset allocation would predict. This observation has led to recent research cautioning that the gains from international diversification might be much smaller than is commonly believed. How do we know which is true? On what factors does the answer depend? This *Letter* will briefly discuss the methods economists use to quantify the benefits from international asset trade. We will do so by attempting to answer the following hypothetical question: How much additional income per year would an investor require to forgo the opportunity to invest abroad?

Using the CAPM to measure the gains

In the early 1960s, William Sharpe (1964) and John Lintner (1965) developed the first formal, quantitative model of capital market risk and equilibrium, the now famous Capital Asset Pricing Model (CAPM). The essential insight of this model is that the risk of a given security has more to do with the covariance of its return with that of other assets than with the variance of its own return. This is because the part of a security's return that is uncorrelated with the return on other assets can be diversified away by holding a portfolio of the assets. If diversifiable risk were rewarded in the form of a higher expected return, investors would in effect receive a "free lunch." Competitive equilibrium in the capital market eliminates free lunches.

While the distinction between diversifiable and nondiversifiable risk provides the foundation for pricing risk in the CAPM, what makes the model useful are the assumptions that Sharpe and Lintner make concerning investors' preferences and beliefs. Sharpe and Lintner show that if investors care only about the mean and variance of the return on their portfolios, and share common beliefs about the future, then in equilibrium they will all end up holding an identical portfolio of risky assets, namely the "market portfolio," which is simply a value-weighted share of all (traded) assets.

The CAPM delivers an elegant, theoretically coherent approach to measuring the gains from portfolio diversification. In the CAPM, the equilibrium trade-off between risk and return is measured by the "Sharpe ratio," which is defined as the ratio of the rate of return on the market portfolio (in excess of the risk-free rate) to the standard deviation of this return. In other words, the Sharpe ratio tells us how much extra return an investor requires in order to take on an additional unit of risk. Thus, to quantify the gains to international diversification, all we need to do is measure how the Sharpe ratio changes when we move from a market portfolio consisting of only domestic stocks to one consisting of both foreign and domestic stocks.

This calculation has been done by Tesar and Werner (1992). They consider stock market returns in the U.S., Japan, U.K., Germany, and Canada during the period 1980 to 1990. Their results imply that (assuming investors expect the future to be like the past) in order to persuade a U.S. investor to invest only in domestic assets, we would have to offer him a rate of return that is 3.2 percent higher than the U.S. market return. Alternatively, instead of offering the investor a higher return, we could simply supplement his income each year so that a "ban" on foreign investment doesn't make him any worse off. This provides a more direct measure of the gains from diversification. Of course, the required compensation will not be the same for everyone. Individuals who like to invest in the stock market will tend to demand a higher compensation than those who invest mainly in safe assets like T-bills. Still, we can get a rough picture of the gains by considering a "typical" investor who puts 25 percent of his wealth into safe assets and invests the remaining 75 percent in the stock market. Using results from Obstfeld (1992), it turns out that this investor would need a 7.3 percent increase in annual income as compensation for a ban on foreign investment. Although this might not seem like a large increase, remember the United States is currently a $6.5 trillion economy. Thus, a 7.3 percent increase in income translates into an annual benefit of $475 billion! The underlying source of this gain is the relatively weak correlation among national stock markets. For example, during this period correlations with the U.S. market ranged from a low of .29 in the case of Japan to a high of .75 in the case of Canada. To the extent that the correlation among stock markets has increased, the gains from diversification have decreased.

The conclusion that the gains from international diversification are large has been the conventional wisdom since the CAPM was first applied to international stock market data. This conclusion presents a puzzle, however. If the gains are so big, why aren't investors more internationally diversified? As noted earlier, despite the large recent flows into foreign equity markets, when expressed as a share of wealth or income, investor portfolios are still strongly biased toward domestic assets. In particular, they don't look anything like the value-weighted shares predicted by the CAPM. For example, the U.S. market constitutes roughly 40 percent of world stock market capitalization. The CAPM therefore predicts that U.S. residents should hold 60 percent of their (risky) portfolios in foreign equities. Instead, according to Tesar and Werner, U.S. residents only hold about 5 percent of their portfolios in foreign equities. Moreover, the discrepancy tends to be worse for other countries, whose stock markets are a much smaller share of the world market portfolio.

Why are investors' portfolios biased toward domestic assets? Unfortunately, quick fixes to the CAPM, like accounting for transactions costs and exchange rate risk, do not seem to work. If investors faced higher (variable) costs of transacting in foreign markets, we would expect them to trade foreign securities less. Instead, the opposite seems to be the case. Tesar and Werner found that turnover rates on the foreign-held component of national stock markets are much higher than on the domestically held component. This casts doubt on the role of transactions costs in producing home bias. Introducing exchange rate risk does not provide an explanation either, since investors can hedge most of this risk in the bond market. For example, consider a U.S. resident who owns Japanese stock. This investor faces the risk that the yen will depreciate, thus reducing the return when expressed in dollars. However, to hedge this risk the U.S. investor can borrow yen and lend dollars. Now if the yen depreciates, the loss on his holdings of Japanese stocks is offset by a gain from his yen loan (that is, he gets to pay back the loan with "cheaper" yen). Thus, exchange rate uncertainty should be reflected in a home bias in bond portfolios, not stock portfolios.

These considerations suggest that something fundamental is missing from the CAPM. Of the assumptions that Sharpe and Lintner make, one in particular is likely responsible for its inaccurate predictions; namely, the standard CAPM assumes that everyone produces and consumes the same goods. This is an especially dubious assumption in an international context because transportation costs and comparative advantage considerations tend to lead countries toward specialization. Interestingly, recent work has shown that relaxing this assumption can dramatically reduce the predicted gains from international diversification.

Specialization, the terms of trade, and the gains from diversification

Cole and Obstfeld (1991) relax the assumption that countries produce identical goods. Instead, they assume that countries are specialized in the production of their own unique good. To incorporate risk, Cole and Obstfeld assume output is random, and therefore individuals residing in different countries want to pool their risks by exchanging equity claims.

Using this model, Cole and Obstfeld make an intriguing discovery. Perhaps the reason why countries are not more diversified internationally is that the gains to such diversification are small. How can this be? The crucial added feature in a world in which countries produce different goods is the possibility of changes in the "terms of trade" (that is, the relative price of foreign goods in terms of domestic goods). Cole and Obstfeld show that market-clearing movements in the terms of trade tend to provide "natural insurance" against domestic output fluctuations: When a nation's output declines unexpectedly, the shortfall in supply tends to raise its price, that is, the nation enjoys an offsetting improvement in its terms of trade. For example, even without equity trade, Brazil is partially insured against a bad coffee harvest, since a bad harvest will lead to higher coffee prices in the world market.

Naturally, the importance of this effect depends on how much the terms of trade adjust in response to relative output fluctuations. To quantify this effect Cole and Obstfeld simulate their model and find that offsetting movements in the terms of trade significantly reduce the gains from diversification. For example, when the terms of trade offset half the reduction in output, so that a 10 percent decline in relative output results in a 5 percent improvement in the terms of trade, Cole and Obstfeld's results imply that the gains from diversification decline by about 75 percent. Compared to the earlier results, this would imply an annual benefit of "only" $119 billion.

Conclusion

What have we learned? First, by the usual standards of cost-benefit analysis, the gains from international diversification are quite large. Second, the work of Cole and Obstfeld suggests that a nation's benefit from diversification likely depends on its economic size. Small countries, whose terms of trade are dictated by the world market, are likely to benefit relatively more than large countries. This is because large countries like the U.S. and Japan tend to receive natural insurance against output fluctuations via offsetting terms of trade changes. Thus, an important topic for future research is to estimate econometrically the actual magnitude of the terms of trade effect in order to obtain a more precise measure of the gains from diversification for large countries like the United States.

Kenneth Kasa
Economist

References

Cole, Harold L., and Maurice Obstfeld. 1991. "Commodity Trade and International Risk Sharing: How Much do Financial Markets Matter?" *Journal of Monetary Economics* 28, pp. 3–24.

Lintner, John. 1965. "The Valuation of Risk Assets and the Selection of Risky Investments in Stock Portfolios and Capital Budgets." *Review of Economics and Statistics* 47, pp. 13–37.

Obstfeld, Maurice. 1992. "Risk-Taking, Global Diversification, and Growth." Working Paper No. 688, Centre for Economic Policy Research.

Sharpe, William F. 1964. "Capital Asset Prices: A Theory of Market Equilibrium under Conditions of Risk." *Journal of Finance* 19, pp. 425–442.

Tesar, Linda L., and Ingrid M. Werner. 1992. "Home Bias and the Globalization of Securities Markets." NBER Working Paper No. 4218.

Interdependence: U.S. and Japanese Real Interest Rates

Over the last decade, Japan's integration into the world economy has increased substantially. Japan became the world's largest capital exporter in the 1980s with net foreign assets rising from $11.5 billion at the end of 1980 to more than $380 billion at the end of 1991. This period was also marked by far-reaching financial liberalization in Japan, the rapid expansion of Japanese financial institutions abroad, and the growing importance of Tokyo as a world financial center. In international trade, Japan is among the world's largest exporters and importers, topping the list in exports of many sophisticated industrial products and several categories of imported raw materials. Japan's growing economic size, importance in international trade, and the magnitude of its capital outflows also suggest that it may be having an important influence over *world* economic developments.

This *Weekly Letter* reports on research (Hutchison and Singh 1993) investigating the extent to which Japan's integration with the world economy has led to greater real interest rate interdependence. It presents evidence that U.S. and Japanese real interest rates are closely linked. It also shows that causal influence runs both ways. Not only does the U.S. have a significant impact on real interest rates in Japan, but real interest rates in the U.S. are greatly influenced by economic developments in Japan.

The real interest rate gap
Highly integrated markets permit more efficient allocation of capital across national boundaries. But these international capital flows also link real interest rates in different countries. Since real interest rates (that is, nominal rates adjusted for expected inflation) are important determinants of national saving and investment patterns, these links make national economies more vulnerable to foreign economic developments and limit their ability to pursue independent macroeconomic policies. With highly integrated markets, for example, a rise in real interest rates in Japan would be transmitted to the U.S. via higher domestic real interest rates, in turn dampening U.S. economic activity.

Given the large gross and net capital flows between the U.S. and Japan in recent years, one might expect little differential between each country's real interest rates. But a number of studies have found large, albeit decreasing, short-term real rate differentials between the U.S. and Japan, for both debt and equity instruments.

To understand why rates would differ between the two countries, consider that the real interest rate differential is the sum of (1) the nominal interest rate differential and (2) the price inflation differential (both adjusted for expected exchange rate change). The nominal interest rate differential reflects the degree of integration of financial markets: Perfectly integrated markets with unlimited arbitrage possibilities lead to a small or zero exchange-rate-adjusted interest differential, controlling for political and default risks. A zero differential is called uncovered interest rate parity (UIP). Increasing liberalization of financial markets in Japan has meant fewer impediments to arbitrage and consequently smaller deviations in UIP. Specific liberalization measures included lifting restrictions on nonresidents' investments in Japanese securities in February 1979 and Gensaki transactions (bond trading with repurchase agreements) in May 1979. Another important step was the enactment of the new Japanese Foreign Exchange and Foreign Trade Control Law (December 1980), which for the first time lifted all restrictions on capital flows unless explicitly prohibited. These measures allowed greater arbitrage opportunities between the domestic and foreign financial markets.

Therefore, it is more likely that the source of the real interest rate differential is in the price inflation differential, which reflects the degree of integration of goods markets. If goods markets in two countries are completely integrated, price levels and price inflation of internationally traded products measured in a common currency should be roughly comparable (after taking into account transactions costs, tax differences, and so on). This is called purchasing power parity (PPP). Big differences in inflation rates that are not offset by corresponding exchange rate changes (so that inflation rates expressed in a common currency also differ) generally mean big impediments to goods arbitrage, which effectively separates national product markets. Clearly, goods markets in the U.S. and Japan are not fully integrated, particularly in the short term when institutional, legal, technical, and informational barriers limit arbitrage possibilities. These impediments include import tariffs, voluntary export restraints (VER or informal quotas), transport costs, restrictive distribution systems, and so on. Thus swings in purchasing power between the U.S. and Japan in the 1980s may be responsible for the short-term real interest rate differentials despite highly integrated financial markets.

A deviation from PPP means that international goods prices are not equal across countries, which in turn may create profitable arbitrage opportunities. Taking advantage of these opportunities in goods markets takes time, but the larger the price differences, the greater is the incentive to find ways around the obstacles limiting international market integration. This is why many studies find evidence that arbitrage works to reduce PPP deviations over longer periods as the economy settles down to "equilibrium." Hence, investigating "equilibrium" real interest rate relationships between countries, where the wedge between rates associated with PPP deviations is less due to arbitrage, should lead to a better measure of the true degree of linkage between Japan and the U.S.

Measuring real interest rate linkages

Prima facie evidence provides some support for the argument that real interest rate deviations tend to disappear over longer periods of time. Figure 1 shows the ex post real interest rate differential (four-quarter moving average) between the U.S. and Japan for the 1981.Q1–1991.Q3 period when international financial transactions were substantially liberalized. The data are quarterly and constructed from short-term (3-month) market determined interest rates (Gensaki rate in Japan; Treasury Bill rate in the U.S.) less realized inflation.

The figure suggests that the real interest rate differential between the two countries varies widely

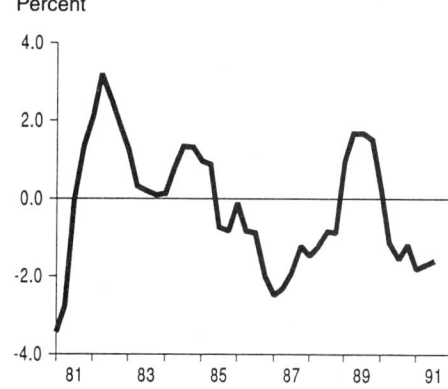

Figure 1
U.S.-Japan Real Interest Rate Differential

over time, but there may be arbitrage pressures bringing it back to zero. Formal statistical tests also suggest that the real interest rate differential is transitory. This means that over longer periods of time there is a tendency for real interest rates in Japan and the U.S. to move closely together. Marston (1992) also finds that real interest rate differentials in the Eurodollar and Euroyen markets (using WPI deflators) vary widely over short sample periods, but that average differentials are close to zero over long sample periods.

How long does it take for real interest rates to reach their equilibrium values? And to what extent do rates in Japan adjust compared to rates in the U.S. following an initial disturbance? To address these issues we estimate a simple dynamic model (an "error correction model") of U.S. and Japanese real interest rates which takes into account short-run adjustment dynamics as well as the tendency for real interest rate parity to hold in equilibrium over the long run. The model is estimated over 1981.Q1–1991.Q3. Simulations of the model allow us to trace out the path of the real interest real differential response to unexpected jumps in the U.S. or Japanese rates. Figure 2 illustrates the behavior of the interest rate differential when U.S. real rates rise 100 basis points (solid line) and when Japanese real rates rise 100 basis points (dashed line). These estimates show that the real interest rate differential adjusts to the long-run equilibrium in about four to eight quarters, regardless of the source of the shock.

Since the U.S. economy is much larger than the Japanese economy, one might expect that Japan

Figure 2
Real Interest Differential Response to Rise in U.S. Rates (solid) and Japanese Rates (dashed)

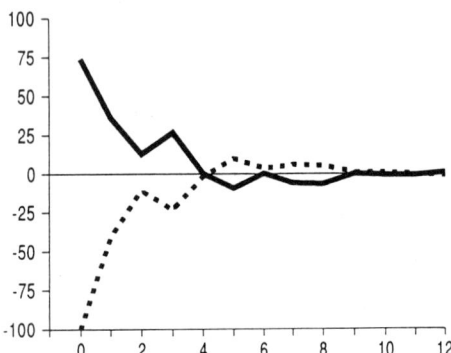

Figure 3
Response of U.S. Real Interest Rates to 100 Basis Point Rise in Japanese Rates

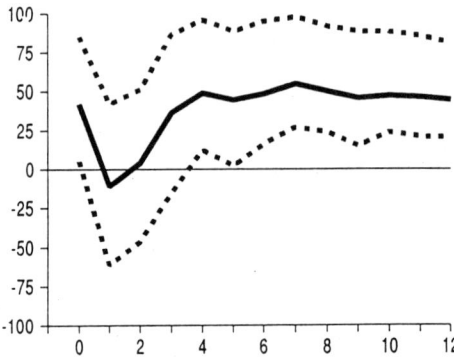

would bear the lion's share of the adjustment when a temporary gap in the interest rate differential opens up. However, additional simulations suggest that the adjustments are more symmetrical. Figure 3 shows the response of U.S. real interest rates given an unexpected 100-basis point jump in Japanese rates. The dashed lines show 90 percent statistical confidence bounds around the simulated path. The simulation indicates that U.S. real interest rates settle down after about five quarters and rise about 40 basis points following a 100-basis point shock emanating from Japan. This is about the same response of Japanese rates to shocks emanating from the U.S. (see Hutchison and Singh 1993).

Conclusion
Our results indicate a very high degree of real interest rate linkage between the U.S. and Japan since the early 1980s, perhaps in response to the financial liberalization measures taken in Japan. Gaps in real interest rates between the two countries also appear to close quickly, and Japan seems to play an important role in the determination of rates in the U.S.

These results are surprising in that they indicate a higher degree of linkage and attribute greater economic importance to Japan than do other studies. Could they be overstated? Perhaps. The period over which markets have been liberalized in Japan is fairly short, which limits the power of statistical tests attempting to measure equilibrium real interest rate differentials. It is also difficult to separate "causal" relationships in real rate movements, which are related to economic importance and interdependence, from simply "linkage" relationships, which are related to arbitrage and economic integration.

In most respects, however, it is not surprising that economic developments in Japan play an important role in the determination of U.S. and world real interest rates. Japan's importance in other areas, such as international business practices, technology development, and international trade, is beyond dispute. The findings here are fully consistent with these other signs of Japan's growing economic importance, as well as interdependence, in the world economy.

Michael M. Hutchison
Associate Professor
University of California, Santa Cruz
and Visiting Scholar, FRBSF

References

Hutchison, Michael, and Nirvikar Singh. 1993. "Long-Term International Capital Mobility: New Evidence from Equilibrium Real Interest Rate Linkages." Working Paper No. 93-06 (April). Federal Reserve Bank of San Francisco, Center for Pacific Basin Monetary and Economic Studies.

Marston, Richard. 1992. "Determinants of Short-term Real Interest Rate Differentials between Japan and the United States." NBER Working Paper No. 4167 (September).

Article 37

The Path to European Monetary Union

By Paula Hildebrandt

In a period of unprecedented change in Europe, European monetary union has emerged as one of the most important new developments. Europe 1992 is already creating a market with more than 320 million consumers and a productive capacity rivaling that of both the United States and Japan. European monetary union would go even further, implementing a unified European monetary policy.

The 12 member-countries of the European Community are currently debating the Delors Report, which outlines a three-step approach to economic and monetary union (EMU) in Europe. The first stage includes the Europe 1992 initiative and has already been accepted. Stages two and three are still being negotiated. They would form a single European central bank and currency.

This article discusses the movement toward monetary union in Europe. The first two sections

---

Paula Hildebrandt is a research associate at the Federal Reserve Bank of Kansas City. George Kahn, a senior economist at the bank, supervised preparation of the article.

lay the historical background for EMU and describe the proposed stages of the Delors Report. The next section provides a detailed description of the European System of Central Banks envisioned in the Delors Report. The article then discusses some of the important issues being debated. A glossary of frequently used terms is included at the end of the article.

Historical Developments Leading to EMU

EMU is not the first attempt to unite Europe. For nearly 40 years, Europeans have sought greater economic and monetary cooperation. From the first "common market" in 1952 to current plans for Europe 1992 and EMU, the Europeans have strived to create a "Europe without barriers."

Foundations of economic union

Economic cooperation in Europe dates back to 1952. France, Italy, West Germany, Belgium, the Netherlands, and Luxembourg banded together to form the European Coal and Steel Community. This "common market" for coal, steel, and iron ore made trade between members easier by eliminating costly tariffs normally placed on these imported goods.

The success of the European Coal and Steel Community prompted members to create the European Economic Community (EEC), formalized by the Treaty of Rome in 1957. The EEC extended the common market to include all goods. By eliminating tariffs, the EEC moved a step closer to economic union.

The European Community (EC), as the EEC was later called, decided in 1969 to pursue complete monetary union.[1] Plans to achieve union were drawn up in the Werner Plan, commissioned by the EC Council of Ministers and adopted in 1971. The Werner Plan established that within ten years exchange rates between EC countries would become fixed and the members would follow a common monetary policy. As an initial step, members were required to keep exchange rate fluctuations limited to designated ranges, called margins. The plan was discarded, however, when the 1973-74 oil price shocks caused many members to abandon the exchange rate margins. The oil price shocks had led to higher and more divergent inflation rates, making the exchange rate margins difficult to maintain (International Monetary Fund).

Momentum for monetary coordination returned in 1978 with the development of the European Monetary System (EMS). The EMS established the Exchange Rate Mechanism (ERM), which bound members to maintain exchange rates within narrow margins. The EMS remains in place today. EMS members include the 12 current EC members: Belgium, Denmark, France, Germany, Greece, Ireland, Italy, Luxembourg, the Netherlands, Portugal, Spain, and the United Kingdom. Currencies for most members currently fluctuate within a $2\frac{1}{4}$ percent band. Two members of the EMS—Portugal and Greece—still do not participate in the ERM. Two other members—the United Kingdom and Spain—only recently joined the ERM and allow their currencies to fluctuate in 6 percent margins. Although realignments occurred often in the early days of the ERM, exchange rates within the ERM have become increasingly stable (Ungerer).

Europe 1992

Trade barriers still existed in the 1980s, although tariffs were gone and exchange rates had become increasingly stable in the EC. Safety and environmental standards in many EC countries, for example, continued to restrict foreign competition. Similarly, subsidies to inefficient industries combined with capital and border controls to impede cross-country trade. These barriers reduced the efficiency of European markets, lowering the potential for economic growth.

Slower economic growth in the Community and strong international competition from the United States and Japan renewed interest in further integration. This renewed interest led to the Single European Act in 1985. Commonly known as Europe 1992, this act was designed to eliminate all barriers to the movement of persons, goods, services, and capital between member-countries by the end of 1992.

Once Europe 1992 is fully implemented, Europeans will enjoy a variety of economic benefits. Both people and firms will benefit from lower costs in transactions. For example, people will be able to travel throughout the EC without being detained at borders. Firms will be allowed to ship goods anywhere in the EC without facing a myriad of safety and environmental standards. Laws will be standardized in many industries, including the telecommunications and automobile industries. Such laws will make it possible for firms to expand and be more efficient in the larger, single market. And Europe 1992 will create a single financial area. A single financial area will allow money to flow freely throughout the Community and allow banks to locate branches anywhere they choose. In short, Europe 1992 will substantially increase economic integration, while providing EC countries with a greater potential for economic growth and a higher standard of living (Bennett and Hakkio).

Economic and monetary union

Europe 1992 and the success of the EMS have renewed interest in greater monetary integration. EC members believe a unified monetary policy will enhance the benefits of Europe 1992 by forcing member-countries to adopt a common anti-inflationary stance and by reducing the costs of exchange rate fluctuations and uncertainty. Hence, members believe monetary union will further increase efficiency and economic growth (Directorate-General).

With momentum building toward economic and monetary union, the European Council formed a committee to develop concrete stages for complete monetary union. In April 1989, the committee presented to the Council the "Report on Economic and Monetary Union in the European Community," commonly referred to as the Delors Report. In June of the same year, the member-states approved both stage one of the Delors Report and the goal of economic and monetary union. Stages two and three have not yet been approved by EC members and are currently being discussed at the intergovernmental conferences on EMU.[2]

The Delors Report on Economic and Monetary Union

The Delors Report offers a concrete, step-by-step approach to economic and monetary union in Europe. According to the Delors Report, *economic union* will occur with the completion of Europe 1992 and the coordination of macroeconomic policies, including policies concerning the size and financing of government budget deficits. *Monetary union* will occur when EC members come to share a common European monetary policy set by a unified central banking system called the European System of Central Banks (ESCB), and when a single currency replaces the 12 member-nation currencies.

The Delors Report outlines three stages to reach unification. Stage one promotes greater economic convergence. Stage two will serve as a transition period by setting up a single European central bank. Stage three will introduce a common monetary policy and a single currency.

Stage one

Stage one, launched officially on July 1, 1990, promotes greater economic convergence by increasing economic and monetary cooperation. A recurring theme throughout the Delors Report is that large differences in economic growth, inflation rates, or budget deficits among the member-states would make integration difficult. For example, the currency of a country suffering rising inflation would be under pressure to depreciate, making the move to fixed exchange rates difficult. Consequently, the EC wants member economies to "converge," or become more similar, before moving to a single currency and central bank. To foster economic convergence, stage one sets goals to encourage economic and monetary cooperation. Stage one will also revise the EC's founding treaty to accommodate new Community institutions.

Four goals of stage one are designed to

promote economic convergence. The first of these is to complete Europe 1992. By eliminating barriers to trade and finance, Europe 1992 will effectively create a single internal market in Europe.

A second goal is for EC members to trim government budget deficits. The EC believes large budget deficits hinder stable exchange rates, making the move to irreversibly fixed exchange rates difficult. To discourage continued deficit spending, the EC's Council of Finance Ministers will assess national economic conditions and policies. During stage one, the Council may only recommend policy corrections; however, national governments are supposed to consult with the Council before making any major policy changes.

A third goal is to provide additional resources for regional and structural development. Stage one allows for financing economic development in the least developed countries, such as Greece and Portugal. For example, if funds are needed to improve roads and railways or to meet new environmental and safety standards to successfully compete in a European market, the EC will offer assistance.

A fourth goal is to promote economic convergence by increasing monetary cooperation. The Delors Report plans to achieve this goal by strengthening the Exchange Rate Mechanism. One way to strengthen the ERM is to have all member-countries participate (currently Portugal and Greece do not). Another way is to create subcommittees within the Committee of Central Bank Governors to monitor foreign exchange, monetary, and bank supervision policies. During stage one the subcommittees will only offer guidelines to national governments, rather than play an active role in policy.

In addition to fostering economic convergence, stage one has another important goal: to revise the Treaty of Rome, which established the European Community in 1957. Because stages two and three require new Communitywide institutions, the Treaty of Rome must be revised to accommodate them. Otherwise, the last two stages of the Delors Report cannot begin. Revisions to the Treaty of Rome and negotiations on stages two and three of the Delors Report are underway at intergovernmental conferences on European Economic and Monetary Union. These meetings, which began last December, are expected to continue through most of this year.

Stage two

The Delors Report identifies stage two as a brief, transitional phase to prepare the Community for collective decision making in stage three. Tentatively scheduled to begin January 1, 1994, stage two would reform existing institutions and create new Communitywide institutions, such as a central banking system. In addition, the Community would continue to promote economic integration by removing any remaining barriers to trade not already eliminated in stage one. Although Europe 1992 is scheduled for completion in stage one, the Delors Report noted that some revisions or improvements in the Europe 1992 program may be necessary in stage two. As the EC continues to integrate, economic convergence will increase, easing the move to a single monetary policy.

The details of stage two are currently being debated at the intergovernmental conferences on EMU. According to the Delors Report, a major goal of stage two would be to establish the European System of Central Banks (ESCB). The ESCB will include the European Central Bank and the 12 national central banks and will be an important step toward a common European monetary policy. With price stability as its main objective, the ESCB will be independent from both the national governments and organizations at the Community level.

During stage two, the ESCB will assume responsibility for the ERM. The exchange rate margins within the ERM will narrow from the current $2\frac{1}{4}$ percent. Exchange rate realignments will be allowed only in emergency circumstances. The 12 national central banks will still be responsible, however, for their individual monetary policies during stage two.

Stage three

Like stage two, stage three of the Delors Report is currently being debated at the intergovernmental conferences. If approved, stage three of the Delors Report would complete economic and monetary union, transferring important powers from national governments to the Community.

Economic union will give the Community three new powers. First, the Community will assume a larger role in allocating funds for economic development. For instance, if a particular country has trouble adjusting to economic union, the EC will offer financial assistance to make the country more competitive. However, the EC may require policy changes before providing funds if it suspects a country's difficulties stem from misguided policies.

The second new power relates to international affairs. New Communitywide institutions will determine international policy decisions for the entire EC, representing a shift in power from national governments to the Community. On international issues, a single Community view will be expressed, instead of separate views for Germany, France, and so on. The Commission believes Europe will have more influence internationally if it speaks with a single voice.

The third new power that economic union will give the Community is the right to monitor national budget policies. While the Community will not set binding rules about budget deficits, the Delors Report proposes that "excessive" budget deficits will have to be avoided.[3] In addition, national governments will not be permitted to finance budget deficits by printing money.[4] Finally, if a country defies the budget recommendations of the Council of Finance Ministers, the country could face sanctions or have Community financial assistance made conditional on economic policy changes.

Monetary union will give the Community two additional powers. First, the ESCB will assume sole authority for monetary policy. National central banks will no longer be able to pursue individual policies; instead, each central bank will operate under a common monetary policy set by the ESCB's governing council. Annual money supply targets, for example, will be set for each EC country by the European Central Bank.

Second, the Community will assume sole authority for exchange rate policy. In the initial phase of stage three, exchange rates of member currencies in the ERM will be irreversibly locked. This system of fixed exchange rates will continue until it is administratively feasible to introduce a single European currency, tentatively called the ECU.

This "new" ECU would be fundamentally different from the current ECU. The current ECU (pronounced ek' coo) is a basket currency used in accounting transactions. Its value reflects a weighted average of the Deutschemark, the French franc, and the rest of the EC currencies. The ECU is at present strictly a unit of account—there is no physical ECU currency.[5] The new ECU will be a physical currency that replaces the existing individual currencies of the 12 EC members as a medium of exchange.[6] The ESCB will issue these new ECUs in accordance with its monetary policy objectives. In addition, the ESCB will handle all foreign exchange interventions against non-EC currencies, according to policies set within the Community.

Organization and Function of the ESCB After EMU

While the Delors Report outlines the basic features and functions of the ESCB, the Committee of Central Bank Governors has worked out the details. The Committee drafted a statute outlining the specific features, objectives, and functions of the system. Presented at the intergovernmental conference on EMU in December 1990, the draft statute is currently being discussed by conference participants. Like the Delors Report, the statute is only tentative. It too must be approved by the member-states before being added to the revised Treaty of Rome.

Organization and principles of the ESCB

The statute outlines a federal system of central banking modeled after the German Bundesbank and the U.S. Federal Reserve System. The ESCB will consist of the European Central Bank and the 12 national central banks. Important in the organization of the ESCB are three principles—independence, accountability, and subsidiarity.

Independence. Independence is a basic element in the plans for the ESCB. The statute states that the ESCB should be independent of both national and Communitywide politics and have "unequivocal commitment to maintain price stability as the primary objective of the System." Such features have been underscored by Bundesbank President Poehl, for example, who has repeatedly stated that his approval of the European Central Bank depends on its being independent and as firmly committed to fighting inflation as is the Bundesbank (Marsh 1990b).[7]

Accountability. While independence of the ESCB is desirable, the Committee recognizes the need for democratic checks and balances. Therefore, the European Central Bank will be required to submit an annual report to the European Council summarizing the monetary policy actions and other activities of the ESCB during the previous year. The European Central Bank will also have to distribute financial statements and other activity reports on a regular basis to interested parties. Finally, independent auditors, approved by the EC, will examine the European Central Bank and the national central banks.

Subsidiarity. Under the principle of subsidiarity, "functions that can be effectively carried out at a subordinate level should be performed by the subordinate rather than by a dominant central organization." In the context of the Community, subsidiarity means that the European Central Bank should only assume powers that require collective decision making. All other powers or responsibilities should remain with the national central banks.

When assigning tasks in the ESCB, the draft statute adheres to the principle of subsidiarity. For example, a single monetary policy and currency could not be maintained if all central banks acted independently—a central decision-making body is essential. Consequently, the European Central Bank will formulate monetary policy for the Community. However, other responsibilities, like supervising banks, could be executed at the national level, provided that Community guidelines are followed.

Functions of the ESCB

The ESCB's functions will include formulating monetary policy, managing reserves, supervising banks, maintaining the payments system, and implementing the Community's foreign exchange rate policy. Three ESCB groups will perform these functions: the Executive Board, the 12 national central banks, and the Council.[8] The Executive Board will consist of six members selected for their expertise in banking or monetary matters. One member will be designated the president and another the vice president of the system. Together, the six members of the Executive Board and the 12 governors of the national central banks will form the Council.

The Council. Formulating monetary policy for the EC will be the main duty of the Council. This duty will include determining monetary targets for each member-country. The Council will also establish guidelines for implementing its policy decisions.[9]

The Executive Board. The Executive Board will be responsible for day-to-day implementation of monetary policy. The Executive Board will monitor economic developments by tracking money supplies, interest rates, and exchange rates. Additionally, by buying and selling securities in the open market, the Executive Board will be able to influence the money supplies to meet monetary objectives set by the Council.

The Executive Board will also perform other duties. For example, the Executive Board will issue the ECU, the new European currency. To obtain ECUs, all member banks will have to deposit a portion of their reserves with the ESCB. The Executive Board will implement the exchange rate policy set by the European Council of Finance Ministers. The Executive Board will also provide regulations on bank supervision and the payments mechanism and will coordinate statistical research in the ESCB. Finally, the Executive Board will delegate responsibilities to the member central banks. For example, the Executive Board may ask the 12 central banks to issue notes or help gather statistical information.

The national central banks. The 12 national central banks will assist the Executive Board in carrying out the operations of the System. The draft states that the national banks should, as much as possible, be the "operational arms of the System." Under the Executive Board's instructions, national banks may participate in activities that include issuing ECUs, managing reserves, supervising banks, facilitating the payments mechanism, and lending to credit institutions. National central banks may even be asked to buy and sell securities in the open market or to intervene in the foreign exchange markets.

The national central banks will have additional responsibilities. For example, as members of the Council, central bank governors will help formulate monetary policy for the Community. Each central bank will conduct research and statistical analysis. And, the draft statute states that national central banks may perform other functions outside those of the System, so long as the activities do not interfere with the goals of the System.

The Delors Report: Issues Under Debate

Not all EC members believe the Delors Report represents the best approach to EMU. In the debate over the details of stages two and three at the intergovernmental conferences on EMU, three primary questions have emerged: What is the best way to implement a unified monetary policy in the EC? How quickly should EC countries proceed with EMU? And, how should national budget policies be coordinated and foreign exchange rate policies be executed?

Implementing a unified monetary policy

Since EMU discussions first began in 1989, the United Kingdom has expressed concern about moving to a single currency and central bank. The United Kingdom opposes the loss of national sovereignty involved in the Delors Report's approach to a single monetary policy, fearing it would lead to a loss of control over

U.K. economic policy. For example, after monetary union occurs, national central banks would be unable to set national goals for monetary policy, thus denying national governments a policy tool for stabilizing the economy.[10]

U.K. prime minister John Major has presented an alternative to stage two of the Delors Report. Commonly known as the "hard ECU" plan, Major's alternative would introduce a thirteenth currency, the hard ECU, to compete in the market with the existing 12 national currencies. The hard ECU's value would be linked to the strongest national currency and would never be devalued—features Major believes would make the hard ECU noninflationary. The hard ECU would be issued and managed by a new Communitywide institution called the European Monetary Fund. Management of the national currencies would remain with the national governments. Because the hard ECU would never be devalued, Major believes it would be relatively attractive to businesses. If so, the hard ECU might eventually eliminate demand for national currencies.

Proponents of the hard ECU plan stress the benefits of the market-driven approach to monetary union. By gradually becoming the only currency used, the hard ECU would avoid the risk of fixing exchange rates before adequate economic convergence has developed. The hard ECU plan would also provide central bankers with experience in a common currency before moving exclusively to a single currency. Moreover, because the hard ECU would never be devalued against national currencies, proponents believe the European Monetary Fund would gain credibility as an inflation fighter (Flemming).

The hard ECU plan initially met with strong criticism. Germany was particularly critical—suspecting that adding another currency to the existing 12 would compound the difficulties of coordinating monetary policy. Bundesbank President Poehl opposes the hard ECU, fearing it would be inflationary, despite Major's claims to the contrary (Alterman).

Other members, while less critical than Germany, have expressed additional concerns about the hard ECU plan. Some question the need to introduce a thirteenth currency when the basket ECU already exists. Others claim the hard ECU plan fails to specify conditions that would allow a move to stage three—that is, they fear the hard ECU plan would keep the EC in stage two indefinitely (Ungerer). Still other critics doubt the hard ECU will be able to eliminate other currencies since member-nations have shown no signs of abandoning their own currencies, even though they now may use the currency of their choice.

Since the intergovernmental conferences began in December, signs of compromise have developed. The United Kingdom has indicated that perhaps the ESCB, instead of the European Monetary Fund, could manage the hard ECU (Buchan and Marsh). In addition, both Spain and France have introduced draft treaties that combine features of the Delors treaty and the hard ECU plan. Both treaties plan to increase the role of the basket ECU currency (as opposed to introducing a new hard ECU), with the belief that it would eventually "harden" and become the single currency (McCune).

EMU timing

Issues have also arisen over the timing of EMU. One debate centers on whether to take a slow or fast approach to EMU. The other centers on whether all 12 EC members should proceed with EMU at the same time.

Slow track or fast track to EMU. While the United Kingdom and Germany disagree about the hard ECU plan, they agree that greater economic convergence should come before moving to complete EMU. Both feel that monetary union before adequate economic convergence would be difficult to sustain (Ungerer). U.K. Prime Minister Major supports a slow, market-oriented approach to EMU, in contrast to the union by legislative fiat called for by the Delors Report. German Chancellor Kohl has insisted that "convergence in economic and budgetary policies" is necessary before moving to a single European currency.[11] To provide more time for convergence and time to prepare adequately for a single currency, Kohl also suggests delaying establishment of the ESCB until 1997—three years later than originally planned (Marsh 1991; *The Economist* 1991).

While the members that favor a slow path to EMU believe economic convergence is necessary for monetary union, other members think monetary union would itself foster economic convergence. France and Italy, for example, would like a quick move to monetary union. In France's draft treaty proposal, stage two would begin January 1, 1994. By the end of 1997, the EC would determine whether a single currency were feasible. If so, detailed plans for the introduction of a single currency would then be devised (BIS).

Two-tier plan to EMU. The "two-tier" plan (sometimes called the "two-speed" plan) raises questions as to whether all 12 EC members need to proceed with EMU at the same time. As noted earlier, the idea that full economic and monetary union requires economies to have similar inflation rates, living standards, and economic growth rates prevails throughout the Delors Report.[12] Because it may take some time to reduce the differences that currently exist between some regions, the "two-tier" plan proposes that countries already sharing similar economic performances—for example, Germany, France, Belgium, Luxembourg, and the Netherlands—proceed with monetary union. The other countries would be left behind until their economies are in better condition for union (Nelson and Roth).

Countries with high inflation rates—like the United Kingdom and Portugal—oppose the "two-tier" approach.[13] These countries fear they might lose power and prestige by not being part of the first group in monetary union. Once the first group experiences the benefits of monetary union, it may be even more difficult for the second group to "catch up." Opponents of the two-tier plan argue the tension it would create between countries would hinder complete economic and monetary union (Marsh 1990a).

Additional macroeconomic issues in EMU

In addition to questions about a single currency and the pace of EMU, EC members have raised other issues. In particular, how much control should the Community have over national budget deficits? And what role should the ESCB play in foreign exchange rate policy?

Budget policies. In the Delors Report, the Community would recommend budget corrections, but not set binding rules on budget deficits. However, some members believe the budget policies outlined in the Delors Report are insufficient. Germany and the Netherlands, in particular, want binding budgetary rules set by the Community. Without such rules, they argue, the stronger members would bear the financial burden of bailing out heavily indebted members (*The Economist* 1990).

Foreign exchange rate policies. The Executive Board's role in exchange rates has also caused some disagreement. In the Delors Report, the ESCB executes foreign exchange rate policy for the single European currency vis-a-vis non-EC currencies, according to guidelines set by the Community. Some committee members, however, believe the Executive Board should play a more active role. Since foreign exchange rate policy and monetary policy affect each other, some members think the Community's exchange rate policy should at least be subject to the approval of the ESCB. Other members go further, suggesting the ESCB should formulate foreign exchange rate policy (Draft Statute).

Conclusion

Intergovernmental conferences are underway to finalize plans for EMU. At the conferences, EC members are debating the Delors Report and a draft statute on a European central banking system.

The Delors Report, the main proposal for EMU, outlines a three-stage approach to economic and monetary union in Europe. By promoting greater economic and monetary cooperation, stage one plans to increase economic convergence, easing the transition to unification. Stage two would serve as a transitional period, setting up the European Central Bank. Stage three would complete EMU. It involves a move to a common monetary policy and a single currency.

Building on the Delors Report, the Committee of Central Bank Governors drafted a statute on the European System of Central Banks. According to the statute, the ESCB would assume sole authority for monetary policy once EMU is completed. The ESCB would be independent and pursue price stability as its main objective. The Council, the Executive Board, and the 12 national central banks would divide the ESCB's responsibilities, which include formulating monetary policy, executing foreign exchange rate policy, managing reserves, supervising banks, and maintaining the payments system.

Debates have begun over several points of the Delors Report. Issues like the introduction of a single currency, the timing of EMU, and the transfer of powers from national governments to the Community must be overcome. But Europeans are getting closer to their goal. After nearly four decades, economic and monetary union is in sight.

A Glossary of Common Terms

Bundesbank. The central bank of Germany.

Council. The decision-making group for monetary policy in the ESCB. The Council consists of the six members of the Executive Board and the 12 Governors of the national central banks.

Council of Finance Ministers. An EC group consisting of the finance ministers of each member-nation. Sometimes referred to as ECOFIN. After EMU, the Council of Finance Ministers will determine the foreign exchange policy for the Community.

Delors, Jacques. President of the European Commission and chairman of the committee that developed the Delors Report.

Delors Report. The general name for the report entitled "Report on Economic and Monetary Union in the European Community," written by Jacques Delors. The report outlines the stages in economic and monetary union.

EC. European Community. The members include: Belgium, Denmark, France, Germany, Greece, Ireland, Italy, Luxembourg, the Netherlands, Portugal, Spain, and the United Kingdom.

ECU. European currency unit, pronounced "ek' coo." The ECU is now primarily a unit of account. The Delors Report recommends that the ECU eventually become the currency used in day-to-day transactions throughout the EC.

EEC. European Economic Community, later called the European Community. The EEC created a common market for all goods traded between members.

EMS. European Monetary System. Formed in 1979, the EMS is the name used to describe the current system of monetary cooperation.

EMU. Economic and monetary union, pronounced "ee' moo." According to the Delors Report, economic union means removing barriers to trade. Monetary union means creating a European central bank (ESCB) and a single European currency.

ERM. Exchange rate mechanism. The ERM provides the rules for setting and realigning exchange rates.

ESCB. The European System of Central Banks. The Delors Report recommends creating a European central bank that would be responsible for setting European monetary policy.

Economic and monetary union. See EMU.

Europe 1992. The EC program that abolishes all barriers to trade, commerce, and travel by December 31, 1992.

European Coal and Steel Community. A common market for coal, steel, and iron created in 1957.

European Community. See EC.

European Council. A decision-making group within the EC. All member-countries have representatives on the Council.

European Currency Unit. See ECU.

European Economic Community. See EEC.

European Monetary Fund. According to the United Kingdom's "hard ECU" plan, the European Monetary Fund would manage the hard ECU.

European Monetary System. See EMS.

European System of Central Banks. See ESCB.

Exchange rate mechanism. See ERM.

Executive Board. One of the three groups of the ESCB. Responsibilities of the Executive Board will include implementing monetary and exchange rate policies and issuing ECUs. The Executive Board will consist of six members selected for their expertise in banking or monetary matters.

Governor. The title for the executive officer of each national central bank.

Hard ECU plan. An alternative to the Delors Report, put forth by the United Kingdom. The plan recommends creating a thirteenth currency, the hard ECU, to compete with and eventually replace national currencies.

National Central Banks. The institution in each of the 12 EC countries responsible for formulating monetary policy. Once EMU occurs, the national central banks will become part of the ESCB.

Single European Act. The 1985 act commonly referred to as Europe 1992. See Europe 1992.

Stage One. The first step of EMU in the Delors Report. The goal of stage one is the continuation of economic and monetary integration.

Stage Two. The second step in the Delors Report. Stage two is an interim stage, used to prepare the EC for moving to collective decision making.

Stage Three. The final step in the Delors Report. Stage three completes EMU with European monetary policy set by the ESCB and a single European currency.

Subsidiarity. The principle of subsidiarity states that national authorities will retain all powers except those that require collective decision making; the latter will be vested in EC-level institutions.

Treaty of Rome. The 1957 treaty establishing the European Community.

Two-tier plan. An alternative to the Delors Report, put forth by Germany and France. The plan recommends that countries with similar economic performance form their own monetary union; other countries are left behind until their performance is similar to the original group.

Werner Plan. The 1970 plan for monetary union. Oil price shocks in 1973-74 led the EC to abandon the Werner Plan.

Endnotes

[1] The EC's interest in monetary union was in part due to growing instability under the Bretton Woods system during the late 1960s.

[2] Since June 1989, the Delors Report has occasionally been revised. This article is based on the most recent version of the Delors Report, which was presented at the intergovernmental conferences in December 1990.

[3] Not everyone agrees that national budget deficits are an impediment to EMU (Mussa).

[4] Even before a single currency is introduced, EC members are strongly urged not to finance their budget deficits by increasing the money supply. Once a single currency is introduced, financing budget deficits by issuing money will not even be feasible. The European Central Bank will issue the currency to EC members.

[5] For example, central banks currently use the ECU as a reserve asset and for settling accounts, while some private investors currently issue international bonds denominated in ECUs.

[6] The new ECU will also replace the current basket ECU.

[7] Bundesbank President Poehl is chairman of the Committee of Central Bank Governors, which drafted the statute of the ESCB. The Committee consists of the governors of the central banks of each of the 12 member-countries.

[8] These bodies are similar to the Directorate, the Land Central Banks, and the Central Bank Council of the Bundesbank and to a lesser extent, the Board of Governors, the Federal Reserve Banks, and the Federal Open Market Committee of the Federal Reserve System.

[9] The Council of the ESCB should not be confused with the European Council. The European Council is an existing Community organization, consisting of representatives of each EC nation. The European Council will appoint the six members of the Executive Board.

[10] Margaret Thatcher was particularly critical of the loss of national sovereignty implied by the Delors Report. Her bitter opposition to EMU contributed to her resignation as U.K. prime minister.

[11] Germany also supports a slower approach to EMU because it is currently preoccupied with its own reunification problems (Riding).

[12] The Delors Report states that large regional differences "would pose an economic as well as political threat to the union."

[13] Not everyone in the United Kingdom opposes the two-tier plan. Some believe a two-speed system might reduce pressure on the United Kingdom to join a complete economic and monetary union (Buchan).

References

Alterman, Simon. 1991. "Latest British ECU Proposals Further Step Towards EC Mainstream," *Reuters*, January 9.

Bennett, Thomas, and Craig S. Hakkio. 1989. "Europe 1992: Implications for U.S. Firms," Federal Reserve Bank of Kansas City, *Economic Review*, April, pp. 3-17.

BIS Review. 1991. "A Draft Treaty on Economic and Monetary Union Presented by the Government of France," February 12, reprint from *Europe Documents*, January 31, 1991.

Buchan, David. 1991. "Howe Warning on EC Split," *Financial Times*, March 1.

_____, and Peter Marsh. 1991. "UK May Offer Deal Over Hard ECU," *Financial Times*, weekend ed., January 5-6.

Committee of Governors of the Central Banks of the EC. 1990. "Draft Statute of the European System of Central Banks and of the European Central Bank," *Europe Documents*, December 8.

Committee for the Study of Economic and Monetary Union in the European Community. 1989. "Report on Economic and Monetary Union in the European Community."

Directorate-General for Economic and Financial Affairs. 1990. *European Economy: One Market, One Economy*, no. 44, Belgium, pp. 11-12.

The Economist. 1990. "Delors' Last Word," August 25, pp. 65-66.

_____. 1991. "The Spoilers," March 9, p. 44.

Flemming, John S. 1990. "British View of the Move from the Single Financial Market to EMU," address presented October 26, in Milan.

International Monetary Fund. 1989. *IMF Survey*, Washington, July 10, pp. 209, 219-22.

Marsh, David. 1990a. "Bundesbank Agrees with Bonn that EMU Will Be 'Two Speed'," *Financial Times*,

November 26.

———. 1990b. "A War of Monetary Nerves," *Financial Times*, October 29.

———. 1991. "Kohl Defends Policy on Monetary Union," *Financial Times*, March 1.

McCune, Greg. 1991. "Hard Basket ECU Will Serve 12 EC Members," *Reuters*, January 30.

Mussa, Michael. 1990. "Monetary and Fiscal Policy in an Economically Unified Europe," unpublished article.

Nelson, Mark M., and Terence Roth. 1991. "Bundesbank Warns Europe on Rushing to a Single Currency," *Wall Street Journal*, March 20.

Riding, Alan. 1990. "Hesitation Now Greets Unity Plans," *The New York Times*, October 1.

Ungerer, Horst. 1990. "Europe: The Quest for Monetary Integration," *Finance & Development*, December, pp. 14-17.

Article 38

K. Alec Chrystal and Cletus C. Coughlin

K. Alec Chrystal is the National Westminster Bank Professor of Personal Finance at City University, London. Cletus C. Coughlin is a research officer at the Federal Reserve Bank of St. Louis. Kevin White provided research assistance.

How The 1992 Legislation Will Affect European Financial Services

THE EUROPEAN ECONOMIC Community (EC) was created by the Treaty of Rome of 1957. Its intention was to create an integrated "Common Market" within which goods, services, labor and capital would move freely. In its early years, the implementation of the Treaty of Rome focused on eliminating tariff barriers on trade in goods between the member countries. Barriers affecting capital movements and trade in services were neglected, while those affecting labor mobility, such as lack of recognition of professional qualifications across member countries, were greatly reduced but not eliminated.

A major initiative to eliminate all remaining barriers to intra-EC trade began in 1985. This is referred to as the "single market program" or "1992," its target date for completion (in reality, the end of 1992).[1] The legislation underlying the single market program affects virtually every product area. This paper examines one key portion of the legislation: the regulatory changes that pertain directly to banking and other financial services.[2]

In 1985, this sector accounted for 6.4 percent of total output and 2.9 percent of employment.[3] Since the sector provides services for other sectors, the integration of EC financial markets will affect efficiency not only within the financial services sector, but also in sectors *using* financial markets.

1992: GRADUAL RATHER THAN SUDDEN CHANGE

The commitment to eliminate the remaining EC trade barriers was formalized in the Single European Act (SEA), which was signed in 1985 and came into force on July 1, 1987. (See the shaded insert on pages 64-65 for additional highlights on EC history and a description of institutions and legislative instruments.) The SEA defines both the goal—"an area without internal

---

[1]For a recent overview of 1992, see Boucher (1991).

[2]Grilli (1989b) summarizes the numerous restrictions affecting international trade and investment transactions in the financial services sector, both in the EC and in other developed countries.

[3]See Emerson et al. (1988) for additional details on the economic dimensions of the financial services sector.

frontiers in which the free movement of goods, persons, services and capital is ensured"—and the target date—the end of 1992. It also incorporates reforms to speed up decision-making within the EC by establishing "qualified majority voting" to decide most issues of the reform process.[4]

In 1985, the EC Commission produced a White Paper entitled "Completing the Internal Market." It listed numerous measures thought to be necessary for the completion of the program, many of which have not yet been adopted.[5] Because of the large number of required measures, all barriers cannot be eliminated at once.[6]

The large number of proposals and the time necessary to consider a given proposal contribute to 1992 being a process rather than an event. Each directive must go through a complex process of discussion, first within the Commission and then in the Council of Ministers. Member state governments must be informed at each stage because they wish to consult with the domestic parties that will be affected. Parliaments of member states, as well as the European Parliament, also comment on each proposal. Finally, each agreement has to be ratified and reflected in the legislation of each member state.

A typical EC directive could take three years from first draft to Council ratification, with another two years or so for full implementation. Only measures close to adoption in early 1992 (or already adopted) will be implemented by the end of 1992; and measures not yet drafted will not be implemented before the mid-1990s.

A SINGLE MARKET IN FINANCIAL SERVICES: THE CORE REGULATORY CHANGES

Before the 1980s, no systematic attempts had been made to reduce trade barriers in financial services. Although services had been addressed when the EC was formed in 1957, the implementation of intra-EC free trade in services had been neglected. Moreover, trade in financial services had not been covered by multilateral negotiations under the General Agreement on Tariffs and Trade (GATT). (This may change in the current Uruguay Round of negotiations.)

More important, many countries maintained exchange controls for capital account transactions long beyond when they liberalized current account transactions.[7] Without a free flow of financial capital to balance the flows of goods between countries, "free" trade is constrained by capital controls. That is, financial services, which include a range of banking, investment and insurance services, cannot be freely provided across borders if access to foreign exchange is restricted.

Thus, an important step before removing specific restrictions on cross-border trade in financial services is to remove all exchange controls. Such a step was provided for by the Council Directive of June 24, 1988—The Capital Liberalization Directive—which removes controls on all capital flows within the EC and, for

---

[4] Key (1989) notes that under qualified majority voting, the number of votes of each member is weighted roughly according to its population. To adopt legislation, 54 votes out of a total of 76 are required.

[5] According to Hill (1991), as of December 1991, 65 of the 282 measures outlined in the White Paper remained to be adopted. A goal of the EC Commission was to have all measures adopted by year-end 1991 to allow member nations to convert the directives into national legislation. Problems with the directives are also occurring at the national level. For example, Italy has converted only half of the relevant directives into national law.

[6] Capie and Wood (1990) stress that gradual deregulation of the financial system is unlikely to cause instability. The history of deregulation, they note, reveals that only rapid changes in regulation threaten the stability of the financial system.

[7] According to Bannock et al. (1972), exchange controls are government policies that attempt to control the purchases and sales of foreign currencies undertaken by the residents of a specific country. For example, the Exchange Control Act of 1947 restricted the purposes for which foreign currencies could be bought by British residents and limited the use and retention of foreign currencies and gold they acquired.

An Overview of the European Community

The European Community (EC) is a grouping of 12 member states.[1] These are the original six signatories of the Treaty of Rome in 1957—France, Italy, Belgium, Luxembourg, the Netherlands and West Germany—plus six countries that joined later—Denmark (1973), Ireland (1973), the United Kingdom (1973), Greece (1981), Portugal (1986) and Spain (1986). Further expansion of the EC to include Austria and Sweden, as well as other countries, is a strong possibility. Key dates and events in the history of the EC, including the recent Maastricht Summit Accords on monetary and political union, are provided in the accompanying table.

EC Institutions

There are four major EC institutions. The *Commission* is the civil service of the EC. It is divided into 23 functional areas (Directorates General). There are 17 commissioners who are responsible for managing these areas. The Commission proposes new laws and policies and is responsible for implementing decisions made by the Council.

The *Council* is the ultimate decision-making authority. It is a committee whose members represent their own national governments. The Council makes final policy decisions based on Commission proposals. Participants at Council meetings vary according to subject matter. For example, if the topic is finance, then the finance ministers of the 12 member nations attend. If the topic involves the external relations of the EC, then foreign ministers attend. Council meetings involving heads of state occur twice a year. The chairmanship of the Council rotates among member states in alphabetical order for six-month periods. In some areas, such as for most labor and taxation questions, unanimity is required; for most single market issues, however, "qualified majority voting" is used.

The *European Parliament* is a chamber of elected representatives from all member states. It offers opinions on most European legislation but it has no formal legislative powers.

The *European Court of Justice* is a body of 13 judges, including at least one from each member country. The Court rules on applications and interpretation of EC laws. Judgments of the Court are binding on each member state.

Legislative Instruments

There are four main legislative instruments. To become effective, legislation generally must be "adopted" by the Council. In some circumstances, however, the Commission may make laws itself. Typically, this will involve legislation that is required to implement previous Council decisions.

One instrument is *regulations*, which are legally binding on all member states whether or not ratified by national parliaments. If a regulation conflicts with national law, the regulation dominates. A second instrument is *directives*, which are legally binding only as to their ultimate effect; it is up to member states to decide how to implement the rules in their own national legislation. Virtually all of the 1992 program is being implemented by directives. *Decisions* are the third instrument. Decisions, which are more narrowly focused than directives, are legally binding on all those to whom they are directed. All decisions with financial implications are enforceable in courts of member states. Finally, *recommendations* (or opinions) have no legal support but merely state a view about some desirable condition or policy change.

EC legislation normally is subjected to a lengthy process of consultation and discussion before it is adopted by the Council. The "right of initiative" lies with the Commission. Once the Commission has drafted a proposal, there are consultations with all affected parties both directly and via the relevant ministries of member states. The European Parliament also has the right to be consulted and is given the opportunity to propose amendments.

---

[1] For more details on the EC, see Rosenberg (1991).

Major Post-War Steps Towards European Integration

1947	Customs Union formed between Belgium, Netherlands and Luxembourg - "Benelux".
1948	Organization for European Economic Cooperation (OEEC) formed to administer U.S. aid for rebuilding post-war Europe.
1951	France, West Germany, Italy and Benelux form European Coal and Steel Community (ECSC) providing for a "Common Market" in these products.
1957	Treaties of Rome establish the six-member (Belgium, France, Italy, Luxembourg, Netherlands and West Germany) European Economic Community (EC) and the European Atomic Energy Community (Euratom).
1960	European Free Trade Association (EFTA) formed to promote free trade between non-EC Western European countries - Austria, Britain, Denmark, Finland, Iceland, Norway, Portugal, Sweden and Switzerland.
1962	Common Agriculture Policy (CAP) started.
1963	Britain's application to join EC vetoed by President de Gaulle.
1965	France boycotts EC in protest at excessive speed of integration moves.
1968	Customs union completed.
1970	"Werner Report" calls for Economic and Monetary Union within Europe - including a single currency.
1972	European exchange rate "Snake" arrangement formed, but the United Kingdom leaves the Snake after six weeks.
1973	United Kingdom, Denmark and Ireland join the EC.
1979	European Monetary System (EMS) formed - establishing the Exchange Rate Mechanism (ERM) and the European Currency Unit (ECU). Britain joins EMS but not ERM.
1979	First direct elections to European Parliament.
1981	Greece joins EC.
1983	Common Fisheries Policy established.
1985	White Paper on completing the internal market published.
1986	Spain and Portugal join EC.
1987	Single European Act comes into force.
1989	Delors Report calls for Economic and Monetary Union - including a single currency. Undertakings for Collective Investment in Transferable Securities took effect.
1990	United Kingdom joins ERM and Capital Liberalization Directive and Second Non-life Insurance Directive took effect.
1991	Maastricht Summit Accords on monetary and political union. The third and final stage of Economic and Monetary Union will begin by January 1, 1999. A single European currency will begin by this date (possibly as early as January 1, 1997). An independent European Central Bank will be set up six months before the single currency.
1993	Second Coordinating Bank Directive, Own Funds Directive, Solvency Ratio Directive and Second Life Insurance Directive take effect. Council Directive on Investment Services in the Securities Field and the Capital Adequacy Directive likely take effect.

The enforcement of EC laws is the responsibility of the Commission. Where breaches of EC laws are suspected, the Commission may issue a formal letter of notice to the governments of member states. Where this procedure proves insufficient, the Commission may refer the issue to the European Court of Justice.

the most part, on capital flows between an EC member and a non-member. For most member states, this directive was to apply from July 1, 1990.[8] The deadline has been met, though several countries, like the United Kingdom, Germany, the Netherlands and Denmark, had eliminated explicit controls before 1988.[9]

Various approaches have been used to quantify the integration of international financial markets. One way to see the effects of the relaxation of capital controls is to examine interest rates on comparable financial instruments in different countries that are denominated in the same currency. The elimination of capital controls should allow capital flows to equalize these interest rates.[10] This is exactly what has happened in the EC countries that have already eliminated capital controls. Figure 1 presents evidence for the United Kingdom, which abolished exchange controls as of October 24, 1979, and undertook a series of domestic liberalization measures in the 1980s. The U.K.'s deregulation has caused the Eurosterling-London Interbank Offer Rate (LIBOR) spread to collapse near zero.[11] Similar evidence exists for other EC countries that have liberalized.[12]

This evidence suggests that most of the effects of liberalizing capital flows for some, but not all, countries have already been realized, reinforcing the point that 1992 is a *series* of changes. There are, however, additional gains possible from the 1992 process. One is that 1992 will make it less costly for financial firms from one member country to be authorized to provide services in other EC countries. New financial services, as well as lower prices for existing services, might also occur. Before discussing these potential gains, we will summarize the major directives that pertain directly to financial services.

MAJOR DIRECTIVES

The major directives of the 1992 program for financial services can be divided into four categories: banking, investment services, undertakings for collective investments and insurance.[13]

Banking. Efforts at EC coordination did not begin with the Single European Act for any of the four categories of financial services. Rather, the SEA has accelerated the process of harmonizing regulations. For example, the First Banking Coordination Directive, which was approved by the Council in December 1977, required member states to establish systems for authorizing and supervising credit institutions.[14]

A second example is the Consolidation Supervision Directive of June 1983, which required that credit institutions be supervised on a consolidated basis. Any credit institution owning 25 percent or more of the capital of another financial institution was to be supervised on a consolidated basis by the authorities in the owning institution's home state. Another provision mandated the exchange of information between supervising authorities to obtain an overview of a consolidated company's affairs. To assist this supervisory cooperation, the Bank Accounts Directive of December 1986 harmonized accounting rules for credit institutions.

In the 1992 legislation, the Second Coordinating Banking Directive (2BD) is the primary banking directive. The 2BD allows any credit institution authorized in one member country to establish branches and provide banking services anywhere in the EC. While this so-called "common passport" allows home-country authorization, the credit institution must conform to all local laws. Thus, the host country's business rules, such as reporting requirements and res-

---

[8]Ireland, Spain, Greece and Portugal have until the end of 1992 to comply, with the latter two having the option to delay compliance until 1995.

[9]According to Blundell-Wignall and Browne (1991), the integration of financial markets internationally began in the mid-1970s with the removal of capital controls in Germany, the United States and Canada. Japan and the United Kingdom relaxed capital controls in the late 1970s, while France, Italy and some other EC countries realized the complete elimination of controls by the middle of 1990.

[10]This result is analogous to the effect of eliminating trade barriers on goods. When a country eliminates a tariff on a specific good, the difference between the price of the good in the country's domestic market and that in the international market should narrow.

[11]The two interest rates are ones charged by banks to other banks for three-month loans denominated in British pounds. The Eurosterling rate pertains to loans made outside the United Kingdom and the LIBOR applies to loans made inside the United Kingdom.

[12]See Blundell-Wignall and Browne (1991) for charts similar to figure 1 for Germany, the Netherlands and France.

[13]See U.K. Department of Trade and Industry (1991) for a summary of EC Directives relating to 1992.

[14]We refer to credit institutions rather than "banks" because these regulations include institutions other than banks. These would include the European equivalent of thrifts.

Figure 1
Difference Between the Three-Month Eurosterling and Libor Rates

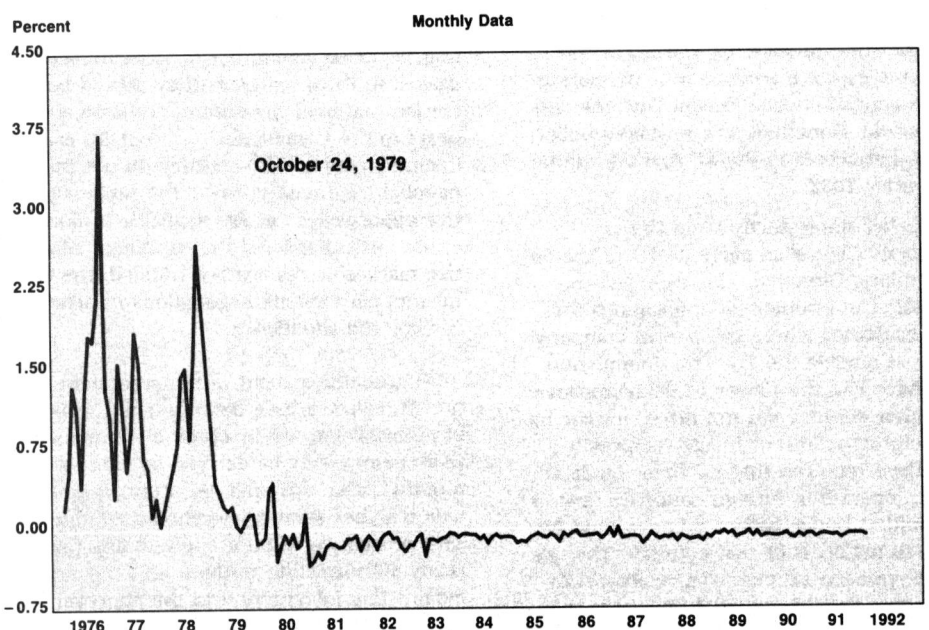

trictions on permissible products and activities, must be followed.

The 2BD also gives the commission some influence in authorizing institutions from outside the EC—the so-called "Reciprocity Clause." The first, but not the final, draft of this clause created much controversy and is partly responsible for the label "fortress Europe" that has inappropriately been associated with the 1992 program. (See the shaded insert on page 68 for additional discussion of this topic.)

The 2BD is supported by the Own Funds Directive and the Solvency Ratio Directive. The former provides common definitions for the components of the capital base; the latter uses these definitions to establish minimum asset ratios to be met by all credit institutions. All three directives become effective on January 1, 1993.

Investment Services. A related, but more problematic, set of measures deals with investment services. This category covers all aspects of the markets in tradeable securities, including investment banking, stock brokerage and the organization of the exchanges themselves. The key elements of the 1992 program are formulated in the Council Directive on Investment Services in the Securities Field and the Capital Adequacy Directive, neither of which has been adopted formally.

Until recently, observers generally thought both directives would begin operation at the same time as the banking directives because the 2BD gives banks (and other credit institutions) the right to do securities business throughout the EC on a single passport basis. As time passes, this simultaneity becomes less likely. If an identical single passport is not extended to non-

The Second Banking Directive and Fortress Europe

One of the great concerns, often heard outside the EC, is that the 1992 program will lower barriers to internal trade but at a cost of higher external trade barriers. The 1992 program does not introduce new barriers to trade in goods between Europe and the rest of the world. Nonetheless, a mistaken belief persists that access to the EC market will be harder after 1992.

This belief stems partly from the "Reciprocity Clause" in early drafts of the Second Banking Directive. This required the Commission to evaluate all applications for new subsidiaries where the parent company was based outside the EC. The Commission would have had the power to delay approval if the other country did not offer "mirror image" reciprocity. Mirror image reciprocity would have required that EC firms be allowed to operate in foreign countries, just as they could at home, before access would be offered to nationals of that country. This would have been very restrictive. For example, because there is no legal separation between investment banking and commercial banking in the EC, it would have required abolition of the Glass-Steagall Act in the United States before U.S. banks could gain access to the EC.

This requirement was weakened in later drafts of the directive. The final directive simply calls for negotiations with third countries (that is, countries outside the EC) in the event that EC firms are denied "effective market access." The critical criterion now is that EC firms should not be discriminated against in third markets—they should be accorded "national" treatment. "Whenever it appears to the Commission . . . that EC credit institutions in a third country do not receive national treatment offering the same competitive opportunities as are available to domestic credit institutions and the conditions of effective market access are not fulfilled, the Commission may initiate negotiations in order to remedy the situation."[1]

If negotiations about unfair treatment in a non-EC country have been initiated, approval of EC market access by credit institutions from that country may be delayed by up to three months. After this time, the Council must decide whether such delays should continue. This procedure will not apply to any firm already authorized to trade in an EC country. Finally, this intervention in the approval process must not contravene "the Community's obligations under any international agreements, bilateral or multilateral, governing the taking-up and pursuit of the business of credit institutions."[2] The general structure of the reciprocity clause in the Second Banking Directive is expected to be copied for the other major areas of financial services, including investment services and insurance.

---

[1] See Title III, Article 9, paragraph 4 of the 2BD. In official documents, the 2BD is the "Second Council Directive of 15 December 1989."

[2] See Title III, Article 9, paragraph 6 of the 2BD.

bank securities firms at the same time, they will be at a disadvantage.

A key problem in formulating regulations in investment services has been that the range of activities covered is much more heterogeneous than in the banking area.[15] Arguments have arisen about which activities to include and how much capital should be required for different lines of business. Initial proposals, for example, incorporated such high capital requirements that some businesses objected strongly. Nonbank securities houses argued that the requirements were so onerous, their business would be driven outside their countries. Universal banks, on the other hand, feared they would be at a disadvantage if securities houses had lower requirements than banks.[16] The latest drafts of the directives incorporate a compromise that appears acceptable to both camps. Banks will be permitted to treat their securities business separately and calculate capital requirements under the investment services rules rather than the banking rules.

Another point of controversy concerns the provision of compensation schemes for investors. A commission recommendation in 1986 suggested the establishment of compensation schemes for depositors (that is, deposit insurance) in credit institutions. In the wider area of investment services, the position of compensation schemes is even less clear. Some countries, like the United Kingdom since the implementation of the 1986 Financial Services Act, have compulsory compensation schemes for investment business, while many others do not. This position raises potential anomalies in cross-border business.

A final sticking point in the Investment Services Directive relates to the monopoly of organized stock exchanges over securities trading. Some countries, like France, have argued for the official stock exchange to have a monopoly. Without a monopoly, the present French system could not be used throughout the EC. Others, especially the British, are strongly opposed.

Undertakings for Collective Investments. In contrast to the banking and investment services directives, the directive governing Undertakings for Collective Investment in Transferable Securities (UCITS), which are open-ended mutual funds, has already come into effect. The Council Directive on the coordination of laws relating to UCITS took effect in October 1989. The directive establishes minimum requirements for authorization of UCITS and permits their marketing throughout the EC. This freedom is subject to the usual proviso that the host state be notified and local marketing rules be obeyed. Minimum requirements are established for adequate risk spreading, the separation of trustees from managers and the specification of acceptable investments.

Before it was implemented, there was some concern that the UCITS Directive would lead to a migration of UCITS managers to countries, like Luxembourg and Ireland, with the most favorable tax treatment. It is too early to determine whether this expectation is correct. To counteract this possibility, however, efforts were made to reduce tax differences. For example, the British budget of 1989 reduced taxes on unit trusts.

Insurance. A final set of directives on financial services deals with insurance. Insurance provides examples of 1992 initiatives already in effect as well as those many years away. The primary directives are the Second Non-Life Insurance Directive and the Second Life Insurance Directive.

The Second Non-Life Insurance Directive establishes freedom of services for cross-border business within the EC. This freedom, however, applies only for large commercial risks. What is

---

[15]Another reason for the relatively faster agreement on banking is that bank regulation had already been well worked out globally—through the Bank for International Settlements and formalized in the Basle Agreement. The 1988 Basle Agreement replaced differing national regulations for measuring capital adequacy by a single, internationally accepted standard. The goals were to strengthen the soundness of the international banking system and remove regulatory differences that affected the international competitiveness of banks. See Blanden (1988).

[16]Generally speaking, EC countries did not have counterparts to U.S. banking regulations that limited their spread geographically or their lines of business activity. As a result, a small number of large banks evolved. For example, German banking is dominated by a small number of banks engaging in normal commercial banking as well as buying and selling stocks for others, underwriting new stock issues and owning stock on their own behalf. In fact, German banks are represented on the boards of directors of many companies. In the United Kingdom, merchant banks specialized in the securities business, while commercial banks had the bulk of deposits. Since the deregulation of British financial markets that began on October 27, 1986, known as the Big Bang, U.K. commercial banks have gone universal in that they have merchant bank subsidiaries and are expanding into insurance services, especially life insurance. Belgium is the only EC country that separates investment and commercial banking.

referred to as "mass risk," which includes most things insured by people other than their lives—theft and fire damage to personal property—remains subject to numerous restrictions. A new, more liberal regime applies to all marine, aviation and shipment risks, and other fire, property and financial risks for situations in which the policy holder is a large commercial company. Here, the insurer has an obligation to notify the authorities (in the insured company's country), but may write the business directly. For all other businesses, the authorities in each country may continue to control the terms of authorization, premiums, policy conditions and reserve assets.

This Directive took effect in July 1990 and, hence, the large commercial risk market has effectively achieved the single market position already. Unlike banking, this directive did not create a common passport. Thus, branching in other countries is not freely permitted, and establishment still requires authorization in each member state. Two draft "Framework Directives" for life and non-life insurance appeared in 1991 and 1990, respectively. These would establish the single passport for insurance; the fact that the first drafts of these directives did not emerge earlier, however, suggests that they will not be in operation until 1995 at the earliest.

Only modest progress has been made on life insurance so far. The Second Life Insurance Directive was adopted in November 1990 for implementation on May 21, 1993. It only goes a small way, however, toward creating a single market in life insurance. A liberal regime is provided for, but only in cases where the consumer takes the initiative in buying a life insurance policy from a firm in another member country. In all other cases, the restrictive regime applies, under which the insurer may be required to obtain special approval (depending upon local law) and the policy terms may be proscribed.

Under the most recent draft of legislation involving life insurance, whose date of implementation has yet to be agreed upon, insurance companies are permitted to advertise, but they may not approach consumers directly. It also is possible that "local" asset backing for the policy may be required. This means that, for example, an Italian firm selling insurance in Germany would have to back its German policies with German securities. This draft of the legislation also restricts the role of brokers. For three years after implementation, member states will be able to forbid consumers from seeking policies from other member states through brokers.

Considerable resistance exists in some quarters to the creation of a genuine single market in life insurance. The basic conflict arises because some countries—notably Germany—have had a very conservative attitude to life insurance, while others—like the United Kingdom—have been very innovative. German insurance companies have typically invested in safe fixed-interest securities, and innovation in the industry has been strictly controlled. The United Kingdom, in contrast, allows its firms to invest across a range of assets including property and equities. Thus, the typical British firm's portfolio is riskier than its German counterpart, but has a much higher average yield, producing significantly lower prices for British products.

The Common Passport

Before discussing the reform process, an important distinction must be made between wholesale and retail financial markets. As demonstrated above, the globalization of international financial markets in the 1970s and 1980s has already led to highly competitive wholesale capital markets across many EC countries. These markets, in which financial firms deal directly with each other, experienced considerable competitive pressures in the past 20 years. Faced with the choice of deregulation or the loss of firms to less-regulated environments in other countries, most nations dismantled much of the regulatory structure in wholesale financial markets.

Retail markets, in which consumers deal with firms to borrow money, purchase insurance and trade stock, are quite different and present the biggest problem for deregulation. These markets retain a myriad of complex regulatory structures and external barriers that are generally justified on the grounds that they protect the small consumer.[17] Regardless of whether

---

[17]For example, the U.K. Financial Services Act of 1986 requires any firm selling investment products in the United Kingdom to register with either the Securities and Investment Board or a recognized regulatory organization. The firm must conform to a complex set of rules, subject itself to inspections and pay membership charges, which include investor compensation schemes.

domestic officials actually believe this or are simply disguising their protection of domestic firms, the abolition of regulations to increase cross-border trade and competition in retail financial markets is the primary challenge of the 1992 program.

Starting with the existing regulatory structures in each member country, the central principle guiding deregulation is that regulators in each member state are competent to judge which firms are "fit and proper" to do business in the industry. Once a firm has been authorized by the regulatory authority in its home country—so-called home authorization—it is automatically authorized to do business in any other member country and is said to have a "common passport."

Previously, many countries have allowed firms from other EC countries freedom of establishment, but this freedom has been subject to a separate process of approval in each country.[18] The abolition of this requirement, therefore, will make it easier for firms to establish subsidiaries in other member countries.

Home authorization, however, is not the end of the story. Firms operating outside their home states still have to obey "host country conduct of business rules."[19] In other words, foreign firms must obey all the local regulations about the nature of acceptable products and the way in which they may be advertised and sold. For example, France does not allow interest payments on checking deposits, while most other EC countries do.

The fact that business rules will continue to differ across countries limits the extent to which there will be a genuine single market. The various rules increase the costs of cross-border activity and are sometimes even anticompetitive. For example, the business rules in some member states define which products can be sold and their respective prices. Thus, one of the main incentives for attempting to enter new markets—the introduction of new products not offered by local firms—is not guaranteed.

Regulatory Complications from the Common Passport

The move to a common passport will complicate the regulatory process.[20] At this point, only hypothetical situations can be offered to suggest the potential difficulties. While firms require authorization only in their home states, the regulatory authorities of other nations have to monitor the activity of these firms within their domain because they are responsible for consumer protection and adherence to business rules.

To illustrate, suppose a German bank establishes a subsidiary in the United Kingdom after 1992 on the basis of its German banking license. It takes deposits and makes loans in British pounds sterling. As the German banking authorities are responsible for prudential supervision, the bank must file the reports required by these authorities. The bank, however, must also register with the Bank of England, fulfill all reporting requirements and conform to all British banking regulations in the United Kingdom—including reserve requirements and banking codes of practice. It must also pay regulatory fees just as any British bank must do.

The lower costs of establishing an office in the United Kingdom may increase the regulatory burden of both the British and German authorities. Suppose, for example, the German bank gets into difficulties, like a run on deposits, or is involved in a breach of rules, like fraud. Clearly, both British and German authorities will have to get involved to resolve the problem. Indeed, a bank with branches (or subsidiaries) across Europe could draw 12 sets of regulators into a dispute over its operations. The number of regulators would rise even further if the

---

[18]For example, Emerson et al. (1988) note that each EC country allows freedom of establishment for foreign banks; however, the conditions under which this may be done vary substantially across countries. High establishment costs make it difficult for a foreign bank to enter and compete successfully with an existing domestic retail bank. Additional obstacles in certain countries, like Italy and Spain, are restrictions on foreign acquisitions and involvement with domestic banks.

[19]For an alternative interpretation of the implications of home authorization in the context of the 2BD, see Key (1989). In our view, home authorization applies to the issue of a license and prudential control, but it does not apply to any behavior that falls under conduct of business rules. Home authorization is much different than home control. Even though a bank is given a license to operate abroad by its home authorities, the bank's subsidiaries will have to obey all the laws attached to banking practice in the foreign countries in which they operate.

[20]Capie and Wood (1990) make a similar point that the Second Banking Directive will make supervision and regulation much more complicated. They speculate, however, that this complexity may cause a change in regulation from detailed supervision to one in which central banks are primarily lenders of last resort.

Table 1
Deposit Insurance in the EC[1]

Country	Limitations (in U.S. dollars as of July 6, 1990)	Coverage[2]		
		Deposits in foreign currency	Deposits in domestic branches of foreign banks	Deposits in foreign branches
Belgium	$14,706	No	No	No
Denmark	39,708	—	—	—
France	72,033	No	Yes	No
Germany	30% of bank's liable capital	Yes	Yes	Yes
Ireland	16,206	—	—	—
Italy	659,385	Yes	Yes	Yes
Luxembourg	14,706	—	—	—
Netherlands	21,486	Yes	Yes	No
Spain	14,789	No	—	No
United Kingdom	35,730	No	Yes	No

SOURCE: Bartholomew and Vanderhoff (1991).
[1]Greece and Portugal have no formal systems of deposit insurance.
[2]The "—" indicates no information was available.

bank's activities spread beyond banking into securities or insurance.

It is also noteworthy that the British authorities have no power to withdraw the banking license if the bank transgresses business rules in the United Kingdom. Even though the Bank of England could stop a bank from trading temporarily, a high degree of communication and cooperation between regulators of the member countries will be required to manage such a problem. Eventually, there might be a formal regulatory agency that operates on a community-wide basis.

The preceding example, which pertains to all member countries, is relatively simple in comparison to the regulatory issues that might arise when services are provided across national borders. Suppose the German bank takes deposits and makes loans in sterling with retail customers in the United Kingdom only by mail or telephone from its head office in Frankfurt. In this case, the German bank need not register with the Bank of England, but has an obligation to conform to British conduct of business rules. This means that the Bank of England must monitor this business in some way. While cases like this may be of trivial quantitative significance (especially in retail trade), they also may generate the greatest regulatory headaches, in terms of allocating regulatory responsibilities for the monitoring and enforcement of standards of business practice.

Such jurisdictional problems may be greatest where deposit insurance is involved. Table 1 summarizes the deposit protection schemes for commercial banks in the EC. The amount of protection for depositors varies substantially across countries. This may influence where a specific deposit may be made. The high level of protection in Italy could attract large depositors. By the same token, the different levels of protection may confuse depositors. A Spanish depositor, who made a deposit in a French branch in Spain that fails, for example, may mistakenly believe that the French deposit insurance scheme applies. Since deposit insurance is politically sensitive, controversy is not difficult to envision. The EC Commission has drafted a proposal, not yet published, for the harmonization of deposit insurance, but any changes are unlikely to take effect before the mid-1990s.

The almost complete harmonization of regulatory standards is inevitable when transactions within an industry are predominantly of an international nature. By itself, however, 1992 is unlikely to make the transactions in European retail financial markets to be primarily international. Thus, the regulation of retail financial markets in Europe involves a compromise between host country control and the creation of a single market. Harmonization of business rules will not be complete and, in some cases, may not be even close.

Product Innovation

The potential gains from removing barriers to the spread of new products across borders seem to be positive and potentially quite large. Lower-cost producers of financial services products would prosper at the expense of less efficient firms that now survive only because of regulations that limit competition by foreign firms. Consumers would benefit from having a greater variety of products from which to choose and would pay lower prices for them.

The basic problem is the resistance by some countries to relaxing domestic regulation of an industry. Frequently, a country's business rules inhibit product innovation. For example, current German regulations restrict the introduction of new insurance products into Germany. Even with a common passport, a foreign insurance firm faces a major deterrent to entering the German market. Taken together, German citizens and foreign insurance firms clearly would benefit from free trade in new products, but it is also clear that some German insurance companies would suffer from the influx of competition.

This is the area where the least progress has been made in the 1992 program. In view of the time required to reach and implement EC decisions, as well as the current controversy about these decisions, the potentially large gains from product innovation and lower prices in many financial services will not be realized any time in the near future.

POTENTIAL BENEFITS OF THE SINGLE MARKET

The preceding discussion raises doubts about how sizable the gains will be from the 1992 legislation in the financial services sector; however, we do not provide an estimate of the gains themselves.[21] These doubts are at odds with the potential gains estimated in the Cecchini Report, the best-known attempt to measure such gains.[22] This report found substantial potential gains from the creation of a single market in many industries.[23] The gains from the liberalization of the financial services sector, which are presented and examined below, were found to be substantial as well.

Financial Services: The Estimated Gains of Eliminating Trade Barriers

The reduction of trade barriers can generate gains via a number of routes, all of which are driven by increased competitive pressures. For example, the reduction of trade barriers will allow firms with lower production costs to expand their production, increasing total output and economic welfare. Other gains can be realized as larger markets increase the opportunities to use certain production technologies that lower per-unit production costs. Finally, increased competition tends to drive down profit margins, eliminate waste and stimulate the development of new products and less costly methods to produce existing products. Ultimately, the competitive pressures will allow consumers throughout the EC to consume (use) more financial services at lower prices per unit.

The competitive pressures resulting from 1992 are expected to narrow the price differences of a financial service across the EC. As part of the Cecchini Report, Price Waterhouse calculated prices across eight EC countries for the 16 financial services—seven banking services, five insurance services and four securities services—listed in table 2. The average of the four lowest prices for each service was chosen as the likely price after the elimination of trade barriers. The potential price declines for financial services are listed in table 3. Exactly how much of this potential decline will be realized is difficult to estimate, so an expected decline (with a plus/minus 5 percentage-point range) was defined as one-half of the potential decline.

---

[21] To reiterate, we are not questioning the gains from the abolition of exchange controls; rather, we are questioning the gains from the common passport in light of the continuation of different conduct of business rules.

[22] In theory, the abolition of trade barriers for goods traded among a group of countries may or may not yield net benefits. An elementary demonstration of this result can be found in Coughlin (1990).

[23] The Cecchini Report estimates that the gains from completing the internal market range from 4.3 percent to 6.4 percent of gross domestic product in the EC. See Coughlin (1991) for an examination of the approach used in the Cecchini Report as well as other approaches used to estimate the economic effects of 1992.

Table 2
List of Standard Financial Services or Products Surveyed

Name of standard service	Description of standard service
Banking services	
1. Consumer credit	Annual cost of consumer loan of 500 ECU. Excess interest rate over money market rates.
2. Credit cards	Annual cost assuming 500 ECU debit. Excess interest rate over money market rates.
3. Mortgages	Annual cost of home loan of 25,000 ECU. Excess interest rate over money market rates.
4. Letters of credit	Cost of letter of credit of 50,000 ECU for three months.
5. Foreign exchange drafts	Cost to a large commercial client to purchase a commercial draft for 30,000 ECU.
6. Travellers checks	Cost for a private consumer to purchase 500 ECU worth of travellers checks.
7. Commercial loans	Annual cost (including commissions and charges) to a medium-sized firm of a commercial loan of 250,000 ECU.
Insurance services	
1. Life insurance	Average annual cost of term (life) insurance.
2. Home insurance	Annual cost of fire and theft coverage for house valued at 70,000 ECU with 28,000 ECU contents.
3. Motor insurance	Annual cost of comprehensive insurance, 1.6 liter car, driver 10 years experience, no-claims bonus.
4. Commercial fire and theft	Annual coverage for premises valued at 387,240 ECU and stock at 232,344 ECU.
5. Public liability coverage	Annual premium for engineering company with 20 employees and annual turnover of 1.29 million ECU.
Brokerage services	
1. Private equity transactions	Commission costs of cash bargain of 1,440 ECU.
2. Private gilt transactions	Commission costs of cash bargain of 14,000 ECU.
3. Institutional equity transactions	Commission costs of cash bargain of 288,000 ECU.
4. Institutional gilt transactions	Commission costs of cash bargain of 7.2 million ECU.

SOURCE: Emerson et al. (1988), p. 102.

Using the expected price declines for financial services, the gains for the eight EC countries examined are estimated to be 21.6 billion ECU, which is 0.7 percent of their gross domestic product.[24] The distribution of these gains across the EC are listed in table 4. One's confidence in these estimates, as acknowledged in Emerson et al. (1988), should not be great. First, the price comparisons themselves can be questioned. Products such as "credit" and "life insurance" have been priced as if the characteristics are the same in each country. For example, no attempt has been made to adjust for theft and mortality differences across countries, and, hence, it is not clear that homogeneous products are compared.

More important, even if price differences exist for identical products, it is far from clear that the 1992 legislation will eliminate such differ-

---

[24]The ECU, which stands for the European Currency Unit, is composed of the weighted averages of the currencies of the 12 member countries and is the unit of account for the EC. Even though much negotiation remains, the ECU is likely to become the single currency of the EC. For a brief history of the ECU, especially recent developments, see Tyley (1991). One ECU was equal to $1.29 on February 11, 1992.

Table 3
Potential and Expected Price Declines for Financial Services

Country	Potential price fall	Range of expected fall
Belgium	23%	6-16%
France	24	7-17
Germany	25	5-15
Italy	29	9-19
Luxembourg	17	3-13
Netherlands	9	0-9
Spain	34	16-26
United Kingdom	13	2-12

SOURCE: Emerson et al. (1988), p. 104.

Table 4
Estimated Gains Resulting from the Expected Price Reductions for Financial Services

Country	Total (million ECU)	Percentage of GDP
Belgium	685	0.7%
France	3,683	0.5
Germany	4,619	0.6
Italy	3,996	0.7
Luxembourg	44	1.2
Netherlands	347	0.2
Spain	3,189	1.5
United Kingdom	5,051	0.8
Total	21,614	0.7

SOURCE: Emerson et al. (1988), p. 106.

ences. The reason is that business rules will continue to differ from country to country, thereby impeding trade in financial services and limiting potential gains to levels below those estimated in the table.[25] Thus, the value of the single passport is diminished considerably by the inability of firms entering new markets to offer a full line of products and services.

Grilli (1989a) has also raised doubts about the estimates in the Cecchini Report on the likely effects of liberalization on wholesale and retail banking throughout the EC. Grilli doubts whether a perfectly competitive market structure is an accurate approximation of retail banking post-1992. Much evidence suggests that banks have market power in their retail markets that will not be eliminated by the 1992 legislation. For example, within the same country, which is already a homogeneous regulatory and institutional environment, the terms of a deposit contract, such as the interest rate paid on a time deposit, frequently vary across banks. In addition, the transaction costs of switching between domestic and foreign bank accounts will remain after 1992, and a business relationship with a local bank will remain less complicated than with a foreign bank. Furthermore, Grilli argues,

the use of other, more appropriate market structures produces smaller estimated gains from 1992 than those based on perfect competition.

The bottom line is that the estimates in the Cecchini Report are probably optimistic. Of course, the absence of better estimates precludes any quantitative statements about the degree of overstatement.

Single Currency

The preceding discussion, including the estimates in the Cecchini Report, has presumed that 12 currencies continue to exist within the EC, albeit tied together by the exchange rate target zones of the European Monetary System (EMS). Thus, far from there being a single market in financial services, there will continue to be 12 quite separate markets at the retail level. Within those markets, firms will operate separable portfolios and most retail customers will stick almost exclusively to their domestic environment.[26]

The creation of a single currency, which was agreed upon at Maastricht, the Netherlands, in

---

[25]Evidence that supports this view was highlighted by Grilli (1989b). For individual financial services, he noted that the price dispersion across countries that had already liberalized, like Germany, Belgium, Luxembourg, the Netherlands and the United Kingdom, was no less than across the remaining EC members.

[26]Separable portfolios means that a bank with subsidiaries in more than one member state will operate a matched deposit and loan book in each currency. For example, a Dutch bank with a subsidiary in Greece will use drachma deposits rather than guilder deposits to fund drachma loans.

December 1991 will induce major changes, irrespective of the regulatory regime.[27] Obviously, the foreign exchange market—and with it the costs of currency conversion—among the EC members will be eliminated. Closely related is the fact that the international accounting of many businesses will be simplified by the elimination of multiple currencies. On the other hand, many contracts will have to be rewritten. For example, a long-term bond contract that requires interest and principal payments in a specific currency, say French francs, will have to be modified.

Generally, retail customers will continue to do business with familiar institutions in their own countries, while wholesale market arbitrage and potential competition ensure that product prices are brought closely into line throughout the EC. These competitive pressures will lead to changes in the regulatory structure so that the conduct of business rules become more similar and, in some cases, identical; otherwise, firms in some countries will be at a competitive disadvantage relative to firms in other countries.[28] It is difficult to predict exactly how business rules will be harmonized for each financial service and, thus, how extensive the potential gains from a "free" single market will actually be. A more homogeneous and unitary monitoring mechanism is likely, although its full implications are equally hard to anticipate. Nonetheless, the gains from a single market are more likely to be realized if monetary union is achieved.

CONCLUSION

The goal of 1992 is to create a single European market, a goal that encompasses the financial services sector. Our assessment is that the 1992 reforms are a small step toward the liberalization of the financial services sector. Clearly, 1992 will contribute to the realization of some gains, especially in countries that have previously resisted liberalization. Nonetheless, serious doubts exist about how extensive the changes will be in the near future and, thus, the magnitude of the gains to be realized overall. In reality, the 1992 legislation will not cause major changes. The reason is that virtually all of the potential efficiency gains in the financial services sector can be (or have been) achieved through the combination of the abolition of exchange controls and the freedom of foreign firms to enter domestic markets. In fact, the former was implemented in July 1990 (in all but Spain, Portugal, Greece and Ireland).

The key innovation of the 1992 legislation is the split between home country authorization and host country conduct of business rules. This dichotomy will create problems. Whereas wholesale markets already are highly integrated, not just within Europe but at the global level, 12 quite different retail markets will continue to exist in the near future. This segmentation means that many existing regulatory burdens will remain; however, regulatory complications may multiply as numerous domestic and EC authorities become involved in the supervision of a single firm. Finally, in some markets, like insurance, rigid regulation of domestic markets will delay any implementation of the current model of a framework directive until well beyond 1992.

The greatest boost to financial market integration, once markets are open, will be the use of a single currency. With a single currency, pressure will mount to revise the regulatory structure so that the conduct of business rules are homogeneous.

Major changes in the regulatory structure lie ahead. It is these changes that will create a single market and allow for the realization of substantial gains in the next century.

REFERENCES

Bannock, Graham, Ron Baxter, and R. Rees. *A Dictionary of Economics* (Penguin Books, 1972).

Bartholomew, Philip F., and Vicki A. Vanderhoff. "Foreign Deposit Insurance Systems: A Comparison," *Consumer Finance Law: Quarterly Report* Vol. 45 (1991), pp. 243-48.

Blanden, Michael. "Ironing Out Those Troublesome Bumps," *The Banker* (February 1988), pp. 56-59.

---

[27] A recent issue of *The Economist* ("The Deal is Done," 1991) characterizes the Maastricht Treaty as important as the Treaty of Rome because it lays the foundation for a much closer union of countries via a single currency, a common foreign and defense policy, common citizenship and a parliament with power. A summary of the Maastricht Treaty as it pertains to monetary union can be found in "Mapping the Road" (1991), page 5.

[28] Not surprisingly, the U.S. legal system has had considerable experience with conflicting laws and regulations across states. The Uniform Commercial Code is an excellent example of states reaching general agreement on numerous laws. See Levine (1976) for additional details.

Blundell-Wignall, Adrian, and Frank Browne. "Increasing Financial Market Integration, Real Exchange Rates and Macroeconomic Adjustment," OECD Department of Economics and Statistics Working Paper No. 96, 1991.

Boucher, Janice L. "Europe 1992: A Closer Look," Federal Reserve Bank of Atlanta *Economic Review* (July/August 1991), pp. 23-38.

Capie, Forrest H., and Geoffrey E. Wood. "Financial Structure in a Changing Regulatory Environment: Europe after 1992," in *Game Plans for the '90s* (Federal Reserve Bank of Chicago, 1990).

Coughlin, Cletus C. "Estimating the Economic Effects of 1992," 1991 International Trade and Finance Association proceedings, forthcoming.

_____ . "What Do Economic Models Tell Us About the Effects of the U.S.-Canada Free Trade Agreement," this *Review* (September/October 1990), pp. 40-58.

"The Deal is Done," *The Economist* (December 14, 1991), pp. 51-54.

Emerson, Michael, Michel Aujean, Michel Catinat, Philippe Goybet, and Alexis Jacquemin. *The Economics of 1992* (Oxford University Press, 1988).

Grilli, Vittorio. "Europe 1992: Issues and Prospects for the Financial Markets," *Economic Policy* (October 1989a), pp. 388-411.

_____ . "Financial Markets and 1992," *Brookings Papers on Economic Activity* (No. 2, 1989b), pp. 301-24.

Hill, Andrew. "EC Leaders Reminded of Single Market Goal," *Financial Times,* December 9, 1991.

Key, Sydney J. "Mutual Recognition: Integration of the Financial Sector in the European Community," *Federal Reserve Bulletin* (September 1989), pp. 591-609.

Levine, Mark Lee. *Business and the Law* (West Publishing, 1976).

"Mapping the Road to Monetary Union." *Financial Times,* December 12, 1991.

Rosenberg, Jerry M. *The New Europe: An A to Z Compendium on the European Community* (Bureau of National Affairs, 1991).

"Second Council Directive of 15 December 1989," *Official Journal of the European Communities,* December 30, 1989.

Tyley, Robert T. "The ECU: A New Global Currency," *International Economic Insights* (July/August 1991), pp. 38-40.

U.K. Department of Trade and Industry. *The Single Market: Financial Services,* March 1991.

U.S. Banks, Competition, and the Mexican Banking System:
How Much Will NAFTA Matter?

William C. Gruben
Senior Economist and Policy Advisor

John H. Welch
Senior Economist

Research Department
Federal Reserve Bank of Dallas

Jeffery W. Gunther
Senior Economist and Policy Advisor

Financial Industry Studies Department
Federal Reserve Bank of Dallas

For Mexico, the details of the financial services portion of the North American Free Trade Agreement (NAFTA) are an important part of a broader program of financial liberalization that has been under development for close to a decade.[1] Not only do NAFTA's details represent a major step in Mexico's recent financial liberalization efforts, but the general framework of the agreement also is important.

NAFTA's financial-sector portion commences with an explication of general principles and subsequently focuses on the expression of these principles through the industry-by-industry details of the agreement. In this regard, NAFTA reflects an attempt to apply trade policy concepts to the financial services sector, an innovation stemming from prior efforts to develop the General Agreement on Trade in Services. Sauvé and González-Hermosillo (1993, 4) note that this approach derives from the recognition that the joint pursuit of "business globalization and trade liberalization requires agreement among countries on a guiding set of rules and disciplines relating to matters of establishment, market access, standard of treatment, transparency of regulations and dispute settlement." By establishing both a general framework for greater foreign participation in Mexico's financial markets and particular rules governing that participation, the agreement represents a palpable reduction in the payoff to protectionist lobbying and an increase in the long-term sustainability of financial reform.[2]

This article provides an overview of the financial portion of NAFTA and includes analysis of its potential impact on the Mexican banking system. NAFTA's general framework, combined with the details of the important financial liberalization that NAFTA sets forth, indicates that the agreement will further Mexico's goal of increasing competition and efficiency in the provision of financial services. Differences in the agreement's treatment of various financial services, together with certain characteristics of financial markets in Mexico, suggest that most entries into the Mexican financial

---

We would like to thank Agustín Carstens and Moises Schwartz of the Banco de México and Yves Maroni of the Board of Governors of the Federal Reserve System for their comments. Of course, all remaining errors are our own and the usual caveats apply.

[1] See Welch and Gruben (1993) for an analysis of the financial liberalizations that occurred in Mexico both over the past ten years and in previous periods of Mexico's modern history.

[2] Also, by increasing the credibility of policy permanence, NAFTA can reduce response time to a policy change. An important reason for having free trade agreements like NAFTA, as Gould clarifies, is that "unlike most legal contracts, enforcement of these agreements is entirely voluntary, and their credibility does not depend on the objectives and interests of only two parties, but on the relative power of competing interests within two or more subscribing countries" (Gould 1992, 20). Incredible policy changes may have neutral or even perverse effects. In the early 1980s, Peru's attempt at trade liberalization lacked credibility. Suspecting that tariffs would rise again, investors imported large quantities of foreign goods and reduced domestic investment (Gould 1992).

sector under NAFTA likely will occur in nonbank areas, especially brokerage. As competition in the provision of nonbank financial services continues to grow, and as more banks—both foreign and domestic—commence operations in the Mexican market, Mexico's banks will be challenged to make strong gains in efficiency.

---

[3] NAFTA also represents much effort to ensure procedural transparency; in fact, transparency is one of the general principles on which this principles-based agreement is founded. In processing applications for entry into its financial services markets, each NAFTA country has committed itself to clarifying its requirements for completing applications, to providing information on the status of an application on request, to making an administrative determination on a completed application within 120 days, to publishing measures of general application no later than their effective date, to allowing interested persons the opportunity to comment on proposed measures, and to establishing inquiry points to answer questions about its financial services measures.

[4] NAFTA countries generally have agreed not to increase current impediments to cross-border trade. However, the United States has declined to make such a commitment with regard to cross-border trade in securities with Canada, even though such an agreement does exist between the United States and Mexico. Likewise, Canada has not committed to such a "standstill" agreement with the United States. While NAFTA countries generally have agreed to permit their residents to purchase financial services provided from the territory of another party to the agreement, the transaction must originate at the request of the purchaser. Active solicitation of business from a seller in one NAFTA country to a purchaser in another is not part of the agreement.

[5] The financial services chapter of NAFTA focuses more on institutions than on products. NAFTA's focus is a departure from that of other agreements, such as the General Agreement on Trade in Services, in that NAFTA treats financial services as institution-specific, so that the rules for one type of lending or deposit-accepting institution are different from those of another. Under NAFTA, the same category of service may face different regulations or restrictions in accordance with the category of institution providing the services.

[6] The term "comparable" is important. Sauvé and González-Hermosillo (1993) note that NAFTA borrows from the General Agreement on Trade in Services in defining national treatment in a *de facto* rather than *de jure* sense. A *de jure* national treatment means that the very same laws apply to foreign firms as domestic.

The Financial Services Portion of NAFTA

One way to facilitate the process of business globalization and trade liberalization, and accelerate the speed of adjustment to a policy change, is to assure that the new policy is easily understood.[3] Accordingly, the two most important doctrines in the financial services portion of NAFTA are relatively simple: each country allows its residents to buy financial services in other NAFTA countries[4], and foreign subsidiary institutions receive national treatment. The first clause implies a promise that Mexico's capital flight restrictions of late 1982, which inhibited foreign financial services' availability to Mexicans, will not reappear. In the second clause, national treatment means that foreign financial institutions[5] are subject to laws, rules, and regulations comparable[6] to those governing domestic institutions in a given host country.[7] The country for which this doctrine signifies the biggest change is Mexico, where NAFTA allows U.S. and Canadian financial services firms to set up wholly owned subsidiaries for the first time in fifty years.

Although the principal tenets of NAFTA's clauses on financial institutions are relatively simple, several complications arise from the past histories of each country's individual financial service industries, such as banking or securities, and from the connections that different countries permit among such industries. Unlike the United States, Mexico permits the same holding company to own banks, insurance companies, stock brokerage houses, funds management firms, bonding institutions, factoring operations, exchange houses, leasing firms, and warehousing firms.[8] As will be seen, these variations in what NAFTA signatories permit invest the agreement with some peculiar clauses. Moreover, under NAFTA, the structure of Mexican financial services firms owned by U.S. or Canadian firms is important. The Mexican firms must be subsidiaries rather than branches of their foreign owners. This rule means that a Mexican bank will have its own board of directors, even if it is owned by a U.S. or Canadian firm. More importantly, these subsidiaries can fail, even when the foreign parent bank does not.

NAFTA phases in liberalization. Mexico will allow U.S. and Canadian commercial banks, insurance companies, brokerage firms, and finance companies their fullest access only after a six-year transition period (beginning in 1994), during which the market will be limited. For example, the capital of foreign insurance affiliates may not exceed 6 percent of the aggregate capital of all insurance companies in Mexico during the first year of the transition period, but that share goes to 12 percent on January 1, 1999, and to 100 percent a year later.[9] Similarly, during 1994, bank capital under the control of foreign investors in Mexico may not exceed 8 percent of the value of all bank capital in the country. In the last year of the six-year transition period, this limit goes to 15 percent.

But even after the phase-in period, NAFTA's characterization of national treatment is limited. Mexico will still be able to treat potential U.S. and Canadian-owned subsidiaries somewhat differently than it treats domestic firms. As an example, consider Mexico's banking system. Each of Mexico's two largest banking institutions, Banamex and Bancomer, accounts for more than 20 percent of total bank capital in the country. Together, they account for about 50 percent of total bank capital. After NAFTA's phase-in period for banks, neither Canadian nor U.S. groups may acquire an institution that accounts for more than a 4-percent share of the aggregate capital of all commercial banks in Mexico. In addition, once the six-year transition period is over, the Mexican government has the one-time option of freezing *temporarily* the total level of capital of Canadian and U.S. banks if that capital reaches 25 percent of total bank capital in Mexico.[10]

The United States, likewise, explicitly restricts what foreign financial institutions of NAFTA signatory countries may do, and some of these restrictions reflect differences between Mexican and U.S. financial institutions. The United States will permit a Mexican financial group that before NAFTA's enactment had acquired both a Mexican bank with U.S. operations and a Mexican

---

A *de facto* standard takes account of the potential inequality of effects that regulatory requirements might have if they were applied identically to domestic and foreign institutions. Accordingly, *de facto* treatment may allow somewhat different laws and regulations to apply to foreigners than apply to locals, "so long as their effect is equivalent and does not place the former at a competitive disadvantage in the host country market" (Sauvé and González-Hermosillo 1993, 13). Of course, not all parties will agree in every future case on what equal effects are. There is a dispute settlement mechanism to address these potential differences.

[7] The host country provision contrasts with that of the European Economic Community, which allows country A's subsidiary financial institutions operating in country B to behave in accordance with country A's regulations instead of country B's.

[8] See Welch and Gruben (1993) for a description of Mexico's regulations pertaining to financial structure. We should note that NAFTA prohibits U.S. and Canadian banks from investing in credit unions, development banks, and foreign exchange firms

[9] NAFTA also allows foreign insurance providers to enter Mexico through a partial equity interest in a new or existing Mexican insurance company. Under this alternative entry mechanism, the share of a Mexican insurance company's voting common stock owned by foreign insurance providers is subject to limits that are relaxed during the transition period.

[10] The freeze is permitted to last only three years and can only be implemented during the period 2000–2004. NAFTA provides a similar option for Mexico with regard to securities firms, but there the aggregate capital percentage that triggers the option is 30 percent, although the same three-year maximum freeze period holds. Note that Canada exempts Mexican firms and individuals from its prohibition against nonresidents' collective acquisition of more than 25 percent of the shares of a federally regulated Canadian financial institution. Canada had already extended this exemption to the United States as part of the Canada–U.S. Free Trade Agreement. Mexican banks are also exempted from the combined 12-percent asset ceiling that applies to non-NAFTA banks, and also need not seek the approval of the minister of finance as a condition of opening multiple branches in Canada. Financial services commitments of Canada and the United States under the Canada–U.S. Free Trade Agreement will be incorporated into NAFTA.

securities firm with U.S. operations to operate both for five years after the acquisitions. The U.S. securities affiliate, however, will not be permitted to expand through acquisition. Moreover, the United States requires that the majority of directors of a foreign subsidiary bank be U.S. citizens.

With regard to start-up operations in Mexico, one of NAFTA's attractions for Canadian and U.S. firms is the opportunity to carry out operations denominated in pesos rather than dollars, which will enable firms to accumulate peso liabilities to offset their peso-denominated assets.[11]

The breadth of opportunities offered by NAFTA is important. For example, NAFTA signifies that finance companies may ultimately establish subsidiaries to provide consumer lending, commercial lending, mortgage lending, or credit card services. During the transition period, such operations are subject to the restriction that they may not collectively exceed 3 percent of the sum of the aggregate assets of all banks in Mexico plus the aggregate of all types of limited-scope financial institutions in Mexico, a phrase that refers to companies that provide consumer lending or commercial lending or mortgage lending, or credit card services. After the transition period, such firms receive purely national treatment, which is to say they will not be subject to the caps that banks will face after the phase-in.

Even during the transition period, some types of auto-related financing are not subject to the caps that other financial operations will face during the phase-in. Accordingly, it should not be surprising to note reports that at least one U.S. nonbank firm is already planning the introduction of auto financing and leasing operations, and that U.S. brokerage firms, meanwhile, are planning cross-border mergers and acquisition activity and the introduction of swaps and options into the Mexican market.

Attractiveness of Mexico for Entry by U.S. Financial Institutions

Are U.S.-based financial institutions likely to be interested in establishing operations in Mexico under NAFTA? A look at the Mexican banking system, as an example, offers an indication of what may make NAFTA attractive to U.S. financial institutions. Mexico's banking system is highly profitable, highly concentrated, not very competitive, fairly inefficient, and somewhat less aggressively oriented toward marketing than some developed-country systems.

Mexican banks are more profitable than U.S. banks and most European banks. In 1992, the net return on assets for Mexican banks was approximately 1.45 percent, versus 0.96 percent for U.S. banks. The return on average assets in 1991 was 1.09 percent in Mexico, compared with 0.53 percent for the United States, 0.41 percent for all of Western Europe, 0.19 percent for Japan, and 1.11 percent for Spain (*Chart 1*). When the Mexican government began to

Chart 1
Bank Return on Assets, 1991

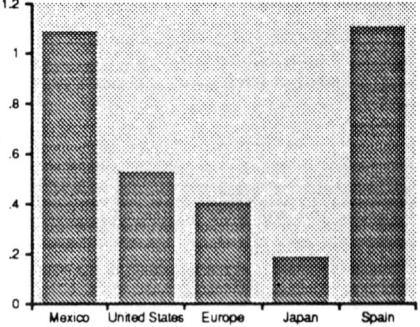

SOURCE: Natella et al.

---

[11] In general, to gain peso exposure, U.S. and Canadian financial institutions must locate operations in Mexico, as offshore peso trading is strictly prohibited. However, certain operations between U.S. and Mexican markets also provide vehicles for peso exposure.

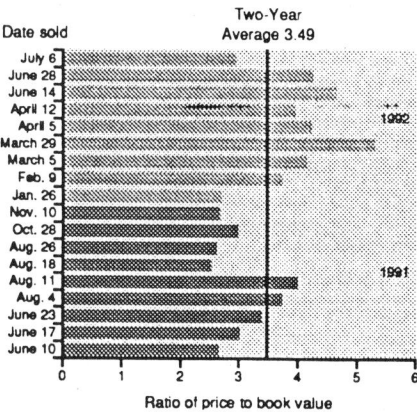

Chart 2
Mexico: Commercial Bank Privatizations

SOURCE: Banco de México.

privatize the formerly state-owned banking system in 1991, some U.S. observers were surprised to see the selling prices of these banks range from 2.6 times book value to 5.4 times book (*Chart 2*). Expectations of future profitability helps explain these prices. Moreover, some observers suspected that privatization would make Mexican banks compete more intensely with one another, paying higher rates on deposits and charging lower interest rates. But instead of narrowing, spreads between interest rates on loans and bank deposits have widened. During the second half of 1990, interest rate spreads averaged about 5 percentage points. During 1992, when inflation rates had declined considerably compared with rates in the 1980s, spreads fluctuated between 7.57 percent and 10.69 percent (*Chart 3*).[12]

The Mexican banking system is currently highly concentrated, especially when compared with the U.S. banking system (*Chart 4*). As of mid-1992, the three largest commercial banks in Mexico—from a total of twenty (counting First National City Bank, or Citibank, and the union-owned institution, Banco Obrero)—held about three-fifths of all Mexican commercial bank assets. In contrast, as of year-end 1992, the three largest U.S. banking organizations held roughly one-seventh of total U.S. bank assets.[13] The level of competition that such concentration implies for Mexico, which lacks a deep nonbank financial market for private debt, may explain why large interest rate spreads persist.[14]

In addition, some indicators suggest that Mexican banks may not have begun to operate very efficiently, at least by commonly applied standards. In 1991, the ratio of noninterest operating costs to assets in Mexican banks was 5.9 percent, versus 3.7

---

[12] In a discussion of this point, Mansell Carstens notes that spreads have remained high and are likely to stay high over the next two years, not only because of the oligopoly power in the provision of commercial bank services, but because "commercial banks have been moving into high yield consumer lending" (Mansell Carstens 1993, 29). She notes that consumers had not had access to credit since the early 1980s; that banks have enjoyed a seller's market in satisfying the backlog of credit demand; that banks will probably expand their credit card, consumer durable, and mortgage lending programs to middle and lower-income groups; and that such operations typically involve large spreads.

[13] The bank assets of individual U.S. banking organizations are approximated by the sum of the assets of their bank affiliates. U.S. concentration measures based on deposits are similar to the asset concentration figures reported here. Note that the national concentration measures used here do not necessarily reflect the degree of concentration within local market areas in either Mexico or the United States.

[14] Concentration, in and of itself, need not preclude competitive provision of banking services. Shaffer (1992) finds that the Canadian banking system, which is comparable to Mexico's in terms of market concentration, still behaves competitively. The historical difference has been the contestability of Canadian markets for the types of financial services that Canadian banks offer. That is, market entry has traditionally been more viable in Canada, and securities markets for private debt are broader and deeper than those in Mexico. Later in this article, we more fully address problems of Mexico's nonbank private-debt markets in providing competition for the banks.

Chart 3
Mexico: Net Interest Margin, 1990–92

Percentage points

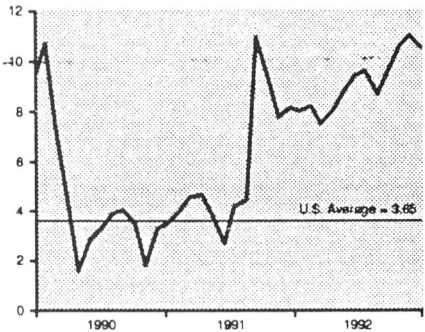

NOTE: Difference between average lending rate and average cost of funds for multibanks.
SOURCE: Banco de México.

---

[15] International comparisons of financial ratios probably offer a general picture of differences between the Mexican banking system and its counterparts in other countries, but care must be exercised and tenths of a percentage point ought not to be taken seriously. For a more extensive clarification of international comparisons of financial ratios in the context of NAFTA countries, see Gavito Mohar, Sánchez García and Trigueros Legarreta (1992). Despite their cautions, those authors still draw conclusions about the essential differences between Mexican and U.S. financial performance, and the conclusions are very similar to those we draw in this article.

[16] See Mansell Carstens (1993) for further discussion of this issue.

---

percent for U.S. banks.[15] It should be noted that Mexico's 5.9 percent in 1991 represents a decline from 6.3 percent in 1990 and that, for reasons discussed below, this ratio will probably continue to fall.

Other evidence suggests Mexican banks may devote less attention to marketing than is common in the United States and Europe. In 1991, Mexico had one bank branch for about every 18,000 people. In the United States, the number was about one branch per 4,000 inhabitants and, in Europe, about one for every 2,000.[16] Nevertheless, as in the case of other bank characteristics, time may not have permitted recent bank behavior to reflect fully the impact of privatization.

Although these factors suggest that under NAFTA Mexico may attract U.S. banks, it is important to emphasize that the Mexican financial system is anything but static. The circumstances implied by the financial statistics and ratios cited earlier will probably not persist.

The first reprivatization of a Mexican bank did not occur until June 1991 and the last, that of Banco del Centro, took place in July 1992. There is much reason to suspect that insufficient time has elapsed for any bank to complete its transition from a public to private entity. In a study of bank acquisitions by holding companies in the United States, Johnson and Meinster (1973) show that an acquired bank's income and balance sheet ratios do not begin to display statistically significant differences from those of prior management until two years of new ownership. Moreover, the full impact of a change in management appears not to be felt until four years after the acquisition (Johnson and Meinster 1975). As of this writing, only two years have passed since any Mexican banks were privatized.

Tenure of ownership is not the only factor contributing to the state of flux in Mexican banking. As of September 1993, applications had been made for the establishment of at least six new (rather than acquired) banks, and five had been approved. Whether or not competition has intensified since bank privatization, the opportunities for intensification are clearly increasing. NAFTA's six-year phase-in to the point at which Canadian and U.S. banks receive their full opportunities for establishment in the Mexican market is likely to offer profound changes in the Mexican financial system, even without any foreign entrants.

In addition to the rapidly changing nature of financial institutions and markets, other factors in Mexico raise questions about the

Chart 4
Asset Concentration in Top Five Banks
(Share of Total Assets)

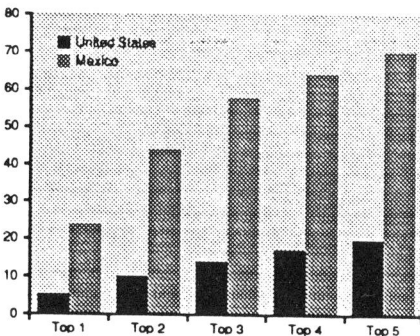

SOURCE: Comisión Nacional Bancaria–Mexico; Reports of Condition and Income.

intensity and rapidity with which Canadian and U.S. banks may choose to enter the Mexican market. While Mexico may be underbranched, and while "rising incomes... are expected to increase the demand for banking services by Mexicans, most of whom live outside the major cities and currently have no banking relationship at all" (Laderman and Moreno, 1992, 3), Mexican banks have well-established positions in the retail market, which U.S.-owned institutions may have difficulty achieving.[17]

With regard to wholesale banking, Mansell Carstens (1993) notes that Mexican banks have faced competition from foreign firms in this sector for years. While foreign banks have not been permitted to establish themselves as banks *per se* in Mexico, they have had representative offices. Moreover, Mexican banks, private and public corporations, and the government have relied for decades on these institutions. Mansell Carstens remarks that "for the wholesale banking sector, NAFTA may be a nonevent" (Mansell Carstens 1993, 37).

A related detail may offer a useful perspective on the extent of competition that Canadian and U.S. financial institutions could face from Mexican entities. Although the Mexican bank nationalization that occurred in 1982 formally removed only bank directors and left other employees at their desks, many of these employees departed for securities firms, which took on a rising share of financial activity.[18] Later, Mexican securities firms turned out to be the major purchasers of privatized Mexican banks. Since many securities industry executives were bankers before the nationalization, the recent financial deregulation has meant a reunification of financial products and personnel. Does this mean that Mexican banks have an information advantage that would make a U.S. bank's entry into the Mexican market a highly competitive event? It seems to suggest that, because of personnel movement out of banking and into the securities business and then back, human capital appropriate to the joint provision of securities services and traditional banking products may be particularly abundant in the Mexican financial system.[19]

Perhaps the main barriers to entry by U.S. banks are the minimum capital requirements and the global and individual maximum market share restrictions on U.S. bank holdings. The initial minimum capital requirement for a new entrant into the banking system is 0.5 percent of total paid-up capital plus reserves in the banking system, while

---

[17] In a discussion of this point, Mansell Carstens (1993) notes that the smallest of Mexico's three largest banking institutions (Banca Serfin) has 596 branches and that both Banamex and Bancomer have more.

[18] See Welch and Gruben (1993) for a description of the Mexican bank nationalization.

[19] The stock of financial experience in Mexico's banks contrasts sharply with that of many U.S. financial institutions in the 1980s. The partial erosion of barriers to competition at that time in the United States led many U.S. thrifts to enter into areas in which they had little or no previous experience. Similarly, the financial deregulation of the 1980s broadened the types of financial controls that U.S. banks and thrifts were required to maintain on their own, leading to substantial financial difficulties at some institutions.

the maximum allowed is 1.5 percent of the sum of total paid-up capital, reserves, and current gross profits.[20] As of December 1992, these requirements convert to about $20 million for the minimum and $90 million for the maximum. Given recent trends in capital growth, these limits easily could rise to $26 million for the minimum and $126 million for the maximum. The minimum capital requirements exclude a number of would-be entrants into the Mexican market (see the box entitled "NAFTA's Implications for U.S. Border Banks"). But the maximum capital requirements are small compared with the rest of the banks in the banking system. If a U.S. firm wanted to buy a Mexican bank, only two of the twenty could be purchased because the remainder have capital larger than the maximum.

The maximum capital allowed for any individual entrant grows to 4 percent by the year 2000. If 4 percent were the maximum today, all but the largest five banks could be bought by an interested U.S. bank. But these five banks command a huge proportion of Mexico's banking system. Hence, the strategy in NAFTA allows U.S. banks to enter in the phase-in period only in a very limited part of the market, mainly in regional retail operations. U.S. banks will essentially have to "grow their own" Mexican subsidiaries because the restrictions on banks that develop a large market share are considerably less stringent.

Current Issues in Mexican Banking

A broader issue involving the development of the Mexican financial system is the connection of this process to other components of Mexico's liberalization programs, which have attracted large influxes of foreign capital into the country. While very little of these international flows have taken place in the form of loans from foreign banks, their implications for banking have been important.

These inflows of foreign capital, and their translation into pesos, have bolstered both the demand for the peso and its rate of exchange against other currencies. Partly as a result of the strong peso (or the weak U.S. dollar), and partly because Mexico has dramatically lowered its barriers to foreign trade in recent years, the United States increasingly has become a low-cost supplier for Mexican buyers. In fact, U.S. producers have begun to out-compete Mexican producers in so many Mexican markets that Mexico's imports from the United States have quadrupled since 1987. As a result of rising U.S. and other foreign competition, Mexican tradeable goods producers have begun to default on their debt to Mexican banks at a more rapid rate than in past years (*Chart 5*). Also, loans with a moderate or higher risk of default rose from 5 percent of total loan volume in September 1991 to 9 percent in September 1992.

Does this mean that increased U.S. sales to Mexico under NAFTA will mean more defaults? In fact, it is hard to separate the various factors that have caused increases in the ratio of past-due loans to overall loans. While foreign competition plays a role, other issues are important as well. A significant portion of the recent rise in troubled assets may be linked to loans booked under the directed credit programs maintained by the Mexican authorities before privatization. The Mexican government created a compensation mechanism, within the privatization program, to reimburse the purchasers of the banks for any initially unreported problem loans. The problem loans associated with these past programs would, in any case, not be expected to reflect accurately any new trends in financial performance generated by the restructured financial system. Nor should

---

[20] Note that the measure of capital used in determining the maximum is different from that used in determining the minimum. This difference results from the fact that the minimum capital requirement was determined by the Law on Credit Institutions of 1990, whereas the maximum is specified by NAFTA. Also, the Mexican authorities have much discretion in determining minimum capital requirements.

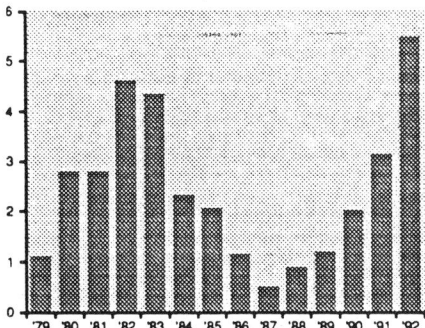

Chart 5
Mexico: Ratio of Past-Due Loans to Total Loans, 1979–92

SOURCE: Comisión Nacional Bancaria–Mexico.

they call to question the solvency or profitability of these banks.

The rise in problem loans also reflects greater risk-taking at Mexican banks. However, some (Garber and Weisbrod 1991) have argued that the important role of banks in Mexico's financial system imparts a substantial franchise value to Mexican banks, particularly those with high market shares and strong reputations. The incentive to protect this franchise value from loss due to failure may partially offset banks' propensities to extend large volumes of high risk loans.

A comparison with recent events in the U.S. financial system helps illustrate the incentive Mexican banks may have to maintain a moderate risk profile. During the 1970s and 1980s, advances in information technology, together with the regulatory restrictions imposed on banks and thrifts, meant savings were more remunerative and borrowing cheaper at other sorts of institutions (Kaufman 1991). The partial financial deregulation that occurred during the 1980s materialized largely in reaction to these forces. In response to the lower charter values brought on by increased competition, U.S. financial institutions took on riskier portfolios (Keeley 1990).

Perhaps similar forces are at work in Mexico. But despite problems of disintermediation qualitatively similar to those in the United States, Mexico's financial reforms occurred in an atmosphere somewhat less hostile to banks. The relatively illiquid nature of Mexico's financial markets continued to offer banks there a central role in supplying liquidity and monitoring the financial condition of borrowers. Moreover, as Mexico's financial markets continue to broaden and deepen, Mexico's relatively unrestrictive regulations pertaining to financial structure offer broader avenues for avoiding the erosion of market share than those afforded U.S. banks in the 1980s.[21] These conditions may help curb the recent rise in problem loans.

Other Mexican Financial Markets

We have suggested that bank concentration need not inhibit competitive provision of banking services but that, up to now, it seems to have done so in Mexico. One reason Mexico's banking system seems to lack competition appears to involve a shortage of contestable markets. That is, the viability of entry by new banking firms or the existence of deep and broad markets for nonbank funding of private enterprise seem not to have been sufficient to discipline banks toward competitive behavior. While stock and securities markets exist in Mexico, and while factoring and leasing operations and other nonbank sources of *de facto* finance for private borrowers have also existed for years, many of these institutions have had problems of their own that have impaired their competitive strength.

Consider the stock market in Mexico. In general, stock markets transfer capital from

---

[21] See Gunther and Moore (1992) for a discussion of the relatively unrestrictive product and geographic expansion laws that distinguish Mexico's banking system from that of the United States.

savers to investors (the primary market), provide liquidity to owners of fixed capital (the secondary market), and improve the efficiency and performance of firms through the market for corporate control (the secondary market). However, the performance of the stock market depends not only on market access but also on the market's ability to discipline its corporate participants.

The Mexican stock market is small compared with those of developed countries. An important reason involves contestable markets, but of a somewhat different sort than those stressed in our previous discussions. Here, the contest involves the threat of takeover when a company's managers behave in their own interests rather than the stockholders'. McConnell and Servaes (1990) provide evidence that self-serving managerial behavior increases with the percentage of insider ownership and that increases in insider ownership accordingly lower the value of stock.

High insider ownership rates are common in Mexico, and the result has been an illiquid market. Under the current Mexican regime of comparatively loose regulation of company performance reportage, in a milieu of heavy insider stock holdings, participants in the Mexican market are suspicious of managers and discount stock values accordingly.

Moreover, the market suspicions that have been inspired by Mexico's longtime corporate issuers naturally contaminate efforts of new firm entrants to fund themselves efficiently in the equity market. Accordingly, Mexico's stock market is less liquid than that of developed countries and offers even less competition with the banking system than do stock markets in developed countries.[22]

Other forms of private-firm securities likewise play a smaller role in Mexico than in developed countries. As an example, consider commercial paper, an open market substitute for bank loans. The ratio of commercial paper holdings to bank lending is less than one-fourth as high as in the United States. And the banks themselves behave as if they are money market mutual funds. They place their own funds and those of the trusts they operate into commercial paper that they themselves market (Garber and Weisbrod 1991).

More generally, until now the overwhelming share of securities traded in the Mexican Bolsa de Valores has been of government issue. Because of the thinness of nonbank financial markets for nongovernmental borrowers, firms that could go abroad for funding have. It has been common for Mexico's great conglomerates to issue fixed-income securities in U.S. or European markets, and it is not unusual for the government to do the same.

Over time, however, the role of government issues in the Mexican securities market has diminished and will probably continue to decline. Recent innovations, expected developments (such as a Mexican options market), as well as a broadening and deepening of existing markets, suggest a diminishing role for traditional lending services in Mexican financial markets, much as has been the case in the developed world. The worldwide revolution in information processing that has increased the abilities of nonbank financial institutions to tailor securitized debt to the special needs of particular borrowers will likely continue to affect Mexican domestic financial markets (Walter 1992). That is, Mexican firms may be increasingly able to offer services at a level of particularity that up to now has been restricted to bank lending.

However, the same is true for Canadian and U.S. brokerage firms that could enter Mexican markets under NAFTA. Moreover, Canadian and U.S. firms already have experience and technology of the types that Mexican institutions are just now gaining. Accordingly, this is the area of the Mexican financial market that may see the greatest foreign penetration. Growth in such

---

[22] For further development of these issues, see Welch (1993).

securities and trading by both Mexican and foreign institutions may prevent the fall in the liquidity of the Mexican financial system Garber and Weisbrod (1991) expected to result from reductions in the number of Mexican treasury instruments outstanding. Private issues may offset those of the government.

Another reason most entries under NAFTA will be in securities brokerage is the agreement's relatively favorable treatment of this industry. As mentioned earlier, during the agreement's transition period, the maximum level of start-up capital for a new entrant into Mexico's banking system is 1.5 percent of the sum of systemwide, paid-up capital, reserves, and current gross profits. That limit increases to 4 percent by the year 2000.[23] The comparable restricted maximum for securities firms is more liberal, starting at 4 percent during the transition period before being removed entirely in the year 2000. Similarly, restrictions on the aggregate capital under the control of foreign investors in Mexico also treat securities brokerage relatively favorably. For bank capital, the aggregate restriction increases from 8 percent in 1994 to 15 percent in 1999, as mentioned earlier. In contrast, the comparable restriction for securities firms is 10 percent in the first year of the six-year transition period and 20 percent in the last. The relatively quick opening of brokerage services should facilitate early foreign penetration into that area.

Another possible role in the Mexican financial system for foreign financial firms is that of an offshore banking center. In July 1990, for example, the Law on Credit Institutions changed to allow Mexican banks to create dollar-denominated deposits for non-resident depositors. Currently, however, several factors discourage foreign institutions from establishing offshore operations in Mexico. First, the Mexican income tax for such institutions is 35 percent, a relatively high level compared with those obtaining in traditional offshore banking centers. In addition, Mexican labor laws require any company in Mexico to share 10 percent of its profits with its workers. Inasmuch as financial institutions in general, and offshore banks in particular, realize relatively high profits per employee, these laws may also dissuade potential offshore bankers from establishing operations in Mexico (Mansell Carstens 1992).

Conclusion

Despite much discussion of Canadian and U.S. banks entering the Mexican market, and despite the likelihood that some will, there is reason to suspect that the Mexican banking market may constitute one of NAFTA's least inviting financial market apertures. The Mexicans have taken special care to protect their banks from foreign competition during the long phase-in period. Because of the capital ceilings, the areas open to U.S. banks are the smaller regional banks, which mainly deal in retail banking and consumer financing. Although these areas are extremely profitable, most U.S. banks are not familiar enough with the Mexican market to compete effectively in the retail area. On the other hand, the more liberal treatment given to brokerage, bonding, leasing, factoring, insurance, and warehousing suggests that equity and bond markets will almost surely prove more attractive.

The complexion of the Mexican banking system indicates that in the next ten years most entry will be in these nonbank areas, especially brokerage. Mexico already imports a large amount of brokerage services from the New York Stock Exchange through the floatation of American Depository Receipts (ADRs) and from world bond markets through the large floatations from PEMEX, some large banks, and also some smaller firms. Hence, brokerage operations with strong links to U.S. investment banks will enjoy a strong position not only for arbi-

---

[23] This 4-percent limit applies only to acquisitions and not to new banks.

trage between the Mexican and New York markets but also to tailor asset and liability products to the needs of firms that conduct business internationally.

Certainly, increasing competition in the nonbank sectors from foreign participation in combination with a number of new Mexican banks will put pressure on banks to improve their efficiency. As we have described, this process is already well under way. The Mexican financial system, although not competitive at present, shows signs that very soon the institutions and markets will offer better financial services at significantly lower cost.

But a number of questions remain. One concerns the role that banks will play relative to securities markets. The remaining statutory barriers to entry in Mexican banking and the problems with the Mexican market for corporate control indicate that banks will maintain a privileged position in the Mexican financial system for many years to come. But the decline of banking in the United States and Europe cannot be explained solely by overregulation, implying that perhaps the importance of Mexican banks may also erode over time. Technological advance in information processing and financial instruments has given securities markets an edge, as witnessed by the major increase in securitization (Kaufman 1991). If U.S. and Mexican specialist institutions can offer nonbank services more efficiently than banks, then one would expect the importance of banks to wane. The favorable treatment of securities brokerage by NAFTA would be expected to promote such a competitive process. These considerations make projections of the future structure of the Mexican banking system extremely difficult. But no matter what the ultimate outcome, the evolution of the Mexican banking system should prove a fertile experiment in financial market liberalization.

NAFTA's Implications for U.S. Border Banks

The greatest opportunities that NAFTA's financial provisions present U.S. firms, at least initially, are outside traditional retail banking. One of the factors that suggests this conclusion is the information advantage Mexican financial institutions have over most U.S. banks in assessing risks and opportunities among Mexico's bank customers. However, because of their proximity to Mexico and familiarity with its markets, U.S. banks along the Mexican border may face a relatively low information hurdle in competing with Mexican financial institutions. Regulatory barriers, not information costs, will limit the capacity of most border banks to enter Mexico under NAFTA.

Border banks' specific knowledge and skills favor their penetration into Mexican retail markets. U.S. banks along the Mexican border generally are familiar with retail banking opportunities in Mexico. The banks' proximity to Mexico enables them to provide deposit services to Mexican citizens, and they extend credit to Mexican businesses. Moreover, the local banking markets on the U.S. side of the border are, in many respects, similar to the banking environment in Mexico.

The familiarity of border banks with Mexican markets should help these banks assess the credit quality of small and mid-size businesses in Mexico. As a result, any information advantage that established business relationships impart to Mexican banks should be reduced. In this regard, the border banks are particularly well-suited for entry into Mexico's growing retail banking market.

Although the proximity of border banks to Mexico enhances their position as potential entrants, other factors suggest that the entry of border banks into Mexico under NAFTA will be limited. Mexican financial companies provide commercial banking, brokerage, and insurance services jointly through an extensive network of branch offices. The established retail market position of Mexican banks increases the difficulty entering U.S. banks will face in attracting a broad base of retail customers. And this barrier to entry may be particularly formidable for border banks, most of which are relatively small.

Perhaps the greatest obstacle constraining the ability of border banks to take advantage of NAFTA's entry provisions is the minimum capital requirement established by the Mexican authorities for new banks. The required minimum level of capital that would apply to new banks established by U.S. financial services providers under NAFTA is, as of this writing, approximately $20 million. Moreover, each of the new Mexican banks recently approved by the Mexican authorities has been established with more than $40 million in capital, suggesting that investments well above the published minimum are encouraged. While this level of capital would not be expected to pose a serious barrier to entry by large U.S. banking organizations, it could represent a problem for smaller institutions along the border that otherwise would be interested in establishing a bank in Mexico.

(Continued on the next page)

NAFTA's Implications for U.S. Border Banks—Continued

The capital levels of Texas banking organizations near the Mexican border illustrate how the minimum capital requirement may constrain the entry of smaller U.S. banks into Mexico. As of year-end 1992, forty-eight banking organizations operated at least one bank in Texas counties along the Mexican border. As shown in the accompanying chart, the minimum capital requirement of $20 million was more than five times greater than existing bank capital at 32 percent of these banking firms.[1] And the minimum capital requirement exceeded 100 percent of bank capital at 86 percent of the firms. To meet the minimum capital requirement for establishing a bank in Mexico, while maintaining an adequate level of capitalization among their domestic banks, these banking organizations would need to raise large amounts of external capital. And it generally is difficult for small banks to raise equity externally. Similar adjustments would be required of all but the largest U.S. banking organizations that currently operate a bank along the Mexican border.

The regulatory constraint posed by Mexico's minimum capital requirement, coupled with the extensive market resources of Mexican banks, suggests that most U.S. border banks will be unlikely to exploit their familiarity with Mexican markets by establishing banks in Mexico. Rather, the factors considered here indicate that NAFTA represents the greatest opportunity for relatively large U.S. banking organizations. The primary benefit of NAFTA for most of the border banks will be an indirect one resulting from an increase in trade and economic activity in the border region.

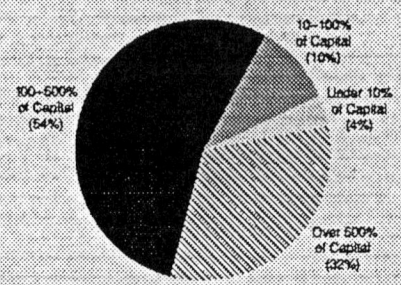

Distribution of Texas Border Banks by Minimum Required Capital Relative to Existing Capital

- 10-100% of Capital (10%)
- Under 10% of Capital (4%)
- 100-500% of Capital (54%)
- Over 500% of Capital (32%)

SOURCE: Reports of Condition and Income.

---

[1] Total bank capital is approximated by the sum of the year-end 1992 capital levels of an organization's individual banks.

References

Garber, Peter M., and Steven R. Weisbrod (1991), "Opening the Financial Services Market in Mexico," (Paper presented at the Conference on the Mexico–U.S. Free Trade Agreement, Brown University, October 18–19).

Gavito Mohar, Javier, Sergio Sánchez Garcia, and Ignacio Trigueros Legarreta (1992), "Los Servicios Financieros y el Acuerdo de Libre Comercio: Bancos y Casas de Bolsa," in Eduardo Andere and Georgina Kessel, eds. *México y el Tratado Trilateral de Libre Comercio: Impacto Sectorial* (Mexico City: ITAM and McGraw-Hill).

Gould, David M. (1992), "Free Trade Agreements and the Credibility of Trade Reforms," Federal Reserve Bank of Dallas *Economic Review*, first quarter, 17–41.

Gunther, Jeffery W., and Robert R. Moore (1992), "Mexico Offers Banking Opportunities," Federal Reserve Bank of Dallas *Financial Industry Issues*, fourth quarter.

Johnson, R.D., and D.C. Meinster (1975), "The Performance of Bank Holding Company Acquisitions: A Multivariate Analysis," *The Journal of Business* 48, 204–12.

———, and ——— (1973), "The Analysis of Bank Holding Companies' Acquisitions: Some Methodological Issues," *Journal of Bank Research* 4.

Kaufman, George G. (1991), "The Diminishing Role of Commercial Banking in the U.S. Economy," Federal Reserve Bank of Chicago Working Paper no. WP-1991-11, May.

Keeley, Michael C. (1990), "Deposit Insurance, Risk, and Market Power in Banking," *American Economic Review* 80, (December): 1183–1200.

Laderman, Elizabeth, and Ramon Moreno (1992), "NAFTA and U.S. Banking," *FRBSF Weekly Letter* no. 92-40, 1–3.

Mansell Carstens, Catherine (1993), "The Social and Economic Impact of the Mexican Bank Reprivatization" (Paper presented at Institute of the Americas, La Jolla, January).

——— (1992), *Las Nuevas Finanzas en Mexico* (Mexico City: Editorial Milenio).

McConnell, John J., and Henri Servaes (1990), "Additional Evidence on Equity Ownership and Corporate Value," *Journal of Financial Economics* 27-2, October, 595–612.

Natella, Stefano, Thomas H. Hanley, Justin Manson, Suhas L. Ketkar, Veronica Dias (1992), *The Mexican Banking System II* (New York: CS First Boston).

Sauvé, Pierre, and Brenda González-Hermosillo (1993), "Financial Services and the North American Free Trade Agreement: Implications for Canadian Financial Institutions," unpublished paper, External Affairs and International Trade Canada and Bank of Canada, Ottawa.

Shaffer, Sherrill (1993), "A Test of Competition in Canadian Banking," *Journal of Money, Credit, and Banking* 25, February, 49–61.

Walter, Ingo (1992), "A Framework for the Optimum Structure of Financial Systems," New York University Salomon Center Working Paper Series no. S-92-47.

Welch, John H. (1993), "The New Face of Latin America: Financial Flows, Markets, and Institutions," *Journal of Latin American Studies*, forthcoming.

———, and William C. Gruben (1993), "A Brief Modern History of the Mexican Financial System," Federal Reserve Bank of Dallas *Financial Industry Studies*, this issue.